Student Handbook

ADMINISTRATION

Carol Carysforth
Maureen Rawlinson

HEINEMANN

NVQ LEVEL 3

Heinemann Educational
a division of Heinemann Educational Books Ltd,
Halley Court, Jordan Hill, Oxford OX2 8EJ

OXFORD   LONDON   EDINBURGH
MADRID   ATHENS   BOLOGNA   PARIS
MELBOURNE   SYDNEY   AUCKLAND   SINGAPORE   TOKYO
IBADAN   NAIROBI   HARARE   GABORONE
PORTSMOUTH NH (USA)

First published 1992
   93 94 95 96 11 10 9 8 7 6 5 4 3

A catalogue record for this book is available from the British Library on request.

ISBN 0 435 45014 X

Designed by Ken Vail Graphics Design

Typeset by Taurus Graphics, Abingdon, Oxon

Printed Clays Ltd, St Ives plc

ACKNOWLEDGEMENTS

The authors would like to acknowledge personally the co-operation, assistance and support of friends and colleagues, whose combined expertise proved invaluable in the writing of this book.

Especial thanks for specialist help and advice are due to David Williams AIDPM, Mavis Williams Cert Ed, AFTComm, Vince Higham and not least to Margaret Berriman for her support and encouragement. Our thanks also go to Stewart Carysforth who put up with many trials and tribulations associated with the writing of this book!

The authors and publishers would also like to thank the following organisations for permission to reproduce copyright material:

The Controller of Her Majesty's Stationery Office
Lowe Bell Communications
Pitman Publishing
The Sunday Times
WordPerfect UK

Contents

Introduction

It seems a pity that today many bright young people are dissuaded from following anything which could even remotely be termed a 'secretarial career' because they have been told that it is a 'dead-end job'. The experience of both authors – and many of their protogées – has been rather different. For virtually all secretaries who have the benefit of a broad-based business training the opportunities are enormous. Many PAs and secretaries move into a wide variety of fields including publishing, personnel management and the media – and are highly valued for the skills they possess. Others become office administrators and move on to management. Their secretarial training is usually easily identified by their impressive organisational skills!

This book is primarily aimed at all office staff who want to rise to a higher position. It is equally suitable, however, for full-time students with a good background of secretarial skills who wish to study to higher level in order to enter the world of work as an administrator or PA. It is assumed that all readers will have a basic knowledge of office procedures, up to NVQ Level 2.

To manage such a position successfully means developing office procedures skills to a more sophisticated level, and the NVQ 3 chapters in this book will enable you to achieve the knowledge and expertise required. However, personal development is equally important – the 'managing' skills you need to possess to enable you to cope successfully with your job, your boss and, probably most important of all, other people. For that reason, between every two main NVQ chapters you will find a short section that helps you to develop these skills. If you find these sections particularly interesting, and want to pursue some topics further, then you should refer to the further reading list at the end of this book for details of additional reading material.

Your future as a secretary, administrator or PA depends very much on what you make it. You can choose the field in which you want to work, and change at a later date if you wish. You can choose the region and, if you are bi- or multi-lingual, the country. If you value your own worth then the world can become your oyster.

To quote from a well-known poem:

'Two men look out through the same bars
One sees mud, and one the stars'[1]

The aim of this book is to bring the stars within reach.

Carol Carysforth and Maureen Rawlinson
June 1992

[1] Frederick Langbridge, *A Cluster of Quiet Thoughts*, 1896, a Religious Tract Society Publication

1 Communication systems

Section 1 – Organising the allocation and despatch of mail

As a PA or administrator your involvement with the intricacies of mail handling will vary considerably depending upon the organisation for which you work and the systems in operation. You will be responsible for the receipt and despatch of mail for your own boss and you will probably also have to organise the work of your junior staff in this respect. In addition, however, you may be expected to organise the mailroom and the work of its staff. Whatever your remit you must make sure that you are aware of the procedures which need to be put into operation to ensure that mail is allocated and despatched in the most effective way.

CHECK IT YOURSELF
If you work for an established organisation you will find that established mailroom procedures are already in force. Check those in operation at your place of work against the considerations given below.

Mailroom systems
Devising the system
- Is the volume of mail sufficient to warrant a specific mail handling office or department?
- If so, what hours will it operate and who will be in charge?
- Will staff be required constantly throughout the day or only during peak morning and afternoon periods? This again will depend on volume.
- If staff from other departments will work in the mailroom only during peak times:
  - should they be junior staff?
  - what incentives can be used to persuade mail staff to start earlier than other staff, so that mail can be sorted promptly?
  - who will supervise their work?
  - who should deal with mid-day deliveries, those made by hand or any special incoming items eg parcels?
- If the organisation has a high volume of mail both inwards and outwards, should a departmental manager be appointed to be responsible for negotiating mail contracts, the purchase and maintenance of equipment and to keep a watching brief on new developments which could be effectively used by the organisation?
- To what degree is it essential for the mailroom to have close links with the computer section, eg for computerised mailshots?

- What range of incoming/outgoing mail equipment should be purchased to ensure the most cost effective operation for the organisation?
- How many specific Royal Mail services will be used which will require:
  - staff training plus specialised knowledge and expertise
  - space for forms, bags, labels, mailshots in progress etc?
- Where should the mailroom be sited and how should it be set out? (Obviously it should be near to the main entrance and spacious enough for staff to work effectively.)
- Is the company large enough to require 'internal' postmen?
- Will *all* mail be opened in the mailroom or should it operate merely as a 'receiving office' so that unopened mail is put into departmental trays and opened later?
- Should the mail be collected by departmental representatives or delivered to departments? Should the procedure be different for senior staff?
- If mail is opened centrally and needs to be seen by several people, should the mailroom be responsible for the distribution or the first department or person mentioned in the document?
- Should departments be responsible for enveloping and sealing their own outgoing mail items, or should this task be undertaken centrally?
- What accounting procedures are in operation, ie will postage costs be calculated centrally and then charged to specific departments; is the organisation a Royal Mail contract user with a mail account which must be checked monthly?
- Bearing in mind the volume of outgoing mail daily, what time constraints would have to be in force so that deadlines could be met? Under what circumstances could exceptions be made? What action should be taken if such arrangements are abused?
- Should messages received by fax or telex be incorporated into the system? What alternatives are available?
- Should parcels be opened by mailroom staff or delivered to addressees unopened? Will mailroom staff have the authority to sign for parcels? Should damaged parcels be refused or simply signed for as damaged?

Operating procedures

Once the system has been set up, your next objective should be to ensure that all staff know how it operates. It is a good idea to issue a set of guidelines so that everyone knows what their duties are (see table opposite).

TAYLOR ELECTRONICS PLC

MAILROOM PROCEDURES

In order that the mailroom can operate at maximum efficiency and effectiveness, users are asked to adhere to the following standard procedures at all times.

Incoming mail

1 This will be opened, date-stamped and pre-sorted into departments within the mailroom. Departmental representatives should collect mail from their basket no later than 0915 hours each morning.

2 Mail which has to be seen by several departments will be copied and distributed by the mailroom or distributed using a standard circulation slip.

3 Remittances will be recorded in the mailroom and sent direct to the Accounts Department. Accompanying documentation which must be seen by other departments will be photocopied and distributed as in (2) above.

4 Lunchtime mail will be sorted and ready for collection by 1330 hours.

5 All envelopes will be retained for a period of 48 hours in case of queries as to their contents.

6 Confidential and personal items of mail will *not* be opened by mailroom staff but, if the named recipient is away from the office, company procedure is that items will be opened by secretarial staff in an executive's absence. This is to avoid urgent items being neglected in error. Whilst this policy may cause some inconvenience to staff, it is generally expected that all mail addressed to the company will relate to business matters.

Internal mail

1 This should be received in the mailroom by the following times:
   ● for sorting and outward distribution by 1330 hours
     – **no later than 12 noon**
   ● for sorting and outward distribution by 0915 hours
     – **no later than 1600 hours**

2 Enveloped items should be sent using the standard, reusable envelopes.

Outgoing mail

1 This must be received by the mailroom **no later than 1500 hrs**. Documents created after this time should be:

   ● dated for the following day if non–urgent
   ● faxed to the recipient if urgent.

   In *exceptional circumstances* only departmental managers may contact the mailroom supervisor to make special arrangements. A log will be kept of such occurrences and action taken if the system is abused by any users.

2 All outgoing mail must be enveloped and sealed within departments with special mailing instructions clearly marked on the envelope. In the absence of other instructions, all outgoing mail will be despatched by second class post.

3 Departmental managers should contact the mailroom supervisor *in advance* if large mailshots are required. The service to be used will be recommended by the mailroom supervisor. Both the departmental manager and the computer section will be expected to liaise closely with the mailroom supervisor so that the organisation can benefit from discounted rates for bulk postage and pre-sorting.

4 Any items of mail which require priority, international or other specialist services must be despatched through the mailroom. The service to be used will again be at the discretion of the mailroom supervisor.

General

1 For security reasons, staff visiting the mailroom must not bring with them any bags or packages which are not directly related to their mail requirements.

2 Staff must not send personal items of mail via the mailroom and only outgoing mail in printed company envelopes will be accepted unless stamped beforehand. The company reserves the right to open any official envelope where there are reasonable grounds for suspicion that the contents are of a personal nature.

3 Items delivered by hand to the company in the reception area will be passed to the mailroom for onward despatch to departments by the normal system. If the item is marked urgent, or has special instructions attached, the mailroom will contact departmental staff who should arrange for immediate collection.

Mailroom organisation and equipment

Check that you have the following essentials:

For incoming mail

- tables and work surfaces where incoming mail can be sorted rapidly
- a range of departmental baskets and trays, clearly labelled
- sacks or waste bags in which discarded envelopes can be placed (and held for a specified period in case of queries)
- letter opener(s)
- date stamp(s).

For outgoing mail

- baskets or trays for:
  - UK mail – first class and second class mail plus priority items such as mail being sent by registered post or special delivery
  - international mail
  - branch or head office mail (and any other organisation or person to whom you regularly send several items daily)
  - packets and parcels (both before and after wrapping)

- space for wrapping packets and parcels (use the tables which you used for sorting mail in the morning)
- a range of wrapping materials
- forms, bags and postage dockets for special Royal Mail services
- plenty of cupboard space
- a filing cabinet to keep copies of leaflets and circulars, postage records and, if your company has an account with Royal Mail or a delivery company, copies of invoices and statements received and checked
- the correct equipment for your requirements from a range including:
  - postal weighing scales for both letters and parcels
  - franking machine
  - folding, inserting and sealing machine(s)
  - parcel tying machine
- sundry items such as staplers, calculators etc.

Organisation

Impress on the staff the importance of tidiness and forward planning. No one will be pleased if their urgent package cannot be sent for two days because there is no wrapping for it.

Note also that the working area should be organised so that there is a 'free' traffic area for people to move around without disturbing anyone else.

SPECIAL NOTE
Some mailrooms contain their own photocopiers (for photocopying incoming documents which must be sent to several people) and/or shredders. The latter can be useful as the strips produced by these make ideal packaging material.

Equipment

A large company which is regularly involved in computer managed mailings (see page 12) may have a whole array of sophisticated equipment, but a smaller company may be content with some weighing scales and a franking machine. A franking machine may be used *less* frequently by a company which regularly undertakes mass mailings, as it is likely to have its own envelopes pre-printed with PPIs (see page 11).

Most organisations today use electronic weighing scales for weighing letters, rather than the traditional type, as these are preset with current postage rates, held on a silicon chip. You need, however, to train your staff to press the correct keys and they will still need to know which priority postal service, if any, must be selected. When postal rates change the manufacturers send a new chip which you insert in the machine.

All staff *must* know how to use a franking machine properly *and* how to change the date, replenish the ink and complete a franking machine control card. You must devise a system to cope with any items which are franked with too large an amount of postage in error, as these can be saved and returned to the Post Office for the amount to be credited to the company's account. If your mail is not collected each day, then your staff should know to place all franked mail in special envelopes and hand these over the Post Office counter. Today most franking machines can have additional units set into them electronically. It would be your responsibility to telephone the manufacturer when these were needed and obtain the special code which must be keyed in to the machine. If your franking machine is an older model, it may need to be taken to the Post Office for the units to be reset manually.

CHECK IT YOURSELF
Obtain a range of literature on mail handling equipment by contacting the manufacturers of the type of machinery given above and compare the functions available.

Training mailroom staff

As their supervisor it is your job to ensure that your junior staff know and clearly understand:

- the procedures they have to follow
- the equipment they have to operate
- the services they are expected to use
- the 'exceptional' cases and problems which should be reported to you.

Incoming mail

Most organisations usually possess a letter opening machine and a date-stamp. Some companies use a machine which also automatically records the time the mail was received.

Make sure your junior staff are aware that:

- envelopes to be put through a letter opener should be tapped gently first (so that the contents are at the bottom)
- they *must not* open confidential or personal items
- urgent mail must be put on the *top* of departmental trays
- remittances must be recorded properly in the Remittances Book, and any discrepancies clearly noted
- recorded delivery and registered mail may be listed in an incoming mail register and must always be signed for on delivery. Once a staff member has signed for an item then he/she is deemed to be responsible for its safe delivery to the recipient!
- enclosures should be securely attached to the document to which they relate and, again, discrepancies should be noted. Make sure that staff are aware that paperclips can 'hook' other documents to them – and thereby create a mailroom nightmare
- *some* documents must never be date-stamped, eg cheques and legal documents
- the company procedures in relation to parcel deliveries.

Incoming mail – problems you may encounter
With your juniors

- Documents reported as 'lost' because they are:
  - left in envelopes in error
  - hooked behind paperclips fastening other documents
  - despatched to the wrong department
  - mentioned as an enclosure but omitted from the envelope and never noticed by your staff.
- Incoming documents damaged because the envelopes have been opened wrongly.
- Confidential envelopes opened in error.
- Juniors taking unilateral action to solve a problem eg hiding a 'problem' document – such as the confidential letter they opened in error – in a drawer!
- Juniors gossiping about something they have read in the post.
- A junior persistently arriving late, when half the mail has been dealt with, despite the fact that all mailroom staff are paid a bonus for early morning working.
- Juniors date stamping *everything* – to the acute annoyance of staff.

TEST YOURSELF
Devise a set of procedures and guidelines which you can implement to minimise the problems given above. How would you deal with *each* problem if you found that your instructions had been ignored – both to a departmental complainant (if applicable) and to the junior concerned?

With the mail in general

- Items which keep being returned to you as 'nothing to do with this department'.
- Personal mail for employees who have now left the company/misdirected mail.
- Circularised mail which falls into a black hole halfway around the organisation.
- The fear that 'suspicious' packages may be received in the mailroom.

Contingency plans for emergencies
Constantly returned mail   Firstly check that the departments which have received it to date were the logical choice! If not then reroute. Is an executive responsible for this type of problem. (If not, should there be?) If you still have no luck then you have two options – bin the item if it is only a circular or contact the sender if it is important and ask him/her for more details.

Misdirected mail   If this is for the company up the road or in the same building then have someone take it round by hand. If the misdeliveries continue notify your local sorting office. Otherwise simply repost with your outgoing mail.

Personal mail to employees who have left *can* be redirected to them (if this is company policy) by simply writing a note on the envelope that they are no longer with your organisation and adding their home address. Repost as before.

Circularised mail   Decide *in advance* whether circularised items have to be returned to a central point – and where this is. Make this the last name on the circulation slip. Further pressure is put on recipients if you include two columns – one for date received and another for date passed on! Keep a list of key items circulated and when they first started on their travels.

TEST YOURSELF
Obtain up-to-date information from your Regional Crime Prevention Officer on recommended police procedures in the case of suspicious packages. Draw up a key list of procedures for all mailroom staff to follow.

Outgoing mail

Throughout the day, mail for despatch will be received in the mailroom. Most of this will be standard first or second class post, and should be sorted upon arrival into two main baskets. In most organisations this has already been enveloped and sealed. If it has not, your juniors should know to:

- check that all letters have been signed and the address on the envelope matches that on the document
- fold the documents the minimum number of times to fit in the envelope
- fold documents to be inserted into window envelopes correctly so that:
  - *all* the address is clearly shown
  - the document is not folded so that it is too small for the space available as it will then slide about in the envelope and the address will disappear!
- make sure any special postage instructions are clearly marked on the envelope
- weigh any envelope containing more than two sheets of paper and note the weight (or the postage charge if electronic scales are used) lightly in pencil on the envelope
- put items over the standard first and second class letter weights in a special tray so that they can be franked separately.

Inter-organisational mail

If your company has other offices, or contacts to which it writes frequently (eg if the company secretary or accountant is located at a different address), it is usual for the mailroom to contain large, pre-addressed envelopes for each of these offices or people. Items for these destinations should be placed in specially marked trays and, at the end of the day, transferred to the appropriate envelope. This not only reduces the postage costs but is infinitely preferable to, say, a branch office receiving and having to open a variety of envelopes from head office each morning!

Parcels and packages

In addition to the standard postal items, you will also have a variety of documents and/or packages which need to be despatched by special mail. Some packages and parcels may need wrapping. A variety of materials should be kept in the mailroom for this purpose. Teach your juniors how to wrap parcels correctly and securely (make them read the Royal Mail leaflet *Wrap up well*) and to address them properly – with both the name of the recipient and the sender clearly shown. Most companies have their own printed labels for this purpose. You should train your staff to write them before putting them on the box. The parcel should then be weighed and the weight, or amount of postage, written on in pencil.

Priority Items

Priority items of mail are those which are to be sent by a particular Royal Mail service – usually because they are valuable or need special treatment. Your mailroom should contain a supply of special envelopes, forms and, in some cases, postage dockets, for the services you use regularly.

Post Office services

The Post Office is divided into three separate businesses: letters, parcels and counters. Letters are the responsibility of the Royal Mail service and parcels are dealt with by the Parcelforce service. This can sometimes cause confusion as to which service should be used, for instance if you have a small parcel to send quickly. You should note that any item under 1 kg in weight can be sent by first class letter post and any item under 750 grams by second class letter post. You can also send heavier items quickly by using the Royal Mail Special Delivery service.

All Post Office services can be divided into:

- those which are used by anyone posting letters or parcels, both within the UK and internationally. You and your staff should be completely familiar with all these services
- those only used by businesses, some of which have a large volume of outgoing mail. These are the services about which you need to know if your company produces mass mailings on a regular basis.

Other service providers

In addition to the Post Office services there are other ways of sending letters and goods quickly. The British Rail Red Star service can be used to send a parcel between any two stations. The sender has the option whether to instruct British Rail to deliver it to the recipient's address (the more expensive option) or whether to ask British Rail to hold it at the destination station for collection. Because British Rail will specify the train on which the parcel will travel, it is possible to ring the recipient with information on the time of arrival of the parcel at the local station.

A further development in recent years, has been the emergence of many private delivery and collection services, virtually all of which offer express delivery and a courier service both within the UK and to countries overseas. They will also give advice and assistance with customs documentation where necessary.

CHECK IT YOURSELF

As a mailroom supervisor you should have at your fingertips up-to-date information on all the most commonly used services:

- Registered post and Consequential Loss Insurance
- Recorded delivery
- Advice of delivery
- Certificates of posting
- Special delivery
- Swiftair
- Airmail and surface mail
- Small packets service
- Business reply and Freepost
- Poste Restante

Plus Parcelforce services:

- Datapost
- Parcelforce 24 and 48
- Parcelforce Standard and Compensation Fee
- International Parcelforce
- Cash on Delivery and Postage Forward Parcel options

and information on the Red Star service and those services offered by private companies with local offices.

If you regularly send documents or packages overseas then you should know the regulations in relation to the completion of Customs documentation and VAT forms. Obtain a copy of the Post Office Guide plus the latest leaflets and *read them*, eg the Royal Mail guide to letter rates and services, the Royal Mail International leaflet and the relevant leaflets on Parcelforce services. Information on Royal Mail services is available from Business Centres around the country *or* for international information you can contact their helpline on 0345-585820. For Parcelforce information ring 0800 224466.

Look in your local Yellow Pages and make out a list of private companies which offer delivery and collection services and find out the services in which they specialise, eg local courier, international express etc.

Business services

Special Post Office services are available to companies which regularly use the mail to promote their company. Those operated within the UK include:

Admail A contract service for advertisers who wish to quote an address in the area in which their advertisement appears, but then have replies re-routed to a different address within the UK. In many cases this address will be that of a 'fulfilment house', ie the company which has been retained to supply the goods or information after an order or enquiry has been received. The Admail service can be used in conjunction with the Freepost service.

Household delivery This service provides the user with a door-to-door delivery service of mail. The targeting of potential customers can be by postcode sector, by TV area or demographically, (so that potential customers are identified by age, location, status, profession, income etc). Deliveries can be as small as one postcode sector up to nationwide. No stamps are required and it is up to the user whether items are enveloped or not. (Note that many private companies also offer this service.)

Mailsort The organisation obtains a discount (between 13 per cent and 32 per cent) for pre-sorting its own mail for delivery. Large quantities then go direct to the nearest Royal Mail delivery offices, smaller quantities to intermediate sorting offices. Users have three delivery options – first class (target next day delivery), second class (target within three days delivery), economy (target delivery within seven days).

Presstream This is a magazine distributions service which is offered solely to members of the publishing industry. As with mailsort, the user obtains discounts for pre-sorting the mail before posting.

Printed Postage Impressions (PPIs) These are the pre-printed alternative to postage stamps or franking machines, used by companies which send large quantities of identical inland or international letters and packets. Time is saved on preparing the post and envelopes or labels can be prepared in advance for special mailings. Accounting procedures are simplified as an account is opened with the Royal Mail Office and the user is billed for the postage against a posting docket handed in with each posting.

Any single PPI posting must comprise a minimum of 4000 letters or 1000 packets and all items in one posting must be the same size, shape and weight, posted at the same class/rate of postage and presented in bundles of convenient size with addresses facing in the same direction.

PPIs can be used in conjunction with a wide variety of Royal Mail services including Mailsort.

Computer managed mailings

Companies which use large volume contract services often use a computer database of addresses containing its mail listings which are organised in a specific way so that, for instance, mailshots are produced by postcode area. Companies can also buy a **Postcode Address File (PAF)**, which is a centrally stored database of every address (not names, except in the case of businesses) in the UK with its appropriate postcode. Residential and business addresses are listed separately. This can be purchased as microfiche (updated annually) or in tape or CD format (both updated monthly) for downloading on to mainframe or microcomputers. The database can be used to check that the company's own address lists are correct and also linked to other software so that the company can plan, automatically target and print its direct mail shots easily and rapidly.

Quite obviously, a company which produces a large amount of computer-managed mailings will also need a range of sophisticated equipment in the mailroom to ensure that the mail is handled swiftly and efficiently. Automatic folding, inserting and sealing machines will process the documents very quickly indeed. If the envelopes are pre-printed with a PPI then a franking machine is not required for these items.

Any company can arrange for its mail to be collected and there is usually no charge. Needless to say, this is essential for companies which regularly produce mass mailings.

SPECIAL NOTE
Companies sending out mass mailings used to use addressing machines which contained pre-prepared metal plates embossed with the names and addresses of their customers. Envelopes passed through the machine were automatically printed with the name on the plate currently in the machine. Although there may be a few of these machines still in existence, the advent of databases and computerised address labels has rendered them obsolete in most organisations.

Accounting procedures

In a small organisation a postage book may be used to record all first and second class mail, as a batch, and then any special mail. Other companies simply use their franking machine account and/or their PPI account as a guide to their postal expenses. The problem with this in a large company can be one of allocation. Unless some method is devised whereby the mailroom keeps a record for each department or user, it is impossible to analyse objectively those who may misuse or abuse the services. Equally, there can be very good reasons why postal charges have increased – obviously a company which decides to start advertising by sending out mailshots will see its postal charges soar. Organisations involved in this type of exercise will usually open an account with the Royal Mail so that they are invoiced monthly for the services they have used – and it may be your task to check this invoice against your records and copies of postage dockets. Within the company, this account may then be broken down and analysed by department.

Outgoing mail – problems you may encounter

With your juniors

- Letters and parcels sent by normal post instead of by the priority service requested (or sent by the wrong service altogether)
- Letters and parcels wrongly addressed and returned by the Post Office.
- A letter put in an envelope addressed to someone else
- Letters and parcels underfranked so that the recipient has to pay the difference in postage *plus* a surcharge.
- Letters and parcel labels overfranked and then destroyed (or hidden in the drawer with the confidential letter opened in error . . .).
- Parcels and packages poorly wrapped so that the contents spill out in the post – and the recipient complains.
- Important forms and dockets put in the wrong place so they are missing when needed quickly.
- Nobody confessing that they used the last jiffy bag last week.
- Equipment being misused so that it jams or breaks at a critical moment.
- Pre-sorted batches of mail for mass mailings being muddled up and having to be sorted all over again.
- No one telling you that there aren't enough units in the franking machine for tonight's post.
- Postage dockets and the postage book wrongly calculated and/or illegible.
- A lack of urgency in relation to postal deadlines.

With the mail in general

- Managers continually sending down items as 'urgent' long after the official deadline has passed.
- Managers marking *everything* to go by first class post – despite a company instruction that routine items must be despatched by second class post.

- Staff asking you to send a personal parcel or letter through the system 'just this once'.
- Staff sending confidential documents to the mailroom for despatch without enveloping them first.
- Equipment breaking down just when it is needed most.

 TEST YOURSELF
As a group:

1 Add as many other possible problems as you can to those given above and on page 7.
2 Suggest procedures and systems which would help to minimise each of the above.

Incoming mail – the role of the PA/administrator

When you receive your mail, plus any overnight faxes or telexes, you have several priority tasks to carry out so that your boss can quickly and rapidly assess the work which must be carried out that day.

- Quickly skim read all the documents and make a preliminary sort into:
  - urgent items
  - documents which are less urgent
  - circulars
  - routine items you can deal with on your own and/or replies to *your* own correspondence which your boss doesn't need to see.
  (See also Chapter 6, Processing correspondence, page 298.)
- Check through again a little more carefully, this time reading the documents more thoroughly to enable you to prioritise the documents *within* each set.
- Date-stamp as you go (if this has not already been done), making sure you do not obliterate any text.
- Get out any files you know your boss will need to answer incoming mail and, depending upon his/her preference, either clip each document to its particular file *or* keep the file folders separate, albeit in the same order as the correspondence.
- Put the mail in order with the most urgent documents on the top. Bear in mind that confidential documents should never be placed on top of the mail inwards tray for anyone visiting the office to read.
- Take the mail to him/her, either leaving it on the desk or in the mail inwards tray. It is usually appreciated if you give some warning of any potential problems you have spotted or very high priority matters which need dealing with immediately.

It is wise to check your boss's preferences about confidential and personal mail. You may have to open both, but in some cases your boss may prefer to receive personal mail unopened. A very important fact to bear in mind is that, at PA level, any breach of confidentiality is a potentially fair reason for dismissal. Your boss should be able to show you confidential documents with impunity – you are *paid* to keep your mouth shut!

If your boss has a meeting arranged for early in the morning, or will be going out of the office on business, you may have to skip two or three of the stages above, so that you can appraise him/her quickly before he/she leaves the office. In this situation, as you skim read *extract* anything urgent from the rest of the pile, stamp these, and take them to your boss. You can sort out the rest later.

Remember that you should *always* read every document thoroughly. Only by doing this can you be completely au fait with what is going on around you and capable of answering queries and questions you may be asked – and reminding your boss when something is forgotten!

When your executive is away

If your boss is away from the office for a few days, or longer, then you need some agreement as to how the mail should be handled. Usually day-to-day priorities are handled, by phone, at a previously arranged contact time (see Chapter 4, Arranging travel, page 183). So that your boss can quickly get to grips with what has been happening on his/her return it is useful if you type three summary lists:

1 **urgent mail** – summary of action agreed by you over the phone, plus what you have actually done. Clip this list to the front of a brown folder containing copies of all documentation (incoming, plus copy of your letters, faxes etc sent in reply) in the same order as detailed on your list.

2 **non-urgent mail** – summary of mail left for your boss's attention (ie name of company, nature of document, brief sentence on its contents). Clip this list to a folder containing the non-urgent mail, again in the same order as your list.

3 **mail you have dealt with yourself** – summary of letters, faxes etc to which you have replied. This list should be clipped to a folder containing copies of incoming documents plus copies of your replies.

Your boss can then go quickly through the lists to get up to date, then methodically work through them, ticking off items as they are dealt with. Make sure you have your own copy of your lists; then you can keep a check on what has and has not been dealt with over the next few days, and give gentle reminders where necessary. Make sure also that you have included this information in your mail reminder system (see Chapter 7, Organising work schedules, page 352).

 SPECIAL NOTE
Rather than include your file copies in your boss's folders, take a spare copy of letters you type in his/her absence which you will need to show him/her later. Mark this copy with your boss's initials. You can then keep your filing up to date, and when the copies are sent through as outstanding work is completed, you can simply destroy them.

Additional items

Throughout the day you can expect additional documents to arrive – the mid-day post will need sorting, together with faxes and telexes which you receive. You *must* be prepared to alter your priorities at any time to deal with such items. If life is very hectic then your skim reading techniques can come in very useful – you can pass on anything urgent and, if this suits both of you, hold on to anything non-urgent until the following morning, when it can be incorporated into the follow day's post. This system means that you are only dealing with 'bulk' items once a day, rather than continuously.

SPECIAL NOTE

It is worth noting the value of the date stamp to the efficient PA, and its drawback for the inefficient! If there is any dispute, at any time, as to how long it took you to respond to a document, the date stamp on the incoming item and the date of your reply should solve the problem. Of course, if you *did* forget to write back for two weeks during your boss's absence – or kept putting it off because you couldn't be bothered to do it – the date stamp will remove any onus from the Royal Mail service and any inventive alibi you might have been considering!

Outgoing mail – the role of the PA/administrator

If you organise your work properly, then you should be producing documents so that you always give priority to urgent items (see Chapter 7, Organising work schedules, page 352). If you follow this type of system then you will have no difficulty in keeping to the system operated by your mailroom, as by the time the deadline approaches all your urgent documents will have been completed long since. The odd emergency is unavoidable, but here the fax machine can come into its own on the majority of occasions (see page 50).

Two rules to remember are:

- it is pointless producing urgent documents quickly if you forget to get them signed!
- if you have a genuine emergency *always* ring down and warn the mailroom. If you abide by their systems and are perceived as helpful and cooperative most of the time and have had the good sense to develop a good working relationship with the staff who work there, you should have very little difficulty.

Any PA worth her salt will always keep a set of stamps in her drawer for last minute items which she can post herself on the way home if necessary. A small set of letter weighing scales is cheap, small and extremely useful in case the Post Office is shut.

If you have a mammoth job in progress, again notify the mailroom in advance. If you regularly send off mailshots from your own customer database do remember to keep this up to date. Make sure you are on the circulation list for letters which arrive in your company notifying a change of address – if you are first on the list then don't forget that other departments will need to know too. There is nothing worse than sending out a mailshot and having half your envelopes returned to you – and there will be many moans about the wasted cost of postage!

Accounting procedures

Depending on the systems in operation in your organisation, it is possible that your department is accountable for all mail sent, and a record is kept of these items in the mailroom (see page 12).

Your manager could easily require you to keep a duplicate log so that costings can be verified – and disputed if necessary. If such a system is in operation then your ability to determine quickly the most cost-effective and appropriate service for despatching your mail is critical. Your carrier may vary prices if time of delivery is important, or the question of insurance is critical. You *must* know the services available and you *must* 'shop around'.

The easiest way to keep such a log is to keep a mini postage book which details the date, the total number of first and second class letters despatched and the total postage cost of these, and then detail any special mail and parcels and the cost of these. Total this per day and carry forward your daily totals for a final total at the end of the accounting period in question.

You can also reduce costs by 'batching' your mail in a similar way to that operated by the mailroom for branch offices. For instance, if you send memos to representatives or several documents to certain companies each week, make your own pre-prepared envelopes to contain all the items you prepare for them over a day (or longer if non-urgent). This will also make you look far more efficient than sending out five envelopes to one person in a day would!

Confidential documents

Confidential documents you prepare should *never* be sent out of your office unless they are securely sealed in an envelope. In some top security establishments, and others which deal with items which are commercially confidential, the documents are not only sealed in an envelope but the flap is sealed, then initialled across the join, and finally sealed with sellotape. Any attempt to tamper with the envelope is then clearly noticeable. The document will probably then be delivered by courier, rather than sent through the usual postal channels.

On a lesser level, you may frequently be typing letters and memos which are confidential. *Both* must be enveloped and clearly marked either CONFIDENTIAL or PERSONAL before they enter your company's mail system.

Individual tasks

1 Devise an instruction sheet which could be used by your junior staff and which clearly shows:

   a how to fold paper *correctly* to fit into envelopes

   b the correct size of envelope to choose for different sizes and volumes of paper

   c how to fold a business letter correctly to fit into a window envelope

   If possible, illustrate your sheet by means of diagrams so that key information is shown clearly and simply.

2 From your investigation of the main Post Office services (see page 9) make out for yourself a short reminder page detailing each service and its main features. If you prefer, you can use the layout of business services shown on page 10 as a guide.

   The display should be such that the page is clear and easy to follow and can be used as a source of reference.

   You should note that if you have access to a word processor you can also include a column for current postage rates which you can update as necessary.

3 Your company is in the process of moving to a new office block a few miles away. Your boss is concerned about mail going astray or being wrongly delivered after the move. You know that the Post Office will redirect mail for a specified period after the move and he has asked you to provide full details.

   Investigate this service and give full details in a short memo.

Individual/group tasks

Case study 1

You have recently started work for the head office of a computer consultancy company. Two directors started the company ten years ago and it has grown very quickly. There are now 50 employees in head office, four branch offices and several external consultants who work from home.

As PA to Sandra Phillipson, one of the directors, you have been given the responsibility of completely re-organising the mailroom and the procedures followed. These have evolved over the years and are now totally inappropriate for the volume of mail received and despatched.

The new mailroom will be situated in a large office, 10 metres square, on the ground floor and two junior staff from the General Office will be delegated to assist for two hours each morning and afternoon. The office you will use is at present completely empty.

Your boss has asked you to:

a Investigate and select suitable new equipment for the mailroom. Detail your recommendations in a memo to her, clearly stating the items you consider are essential, the specific machines you recommend, the cost and your reasons for selecting these particular models.

b Devise a suitable layout for the mailroom to maximise work flow. Your diagram should clearly show the siting of all furniture and equipment and where electrical sockets will be required. Attach a short rationale on your proposed layout to your diagram.

c Make a list of the standard procedures you consider users must follow for your mailroom to function effectively.

d Draft out a short training programme for the two juniors showing clearly the topics you think must be covered and the time allocation for each.

Case study 2

You work as PA for David Malkovich, the Marketing Manager of a large polytechnic. From next month, all departments will be accountable for their own postage charges and this will be set against their budget for the year. David Malkovich is concerned that there will have to be some system of record keeping in his department. He regularly sends advertising displays to exhibition organisers, schools and colleges, many of whom request information at the last minute. He is also responsible for all direct mail shots and all student enquiries.

He has asked you to:

a Devise a simple, easy-to-follow accounting form on which you can record the postage used. Make sure that the totals can be carried forward for a grand total to be taken at the end of each month.

b Test your form by entering and totalling the following items sent at *today's postage rates*:

- 15 first class letters
- 33 second class letters
- 2 letters by registered post, one for compensation of £500 and one for compensation of £2000
- 5 recorded delivery letters sent by first class post one of which is accompanied by an AD form
- 2 airmail letters, both weighing 20 g to Spain and the USA (the latter was sent Swiftair for speed)
- a parcel weighing 3 kg sent to Australia by the International Datapost service.

c David Malkovitch is concerned that student enquiries sometimes go astray or get into the administrative mail by mistake. The polytechnic address is long and there is a similarly named college nearby. To solve the problem he is considering taking out a PO Box so that this number can be easily quoted on advertising literature and enquiries will be kept separate from the main mail.

Investigate this service and provide full details, including cost, in a short memo.

d To date the polytechnic has always used Parcelforce services to despatch advertising displays. To keep costs to a minimum David Malkovitch has asked you to obtain information from local private delivery services and draw up a comparative table showing their charges, together with those of Parcelforce and British Rail. Make sure that your table also includes an assessment in terms of speed of delivery and insurance cover.

Section 2 – Using the telephone system to the full

Today, the vast majority of people have a telephone in their own home. Yet it is amazing how many have difficulty in coping with even the simplest telephone calls in a business situation. As a PA your competency on the telephone is *essential.* Your ability to deal with a wide range of people – and difficult situations – courteously and effectively is an integral part of the job and your mastery will be long remembered even after you have moved on to higher things. Equally, your inability to cope will never be forgiven or forgotten. The telephone is a potent weapon – in the hands of someone who is accomplished and skilled it can be used to charm, inform and even flatter to deceive. Equally, it can assist you in alienating an important customer or even the MD in five seconds flat. Your mastery of this instrument is therefore essential, not only to your future progress but also to your present survival!

There are two ways in which you can develop and improve your telephone skills.

1 Know the telephone system, its features and the related equipment in your organisation *backwards.* This is especially true if, as part of your job, you are operating a multiline telephone system yourself which receives incoming calls to the company.

2 Develop an impressive array of telephone techniques which will enable you to deal with any caller – from the chairman to a tricky customer to the tea-lady – with skill and aplomb.

Telephone equipment

There is a huge range of telephone equipment on the market, and that owned by your organisation will depend upon the volume of business carried out over the phone (which will determine the number of outside lines) and the size of the organisation (which will determine the number of extensions). There are basically two types of telephone system:

- a private automatic branch exchange (PABX) – the very large switchboard which is permanently manned by an operator
- a key telephone system or multiline, which is often used by smaller companies – though systems can be purchased which incorporate up to 80 extensions.

Also available are 'modular' systems which enable an expanding company to add on other elements to a basic key system. Additionally, many of the functions previously found only on PABXs are now available on many key systems – together with a few more which are quite inventive, eg an automatic door locking/unlocking facility.

The type of system installed can affect you in one of three ways.

- If a PABX is installed, and especially if this is digital (as most now are), there will be a range of functions you and your boss can use as extension holders. Many PAs never bother to master most of these, yet each one can help you to do your job more effectively.
- If a key system is installed then you may be working as an administrator in a small company, and part of your duties may involve operating an extension which is designated to act as the switchboard. In this case you will not only be screening calls for your own boss, but also for other senior staff.
- If the key system is large, it may warrant its own switchboard operator. In such a case you are once again a user – and need to know the features available on your system.

Finally, of course, many organisations have manager/secretary linked telephones for PAs or administrators and their bosses. This means that normally you will receive *all* incoming calls (unless you are out of the office), and are the initial point of contact for anyone trying to reach your boss. At the very least you must be able to put calls through quickly and efficiently – and know the range of correct responses to enable you to deal with a variety of situations.

Systems and features

All digital telephone systems contain a microprocessor which enables them not only to handle calls but to remember what they are doing and tell the operator by means of a small VDU screen; equally some systems can be linked to a full size VDU. In addition, extension users have a variety of facilities which were not previously available, eg all extension users (unless barred) can make their own outside calls, and contact other extensions direct, thereby leaving the operator free to concentrate on incoming calls and enquiries.

On the basis that there is nothing more offputting for a caller than to keep hearing the engaged signal – or to have to wait for ages in a queue to be answered – efficient switchboard operation is vital to the success of the organisation. For this reason, in very large organisations, one executive may be designated to oversee the management of the telephone system in terms of facilities for users, number of extensions and outside lines etc. He/she will be involved in any discussions whether to upgrade the equipment, and whether it should be bought, leased or rented. The advantage of leasing or renting is that equipment may be able to be changed or upgraded when required and the old machine doesn't have to be written off – nor do changes involve large amounts of capital expenditure. You may like to note that many modern switchboards can be programmed to record and monitor all usage, eg numbers of incoming calls and the days and times these were received. Such a record can help a manager decide whether or not the current system is becoming congested and a larger one is required.

Switchboards and key systems can be bought from a wide range of manufacturers and the latter are often sold by office supplies companies. An astute manager will obtain many quotations and compare the benefits and limitations of each system, together with full details of the installation and maintenance services and the ability to upgrade or change the equipment at a later date. The eventual decision to purchase is likely to be influenced by factors such as:

- the size of the company and whether or not it is expanding
- the volume of calls handled in an average day
- the total telecommunications requirements of the company
- the extent to which call logging is required
- the cost of the system and the budget available.

An expanding company can purchase a digital system which the operator can reprogram herself, eg by making new extensions and allocating a number to them (provided the switchboard isn't used to full capacity), by altering extension numbers, by making extensions inactive (eg if a room is converted for another use) and by taking exchange lines or private circuits out of use.

In addition, some models can be networked (linked) to fax machines, word processors and computers, and voice and fax messages which come in overnight can be stored and retrieved.

Finally, the manager must consider whether the network the company uses should be that operated by British Telecom (BT) or that operated by Mercury Communications.

SPECIAL NOTE

Many switchboards are operated by people who are visually handicapped. This is possible because modifications can be made to a switchboard eg tactile indicators (which make the keys easier to find), meters with braille markings, and a voice synthesiser so that a computer 'voice' keeps the operator aware of the status of all calls. In addition a talking address book system is also available on which can be recorded addresses and telephone numbers.

Applications for switchboard modifications are handled by the Royal National Institute for the Blind under the Aids to Employment Scheme and not by the telephone companies.

Telecommunications companies

There are now two telephone companies in the UK which compete in offering a wide range of telecommunications services, including a telephone network – BT and Mercury Communications. Both offer a public phone network and private circuits for companies who wish to have an exclusive line or lines (eg to branch offices). In this case the organisation pays for the rental of the line but *not* for calls made.

BT has the advantage of being the company most people think of first; having full operator services and a more widely accessible public network. In addition it has a sizeable marketing operation to keep its name in the public (and business) eye. For its part, Mercury claims its long distance calls are 20 per cent cheaper and its international calls are 14 per cent cheaper. In addition, Mercury charges only for the exact duration of the call, instead of rounding up the charge as BT does. Both provide fully itemised bills – BT only on request.

CHECK IT YOURSELF
Obtain a copy of the latest business catalogue from BT and information on the services provided by Mercury Communications. Both are 0800 numbers so your call is free. Dial 0800 800 855 for BT and 0800 424 194 for Mercury. Then compare the services each company offers.

Systems jargon

The range of facilities for both PABX extension users and key system users is comprehensive and known by its own jargon. Whilst this may vary a little from one system to another, below is an overview of the features you may have on your system.

Abbreviated dialling   Provides a shortened (coded) version of commonly used numbers. Keep these to a minimum (or keep your list handy) or you'll forget them. Use mainly for long IDD numbers.

Callback   Recalls an engaged extension as soon as it is free. Don't set this up and then wander out of your office without cancelling it!

Call barring   Enables a PABX operator to prevent certain extensions making certain types of call, eg IDD, directory enquiries etc. Frequently used when the company is economising but invaluable if many extensions could be 'open access'.

Call forward   Routes all calls on a specific extension to another (may be called *Follow me* – which is usually a more appropriate description)

Call logging   A system of telephone management whereby all calls from extensions are recorded, together with the units used, for costing purposes (see page 32).

Call sequencing   A system which can be connected to your telephone system and which automatically greets every caller with a pre-recorded message and then queues them. A further message is given if the caller is still holding after a specified time. The problem for the *caller* is that he is paying for the call from the moment the call is answered – yet still can't talk to anyone!

Call storage   Useful if you accept a call in an office other than your own – you effectively hold the call in the system until you can retrieve it again from your own phone.

Call waiting   A tone which signals to an extension user that another caller is trying to get through.

Conference calls   Enables several users (usually up to four) to speak to each other simultaneously.

Distinctive ringing   The difference in the ringing between external calls, internal calls and the diverted ringing signal.

Distinctive tones   Tones you hear on your system which confirm that certain facilities are in operation, eg call waiting, your call has been diverted etc. Know yours well or you won't understand what is happening.

Diversion   Can be used for all calls, for when there is no reply from your phone or if your phone is engaged. Rather than *you* operating the divert facility to anyone it is more likely that you will be on the receiving end if your boss is busy. Train him/her to warn you first! If an emergency occurs, on most systems the operator can override this and ring him/her anyway! NB if you work for several executives, try to avoid them all diverting their calls to you simultaneously!

Do not disturb   Shuts down an extension temporarily (see also *Diversion*).

Door phone   The ability of some key systems to be linked to a microphone on a locked door. Usually linked with a **door lock** so that the operator can unlock the door once the caller has been identified. Very useful for security when the reception area is a long way from the front door.

Earth recall key   The 'R' key which enables an extension user to put a call on 'hold' whilst making another call or transferring the call to another extension. Pressing the key a second time usually returns the caller to you – but check your system carefully for how this operates! Apart from any possible harm to your image there is no need to panic if you cut a caller off by mistake. With most systems the call will automatically be rerouted back to the switchboard.

Group hunting   The phone system searches through a number of phones linked as a specified group until one is free. Most systems can be programmed to hunt cyclically or sequentially. With the former the calls are spread evenly over all extensions in the group; with the latter the hunt always begins at the same phone (try to prevent this being yours!). The main point to remember is to keep group numbers small – otherwise the caller may be subjected to continuous ringing whilst the system keeps hunting!

Group listening   The ability to transfer an incoming call from the handset to a loudspeaker. Extremely useful if you're trying to speak to someone and find a relevant document at the same time (see also *Hands free*).

Hands free   The ability to make or receive calls without picking up the handset because you speak and listen through a loudspeaker instead. Not advisable for confidential calls!

Intrude   The ability of the operator to cut in to a call if something urgent occurs. An extension can be barred from intrusion – usually for reasons of confidentiality. Intrude is a useful facility to request of your operator if you are making a very urgent outside call to your boss and his/her phone is busy. Whether the operator complies or not will probably depend on the likely reaction of your boss!

Last number repeat   Automatically redials the last number you called.

Music on hold   Theoretically supposed to comfort the caller as he knows he has not been disconnected. In reality often an irritant. Very little soothes a caller who is kept waiting too long.

Night transfer/night service   The night system which operates when the switchboard operator has left and selected extensions are programmed to receive incoming calls. If you are in charge of the switchboard and forget to put it on to night service as you leave, no calls can be received by your company!

Notepad memory   A feature which enables you to store the next number you need while you're still on a call. Useful if your boss rings you, asks you to call someone and quickly gives you the number.

On–hook dialling   The ability to make a call whilst the handset is still on the hook, and to pick it up only when the person at the other end answers. Enables you to keep typing until the last possible moment!

Paging   The ability to access nominated extensions with a tannoy message. On some key systems the message comes through the loudspeakers of all extensions which are not in use – a feature which may or may not be welcomed.

Pickup group   A number of phones linked as a specified group where a call to any extension in the group can be answered by any other extension in the same group. Useful for a departmental office where it doesn't matter who answers. Equally you and your boss can be a group of two then you can pick up any calls from his/her phone if he/she is out of the office, by dialling a short code (and vice versa).

Secrecy button   Press this before you discuss your current call with someone else in the room. Putting your hand over the receiver is almost useless.

Shuttle   Alternating between two people by means of the recall key.

Trunk queuing   A feature whereby callers are placed in a waiting queue if the incoming lines are busy. See also *Call sequencing*.

Wait on busy Sending a signal to another extension user, who is in the middle of a call, to indicate that you want to speak to him. With most systems the trick is to keep holding until he answers you – if you put your phone down he'll have no-one on the line when he does.

SPECIAL NOTE
Training your boss to know the phone system will depend largely on how keen he/she is on gadgets! A natural enthusiast will play with the system for hours and probably show you a trick or two. If not, then you might have to do a little coaxing. Introduce the features one at a time, and then make out a quick reference sheet (such as the one you have just produced above) which your boss can keep in a handy place. Anyone who starts to use such a system well, yet normally avoids equipment and machinery like the plague, usually feels very proud of this type of achievement. Encourage this type of independence – it pays dividends. With luck, in a few weeks, your boss will not only be making his/her own telephone calls but also sending faxes *and* making photocopies when you're busy (see also Managing your boss, page 291).

Health and safety considerations

If you use any type of telephone system then there are certain facts you should bear in mind in relation to health and safety.

- Most switchboards have a series of air vents. Don't cover these up, poke about in them or spill liquid into them if you expect the equipment to continue functioning.
- Several headphone designs are available, and they can usually be connected to the switchboard at either side. Alternatively there are those which can be worn in the ear. An operator should be able to choose the design she feels most comfortable with. Needless to say, the headphone should be kept spotlessly clean. If there are several operators check if the sponge or section at the end of the headphone can be changed.
- Office telephones are used by many people and it is therefore important that the receivers are kept clean and disinfected regularly. There is a variety of sprays on the market for this purpose. Some companies have a contract with a telephone cleaning company to clean all their phones regularly.

SPECIAL NOTE
Organisations which operate in a security sensitive area and are worried about bugging or industrial espionage, can buy an add–on system which links their telephones to a cryptographic device. This scrambles all calls and makes them unintelligible to eavesdroppers.

Additional telephone equipment

In addition to the basic telephone system, you are likely to be involved in the operation of other related equipment, eg:

- bleepers or pagers to contact someone out of the office
- a telephone answering machine to enable you to give and/or receive messages when the office is closed
- a mobile phone which is used by your boss when travelling.

Modern equipment is so sophisticated that in many cases the systems can be linked, eg your boss can call in to the office answering machine via a mobile phone and access any messages and even reset the tape. Alternatively the answering machine can be programmed to page your boss after a message has been received. This is a very useful facility if an urgent and important call is expected.

Bleepers/pagers

Today the terms *bleeper* and *pager* are virtually interchangeable – and there is a wide range on the market. Some pagers are tone-only, but can emit a range of up to four tones to distinguish between callers, eg one tone each for home, general office use, PA and customers. Others give a numeric only display. A further type displays an alpha-numeric message. Pagers come in all shapes and sizes and are designed to clip onto jackets or fit into pockets – one is even designed as a pen with a tiny VDU screen on the barrel. Some are silent – instead of bleeping they vibrate – so that important meetings or even social occasions aren't disturbed.

Tone-only pagers are generally used for people who understand the bleep to mean 'call me'. These are the cheapest type available. Numeric display pagers are often used in conjunction with a PABX system. A person is paged automatically by the system when an extension user keys the special pager number and follows this with his/her own extension number. The pager will bleep and show the extension number the holder should call.

If your boss carries a numeric pager when away from the office, it is useful to set up a code system so that the type of message can be identified from the code received, eg:

- 0 + number = ring that number
- 10 = call office
- 20 = call answering machine
- 30 = call home etc.

Other details can be added such as:

- 90 (+ time and date) = meeting arranged for that time/date
- 91 (+ time and date) = meeting for that time/date cancelled.

In addition, a severity code can be added to give some idea of urgency, eg:

- 101 call office (panic!)
- 102 call office within the next hour
- 103 call office some time today.

This saves your boss from screeching the car to a halt at the nearest telephone box – or rushing out of an important meeting, only to find that you wanted to issue a reminder about a dental check-up at 9 am the following morning.

Finally, customers can be allocated their own code number, so that the person with the bleeper can identify which customer has to be called. Again a further digit can be added to denote the panic level – ad infinitum.

Alpha-numeric pagers do not need a code because the message can be sent in words. The most sophisticated model not only holds up to 56 messages, but can also be programmed to display share updates, weather information and latest flight information automatically from different sources. The message can comprise up to 90 characters (about 15 words) which are displayed on a small screen.

Users of BTs numeric or message pagers can access a free service called Message Confirmation which can help them collect messages they have missed while they were outside a coverage zone, travelling on the Underground or moving around with their pagers switched off. By telephoning 0345 010555 at a local call rate from anywhere in the country, paging bureau customers can have all their messages for the past three days relayed to them.

! **SPECIAL NOTE**
It is never advisable to give a customer your boss's pager number – *always* act as the 'go-between'. Otherwise you will find that without a screening process in place, some customers will be in contact any time, day or night, even with non-urgent queries.

Equally, don't use 'panic' mode unnecessarily – otherwise your boss will become attuned to this and often keep you waiting before calling, assuming that you are simply flapping again! Rather like the boy who cried wolf, on the occasion that it *is* really urgent, you have only yourself to blame if there is no immediate response to your calls!

Contacting a pager
There are two methods of contacting a pager:

- a bureau
- direct input.

Both BT and Mercury operate a **pager Bureau Service**. You contact the bureau, ask for the pager number and give the message – in code or words depending on the type of bleeper.

The bureau contacts a central computer which signals all transmitters in the area. The computer is programmed with codes for each bleeper and therefore knows the zones or regions to which it must transmit the message. The zones are specified when the pager is first purchased.

Direct input means that you are contacting the computer direct and this can be done from an MF (multi-frequency) telephone (the type with star and gate keys), telex, packet switching (see page 236) and other services such as Datel and Keypage. You communicate with the computer by keying in codes of figures, star and gate. A computer voice acts as a guide. If you are going out of the office, you can program the answering machine to do the job for you! See below.

SPECIAL NOTE
If your boss frequently travels to Europe you can *rent* a pager from BT which is compatible with European paging regions (called the Euromessage Pager). There is a Message Confirmation service also available for Euromessage pager holders if they wish to collect messages they may have missed.

Answering machines

These are now common features in many offices. Whilst their obvious purpose is to play a short pre-recorded message and then tape the caller's response, today's machines offer a wide variety of features and some are even combined with a fax machine (see next section).

Announcement only mode   Gives a pre-recorded announcement without allowing the caller to leave a message.

Call screening   Enables you to listen in and decide whether to answer personally.

Handset listening   Messages can be listened to over the handset rather than through a loudspeaker, for privacy.

Memo message   Allows you to leave a message for your boss (or for him/her to leave one for you – even from a remote location).

Message forward   The machine can be programmed to forward a coded message to a specific telephone number. If the number relates to a numeric pager, the machine can relay a code set up to tell the user to contact the answering machine as soon as possible. (See *Tone remote control*.)

Tone remote control   Means the answering machine can be activated from a remote location by using the buttons on an MF telephone.

Two-way recording   Enables you to record both sides of a telephone conversation.

User codes   Usually used with *tone remote control* the code must be keyed before the machine will activate – to prevent unauthorised access.

Voice synthesis   Prefaces each message with the time and day, may also be capable of reading out telephone numbers in memory, prompting an executive contacting the machine from a distant location etc.

SPECIAL NOTE
If your boss travels abroad to countries where MF phones may not be available, it is a good idea to purchase a special keytone device which, when held over the mouthpiece of a non-MF phone, enables the user to gain access to the machine.

Mobile phones

More commonly known as 'car phones', these too are growing in popularity. All operate by means of a cellnet system through which they are signalled. There are two rival companies – Vodafone and Cellnet, both of which operate their own cellular network. Some mobile phones are very small, and can fit into a pocket or briefcase. These are known as **hand portables**. Many of the phones which are permanently fitted into cars are slightly larger and have a separate charging unit which can be used to recharge the batteries.

   Mobile phones incorporate many of the features of other telephone systems, eg abbreviated dialling, divert, last number repeat, notepad memory and conference calls. All mobile phones designed for use in a car offer the hands-free option so that a driver needn't pick up the handset to listen to an incoming call – which could obviously be dangerous. Instead he/she can speak through a microphone attached to the sun visor or dashboard.

   The latest mobile phones now offer a message taking facility, which operates if the cellphone is busy or switched off. In effect, this is a mobile phone and answering machine combined.

SPECIAL NOTE
If your boss regularly uses a mobile phone – especially one without a recharger – always keep a spare battery in your desk drawer for emergencies. Alternatively, try to persuade him/her to keep one in his/her briefcase.

Telephone services

There are several telephone services which can be used both by you and by your company and many are given in your Phone Book. Start by reading the information pages and noting down the numbers that business customers should call for advice or information.

   Other services business may use or require include:

For customers

0800 and International 0800 numbers   An 0800 number enables potential customers to call the company free of charge to ask for product information.

0345 numbers   These numbers enable potential customers to telephone for the price of a local call – regardless of their location.

Freefone   In this case the customer contacts the operator and asks for FreeFone plus the name of your company. The operator logs the calls including their location thereby supplying a market research function for the company.

 SPECIAL NOTE
Are you using 0800 numbers properly yourself? If you are asked to undertake any research on particular products, then before you start hunting for addresses of major suppliers, telephone the operator and ask if there is an 0800 or freephone number for that company. In the course of a year you can save your company a considerable amount of money in your search for information – and find it more quickly!

For executives

Chargecard   This enables an executive to call from any telephone, either in the UK or overseas, and charge the call to the company's account with BT. The international traveller can use the card in conjunction with the UK Direct service which resolves any possible language problems (see Chapter 4, Arranging travel, page 221).

Voicebank messaging   This enables a cellphone user to have a voice mailbox (similar to Telecom Gold – see next section – but for voice messages only) which can be accessed via a PIN number to leave or retrieve messages.

For you

Directory enquiries   This service is now free only from a payphone and for blind and disabled people who cannot use a printed phone book. Companies who do not wish to run up a huge phone bill with the directory enquiry service have three choices. They can:

- buy directories for the areas they need
- subscribe to Phone Base, which gives the operator access to BT's database of names and addresses via a PC. A charge is made each time the database is accessed.
- buy a Phone Disc – a compact disc holding all the listings of the UK Phone Books. Users need an IBM compatible PC and a disc reader attachment.

Information services   The only information service operated by BT is the speaking clock – all the others are operated by private companies.

International   See page 35.

SPECIAL NOTE

It is useful to collect numbers for information services you may use regularly, eg motoring information (or the latest cricket scores!) In addition, add to these other phone services which you could find useful, eg the Interflora Flowerline – so that you can order a bouquet of flowers to be sent to another part of the country without stirring from your desk – at times when your local florist would be closed.

Telephone management and accounting systems

All the facilities available from telephone companies assist an organisation to maximise its communications with its own staff and the outside world. However, they all cost money – and telephone accounts for large companies can run into many thousands of pounds per quarter.

Different accounting systems are available in different organisations. In one organisation the account may be settled and the total amount split equally among departments in terms of costing. In another, each department may be responsible for its own expenditure. Either way, the emphasis will be on:

• keeping costs to a minimum
• monitoring the calls made and services used – for cost allocation and/or to observe usage and take remedial steps if there is obvious wastage.

Many call logging systems are available which can be connected to both PABX and key systems. These enable a report to be generated at regular intervals of all usage, together with details such as department, extension number, number called, duration of call, units used and total cost. The exact format of the report can be determined by the company.

Many switchboards will give the same, or similar information, but only on the VDU – not as a print-out. If you do not have separate call logging equipment then you may have to devise a form on which you can enter the information. You should note that most switchboards have a limit as to the number of calls they can retain in memory and you obviously need to access these before the memory is full – or recent information will no longer be stored. After accessing the information you must remember to reset the metering facility to zero for the next accounting period.

A final point to remember is that VAT can be reclaimed on all telephone accounts. Therefore, if your executives use a BT Chargecard (so that the calls are billed on the normal account) this amount is easier to identify and reclaim. VAT cannot be reclaimed just on the word of an executive and an expense claim form!

As a PA, you will obviously be expected to know all the tricks of the trade to keep your call charges low! This topic is dealt with in more detail on page 44.

Using the telephone

The telephone is an important tool of the trade and it is important that you learn to use it skilfully. Your manner and telephone technique can make all the difference when it comes to soothing an irritated client or passing on 'tricky' information. In addition, you should be a superb role model for your junior staff – so that *by example*, as much as by training, you set the standards for how telephone calls are dealt with in your section.

CHECK IT YOURSELF
If you are concerned about your own telephone technique, worried about how to make difficult calls or how to get rid of callers who simply won't say 'goodbye', then send for the BT booklet *Be your own boss* by phoning 0800 800 878. It contains useful information and hints and tips on all these problems.

Making telephone calls

You will have to make a wide variety of telephone calls as an integral part of your job, both on your own behalf and on behalf of others, including your boss. The calls may be to internal extensions, or external – either national or international. Your boss may prefer you to make all outgoing calls – and only put calls through once the person to whom he/she wishes to speak is on the line.

SPECIAL NOTE
If people to whom you want to speak are unavailable then try to find out when they will be back. If possible arrange that you will call them again later rather than leave a message for them to call you. This is an old PA trick and has three advantages:

- It enables you to cope with the unreliable types who never respond to messages!
- You can give your executive details of exactly when the person should be available – rather than have both of you hanging on for a call which doesn't come
- You keep the initiative – and therefore retain control of the situation.

This strategy is just as relevant (if not more so) for external calls.

External calls

There are several 'golden rules' for making effective telephone calls.

- Make sure you have the right telephone number and know to whom you want to speak and, preferably, their extension number.
- Have all your facts to hand – relevant documents, files etc.
- Jot down headings for what you want to say so that you won't forget anything. Make sure your topics are in a logical order or you will confuse the listener completely!

- Only make the call when you have your shorthand notebook in front of you and a pen in your hand.
- If your call is answered by a switchboard ask for the person or extension you want. Most operators today don't ask 'who is calling' – this type of screening is usually undertaken departmentally. However, the operator may screen calls for senior staff – so be prepared to give your name, title and name of your company. Know your telephone alphabet so that you can spell any difficult letters if you have an obscure name (see page 41).
- Have a strategy as to what you will do if the person you require is unavailable eg ask for someone else or call back later (as above).
- Be prepared to leave a message on an answering machine if necessary. Don't start talking until after the bleep! Keep your message short and to the point or the tape may run out and you will be cut off. *Don't* forget to leave your telephone number!
- When you are through to the person you require (or their PA) clearly identify yourself (as above) and state the reason for your call.
- Be prepared to check and question anything about which you are uncertain or for which your information is incomplete.
- If anything complex is discussed, or if names, dates and figures form part of the conversation, always 'review' these at the end of the call to check they are correct.
- Remember that the person who initiates a call should, technically, be the person who ends it. This is you! After the review of information it is fairly easy to thank the person for their help and say goodbye.
- If you have to take a message on behalf of your boss, write or type it out immediately you complete the call – while it is fresh in your mind.

 SPECIAL NOTE

You are doing your own image no good at all if, the next time you are trying to reach an executive in another company for your boss, you refuse to connect him/her to the PA if the person wanted is away. If the PA is worth her salt she can cope with the call and process it – even if she has to check with her own boss and call back later. If you imply she isn't worth speaking to, what does that make your boss think about you?

Internal calls

Make sure you have a complete list of internal extension holders close to hand. Obviously your tone and manner to colleagues will be more informal – though be careful you don't appear too chatty with senior staff. If the person you are trying to contact is senior to your boss (eg the MD) be prepared to connect him/her with that person's PA, rather than expect the MD to come on to the line and then wait for your boss to be connected!

A difficulty frequently encountered is where two PAs 'clash' over who is to be put through to whom! It may sound amusing to hear two PAs trying to gain some sort of moral ascendancy by insisting that their executive takes precedence and it is therefore the other PA's executive who has to wait, but in reality it can cause needless arguments. In cases where the hierarchy is clear, the general rule is that the more senior person never has to wait. The difficulty arises where the two executives are of equal status, eg the Sales Director and the Purchasing Director, neither of whom wishes to give precedence to the other. The best solution is for the two PAs to persuade their bosses to contact each other direct. If not, the PAs must try to come to some agreement themselves (a rota basis?). No solution is entirely satisfactory in such circumstances.

International calls

International Direct Dialling (IDD) has actually made life worse for those PAs who dread making international calls. At least when all calls were connected by the international operator there was always help at hand if it was required. Today, unless you deliberately use the operator service (which is more expensive) then you are on your own for most places in the world!

Common fears are:

- you can't recognise the tones you hear – and don't know whether the phone is ringing, engaged or even unobtainable
- the person who answers cannot speak a word of English (the biggest worry of them all!).

There are ways round both these problems – see the list below.

Useful tips for phoning abroad

Don't do *anything* until you've thought through the possible problems.

- Check the time difference (use the Phone Book) and don't forget to allow for British Summer Time if it is in force. You will make yourself very unpopular if you ring one of your American representatives at home in the middle of the night.
- Check the tones you will hear (see below).
- Consider if language is going to be a problem, and to what extent. Non-English speaking countries fall into three categories:
  - those whose language someone in your company can speak fairly fluently
  - those whose language is vaguely recognisable (if simple words are used) because someone has visited them on holiday
  - those whose language is beyond everyone.

In addition, you need to consider the country and the region you are calling. Some countries (eg Holland) take pride in the fact that virtually every inhabitant speaks English. Others do not. Equally, if you are ringing, say, France, there is a vast difference between the likelihood of a switchboard operator for a large multi–national in Paris speaking English and the hotel proprietor of a small inn in the Dordogne!

If language is a problem what can you do? You have three options.

1 Hope that someone speaks English and have a list of how to say 'Do you speak English, please?' in a variety of languages so that you can cope with the person who answers. If you feel brave enough, start with 'Good morning' – but don't worry too much about this – 'Hello' is recognised almost the whole world over.

This idea isn't as silly as it sounds and frequently works well. If you need the phrase for a language you never use then write it phonetically – it's your pronunciation which is going to matter here, not your spelling! For a response listen intently for anything which sounds vaguely like the word 'moment' in English – which is also commonly used – especially on the Continent. This usually means the operator cannot speak English herself – but is finding someone who can. Be patient. Usually your lifesaver is next on the line!

You should note that it is normally not advisable to increase your list of phrases, eg by adding 'Can I speak to Mr . . ., please'. If you do, you are in dire peril of the operator gaining the mistaken impression that you are fluent and answering you with what seems to be a stream of unintelligible gibberish.

2 If you are ringing a customer, find the representative who deals with this area. After all, presumably he must survive when he visits them. Either have him by your side when you make the call or ask him for the name of his English-speaking contact and place a person to person call via the operator.

3 In cases of dire need, use BT's interpreter service. In addition to providing on–line interpreting, the service can also be used to translate documents, letters and contracts and interpreters are also available on a face-to-face basis. If you want to be cost conscious then ring round your local translation bureaux for one which provides a similar service and set up a three-way conference call.

If you do speak to someone direct, even if their English seems faultless remember that they are a foreign national and avoid slang, colloquial and regional expressions and long or complicated words. You are trying to establish communication – not test linguistic skills.

Beware also of assuming that talking to your contact in another English speaking country will be plain sailing. For instance, someone once said of the UK and the USA that they were 'two nations separated by a common language.' Think how the simple sentence 'I was mad about my flat' would be interpreted on either side of the Atlantic (bearing in mind that both the words 'mad' and 'flat' have different meanings!).

Your other problem area could be line faults and difficulties getting through. If you have a bad line hang up and try again – don't struggle on – these days a good international call sounds as if it is coming from just down the road. Bear in mind that if your caller is very far away then you will have a slight delay on the line. This becomes apparent the second you try to interrupt one of their sentences – only to realise they hadn't finished speaking! The way to cope with this is mentally to count to about five before you start to reply. You'll soon get used to this and it will save any embarrassing moments.

If you have difficulties getting through then check the number with International Directory Enquiries on 153 or dial the international operator on 155.

> **CHECK IT YOURSELF**
> BT produce a handbook called *Phoning Abroad* which is invaluable to anyone who has to make international calls. It also contains a list of all the tones you may hear for each country of the world. The booklet is free if you call 0800 800 878.

Training your juniors to make calls

Start slowly! Make sure your juniors know the basics of good telephone technique and then entrust them with a simple call (preferably an internal call to an understanding colleague) where the outcome isn't very important. Make them prepare well and check their notes. Then move away – or you will inhibit them completely. Afterwards give praise where it is due and constructive advice, tactfully, if necessary. You are wise to refrain from asking your junior staff to initiate calls until they have had considerable practice in receiving them (see below).

Receiving calls

Both you and your junior staff must be capable of dealing with a wide range of callers and visitors – both over the telephone and face to face. *Your* telephone technique must be first rate as *you* are the one who will have to deal with all the difficult calls, the senior staff both within and outside the organisation and receive your boss's calls. Probably more important to you as a supervisor is that your junior staff must be similarly capable. This will have two benefits – your section will be praised, not criticised *and* there will be fewer callers passed on to you because your juniors can't cope or don't know what to do next. It is essential that your juniors are fully conversant with the telephone system in use and all the services which are available to them.

You must take (and make) time to train them in the correct telephone technique. Remember, however, that many junior staff in particular are nervous about answering the telephone and that it is therefore essential that you try to build their confidence in this respect.

Try not to say 'Slow down, will you'; choose instead to say 'You've got the right approach – but can you take it a little more slowly?'.

 SPECIAL NOTE
Telephone users are sometimes encouraged to smile when answering the telephone in the hope that they will sound pleasant and friendly. The reverse side of the coin is to encourage them to stand up when taking calls (particularly internal calls from people they know) which is meant to discourage them from talking too long. Be careful in instilling this practice into junior staff, however, – you don't want them to bang down the receiver on the Chief Executive!

External calls

There is a sense of the unknown about external calls – the call could be coming from down the street or the other side of the world (though it helps if you can at least recognise the ringing tone which differentiates it as an outside call!). The person with whom you are dealing could be of high or low rank, their business may be simple or complicated. First two rules – be prepared for anything and never answer a telephone without a pen in your hand and a notepad by your side. Teach your juniors to do the same. Then train them steadily in the standard responses to make and the situations they may encounter.

Standard opening

You should make sure that your staff are aware of the standard opening. Much depends on your organisation's ethos. Some prefer a light-hearted approach such as 'Hi, I'm Julie, can I help you?'. Others, who prefer a more traditional approach, may collapse on the spot if they hear your staff give such a response. If there is a standard approach such as 'Good morning, Whitehall Carpets Ltd' or 'Sales Department, Margaret Douglas speaking' train your staff to use it automatically.

Do encourage your staff to identify themselves (even if sometimes they are reluctant to do so in case a complaint is made about them).

Screening calls

Make sure your staff know how to obtain any relevant initial information eg:

- 'May I have your name?'
- 'To whom do you wish to speak?'
- 'On what matter?'

This last question sometimes causes problems. Some callers will not want to state their business – either because they want to 'bluff' their way into talking to an executive (in the case of a salesman, for instance) or because they do not wish to tell a junior (or even you) their business.

TEST YOURSELF

Discuss as a group what action should be taken in such circumstances. Consider such factors as:

- your boss's preferences – does he/she strongly object if a caller is put through whose business is unknown – or is he/she prepared to accept that you may have difficulties in this area and is willing to help you out on occasions?
- the possibility of asking the caller to write in for an appointment (although this could offend a potentially important client).

When your boss is not available

Ensure that everyone knows who should deal with a situation when the person to whom the caller wishes to speak is unavailable (either genuinely or otherwise!).

One of the following approaches is to be recommended:

- 'I'm sorry, Mr Darken's extension is engaged. Do you wish to hold on?' (provided you know that Mr Darken will speak to the caller eventually).

  Note that allowing a caller to wait indefinitely is not good practice – even if your telephone system does attempt to soothe him by playing musical selections during his wait. Refer back to him if the wait is prolonged to see if he wishes to accept an alternative approach.
- 'I'm sorry, Mr Darken is out today. May I take a message?' (if he is actually out or does not want to speak to the caller).
- 'I'm sorry, Mr Darken is not in at the moment. Can I ask him to ring you back?' (if the caller is known, important or someone to whom Mr Darken is anxious to speak).
- 'I'm sorry, Mr Darken is in a meeting at the moment. Can someone else help you?'

  This is one of the most useful tactics to use – provided, of course, that someone else *is* willing to speak to the caller. Why not you? As a PA you should be able to deal with many matters yourself and it is very helpful to the junior staff if they know they can make this response and then transfer callers to you. Remember, too, that it is sometimes psychologically sound to arrange for a call to be put through to you rather than to answer it direct – it increases your importance and makes the caller feel he/she is not being 'fobbed off' by someone very menial.

TEST YOURSELF

If your boss is in an important meeting and a telephone call comes through from someone to whom you know he/she wishes to speak, what should you do?

What if the caller insists it is urgent but you are not sure whether or not your boss wishes to be interrupted? (See Chapter 8, Servicing meetings, page 386 for details on how best to pass on information to an executive taking part in a meeting.)

Taking a message

Your staff should be able to take a message correctly. Make sure that they know how to complete a telephone message form (see the illustration below for an example) and emphasise that a telephone message pad should always be kept by the telephone – otherwise their desks will be littered with odd scraps of paper covered in scribbled notes.

Pay particular attention to getting them to give *all* the details – not just some.

EXAMPLE OF TELEPHONE MESSAGE FORM

```
MESSAGE FORM              DEPT: . . . . . . . . . . . .

TIME: . . . . . . . . . . . . . . . .   DATE: . . . . . . . . . . . . . .

CALLER:

COMPANY/ORGANISATION:

TEL. NO.                            EXT. NO.

Telephone                          ┌─────────────────┐
Returned your call                 ├─────────────────┤
Called                             ├─────────────────┤
Sent in a message                  └─────────────────┘

Would like you to return call      ┌─────────────────┐
Wants to see you                   ├─────────────────┤
Send message through reception     └─────────────────┘

Will telephone again               ┌─────────────────┐
Will call in again                 └─────────────────┘

Message:       . . . . . . . . . . . . . . . . . . . . . . . . . . . . . . . . . . . . . . . .
               . . . . . . . . . . . . . . . . . . . . . . . . . . . . . . . . . . . . . . . .
               . . . . . . . . . . . . . . . . . . . . . . . . . . . . . . . . . . . . . . . .
Taken by:      . . . . . . . . . . . . . . . . . . . . . . . . . . . . . . . . . . . . . . . .
```

TEST YOURSELF

You have been out of the office all morning. When you return you find that your newest junior has left you the following messages.

   a S Jones called about late delivery of order. Ring back.

   b Mr Lionel Foster rang – very angry. He wants you to ring him back within the hour on 0345 62310.

   c José Ramirez returned your call. He says 'yes'.

   d Louise Tenby rang about the price of the new accounts software package – she says she wants more details of the other one.

1 What important information has she omitted in each case?

2 In each case, can you identify the action you *could* have taken prior to contacting the caller, had you received more information, or the extra work you will have to undertake *because* important information was omitted?

Lucid message taking

Start by pointing out the importance of writing down proper names and figures correctly.

Proper names

Junior staff can become easily embarrassed when they do not hear a name correctly on the first occasion. Train them not to guess but to ask the caller to repeat his/her name and, if necessary, to spell it out.

To help them you could arrange for a copy of the standard telephone alphabet to be available within easy reading distance of the telephone, ie

A	Alfred	N	Nellie
B	Benjamin	O	Oliver
C	Charlie	P	Peter
D	David	Q	Queen
E	Edward	R	Robert
F	Frederick	S	Samuel
G	George	T	Tommy
H	Harry	U	Uncle
I	Isaac	V	Victor
J	Jack	W	William
K	King	X	X-ray
L	London	Y	Yellow
M	Mary	Z	Zebra

It is also a good idea for you to encourage them to write down phonetically any unusual names of callers – particularly if they have to put them through to someone else, eg if a Jacques Mitterand telephones, your junior could jot down 'Zhak Meeteron'– even if the pronunciation isn't great, at least it is better than a meaningless mumble to the recipient of the transferred call.

Figures

Emphasise the importance of absolute accuracy when writing down figures. Make sure that your juniors aren't reluctant to double check figures, preferably by using the British Telecom technique, ie:

- pronounce 5 as 'fife' (emphasis on the 'f')
- pronounce 9 as 'nine' (emphasis on the 'n's)
- pronounce 0 as 'oh' when it occurs singly in a group of other figures, eg 102. Where it is used more than once, however, '100' is read as 'one hundred', '2000' is read as 'two thousand' etc

- where a long string of numbers has to be read out, it should be read in groups of two, preferably with a single number at the beginning, eg 987654321 should be read as 9, 87, 65, 43, 21
- if there are two '0's in the middle of a long string of numbers, eg 60032 they should be read as 'double oh' etc (unless it splits up a pair, eg 6500321, which should be read as 6, 5 'oh', 'oh' 3, 21).

Key facts

Train your staff to recognise the key facts in a conversation as the essential components of a message and distinguish these from waffle and pleasantries.

SPECIAL NOTE
- An alternative way of coping with the figure 0 is to read it as 'zero' rather than 'oh'. This is completely unmistakable over the telephone and is now becoming common practice in many organisations.
- Do make sure your juniors know they need to check that urgent messages have actually been received and do *not* just leave them on desks if the occupant is absent – especially if you aren't around to keep a weather eye on the situation. One executive had a fruitless 150 mile round trip one night to a non-existent meeting, all because a junior member of staff had never checked that he had received a frantic message saying the meeting was cancelled

Verbal messages

You are too experienced ever to pass on certain messages from your boss to a caller without first 'translating' them, eg 'Tell him to clear off; I'm busy,' or 'Tell him to get up here right away.' Make sure your juniors know they must do the same!

TEST YOURSELF
Re-translate the following comments into a more diplomatic form.

1 'Tell that idiot to get that report on my desk by this afternoon – or else.'

2 'I don't care if she does want to speak to me – tell her I'll not be available until hell freezes over.'

3 'Tell him that if he phones once more pestering me for an answer he'll get very short shrift.'

SPECIAL NOTE
For new juniors a telephone check list is helpful. It can be used as the basis for initial training and as an 'aide memoire' for later use (see the illustration opposite).

Internal calls

In some respects your staff will find calls from internal staff easier to handle. They will know who they are, what position they hold in the organisation – and their various personalities. (If they don't, then appraise them quickly!) In general the information can be more

```
TELEPHONE MESSAGE CHECK LIST FOR JUNIOR STAFF
```

1 Make sure that a telephone message pad and pencil are
  always available near the telephone. Use the pre-printed
  form as an aide memoire when you take a message.
2 Your message should contain the following information:
  ● the date and time it was received
  ● the name and department/division of the person to whom
    it is addressed
  ● the message itself including the name of the sender,
    the name of the company (where applicable), the
    telephone number (plus extension) or fax number, as
    detailed an account as possible for what is required.
3 Remember to ask for any words or information which you
  have not quite understood to be spelled out.
4 On pre-printed forms, make sure you tick the correct
  box(es). If the sender is awaiting a return call and you
  forget to tick that box, he will be justifiably annoyed.
5 Write clearly. Remember to take particular care over
  numbers and amounts: it is easy to write a 3 which looks
  like an 8 and vice versa.
6 Pass on all messages as quickly as possibly, normally in
  chronological order – unless one is so important that it
  takes priority. (If in doubt, ask your PA.)

informal (bearing in mind the seniority of the caller) though your juniors should be discouraged from being too chatty, personal or even casual with internal callers. There are usually fewer problems for you in deciding whether or not the call should be transferred to your boss. Even so you should be aware of any 'priority' system which exists (either officially or unofficially). In some organisations the MD expects to be connected immediately even if the person to whom he wishes to speak is already talking to someone else. If this is accepted policy you may have to use the 'intrude' or 'override' facility on your telephone system to alert your executive.

There may also be a problem in deciding who is and who is not allowed to have an outside line for personal calls (though this is more likely to affect any of your staff who operate the switchboard, rather than those who work on reception). Even if a company policy exists, there is always someone who will try to 'beat the system'.

You should ask your juniors to report constant requests, any type of pestering or even emotional blackmail to you, as you are in a better position to raise the matter with the member of staff concerned than they are. If your informal approach of reminding them pleasantly of company policy does not work, then a quiet word to your boss may help. (You're not telling tales – merely trying to avoid your junior staff becoming involved in embarrassing arguments.)

TEST YOURSELF

If it is company policy that personal calls cannot be received by employees, you may have to be tactful in dealing with an outside call which is of a personal nature. What should you say in such circumstances? What would you do if the caller says it is an emergency?

Keeping costs down

In most organisations there is considerable emphasis on keeping the costs of telephone calls down. You will have to train your juniors well in this respect by making sure they know the cheapest times to make both national *and* international calls (which depends on the country being called). The duration is important – teach them how to end a call, and *not* to hold on for someone who is engaged. Equally they should show the same courtesy in return. If there is a need to find additional information to answer an enquiry then it should be company policy to call back later, rather than expecting the caller to hold on whilst they find it.

Be very firm with junior staff who try to use the telephone to make personal calls. Most companies these days have a payphone installed for this purpose. Tying up company lines to chat to a friend is not acceptable behaviour.

Difficult calls

These may come from outside or inside the organisation – and you may have to make them or receive them. Typical ones are given below.

1 The MD pressing for a report your boss should have completed yesterday. You are asked to stall him/her for now!

2 A caller pressing for confidential information he/she claims your boss promised yesterday. Your boss is out until tomorrow.

3 Your boss asking you to ring the MD and say he/she would prefer not to attend Friday's Board Meeting because of a conflicting appointment. However, your boss doesn't want to upset the MD so wants you to 'read the signals', back off and agree to his/her attending if the MD sounds irritated.

4 The Press calling for information following the dismissal of an employee who is now claiming sexual harassment.

5 Your most important customer ringing to complain that she is having dreadful problems and if she doesn't speak to your boss immediately she will cancel negotiations for the new contract. At that particular moment your boss is in mid-air on the way to Vancouver.

TEST YOURSELF

Before you read further make notes on how you would deal with *each* of the situations given above.

Strategies for action

No book can ever detail the full range of difficult situations you are likely to encounter – or give you definitive answers. Much depends on the situation, the relationship with the caller and the background. Facts you might like to consider are given below.

- People who complain should always be allowed to run out of steam before you intervene. Take down all the details, be sympathetic but non-committal and, if your boss is absent and they are important, ask another executive to call them back – pronto.
- Developing a sixth sense so that you accurately represent your boss takes time and experience – and is easier if your boss plays a straightforward rather than devious game. The only trick you can try is to remain fairly ambivalent until the last moment, when you will have more clues with which to weigh up the situation. Only then commit yourself. (On the basis that attack is often the best form of defence, if you have to handle very difficult situations and they go wrong, you could always claim it was unfair that you were asked to do the job in the first place!)
- Always err on the side of caution in respect of confidential information. Far better that someone is inconvenienced for a day or two than you reveal a 'state' secret! So far as the Press are concerned there is a phrase many people use called 'off the record'. If you make it clear that you are speaking off the record nothing you say *should* be quoted - but don't bank on it and don't get labelled 'company spokeswoman' unless you are reading an *official* statement.

    Assuming you try, 'Completely off the record I'm not the person who should be dealing with this as I know absolutely nothing about it. You would have to speak to my boss personally and, no, I don't know where he is at the moment.' Tomorrow morning you read in the press 'Mr Glover, the executive involved in the case, was not available for comment. It is understood he has gone away to an unknown destination.'

    Draw your own conclusions.

For all these reasons you will have to use your own judgement and initiative. Wherever possible try to keep your communications with other people simple, straightforward and unambiguous but be very aware of the 'tone' and 'mood' of the conversation and the way in which a recipient *might* interpret your message. With practice and perception, you can develop a wide variety of skills which will help you to negotiate not only with people in business, but in many situations you will meet in your personal life as well.

ACTIVITY SECTION

Individual tasks

1 Your organisation exports many goods to the USA and Canada and frequently makes calls to both its customers and area offices. Recently operations have been extended to include Bermuda and the Bahamas and agents have been appointed to cover each territory.

Your executive is concerned that no one knows the cheapest time to contact these areas. In addition, a junior clerk recently upset an American representative by telephoning in the middle of the night.

He has asked you to:

a obtain a copy of the latest business charges leaflet

b from this, work out the times of cheap, standard and peak rate calls

c to note the local time for the following areas against each charge rate: Calgary and Toronto; Chicago and San Francisco; Bahamas and Bermuda

d type your information in a simple table for the benefit of all staff.

2 You are eager to delegate the making of telephone calls to your junior, but concerned that some types of calls may be too difficult for her to cope with. From the list of calls given below, state:

a whether you would give her this job immediately, later or never

b the training you consider she would need beforehand

- booking hotel accommodation
- ringing the production department (weekly) with summarised information extracted from the weekly sales report
- ringing the MD's office to try to change an appointment time
- ringing the photocopier company to report a fault
- complaining to the photocopier company when no one has appeared after 24 hours
- booking a table in a restaurant
- ringing the tax office to give them information they have requested about a director's expenses
- contacting your boss urgently to ask him/her to call in to see a customer about an emergency on the way back to the office
- ringing around all representatives to try to find the best date to hold an urgent meeting, without any representative having to cancel a crucial appointment
- ringing the Press to read out an official statement following an employee's successful claim for unfair dismissal.

3 Read the following telephone conversation.

Ramon (*your office junior*)	'Hello.'
Caller	'Have I got the right department?'
Ramon	'Depends on who you want.'
Caller	'I wanted the Management Department.'
Ramon	'You've got it – what do you want?'
Caller	'Well, I'd like some information about an accountancy course.'

Ramon	'We've lots of them – can't you give me more of a clue?'
Caller	'Well, not really – I've an AAT intermediate qualification but I took the exam a few years ago now and I'd really like some advice as to what to do next.'
Ramon	'Well, I'm here.'
Caller	'Yes, but I need some professional advice'.
Ramon	'I do work here you know – I'm not just passing through for a visit.'
Caller	'I didn't mean to offend you – it's just that I'm rather nervous about the thought of coming back to College.'
Ramon	'Nothing to be nervous about – provided you get someone decent to teach you. The Accounts section is OK though.'
Caller	'Should I write in for some information?'
Ramon	'That's probably best. Bye.'

You may have spotted one or two errors in Ramon's telephone technique! Assume that you have overheard him and feel that you must talk to him about what he has done wrong. Prepare a brief outline of what you would tell him and how you would go about it.

Individual/group tasks

Case study 1

You work as PA to the senior partner in a local firm of architects which has gone from strength to strength in the last few years. The company is now moving to larger premises and your boss, Brian Whiteside, wishes to review his communications systems and to make sure also that there will be no inconvenience to actual or potential clients during the move. After that time a new junior member of staff will be appointed to help you.

Brian Whiteside has decided to install a key telephone system in the new premises and for the junior to use the extension which will be designated as a switchboard. He also wants him/her to be responsible for transcribing any messages left on the answerphone when the office is closed.

He has asked for your help in the following ways.

1 Obtain details of the services offered by BT to intercept or divert calls when a business is in the process of moving and detail these in a memo.

2 List the features which you feel should be incorporated into the new key system to assist staff. Find information on at least three key systems which meet your requirements.

3 Devise a schedule of callers which will act as a record for your junior. Use headings which will act as a check to you of her actions in dealing with incoming callers over the first few weeks.

4 Make a checklist of the action she should take to enable her to transcribe answering machine messages efficiently and accurately.

Case study 2

You are PA to Helena Scott, Chief Accountant of a carpet manufacturing company. The company is quite large with six departments – Sales, Production, Accounts, Personnel, Purchasing and Administration (which includes Computer Services). The Board of Directors have recently been very concerned about rising costs in the industry and it has been decided that a determined effort must be made to reduce these across all areas. Your executive has noticed that telephone accounts for the company have virtually doubled over the last two years and cannot believe that this increase is justified. She considers that staff have little appreciation of how to keep costs down – and many are using company telephones for private calls. The company has a modern digital PABX installed.

She has asked for your assistance in trying to reduce the costs associated with telephone communications.

1 Investigate the type of payphones on the market which could be sited around the building for the use of staff. Give the advantages and disadvantages of at least three models together with the current cost of rental. Recommend the one which you feel would be most suitable and justify your decision.

2 Draw up a ten point list for all staff on how to use the telephone to keep costs to a minimum. This should fit on a single A4 sheet and be well-designed and easy to read.

3 The PABX already in use will give details for call logging, although it has not been used for this purpose before. The display screen on the equipment is only small and details of length, duration, units used, extension number etc would have to be transferred daily to a call logging sheet for analysis by your executive. Draw up such a sheet, with suitable headings, which will be easy for your operator to use and clearly show the information required by Ms Scott.

Section 3 – Transmitting and receiving information using electronic equipment

It used to be standard practice in many PA interviews to include several questions designed to see if applicants could 'think on their feet'. One always involved the scenario that, whilst the boss was away from the office a major crisis occurred. On the basis that her boss was beyond reach, what would she do?

Today that question is defunct. Whether in Russia, Hawaii or Australia, or on a day trip to Bridgend, her boss is constantly within reach by means of a whole host of electronic equipment. No longer does a PA need to chew her fingernails as she tries to work out what time would be best to ring with an urgent query when her boss is on business in New Zealand. Her smart answer to the question 'what would she do?' would probably be to leave a message on the electronic mail outlining the problem. Because they had arranged for her boss to access the electronic mailbox daily via a portable laptop computer with built-in modem, he/she would have responded with the action to take by the time she arrived for work the following day. Crisis over!

Telecommunications equipment

In most organisations this is likely to include:

- a fax machine
- a telex machine – to reach those customers not yet on fax and to transmit 'special' documents
- electronic mail
- paging equipment, bleepers and mobile phones.

A company which needs to set up a permanent communications link with a branch office or distributor can arrange to have its own national or international private circuit over which to transmit either voice or data. In most cases, however, organisations use the standard public network (see section 1 of this chapter).

It is your responsibility not only to know how electronic equipment functions, but to be able to determine quickly which would be the best to use for each particular message, bearing in mind the priority level, the cost and the degree to which security is a factor. As a supervisor you must be able to train and monitor junior staff who will use the equipment. You will be the one who will be expected to solve all the problems – the paper jammed in the fax, the unobtainable telex number, the 'frozen' computer screen when your junior is trying to send a message by electronic mail. Knowing which problems you should be able to rectify yourself and those with which you will need professional help from the outset enables you to take the correct action without hesitation – and not run the risk of calling out an engineer or computer specialist who discovers that the only reason your junior can't see anything on her computer is because someone has turned down the brightness control!

It will not only be your junior staff who ask you for help and advice. Your boss, too, unless he/she is a whiz kid at telecommunications, will expect you to know more about the systems than he/she does and may ask for your opinion on the best way to make urgent contact with a customer or an absent member of the organisation.

Becoming something of an oracle on this subject is therefore not an 'optional extra' but essential if you are to do your job properly in an age where instant information, any time and anywhere, is the name of the game.

Fax machines

Fax machines are the fastest growing sector of the telecommunications market. According to the BFICC (British Facsimile Industry Consultancy Committee) one in three businesses in the UK now has a fax – and the number is growing daily as businesses realise the benefit of being able to transmit text, graphics, photographs and anything else which can fit onto a sheet of paper quickly, easily and cheaply to almost anywhere in the world.

The price of faxes has fallen to bring them within the reach of even the smallest businesses. There are portable faxes (which can be used on a train or carried in the car and then carried in a purpose-built shoulder case), faxes and answering machines combined, coated paper and plain paper faxes and larger models which can call other faxes on their own without your help!

What to buy and which features to select will depend very much on the requirements of an individual organisation.

Fax facts

A fax machine works by scanning a black and white document and converting what it sees into a signal which it transmits down a telephone line.

Faxes are known by CCITT (the Consultative Committee for International Telephone and Telegraphy) international groupings, the majority currently in use now conform to Group 3 and Group 2 standards. The groups are based on the average time it takes to transmit a single A4 page. Group 2 are therefore slower than Group 3. Group 4 machines are state-of-the-art technology and can transmit an A4 sheet in just a few seconds! When two machines connect there is a brief 'handshake' period in which they identify each other's grouping. Bear in mind that transmission speed is always governed by the slower of the two machines, and the longer it takes to transmit the message the more it costs.

Although a phone/fax switching device can be purchased to enable a small business to use the same line for both phone calls and fax messages, most businesses have a separate incoming line for each of their fax machines which does not connect with the main switchboard or phone system.

Fax features

The basic difference between the cheaper and the more expensive fax machines is the number of features available. All the cheaper models use coated (thermal) paper which is heat-sensitive. The paper is provided in a roll which fastens inside the machine. The disadvantages of this paper are:

- its price (more expensive than plain paper)
- the fact that faxes tend to curl up in the direction the paper was wound on the roll (especially faxes which are produced when the roll is nearly empty)
- the dangers of the roll running out overnight
- the fact that fax messages printed on this paper tend to fade over time or if pinned on a notice board.

The alternative is to buy a plain paper fax machine but these are usually much more expensive. However they do have the advantage of doubling as plain paper copiers when required and the paper costs are less, though it can take some years before you would get your money back! In addition all faxes are printed out as A4 size and are therefore easier to file.

All fax machines have a liquid crystal display (which helps to guide you along), a key pad (usually with raised notches for the visually handicapped) and *most* have their own telephone handsets, which saves having to install a separate telephone alongside.

Many facilities are common to all fax machines, eg the ability to store customers' names/fax numbers in memory (though the size will vary with the cost of the machine), shortcode dialling, an automatic paper cutter and the ability to operate as a copier (though usually not at the speed of your usual photocopier!). Other features will depend very much on the price you are prepared to pay, and may include:

Activity logging   The machine can be pre-set to print out a report on everything it has been sending/receiving and the result.

Automatic dialling   The fax machine automatically starts to transmit a document once the connection is made.

Broadcast facility   The fax will send a specified number of pages to several different numbers automatically.

Deferred dialling   The fax machine is programmed to transmit documents at a pre-set time during the day or night.

Document carrier   For holding small or flimsy originals.

Document feeder   Stores documents for transmission (size of feeder will vary with price).

Fax header   Automatically prints your name and number on the top of all faxes you send, plus date, time and page number. It will only do this correctly, of course, if you set the time and date correctly in the first place and remember to alter this when the clock changes.

Half tone mode   Basically enables the fax machine to understand grey as well as black and white. You need this option if you intend to transmit photographs (see also *Photograph transmission*).

Loudspeaker facility   Enables you to hear what's going on from across the office, eg if a number is engaged and you have set the fax to keep trying.

Network capability   Can be linked to receive fax messages direct from any PC on the network and transmit them as instructed (for networks see Chapter 5, Preparing and producing documents page 233).

Number memory   A memory for storing regularly used names and fax numbers and dialling these by pressing a short code number.

Number search   Enables you to look through the number memory for information you require (eg if you've forgotten the code number to dial!).

Page editing   Enables you to recall messages stored in memory and amend these as required (see *Page memory*).

Page memory   Enables you to store messages in memory and send them later. Conversely incoming messages can be stored for printing out later.

Paper out warning   Signals when the paper is running low (in case your junior thinks the red lines now appearing are part of the design).

Password/passcode   Used to restrict access for sending faxes, retrieving faxes stored in memory (either in your machine or someone else's) or *polling*.

Polling   The ability of a fax to call another fax machine and 'collect' messages left for it.

Photograph transmission   Enables photographs to be sent and received. The more shades of grey your fax can handle the better the quality of photographs sent or received.

Repeat dialling   If the number required is engaged, the fax machine can be programmed automatically to keep trying until contact is established.

Resolution mode   Most machines operate on standard or fine resolution. Some machines also have a superfine setting. Adjusting the resolution slows down the scanning speed so quality is enhanced. It is not usually worth the additional transmission cost unless sending very intricate drawings or tiny print.

Signature storage   Enables a previously stored signature to be reproduced at a specified point.

Transmission report   An optional print-out after each fax is sent or received which gives details of time, date, sender, receiver, number of pages, duration and result (eg OK or not OK!).

Transmission reservation   Enables a 'busy' fax (ie one already receiving a document) to be programmed to send your outgoing message as soon as it's free (thereby saving you having to stand over it while a 20 page document is arriving).

Turnaround polling   Enables the machine to send a fax and poll the called machine in the same call.

Verification mark   A small 'x' mark automatically printed at the foot of each transmitted page (useful for reference if you can't remember whether you've sent it or if you're not sure whether transmission broke down part way through).

Voice contact   Enables you to discuss a fax with the person at the other end over the telephone handset. Some machines now enable you to do this *during* transmission.

White line skip   The machine is set to ignore white spaces altogether to speed up transmission time.

Using a fax

The most difficult part of using a fax is setting it up when it is first purchased. If you are ever in a position where you order a new fax, make it a condition of purchase that the shop sets it up for you – unless you or your boss really enjoys staring at sometimes unintelligible manuals and playing with keys and codes for hours.

The quality of manuals can vary enormously and they can be a real help or hindrance. If it is very difficult to read (or long-winded) then you are recommended to translate some of the manufacturer's instructions into a simple, idiot-proof format for staff in the office who haven't the time to plough through three pages on 'fax transmission procedures'.

There are three operations involved in using a fax:

- preparing the documents to transmit
- sending documents
- receiving documents.

Preparing documents to transmit

Remember that faxes only understand black and white (and shades of grey, in some cases). Therefore your coloured advert (or photograph) is going to cause problems, as is writing in red or green, because the colour definition is poor. If you are trying to transmit anything other than a standard black and white document start by photocopying it first and adjusting the density on your photocopier until you have the best possible original you can produce. Only a few faxes will enlarge or reduce, so again this should normally be undertaken on your photocopier if the original is too small to be read easily or too large to fit in the fax in the first place.

Train your staff to put flimsy or precious documents in the document carrier to prevent damage or automatically to photocopy them before transmission. Books, passports and any other documents which cannot be fed into a machine obviously need photocopying, unless you have a more sophisticated fax with a hinged lid like a photocopier.

Many organisations have printed fax paper on which messages can be written or typed. These have printed headings which the sender then completes. The essential information most organisations include is shown by the headings given on the next page.

Remember that the time of transmission will be printed on automatically by the fax, as will the name of the company. However, as this is only small, many companies prefer to send their fax messages on letter headed paper so the receiver can easily see the sender's name. You should note that the page number is shown in a different format to other documents. Stating which page number is being sent, and the total number in the transmission, means that the receiver is alerted to

```
┌─────────────────────────────────────────────────────────┐
│                      FAX MESSAGE                        │
├─────────────────────────────────────────────────────────┤
│                                                         │
│  TO        Paula Wainwright                             │
│                                                         │
│  FROM      Martin Phillips                              │
│                                                         │
│  DATE      14 February 199-                             │
│                                                         │
│  PAGE      1 of 2                                       │
│                                                         │
│  VISIT SCHEDULE                                         │
│                                                         │
│  I confirm that we shall be arriving at your            │
│  premises at 1030 hours tomorrow as agreed.             │
│  Attached is a full list of delegates and the name      │
│  of the company each represents.                        │
│                                                         │
│  I look forward to meeting you again.                   │
│                                                         │
│  Regards                                                │
│                                                         │
└─────────────────────────────────────────────────────────┘
```

the number to expect and can check at the end that all have been received.

The style and tone of faxes is usually relatively informal, although this obviously depends on the circumstances. It is usual for the sender to *sign* a fax (unlike a memo) but this may vary from one organisation to another, so do check.

Sending a fax

If you are showing your juniors how to operate a fax you are wise to concentrate on the following aspects:

- the importance of dialling the right number – and what to do if they dial the wrong one (ie how to cancel a call quickly!)
- how to use the UK Fax Book to look up numbers they don't know, and the number to dial to find out international fax numbers (153)
- which way up the paper must be inserted into the machine (or you will suddenly find you are transmitting blank paper around the country)
- setting the document guides so that the paper will go in *straight*. Paper put in so that it is crooked is very likely to be so askew by the time the end of the document is reached it jams in the machine
- letting the machine eject the master *itself* and not pulling or tugging it out in haste. (The document will probably come out all right – with luck – but the verification mark will be missing. Too late your junior will hear the dull 'clunk' from inside the fax as it desperately tries to mark a rapidly disappearing piece of paper.)

- the importance of sending multi-page documents in the right page order. Doubtless if the pages are numbered the receiver can work this out for himself but it does aid working relationships with other companies if there is some semblance of organisation about the transmission.

Apart from the above, sending faxes is so easy that even your boss can be trained how to do it! Delay teaching your juniors other techniques, such as delayed/repeat dialling, changing the date/time and replenishing the paper roll until you are happy that they can send straightforward faxes without difficulty. Then work up to the really complicated stuff such as polling, working in memory and deferred dialling and *check* their actions on this carefully. The last thing you want is 14 strangers across the world receiving unexplained fax messages overnight from your company.

After transmission is complete the document should be returned to its originator. Most organisations attach the transmission report as 'proof', though some keep these centrally for costing purposes (see below).

SPECIAL NOTE

The major problem you can experience when transmitting faxes is that of transmission breakdown part-way through. This is far more likely to occur on multi-page than single page documents and it can be difficult to spot exactly where the transmission broke down. Train all your staff to examine the verification report at the end to check that the result is OK. Other signals might show that either their machine or yours failed during transmission, *or* your paper or theirs ran out, *or* your machine overheated when you were sending a document with a high percentage of black or during a very long run. Examine all the pages to find out where the verification marks stopped, then go back a page (to be on the safe side) and try again. It is courteous if you preface your repeat message with a short note to say why you are resuming contact.

Receiving faxes

Most fax machines are left on 24 hours a day, seven days a week to receive incoming messages. Identifying incoming messages very much depends on:

- where the fax machine is sited
- whether or not incoming messages are stored in a paper tray.

The biggest danger is that the fax machine is placed on a desk and incoming messages (which are automatically cut after every sheet remember) simply spill out on to the desk overnight. Your cleaner or junior may spot the two or three pages of rolled up paper and think they are being helpful by throwing them away. Do *warn* juniors that any paper lying about near the fax should be examined carefully – and ban your cleaner (nicely!) from tidying up that area.

Specially adapted workstations are now available for fax machines, which have space to carry the electrical wiring and to store the incoming messages. Shelves above and below can be used for directories and paper supplies.

Your juniors should be trained to deliver incoming faxes *quickly* – the whole idea of using fax is to give instant information! You must devise a system for coping with incoming faxes for executives who are out of the building – if necessary insist that you scan all incoming faxes prior to delivery. Not only will this enable you to decide the best course of action to take if someone is absent or away, but it will also keep you extremely au fait with what is going on!

Trouble shooting and maintenance

The back of your manual will contain a trouble shooting guide which you should read the day you buy the machine. Needless to say, if anything doesn't work, a few basic checks must be carried out, eg is it plugged in, switched on, is the cover closed etc. Look on the LCD display: most error messages are shown on this and tell you what to do to rectify the fault (including ringing the engineer if necessary). Some self-diagnostic machines contact their own base when they know they have a problem!

Learn how to rectify paper jams. If an alarm sounds when you lift the cover don't panic – it can usually be silenced easily by means of a reset key.

Remember that all faxes have batteries which are required for the time and date facility and also enable them to operate for a short time in the event of a power cut. Keep spare batteries in your drawer and learn how to fit them.

In addition, read the instructions on how to clean the machine, and not just on the outside. If the document rollers inside become grubby they will mark all the messages you transmit and render some unreadable. Alcohol, such as methylated spirits, applied with a lint-free cloth, is all that is needed to wipe the rollers clean.

The cost of faxes

Fax machines are cheap to buy and transmission costs the same as a telephone call; it is therefore influenced by factors such as time of day, distance and the duration of the transmission. Keeping words to a minimum helps as the 'blacker' (or lengthier) the fax the longer it takes to transmit. More expensive machines often have higher transmission speeds which again can help to save money.

Using deferred dialling or polling means that your machine can be set to transmit or access faxes during cheap rate periods.

If an organisation uses fax facilities almost constantly it can consider the option of having one or two sophisticated fax machines which are linked to networked PCs. A message typed on any of the micro-computers in the network is automatically sent into the memory of the fax machine for transmission at a specified time. Documents produced on a variety of packages – spreadsheets, desktop publishing, word processing, graphics etc can therefore be downloaded to the fax machine at the touch of one or two keys. Security is enhanced as no paper original is required for the fax machine and there is higher copy quality as each message is electronically generated rather than scanned. This is a more cost-effective option than multiple fax machines with multiple telephone line charges. Additionally it reduces operator 'waiting time' in printing out the message, taking to it a fax machine, waiting whilst it is transmitted etc. A further option is to have smaller fax machines linked to a more powerful model which can automatically receive and relay messages to take advantage of cheap and local call rates.

Most fax machines will print out a regular transmission report which can be used to assist costing. Some will incorporate a departmental code automatically; otherwise you will need to keep a record of all senders. The basics you need to know are date and time, number dialled, duration of call, and the result. You can then calculate the cost manually if necessary, by means of an up-to-date telephone charges booklet.

Security

The major problem with fax machines initially was that everyone who used them saw the messages being sent/transmitted. This has now changed with the introduction of a range of features, many of which have already been mentioned, such as passwords, pass codes, and downloading messages prepared on a PC. Companies which want an even higher level of security can buy fax machines which can interconnect with cryptographic equipment to stop users copying or transmitting messages and to prevent connection to a non-secure telephone network when sending sensitive data.

Telex machines

As fax machines have increased in popularity, the use of telex machines has declined. That does not mean to say that organisations don't use telex any more – they do – because telex is still useful in a some situations where fax facilities are either not suitable or not available.

The critical difference between fax and telex is that because the answerback code of both the sender and receiver is printed at the top of the telexed document *and* at the end, there is proof that transmission took place and was completed. A telex is therefore recognised as a legal document in most countries of the world – the position is less clear as regards fax messages. If, therefore, you are contacting a company to ask them to agree to accept new terms of delivery you would be well advised to send the communication over telex, rather than fax – and to ask them to reply in the same way.

It is also advisable to use telex in any situation where you want unqualified evidence that you were in touch, eg when booking your boss a hotel room halfway across the world (make sure he/she takes the copy telex with him/her!).

Telex features

There is little difference today between a telex machine and a PC – except that the former will transmit a typed message to another location. There is even less difference between a telex and a *communicating* PC (see electronic mail, page 64) except that the former transmits information via telegraph lines and not over telephone lines. National and international telex networks are used solely for telex traffic and are available in many remote corners of the world where fax isn't as common as in the UK. Indeed a PC can easily be used to send telexes (in much the same way as faxes) by preparing the document on screen and transmitting it over a network eg via Telecom Gold or Prestel (see next section). One system on the market allows network users both to send and receive fax and telex messages on their PCs. This system will also store letterheads (and logos) in memory which can be automatically printed at the top of each document to be transmitted. Equally, dedicated telex machines can be used as a word processor when not in use as a telex and can be interfaced to link with other communications equipment. The features on a telex include:

Automatic date/time stamp   Inserted automatically upon every telex sent.

Automatic transmission   Messages stored in memory can be programmed to be transmitted at a predetermined time. If the line is busy the machine will keep trying.

Delayed dialling   The machine will redial busy numbers automatically.

Multiple transmission   The machine will automatically send the same telex to several numbers.

Short code memory   The machine will store commonly used telex numbers against a code.

Simultaneous preparation and receipt   Incoming messages are automatically stored in memory until the operator is ready to receive them.

Text discrimination   Incoming text is printed in red, outgoing text in black.

Text memory   The ability to store pre-prepared messages in memory to be recalled and transmitted later.

Using telex

If you are instructing someone who has never used a telex machine, you have two areas to cover. One is machine operation – and the functions and keys peculiar to telex equipment; the second is that of 'telex conventions'. Both the layout and wording of telexes are understood worldwide and if tradition is followed there will few, if any, misunderstandings. Additionally, if your operator needs to contact the telex operator it will be necessary to understand some of the basic abbreviations which may be shown on screen. Because telex has always been charged on the length of transmission time, many abbreviations have emerged, which are understood the world over. Some of these are operational; others relate to the message itself. It is not advisable to introduce a few of your own if you want to aid international understanding!

Special keys

Here is   Transmits your answerback.

Who are you   Transmits the answerback of the telex with which you are connected.

Bell   Calls the operator to the machine.

Call   Starts or ends a call.

Store   Puts messages into memory for later transmission.

Telex run*   Transmits the message on screen.

Transmit from memory   Transmits from memory.

Layout

A typical layout is shown. Note the exchange of answerbacks (ie the recognition code of each machine), at both the start and the end of the message. The letter G at the end denotes a machine in the UK. All telexes are printed in capital letters; otherwise they would not be compatible with older machines still receiving messages all over the world.

Below the answerback you should key in the name and address of your company *if* you will not be recognised by the recipient, followed by any internal reference number you are using for telexes, and the date and the time (if this is not printed automatically by your machine). If the telex is urgent make sure this word is prominent and the name of the recipient is clearly shown.

It is usual practice to repeat any figures at the end after the abbreviation COL or RPT (see below). Equally, it is standard practice, if you quote an important monetary figure (eg the price of contract), to put it in figures first and then repeat it in words within the text itself. The four crosses at the end denote the message is ended. If you are sending several messages to the same company, end each individual message with one cross and end the transmission with four crosses as shown.

* or similar

Note that at the end of the telex the answerbacks are deliberately reversed – so that you can ensure that contact with the recipient was retained until the very last line.

Abbreviations

The message below contains several abbreviations of which you should be aware. There is one abbreviation which denotes that this telex must have been transmitted 'live' – which can happen – particularly if you have been called (by the bell) to respond immediately. Find the mistake in the message and note how the operator coped with the situation. Knowing what to do if you make an error is vital!

```
OCC

OCC

248173 XPRESS G
572637 HARLCO G

OUR REF 1060     14.06.92     15:30

U R G E N T

ATTN JOHN EVANS
ADVISED GOODS NOT RECD BY CLIENT - OUR ORDEG E E
E ORDER 9/1928 REFERS. PSE DELIVER ASAP AND CFM.

PAULA KING

COL 9/1928
+ + + +

572638 HARLCO G
248173 XPRESS G
```

Sending a telex

You must study the instruction manual for your particular machine or, if you are downloading via a PC, be certain you know exactly what you are doing at the outset. Only when you feel confident and capable should you start demonstrating what to do to other people. On all modern telex machines the message is typed on screen, checked, edited and stored in memory if it is not being transmitted immediately.

CHECK IT YOURSELF

In the list given below, try covering up the right hand column and see how many abbreviations you can guess – purely from the letters used.

Operational abbreviations and those used by operators/your recipient

ABS	Absent subscriber or office closed
DER	Subscriber's telex out of order
GA	Go ahead and transmit
INF	Subscriber temporarily unavailable – call the enquiry service
MOM	Wait a moment (MOM PSE used when calls are being queued)
NC	No circuits (ie lines are busy)
NP	No party (the person you are calling is no longer a subscriber)
OCC	The number you are calling is engaged
P*	Stop transmitting
RAP	I shall call you back
WRU	Who is there?

* the letter P is repeated continually until transmission is stopped. It usually means they've run out of paper or had a disaster at the other end!

Message abbreviations

CMF	Please confirm/I confirm
COL	Please repeat/I repeat (used for unusual words or figures)
E E E	Error (only used when transmitting live)
FIN	I have finished my message
MNS	Minutes
OK	Agreed/Do you agree
PSE	Please (SVP is also used)
RPT	Another version of COL (easier!)

It is usual to keep a special telex index of those numbers you call regularly (some telex machines will hold a specified number in memory and automatically call these as required). If the company is unknown to you then look up the number you require in the BT Telex Director. Note *both* the number *and* the answerback. (BT also does an answerback directory for when you receive a telex and don't know who sent it!)

The procedure from then on is simple. Press call, check the answerback is correct (it prints automatically), transmit your message and wait until the answerbacks have automatically exchanged at the end of the message and the line has cleared before either switching off or starting another message.

If you store a message in memory the machine allocates this a number and adds it to a directory which you can access at any time. You need the message number to download a stored message.

International calls are made via the International Operator who is accessed by dialling the appropriate number for your machine (look in the BT reference book). The automatic exchange sends a reference and the time, takes your answerback and then sends KEY. You respond with the country code as given in the BT list and the number and a plus sign. You then wait for the answerback, just as for a UK call.

If you have any queries access the telex operator and ask for help.

Receiving a telex

Do not worry about incoming messages 'clashing' with yours if you are trying to prepare one on screen; most machines give you warning a message is coming in and you can stop to let this show on screen or have it stored in memory and access it when you have finished preparing your own. The options you have will depend on your equipment.

Possible difficulties

You and your junior staff may be somewhat hampered by line faults, particularly if you are trying to make a connection with a far-flung destination – eg China, Kurdistan or Malawi. Either you cannot get a line, so that you are still trying to transmit your message when everyone else has long gone, or the transmission cuts off part-way through.

If the transmission cuts off then you will have to try again. If you regularly have trouble making a connection you either need a telex which can be programmed to keep trying calls automatically or to persuade your boss to subscribe to Telex Plus, a pay-as-you-go service which will undertake certain jobs for you eg:

- repeated delivery attempts to difficult numbers
- broadcast a telex to up to 100 different addresses.

Security

Possible breaches in security are obviously reduced on telex if messages are created on a modern machine or PC where they can be created on screen, stored and then transmitted, provided that documents in the directory are not available on open access. You cannot, however, determine security at the receiving end – in some parts of the world older telex machines are in operation which print out the text for all to see (unless you devise a coded method of sending your message). An easier way in an emergency is for your boss to be at the other end of the line, you can then have a 'live' conversation if necessary to resolve a crisis.

TEST YOURSELF

Unlike fax machines, where 'master' documents are returned to the originator and there is no print-out, telexes are usually printed out in duplicate – the top copy for the originator and the bottom copy stored firstly by the operator in case there are any queries over the next few days and then moved to the main files.

What *short-term* method of filing would you use to store telexes you have sent on behalf of your executive, prior to their transfer to the main system?

Trouble shooting and maintenance

Again check your manual for details. Most problems are caused because some routine operation is required, eg:

- replenishing the paper roll
- adjusting the paper roll (if the person before you didn't fit the paper correctly)
- fitting a new ribbon in the printer (if one is used)

You are always advised to switch off a telex before you change the paper or the ribbon. Regardless of modern safety backups which may divert or store incoming messages if your printer is offline, it is always as well to be safe, rather than sorry.

Telex costs

The greatest difference between a fax machine and a telex machine is operator cost. Each document to be sent by telex must normally be keyed in, even if it was received by the operator in typed format. The exception is when a PC, with a telex facility, has an attached document scanner, but this combination is rare and usually unnecessary, as telex messages are seldom long enough to be worth it.

Dedicated telex machines are much more expensive than fax machines, but can be rented or leased to reduce capital outlay. In addition, transmission costs are higher – especially on the more remote routes.

Telex versus fax

Most organisations have opted for fax because of its ease of use, cost and the variety of documents which can be transmitted. You can't send a completed form, signed order or signed contract by telex. One of the biggest drawbacks of telex is encountered by companies which regularly trade internationally. If your organisation regularly has documents translated before transmission, there seems little point in having an operator key in the text all over again, especially if it is in a language she doesn't understand. Additionally there may be the problem of missing accents on a telex. With a fax, the company can simply transmit the translated document in the form in which it was received – or ask their translation bureau to do it.

Telex's one advantage over fax is in proof of transmission and receipt.

Electronic mail

Electronic mail (or Email) is a messaging system whereby documents prepared on a PC are then transmitted to another PC via a 'mailbox' system. The mailbox stores messages until the user is ready to access them. The user can reply, store or delete messages, print out, redistribute and even check if the messages he sent have been read by the recipient.

Electronic mail systems are becoming more and more common as *in-house* facilities for organisations which have networked their PCs (see Chapter 5, Preparing and producing documents, page 233). This relieves the load on the mailroom considerably, as internal messages, and those to branch office/head office (if they are on the system), can be transmitted instantly via the network.

In addition, to contact those outside the internal system, the company can subscribe to either Telecom Gold or Prestel (or both) to send messages to customers, suppliers etc.

The advantages of any electronic mail system are that:

- all forms of data can be transmitted (graphics, text, spreadsheets etc)
- there is complete confidentiality as only the user can access his own mail by means of his password or ID
- a recipient who wishes to incorporate information received by electronic mail into another document stored on his computer does not need to key it in for a second time
- messages can be sent to several mailboxes simultaneously
- travelling executives can access their mailbox via a laptop computer from virtually anywhere in the world.

Internal electronic mail

This is usually installed via 'off-the-shelf' software which may also comprise additional facilities such as an electronic diary and scheduler (see Chapter 7, Organising work schedules, page 357).

To give additional security, users normally have to key in a *second* password to access their mail, in addition to the one used to log on to the network in the first place.

Features

These usually include:

Blind copy   The ability to send a copy of a message to other users without the main recipient or other users knowing what you have done.

Carbon copy   Again a copy of a message is sent to another user (or users) but this time all the recipients know to whom copies have been distributed.

Cancel   If you change your mind about sending a message.

Delete   To delete messages you've read and don't need again – otherwise they will clutter up your mailbox. On some internal systems all messages are purged after a specified time (eg a month) to save space in the system. If you want to prevent this happening to a special message you'll have to store (or save) it.

You can also use delete to erase a message you have already sent to a mailbox *provided that the recipient hasn't yet read it.*

In mailbox   The mailbox in which incoming mail is stored. Mail is displayed in 'envelopes' on your screen. Unread mail is usually differentiated in some way on both your screen and your sender's screen. When you 'open' an envelope the colour or mark changes. This is one way in which the sender can tell whether or not it has been read.

Mail forward   Enables you to send on a message you have received to another user or group of users who you feel should receive the information.

Mail message   This, or a similar command, gives you access to the screen for typing/editing messages.

Out mailbox   The mailbox in which your outgoing mail is stored. You can tell by the colour of the message summary whether or not your messages have been read.

Phone message   An optional screen available on some systems with a pre-printed phone message form for easy completion.

Print   Enables you to print the contents of messages, lists and 'help' information.

Read message   The option to select if you want to see what is inside the envelopes listed in your *In mailbox.*

Reply   Used to send a reply to a message you have received. Because this is a reply the recipient's name is included automatically in the heading.

Send   The command which transmits the message. With some systems you can arrange for recipients to be 'beeped' the next time they turn on their computer.

User groups   These can be set up centrally. If the message is addressed under the group name then all members of that group will receive the message simultaneously. In addition 'personal user groups' can be set up by individual users. If you forget who is in which group you can usually access these with a list command.

External electronic mail

You can access external electronic mail if your organisation subscribes to either Telecom Gold or the Prestel Mailbox service. In addition you will need a PC, a modem and communications software installed in your machine. This is the 'link' between your PC and the outside world and enables you to dial out, store numbers, save pages to disk etc.

A separate telephone line is preferable (as for fax). Otherwise constant outgoing calls would cause congestion at the switchboard. In addition it would be more difficult to cost usage. Electronic mail users have *two* accounts to pay – one for the phone call and the second for the time of connection and any additional charges. Because connection time can be expensive (as can access to additional facilities) it is important to know exactly what you want to do *before* you start using the system. There is an additional charge for mail which is stored or saved.

Telecom Gold is more sophisticated, has more subscribers but is more expensive and more difficult to use (although there is an in-built tutor to help). Users are given a mailbox ID in the form of a number of characters *plus* a password which they are free to change at any time. The ID is not alterable as this is the mailbox number. In addition to electronic mail, users also have automatic access to a wide range of information pages which are charged at a variety of rates (some very expensive) eg company information, financial information, news and market information, credit ratings etc. Users can also send telexes and faxes via Telecom Gold from anywhere in the world.

Prestel Mailbox is accessed through the standard Prestel network. Subscribers also receive an ID number and a password. Information pages are also available on Prestel – indeed it is for this service Prestel is best known (see Chapter 2, Researching and retrieving information, page 75). The difference between the two systems is that Prestel operates a system of closed user groups (travel agents are a typical example) who will have access to information which other users do not (unless they pay an additional subscription). Charges are less (see page 68) and may be shown as a frame charge (for viewing a particular page) or a time charge (for the length of time you keep that page on screen). There are no 'premium' charges to view special pages. Telexes, but not faxes (as yet), can be transmitted via Prestel.

Additional features
These may include:

Acknowledge Receipt of message is automatically acknowledged to the sender.

An editor Allows the creation, editing and revision of documents – often used in conjunction with a personal directory.

Express mail Mail sent express is always stored at the top of the mailbox.

File mail Saves the message in a specified 'file' for later retrieval.

Forward with comments Self-explanatory.

Personal directory Used to set up specific distribution lists.

Quickscan   Condenses *Scan* information still further – useful if there are a lot of messages and your boss is in a rush.

Scan mail   Quickly previews the contents of the mailbox eg sender, date/time message was sent, the number of the computer from which it was sent, size of message and subject.

Using electronic mail

Before you even attempt to instruct *anyone* how to use electronic mail you must be familiar with the system yourself. This means reading carefully any instruction books which are issued with external systems or any in-company manual relating to internal systems.

If you have any choice in the matter you are advised to start with an internal system – there is less chance of a major disaster if you make a mistake and it is cheaper for you to play on! Remember that Prestel is the next most user-friendly with basic options of 'send', 'acknowledge', 'store' (or all three at once) or 'cancel'. Before you try transmitting any documents on Telecom Gold either find a mentor who will carefully and clearly show you how – or use the tutor to help you.

Make sure you know how to log out or exit the system *properly* so that the phone link is disconnected.

A word of warning! If you are registered as a mailbox user then *do* check your mail regularly (or that of your boss if you have permission to access his/her mailbox). There is nothing more frustrating for other users than to notice that their urgent messages are still unread after several days!

Trouble shooting and maintenance

Provided all the networks are functioning (and so is your PC!) you should have few problems operating electronic mail. One problem you may encounter is if you either receive 'rubbish' on your screen or if the system 'locks out' on you whilst you are still connected (ie your commands are ignored). The critical fact to remember is that you are still connected via the phone link – so don't just switch off your PC and walk away! On some modems you can press a button to cancel the call. On others the secret is to switch off your PC (assuming you can't log out as normal) and then re-enter and, via your communications software, instruct your phone to hang up. Then try again.

Both Telecom Gold and Prestel operate a user help line for subscribers who are experiencing difficulties.

Electronic mail costs

Internal electronic mail is free – because a private network is used to transmit the messages. External Email is expensive – so you need to know what you are doing.

Telecom Gold operates two membership schemes – Club membership for users who only require one mailbox and Corporate membership for organisations which require an unlimited number. There is an initial registration fee and then a standing charge per month, plus connection and storage charges. The former vary depending on time of day. Additional charges are levied for sending telexes and faxes and accessing information pages, and some of these are very expensive.

Prestel users also pay a standing charge – this time per quarter – and this is more expensive for business users than residential customers. There is no registration fee. Connection charges are usually cheaper than with Telecom Gold.

There are several ways in which you can reduce the cost of accessing the system:

- know what you are doing before you start
- prepare messages 'off-line' and then download them if your system will let you
- save a page of information you need to study to disk and view it off-line, if your software allows
- save your messages on your own disk, if possible, rather than in store in your mailbox.

Pagers, bleepers and mobile phones

These are dealt with in full in the last section, pages 27 to 30.

ACTIVITY SECTION

Individual tasks

1 Using your manual as a guide, draw up an easy to understand list of instructions for your junior to enable her to change the paper roll on *either* your fax *or* your telex machine.

2 You are 'holding the fort' for your organisation's sales section as most of the staff are away on business today, either in the UK or abroad.

   You have the following messages and documents to relay urgently. Which method of transmission would you select in each case (assuming that equipment is no problem)?

   a a wiring diagram to be sent to a customer in Munich

   b details of the conditions of an agency agreement to be sent to your new agent in Athens

   c an urgent message for your executive who is driving between Perth and Aberdeen

   d an urgent summons for your MD who is at present showing guests around the shop floor

   e a publicity photograph for your office in Melbourne

   f an urgent message to your Sales Director who is at present attending an important meeting in the Board Room of another company

   g an important order to be confirmed to a company in Zimbabwe

   h your executive's monthly update to be sent to three members of staff away from the office until next week.

Individual/group tasks

Case study 1

Your brother has recently set up in business as an independent Financial Adviser. He is doing well but is concerned that he is lacking the necessary electronic equipment which would enable him to operate more effectively.

In particular he is concerned that:

- he has no way of sending or receiving documents quickly
- there is no way his young assistant can contact him quickly when he is out on the road.

He knows you are an expert in this type of equipment and has asked for your help.

1 Identify the best type of machine he could purchase to solve his document problem. Collect information on at least four models which you think may be suitable; analyse the features of each and recommend one for purchase. Justify your decision.

2 On a separate sheet, identify the advantages and disadvantages of your brother purchasing:
   a a pager
   b a mobile telephone
   in terms of flexibility, features available and price.

Case study 2

You work for a large organisation which has just introduced its own electronic mail system for all staff. Your junior staff have all been allocated mailboxes. In the past two weeks, however, you have received the following complaints:

- messages sent to senior staff, eg telephone messages, omit essential facts and are too 'chatty' in tone
- some staff aren't even bothering to switch on their machines each day with the result that urgent messages are unanswered.

From what you can see, few seem to have much idea of the facilities available, nor how these should be used. You have therefore decided to hold a short training session to make sure that, in future, your staff will be able to operate the system properly.

1 On the basis that the training session will last one half day, draw up a schedule with times and topics to be covered.

2 Draft out a message which can be used as an example of how to use the correct tone and style for senior staff. The content of the message is up to you.

3 Design a small user handbook which covers the main points of the system and which your staff can use for reference.

Managing yourself

What do I really want out of life?

Before you can even think of 'Managing yourself' you first need to know something about yourself. 'Know thyself[1] (or in modern terms, self-awareness) has been talked about for years. In terms of your personal self-development it is critical; not knowing what you like to do, or what you want, is rather like going on a journey without knowing where you are starting from or where you want to end! From that point of view, you will also never know when you've actually arrived! So a little self-analysis and psychology is a good starting point.

People are often fascinated and intrigued by self-analysis which is one reason why, especially in America, people pay a fortune to have their own 'analyst' to help them to identify what they want out of life and what they can realistically hope to achieve.

RULE 1
Self-awareness helps you to promote a positive self-image and go forward in life.

You – your 'self'

We all regularly use the words 'myself' and 'yourself' in everyday conversation, but very rarely consider what these terms actually mean.

According to Freudian psychologists your 'self' has two parts – the unconscious self and the conscious self. As a whole your 'self' comprises all your values, needs, abilities, beliefs and feelings. Some of these you are not aware of, ie they are unconsciously held, inherited from your parents and others who influenced you when you were a child. Your conscious self is that part of yourself of which you are aware, ie your self-concept. This is the perception you have of yourself – how you would describe yourself to other people.

The reason why your description of your 'self' might not match their opinion is that they also see the behaviour which is determined by your unconscious self – of which you are not aware.

RULE 2
Because everyone's behaviour is determined by two factors – their unconscious and conscious 'self' – no one is totally aware of how they appear to others or why they always act as they do.

Sigmund Freud was a famous Austrian psychologist who lived in the 19th century. Many consider he was the father of psychoanalysis. Freud

[1] Variously attributed to Juvenal, Cicero and Diogenes Laertius, it is generally agreed that this inscription was written on the wall in the temple of Delphi in Ancient Greece.

frequently referred to a person's **ego**, ie their ability to make rational decisions to make the most of what they have and what they want.

In addition, Freud considered that we also have an **ego-ideal**, or **self-ideal**. These are the goals and values we aspire to and the criteria we use to measure ourselves. They reflect the values our families taught us. If we undertake an activity which links with this, and are successful then we enhance our self-esteem. Therefore, to help our self-development – and to increase our self-esteem, everything we try must be relevant to our needs and must make us feel successful. How this works is shown below:

	Activity fits with what you want for yourself	Activity doesn't fit with what you want for yourself
Success	Esteem increased – feel great	Feel OK but nothing more – activity tedious
Failure	Feel thwarted but can't wait to try again	Feel deflated and fed up – activity pointless

TEST YOURSELF
Think of several different activities you have undertaken in your life – tennis, golf, acting, car maintenance etc. If you are still pursuing that activity today, it is probable that it falls into the middle box – it 'fits' your mental image of yourself and you have been successful. Now try to think of activities which fit the other boxes. What have you tried to do and then given up, regardless of how successful you have been?

> **RULE 3**
> You can develop your self-esteem by trying new things which 'fit' your self-perception. The only condition is that the goal you set yourself should be realistic and yet challenging.

Setting your goals

Usually if we identify the right goals then we can devote psychological energy to trying to achieve them. This is the energy which seems to come from nowhere when, after a hard day, we suddenly feel lively enough to go out with our friends or dance the night away!

To harness your psychological energy at work you need to consider:

1 What are the activities and interests in which I am really keen? What are my goals?

2 How can I strive for these realistically?

3 What are my strengths and weaknesses?

4 How can I build on my strengths and eliminate my weaknesses to help me to achieve my goal(s)?

Any form of personality quiz can be misleading, as it is apt to make you think in black and white categories and label yourself introvert or extrovert, sociable or shy, aggressive or defensive, patient or intolerant, when most of us can *vary* depending upon the circumstances.

However, if you have chosen to be an administrator or PA then there are undoubtedly certain attributes and abilities which will help you to do the job more easily. If you detest working with people, and like working in the open air then it is hardly likely that you are tailor-made for the job!

Below is a list of questions you may usefully work through to discover a little more about yourself. Bear in mind there are no right and wrong answers; the questions are there purely to provide you with an opportunity to reassess yourself. You may find it interesting to answer the questions yourself, and then see if an honest and loyal friend can 'second-guess' your answers correctly. This will at least highlight areas where you do not give out the same 'signals' as perhaps you think! Consider what evidence you can offer to back up with your answers – and be honest!

RULE 4
Remember that self-deception is exactly what it says – the only person you fool is yourself!

Have you the personality for the job?

Work profile
Do you like work which calls for accuracy and detail? Do you like thinking and planning out a job? Are you well organised and find what you put away? Do you like a known routine or do you like new challenges on a regular basis? Are you observant? Do you consider you have a good memory? Do you work quietly or make a lot of fuss? Are you sometimes 'difficult' to work with – and in what way? Are you always punctual?

Achievement profile
Are you a hard worker or do you get tired easily? Are you highly competitive – or very laid back? Can you cope with constant interruptions? Do you enjoy responsibility? Are you constantly striving for something new or do you rest on past glories? Are the targets and goals you set yourself realistic? How do you react to failure? Are you ever tempted to blame someone (or something) else for something you have done? Do you give up easily? Would you cheat to get what you want?

Leadership profile

Do you like telling other people how to do things? Do you find it easy to get people to do what you want them to do? Do people consider that you are bossy? Does it annoy you if people disagree with you? Do you *think* before making a decision or are you impulsive? Do you change your mind frequently – or never? Do people often ignore you and/or your opinions? Can you make it clear to people what you want without causing any offence? Do you expect more from other people than you are prepared to do yourself? Can you motivate other people to work hard? Can you keep a secret?

Emotional profile

Do you get upset easily? Are you soon bored – if so, do you show it? Are you easily elated or depressed? Do you enjoy arguing or are you nervous if challenged by someone in authority? If someone 'takes you on' do you jump onto the defensive? Do you consider that you are tactful and/or diplomatic? Are you prepared to compromise with other people when necessary? Do you sulk or bear grudges? Do you ever lose your temper? Do you think before you speak?

Social profile

Do you value your close friends? Do you like a hectic social life? Do you always want to be 'in' with the crowd? Do you like working on your own? Do you consider you are always friendly? Do you share confidences easily? How do you cope if you find out someone doesn't like you? Could you make an unpopular decision if necessary? Do you mix with people easily? Are you a good judge of character or easily impressed?

Followership profile

Do you like to be told exactly what to do, or prefer to use your own initiative? Do you want to please people in charge of you? Do you follow rules to the letter – or ignore them? Are you a willing workhorse who finds it difficult to say 'no'? Could you cope with a moody or uncommunicative boss or do you need a lot of encouragement? Do you need constant supervision? Can you stick up for yourself without upsetting people?

Life profile

Are you always 'on the go' or in a rush? Do you burn the candle at both ends? Do you like to keep fit? Do you work quickly? Do you know what you want out of life? Do you quickly grasp what is required in a situation – or need it spelled out for you? Are you self-confident or a worrier? Do you find it difficult to relax or even harder to get started?

TEST YOURSELF

1 Under each profile area, discuss as a group the personal attributes you feel are essential for a first class PA/supervisor.

2 Individually, highlight those you feel you already possess and on which you could build quite easily.

3 Now highlight those qualities which you feel you are lacking. Divide these into:
   a those which are essential (eg punctuality) and to which you could adjust with a little self-discipline
   b those which are important but are really not 'you', eg liking to meet new people.

Managing yourself

You are now on the way to learning to manage yourself. Under question 2 above you should have a list of your strengths – qualities you possess which are important to your chosen job. You have to 'manage' these by making sure that you continue to concentrate on these areas until they are second nature.

Under question 3a you have identified tougher areas – your weaknesses in relation to your chosen career. Come to grips with these one at a time over the next few months – if you normally fuss a lot when given something to do try keeping quiet about it instead. Congratulate yourself as you achieve each goal. Don't give up if, at first, you slip back occasionally.

Under question 3b you have identified areas about which you feel unhappy and it is important for you to work in a job where these skills wouldn't be essential.

In time you will find that your areas of emphasis and your strengths and weaknesses will change. What is a problem one year may be of no significance the next, as you gain in experience, knowledge and self-confidence.

RULE 5
Review your self-development profile at regular intervals throughout your career and adapt both this, and your goals, as necessary.

If you do this then not only will you come to know yourself better, but you will also gain greater satisfaction from your achievements than if you merely 'drift' through life. In this way you can be said to be truly 'managing' yourself.

2 Researching and retrieving information

Section 1 – Using and developing manual and computerised filing systems

Consider the following statements. Are they true or false?

- *I've far more important things to do than file.*
- *I'm a PA – I shouldn't have to deal with filing.*
- *Filing's old-fashioned – what about the paperless office?*

All false!

As a PA you should have in mind the image you want to present to the world – in this case the working world. Do you want others to see you as disorganised, dishevelled and untidy? Obviously not! In that case, why spoil your image by having a disorganised, dishevelled and untidy office with systems to match?

Remember that filing covers a variety of tasks. Do you want to make work for yourself? A well thought out filing system saves you time – and often preserves your sanity in times of crisis when everything is wanted *now*.

Remember also that although you, as a PA, will be able to delegate day to day filing duties to others, you are the one to make the decision as to what information is stored, how it is stored and how long it is kept. If a paper cannot be found then that is your responsibility, not that of your office junior.

Do you *really* think that you will be in a position (at least in the next few years) where you will never handle a piece of paper and that the computer will replace altogether the filing cabinet? Even if it does, you will still need to know how to deal with a computerised filing system – and how to cope when all the computers go down just when something urgent is needed!

Setting up the system

Will you be expected to operate within a centralised or departmental system of filing?

If you are new to a particular job the first question for you to ask about your filing system is where it is! If the system is within your own working area then you, as PA/supervisor, will probably be given the responsibility for organising and controlling it. If, however, the firm has decided upon a centralised system, then you will find that your files, together with those of all other departments in the firm, are stored centrally in one location with its own specialist staff.

There are obvious advantages in centralising the system:

- **economy of scale** – if all filing is concentrated in one place it is possible to instal better and more expensive equipment (eg automated filing equipment, see page 79)
- **standardisation** – one set of procedures only is required and duplication of record-keeping can be avoided
- **specialist staff** – up-to-date and efficient procedures can be implemented more easily if filing is not left to either the newest (or most weak-willed) member of staff
- **better supervision** – it is difficult for staff to say they are too busy to file or that they have other more important work to do if their only job is filing
- **cover for absence** – filing won't be left to accumulate during the period someone is off sick or on holiday.

 TEST YOURSELF

Suppose that you are a PA in the Architects' Department of a large local authority. Your duties include:

- dealing with a large number of telephone queries
- organising the work of your office junior
- keeping personnel records up to date
- coordinating the site plans and designs for a number of different architects.

Your department is situated in the annexe 250 yards from the main building in which the centralised filing system is located. What difficulties do you think you may experience with the system? List all the reasons you can think of before reading further.

Your answers will probably include these points.

- You may not have the information readily available when answering the telephone or dealing with unexpected queries. You might try to beat the system by keeping a duplicate copy of any frequently used information but this obviously defeats one of the objectives of a centralised system.
- Your office junior is not gaining any filing experience, nor can you use filing as a routine 'time filler' if other work is not available. Indeed, it may also be a possibility that although your junior is sometimes underemployed, extra staff are being employed centrally.
- You are concerned about the confidentiality of certain information.
- You cannot use the type of filing system best suited for the architects' plans and drawings.
- You are frustrated by the time you or your junior spends in walking to and from the centralised unit (unless the information can be called up on a VDU via a centralised computer system – and then there may be problems printing it out).
- Some of the architects also try to beat the system by withholding documents or plans they think may be needed again in the near future.

You should note that some of these problems can be solved by the use of a half-way approach whereby:

- **active** (ie currently used) files are stored departmentally and **dead** (ie no longer used or reserve) files are stored centrally
- certain types of documents, eg personnel records, or documents which are exclusive to one department eg the architects' plans, are again kept in the department.

If the system is a departmental one, where will you store the information?

If, as is likely, you are asked to organise your own or your boss's filing system, you will probably find the documents stored in one of a number of different types of filing cabinet.

The choice may have been made for you. If you like the choice – good. If not, try to persuade your boss to let you change it. If you can't, try to work round it.

The factors which should have been considered are:

- the nature of the material to be filed: general correspondence, specialist material, confidential records etc
- the quantity – five documents per day, or 500?
- the space available
- the money available
- how quickly the information is required; if, for instance, you are dealing with the general public you want the information very quickly; if you are engaged on research for your boss then you can afford to take more time
- the number of people using the system; a word of warning here – whilst the reputation of being the 'office dragon' is not good for your image in general, a little firmness here is an advantage. If everyone uses the system without any control, you have problems – see page 94
- the length of time for which the material needs to be kept (see page 93 for information on records retention systems)
- the confidentiality of the records
- the location of the storage equipment – is it in your own office or is it in a public area?

What different methods of storage can you use?

In the case of traditional storage systems (as distinct from computerised systems) you may wish to consider the following:

Vertical filing cabinets

The document folders are placed one behind the other in a filing cabinet with 2–6 drawers. The drawers may be fitted with suspension pockets into which the document folders can be placed. (Note that although 4-drawer cabinets are the norm, a 2-drawer cabinet can be useful in your immediate work area for documents which are either in constant use or needed when you are using the telephone.)

Very large documents can be stored vertically in a chest plan file where the documents are suspended, either one behind the other or in stand-alone dividers.

Advantages
- They are traditional – most people know how to use them.
- They are convenient to use and the files are easy to label.
- Closed cabinet drawers can conceal a multitude of sins from the outside world!

Disadvantages
- A large amount of floor space is used.

CHECK IT YOURSELF
Discuss with your tutor any safety hazards this type of cabinet may present – particularly if someone is in a hurry to collect information from a number of different cabinets. What safety features have manufacturers now built into the equipment to prevent accidents occurring?

Lateral filing cabinets

Documents are contained in files which are placed side by side in a cabinet, again usually in suspended pockets.

A variation is the use of a lateral multi-purpose cabinet which allows a combination of both lateral and vertical filing and which includes other features such as shelves and storage space for computer materials – print wheels, cartridges, disks, print-out paper etc.

Advantages
- Best use is made of floor space – it is possible to store records virtually from floor to ceiling.
- More than one person can access the files at the same time.
- Every file within the cupboard can be seen at once.

Disadvantages
- They are not as easily accessible as vertical filing cabinets.
- It is more difficult to keep the system presentable – many lateral filing systems are open systems and are only concealed from public view at the end of the day when the dust covers are lowered.

TEST YOURSELF
Discuss the safety hazards there may be with this type of system – particularly if the filing clerks are small!

Horizontal filing cabinets

Documents are stored flat, one above the other.

Advantages
- They are useful for awkward documents such as plans, drawings or photographs.

Disadvantages
- They are too specialised for general use.
- There are difficulties in extracting and returning documents.

TEST YOURSELF

1 What other types of container can be used for this type of document?

2 There are several variations on these standard systems and much depends on the size of the organisation as to which are used. Two further systems are given below. Add to these by producing your own information sheet on rotary filing.

Variations
Mobile filing

Suspended file holders are incorporated into trolleys so that they can be easily moved from place to place. These are particularly useful in open plan offices.

Automated filing

The files are contained in automated units and the operator obtains the information by pressing a button. The units move around automatically until the relevant document is reached.

Some firms specialise in transforming work environments by installing automated filing which operates on a vertical **carousel** system from floor to ceiling. One firm of London solicitors compressed 290 4-drawer conventional filing cabinets into 54 square feet of space by means of just such a system.

A variation on this system can be found in college or university libraries where reference material such as magazines and journals are stored in aisles on large shelving units which can be moved automatically to close one aisle and open up another.

TEST YOURSELF

Given that different students may wish to consult reference material on two or three different shelves at the same time, what do you suggest the system should incorporate to prevent someone from being trapped in an aisle?

Would you know how to use an electronic filing system?

Even the most modern offices seem to handle an increasing quantity of paper. Recent research indicates that, despite the increase of computerised information-handling techniques, more than 95 per cent of business communications still arrive in paper form. Even so, most offices are now taking some steps to reduce their volume of paper work by use of computerised systems.

As an example, a recent user is the Inland Revenue which is now operating a system capable of storing and retrieving over a million A4 documents. Although the cost of installation was about £30 000 this has to be balanced against the saving in floor space and consequent saving in office rental.

There can be a three-way approach to the introduction and implementation of electronic filing:

- the use of word processing
- the use of a database
- the integration of all information into an electronic filing system, sometimes referred to as **total document management**.

Word processing

If you use a word processor, the material you produce is stored on disk until you wish to print it. When you want to find a

Compulsory weight-training

Time-consuming and boring

Hard to get at

document you have already prepared you call up the **directory** on the word processing system and retrieve the information either on to the screen or on to hard copy (ie in paper form) via the printer. There is little difference here from your storing and then retrieving a document from a filing cabinet.

With new electronic filing

13 000 pages on one compact disk

Automatic and fast

Indexing finds the file at the touch of a button

Database

You may find that in addition your computer terminal has a database which contains a set of data (or information) about a particular topic or topics which is intended to be used in the same way as any other filing system, ie as a source of reference. You may be allowed only to 'read' the information (ie to call it up on screen or print it out on hard copy) or, if you are authorised to do so, you may be able to amend it and input further information.

For instance, a Sales Manager may wish to store on his database:

- the names of his customers
- the areas in which their firms are situated
- the products they order.

Not only can he do this but he can then retrieve the information in different ways.

- He may wish to find out how many customers he has in the Manchester area.
- He may want to know how many customers buy a certain product.
- He may want to know in which areas a product is or is not selling.

With this information he can then start to plan different targeted sales campaigns, mail shots etc.

SPECIAL NOTE
Many commercial firms now supply tailor-made databases. For example, there are computer personnel packages which cover the storage and retrieval of personnel reports, routine correspondence, absence statistics, graphical analysis and which are capable of being integrated with training and recruitment files.

Total document management

You may work in an organisation where electronic filing is used to store the vast majority of files used during the working day.

In such cases, certain procedures have to be followed.

- The material may be input to the computer (which can be stand alone or networked) by means of the keyboard. The difficulty here, however, is that:
  - a lot of time is spent on inputting the information. It is estimated that a good typist, working at a steady 60 wpm will take about 10 minutes to type the text of a full A4 page.
  - there may be details which cannot be input easily, eg photographs, drawings, charts or diagrams.

  Fortunately an alternative is available. If the material already exists in hard copy it can be scanned direct into the computer memory by means of a **document scanner**. This operates in tandem with special computer software which uses **Optical Character Recognition** (OCR). You may find this referred to as **Document Image Processing** by some companies.

- Once the information is stored it can then be retrieved in the same way as from a word processor or database, ie you key in the appropriate code and the data is displayed on the VDU for reading or printing. With many document management systems you are now also able to fax the material direct from the computer to its destination or reproduce it on to microfilm or microfiche using a technique known as **Computer Output to Microfiche** (COM).
- Because the volume of records in such a system is normally large, you may find that special optical or laser disks are used to store the material. These look like compact disks and can store up to 175 000 pages of word processed material on a 12″ disk (thus replacing – so the salesmen claim – the contents of 30 ordinary filing cabinets!). Originally, one supposed difficulty with this method of storage was that information stored on disk could not be overwritten. Recent developments, however, have resulted in the rewritable disk which can be altered.

The advantages of the system are apparent, ie:

- the volume of material which can be stored
- the fact that more than one person at a time may consult the documents in a file

- the ease of keeping track of files
- the standardisation of filing procedures
- the possible multi-use of the computer equipment.

However, there are corresponding difficulties, ie:

- expense (both in relation to capital investment and running costs)
- reliability of equipment – computer failure means no documents are accessible
- confidentiality (the notes of a staff disciplinary interview should not be open for all to see!)
- staff reaction (not all people are 'high tech' minded)
- groups of people requiring the same information at the same time, eg at a meeting, must view the same screen simultaneously
- the fact that people will insist on taking a hard copy of most of the information on disk (to take home, for reference or simply to make notes on) – thus setting up a rival filing system.

Do you know what the legal restrictions are on electronic filing?

Any storage of information on computer is now subject to the legal restrictions outlined in the Data Protection Act 1984.

CHECK IT YOURSELF

Suppose you have been asked to take charge of an electronic filing system in the Personnel Department of a large organisation. The system is only in the process of being instituted but, even so, certain procedures are beginning to worry you, ie:

- everyone in the department is anxious to see the job completed so that they can have full access to the files as before
- most of the Personnel staff are a very close knit group who have worked together for years. They are very conscious of their responsibility as regards confidentiality and intend to continue the normal practice of allowing no one but themselves (or a senior manager) to see the files
- they are also anxious that the information is as complete as possible. The older members of staff can point to numerous instances when information was required about staff who had left the firm ten years previously and they are pressing for complete records of employment to be transferred, even though some of the information is rather old and out of date
- it is common practice for senior managers to add a note to a staff file that the person concerned should be considered for any future promotion.

Check the provisions of the Acts as outlined in the box below to see if you have a genuine cause for anxiety.

THE DATA PROTECTION ACT 1984

The Act requires employers using a computerised data system to register as data users. They must state:

- what information is being stored on computer
- why it is stored in such a way
- how and from where they have obtained it
- to whom it will be disclosed.

The Data Protection Registrar must then try to ensure that personal data:

- is obtained and processed fairly and lawfully
- is held only for one or more specified and lawful purposes
- is adequate, relevant and not excessive
- is not kept for longer than necessary
- is stored in a way which prevents unauthorised access or accidental loss or destruction.

Additional safeguards are required in respect of personnel data covering:

- racial origin
- political opinions or religious or other beliefs
- physical or mental health or sexual life
- criminal convictions.

Note Employees have a *right of access* to all computerised information held about them and may claim compensation for damage and distress if the information is inaccurate.

Exemptions
The provisions of the Act do not apply to data held for:

- the purposes of national security
- the detection or prevention of crime
- calculating payroll or for keeping accounts
- household affairs or recreational purposes
- the subsequent preparation of text (such as documents held in a word processor)
- the purposes of recording the 'intention' of the data user.

Note Although at the moment UK law covers only information in a computerised data system, the European Commission is now considering a proposal to extend this protection to all files whether computerised or manual.

Do you know how microform storage operates?

An organisation with a large number of documents to store and with a limited amount of floor space may use a system of microform storage whereby documents are reduced in size on film so that they can be stored in much smaller units than would otherwise be possible.

The equipment required includes:

- a **camera** – to photograph the information
- a **duplicator** – to reproduce additional copies of the film taken
- a **reader** – to enable users to read the filmed information
- a **reader/printer** – to enable users both to read and print the filmed information.

The type of storage media which can be used includes:

Roll film – like a normal film for a camera.

Advantages

- Gives maximum storage capacity.
- Is relatively inexpensive to prepare.
- Continuous roll format ensures minimal misfiling.

Disadvantages

- Difficult and costly to update.
- Sequential access (rather than random access) means information is difficult to locate quickly.

Microfiche – a rectangular sheet of film containing several images

Advantages

- Preparation is quick and inexpensive.
- Is convenient to post.

Disadvantages

- Is difficult to update.
- Quality can be inferior.

The use of jacket microfilm is a combination of the traditional film strip and microfiche. Short lengths of film are slotted into holders for quicker reference and ease of handling.

Apart from the advantage of space saving, micro-form storage offers other advantages. It allows for:

- savings in filing and indexing equipment
- the safekeeping of very important documents which, after filming, can be stored in a high security area such as a bank
- the removal of the need for weeding out old files
- durability (film lasts longer than paper).

However there are some disadvantages:

- It is inconvenient – use of a reader is always necessary.
- Difficulties in locating exact frames on a film.
- Problems of poor processing resulting in illegibility.
- There are occasional difficulties in filming – if the documents are on coloured paper etc.
- Time is spent in preparing documents for filing (removing staples etc).

SPECIAL NOTES

1 A microfilm bureau will undertake much of the work for you. Many organisations batch their documents and send them to a bureau for processing, rather than bother with doing this themselves.

2 The Civil Evidence Act 1968 allows microfilmed records to be produced as evidence in court subject to certain conditions. Two certificates should be photographed with the documents on each roll of film.
- At the beginning of the roll there should be a **Certificate of Intent** which identifies the nature of the documents to be photographed and declares the intention to destroy the originals after the film has been inspected and found satisfactory.
- At the end of the roll there should be a **Certificate of Authenticity** which declares that the images in the film are true and correct.

Both certificates should be dated and signed by the camera operator and by a senior official of the organisation. You should note that computer disk print-outs are now also admissible as evidence.

TEST YOURSELF

Do you think that such certificates are necessary for all microfilmed documents? List the documents you think should be covered by these certificates. From what you know already, how should the most important documents of an organisation be treated once they are microfilmed?

What can you use to store documents within conventional filing cabinets?

There are several ways in which documents can be stored within a filing cabinet or storage unit. Either at your workplace or training office check to see whether you use:

- shelf filing wallets (used independently or as part of the system)
- filing folders (with or without clear plastic title holders)
- individual suspension folders (in which wallets or filing folders can be placed)
- continuous suspension folders
- lateral suspension folders
- tabbed insert files.

In addition, as a PA/office supervisor you may want to store certain documents on your desk or working area. You could choose:

- a ring binder
- a lever arch file
- a box file
- an expanding or concertina file
- a multipart file
- document (or envelope) wallets.

The factors determining your choice may be:

- low cost
- durability
- size and capacity
- ease of removal of out-of-date documents
- retention of pages in a pre-determined order
- ease of inserting pages to fill gaps while still retaining the overall order.

CHECK IT YOURSELF

Look through some business supplies catalogues and state which type of folder you would use for the following. Note that there may be more than one which is suitable in each case.

- booklets and catalogues
- copies of invoices received
- minutes of meetings
- day-to-day reminders

In what order should you place files in your storage system?

There is little point in buying expensive storage equipment if the documents are then going to be stored in them without any thought as to the order in which they should be stored. Depending on the type of documents with which you are dealing, you can choose from a number of systems, normally known as **methods of classification**.

Alphabetical

This method refers to the filing of the documents according to the first letter of the name, normally the surname of a particular person.

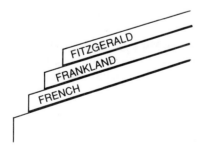

Advantages

- It is simple to understand (if you know the rules for alphabetical filing!).
- It is a direct method requiring no index.
- It is useful for miscellaneous papers (a file can be opened for every letter of the alphabet).

Disadvantages

- It is more difficult to operate in a large filing system.
- It is more difficult to estimate space requirements.
- Confusion or congestion may arise with common names or frequently used letters.

Numerical

In this instance documents are arranged in number order and filed in serial number order (1, 2, 3, etc).

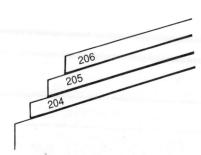

Advantages

- It is capable of unlimited expansion.
- Each document can be given a unique number.
- Greater accuracy should be possible (but see also disadvantages!).
- The file number can be used as a letter reference.
- The index can be used independently (for addresses, telephone numbers etc).
- It can help confidentiality.
- Individual departments can be given a specific block of numbers for easier identification (eg the Personnel Department can be allocated 1–999, the Purchasing Department 1000–1999 etc).

Disadvantages

- There is no direct access – an index is always required.
- There is always the possibility that figures may be transposed, eg 312 can easily become 321 and the file is then very difficult to find.

CHECK IT YOURSELF

A further disadvantage with numerical filing is that miscellaneous files can be difficult to initiate. Discuss with your tutor why this is the case and suggest, as a group, ways of overcoming this problem.

Terminal digit

This is a variation of the numerical system in which the files are arranged numerically from right to left, each two digits representing a piece of information. For instance, a file numbered 146321 may indicate that:

- 21 is the drawer number
- 63 the file number, and
- 14 the number of the document itself.

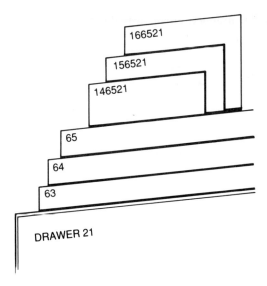

Normally terminal digit systems are only used in organisations with a very large number of files or where pinpoint accuracy is required (eg a hospital).

Advantages

- It is useful where the precise location of individual documents is important.

Disadvantages

- It is complex and time-consuming.
- It is not a direct system of filing – an index is required.

Subject

Subject classification requires documents to be arranged, usually in alphabetical order, according to the subject matter. Under 'A' for example, there could be a number of files relating to Accounts, Annual Reports, Architectural plans, etc.

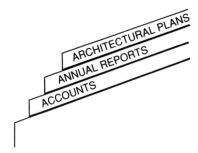

Advantages

- It is an easy system to understand.
- The papers relating to one topic are filed together.
- Direct access is possible.
- Unlimited expansion is possible.

Disadvantages

- When more than one person is using the system, it may be difficult for users to read someone else's mind and to work out the exact subject title. If you are asked to file some documents relating to a visit to Poland you may want to file them under Poland but someone else may wish to file them under Travel Arrangements, etc.
- There may be too many files covering a number of related topics.
- It is difficult to estimate space requirements.

Geographical

In this system documents are arranged, again usually in alphabetical order, according to their geographical location.

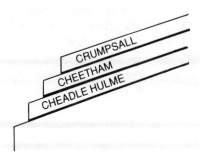

Advantages

- It is a convenient system where the location is known.
- It is useful where regional information may be required.

Disadvantages

- It is too specialised for general use.
- There is the possibility of error

if the user's geography is weak, eg is Richmond in Surrey or in Yorkshire – or both?

Chronological

Here documents are arranged according to date.

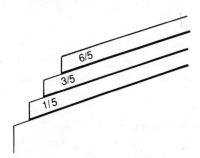

Advantages

- It is useful where a date has some special significance.
- It can be used as a part of an overall system (such as the filing of applications for shares where they are to be allocated on a first come, first served basis).

Disadvantages

- Again, it is too specialised for general use.
- It is meaningless without an index.

 SPECIAL NOTE

As a PA/supervisor you can choose more than one system of classification. For instance, it is often useful to combine alphabetical and subject methods of classification.

It is also possible, in some circumstances, to integrate two systems completely – particularly in the case of an alpha-numerical system in which:

- the files are initially grouped alphabetically, but
- within each alphabetical division each file is given a number.

The system is supposed to combine the advantages of both alphabetical and numerical systems – but is apt to contain some of the disadvantages of both as well!

TEST YOURSELF

Suggest a suitable method of classification for:

- a solicitor's list of clients
- staff records in a Personnel Department
- a client's documents held by a travel agent
- sales invoices and orders
- minutes of a committee meeting
- details of sales territories allocated to a number of sales representatives
- documents relating to a fixed term research project covering a single topic area

Are you going to have an index system?

Although many filing classification systems depend on an index, an index can also be useful in its own right to record information such as telephone numbers and addresses. In addition, other facts may be included eg the name of the representative responsible for that account, the credit limit etc. Often the same index system can be used for both purposes, particularly when a numerical system of classification is used.

You can choose from the following.

Vertical card index

This consists of a number of cards, each concerned with one item of the index. The reference heading is written along the top edge of the card and the remainder of the space can be used for other information.

The cards can be arranged vertically in a drawer or small container and tabbed guide cards can be used for easy reference.

A variation on this theme is the use of an automatic card index where trays of cards are suspended from revolving mechanisms to allow the user to obtain quick access to a large number of cards.

Strip index

This consists of a frame into which 'strips' of card containing one or at the most, two lines of information, can be fitted in any required order. The frames can be fixed to the wall, made up into book form or arranged on a rotary stand. Strips of different colours can be used to differentiate different types of information.

Visible edge card index

This consists of a series of index cards arranged so as to overlap, leaving a strip of each card exposed. The exposed edge is used for the reference heading and the remainder of the card for the other information. Again the cards can be housed in a cabinet or kept in book form.

SPECIAL NOTE

You would locate files stored in an electronic filing system by means of the database menu. No other indexing system is required unless you are storing the disks yourself, in which case you would have to index the disks, normally numerically.

TEST YOURSELF

The type of index storage container you choose wll normally depend on:

● the number of index references
● the amount of information you want to include in the reference
● the speed with which you may require it.

Bearing these factors in mind, which do you consider would be met by:

a a vertical card (visible edge) index system
b a strip index system?

Operating the system

Let us assume that you have sorted out your filing equipment and arranged your files in a logical order. However, as a PA/supervisor, even more is expected of you!

A filing system can only be really efficient if:

● the systems and procedures for operating it are clear *and*
● the operators are properly trained.

If your responsibilities do include the effective operation of the organisation's or department's filing system then you should check that your staff:

● know the general rules of filing
● know what to keep and what to throw away
● can cross-reference documents
● can trace documents which have been borrowed
● are aware of the procedures for dealing with confidential documents.

You can help them by:

● giving them some training in how to file *and*
● instituting procedures relating to
  – records retention
  – cross referencing
  – follow up systems
  – security of files.

How to file

You may have to help your staff by giving them the following hints.

● Make sure they know how to file alphabetically (use the telephone directory as a guide).
● If there is a batch of documents to file *pre-sort them first* (a concertina file is ideal for this). They should not file one document at a time or they will be constantly moving from one cabinet to another.
● File documents in date order within each folder; the most recent document should be placed in the front or on the top of the papers in the folder.
● Keep files tidy (staff should remember their image!).

- Do not let files become too overcrowded (see below for information on records retention).
- Have some procedure for recording the borrowing of files (see page 94 for details on follow-up systems).
- File regularly – every day if possible.

Records retention

You can take one of three courses of action:

- transfer old records to reserve filing
- destroy all unwanted documents and leave the rest of the file intact (but be careful!)
- microfilm all documents.

The factors influencing your choice may be:

- the amount of low cost space available – if there is plenty you might want to retain documents for longer periods
- the volume of individual records – if small, they may be kept for longer periods
- frequency of reference – how far is reference back necessary and how often it is carried out
- legal requirements – certain documents must be kept for a specific period of time, eg contracts and VAT documents must be kept for six years, contracts under seal for 12 years.

What *you* must do is to set up a specific policy for others to follow.

- You should first of all decide which papers need to be retained, which destroyed and which placed in reserve storage.
- You should lay down guidelines for various types of documents and make out a programme listing the records under headings such as '1 year', '2 years', 'indefinitely'.
- You can distinguish documents with an indefinite retention life by keeping them in separate folders or you can subdivide them according to the retention classification of their contents (by a note attached to the cover, colour coding etc).
- You should decide on the timing of the periodic checks, eg three months, six months etc and use your follow-up system to remind you. (See page 94 for further details.)

Cross referencing

Some systems of classification require more cross referencing than others. If, for instance, you decide to use subject classification you may find that you use cross-referencing frequently because one document may contain information on several subjects.

In one morning's post, for example, there may be

- a letter from a builder containing information about three separate contracts

- a letter from an important client covering two accounts
- a letter from a publisher referring to two books.

Unless you train your staff carefully you may find that the letters are put in one file only, thus leaving the other relevant files incomplete. It may be a good idea for you to institute a cross-referencing system so that:

- the original document is placed in the 'master' file *and*
- there is a brief note made of its existence on an index card which is then placed in the 'secondary' file or files.

CHECK IT YOURSELF
Modern office juniors may argue with you that the use of a photocopier now makes this system outdated. In many cases this is so, but in what circumstances (and in relation to what sort of documents) would you suggest it is still necessary?

Follow up systems

You *must* ensure that you know where your files are (and who has them!). Electronic filing can solve many of your problems in this respect but if you are operating a manual filing system then you must establish a system which both records the removal and return of files and reminds the filing clerk to check up on their whereabouts after a certain period of time. Much depends on the size of the filing system, of course, and in some cases a note in your office diary followed by a further self-reminder note a week later will be sufficient. In most cases, however, you need a more formal procedure.

A **pro-forma card** index system can be used containing details of:

- name/reference number of the folder
- date of removal
- name/department of person to whom the folder is given
- projected date of return.

You should note that normally it is far better to allow the full folder to be borrowed (unless some of the information it contains is too confidential to be released) rather than a single document. It is easier to lose one document than a bulky file!

Once the card has been completed it can then be placed in the folder from which the file has been taken or it can be placed in an index card container and an OUT marker placed in the folder itself. Obviously the latter method makes it easier for you to follow up the missing files as the cards can be placed in date order and the system checked each day to see what documents have not been returned.

TEST YOURSELF

Following up absent files is one task which, in theory, is simple for you to delegate to your office juniors but in practice can cause them some difficulty. Why do you think this may be the case?

Security of files

Confidentiality of information is the buzz phrase at the moment – remember the Data Protection Act. You as supervisor will be well advised therefore to lay down some basic rules to protect the security of your files.

- It is naive to think you can *entirely* prevent leakage of information – determined office gossips can be very inventive in thinking up ways to gather information – but you can cut down the opportunities you give them.
- One of your most important lines of defence is your staff – you must impress upon them the need for confidentiality and put in place certain procedures to help them.
- An obvious safeguard is the locking of filing cabinets and the rooms in which they are kept. If files are particularly confidential other procedures must be instituted such as the authorisation of the taking of photocopies.
- If you file electronically, you can make use of a password to which only authorised users have access. In some cases there may be several levels of user. Some will be allowed access via a password to sections of information: only a few will be allowed access via an additional or different password to all the information. As an extra precaution passwords can be changed at regular intervals.

CHECK IT YOURSELF

All the above procedures protect the security of the files and their confidentiality. They do not protect them from physical hazards such as fire or water. Investigate as a group the precautions which could be taken to protect files from such risks.

ACTIVITY SECTION

Individual tasks

1 You are in charge of a centralised electronic filing system. The Training Office has asked you to give a five minute talk to a group of new employees about how it works.

   As a group research the topic and prepare some relevant notes. Give the talk with each member of the group having an equal input.

2 Divide into two groups. Group A has to prepare and present a case outlining the advantages of the proposed change in the legislation allowing employees to have full access to their records. Group B has

to prepare and present a case outlining the disadvantages of this initiative.

Debate the issue and note your conclusions.

3 One of your juniors cannot get used to the terminal digit system of classification. You prepare the following exercise for him. Make sure you know the answers!

EXERCISE

You are operating a terminal digit system of classification in which each file drawer is given a number, each folder is given a number and each document is given a page number, eg

Document	**File folder**	**Drawer**
21	14	01

Remember that the numbers are read in pairs from right to left.

a You are asked to start a new file. What will be the reference number of the first document in that new file (assuming that the drawer is not full)?

b If the current situation in drawer 01 is as shown above, and you want to file a new document in file folder 14, what number will you give it?

Individual/group tasks

Case study 1

1 When you begin your new job as office supervisor in an engineering firm you are faced immediately with the problem of an inefficient centralised manual filing system.

The major complaints from senior managers appear to be that:

- every time a file is requested a different clerk goes to look for it (normally the newest member of staff) – the time spent waiting for files to be found is therefore excessive
- quite often a file cannot be found because someone else has borrowed it and forgotten to return it
- sometimes it just cannot be found!
- occasionally the material required is contained in three or four different files
- it is often difficult for the clerk physically to extract the file because there are too many files in one drawer
- very recent documents are generally found only after a hunt through the filing basket
- most of the filing folders are old, dirty, torn and over-full.

You have to sort this out. Draw up a schedule indicating what action you will take and in what order you will take it.

2 After you have been in your new post a week, one of your juniors comes to see you to discuss some problems she has been experiencing with various members of staff. She gives you the following information.

- Mr Frankland is always trying to beat the system; he comes in at all hours of the day and tries to persuade whoever is available to stop work immediately and give him the file he requires.

- Miss Waterhouse pulls rank. She is the Sales Manager's secretary and demands that she is given priority whenever she wants any information. Your predecessor had difficulty in trying to prevent her from doing this because if she was not given special treatment she complained to the Sales Manager (who normally took her side).
- Mr Jayasuria is pleasant but scatterbrained; he never returns a file despite repeated reminders.
- Mr Heap does return files but there are sometimes one or two papers missing from them or they are in the wrong order.
- There is no actual proof, but every time Mrs Roberts borrows a file containing any confidential information, this information becomes common knowledge very quickly.

How would you try to solve these problems?

3 You feel that there should be a radical change to the centralised system of filing. You discuss the matter with the Managing Director who wants to retain a centralised system of filing but is willing to consider the use of:

- automated filing and/or
- microfilm storage.

He asks you to prepare a report outlining the benefits of each system.

Case study 2
Read (or enact) the scenario below and then answer the questions which follow.

John I've got to find that letter. Peter Dobson has been in three times already asking for it. (*starts looking through papers in filing tray*)

Salma Have you looked for it in the filing cabinets?

John (*sarcastically*) Do you know I never thought of doing that – (*snaps*) of course I've looked in the filing cabinets! Where do you think I've been looking – in one of the plant pots?

Salma From the look of that cabinet you might as well.

John (*pathetically*) Well, I've been busy lately. You know how it is.

Salma Well, frankly, no – and whilst you're looking for Mr Dobson's file, could you get out the papers for Mr Andrews. He has a meeting at 11.30 this morning and he rang you up about it yesterday.

John (*in a rage*) Look, I'm fed up with this! It's always my fault when something gets lost – I'm sick of taking the blame.

Salma Well, you're the filing clerk, aren't you? I thought that meant that you were supposed to be good at filing papers – not just your nails.

John Oh, very amusing. Look, there's nothing wrong with my filing. I file things perfectly (*hesitates*) – I just can't find where I've filed them sometimes.

Salma (*exasperated*) Oh, let me have a look will you – I can't do any worse! (*dusting a file*) What a mess! Some of these papers go back years. Don't you ever clear them out?

John (*simply*) No.

Salma Well, what do you do when you can't get anything else into the cabinet?

John Ask for another.

Salma But surely . . . (*gives up and starts looking through cabinet*)

Telephone rings

John (*picks up receiver*) Hello – look I'm busy at the moment, I'll ring you back. Yes, I know it's my job to look after the files. Yes, I know I should be able to lay my hands on a file at a moment's notice. Yes, I know all that. (*loses temper – snaps*) Look, do you want a pint of blood at the same time? (*calms down – wearily*) All right, all right – what name is it again? Oh, the Thompson file . . . well why didn't you say so . . . you didn't, you know . . . you said Johnson . . . (*more emphasis*) . . . you did, yes you did. (*pause*) Well, I'm not going to argue – OK. It's the Thompson file. I'll send it up as soon as I can. Anything else? The ABC Company file? OK. I'll check for you. (*puts hand over receiver – to Salma*) Look for the ABC Company file will you? (*looking through files*)

Salma I can't find it. Are you using the alphabetical system?

John Of course I am. It must be there. You're not looking properly.

Salma I've been through all the A's

John Well, that's it then – try the C's.

Salma Why?

John Because I tell you to, that's why.

Salma No, I mean why C and not A?

John C for company of course – do I have to spell everything out for you? Look, hold on, (*to telephone caller*) you'll have to wait – I'll send that file up too. (*puts phone down*) If you can't find it in the Cs look in the miscellaneous file, will you?

Salma (*takes out a very large, untidy file*) It'll take hours to go through this.

John I never bother.

Salma But what's the point of having a miscellaneous file if you don't use it?

John (*sorting aimlessly through files on desk*) Gets things off the desk, doesn't it? Hang on, I think I've found one of them at least – that should shut the old fool up for a while. Just chuck it in the out basket will you?

Salma Is that all you're going to do?

John (*engrossed in reading another file and only half listening*) What else should I do . . . Hey, look at this . . . I didn't know Jim Redding was as old as all that . . . his wife must be only half his age . . . and just look at how much he earns. I'm getting a pittance compared to him – wait until I see him.

Salma (*reading a leaflet*) Have you seen this? There's an in-house training course about the use of computers for the storage and retrieval of information. Why don't you ask to go on it?

John   Because I don't want to know anything about storing and retrieving information.

Salma   But that's what you're paid to do.

John   It isn't you know! I'm paid to file (*smugly*) – and I reckon I'm doing a pretty fair job.

1 What basic filing rules do you consider the filing clerk has forgotten (or never been told!)?

2 What do you consider is the difference between simply 'filing' and 'the storage and retrieval of information'?

3 Despite your annoyance and impatience with John, your boss is concerned that lack of training could be the problem. If this is the case, it is the company's responsibility to try to put things right. He has asked you to draw up a comprehensive training programme to cover the main points and note down the factors you would include.

4 How would you persuade John that he should not only attend the training sessions but put what he learns into practice?

Section 2 – Locating and abstracting information from unspecified sources

Facts can't lie? Unfortunately they do sometimes. When trying to obtain information from any source, don't be too ready to accept anythng you read or are told. Reference books can be out of date or incomplete; so too can computer databanks. People can be in too great a hurry to be bothered to give you the information you require. The Public Relations Officers of some organisations may wish to confuse you deliberately (or at least give you some biased information) – try contacting ASH and the Tobacco Advisory Council for facts on the effects of smoking and compare the different sets of information!

With that warning in mind, however, there are certain major sources to which you can refer as a first step.

Personal and office files

You are often your best source of information and therefore your **personal** files should be comprehensive, up to date and tailor-made to your own particular needs. Most PAs, however, would find it useful to have readily available information on:

- names, addresses and telephone/fax numbers of clients (plus, where relevant, the name of their opposite number PA)
- internal telephone users
  – names, titles, extension numbers of everyone in the organisation

- 'help' agencies
  - travel
  - employment
- sources of supply
  - office stationery and equipment
- maintenance services (either within or outside the organisation)
  - electrical
  - plumbing
  - heating
- local restaurants/hotels/caterers
- local garages.

Your next step would be to consult your **office** files. They should supply you with most of the information you need about your own organisation and its contacts.

Outside sources of reference

Before you start your enquiries outside your own particular company, remember that most outside organisations are not paid to help you. If you want information, therefore, be persistent but tactful. If you don't know the name of the relevant person, either ask for the Public Relations Department, or rely upon the receptionist to help – be prepared with a brief summary of your requirements. Remember also to thank anyone who has been helpful; not only is it good for public relations but it may also pay dividends should you seek their help again!

Outside organisations

Much depends, of course on your particular query as to the organisation you will contact.

Examples of **general** sources include:

- local government and town hall departments
- the Post Office
- newspaper information services eg *The Times, The Daily Telegraph*
- consumers' associations and consumer watchdogs, eg OFTEL
- individual advisers, eg solicitors, accountants.

Outside organisations which may be able to help you with a **travel** query are:

- embassies and national tourist offices
- local tourist information centres
- travel agencies
- AA/RAC
- airline offices/shipping offices
- British Rail
- local car hire firms
- passport offices

- local Customs and Excise Departments
- hotel booking services.

Business queries tend to be more specialised, but useful sources include:

- the public relations departments of large firms
- local Chambers of Commerce and Industry
- London Chamber of Commerce and Industry
- British Institute of Management – its information centre in London houses one of the world's largest management libraries
- professional bodies. (A full list is given in Whitaker's Almanack – see page 113 for further details)
- trade associations (useful information is provided in their annual handbooks)
- HMSO (see page 118 for details of its publications)
- British Standards Institute (for approved standards of production etc)
- Industrial Society (for advice on and training in management and industrial relations)
- Advisory, Conciliation and Arbitration Service (ACAS) (Its Work Research Unit provides details of published articles on all aspects of employment.)
- the Department of Trade and Industry (particularly for information about registered companies)
- the Commission of the European Communities (background report sheets are available on a wide range of topics of interest concerning the EC).

Staff welfare

You should be aware of sources of reference which could assist you with **staff welfare** problems. As PA/supervisor you could be responsible for a number of staff. Part of your terms of reference should be a concern for their welfare and a willingness to listen to any personal difficulties which may be affecting their work. However, you are not likely to be able to give expert advice if, for instance, one of your staff says that:

- her husband cannot understand why he is not entitled to unemployment benefit even though he is unemployed, or
- she is having problems with her neighbours whose son plays loud music late at night, thus preventing her from getting to sleep

and so on.

What might be useful to you is to be aware of what professional help there is available in these or similar circumstances.

The reference library

Obviously the outside organisations which could be valuable sources of reference to you are almost as numerous as the reference books. What you need, therefore, is a starting point and that starting point is normally your reference library. Your organisation may choose to pay a subscription to obtain the services of ASLIB (Association of Special Libraries and Information Bureaux) which will:

- undertake searches for specialist technical and commercial information
- locate reports and articles
- trace references and search for other bibliographic information.

It also maintains an index of English translations of articles originally in foreign languages and a register of translators with an indication of their qualifications and specialised subjects.

SPECIAL NOTE
The Guide to Government Departments and other Libraries, published bi-annually by the British Library, lists a large number of specialist libraries, as does *Libraries in the UK and Republic of Ireland*.

Using the library
Remember that librarians are there to help you. Ask them what you want to know!

If, however, you want to look at a range of reference materials on a particular topic it is useful if you know the indexing system used in most libraries – commonly known as the **Dewey Decimal System**.

THE DEWEY DECIMAL SYSTEM

A A numerical designation is used to indicate the subject of the book and its shelving position. There are ten main classes:

000 General Works
100 Philosophy
200 Religion
300 Social Sciences
400 Language
500 Natural Science
600 Applied Science or Useful Arts
700 Fine Arts and Recreation
800 Literature
900 History, Biography and Travel

B Each of the main classes is divided into ten sections. For example 600 is divided as follows:

610 Medical Science
620 Engineering
630 Agriculture
640 Domestic Economy
650 Commerce
660 Chemical Technology
670 Manufacturers
680 Mechanic Trades
690 Building Construction

C The sections can be further subdivided as follows:

650 Commerce
651 Office Economy
652 Typewriting
653 Shorthand
654 Telegraph, cables etc
655 Printing and Publishing
656 Transport
657 Book-keeping and Accounts
658 Business Methods and Industrial Management
659 Advertising

D It is possible, by using decimals, to break down the subsections still further if required, eg
Advertising
659.1 **Newspapers**

CHECK IT YOURSELF
Using the information in the table on page 103, as a guide, check in your nearest library what general information is contained in the books classified under the following index numbers:

331.1   658.322
331.88 658.386
347.7   658.800

NOTE   All are connected with business or industry.

Reference books

Reference books and journals can be very useful if they are used with caution. Remember always to:

- look at the date of the book (old editions can confuse or – even worse – give false information)
- check on the country of origin (if, for instance, you are looking at an American reference book you may find that the information given relates solely to that country).

Although in most cases you can make use of the reference material in your nearest reference library, you may also need to buy some books. If possible, choose those which are in loose leaf form in a binder so that they can be updated (eg *Croner's A – Z of Business Information Services*). In such cases the publishers will provide a regular updating service in return for an annual subscription. A further option is to subscribe to a weekly or monthly journal on the topic.

A single list of reference books is often meaningless, unless the index of the entire contents of the British Library is reproduced! However, it is possible to classify the major reference materials into these sections:

- Books about books
- General reference
- People
- English usage
- Travel

- Business – at home
- Business – overseas
- Government publications
- Statistics

CHECK IT YOURSELF
Rather than just reading through the list in the Appendix at the end of this section – you'll never concentrate for so long – take it to your College or nearest town library and check to see how many are on the shelves or in stock. (Remember that some libraries keep certain reference books in **reserve storage** to be handed over only on request.) Remember also to use the library index!

Read the Appendix on page 112 and then try the questions which follow.

1 Name at least two books from the list which give information on:
   a synonyms
   b forms of address
   c hotels
   d stocks and shares
   e British companies
   f European companies
   g trade marks
   h MPs.

2 Find out the following information. In each case give the name of the book as well as the correct answer.
   a half day closing in Malmesbury
   b the area in square miles of Algeria
   c the MP for Kilmarnock
   d the meanings of *iodoform* and *ultrasonic*
   e when *lunch* and *luncheon* should be used
   f a four star hotel in Salcombe
   g the monetary unit of Australia
   h the difference between notable and noted
   i the additional charge for a personal call

Business periodicals/journals

Although the use of types of journals depends very much on the specialised area in which you work, certain journals are of interest to almost anyone working in the business sphere, eg:

- *Business Equipment Digest*
- *Computing*
- *European Management Journal*
- *Financial Management (US)*
- *Industrial Society Magazine*
- *Industrial Relations Journal*
- *Information and Software Technology*
- *The Journal of Marketing*
- *Management Accounting*
- *Management Today*
- *Modern Management*
- *New Statesman and Society*
- *New Scientist*
- *The Spectator*
- *Office Equipment News*
- *Personnel Management*
- *Training.*

Databanks

An increasing amount of information is now held in computer **databanks.** This is the name given to a database which contains a large quantity of reference material.

Some information is stored on **public computer databanks** to which you pay a subscription. The information can be recalled in the usual way on to a computer VDU or an adapted television set. Such databanks include the following.

Teletext

A **one way** communication system by which the user can request information but cannot transmit any. In the UK, Teletext is known as **Ceefax** (available on BBC) and **Oracle** (available on ITV). It is essentially a free service although the user must purchase a television with Teletext included or an add-on Teletext facility for an existing television etc. When Teletext is accessed an index is displayed on the screen and, with the aid of a hand-held digital unit, the user is then able to request the pages (or **frames**) of information required. Information available includes subjects of general interest.

Videotext (or viewdata)

An **interactive** system through which users can both request and transmit information. A keyboard and a modem are required to enable the user to communicate with viewdata and the viewdata equipment is connected to a telephone line.

One form of viewdata is a public system known in the UK as Prestel. To access the **Prestel** service the user dials a given number and then enters his/her identity and personal password. An index is displayed on the screen and there is also a Prestel directory which can be consulted. Users pay a quarterly charge for the service, the charge of a local telephone call to access the system and a charge for computer time during business hours. Most of the information is available to all users but some is restricted to **closed groups**, ie specified users.

Information provided includes both general and specialist topics. The following services are also available:

● an electronic mail service (see Chapter 1, Communication systems, page 1)
● a telex link.

What you may also find, however, is that you have access to a **private viewdata system**.

Private viewdata

A complete private viewdata package usually includes a computer, a number of viewdata terminals and the viewdata software. The normal procedure is for an organisation to create and maintain a private database for certain specific applications, access being available to both staff and clients. Tour operators, for instance, often allow travel agents to access their system. In addition, travel agents can participate in the *Gallileo* system which enables them to access a wide range of travel information and produce their own tickets.

It is also possible for the Prestel and the private viewdata system to be interlinked by means of the **Gateway** system so that you can make use of both systems.

SPECIAL NOTE
If your organisation does not want to set up a system for its own use but wants to access other subject specific systems, there are now a number of such services available. If, for instance, you work in exporting, you might want to make use of an organisation such as **Export Network**, an information system for exporters which covers areas such as marketing, business contacts, local agents and distributors, finance and insurance regulations, documentation, freight, transport and communications. The information is accessed via a computer terminal and modem through a telephone line.

Library databanks

Also useful for you to note are the databanks now used by many libraries. These contain a wide variety of information on any number of topics and are normally designed to list the titles of any publications relating to your specific inquiry. In addition, some databanks will provide you with summaries of book contents or journal articles. Examples include:

- MARC (Machine Readable Cataloguing) – details of books and journals published worldwide
- DIALOG – details of publications from a wide variety of general sources
- TOXLINE/medline – specific information on medical matters
- LEXIS – legal information.

Note that although you may be able to gain direct access to a library databank, it is also possible to ask the library to institute a search for you (normally for a fee).

Copyright

You and your staff would probably be lost without your photocopier. What you have to remember, however, is that it is likely to be your responsibility to see that you do not break copyright law by allowing unrestricted photocopying of certain documents.

If someone writes a book, composes a song, makes a film or creates any other type of artistic work, the law treats that work as their property (or copyright). Anyone else who wishes to make use of it (by, for instance, taking a photocopy of it) must get permission to do so and – on occasions – must be prepared to pay a fee.

One difficulty for authors and composers in the past has been how to collect the fees owing to them. Today, however, there are a number of collecting agencies which have been established to ensure that such payments are made, ie:

- The Copyright Licensing Agency (CLA)
- The Performing Rights Society (PRS)
- The Mechanical Copyright Protection Society (MCPS)
- The Phonographic Performance Ltd (PPL)
- The Video Performance Ltd (CPL)
- The Design and Artists Copyright Society (DADS)
- The Educational Recording Agency Ltd (ERA).

In most cases, therefore, authors or composers will entrust the administration of their copyright to these societies in return for a percentage of the fees collected. What the societies will also do is to grant a blanket licence to both public and private individuals to give them the right to photocopy certain publications on the payment of a fee. Such licences now cover most educational institutions and negotiations are currently taking place with Government establishments, industry and commerce.

It is important, therefore, that you know what you can or cannot photocopy. Look at the following table which gives details of the relevant Sections of the **Copyright, Designs and Patents Act 1988**.

THE COPYRIGHT, DESIGNS AND PATENTS ACT 1988	
Works protected by copyright • literary, dramatic, musical and artistic works • sound recordings, films, broadcasts and cable programmes • the typographical arrangements of published editions (ie the whole layout of the printed pages of a published edition of a work)	
Length of copyright period Literary, dramatic musical and artistic works	copyright expires at the end of the 50th year after the year in which the author died
Sound recordings and films	copyright expires at the end of 50 years from the end of the year in which the work was made or released
Typographical arrangements	copyright expires at the end of the 25th year after the year in which the edition incorporating the arrangement was first published.

Rights of the copyright owner

The owner has the *exclusive* right to

- copy the work
- issue copies of it to the public
- perform, show or play the work in public
- broadcast it or include it in a cable programme service
- adapt it.

Specific exceptions

Copyright will *not* be infringed if the work is used for certain specific purposes such as

- research or private study
- criticism or review of a work provided the identity of the author and the title of the work are acknowledged
- the reporting of current events provided the identity of the author is acknowledged
- incidental inclusion of any work in an artistic work, sound recording, broadcast or cable programme, eg a shot in a film showing a book lying on a table with its title visible
- educational use

  Note If a licence has been negotiated, such exceptions do not apply.

- libraries and archives – specific regulations are contained in the Copyright (Libraries and Archivists) (Copying of Copyright Material) Regulations 1989
- the reporting of Parliamentary or judicial proceedings, the proceedings of a Royal Commission or statutory enquiry
- abstracts – the copying of an abstract (summary) or an article on a scientific or technical subject published in a periodical containing the abstract or article.

Other exceptions relate mainly to the use of sound recordings and artistic designs.

TEST YOURSELF

You have made yourself aware of the provisions of the Act. You want to make sure that your juniors also know about them.

1 Prepare a brief summary of the relevant provisions of the Act for them.

2 Discuss with your tutor what procedures you could institute to ensure that your juniors do not breach copyright by accident. Consider points such as:

- what paperwork needs to be carried out
- an audit of the types of document normally photocopied (and the quantity)
- the classification of documents into high/medium/no risk areas
- the use of forms to be completed and signed by individual users stating the purpose of the photocopying
- the use of training sessions to raise the awareness of your junior staff
- your role as PA and your responsibility for any decision taken in this area.

Individual tasks

1 What you choose as your major reference books depends on the nature of your employer's business. Look at the requirements of two PAs working in very different areas.

Case 1

The PA to the chairman of a national newspaper listed her most frequently used reference books as:

A dictionary
Who's Who
Vacher's Parliamentary Companion
Stock Exchange Official Yearbook
Directory of Directors
Whitaker's Almanack
AA Handbook
Essential Law for Journalists
Facts and how to find them.

Case 2

The bilingual PA working in the scientific, education and information department of an international space research organisation in Paris makes frequent use of

A French dictionary
Modern English Usage
Atomic Data Processing Glossary
Dictionary of Technical Terms for Aerospace Use
Dictionary of Economics and Commerce
Chambers Dictionary of Science and Technology

Assume that you are working for:

a a sales manager
b an MP
c a hospital consultant.

List the reference books you would find the most useful in each case.

2 Discuss with your tutor the *sources* of reference (not just the books) you would most require if you were PA to *each* of the following people:

a the Public Relations Officer of a cosmetics company who is involved in setting up exhibitions both in the UK and abroad. He needs frequent updating on rival companies' products and the progress they are making.
b the Director of an animal welfare charity who is responsible for mounting fund-raising campaigns and increasing public awareness of the charity. She is also much in demand as an after-dinner speaker.
c a university professor whose particular field of research is Industrial Relations. He has frequent contacts with Trade Union officials, Personnel Directors and ACAS. In his spare time he 'dabbles' on the Stock Exchange.

Individual/group tasks

Case study 1

Your employer arrives at the office in a temper. His car window has been smashed and he wants a replacement urgently. It's over to you to find someone who will come and do it.

In the morning post he receives an acceptance of his invitation to the local MP to open the company's new annexe. He wants you to find out the MP's biographical details so that they can be included in the company publicity for the event.

The MP will require overnight accommodation at a local hotel and would like to stay somewhere which has a health and fitness club.

Some disciplinary problems have arisen in one department and your employer wants an up-to-date copy of the ACAS Code of Conduct on Disciplinary Procedures. He thinks that staff shortages may be at the root of the problem and asks you for a list of local agencies supplying temporary workers particularly in the clerical area.

He remembers that he has promised to contribute an article on staff appraisal systems to a management journal and asks you to find some abstracts on the topic from various books and journals (plus any information there may already exist in the company).

His parting shot as he leaves the office at the end of the day is that his grand-daughter is coming for the weekend and he wants you to find out what films (with a PG classification) are showing at the local cinemas and the times of the performances.

Provide the necessary information for him.

Case Study 2

You work for Morag Braidy, Personnel Director of your company. Morag's speciality is employment law and she is very interested in equal opportunities for women. She is also very interested in the role of women in history and often writes articles for leading magazines and gives talks and lectures to societies, colleges and your local business school.

Morag has recently been asked to give a talk at a local college for students doing politics 'A' level. Her theme is 'Women and politics in the 20th century'.

For her talk she wants to research the life and work of four women politicians

- Nancy Astor
- Barbara Castle
- Shirley Williams
- Margaret Thatcher.

Morag has asked you to visit the library and find out the following information on each woman

a date and place of birth
b date first entered Parliament
c constituency and party represented
d the major achievements for which they are known
e the date they left Parliament – if applicable
f any titles they hold (or held)
g their current occupation (if relevant).

Appendix

MAJOR SOURCES OF REFERENCE MATERIAL
1 How to find out about books British National Bibliography Whitaker's Cumulative Book List The Bookseller (published weekly and brought together quarterly in Whitaker's Cumulative Book Lists) Management Bibliographies and Reviews Current British Directories Directory of Information Sources in the UK **2 How to find out about periodicals and newspapers** British Humanities Index Guide to Reference Material (Library Association) British Sources of Information (Jackson P) Facts in focus (Central Statistical Office) ANBAR Abstracts (various) Willing's Press Guide UK Press Gazette (Trade Press – mainly for journalists) Ulrich's International Periodical Directory

GENERAL REFERENCE
Telephone directories ● Main telephone directories ● Classified business (Yellow Page) directories ● Local alphabetical directories ● Business to business directories listing businesses in classified order which are of predominant interest to the business community The information contained includes: ● names, addresses, businesses, telephone numbers ● details of services such as conference calls, freephone, star services etc.
Royal Mail Guide ● information on all Royal Mail departments ● principal services and regulations Both inland and international charges for letters and parcels are produced in separate leaflets.
British Telecom Guide ● Telecom services and facilities

UK Telex/Fax directories
- names, addresses and numbers of subscribers
- (telex only) – details of answerback codes, charges and services

Whitaker's Almanack
- world organisations and events
- areas and populations of the world
- lists of MPs/peers
- lists of government offices/professional bodies/embassies/legations/trade unions/insurance companies/building societies
- forms of address

Keesing's Record of World Events
- reports and statistics summarised from newspapers/periodicals/official publications

Encyclopaedia Britannica
- a standard work of general knowledge

PEOPLE

Who's Who
- short biographies of living contemporaries in all walks of life

Specialised versions include:

Who's Who in Art
Who's Who in Education
The International Who's Who
Who's Who in the Theatre
The World of Learning
The Academic Who's Who
Who's Who in the World of Oil and Gas
Who's Who in the City

Note also Who was Who – prominent people who have died

Debrett's Peerage, Baronetage, Knightage and Companionage/Burke's Landed Gentry/Kelly's Handbook
- biographical and genealogical information on the peerage
- correct forms of address

Dictionary of National Biography (up to 1985)/Chamber's Biographical Dictionary
- biographies of prominent people past and present

Civil Service Year Book
- members of royal households, public departments, Commonwealth representatives and others

Diplomatic Service List
- British representatives overseas and civil servants connected with diplomacy

Vacher's Parliamentary Companion
- members of the Houses of Commons and Lords, government ministers, staff of government and public offices.

The Times Guide to the House of Commons
- biographical details and photographs of present MPs
- texts of party manifestos
- unsuccessful candidates of the corresponding general election

Dod's Parliamentary Companion
- biographies of peers/MPs
- forms of address
- constituencies
- parliamentary terms

Specialised reference books relating to particular professions, eg
The Army List/Navy List/Air Force List
The Medical Register
The Dentists' Register
The Law List/Scottish Law Directory
Kemp's International Music and Recording Industry Yearbook
Retail Directory
Insurance Directory and Year Book
Education Authorities Directory and Annual

ENGLISH USAGE

Dictionary
- spellings, pronunciations, parts of speech, meanings, derivation, cross reference to related words, plurals.

Note the use of specialised dictionaries such as

- *Chambers Dictionary of Science and Technology; Dictionary of Economics and Commerce; Black's Medical Dictionary; Dictionary of Architecture; Dictionary of Music; Authors' and Printers' Dictionary; Dictionary of Legal Terms.*

Roget's Thesaurus/Webster's New Dictionary of Synonyms
- synonyms

Modern English Usage (Fowler)/Usage and Abusage (Partridge)/ The Hamlyn Guide to English Usage/An ABC of English Usage (Treble & Vallins)
- points of grammar, style and accepted usage

The Complete Plain Words (Gower)
- the way to communicate in unambiguous language

The Spoken Word – a BBC Guide
- pronunciation, vocabulary, grammar

Dictionary of Acronyms and Abbreviations/British Initials and Abbreviations/World Guide to Abbreviations of Organisations
- acronyms, abbreviations

Oxford Dictionary of Quotations/Oxford Companion to English Literature
- quotations, sources

Pears Cyclopaedia
- dictionary/gazetteer/ready reckoner
- synonyms/antonyms
- foreign phrases

British Qualifications
- degrees granted by British universities
- professional qualifications and what they mean

TRAVEL

Atlas
- maps of various continents/countries

Gazetteer
- geographical dictionary of countries/towns/populations/chief products/national incomes

AA Members' Handbook/RAC Guide and Handbook/Michelin Guides
- maps/gazetteer section
- hotels
- garage facilities

The AA and RAC also produce their own Guides for Motoring in Europe.

AA Guide to Hotels and Restaurants in GB and Ireland/Hotels and Restaurants in GB
- hotels and conference facilities

National Express Service Guide/ABC Railway Guide/ABC World Airways Guide/ABC Shipping Guide/Worldwide Guide to Passenger Shipping/ABC Air/Rail Europe/ABC Guide to International Travel/Cook's International Timetable
- timetable services both in the UK and abroad

Travel Trade Directory
- forms of travel
- details of various travel operators/specialist travel services
- addresses of passport and visa offices

World Calendar of Holidays
- chronological and alphabetical details of public holidays of each country

Travel Information Manual (information accessible by airline computer terminals)
- data for all countries on requirements in respect of passport, visas, health regulations, airport taxes, customs and currency

Executive Travel/Business Traveller (published monthly)
- items and articles of general interest for regular travellers

---

BUSINESS AT HOME

Directory of Directors
- directors of all the principal companies of the UK and of a large number of private companies

Stock Exchange Official Yearbook
- details of organisations and membership
- lists of groups of securities and companies
- short history and description of each company

Federation of British Industries Register of British Manufacturers
- addresses of companies, firms and trade associations
- description of products and services
- branch and trade names
- trade marks

Kelly's Business Directory
- alphabetical list of manufacturers
- classification of all companies into trade sections

British Rate and Data (BRAD) (published monthly)
- data and information of rates for all British media trade journals and magazines

Guide to Key British Enterprises (Dun and Bradstreet)
- factual information about prominent British companies

Who owns Whom
- information on British companies owned by American firms and information on the American firms owning them

UK Trade Names/Patents, Designs and Trade Marks/The Trade Marks Journal
• trade marks

Kompass UK
• lists of products and services • company information listed geographically and alphabetically

Croner's A–Z of Business Information Sources/Croner's European Business Information Sources
• major sources of business information

Advertiser's Annual
• companies and their advertising or public relations agencies

Investor's Chronicle (published weekly)
• prices of stocks and shares • news about investment

The Financial Times
• share prices and rates of exchange

BSI Standards Catalogue
• details of the British Standards Institution

Note: **Extel Statistical Services Ltd** produce annual Extel cards stocked by many public libraries which contain details of a large number of quoted British companies including the directors, capitalisation, activities, subsidiaries, profit and loss accounts and balance sheets. A similar service exists for European and North American companies. Note also Macarthy Cards which contain details of newspaper articles about major companies.

BUSINESS OVERSEAS

Statesman's Yearbook
• current information on each country of the world • information on international organisations

Janes Major Companies of Europe
• information on major European companies

Kelly's Business Directory
• information relating to products, subdivided by countries within continents

Yearbook of International Organisations
• information on international organisations

A Yearbook of the Commonwealth
- production and trade statistics for Commonwealth countries

Europa Yearbook: A World Survey
- international organisations in Europe
- as above in Africa, America, Asia and Australasia

Croner's Reference Book for Exporters/Croner's Reference Book for Importers/Exporters' Yearbook/Exporters' Encyclopaedia
- information on exports/imports

British Exports
- products
- technical data

Trade Directories of the World/Anglo–American Trade Directory
- general trades information

GOVERNMENT PUBLICATIONS
(published mainly through the HMSO and available from Government bookshops in London and other large centres, official agents throughout the UK or major booksellers)

Parliamentary papers
- individual reports of Royal Commissions and other inquiries and statements of Government policy, eg Report of the Committee on Data Protection, CMND 7341
- votes and proceedings of the House of Commons and Minutes of Proceedings of the House of Lords, ie concise records of the business transacted each day
- daily or weekly editions of the verbatim reports of debates in both Houses published in Hansard
- House of Commons papers, eg annual reports from Government Departments and reports from Government Committees
- reports from House of Lords Committees
- Acts of Parliament, eg Health and Safety at Work Act 1974

Non-parliamentary papers
- *Civil Service Year Book* – a summary of the functions of Government Departments
- *Britain: An Official Handbook* (annual) – details of legal institutions and financial structures
- individual Government Departmental publications
- publications by international organisations such as UNO
- various catalogues of Government publications published monthly, annually and every five years.

The Central Office of Information (COI) prepares and supplies publicity material on behalf of the other Government departments.

STATISTICS
Government Statistics – A Brief Guide to Resources • guide to statistics available from all official and important non-official publications
Annual Abstract of Statistics • statistical surveys of the social and economic life of Britain in all aspects (supplemented by the Monthly Digest of Statistics)
Business Monitors • business trends • progress of a particular product • rating of companies' performance against the industry as a whole
***Employment Gazette* (published monthly)** • statistics on manpower, wages, hours of work, index of retail prices
Statistical Yearbook • international statistical data collected by the UN Economic and Social Affairs Statistical Office
The HMSO also publishes a variety of specialised statistical booklets eg: *National Income and Expenditure* *Family Expenditure Survey* *Monthly Digest of Statistics* *Financial Statistics* *Overseas Trade Statistics of the UK* *Statistical News* *International Financial Statistics Yearbook (up to 1987)* *Economic Trends* *Social Trends* *Sources of Unofficial UK Statistics (University of Warwick Business Information Service)*

Section 3 – Organising and presenting information in a variety of formats

There are normally three stages in the processing of information:

- finding it
- storing it in such a way that it is easy to relocate
- *using* it.

If you are an effective PA, your boss should be able to rely upon you to carry out all three stages. In some cases you will have to do little more than open a filing cabinet drawer or key in to a computer database to obtain the relevant information which can then be relayed as hard copy or from screen to screen.

In other cases, however, you may find that much of the information you obtain will need amending, abbreviating, re-writing or re-displaying in a different format. The more skilful you become at doing this, the more effective will be your partnership with your executive.

Basic techniques

Your job will be easier if you learn to adopt certain basic techniques in relation to:

- the collation (or drawing together) of all the material collected
- the preparation of the relevant document
- its overall presentation.

Collation of the information

An overall plan of action is essential.

1 Check with your boss as to the format required (is it a summary, a report, a set of statistics etc?).

2 Assess what time you have – is the information required for the next day or have you a couple of weeks before it is needed? In the latter case you have much greater room for manoeuvre (although a better finished result may be expected!).

3 List the sources from which you are going to obtain your material; from that list you can then ascertain how long it is likely to be before you can start work. If, for instance, you are able to obtain all the information from a library you can estimate fairly accurately the length of time you will need. If, however, you are relying on other members of staff or outside organisations to supply you with some information you may encounter problems – you have to work to their time schedule, not yours!

4 Remember the old trick of setting a deadline for the return of the information you need a few days before you *actually* need it (but don't overdo it – otherwise everyone will realise what you are doing!).

5 Once having collected the information, re-check your terms of reference with your boss. (If you are in any doubt you should make a rough draft of what you *think* is wanted and show it to him/her.).

6 Make some 'quiet' time for yourself. Make sure also that you have all the material to hand before you start your first draft.

7 Make certain that the required reprographic/desktop publishing facilities will be available when you need them. A one page document for limited circulation is normally no problem; a detailed high profile report to the company shareholders will require more attention both as to the numbers produced and the standard of presentation.

TEST YOURSELF

Consider the following situations.

a A senior manager is becoming irritated at your repeated requests for some statistical information.

b A manager keeps promising you the information you have requested but never actually produces it.

c A manager responds to your request for information but never gives it in the correct form or amount.

What action would you take in each case? Bear in mind factors such as:

- alternative sources of information
- appeals to other people (either lower or higher in the organisation).

Preparation of the material

1 Draft out the document. At this stage do not be over-concerned about detail but concentrate instead on the correct framework. Make a note at the appropriate place of any charts/tabs/diagrams etc which may be required. Note that if the information is to be displayed in a relatively complicated format, eg a report incorporating graphics/illustrations etc it is likely that you will need to prepare a number of drafts before the final document is produced. In such cases remember to number each draft.

2 Use short rather than long sentences and simple rather than complicated sentence and paragraph structure. Remember your 'audience' – is the report for the Board of Directors, for customers or for your junior staff?

3 Check the draft to see whether:
- the facts are accurate and complete
- it is properly punctuated and grammatically correct
- the vocabulary is clear and easy to understand (Any technical terms or initials should be explained where necessary, eg not everyone will be aware that BTEC stands for Business and Technology Education Council.)
- it is not too long
- the charts/graphs/illustrations are appropriate.

4 Check that the numbering system is appropriate (see page 122 for further details).

5 Remember that another opinion can be valuable, particularly if you are anxious about the style, spelling, grammar etc. Unless the material is confidential ask another PA to read through and comment on your draft.

6 Correct the draft and check with your boss; ask for constructive comments.

7 Prepare the final document and make certain at this stage that your proof–reading is really thorough. Again, if you can, make use of someone else to proof read a second time (see Chapter 5, Preparing and producing documents, page 232). Remember to use your spellcheck!

Presentation of the material

You may have to follow house style. If not adopt your own (and persuade your junior staff to follow suit). Bear in mind:

The numbering system

There are two standard systems from which you can choose. One is to use a combination series of figures and letters, eg

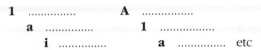

Another approach is to use the decimal system of numbering, eg

1.0 ....
    1.1 ....
    1.2 ....
2.0 ....
    2.1 ....
    2.2 ....
        2.2.1 ....
        2.2.2 .... etc

General layout

Remember to check what reprographic or computerised equipment is available to you in respect of the following:

- varied typeface or fonts (italic, bold, courier etc)
- change of pitch (elite, pica, micro etc)
- emboldening
- line spacing
- graphic symbols (bullets, asterisks, leader dots etc)
- use of capitals/underscore/boxes etc.

Remember, too, to make use of any additional equipment available for binding, stapling and laminating (see Chapter 5, Preparing and producing documents, page 232).

Application to specific formats

Your boss will normally have in mind the format in which the material is to be presented. In general you will be required to:

- summarise the information as one continuous narrative, or
- put it into report form, or
- display it in tabular or graphic form, or
- use a combination of formats.

Summarising the information

Unless you are naturally gifted in this area your heart will probably sink at the sight of this heading. Don't despair – summarising information for business purposes is not as difficult as you may think particularly if you follow certain basic procedures. Suppose, for instance, you have been asked to summarise an article for inclusion in a sales report. What you should do is to break down the task into several stages.

Stage 1

- Skim read the document – don't try to take in every detail the first time through.
- List the main points in note form – don't bother to rearrange any material at this stage.
- Check your list against the original document to see that you have included all the main points.
- If your list indicates that the original document has made several 'scattered' references to one item of information, link them together.
- Check that the names (and titles) of people are included if their identity is relevant.
- Draft out a heading for the beginning of the summary and an indication of its source – the name of the author, the title of the book or journal title, the publisher and the year of publication (if relevant) and the page number(s) of the original document.
- Draft out your summary from your notes – *not* from the original document. Try to keep your sentences short but not too disjointed. Remember to use 'joining' words where relevant.

Stage 2

- Check that the summary is factual and does not include your *opinions*. You don't have to agree or disagree with what is written – merely to record it accurately.
- Check your draft against the original and add or delete information as necessary.
- If you know you have a particular weakness in an area such as spelling try to keep to the vocabulary of the original document as far as possible – and check the rest.
- Check the tense. Use either the past or the present throughout the summary – not a mixture of both.
- Learn to recognise the difference between sentence form and note form, eg:

  Sentence form   The company's sales figures for the past five years showed a steady increase.
  Note form   Steady increase in company's sales figures over past 5 years.

TEST YOURSELF

Change the following notes into sentence form

1 Few department stores opened on Sundays last December. Large increase in the number now doing so.

2 Monopolies and Mergers Commission report – British motorists pay too much for cars – should be a radical change in pricing policies.

3 Pensions – divorced women likely to be in poorer position than married women or widows.

SPECIAL NOTE

In an office it is unlikely that you will be asked to summarise information in a stated number of words. It is more usual for you to be asked to 'cut it down to a couple of paragraphs' or to 'list the main points'. If, however, your boss asks you to make your original summary shorter or longer try to resist the temptation of cutting out or adding odd words. It is far better to rewrite a complete paragraph in order either to shorten or lengthen it.

For instance, if your original paragraph reads

Two distinguished legal writers have compiled a practical guide to quick and effective Court procedures for recovering debts in each EC Member State including procedures to obtain interim and final judgements.

you could abbreviate it to read

A practical guide has been compiled which outlines the Court procedures involved in recovering debts in each EC Member State.

A practical example

Look at the following example which gives you a run through of the steps which you would take in preparing a specific summary for your boss.

Suppose she is the editor of a small local newspaper. She has read the newspaper advertisement opposite and wants you to summarise it so that she can use it as part of her 'selling' campaign to local retailers.

Assume you have read the article and are at the stage of preparing a list of relevant points (in note form). Your list could read

- TV advertising expensive but thought to be a good investment because of audience size and the way in which it 'intrudes' into the home.
- Figures based on assumption that when TV switched on people are watching it.
- Research by Dr Peter Collett, a research psychologist, proves assumption incorrect – 20 per cent of TV commercials play to empty rooms. If, therefore, £10 million is spent on an advertising campaign, £2 million of it is wasted.

You were happy to spend a fortune advertising on TV. Then you had to go and read this.

NO-ONE can deny that television advertising is expensive. The reason advertisers are willing to pay up is because they've been told time and time again – and have had no reason to doubt – that television is a good investment.

Given the huge audiences and the 'intrusive' nature of the medium, for those who can afford it there is no real alternative.

We may think of this as the accepted wisdom. In fact it's the accepted folly.

The figures that make the case for television advertising are based on a method of research which records the times at which viewers turn their sets on, change channels and switch off.

There is also a 'people meter' that records who is in the room, provided they remember to press the button.

This method asks us to make a rather important assumption.

That when people are in a room with the TV set switched-on, they are actually watching.

Everyday experience, common sense and a little elementary sleuthing will show us that this assumption can't be entirely accurate.

Just how wildly inaccurate has recently been demonstrated by research psychologist Dr. Peter Collett, who used the unassailable method of videoing people watching commercials by hiding a camera in their TV sets.

His findings make uncomfortable reading for anyone who spends large sums on television advertising. Let's assume that you 'invest' £10 million. Dr. Collett saw (literally) that 20% of commercials played to empty rooms. Bang goes £2 million.

The video-tapes also revealed that advertising breaks were the cue for people to escape the commercials.

Some people left the room. Others used their remote-control 'zappers' to sample the action on other channels.

As a result, another 10% of commercials (and £1 million of your budget) were lost.

Only 70% of commercials had any audience at all. But the tapes show people talking, reading, sleeping. Some, who evidently forgot they were being filmed, even down to some serious canoodling.

Half the time, no-one was actually watching the TV set.

In effect, only one third of all commercials had the viewers' attention. £7 million of your £10 million was totally wasted.

Whichever way you look at it, television advertising is less than half as effective as you thought it was. Or more than twice as expensive.

In publishing this newspaper advertisement, we do not wish to imply that your television budget is wasted. Just two thirds of it.

Of course we're not suggesting that you stop using television, only that you stop to think about what other, powerful options are available. Newspapers, for example.

You cannot read a newspaper whilst behaving as if it isn't there.

If you put down your newspaper to make a cup of tea, the ads will still be there when you come back. (It is probably impossible to canoodle while reading a newspaper, but if Dr. Collett's research teaches us anything, it is not to be dogmatic.)

Some of the most famous campaigns in advertising history have been conducted in newspapers. We've already featured several of them on these pages. This advertisement contains two more examples.

Newspaper advertisements can be intrusive, powerful and compelling.

You've spent three minutes on this ad already and read every word so far. How much would it cost you to hold someone's attention on TV for three minutes? (Don't forget that TV is more than twice as expensive as you thought it was.)

If you'd like more information, please telephone 071–433 1500.

- Research also reveals that many people leave the room during the commercial break – or switch to another channel. Another 10 per cent of the budget or £1 million is therefore lost.
- Only about 70 per cent of commercials attract any audience at all – and that audience may not be giving them their fullest attention. Only about 1/3 of commercials actually hold the viewers' attention – therefore £7 million of the budget is wasted.
- Proves that TV advertising is less than half as effective (or more than twice as expensive) as is generally thought.
- Cannot both read and ignore a newspaper. Even if the reader has a break, advertisement still there when he comes back.
- Many famous and successful newspaper campaigns in the past.

TEST YOURSELF 1
Develop the list into the required summary. Remember to include a heading and note of the source of reference.

TEST YOURSELF 2
You work for the junior partner of a small chain of antique shops. She feels that there is a market for old toys but needs to convince the other partners (and the bank manager) that she is right. She is preparing a report to present it to them and, when she sees the following newspaper article about the value of old teddy bears, asks you to summarise it for inclusion in her report.

Old teddies bear up well

Collector's file
Peter Johnson

THE Ultimate Teddy Bear Book has been in The Sunday times bestseller list for nine weeks, evidence of the remarkable appeal of the world's most famous toy.

Such attention is good news for teddy bears, you might think, but fame has a price. Once upon a time, although family misfortune might bring out the silver for sale, the resident teddy was the last treasure to be considered for the market. No longer. For 10 years he has been an auctionable commodity, sometimes achieving surprising prices no matter how threadbare – or "well loved", as some catalogues like to put it.

Ever since a plush aristocrat from Baden-Württemberg reached £55,000 at Sotheby's in London in 1989, no bear has been safe. Toy cupboards and attics have been raided in the hope of a killing – though the

market does not expect a repeat performance in the foreseeable future.

The success of the teddy-bear book, by Pauline Cockrill, which has even been No 1 among the general hardbacks, partly reflects the universal triumph of the teddy. There are bear clubs, meets, fairs and, of course, picnics. Ronald Reagan, when president, and Pope John Paul refused to lend their teddies for such events, but Margaret Thatcher allowed her bear, Humphrey, to help a good cause. So did the Princess Royal.

Cockrill spent seven years on the staff of the Bethnal Green Museum of Childhood in east London. "I became a professional arctophile [arctos, Greek for bear] by accident," she says. "An art historian by training, I found that teddy-bear inquiries seemed to make their way to my desk. Before long I was receiving letters addressed to The Lady Who Loves Teddy Bears. I began to build up the museum's

collection of bears. Many donors came with their teddy bears to make sure that they approved of their old companion's final resting-place."

The teddy bear occupies a territory where fantasy meets hardheaded commerce. People used to write to the BBC asking for the autography of Brideshead's Aloysius. And yet a toy-cupboard veteran can fetch the same price as a find old painting, even though no teddy is yet 90 years old.

Teddies owe their name to Theodore (Teddy) Roosevelt, 26th president of the United States, who was a keen big-game hunter.

In 1902, when he was involved as "referee' in a boundary dispute between Mississippi and Lousiana, a newspaper cartoonist, Clifford Berryman, depicted him refusing to shoot a button-eyed bear cub that represented the easy political option.

The cartoon inspired Morris Michtom, a Brooklyn toymaker, to produce a cuddly toy in brown plush. He is said to have received permission from a bemused president to call it after him.

Simultaneously, in a toy factory at Giengen, near ulm in south Germany, Margarete

Steiff, the owner, saw a copy of the cartoon, and Steiff bears were born. Her bears, ungainly, sometimes fierce creatures with sharp teeth, broke into the American market with an order of 3,000; by 1908 her output was nearly 1m.

Steiffs, characterised by a tiny metal name-button sewn into the ear, are today the most highly prized. Among them are world-beaters such as Happy, the 1926 specimen that made £55,000 two years ago. Happy had unusual qualities and was in superb condition, but still it was a crazy price – paid by a Californian tycoon as a wedding anniversary present for his wife.

Most old Steiffs are in the £300– £5,000 range. Some British bears, more round and cuddly than their Teutonic competitors and mad by firms such as Chad Valley and Dean in the 1920s and 1930s, have reached £300–£500. Arcto-philes can test the market on Tuesday when a score of teddies come up at a toy sale at Sotheby's saleroom in Billingshurst, West Sussex.

The auctioneer''s gavel now even hovers over Pooh, Rupert, Sooty, Paddington, Yogi and Fozzie.

Is nothing sacred?

Note that if you wanted to reproduce the entire article in the report or to include part of it verbatim, you would have to seek permission from the owner of the copyright – unless the document was required either for research purposes or purely for internal use. (See pages 108–109 for details of the Copyright, Designs and Patents Act 1988.)

SPECIAL NOTE

On very odd occasions you may be required to summarise a series of correspondence between your executive and one of his business contacts. The same rules apply but in addition you should remember to:

- include the exact dates of all items of correspondence and summarise them in chronological order
- provide a comprehensive title, eg:

Summary of correspondence between Arthur Jensen, Managing Director of Longman Cybernetics Ltd and Diana Maddox, Sales Director of Maddox Computer Services on the subject of the late delivery of networked computer system.

TEST YOURSELF

Discuss with your tutor the circumstances in which you may need to summarise correspondence.

Writing a report

Most reports fall into one of the following categories:

Research reports   where the writer has collected together some information and has presented his/her findings together with some possible conclusions and recommendations, eg if you as a PA are asked to report on the staffing levels in your department.

Work reports   where an account is given of work which has been accomplished during a given period together with an indication of future plans, eg a report written by a sales representative to his head office on the calls he has made during the period covered by the report, potential new customers, increases or decreases in sales, number of new orders, quality issues etc.

Eye witness reports   where a brief account of an incident is required.

Work reports and eye witness reports are normally no more than summaries and are often set out on pre-printed forms. Research reports, on the other hand, require a different format, ie:

The long formal report

A long formal report is normally laid out in several well defined sections:

- the front page – containing the title, the author, the date (and possibly the circulation list)
- table of contents – listing the headings section by section

- the body of the report – including appendices and sources of reference.

The short formal report

The short formal report is similar in layout but is normally displayed in a somewhat abbreviated form and often omits the front page and table of contents.

The brief informal report

This type of report may be little more than a summary in three sections, ie:

- an introduction to the problem
- an analysis of the problem
- a proposed solution.

 SPECIAL NOTE

A **factsheet** may be used as an alternative to the summary or report. Note that:

- it is brief
- it is written in the form of a number of short points rather than a continuous narrative
- it is intended as an 'aide memoire' for the reader

For example:

PROPOSED INTRODUCTION OF TRAINING MODULE/ INTRO-
DUCTION TO OFFICE TECHNOLOGY
1 Existing training
  1.1 General unit in all induction training
      programmes
  1.2 In-house one day course for junior clerical
      staff
  1.3 In-house two day courses for senior PAs
  1.4 External short courses on specific IT areas

2 Proposed additional training in the form of a
  supported open learning unit in office technology
  2.1 Microcomputers
      2.1.1 How to set up a microcomputer and run
            programs
      2.1.2 Essential terms and concepts
      2.1.3 Computers in the office – what they can
            do and how they can be used etc

 TEST YOURSELF

You have been asked to provide some information for the following occasions. For which topic(s) do you think a fact sheet would be the most appropriate form of communication? (Aim for communications where a short list of key points *only* would be required.)

1 A brief summary of the possible effects of wages increases on profits – intended as a working document for a meeting of the Joint Consultative Committee of management and trade union representatives.

2 An investigative report on possible replacement of stand alone computer equipment with a networked system for the Board of Directors.

3 An in-depth article for a journal on recent European legislation relating to occupational pension schemes.

4 Background information to be used as the basis for a handout to visitors attending a launch of the latest model of a car.

Standard report layout

Many companies have their own house style of report and during your induction programme you may be given an outline of how reports should be presented. Whatever the layout required, however, it is likely that there will be certain similarities eg:

1 Terms of reference

Sometimes a heading will suffice:

```
Report on the proposed
installation of a new
vending machine in the
reception area
```

On other occasions you might have to give more details (Note – you may also be expected to give the name of the person who has requested the report.):

```
As requested by the
Managing Director I give
below a report on the
proposal that the present
vending machine in the
reception area be replaced
by a larger machine which
contains both food and
hot and cold drinks.
```

Note that at this stage you should check on the confidentiality of the document; this will affect both your subsequent investigations and your circulation list.

2 Procedure

In most cases you have to state from which sources you have obtained your information – there are normally three approaches.

Direct eg watching the demonstration of a piece of equipment, checking personally on a situation etc.

On Monday, 13 July I visited the reception area on a number of occasions between 10 am and 3.30 pm to make a series of spot checks on the existing vending machine.

Personal eg what you know already or the information you have obtained from talking to someone else

I spoke to five members of staff at random and asked their opinions as to the quality, cost and selection of drinks obtained from the machine. I also spoke to the receptionist on duty.

In addition, I discussed the matter with the Catering Manager whose job it is to keep the machine stocked and to arrange for its maintenance.

Written eg what you have obtained from a previous report or other information on file, what you may have obtained from outside sources

I wrote to four vending machine suppliers and obtained details of their up-to-date provision

TEST YOURSELF
Why should this section be included in a report? Isn't it sufficient for you to state what you have discussed rather than how you have discussed it?

3 Findings
Summarise the information you have obtained (see page 123 for details of how to summarise).

3.1 During the period in question I discovered that between 10 am and 11 am, 12 noon and 2 pm and 3.30 pm to 4.30 pm there was an average of six people queuing up to obtain a drink.

3.2 Of the five members of staff to whom I spoke, only one appeared content with the pro-vision offered. The

complaints made by the
other staff were

3.2.1 no food was
available

3.2.2 the range of hot
drinks was limited

3.2.3 time was wasted in
queuing at peak
periods.

No one seemed to con-
sider cost an issue.

3.3 The receptionist com-
mented that the posi-
tioning of the machine
at the main entrance
caused problems for
visitors when they first
arrived, in that some-
times they had to push
through a number of
employees waiting at the
machine in order to
reach the reception
desk.

3.4 The Catering Manager
expressed concern at the
difficulty he found in
both maintaining the
machine (which is now
several years old) and
in keeping a check on it
when it was not within
the immediate vicinity
of the canteen.

3.5 All four companies
contacted sent me
details of their equip-
ment including the cost
of installation and
maintenance and possible
leasing arrangements
(See Appendix 1).

At this stage you may have completed the work asked of you, in which
case you sign and date the report and hand it to your boss. However,
your opinion may also be needed, particularly if the report has some
relevance to your work, the work of your staff or the organisation of

the office. In such circumstances you may be asked to add your conclusions and/or recommendations.

It is quite common to read a report in which a conclusion is followed by a recommendation which contains almost the same information. Try to distinguish between the two by keeping your conclusion short and your recommendations more detailed.

4 Conclusion

One or two sentences should be sufficient:

> The present vending machine is limited in the provision it makes and is situated in an inconvenient area of the office.

5 Recommendations

The recommendations should be more detailed and, where relevant, should follow the same order as the findings:

> I therefore recommend that consideration be given to
> 5.1 the replacement of the existing machine with either one or two new machines containing a variety of food and drinks
> 5.2 the possible leasing of the equipment rather than its outright purchase
> 5.3 the re-positioning of the machines either inside or immediately outside the canteen area.

6 Signature and date

It is usual to sign and date any report.

Note that in most reports you are able to use relatively informal language, ie 'I recommend that . . .' rather than 'it is recommended . . .' Make sure, however, that you have established which approach is required before you begin the report.

7 References

If you want to make a general reference to some more detailed information in another source remember to make use of the footnote. If, for example, you refer to the Health and Safety at Work Act in your main text, you may want to put a more detailed reference either at the foot of the page or at the end of the report, eg the main text could read 'Attention should be paid to the relevant provisions of the Health and

Safety at Work Act 1974[1]. The corresponding footnote would be displayed as shown at the bottom of this page.

8 Appendices
If the information to which you want to refer is extensive a footnote would not be sufficient. In such cases you would make use of an appendix attached to the report, eg 'A list of names and addresses of potential clients is contained in Appendix 1'.

9 Bibliography
In some cases details of books, journals, magazine articles etc for which some material has been obtained for use in the report are normally listed at the end. (As an example, check the layout and style of the Further reading list at the end of this book.)

10 Circulation list
If required, put the circulation list at the end of the report, either by individual name, eg R James, Technical Director, or by group, eg Members of the Staff Welfare Committee.

! SPECIAL NOTE
You could be asked to present the same information in a memorandum. If so, use the normal layout (see Chapter 6, Processing correspondence, page 298) and then follow the report format with or without the headings.

Review your work
After you have completed a draft report – particularly if you are new to the job – it is sometimes helpful to cast your eyes down a checklist to see that you have covered the main points. Questions you should ask yourself are given below.

- Why have I been asked to write this report?
- Are the terms of reference clear?
- Do I have to give my findings only, or have I to state an opinion, ie come to a conclusion and make a recommendation?
- For whom am I writing the report? Do they have some prior knowledge of the topic or do they have none at all?
- Have I checked all the relevant sources of information?
- Have I considered the possible repercussions – financial/legal etc?
- Do I know whether or not it is confidential?
- Is my report arranged logically – do the conclusions follow on naturally from the findings etc?
- Is the style acceptable – is it too informal/too formal/too full of jargon?
- Are the spelling, punctuation and grammar all right?

[1] ss 3 – 5

- Could I have presented any of the information in a different form, eg in a diagram/tab etc? (See below for details of different methods of presentation.)
- Have I included all the necessary footnotes/references?
- Have I included any relevant appendices, bibliographies, circulation lists?

Preparation of tabular information

Some information is better presented in tabular rather than narrative form. There is little point in writing:

> The number of road accidents in the town in 1990 was 312, in 1991, 405 and in 1992, 410. 15 cyclists were injured in 1990, 23 in 1991 and 30 in 1992

when the information could be more clearly displayed as a table.

Year	Number of road accidents	Number involving cyclists
1990	312	15
1991	405	23
1992	410	30

In many cases you will be required simply to reproduce tables from other sources such as technical journals or official reports. Other than making sure you have obtained the necessary copyright permission, your job will end there. In some cases, however, you may want to put the information you have obtained from various sources into one tabular statement.

TEST YOURSELF

After several complaints from staff, your boss has asked you to prepare a brief report for him on the number of non-employees using the company's car park. The caretakers have reported that during the previous week they found that on Monday 15 out of the 60 available spaces were being used by 'unofficial' parkers, on Tuesday 12, on Wednesday 17, on Thursday 15 and on Friday 25. They have also discovered that many of the unofficial parkers are employees at the nearby entertainment centre and it is their vans and cars (clearly marked with the centre's logo) which are causing most of the problem. 12 were identified on Monday, 10 on Tuesday, 13 on Wednesday, 12 on Thursday and 15 on Friday.

Write the report and include, where relevant, a tabular presentation of some of the information.

Graphs and charts

Another method of presenting information is in pictorial or graph form which can be very effective in illustrating certain points in a report or summary.

Examples include

Pie charts

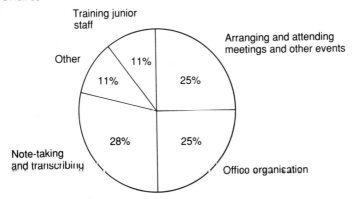

Training junior staff

Arranging and attending meetings and other events

Other

11%

11%

25%

28%

25%

Note-taking and transcribing

Offioo organieation

Analysis of work carried out by a
PA during the course of a week

A circle is divided into proportional segments (usually expressed in percentage terms). The circle can also be shaded in different colours or otherwise distinguished to represent different areas.

Rules of construction

- Draw the circle. (Easier said than done! Use a pair of compasses.)
- Work out the percentage that each subdivision will represent. (Remember they will all total 100%.)
- Calculate the angle for each subdivision by multiplying the percentage by 360. (A subdivision representing 30% will need an angle of $\frac{30}{100} \times 360 = 108$.)
- Subdivide the circle as necessary, using a protractor for the angles.
- Decide on what colours/shading you are going to use.
- Shade as required.
- Add a key if necessary (sometimes the information can be written on the chart itself).
- Add an explanatory title.

Advantages
- simple
- eye catching.

Disadvantages
- unsuitable for presentation of detailed information.

Line graphs

The readership of the daily Recorder from January to June

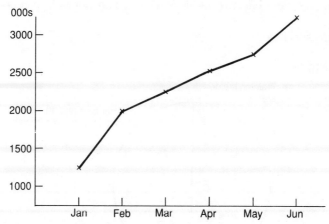

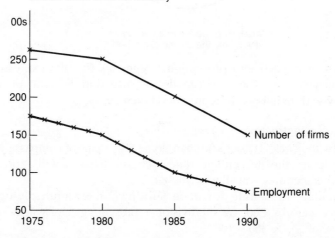

Employment trends compared with numbers of firms in the footwear industry

Line graphs may be single or multi-line and are normally used either to show comparisons or to indicate a trend.

Rules of construction

- Look at the statistics you have to include on the graph and select a suitable measurement – decide whether you are going to work in 10s, 100s or 1000s etc.
- Draw and label the axes. Remember that time is normally shown on the horizontal axis reading from left to right (the *x*-axis). It is also usual to have the lowest number at the foot of the vertical axis (the *y*-axis) and to move upwards.
- Decide on what colours or different types of line you are going to use for a multi-line graph.
- Put in each dot in pencil and *then* join up the lines.

- Add the key.
- Add the title.

Advantages
- detailed comparisons can be made
- detailed information can be displayed.

Disadvantages
- can be time-consuming to compile
- can be over-complicated for some purposes.

SPECIAL NOTE

A Z chart is a form of line graph so called because its shape resembles a Z. It is used in areas such as sales or production to indicate (a) moving totals, (b) cumulative figures for the whole period and (c) individual figures (eg current sales).

Chart to show sales for week ending 7 July

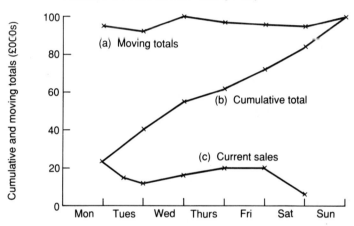

Bar charts

These charts can be displayed either horizontally or vertically and with single or multiple bars.

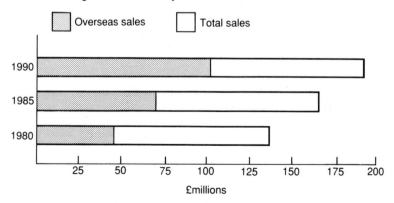

Sales of agricultural machinery

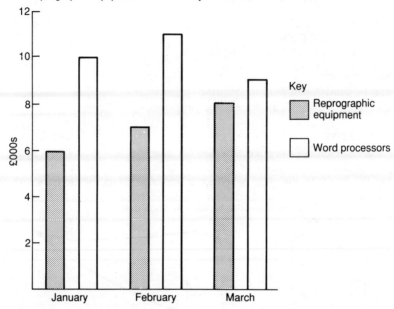

Sales of word-processing and reprographic equipment from January to March

Key
Reprographic equipment
Word processors

Rules of construction

Much the same rules of construction apply as to line graphs but bars (all the same width) are used to represent individual items of information. The bars may be close together or separated by small, even spaces. Shading or colour can be used and it is normal to include a key.

Advantages
- eye catching
- effective in indicating comparisons
- more detailed than a pie chart

Disadvantages
- sometimes a more cumbersome method of presenting information than a line graph.

Variations

Other types of bar chart include

the compound bar chart which consists of bars which are themselves divided by shading or colour to illustrate the proportional parts that make up a bar.

the histogram which is similar to a bar chart but the information is related to the area of the bar, not just its height.

the Gantt chart which is a specialised type of bar chart used to show a comparison between work planned and work accomplished in relation to time schedules. It compares the actual performance against

The compound bar chart

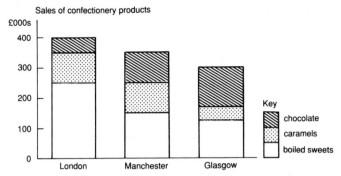

Sales of confectionery products

Key
- chocolate
- caramels
- boiled sweets

The histogram

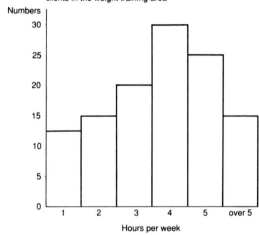

Barton Street Leisure centre
Results of questionnaire on number of hours spent by clients in the weight training area

The Gantt chart

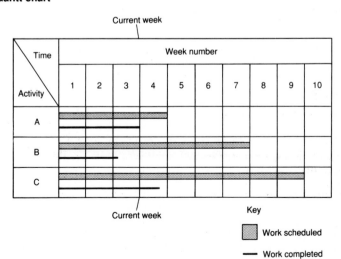

Current week

Current week

Key

▨ Work scheduled

— Work completed

the planned, anticipated or target performance. In a Gantt chart the bars are drawn horizontally.

Pictograms

These charts display information pictorially or symbolically. One picture or symbol can represent a certain number which can then be made larger or smaller to represent an increase or decrease in that number. An alternative is to keep the pictures the same size but to add to their number to indicate an increase. It is usual to choose a picture or symbol which is relevant to the infomation being displayed.

Increase in the number of employees electing to enter
the Company profit-sharing scheme between 1970 and 1990

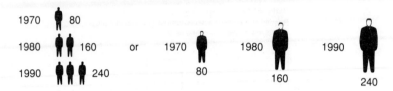

Advantages
- a very individual form of presentation
- eye catching.

Disadvantages
- unsuitable for detailed information.

More specialised pictorial representations include:
the flow chart which portrays a series of steps either in a course of action or in the progress of a document. It breaks down an otherwise complicated operation into a series of simple actions.
the algorithm which is similar to the flow chart but which requires a yes/no answer for every stage.

Computer graphics

First of all, find out what your computer can do. Apart from anything else you will probably need to advise your boss as to which types of graphics are possible and which are not. In most offices you will probably be expected to prepare only relatively simple charts such as basic line or bar charts. If you have access to a spreadsheet package then you can create a basic chart or graph on your computer. If your spreadsheet is also compatible with your word processing package then you can **import** your chart or graph into your typed report for a professional result.

More complicated diagrams or illustrations are normally prepared by more technically qualified personnel. If, however, you have access to a graphics application software package, you may have a much greater opportunity to display the information you collect in a variety of ways.

Most graphic packages allow you to create line graphs, bar charts, pie charts or even pictograms. You will normally be able to use a range of colours together with a variety of fonts and images accessed from scanners. (Remember that you would need a colour printer to be able to generate a coloured chart or graph.)

In addition you will be able to:

- 'explode' pie charts, ie separate certain wedges from the whole

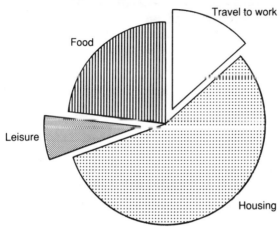

Exploded pie chart of a young woman's spending,
emphasising 'Travel to work' and 'Leisure'

- create a 3D effect on a bar chart or pie chart

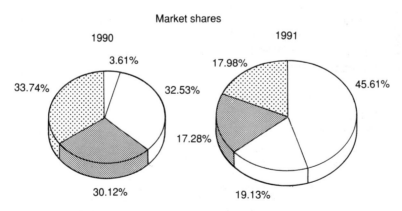

Market shares

1990

1991

Model A
Model B
Model C
Model D

- incorporate copyright-free published drawings (called **clip art**) into pictograms, eg houses, cars etc.

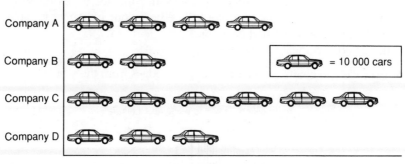

Sales of cars in 1991

Major areas of use of charts and graphs

Charts and graphs are used in many departments of a company. Examples include:

Sales   comparisons of sales in various areas, at various times, of various products etc

Marketing   analysis of results of research, eg share of market compared with that of competitors; consumer demand; publicity material etc

Accounts   analysis of profits; breakdown of costs; salary increases etc

Production   rates of production (including actual as against anticipated targets), operating costs etc

TEST YOURSELF

Discuss as a group the sort of information which could be displayed pictorially or graphically if you were working in

- a Personnel Department
- a library
- the office of a large garage.

ACTIVITY SECTION

Individual tasks

1 You work for the Sales Director of a company which manufactures office planners. The three major lines are

- year planners
- job progress planners
- holiday planners.

You have branches all over the UK, ie in Glasgow, Newcastle, Liverpool, Sheffield and London.

   Your boss has been asked to prepare a six monthly sales report for the Board of Directors. You have obtained for him in tabular form the number of sales of each planner in each area over the past six months (see table opposite) but he is now wondering whether certain information would look better in graph form.

		NUMBER OF SALES			
		JANUARY – JUNE			
Planner	**Area**	**Period**			**Total**
		Jan – Feb	Mar – Apr	May – Jun	
Year	Glasgow	169	130	119	418
	Newcastle	166	136	126	428
	Liverpool	155	130	118	403
	Sheffield	148	126	136	410
	London	203	145	192	540
		841	**667**	**691**	**2199**
Job Progress	Glasgow	134	126	140	400
	Newcastle	138	119	127	384
	Liverpool	150	115	129	394
	Sheffield	121	112	118	351
	London	188	148	172	508
		731	**620**	**686**	**2037**
Holiday	Glasgow	117	114	116	347
	Newcastle	121	119	123	363
	Liverpool	135	120	139	394
	Sheffield	116	111	114	341
	London	166	126	129	421
		655	**590**	**621**	**1866**

He asks you to draft out:

a a line graph to show total home sales for each of the three planners

b a bar chart to show the total sales of each appliance

c a compound bar chart showing the proportion of total sales of each planner to the overall sales for each of the five areas.

Note   you don't need to draft to scale.

2 You work for the Director of a charity involved in raising money for impoverished Developing World countries. You are asked to prepare a publicity leaflet in which brief biographies are to be given of a number of influential sponsors including Bob Geldof.

From the bibliographic information contained in a suitable reference book prepare a one paragraph summary of his biographical details.

3 Your executive is responsible for financing and running the company creche. She wants you to put a summary in the Staff Handbook of the extent to which its use has increased over the past few years, ie 20 children in 1984, 30 in 1986, 50 in 1988, 70 in 1990 and 80 in 1992. The creche is open from 8 am to 5.15 pm. There is a staff of 15 (not including cleaning and clerical staff). It has been visited by Prince Charles in 1988. It has also won several awards.

Prepare the summary for her and illustrate as a pictogram the increase in the number of children being cared for at the creche from 1984 to 1992.

Individual/group tasks

Case study 1

You work for the Chief Librarian of a large public library which is situated in a busy town centre. Over the past six months there has been an increasing number of thefts and incidents of vandalism and the librarian is therefore anxious to introduce certain security measures. She feels that closed circuit television may be one possibility. An alternative would be the employment of part-time security guards.

She wants to put a case for extra funding to the Library Committee which meets every quarter and, in order to make the strongest possible case, she has asked library staff to make a note of every incident which they have observed during the course of one week.

She has received the following replies.

Reply 1

Monday, 2 March – 10 am
Saw two young boys throwing magazines around. They ran off when I went over to stop them.

Wednesday, 4 March – 2.15 pm
Middle-aged man spotted putting copies of today's *Daily Mail* and *Daily Mirror* into his bag. He gave them back when requested to do so but was rather abusive.

Thursday, 5 March – 11 am
Group of children constantly running in and out of the main doors. They went away when I told them to do so but kept returning.

Richard Prescott
Assistant Librarian

Reply 2

Monday, 2 March – 10 am
Old lady nearly knocked over by group of youths running about the reference area.

Monday, 2 March – 7 pm
Man (very much worse the wear from drink!) fell asleep at one of the tables. When woken up and asked to leave he refused to do so (even when threatened with the police). Remained in library until closing time.

Thursday, 5 March – 7.15 pm
Four books found torn up in the non-fiction area. Estimated total replacement value £55.

Carolyn Lee
Assistant Librarian

Reply 3
Wednesday 4 March – 6.30 pm
Fight in the foyer between a group of youths. Police called but did not appear until 20 minutes later by which time the youths had gone.
Friday, 6 March – 6 pm
Check on magazine racks revealed that current copies of six of the most popular magazines were missing.

Mohammed Hanif
Library Assistant

You are asked to draft out a brief report of the incidents for your librarian to present to the Library Committee. Remember, where possible to present the information in tabular form for easy reading.

Case study 2

You work for Patsy Alexander, Sales Director of a large distribution company. Ms Alexander has asked you to investigate the possibility of turning the department into a 'no-smoking' zone. Accordingly you have:

- gathered together some statistics relating to the dangers of passive smoking; recent figures indicate that people with respiratory and bronchial illnesses are particularly affected. One survey compared absences of staff with such illnesses in two departments of similar size over a three month period. One was a smoking and one a no-smoking department. In the 'smoking' department there were 15 absences in January, 10 in February and 5 in March. In the 'no smoking' department the figures were 6, 2 and 1 respectively.
- prepared and circulated a questionnaire to all members of staff asking whether or not they preferred to work in a no–smoking zone. Out of 30, five objected strongly, 10 had no strong views and the rest favoured the proposal.
- checked in a number of personnel journals for articles describing ways in which other companies have overcome the problem: some have used union influence; some, peer pressure; others have set aside a small room for smokers to use at specific times.

You are now in a position to prepare a report for your boss giving her your findings and recommendations Use a line graph to indicate the correlation between an increase in the respiratory related infections and the presence of smoking in the office.

Managing the job

If – you can keep your head when all about you, are losing theirs and blaming it on you . . . [1]

The term 'competence' is difficult to describe, especially when related to a specific job. What is it that makes some people extremely capable at doing their job and others merely mediocre?

Many training courses for secretaries, PAs and administrators start by listing the skills required for proficiency, and continue by identifying a list of traits which have more in common with an archangel than any normal human being. Whilst technical skills are undoubtedly important, we all know people who are excellent at their jobs but may not live up to 'textbook' descriptions in terms of abilities and attributes. So what have they have got which others have not? What is that indefinable 'something' which they bring to their job and yet cannot describe to anyone else?

RULE 1
All jobs have two aspects:

- technical knowledge and skills
- personal skills, abilities and experience which lead to operational competence.

The first can be learned by training. The second is more intangible as it involves judgement and techniques for coping when things go wrong.

To be able to 'manage your job' you first need to be able to analyse it in terms of its components. Then you need to identify the intangible aspects which go towards making all the difference.

Technical knowledge and skills

The duties and responsibilities of a PA or administrator vary tremendously from one job to another. Much depends on the organisation or department, the way it functions, the nature of the job itself and the status and attitude of the boss(es). There are, however, certain key skills which are always required.

TEST YOURSELF
List the skills you consider are essential for a *professional* PA or administrator and the minimum level of competence you think is acceptable.

---

[1] Rudyard Kipling, *If*

Essential abilities

Although your list may be slightly different from ours, you should have included the following:

- good command of the English language – when writing *and* speaking
- thorough knowledge of standard office procedures and clerical duties
- the ability to deal with a wide range of people at all levels
- management skills – to plan and organise the work and motivate those staff for whom he/she is responsible
- keyboarding/proof-reading so that the production of accurate and well-presented documents is rapid and second nature
- accurate and speedy transcription skills from shorthand and/or audio
- efficient operation of all types of office equipment
- good numeracy skills.

How would you score yourself on each of the above, on a rating of one to ten? If you are low on some areas you have a choice – either improve them or choose a job where they don't matter.

RULE 2

No one is competent or incompetent as such – only in relation to particular activities. Make sure you choose a job which requires your particular strengths, not your weaknesses.

Administrative attributes

You can roughly divide these into two types, those required for *specific jobs* and those required for *all* administrative or secretarial work. In addition, the more you climb the ladder the more important some become eg diplomacy, tact and discretion.

It is possible to get too carried away when considering this aspect. If you consider that *all* good PAs are patient, loyal, adaptable, reliable, tolerant, have a good memory, an eye for detail and a sense of humour 100 per cent of the time then you begin to get the idea that PAs are born not made! Such a paragon of virtue can also become extremely irritating for other people to have to deal with. Therefore whilst some qualities are obviously useful and should be cultivated, remember to play to your strengths not your weaknesses.

RULE 3

No one functions more effectively by trying to be something they are not.

The intangibles

Even if you are now certain that you understand what a top administrative or PA job entails in terms of content and attributes required, does that mean you will be super-efficient? In a word, no. Just as reading about woodwork cannot make you a master craftsman, neither can reading about – or training for – a top office job. Why? Quite simply because the intangible aspects are missing and it is *these* which really determine whether you can manage your job.

The best way to identify these intangibles is to isolate some of the characteristics of the really competent PA or administrator, eg one who:

- can handle change positively
- can move to a different organisation and work out quickly how to make the best of the new circumstances
- can tackle the work in a variety of different ways
- knows when to stand up for herself and when to keep quiet
- knows when to take risks and when to play safe
- copes and deals with the problems of the job smoothly and efficiently
- always gets the best out of people.

RULE 4
Those with operational competence always find it difficult to put what they know into words, mainly because operational competence usually relies on awareness and judgement.

Learning operational competence

So how do you learn awareness and judgement? Undoubtedly much of this is learned by experience, but some aspects can be identified, eg:

- knowing your organisation – its rules (both written and unwritten), its methods of operating and its style, image and culture
- knowing the people – who has power and must be kept happy, the background behind relationships, the idiosyncrasies and temperaments of those involved
- knowing the climate – expanding or contracting, reactive or proactive, defensive or open
- knowing the issues – what is top priority at present, what can be ignored, who is involved and why, who is in favour and who is not, the political aspects of a situation.

All these factors may alter the way in which you do your job and the way in which you approach different tasks. Prioritising tasks takes on a whole new meaning when you consider some of the factors given above, so does 'dealing with others'. If you find out that Keith, a rather cantankerous colleague in a nearby office, is the MD's golf partner every Sunday morning, it will probably influence what you tell him and how you deal with him!

RULE 5
In any new job find a mentor – someone who will quickly put you wise to the aspects of the organisation you won't find in any written handbook!

Problems and conflict

Probably the key area which distinguishes the super PA or administrator from the average is the handling of difficulties, crises, disturbances and dilemmas. The good PA copes when all goes smoothly. The super PA comes into her own when things get rough, and because of this people rely on her to solve their problems – quietly, efficiently and effectively. Some of these may be everyday routine difficulties, eg finding out obscure information or contacting someone urgently. In other cases they may have more serious implications and require skilled judgement to decide on priorities and action. In this case the average PA may rush in where angels fear to tread – and actually make things worse!

RULE 6
Develop an empathy with your boss's style, preferences and modes of operation. The more you can identify with this the more likely you are to 'second-guess' what he/she would want you do in any given situation.

Developing your skills

If you are working, start by trying to analyse your current role. It is likely that this will include:

- operating as a member of a team in your section or department
- managing your own and your boss's time
- acting as a communications link between your boss and other staff/outside organisations
- planning and organising
- making decisions
- supervising others – either formally or informally.

This book, and the course you have undertaken, will help you to understand the skills required in many of these areas. Developing these can only occur through practice and by trying to do your best – even if this occasionally means making mistakes.

RULE 7
A mistake is only a disaster if you fail to learn anything from it. Reflect on what happened *without* blaming anyone else or the situation in general.

Finally, learn to acknowledge your own potential and abilities. Have as your top priority the development of the technical skills you need to do your job efficiently and think positively about how you can best contribute to the future development and growth of your organisation. Be aware of the intangible aspects inherent in the job and develop a sixth sense for hidden factors which the less experienced may miss. In this way not only will your own organisation be strengthened by your foresight but so will your own ability to 'manage the job'.

3 Reception

Receiving, screening and assisting visitors

As a PA/supervisor, you have a dual responsibility in the area of reception duties. Not *only* will you have to make use of your all-important personal skills in your dealings with important clients, concerned customers, irritated senior members of staff etc, you will *also* have to make sure that your junior staff exercise the same skills.

If you are beginning a new job you should first of all take stock of your reception area and your staff to establish how effective both are. You will then be in a position to establish your standards (if you need to) in relation to:

- the working environment
- individual personal skills and reception techniques.

The reception area

In many cases there are two reception areas which you may have to look after – the central area and your own particular area. It is likely that the central area will be larger and more comprehensively equipped and staffed than your area but the same principles hold good, ie that a reception area should:

- be welcoming
- create a good first impression of the organisation
- form an effective working environment for the staff.

In addition, however, most organisations want their reception area to reflect their image, whether it be traditional, modern or high tech. Indeed even those organisations which are not particularly public relations conscious will often be prepared to spend time and money on a reception area to achieve this effect.

Some considerable thought should be given to the planning of such an area.

Planning reception

Nowadays there are companies which specialise in the planning and furnishing of reception areas to meet specific client needs.

The general first questions which they normally ask are:

- Is it at street level or is it an annexe to a suite of offices in a large building (ie a 'deferred' reception)?
- How large is it?
- What are the permanent fixtures – lifts, stairs, windows etc?
- For what purpose is it intended – the general public, the organisation's clients etc? Is it going to need a meeting area as well as a reception area?
- How long will visitors be expected to remain in the area?

- How many staff are going to work there?
- What level of security is required?
- What legal requirements are there (eg in relation to access for the disabled in public buildings such as libraries etc)?

Furnishing the area

Much depends on whether or not the area is at street level. If it is, the planners must take into account factors such as:

Dirt

A light coloured carpet with no protective mats or other covering is not going to last very long if members of the general public have access to it directly from the street. Remember too that – somewhat depressingly – there may be a need in such circumstances for measures such as vandalproof paint and non-removable displays and fittings.

Window areas

It is surprising how few people want to be visible from the street, no matter how innocent their business may be. Indeed in some cases they may be deterred from entering the building if they know they can be seen when inside. Job Centres and DSS offices and even solicitors, for instance, would be unwise to have a reception area from which their clients can be seen from the street. In such circumstances, blinds, curtains or tinted windows are a must. So, too, is double glazing if the noise from the street is excessive.

Doors

Both visitors and staff are going to complain if they are sitting in an area where every time the door opens there is a blast of cold air. Solutions include swing doors which cannot be left open, automatic doors, double sets of doors or an **air curtain** – a warm draught of air immediately inside the door.

Heating

Visitors may be in outdoor clothes; the reception staff will not. It is wise therefore to have some extra 'local' heat for the reception staff.

Fixtures and fittings

Wherever the area is situated, the planners should pay particular attention to certain features, depending, of course, on the budget they have at their disposal and on the image the company wishes to present. Traditional organisations may still prefer 'restful' shades such as green, blue or cream. High tech companies may go for combinations of black and silver, red and blue etc. Basic requirements include:

Lighting

Are ceiling lights to be used? If so are they to be recessed and angled to give a softer effect? Should there be spotlighting over displays of the company's products etc? Does the reception desk require additional angle poise lamps? (If so, the VDU must be positioned so that the light does not shine directly upon it, otherwise the reception staff will be complaining about eyestrain.)

Flooring

Is image or durability the main factor? 'Hard' flooring such as rubber, linoleum, vinyl or cork is easier to keep clean (although more prone to show cigarette burns and marks from high heels). 'Soft' flooring such as carpeting is quiet, comfortable and warm but tends to show the dirt and must, of course, be fire resistant (and anti-static if made of man-made fibres). One compromise is the use of carpet tiles which can be replaced on an individual basis if there is any damage – although be prepared for a slight colour mismatch whatever the manufacturers claim!

Furniture

Many office supplies companies now provide furniture which is in modular form. This allows you to buy certain basic items initially and then to add on whatever you wish and whenever you wish. It also enables you to change the furniture arrangement very easily.

Much depends on the size of the area and the uses to which it is to be put but certain items tend to be fairly standard, ie:

- **a reception desk** which can act both as a counter which visitors approach and an area on which other work can be carried out – keyboarding, telephoning etc. In large areas it has become usual for an 'integrated' desk to be used which has a counter top at two different heights so that equipment can be stored behind the part where the desk is at its maximum height. See illustration opposite.
- **easy chairs and small tables** which are normally arranged in clusters but in such a way that a receptionist can keep a check on visitors' arrivals and departures. Chairs should be covered with fabrics which blend in with the general decor but which are stain resistant and fireproof. Glass-topped tables are less easily marked with cups of coffee but do show every fingermark.
- **office style tables and chairs** which are suitable for small meetings if the reception area is to be used for that purpose.
- **display cabinets and boards** which can be used for booklets, leaflets and posters relating to the organisation or as a means of displaying examples of the organisation's products.

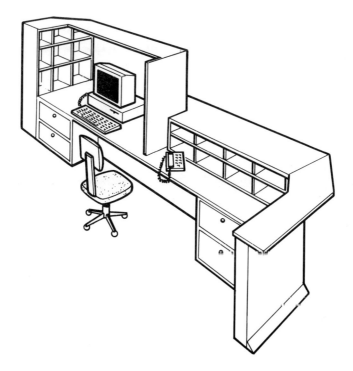

Both cabinets and boards can be free standing or wall mounted, framed in wood or metal and possibly screened with glass. The boards can be made of cork or a synthetic fabric resembling felt and used in conjunction with different types of colour coordinated accessories – labels, mapping pins etc.

In some cases the boards are plastic based and letters can be clipped into small holes.

TEST YOURSELF

For what purposes would you use this latter type of board? What are the dangers of using it in preference to any other board?

SPECIAL NOTE

In these days when environmental issues have assumed considerable significance it may be that your organisation will want to buy furniture which is manufactured in ways that have not threatened the environment. Many suppliers of office equipment claim that their products are now made either of man-made laminates or from wood veneers which are produced from farmed timbers without threat to the rain forests.

Accessories

Do they create a warm rather than a technically correct but clinical impression? Examples include:

Glass screens or mirrors

Glass is often used to complement a colour scheme but care has to be taken to avoid its use becoming somewhat of a safety hazard – in a small reception area in particular, it may be quite easy for a visitor to bump into a glass screen or mirror.

Flowers

Formally arranged flowers are 'out': so too are displays of artificial flowers (unless, perhaps they are country style displays in baskets or similar containers such as the type you may see in upmarket dress shops). A bunch of fresh flowers arranged informally in a glass or pottery container is now the most well-used option. In many instances the organisation will employ professional florists to supply the flowers and they can generally be depended upon to recognise and follow prevailing trends.

Plants

Plants are often a good alternative for providing greenery. In a reception area make sure that these are low in height (or site tall plants in corners), otherwise you won't be able to see your visitors! Select a plant which will thrive in the atmospheric conditions which prevail in your reception area.

Pictures

Pictures are difficult to choose because they are so much a matter of personal taste. The modern approach is to err on the side of caution and to choose sketches, illustrations and line drawings (or possibly enlarged old photographs relevant to the organisation or area). Reproductions of 'Old Masters' are not to be recommended (unless you have a Managing Director whose particular favourite is *The Hay Wain* or *The Laughing Cavalier!*).

Magazines

Magazines and newspapers are important and you should try to maintain a balance between 'serious' reading material such as the financial daily newspapers and some light relief. Obviously all issues must be current; in some very busy reception areas a duplicate copy of all the reading material is kept at the reception desk so that the receptionist can replenish stocks if someone walks off with a paper or spills coffee on it. If you regularly have foreign visitors from specific countries it is both courteous and thoughtful to have some magazines printed in the relevant languages. The trick is to put yourself in the shoes of the clientele and think about what would interest them.

 TEST YOURSELF
Assume you have a weekly budget of £30 to buy magazines and papers in the reception area of a large firm of accountants. What would you buy?

Personal skills

Even the most effective reception area will not compensate for reception staff who are unhelpful, inefficient and sloppy. Personal skills are among the hardest skills to learn – and to teach! Some people are naturally endowed with charm and can be diplomatic, persuasive or conciliatory almost without effort. However, they are few and far between – most people need to practise such skills.

 TEST YOURSELF
Look at the table below. Read the questions carefully and circle the answer which you think is most true of you. Then check your score with the score sheet at the end of this chapter. If you score very highly, you can ignore the rest of this section!

PERSONAL SKILLS QUESTIONNAIRE

1 I always treat all customers/clients the same, regardless of how they are dressed or how well they speak.
  a Yes   **b** Usually   **c** No

2 I am often late when meeting people.
  a No   **b** Sometimes   **c** Usually

3 I sometimes say things to people in haste which I regret later.
  a Yes   **b** Sometimes   **c** No

4 I work best under pressure.
  a Yes   **b** Sometimes   **c** No

5 I never panic.
  a Yes   **b** Sometimes   **c** No

6 I prefer to work as part of a team.
  a Always   **b** Sometimes   **c** Never

7 I would enjoy public speaking.
  a No   **b** Perhaps   **c** Yes

8 I don't like it when people expect me to make a decision.
  a True   **b** Sometimes   **c** False

9 I feel uncomfortable when I think people are looking at me.
  a No   **b** Sometimes   **c** Yes

10 I enjoy dealing with people face to face.
  a No   **b** Sometimes   **c** Yes

11 I can always find things I put away.
  a True   **b** Sometimes   **c** False

12 I don't see why people get so worked up about things.
  a True   **b** Sometimes   **c** False

---

13 I feel very embarrassed and uncomfortable when people criticise me even slightly.

   a Yes   **b** Sometimes   **c** No

14 I like flexible hours.

   a Yes   **b** Sometimes   **c** No

15 I never gossip.

   a True   **b** Sometimes   **c** False

16 I find it difficult to deal with handicapped people.

   a True   **b** Sometimes   **c** False

17 I am sometimes moody.

   a True   **b** Perhaps   **c** False

18 I would love to be on a TV chat show.

   a No   **b** Perhaps   **c** Yes

19 I feel there is no room for improvement in my performance of my job.

   a True   **b** Perhaps   **c** False

20 I feel there is no room for improvement in my colleagues' performance of their jobs.

   a True   **b** Perhaps   **c** False

Identifying personal skills

The first (and easiest) step is to identify what skills are required.

Appearance and image

The adoption and maintenance of the correct image is a skill in itself. You *can't* help being tall or short, fair or dark etc – but you *can* dress and behave to suit what image is required. (See sections on Managing yourself, page 70, and Managing your career, page 527.) Much depends on your working environment (and to a certain extent, peer pressure) as to the way in which you dress. Working in a merchant bank, an office adjoining a factory workshop or a firm of fashion designers will each require a different approach.

Unfortunately, even if you are naturally non-conformist, in most cases you will have to try to curb that tendency. Dressing in jeans when others are in suits (or vice versa) is acceptable in some environments but not in the business world. Indeed in one case which went to an Industrial Tribunal a young man was held to have been *fairly* dismissed for refusing to comply with company regulations that he should wear a tie!

Remember, too, that dressing for a particular image can be quite entertaining – even though you may have to act uncharacteristically. 'Power dressing' (suits with padded shoulders, low heeled shoes, discreet jewellery for women; dark coloured suits, 'conservative' ties for men etc) is now losing some ground in favour of a softer approach but in the office it is advisable that you should be a follower of fashion rather than one of its leaders! (See also Managing your career, page 527.)

Voice

Your voice is important. Whatever your accent, you should concentrate on making yourself clearly understood and fluent. If you have difficulty in this respect – and many people have – ask your tutor for some practice in role-playing exercises or in making presentations to the rest of the group. It can be a nerve wracking experience, particularly at first, but you will experience a great sense of achievement when you find yourself beginning to improve.

It is, of course, possible that you will be called upon at a moment's notice to give a reasoned explanation of your boss's absence or to relay a complicated message etc. What you may need to practise, therefore, is talking on a particular topic with very little, if any, preparation time.

TEST YOURSELF

1 Start by each member of your group thinking of a topic for a one minute talk to be given by another member of the group. Remember not to be too clever in thinking up a very obscure title (eg how long is a piece of string?) – the others may take their revenge when it is your turn.

2 Choose one of the following topics and prepare a five minute presentation for the rest of the group.
   a My strengths and weaknesses
   b The role of a woman in a male-dominated society
   c The role of a man in a matriarchal society
   d A woman I would choose as a role model
   e A man I would choose as a role model
   f Why a sense of humour is important to a PA
   g Is it possible to be successful without being ruthless?

Mannerisms

These are generally quite easy to overcome although, unless a kind friend (such as a fellow PA) tells you about them, you may be completely unaware that you are constantly fiddling with your hair, tapping your pen on the desktop, whistling etc. Watching yourself on video can be instructive and it may be that your tutor will be able to arrange for you to make one of your presentations in front of a camera. Your more obvious irritating mannerisms will then be easy to spot.

Training junior staff

An important point to remember is that you, as a PA/supervisor, should listen carefully to the way in which your junior staff speak. To a certain extent this is an easier task than trying to appraise your own style (even with the aid of a tape recorder). Apart from obvious incoherencies, check that they don't fall into the habit of 'sloppy' speech, eg 'OK' instead of 'yes' or 'certainly'; 'Ta' instead of 'thank you'; 'yep/yeah' instead of 'yes' etc. Discourage (if you can) the use of catch phrases such as 'brill' or 'ace' and the use of modern expressions, where the receiver will interpret the word rather differently. If your junior says someone is 'sad', she should mean they are unhappy – not useless.

In addition, it will be your responsibility to tell them (tactfully!) if *they* have any annoying mannerisms which may be irritating to visitors – and possibly introduce your own 'rules' if necessary, eg to ban chewing gum. You should also be particularly vigilant that your junior staff do not give any appearance of boredom. Reception staff who are yawning, staring into space or constantly glancing at their watches are destined to give a very bad first impression to visitors. If your junior *is* bored (and there can be peaks and troughs in reception work) find her some other work to keep her occupied. If the reception area is well designed you should be able to give her some keyboarding, some filing, some preparatory work on displays etc.

Reception techniques

Even if you look good and have a pleasant voice, you still won't be regarded as a riotous success if you are telling the visitors all the wrong things! You are not meant to be purely decorative but also functional.

RECEPTION CHECK LIST		
Person observed (bank clerk/shop assistant etc) .... Organisation .... Date .... Time .... Period of observation		
Skill	**Max score**	**Actual score**
General appearance (clean/tidy/ suitable hairstyle and makeup etc)	10	
Voice (clear/pleasant)	10	
Manner (pleasant/helpful/ welcoming etc)	10	
Clothes (appropriate/smart etc. If a uniform is worn, does it look as if it has been cared for?)	10	
Shoes – if you can see them (clean/ non-scuffed/not too low/high/casual)	5	
Hands (clean/unbitten nails. If nail polish is used, is it a suitable colour, unchipped etc?)	5	
	50	
If the score is less than 40 out of 50, the organisation concerned has a problem – and possibly needs to review its training schedules!		

Understanding the organisation

One of your first, though possibly little recognised tasks, is to make sure that your staff are familiar with the structure of the organisation and the products or services it sells or provides. It is a good idea for them to have near at hand, preferably on a notice board by the telephone, an organisation chart giving details of departments or sections, names, titles and extension numbers. During their induction course they should have been given some indication of what the organisation does; alternatively much of the information may be contained in the staff handbook. If not, you should try to arrange some visits to major areas of the organisation and possibly to persuade key members of staff to give your juniors a brief outline of different functions within the company. This information is vital whether they will be meeting visitors in person or speaking to callers over the telephone. (See Chapter 1, Communication Systems, page 1.)

Anyone regularly dealing with callers or visitors to an organisation should not only be prepared to answer routine queries but should also know the person to whom to refer a visitor about a particular product or aspect of the service. It is usual for most organisations to have a range of professionally printed brochures and leaflets which can be used for reference and given to enquirers. Make sure that stocks of these are adequate and displays are replenished regularly. Bear in mind that some organisations offer confidential services and, if you work for one of these, be sensitive to the type of discussions which should only be held in private. This is equally the case for commercial companies if, for instance, you are discussing appropriate methods of finance or terms of payment – or innovative products or processes etc.

Telephone callers

Telephone callers are dealt with in full in Chapter 1 on Communication Systems (page 37 to 45).

Personal callers

Most visitors can be divided into those who *are* expected and those who *are not*. In the former case plans can be made for their visit; in the latter case you have to prepared for any eventuality. The first – and most important – rule is to make friends with the receptionists in the central reception area, the commissionaire/doorman or the security guard at the gate house. They can make life much easier for you if they are on your side.

Expected visitors

Although each organisation tends to have its own set of rules as to the way in which visitors are received, there are certain standard procedures which are common to most organisations.

Appointments schedule

Both you and the receptionist at the central reception area should know who is coming and when, from the daily schedule of appointments.

Checking in

It is important to establish whether the staff at the central reception area or your departmental staff are required to carry out initial checking-in procedures. In smaller companies, of course, you and your staff will be the only people available to do this. Nowadays, it is normal procedure to issue visitors with some form of identification, label or badge. In cases where the visit is to be made to the factory floor or building site etc it is also normal at this stage to issue some form of protective clothing/headgear etc. In such circumstances you should, of course, have checked the visitor's height, size, shoe size etc.

It is also common practice for details of the visitors' name, organisation and the people with whom they have the appointment to be entered in a visitors' register (or keyed into a computer terminal). This type of information is useful if someone has parked in the wrong place and vital in the case of a fire! Some organisations even have a 'welcome board' in reception with the names of the day's expected visitors.

EXTRACT OF A RECEPTION REGISTER

Date	Time of arrival	Name	Organisation	To see	Time of departure*
26/1	0930 hrs	Ann Bell	DNP Co Ltd	Rose Dean	1230 hrs

* In some cases the last column will be used only in a central reception area so that the reception staff can keep a check on both the arrival and departure of visitors. In such circumstances the visitor's car registration number is also required.

It may also be company practice for a separate register to be kept at the reception area to record the arrivals and departures of staff (see below), though in small companies an individual record can be kept for each member of staff on a weekly basis.

STAFF IN AND OUT REGISTER
Date ....

Time	France	L Smith	D Poirot
0900 hours		↑	
1000 hours		↓	
1100 hours			

Key out of building

Directions to visitors

If visitors have to report first to a central reception area the receptionist there may direct them to the person with whom they have an appointment. More correctly, the appropriate PA should be contacted and asked to come to reception to collect the visitor. It is less of a security risk and also more welcoming.

Initial welcome

You must be prepared to smile, look pleasant and greet your visitor by name. Encourage your juniors to do the same. If the visitor has an unusual name, you should have pointed this out to your junior beforehand when you went through the appointments list for the day and emphasised (as in the case of telephone calls) that she should ask the visitor to spell out the name if necessary.

Without becoming embroiled in an unseemly struggle, help all visitors with their coat, briefcase, umbrella etc. Ask them to sit down even if you know your boss is expecting them. You want to make your visitors feel at ease and they will be less likely to do so if there is some uncertainty about what to do next. In any case, a visitor who is sitting down has less opportunity to wander about your room looking at confidential papers or noticing unwashed coffee cups behind the blind on the window sill!

 SPECIAL NOTE
- If several visitors arrive at once – to attend a meeting for instance – train your junior staff not to 'guess' who they are from the appointments list but to ask them individually for their names.
- If a visitor arrives straight from the airport or railway station complete with baggage, arrange to have this stored somewhere safe and secure. Do make

sure the visitor and your boss know where it is. If they need to leave urgently to attend a meeting together whilst you are at lunch, they won't be too keen on playing 'hunt the suitcase' for half an hour beforehand.

Notifying your boss

It may be company practice to telephone through to your boss to announce a visitor's arrival. However, this leaves neither of you any room for manoeuvre if your boss wants to ask you about something he/she has forgotten or you want to pass on some last minute information. It is preferable actually to go into your boss's office to say that the visitor has arrived.

 SPECIAL NOTE
You are wise if you develop a code system with your boss if he/she regularly needs rescuing from clients whom he/she has difficulty in persuading to leave. One executive actually moved the desk to a position where it was possible to kick the adjoining wall with the PA's office with one foot when desperate. This was the PA's cue to enter with a file and the line 'I'm sorry to interrupt, but have you forgotten the time? The meeting with the MD starts in 5 minutes.' Make sure such 'help' operations work both ways when necessary! (See Chapter 7, Organising Work Schedules, p 352.)

Introductions

Getting your visitor into your boss's office is sometimes difficult. There are a number of approaches you can take, eg:

- if the visitor is well known to your boss or a member of the organisation, it may be sufficient for you simply to leave your boss's office door open and say to the visitor, 'Ms Jones will see you now', leaving him to go straight in.
- If the visitor is well known but important you may want to allow him to precede you through the door but to accompany him and announce his name. 'Here's Mr Wood, Ms Jones'.
- If the visitor is unknown you may have to effect an introduction. Nowadays the strict rules of etiquette need no longer be followed provided you make sure that both your boss and your visitor know who the other is. If you are in any doubt, however, the normal procedure is that:
  - men are introduced to women (although in these days of female executives this rule may be difficult to apply)
  - juniors are introduced to seniors (ie mentioned last)
  - the lesser important are introduced to the more important
  eg: 'Mrs Parsons, may I introduce Bill Robinson.'
    'Mrs Parsons, may I introduce our new receptionist, Alison Whittle.'
    'Chairman, this is James Leibovici, the latest recruit to the Sales Department.'
  Do not hurry introductions, even though you may wish to do so (and

your junior staff most certainly will wish to do so). You are giving the other people the opportunity to establish an initial rapport and to learn each other's names.

Making conversation

If your boss is not immediately available you may have to spend some time making conversation with the visitor. Although you are probably sufficiently experienced to do so without any real difficulty no matter who the visitor may be, your junior staff may not be so confident. Help them by giving them some guidelines, such as the ones listed below.

- Some visitors are quite content to look through papers or to read a magazine – if so, leave them to it. (This is where a separate reception area is an advantage.).
- If, however, it is apparent that they wish to talk, you should be prepared to respond. It is easy to *say* that the other person may be as nervous as you are and that it is therefore up to you to try to put them at their ease – but less easy actually to *believe* it. Even so, many visitors *are* nervous – if they are to be interviewed for a job, are trying to sell something, have a problem they wish to discuss etc. Even if they are not, most of them will appreciate any attempt on your part to be pleasant.
- Introduce yourself clearly, eg 'Hello, my name is Joanne. I'm Mrs French's PA' etc.
- Think of an opening gambit – even if it is the distance travelled, the time of year, eg 'have you been/are you going on holiday?' etc. *Listen* to that response and try to pick up a lead from that. 'I've never been to New York. Is it as exciting as it sounds ...'.
- Avoid controversial subjects. The old adage is that you should never talk about religion, politics or sex (ie personal relationships) but although you are not likely to introduce those topics your visitor may do so. Be non-committal; a nod in apparent agreement often works.
- More important, avoid being drawn into a conversation about your boss or the work of the organisation. General comments are fine – 'Yes, business is good this year' or 'The MD has just come back from a conference in Brussels' – but beware of saying anything which is even indirectly critical or pessimistic. Obviously you know better than to tell the visitor anything confidential but remember that it is not unknown for a visitor – particularly someone from inside the

organisation – to assume a knowledge he/she doesn't have and to try to trap you into agreeing or disagreeing. A visitor may, for instance, open the conversation by saying 'Pity about Eileen Parkinson in Accounts – I would never have thought that she would have been made redundant.' Whether you know that the comment is true or false, it would be unwise for you to indicate any agreement or disagreement. If the visitor is 'fishing', you have told him/her what he/she wants to know. In such circumstances, turn the situation to your advantage. Ask what he/she knows and how he/she knows it. Express a genuine interest at the answer – you may actually learn something useful.

- If you are interrupted during the course of the conversation or want to see your boss, don't break off in mid-sentence. Wait until an appropriate break and then tell the visitor what you intend to do and leave him/her with some papers or magazines to read.

- **Remember** that making conversation is only one of your duties and should not occupy you all day. If visitors are spending too much time in your office there is something wrong with your appointments system!

SPECIAL NOTE
A top PA continually astounded visitors and her boss by her ability to remember even the smallest details of previous conversations she had held with regular clients of her organisation. She impressed everyone with her ability to open a conversation by referring to topics discussed during their last visit – even though this might have been six months before – eg 'Mr Tate, how nice to see you, and how was your holiday in Canada?' or 'Mrs Sharples, do sit down. Tell me about your daughter's wedding, how did it go?' etc.

Clients thought she was wonderful; each one felt special and important. Her boss was convinced he had found a combination of Wonder Woman and Mastermind. What nobody knew was that stored safely in her top drawer was a small set of index cards. On each one was the name of a client. After showing the client through to her boss, the PA would spend just two or three minutes jotting down facts clients had mentioned which she knew were important to them. The next time they were due, she simply glanced at the card just before they arrived and voila! She soon gained promotion – but her boss never did find out how she managed her memory trick!

TEST YOURSELF
The following people arrive at your office during the course of the day and are asked to wait. Work in pairs, one taking the receptionist role and the other the visitor role and 'make conversation' with each other for at least five minutes.

1 Alan Zorbe, the Head of Computer Services wants to talk to your boss about installing an electronic mail system throughout the company. He has two daughters about whom he is always speaking. One is taking her GCSEs this year; the other has just passed her driving test after several attempts.

2 Kim Lee Sung, a representative from a company specialising in refurnishing reception areas, has an appointment to see your boss. She has travelled

some distance and has brought along a portfolio of sketches and photographs of reception areas which she has recently refurnished. She is very well dressed and seems very interested in the fashion magazines in the reception area.

3 Patrick McNair, the Chief Administration Officer, wants to discuss the installation of certain security measures in the organisation. He has been advocating for some time the use of a CCTV system controlled from the gatehouse and also the issuing of 'walkie talkies' to all caretaking staff. You notice that he has a Manchester United football ticket sticking out of his pocket.

Unexpected visitors

You must be ready for the 'unexpected' visitor even though it is always difficult to plan for the unexpected! It is tempting to hold to the view that any visitor who has no appointment must be persuaded to make one or to go away disappointed. That may be one line of action to take; at least the visitor will leave feeling that something has been achieved. In some cases, however, the visitor is either so important or has something so urgent to impart that such an action is impolitic or inadvisable. On the other hand, no one in the organisation may be prepared to see this particular person in which case you cannot offer an appointment.

If you work in an organisation with a central reception area, the initial problem will be identified there and, although the receptionist will probably contact you for advice, at least you are given some time in which to make a decision. If not, you have to make the decision there and then. Whatever the situation you should take the following steps.

- Obtain as much information as possible from the visitor (including, where relevant, a business card).
- If possible do not give any indication that your boss is in (and ask the central area receptionist to do the same). Try not to be too specific about this. The visitor may know your boss and have caught a glimpse of him/her – or may have spotted his/her car in the car park.
- Follow much the same procedure as for telephone calls (see Chapter 1, Communications systems, page 1). Try to contact your boss (without the visitor being aware that you are doing so) unless you are sure he/she will not want to be disturbed. Avoid, however, getting into the habit of automatically refusing to let *anyone* see your boss – use your judgement in each individual case.
- If your boss is willing to see the visitor, your problem is solved. If not, you can:
  – offer the visitor another appointment (as previously discussed)
  – ask if you can deal with the matter yourself
  – ask if the visitor would like to see someone else (having previously checked up that someone else *will* see him/her).

- Whatever the situation, do not allow a visitor such as a salesman to keep returning to your office by making vague promises that your boss may be available 'some time next week' etc. It is both unkind and time wasting.

SPECIAL NOTE

One of the most difficult unexpected visitors to deal with can be a good (male) friend of your boss – someone with whom he plays squash or golf or sees on a regular basis – especially one who adopts either the hale and hearty approach or the Don Juan alternative, eg:

'You'll have to watch Tom you know, he's a terror to work for. I bet he keeps you on your toes.'

(or, even worse),

'Where's Tom been hiding you then? I bet he finds it difficult to concentrate with you around the place. No wonder he's been working late recently.'

Unless you are absolutely excellent with the one line riposte, which cuts such a conversation stone dead in an instant, bite your tongue. Whatever you do, don't respond in kind. The 'Oh, sorry – I wasn't listening – I must finish this before I leave' is a fair put-down and doesn't invite further conversation. If you are still having trouble, change the subject: ask if it's still raining! If the person concerned is a regular caller, and is a real pain, arrange for him to wait elsewhere and tell your boss why.

TEST YOURSELF

Not all unexpected visitors are external. You may find some difficulty in dealing with the following situations.

1 A senior executive arrives and wishes to see your boss albeit that he/she is in a meeting or is talking to another visitor.

2 The 'office snoop' (who is junior to your boss but senior to you) arrives for a chat.

Discuss as a group what action you would take in each case.

Related duties

Refreshments

Much depends on what is expected of you. As a PA you will probably have facilities to make your own tea and coffee and, whilst this is very convenient for you, it becomes less convenient if you are expected to make tea or coffee for not only your boss but also every visitor to the office. If you have a junior, she should be able to take some of this work off your shoulders although even she may begin to object if she is making drinks all day long. If you have a canteen service your problem is solved provided you make sure you are on a good footing with the canteen staff! If you have a tea lady treat her as if she was the most valuable possession you own – she probably is! The more likely situation today is that you have another option to making the drink yourself – use the vending machine. Many companies now have these installed for use by both staff and visitors. At top level, however, a drink out of a plastic cup may not present the image your boss desires! If that is the case he/she may be more receptive to any pleas you make for additional facilities (or the appointment of/reinstatement of the tea lady!).

If you are expected to look after these facilities yourself, ideally they should include access to a small kitchen area with hot and cold water and sufficient storage space (including a lockable unit for wines and spirits) – although, regrettably, these may not be available in all organisations (particularly the smaller ones). If they are not, you should put pressure on your boss to see what he/she can negotiate on your behalf.

You should also have available:

- a coffee machine
- a kettle
- high quality china (Forget mugs or beakers.)
- glassware (Don't economise and buy glasses which are so thick that you think you are taking a bite out of them every time you sip your drink. Have a range of glasses for sherry, wine, spirits, beer and soft drinks)
- cutlery
- trays of varying sizes
- a microwave – possibly not essential but useful if you are expected to serve a light snack with drinks
- a small refrigerator – again not essential but very useful (Warm white wine tastes dreadful and most people like to have the choice of ice with their drinks. If you have American guests then cool the beer too!)
- adequate cleaning materials.

 SPECIAL NOTE
Linen napkins and cloths look more stylish than their paper equivalents but if you choose this option make sure that you know who is expected to launder them! (The same goes for any tea-towels if you are expected to do the clearing up!)

Preparing the refreshments

Whether you are expected to prepare the food yourself, order it from the canteen or from outside caterers, or call at in the nearest sandwich shop, you must first determine what exactly is required and whether the visitor has any dietary restrictions (because of health, religion etc). If there is any doubt, avoid the use of meat, fish or even cheese and concentrate on salads or eggs (although even this is a problem if your visitor is a vegan). If you arrange a buffet your problem decreases in that you can provide a variety of food, some of which at least should be acceptable to the visitor.

You can normally make certain assumptions ie:

- that brown bread will be preferred to white, and possibly a low fat spread will be preferred to butter (It used to be de rigueur to crust the sandwiches; this is no longer as necessary – particularly if you are in a hurry.)

- that both sugar and sweeteners will be required
- that cream will be required for coffee and milk for tea (although nowadays again non-fat milk may be preferred)
- that if alcoholic or soft drinks only are being served 'nibbles' should be provided (and normally in this case, ashtrays).

SPECIAL NOTE
You must bear in mind the cost of this provision. The initial outlay may be covered by a fixed sum of money allocated to you out of the departmental budget. You must also take into account, however, the on-going cost of consumables. If all refreshments are ordered and prepared on a centralised basis, you will probably be expected only to complete a 'hospitality' slip each time you require something. The cost will then be deducted from the departmental or other relevant budget. In another organisation you may be expected to take the relevant sum from petty cash or even to buy the provisions yourself and claim a refund against your voucher and attached receipts. If the amount allocated is limited then you must set up an appropriate costing system so that you stay within your budget – or have a good argument ready for needing more funds.

Serving the refreshments

Unless the visitors are well known to you or extremely important (or your boss is entertaining a group of visitors) this is a job which could be left to your junior – provided she is confident enough to do so. Let her assist you in the beginning rather than expecting her to take over from you immediately. Make sure too that you give her some guidelines, such as those listed below.

- If relatively elaborate refreshments are required it is preferable to have all the cutlery/china etc laid out beforehand in the meeting room (if that is where the meal is to take place). This prevents your having to interrupt the possibly vital introductory part or closing stage of a meeting.
- Four hands are often better than two. If someone is there to open doors and to carry in some of the refreshments, so much the better.
- Establish beforehand whether you are expected to serve the food or pour the drinks. Some executives prefer to take over at this stage. (If the meeting is a celebratory one and champagne is in evidence, play coy and ask a male present to open it. Have a glass close by. If it goes off with a bang and champagne pours all over the papers then it's his fault and not yours!)
- If you are expected to remain, remember not to interrupt the conversation too abruptly by asking visitors what they want to drink or eat – your boss should assist you by stopping the conversation at that point. Indeed if you wait long enough there will be no alternative.

- The basic rules for serving drinks (tea, coffee, wine) are that:
  - they should be served from the visitor's right hand side
  - if two people are sitting close together preventing access a polite 'excuse me' is preferable to something akin to a shoulder charge to separate them
  - glasses should be filled to only two thirds of their capacity (to prevent spillage); so too should cups (although you may find in this instance that some visitors will ask you for a full cup)
  - tell visitors what is available – sherry, wine, Perrier? – rather than having them ask for something you don't have.
- Most visitors will probably want to help themselves to food and at this stage you may be able to go back into your own office. It may be, however, that you are expected to act as hostess, particularly if there are several visitors or other executives.

SPECIAL NOTE

Even the best trained junior (or – perish the thought – even you) can drop a plate of sandwiches or a cup of coffee. Avoid falling into a John Cleese type faint or bursting into tears. Smile, apologise briefly and clean up as quickly as possible (but don't get down on your hands and knees to scrub the carpet – sort out the stain later). Obviously you would cover for your junior if she was the one who had caused the accident. If she looks upset ask her to fetch you something from the other room or get her out of the office on some pretext until she calms down. If your boss is the culprit, take the blame. That's what you're paid for!

Out for lunch

A variation on the catering theme is that

- your boss takes the visitor out to lunch
- your boss asks you to accompany them – either as a social gesture or because you can either take notes or give moral support on an issue
- your boss is held up and asks you to take the visitor out to lunch yourself.

In each case you will be expected to book the table. Your boss will have a preference for certain restaurants, usually within walking distance of your office if possible. The type of restaurant will vary depending on the importance of the visitor. If you use one or two regularly they will get to know you – and if you play your cards right and develop a good relationship with the receptionist or head waiter you will be able to get bookings at the last minute when necessary.

Accompanying your boss usually only assumes nightmare proportions the first time you are asked to go along – particularly if the invitation is unexpected. Remember, this is the time to listen a lot, talk very little and toe the party line throughout. Stick to non-alcoholic drinks or, at the most, *one* glass of wine.

Taking someone out yourself is not as frightening as it seems, purely because they are the one not expecting *you*, rather than the reverse. Try to choose somewhere where the service is fairly rapid as this lessens the ordeal. Don't forget that *you* must ask for the bill at the end of the meal (make sure you have the means to pay on you beforehand, or get the money from petty cash). Keep the bill – you'll need it for the Accounts Department.

Collecting visitors

A variation of the 'you're on your own' theme is if you are a driver and are being asked to meet a visitor at a railway station or airport. The latter is the easier of the two as everyone exits from the same direction and you know when the right plane has landed. Trains can be more difficult if three arrive at once on different platforms. It's also more difficult to get information on train delays than flight delays before you set off!

Make sure you arrive in good time, stand at a central point and, if the visitor is unknown to you, hold up a card with their name clearly printed on it as passengers start to appear. Don't panic if everyone seems to go away and you're left standing there. Go to the information desk and arrange for a paging announcement to be given out, calling your visitor to the desk, before you ring back to base to check if any update on the situation has been received.

Having established contact the journey back is usually relatively easy – provided your driving is up to scratch! The 'Have you had a good journey?', 'Whereabouts in Germany do you live?' type of conversation can last quite a while.

Receipt of goods or cash

Both central and departmental receptionists can be called upon to accept goods (including cash). This is normally the job of your junior and you should make certain that she is aware of the correct procedures. You don't want to have to sort out a situation in which another company insists that some documents or goods have been delivered and your junior says she can't even remember having seen them (see Chapter 9, Office resource administration, page 420).

- Categorise first of all what 'goods' are likely to be delivered, eg parcels, large envelopes, padded bags brought in by private delivery services, British Rail Red Star, Datapost or personnel of other organisations. Remember, too, that the mailroom personnel will send up urgent items received throughout the day (see Chapter 1, Communication Systems, page 1).
- Most deliveries require a signature and your junior should also know not to accept (or sign) for goods without first having:
  - checked that the label is addressed to the company
  - read the Delivery Note and located the company's official order number (or, if this is not possible, checked with the person responsible for the ordering)

- checked that the goods contained are as listed – although this can be difficult in the case, say, of a large order of stationery. (If the goods cannot be examined the delivery note should be marked 'received, not examined'.)
- recorded any discrepancies (in ink) on the delivery note
- retained a photocopy of the delivery note or completed a goods received note.

Emphasise that these procedures, although time-consuming *must* be carried out. Your junior can quite easily be deterred by an impatient delivery man. If you think that may the case, let her know that in such circumstances she should contact you.

Equally important, however, is to make sure that you train your junior *not* to hand over goods to just *anyone* who calls to collect them (even if they are cloaked in apparent authority, eg are wearing a uniform). Again it is difficult for her to distinguish between a genuine and a bogus caller. Some proof of identity should always be asked for, however, and a signature (for what it's worth) obtained. A confirmatory telephone call to the organisation in question is sometimes advisable.

Note that you or your junior may not only be expected to handle petty cash for items such as the payment of window cleaners, the buying of tea or coffee etc but also, on occasions, to receive sums of money. Try to discourage this practice wherever possible – there can be too many repercussions. If, however, you work in a small office and someone calls in with a sum of money in an envelope as payment of a bill, make certain they have a receipt which states *exactly* what you have received, eg 'one brown sealed envelope on which is written on the front £500 as payment of John Raeburn's account' rather than '£500 from John Raeburn'. Unless you are actually allowed to count the money in front of him, you cannot be sure that the envelope contains that amount. Do not, of course, open up the envelope afterwards other than in the presence of someone else. Otherwise Mr Raeburn could accuse you of tampering with the sum.

Even if the cash handed over to you has been found in the Ladies' Room, for instance, and is destined for Lost Property, make sure that the person who has handed it over to you has seen you enter the amount in the Lost Property register (and preferably counter-initialled the entry).

Obviously, if money is going to be kept even for a short time in the reception area, it should be put into a safe or, at the very least, a lockable petty cash box in a lockable filing cabinet.

Lost property

If one of your junior's jobs as receptionist is to handle items of lost property, make sure that you establish a procedure for her to follow. Train her to:

- attach a tag to each item stating when and where it was found

- enter a brief description of it in a Lost Property Register
- enter also into that Register a brief description of any 'lost' article (at the back of the book)
- make regular checks between the 'lost' and 'found' entries
- store the items in a secure, lockable cabinet
- check with you every six months about what to do with those items still unclaimed (donate them to Oxfam etc).

SPECIAL NOTE

Train your junior to use her own initiative in identifying the best course of action to reunite important items with their owners, eg credit cards, wallets, a briefcase, a passport etc – and not just to tag them and leave them! Remember that you should hand over all valuable items to the police as soon as possible. Apart from the fact that this lessens the security risk on your premises, they are probably the first people the owner would contact.

First aid procedures and fire precautions

First aid

In a large organisation medical facilities are normally available on a centralised basis. In a smaller organisation they are sometimes minimal, other than perhaps the training of some people in first aid skills and the provision of a first aid box. (Note that the Health and Safety at Work Act 1974 lays down minimum health and safety requirements in this respect – see Chapter 10, Health and safety at work, page 488.)

It is common practice to keep the first aid box and Accident Book in the reception area and the receptionist is often the first port of call in the case of a minor accident or illness. Ideally either you or your junior should be trained in first aid.

CHECK IT YOURSELF

The St John Ambulance Brigade runs a series of such courses. Contact your local branch to see what is available. You might then want to persuade your boss to allow you to attend such a course.

Remember, however, that here the watchword is caution! You are not a qualified medical practitioner (even after a first aid course!). If you are in any doubt, call in the experts.

Fire precautions

Similarly many reception areas are regarded as the focal point in the case of any fire alarm procedures and the receptionist may be the person delegated to call the Fire Brigade in the case of any alarm. Make sure that you and your junior are aware of company policy for fire drills and what procedures should be followed if, for example, a telephone call is received from someone who tells you there is an incendiary device or bomb in the building.

Individual tasks

1 You work for a company of computer specialists. during the course of one day you have a number of unexpected visitors:

- a sales representative who says that his computer consumable products are far cheaper than those of any other supplier
- an unemployed person looking for work who says that he is particularly well qualified as a systems analyst
- a solicitor seeking information on behalf of an ex-employee who says that she has suffered eye damage because of prolonged exposure to a VDU
- an irate member of the public who says that a plant pot has just fallen on his head – and that he saw it fall from one of the company's window sills
- a young man who has difficulty in speaking English and who cannot tell you clearly what he wants
- someone who is apparently profoundly deaf

Assuming that the particular executive in question is either out or not available state what action you would take in each case.

2 In the film script on the following pages the receptionist does so much wrong it is unbelievable. Assume that the film is to be in two parts – 'bad practice' and 'good practice'. Rewrite the script to change bad to good practice.

SCENE 1

(*untidy desk: visitors' register hidden; shopping bag on desk; receptionist looking out of window – yawning*)

Relief   Are you the receptionist?

Receptionist   What's it to you?

Relief   I am the relief receptionist. I take over from you next week when you're on holiday and I wondered if you could explain what I should do.

Receptionist   Will I be glad to see the back of this place for a fortnight . . .

(*Telephone rings – receptionist answers*)

Receptionist   He's not here! – (*puts down receiver; to visitor*) – Now what do you want?

Relief   Well, what should I do about the visitors' register?

Receptionist   (*looks through papers on desk*) It's around here somewhere. I don't bother with it much – I've a good memory. If you must have it, I'll look it out for you before you come next week.

Relief   Thank you. You know I've never been a receptionist before and I'm a bit anxious about it – what do I do when visitors arrive? Do I have to ring the secretary and let her know who's come?

Receptionist   Whadda you mean?

Relief   I thought that was the normal procedure.

Receptionist   Not here it isn't. I give them a few directions and tell them to find their own way up. Nobody ever bothers. Anyway I'm not jumping up and down all day – if anyone says anything I just say they slipped past me.

(*picks up apple. Telephone rings. Receptionist answers, still eating*)

Hello – (*pause*) – Well I suppose I can take a message if you want me to – hang on. (*gestures for a pencil*)

Relief
Receptionist

Here's a pencil. Where's your telephone message pad?

Never had one.

(*opens folder, takes out a document, rips it in half and begins to write on it*)

Drat. Find some sellotape will you. (*to caller*) What's that again – (*writes on hand*) – hey, that's a funny name. OK. Got it. Bye.

(*puts receiver down, rubs hand*)

I'll not bother with that. I couldn't understand a word he was saying – something about a delayed order. If it's that important he'll ring again. Now what else did you want to know?

Relief

What happens if a visitor has to wait?

Receptionist

Whatever you do don't offer anyone a drink – you'll never get rid of them if you do. We used to have some magazines but I took them home last week.

(*telephone rings*)

Ignore it – I've just about had enough. If you're not careful you'll be pestered all day. That's about it then. Nothing to it really but don't take any lip from anyone.

SCENE 2
(*visitor enters*)

Receptionist

(*to relief receptionist*) Haven't you done anything like this before?

Relief

I think this gentleman wants to speak to you.

Receptionist

Well, he'll have to wait – (*to relief receptionist*) I don't think I've seen you around – have you been here long?

Visitor

Excuse me please.

Receptionist

Can't you see I'm busy – sit down over there will you. I'll give you a shout in a moment. (*to relief receptionist*) OK then? Nice meeting you. (*relief receptionist leaves*)

(*to visitor*) What do you want then?

Visitor

I've an appointment with Mr Sanderson for 3.30 this afternoon.

Receptionist

(*flicks through register*) What do you want him for?

Visitor

I don't think its any of your business. Just tell him I'm here will you.

Receptionist

He's not in . . . (*pause*)

Visitor	Well what do you propose to do about it?
Receptionist	What can I do about it? I can't make him appear.
Visitor	But I have an appointment.
Receptionist	Makes no difference. When he's out playing golf there's no knowing when he'll get back. He comes in when he feels like it.
Visitor	This whole set-up is absolutely disgraceful.
Receptionist	Well don't get stroppy with me – it's not my fault. Why don't you have a walk round and come back later?
	(*telephone rings – receptionist answers*)
	I can't talk to you now – I'll ring you tonight. (*puts down the receiver*)
Visitor	Is there anyone else who can help me?
Receptionist	How should I know? I'm not paid to make decisions like that
Visitor	Very well then – I'll have to leave it. But you haven't heard the last of this.
Receptionist	See if I care.

(*visitor departs*)

Individual/group tasks

Case study 1

Amanda Daley is the PA to the Managing Director of a small engineering company. One lunchtime when she is alone in the office a journalist appears unexpectedly and asks to see the MD. She greets him pleasantly and asks him if he has an appointment. He hasn't but insists that the matter he wishes to discuss is urgent.

She asks him the nature of his business and he tells her that he has heard that there has been some trouble between one of the foremen and a shop steward. She asks him how he found out about the dispute and he gives a vague reply. He insists on waiting. She knows she cannot contact her MD as he is on the shopfloor at that moment trying to sort out the problem.

She asks the journalist if she can help. He tries to get her to confirm that there is a problem and she is uncertain how to reply. He is trained to spot uncertainty and presses her. She counters by offering to find someone else, more senior than her, to talk to him. During the conversation the telephone rings. She answers it only to find that it is the MD on the line wanting some information about the two men involved in the dispute. She finds the appropriate files and gives her executive details of the job descriptions of both men. She remembers not to say their names out loud.

She tries to contact the Personnel Manager over the phone to see whether or not he will see the journalist. He is on the other line and she decides that it would be better for her to go to his office to tell him in more detail what has happened. She gives the journalist a cup of coffee and says she will not be long. Fortunately the Personnel Manager will see the journalist and, on her return to the office, she thankfully directs him to the Personnel Department.

Amanda has not been totally inefficient given the difficult circumstances in which she has found herself but she has made one or two errors.

1 List what she has done correctly.

2 List her mistakes.

3 Say how you would have acted differently in those circumstances.

Case study 2

You work for a large, prestigious firm of solicitors in Chester as PA to one of the most senior partners – Charles Roebuck. The firm is in the process of moving offices to a recently refurbished building just outside the city centre.

The new reception area is large and spacious and two new receptionists have been appointed to greet visitors on arrival and either direct or escort them to a partner's office. There are 12 partners, who specialise in different aspects of the law – litigation, taxation, matrimonial and divorce, conveyancing etc. The firm has several important clients, including large companies in the city, but is anxious to attract new members of the public in what it calls its 'bread and butter business' eg making wills, buying and selling property etc. For this reason there is a free Saturday morning advice clinic which anyone can attend.

The opening ceremony for the new offices is planned for six weeks' time and will be an elaborate affair. The offices will be opened by the Duke of Westminster. Two high court judges will be attending, together with several QCs, the Lord Mayor and other local dignitaries.

Mr Roebuck has asked for your assistance in several areas.

1 He is anxious that the two receptionists are trained properly to be able to deal with all clients effectively.
   a List the type of information which should be available in reception to enable the receptionists to cope with basic enquiries they receive.
   b Design a straightforward system which the receptionists should follow in the early days which will enable them to deal effectively with callers both with and without an appointment.
   c In the past, partners have kept lists of their appointments in their diaries, with no central list at reception. In a short memo to Mr Roebuck detail the record keeping system you feel should now be adopted and justify your recommendations.

2 Over 30 guests have been invited to the opening ceremony, plus the press, and Mr Roebuck is concerned that everything will run smoothly. In particular he is concerned that many staff will not know how to address important visitors at the buffet after the opening ceremony. Look up the information required and draft a short memo to all staff giving them the information.

Key to personal skills questionnaire

SCORING						
1	a	2	b	1	c	0
2	a	2	b	1	c	0
3	a	0	b	1	c	2
4	a	2	b	1	c	0
5	a	2	b	1	c	0
6	a	2	b	1	c	0
7	a	0	b	1	c	2
8	a	0	b	1	c	2
9	a	2	b	1	c	0
10	a	0	b	1	c	2
11	a	2	b	1	c	0
12	a	0	b	1	c	2
13	a	0	b	1	c	2
14	a	0	b	1	c	2
15	a	2	b	1	c	0
16	a	0	b	1	c	2
17	a	2	b	1	c	0
18	a	0	b	1	c	2
19	a	0	b	2	c	1
20	a	0	b	2	c	1

34 – 40	A paragon, an optimist in the extreme – or 'economical with the truth'?
26 – 33	In the right job
18 – 25	In need of more confidence/experience
10 – 17	Improvement needed
0 – 9	Give up!

Managing other people

I am reasonable, it's other people who aren't . . .

As you move up the ladder, there will be more and more occasions when you have to lead other people – either individually or in a team – and try to get them to do what you want them to do. At this point it is worth noting a two basic facts.

1 Anyone can get someone else to do what they *want* to do, it is much harder to get them to do something they are not so keen on!

2 If you persuade someone to do something they didn't want to do originally, it is harder still to make them feel happy about it!

Managing other people is a complex business and involves enough to fill several books on its own. This brief section only gives you pointers and ideas on which to work – if we whet your appetite then it is a good idea to study some other books which deal with this topic specifically.

RULE 1
Whilst other people's behaviour may seem illogical and irrational to *you*, it will always seem perfectly reasonable to *them*.

Motivation

Any management book will contain much information on the topic of motivation, ie what makes people go to work and – even more important – what makes them work hard when they get there.

There have been many theories about this, and the main ones are given in the table opposite. The important point is this – we often ascribe *different* reasons to other people than we do to ourselves, eg we may consider we are motivated by achievement, an interesting job and being made to feel important. We think others are motivated by money, status, security. Why?

RULE 2
Key aspects of your job that make you feel good work for other people too!

Theories of motivation

Our style of leadership is strongly influenced by our assumptions about motivation and these theories are not mutually exclusive[1].

---

[1]Taken from the work of Taylor, Mayo, McGregor, Maslow, Herzberg and Schein (see Further reading section, page 537)

Research has shown that there are four main groupings, each defined by different factors. Frederick Taylor, sometimes termed the 'Father of Management', was successful in increasing productivity by offering payment incentives and accentuating the division of labour in organisations in the 1920s. He believed that people were motivated mainly by money and self-interest. About ten years later, research by Elton Mayo and his colleagues, in the famous Hawthorne study, showed that people are influenced by the social aspects of their job. Other findings by such writers as Maslow, McGregor and Herzberg all focused on the individual and his/her needs. A further viewpoint is that put forward by Schein, who argued that the reasons for motivation change and can be different from one situation to another.

Rational/ economic man	Social man	Self-actualising man	Complex man
Factors: Money Self-interest	Groups Working with others	Self-esteem Recognition Achievement Self-fulfilment	Depends on situation and experience therefore can change
Therefore: Provide controls and monetary incentives	Help satisfy social needs – link these to company goals.	People naturally behave responsibly and enjoy a challenge. Encouragement vital.	Respond to people individually bearing in mind the circumstances

CHECK IT YOURSELF

1 From the following list of motivating factors, write down (in descending order) those which you consider most important to you, then to your boss and then to a junior employee in your company. Then compare your lists!

- Achievement
- Advancement
- Job growth
- Status
- Responsibility
- Salary
- Recognition
- Job interest
- Power
- Social contacts

If your lists don't match, consider whether you are correct or your assumptions about other people perhaps need re-evaluating!

2 As a group, hold a brainstorming session to discover as many additional factors as you can.

3 Read more about the work of the writers mentioned (see Further reading section).

Leadership

> **RULE 3**
> Good leaders are made not born. The most general theory is that we choose
> as a leader someone who, in a given situation, will help us to achieve our
> objective.

There have been many theories about leadership but the general
findings are that a good leader is *not* some special creature, born with
special attributes not given to the rest of us. You can *learn* to be a good
leader by watching those people who you consider to be effective at
leading others – and noting how they do this. You can *judge* good
leaders by their ability to increase work output *and* keep their
subordinates happy at the same time! The situational theory suggests
that in different situations we would choose a different leader: the
person best suited to help you to set up a new computer system may
not be the one who would make the best leader on a camping
weekend in the Lake District!

CHECK IT YOURSELF
Think of a good leader you know and note down all the factors you think
contribute to this. Now think of someone you know who is not a good
leader and list down the important factors here. What can you learn from
the exercise about your own style of leadership?

The key aspects of leadership

Whilst there are no all-encompassing qualities which make a good
leader, some key aspects are given below. Check how many appear on
your list – though you may have thought of several other good points
not shown here.

- An interest in people at least equal to a desire to get the job done.
- A good listener who *takes note* of another individual's view and,
  wherever possible, uses it.
- Decisive but makes decisions on sound reasoning not impulse.
- Owns his/her own problems – never places the burden of these on
  subordinates.
- Sets high standards but also sets a good example to be followed.
- Sensitive to the needs and expectations of others.
- A good communicator.
- Knows what motivates each individual and uses this to gain
  cooperation and interest in a job.
- Gives praise and recognition for a job well done. Offers help, rather
  than criticism, if the job is not well done.

Assumptions, theories and actions

Start by reading Situation 1 below.

Our assumptions about people and events are coloured by our own views on the world which, in turn, are affected by our experiences, attitudes, values and expectations. It is therefore hardly surprising that we view the same events in completely different ways.

The problem is that we all think that our own view of reality is correct – and, indeed, is the only one available. In truth, we may often be wrong and can learn much by comparing our own view of a situation with someone else.

For the same reason that we are not aware of alternative versions of an event, unless we really sit down and think about it, we are also not aware that the assumptions we make about a situation affect the way we act. Chris Argyris, a well-known management writer, called this our **theory of action**, but pointed out that it often differs from what he called our **espoused theory**.

RULE 4

What we *say* we believe in and will therefore do, and what we *actually* believe in and therefore do, are often completely different – and are noticed by others far more than by ourselves!

In a leadership situation, you may therefore have an espoused theory which allows for delegation, praise of subordinates, helping them if they are in difficulty etc. However, your theory of action may be completely different – or at least be perceived by them to be different. They may see you as autocratic, bossy and only concerned that a task is done – not with how they feel about it.

Self-fulfilling prophecies

From what you have read, you should now realise that our behaviour is
always influenced by the way we see the world and that we are not
always aware of how this affects other people. A further point is that if
we treat a person in a certain way, we can always justify why we have
done this in terms of their response. For instance, if you think John is
always unreasonable, this will affect the way you approach him
(probably in quite a bossy way!) and *your* attitude will affect his
response! As he sees you as bossy he will therefore act unreasonably.
You will see this as further proof that you were right in the first place,
and will continue to be bossy!

RULE 5
We can actually create a deadlock situation by our own behaviour. By acting
in a way which is determined by your expectations, you actually create the
situation you first thought of.

The one to break the deadlock is *you*. Next time, approach him on the
basis that he is a very pleasant, reasonable individual and speak to him
accordingly. It might take a while to work – he may be suspicious of
the change for a while – but persevere and watch how, as he changes
his assumptions about you, so you can also change yours about him!

Finally, if you are in a situation where you are having problems with
subordinates, it is worth sitting down quietly and working out why, *in
their view*, they are acting as they are. Think about the historical factors,
the people as you know them, the situation, other people concerned
and, most important, your own involvement and how this has
influenced events. Try, as much as you can, to put yourself in the other
people's shoes and then work out what approach would be the best
one to use. Bear in mind that the way you think about a situation is
critical to what will happen next.

RULE 6
Trying to analyse a situation from someone else's point of view won't always
solve the problem, but at the very least you will have tried to treat each person
as an *individual* and have attempted to find the best way to deal with them.

4 Arranging travel

Section 1 – Arranging travel and accommodation

Today many companies view the world – not just their immediate locality – as their market place. The result has been a growth in the number of organisations operating on a multinational basis, and a corresponding rise in business travel.

Therefore the PA or secretary who is never involved in making travel arrangements is a rarity. Even if the executives in your organisation are not international travellers, they are likely to travel within the UK – and with the Single Market, European travel will become more commonplace for all business people.

Arranging travel has two aspects – firstly, making the actual arrangements and secondly, coordinating these with the type of visit which has been planned, eg an exhibition, a conference, a business meeting, or a sales trip. This section covers the first aspect and the second section of this chapter relates to the content of the trip.

If you are responsible for planning travel then you can tackle this either in an amateurish, just-do-what-is-needed way or with a professional, well-organised approach. The difference lies in the **detail**. Anyone can ring a travel agent but a good PA will check the fine print, make sure the trip doesn't coincide with local holidays and have information to hand on climate, local customs, and medical precautions. The good PA will also be capable of coping with group bookings, liaising with those who are away and keeping the office well organised in their absence. Finally by knowing the full range of services and alternatives available and who to contact for more information, a good PA will keep the costs of business travel within or below budget.

To help you to become well-organised, after each practical section of information in this chapter you will find a **Hints and Tips** section on organisation and costs. The aim of these sections is to give you some of the practical knowledge used every day by secretaries, PAs and office administrators experienced in planning travel.

Preliminary arrangements
Before anyone can travel abroad they need a valid passport. For some countries a visa is required and/or a current vaccination certificate.

Passports
The style of British passports is changing to the same format as European passports. The words *European Community* are printed on the front cover and the passport itself is printed with machine readable characters. The aim is to take advantage of modern technological

developments in the use of passport-reading equipment to reduce delays at frontiers throughout the European Community.

Annotated example of a Machine Readable Passport

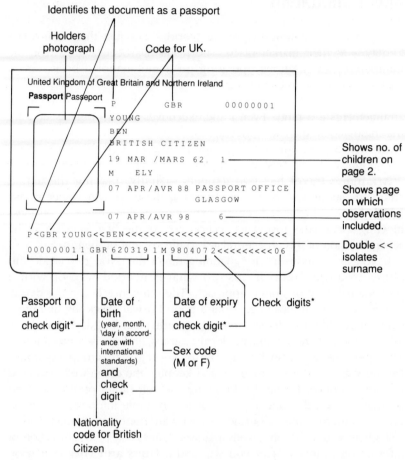

Identifies the document as a passport

Holders photograph

Code for UK.

United Kingdom of Great Britain and Northern Ireland
Passport Passeport

P　　　　GBR　　　00000001

YOUNG

BEN

BRITISH CITIZEN

19 MAR /MARS 62 1 ——————— Shows no. of children on page 2.

M　ELY

07 APR/AVR 88 PASSPORT OFFICE
　　　　　　　　GLASGOW

Shows page on which observations included.

07 APR/AVR 98　　6 ——————

Double << isolates surname

P<GBR YOUNG<<BEN<<<<<<<<<<<<<<<<<<<<<<<<<<<<

00000001 1 GBR 620319 1 M 980407 2<<<<<<<<<06

Passport no and check digit*

Date of birth (year, month, \day in accordance with international standards) and check digit*

Date of expiry and check digit*

Check digits*

Sex code (M or F)

Nationality code for British Citizen

NB:
Unused spaces are filled by character '<' to enable the reading equipment to calculate its position on the line whilst reading.

*Check digits enable the machine to check that it has correctly read the passport.

Application forms for passports are available from the Post Office or travel agents as well as from passport offices in London, Liverpool, Glasgow, Peterborough, Belfast and Newport (Gwent). There are several different passport forms but the usual one is form A. Two photographs must accompany the form (those from photo booths are quite acceptable) and must be endorsed by a British subject who is of professional standing and has known the applicant for at least two years. In addition the applicant must enclose his/her birth certificate (and marriage certificate if the applicant is a woman who wants her passport in her married name). The passport is valid for ten years and an extra large 'jumbo' version is available for people who travel frequently.

Whilst it is usual to apply for a passport by post, in an emergency you can visit the passport office in person and wait for the application to be processed. In some cases a business traveller may need two passports – eg if travelling to an Arab country which will refuse admittance to anyone whose passport contains evidence they have visited Israel, or if submitting a passport to obtain a visa for a future trip at the same time as a current trip abroad is being scheduled. In these circumstances the Passport Office will give you details of how to apply for a second passport.

Once the passport is received make a note of the number and date and place of issue and keep the information in a safe place. If your boss has credit cards insured by a 'card safe' company (see page 200) then the passport details can also be registered with them. If the passport is lost or stolen in the UK notify the card safe company, the police and the passport office. If it is missing abroad then notify the police and contact the nearest British Embassy or Consulate which will arrange for the necessary emergency travel documents to be issued for the return journey home.

Visas

Visas are required by many countries and are usually just a formality. They are obtained from the Embassy or Consulate of the country concerned. Staff there will give you details of the cost, how to apply, the length of time for which the visa is valid and how long it usually takes for one to be issued. Again in an emergency you can apply in person.

Your travel agent will make any visa arrangements for you; this means handing over the passport whilst the visa is issued. The visa is stamped on a page in the passport and states clearly the date of expiry. If your boss needs several valid visas on an almost permanent basis then keep a note of the date of expiry of each so that they can be renewed in good time.

Health

Frequent business travellers to foreign countries should be regularly checked by the company doctor who must be informed of the countries which have been/will be visited. More and more companies are operating preventative health care policies so that travellers are briefed on any health dangers endemic to the area they are visiting - and can also be counselled on the stress involved in making frequent trips. Illness abroad can cause havoc to an important schedule as well as distress for the person involved. In addition, nearly 2000 people return to the UK each year with malaria, others suffer from diseases such as hepatitis, typhoid and even AIDS. Companies which do not have their own doctor and which want expert advice can contact any of the British Airways Travel Clinics, MASTA (the Medical Advisory Service for Travellers Abroad) or the Thomas Cook Medical Centre in London.

Inoculations and/or vaccinations are either essential or recommended for many countries and most can be administered by a GP. All GPs and travel agents should keep an up-to-date list of vaccination requirements but must be contacted *in advance* of the trip – it is several weeks before some vaccinations are completely effective. In addition the Department of Health produces two leaflets on health: *Before you go* (SA 40) and *While you're away* (SA 41) which can be obtained from the local Social Security office or by ringing 0800 555 777.

All travellers should be aware of basic health rules whilst abroad and take basic precautions such as those given below.

- Remember to take vaccination certificates with them. The best place is inside the back cover of the passport, fastened with a rubber band.
- Carry a small first aid kit which includes sterilisation tablets, antiseptic cream, plasters, insect repellent and remedies for travel sickness, headaches, stomach upsets, and insect bites and stings. Remember to take any medicine needed regularly. Visitors to more remote places should include anti-malaria drugs. In addition special kits are available with sterilised and sealed items of equipment which may be required by a doctor or nurse in an emergency. There are also special AIDS kits, containing sterile syringes and dressings, for travellers to high AIDS-risk areas. If sexual contact is likely then condoms are essential.
- Do not drink the water (or use it for cleaning teeth) unless it is known to be safe – bottled water should be used instead.
- Avoid raw vegetables, salads, unpeeled fruit, shellfish, ice cream and ice cubes.
- Have a dental check-up before travelling as treatment can be difficult or costly abroad.
- Remember that a severe attack of diarrhoea or vomiting causes dehydration. Anti-diarrhoea medicines are not, in themselves, a cure. In addition the sufferer should stop drinking alcohol and eating solid food and replace body fluids by drinking a rehydration solution (eg one level teaspoon salt and four heaped teaspoons of sugar added to safe drinking water). If the attack lasts longer than three days see a doctor.
- Carry a medical card which states their blood group and any special medical condition from which they suffer.
- Make sure they have adequate health insurance *in addition* to the standard European cover (see page 198). This is *vital* for countries where treatment must be paid for and is expensive, eg the USA and Canada.
- On returning home, report any strange symptoms immediately to their doctor (and remember to say where they've been).

Methods of travel

Because time is money in business, it is usual for business travellers to want to reach their destination the quickest way possible. For European and intercontinental journeys this usually means travelling by air. Within the UK, air travel may be less convenient as time has to be allowed for travelling from airport to city centre – and the cost is higher than by rail Within the UK rail may be preferable to road travel for long journeys as it is quicker, less tiring and work can be done en route. Sea travel is the least popular method of travel abroad unless, for some reason, your boss wants to take a car abroad.

Air travel

Essential for planning air travel are either the *ABC World Airways Guide* or timetables from airlines you use regularly. Alternatively, you can ring your travel agent for details, but you are then restricted to their choice and opinion on flights and not your own.

You must be able to read a timetable without difficulty, know your airlines (and the ones your boss loves/likes/detests), and understand the terms used, some of which are specific to the airline industry. You should also keep yourself informed about new developments and promotional offers. Many airlines are currently considering installing laptop computers, telex and faxes in onboard work stations on airplanes and payphones, powerful enough to make calls worldwide, are now fitted in many American planes. Callers insert a credit card to release the handset and then return to their seat to make their call. The phones are for outgoing calls only so you cannot consider this a quick and easy way of contacting your boss whilst in transit (unless the company has a corporate jet). On the ground Swissair is testing self check-in procedures in Paris and Geneva to speed up the time taken to board the plane. Such information not only enables you to keep up to date but also to offer your boss the best choice available.

Facts you should know

Airport There is often more than one in a city (think of London which has Gatwick, Heathrow, Stanstead and City airports). Make sure your boss knows to which one he/she is travelling, try to use the one nearest to where he/she will be staying or visiting. *Always* check that connecting flights from a city arrive/leave from the same airport or allow plenty of time for the transfer (see also *Minimum connection times*). All airports are identified by a three letter code, eg LHR London Heathrow, JFK New York, John F Kennedy airport. Be careful when there are two of the same name, eg Birmingham UK (BHX) and Birmingham (Alabama) USA (BHM).

Business class   The class of travel most often used by business people – cheaper than first class and better than economy. Sometimes called **Club Class**.

Carrier   The name of the airline, again identified by a letter code eg BA British Airways, AA American Airlines.

Check-in time   The time before a flight when the passenger must book in at the airline desk at the airport. For connecting flights travellers do not have to check in again at the next airport unless, for some reason, baggage has to be collected in transit.

Computerised booking system   The most common system used by travel agents is the **Travicom/Gallileo** system which not only makes the booking but also issues the tickets.

Domestic flight   A flight within one country.

Frequent flier programmes   Virtually all airlines have a 'club' for their regular business travellers – the names vary (eg Diamond Club (British Midland), Raffles Class (Singapore Airlines), Le Club (Air France). Rules for membership vary and may be based on miles flown or payment of a membership fee (check with the airline or your travel agent). There are many benefits from membership – valet car parking, priority check-in, business lounges (with fax, photocopiers, phones etc), plus discounts and special offers.

Jet lag   The problems of tiredness and fatigue associated with travelling across several time zones, exacerbated by lack of sleep and short nights. Normally worse from east to west, it can severely impair anyone's ability to do business for several hours (so *don't* time the first appointment immediately after arrival!).

Long-haul   The term used for long intercontinental flights, eg UK to Australia. Long-haul flights have **stop-overs** for refuelling.

Minimum connection time   The minimum amount of time which must be allowed between connecting flights. This will depend on whether the incoming/outgoing flight is from the same terminal or different terminals – or even different airports. You will not be allowed to make a booking that breaks the rules on this. Details are given in the *ABC World Airways Guide*.

Non-transferability Most airlines insist that tickets are non-transferable. Therefore if your boss is ill at the last minute you can't send along a substitute with the same ticket. The airline is likely to insist that the booking is cancelled and a new reservation made – if there is still space!

Open-dated return A pre-paid return ticket with no specified date for return travel. The traveller is then free to book the return flight when ready to do so.

Red eye The overnight flight from New York to London.

Short haul The opposite of long-haul, eg European flights.

Shuttle The walk-on domestic UK air service - no booking needed.

Terminal The specific airport building at which the flight arrives or from which it departs. In large airports there are often several, identified by number, ie Terminal 1, 2 etc. *Always* note down the number – both for the traveller and anyone meeting him/her.

Time zones The hourly segments into which the world is divided. West of Great Britain is earlier than GMT, east is later.

TOD Ticket on departure system for last minute bookings. Becoming more common as a service to business passengers.

Wait list The 'reserve' list for a scheduled flight; on European flights there is a high rate of cancellations so it is always worth booking on the wait list for the flight your boss prefers. Book a second choice alternative in case the wait list doesn't come up and cancel this option if it does.

TEST YOURSELF
Bearing in mind that if you travel from New York to London you are travelling eastwards, and from what you should understand about time zones, why do you think the overnight flight *in that direction* is called the 'red eye'?

Hints and tips on organisation

- Organise business appointments *first* then look to see which flights are the most convenient.
- Keep a 'rating' guide of airlines from your boss's experiences. Try a star system (5 stars = excellent, 0 = awful). Devise a simple scoring system based on food, in-flight service, delays, leg room on board and any other categories your boss thinks appropriate.
- Register your boss with the frequent flier programme of the airline he/she likes best. When booking always remember to give the frequent flier registration number.
- Many flights today are non-smoking. If this will be a problem for your boss you may have to investigate alternative airlines/routes.

- Most seats on airlines are pre-bookable. Find out if your boss wants smoking (if available) or non-smoking, aisle or window. Bear in mind these choices may vary with length/time of flight, eg an overnight choice may be for an aisle seat whereas for a short daytime flight a window seat may be preferable.
- If your boss isn't a seasoned air traveller remind him/her that:
  - alcohol increases jet lag. Mineral water prevents dehydration and therefore is much better
  - loose clothes should be worn as the body expands at high altitudes
  - long-haul travellers in first class are given oversocks (feet swell too) so that they can remove their shoes, and eyemasks. These items can be bought pre-flight (together with ear plugs if the noise might be disturbing)
  - a suitcase with jazzy stickers is easy to identify in a busy baggage hall
  - fountain pens leak at high altitude
  - permission *in advance* must be obtained from an airline before a laptop computer can be used in flight – in case of interference with vital communications equipment. Because putting a laptop through an X-ray screening device at an airport may erase the data stored on the disk the traveller can ask for it to be lifted around the machine. However, the security authorities at the airport have the right to examine it if they wish.
  - keep baggage tags carefully (they should be attached to the ticket); the number on these is needed if baggage is lost.

Hints and tips on cost

Calculating fares is complicated and better left to the experts. If you make many bookings your company may send you on a special travel course to learn how to do this. Even without this information you *can* save your company money.

- Watch out for special offers. During certain promotional periods frequent fliers may be able to upgrade a class – which can make all the difference on an overnight flight.
- Alternatively a special offer may be available if you re–route the trip, eg London to Boston via New York instead of direct.
- Some frequent flier programmes offer free trips after so many miles travelled. Try to coordinate bookings to log up the miles required and, if the rules of membership allow for this, centralise offers received by the company so they can be used by *all* executives for the benefit of the company as a whole.
- The magazine *Business Traveller* gives recommended price lists for all classes of travel; check these against any prices you are quoted.
- Check your company's policy on this, but on long-haul flights some organisations prefer to pay for first class travel (so the executive can get a fairly decent night's sleep) rather than schedule a day off into the itinerary.

TEST YOURSELF

- Can you find out the names of the following airlines from their identification letters and state for which country they are the flag carrier? What is the capital city of each country you have listed?

  LH SN QF KL AZ EI OA SR PA IB

- The following are all American airports. Can you name them?

  BOS IND LAX SFO SEA PHL LGA LAS

Travelling by road

Motoring – at home and abroad

Bear in mind your boss may want to travel by road abroad, either by taking a car to Europe or flying to the destination and then hiring a car. All travellers using their own car should be members of a motoring organisation ie the AA or the RAC. These organisations not only offer breakdown and 'get you home' services in the UK but also advice and information on driving abroad. The AA also operates a computerised route planning service for both members and non-members, which can take the work and worry out of planning a trip to take in three cities in Germany, a visit to Belgium and an overnight stop in Holland by the best route possible.

Car ferries

The most usual method of transporting a car across the water is by ferry. Alternatives for passengers travelling from Dover are by hovercraft, Seacat and jetfoil – all of which are more expensive but halve the travelling time. (The jetfoil service is passenger only.)

When you make the booking you will need to know the make/length/registration number of the vehicle. On ferries you can book a cabin – in some cases for day journeys as well as night crossings. You must specify if private facilities are required.

Some ferry companies, eg P & O, have now introduced an Executive Club class on some routes if the ticket holder pays a supplement. Members can use the Club class lounge which contains desks, telephones and fax facilities.

All travellers must check in at the Ferryport before sailing; times vary (the average is about one hour before sailing) so check the ticket or ask your travel agent. For last minute bookings you can arrange for the ticket to be ready for collection on departure from the Ferryport.

Hints and tips

- Remember it may be much easier and quicker for your boss to cross from the east coast if he/she is visiting northern Europe.
- It takes time to load and unload a ferry. You therefore need to take account of the waiting time for embarkation and disembarkation when planning the schedule.
- A longer ferry journey can often reduce the driving required. Although longer ferry journeys are more expensive they are cheaper per mile than short crossings.
- If you time arrival for early morning (and book a cabin overnight) driving time is maximised.
- If your boss regularly takes a car abroad then watch for off-peak reductions – especially if the day of travel is variable. By planning the journey for a quiet day and time – and sometimes for a specified length of time – substantial reductions can be obtained out of season.

British cars abroad

The regulations for British cars taken to Europe vary from one country to another. Most countries require:

- headlamps which point towards the nearside to avoid blinding oncoming traffic (Rather than adjusting the headlamps it is easier to fit temporary headlight converters.)
- a spare set of headlamp bulbs
- a warning triangle to be displayed if the car breaks down.

The AA recommends that the driver takes a spare clutch/accelerator cable as these are different for right hand drive cars and obtaining a spare on the Continent can therefore be very difficult.

All British cars should also carry an approved GB plate on the rear of the vehicle.

Documents required include the driver's licence (in Spain an International Driving Permit is required), the vehicle registration documents and a Green Card or International Motor Insurance Certificate. The latter extends the driver's insurance to cover European countries and is issued by his/her insurance company. In Spain a Bail Bond is also required which covers the driver if he/she is taken into custody after an accident. This is available from the AA, RAC and Europ Assistance – a company which specialises in comprehensive cover packages to Europe.

The quickest way to take a car a long distance is often by **Motorail**; the car travels by train and the driver can relax in a sleeper or couchette. Motoring organisations have full details for each country – which saves having to contact separate railway organisations. Note that you must notify the insurance company so that the car is covered for any damage during the rail journey.

Hints and tips

- Make sure the driver knows which roads are toll roads – and has some small change available in the relevant currency.
- Money can be saved by filling up with petrol on the cheaper side of the border.
- Keep a list of the main driving regulations per country on either a country fact sheet (see fact sheet on America in the next section) or on a card index file. Photocopy the card and give it to the driver before departure.

Hiring a car

First rule – beware unknown or backstreet companies which hire out cars which are unfit for the road. Quite apart from the problems of possible breakdowns, if a driver is stopped for driving a car which isn't roadworthy the police will charge the driver, *not* the hire company! Therefore insist on a relatively new vehicle with a low mileage. However, note that in the case of mechanical breakdown it is the hire company which is legally responsible, *not* the driver. To be on the safe side hire a vehicle from a member of the British Vehicle Renting and Leasing Association (BVRLA) whose members have to operate to a specific code of conduct.

The driver has to produce a current driving licence (and may be refused if the licence has been endorsed for a motoring offence) and will probably be asked for proof of identity. The driver must have been driving for a minimum of one year (often longer for more expensive cars) and must be at least 21 years of age (23 in some cases).

Cars are hired out either on an unlimited mileage basis – the most common method – or with an additional charge for mileage above a specified limit. The best way to pay is by credit card which means no deposit is required and there is no restriction on the choice of cars.

In Britain there are four multinational car companies – Avis, Budget Rent-a-Car, Europcar and Hertz as well as the independent large companies eg British Car Rental, Kenning and Swan National. These companies offer one-way hire so that 'quick drop offs' can be arranged at many airports and railway stations.

Hints and tips

- When you book, check the procedure in case of an emergency breakdown or accident; has the company a 24-hour emergency call-out number?
- Although the standard of car hire vehicles from local firms is more variable than from national firms it is well worth shopping around as often their prices are much lower.
- Always check whether or not the price you are quoted includes VAT.
- Many large car hire firms have their own credit cards which enable the user to claim up to 20 per cent discount. It may also enable

him/her to collect in one place and drop off in another without any surcharges.

- If you find a good local firm, and hire cars often, try to negotiate a better deal. Even with national firms local branches are often allowed to set their own charges.
- Hiring a car in major cities and at airports is more expensive as 'national tariffs' are charged, as opposed to the out-of-town rates charged elsewhere. If cost is a major consideration it can be worth using a *good* rail link from an airport to get to a local depot.
- Although the basic hire charge includes insurance against passenger liability and third party risks, extra charges may be levied. Collision damage waiver covers damage done to the vehicle and there may be an additional charge for personal accident insurance. Check the charges for both of these as rates can vary considerably.
- Car hire abroad can be much cheaper than in the UK and may be offered at premium rates and/or linked to frequent flier programmes and rail bookings (check with the airline, your travel agent or the rail company).
- Check the basics of the vehicle upon collection – tyres, fluid levels, lights, wipers and how much fuel is in the tank. Drive around the block and check the brakes, instruments and clutch function properly. Make sure the handbook is in the car.

Coach travel

Coaches are rarely used for business travel but it is not inconceivable that you will have to book a coach journey at some stage – if only for a relative of your boss who wants to visit Europe but hates flying! The best people to contact are National Express at Eurolines, 52 Grosvenor Gardens, Victoria, London SW1. In addition National Express has enquiry centres all over the UK and will send you a timetable, answer your queries and accept credit card reservations. The fare includes coach travel, ferry crossings and additional charges such as road tolls. Note that insurance is not included – not even for passenger luggage or belongings.

Rail travel

Most business travellers in Britain use the InterCity service to go from one city centre to another and most main railway stations have a Travel Centre with staff who can deal with enquiries and reservations. In addition they stock maps, timetables and booklets on a variety of services. If your nearest station is too far away, then your local Rail Appointed Travel Agent can offer the same service.

British Rail operates a Business Travel Service which includes travel advice and reservations for rail and car-hire. The Hertz InterCity Drive service includes car collection at most mainline stations, a computerised route planning service, mobile telephone rental and 24 hour AA service cover. Companies can open their own Rail Travel Account so that all reservations can be made by telephone. In addition they can arrange to issue a rail warrant to their staff which is presented at the booking office and exchanged for a ticket. British Rail then sends the company an account at the end of the month for the tickets/warrants issued.

There are two main categories of travel on British Rail – Standard and First Class. A variation is Silver Standard – offered in the specially marked coaches on main business trains. However, many executives prefer to travel First Class. Always look to see if a Pullman train is an option: the service is better, as are the facilities, which include an 'at-seat' catering service and a restaurant car offering an extensive menu. If you purchase an Executive ticket then in addition to the first class ticket and seat reservations you also receive refreshment and car parking vouchers, a London underground Zone One ticket and the ability to add and pre-pay for meals and/or sleeper reservations. The Scottish Executive ticket includes sleeper travel in either direction and can be combined with the Motorail service. Both First Class and Executive ticket holders can use the Pullman Lounges at Edinburgh, London (Kings Cross and Euston), Leeds and Newcastle which are equipped with telephone, television/teletext, a photocopier and, in London, a fax machine.

For European countries you need to make enquiries with the specific rail company involved: most have London offices, eg DER, the Germany railway company, and SNCF, the French railway company. Contact the latter for details of the very fast Continental TGV train service. Bear in mind that in Europe an alternative to booking a sleeper on overnight routes is to reserve a **couchette** – the seat converts to a bed and the traveller is given a pillow, blanket and towel.

In Germany, Lufthansa (the German airline) has started a fast rail service between the main German cities. Passengers are given boarding cards and are served by Lufthansa cabin staff. The change has helped to reduce the demand for domestic air flights as it means quicker and easier travel from one city centre to another.

In general, in Europe, rail links are getting quicker – therefore narrowing the gap between rail and air travel. Paris to Geneva takes 3.5 hours by rail as compared to 65 minutes by air yet is less than half the price and is city centre to city centre. Again Motorail can be a useful option, especially for long journeys to southern Europe.

Hints and tips

- Whether your boss travels First or Standard class *always* make a seat reservation. Check whether he/she prefers to travel in a smoking or non-smoking compartment and facing the front or rear of the train (or has no particular preference).
- Make sure your boss carries a phone card – most trains these days have card phones.
- Register with the British Rail Business Travel Service by dialling 081 200 0200 and you will be sent a comprehensive guide to InterCity services and a new guide whenever timetables change.

- Keep a full set of British Rail timetables for the routes your boss uses or have your own copy of the *British Rail Timetable* or the *ABC Rail Guide*.
- If your boss is travelling to a major city by rail and staying a few days it may be worth checking if any company operates an inclusive short-break package – which can be much cheaper.
- Make sure you are on the mailing list of any rail company you use regularly, so that you are advised of special offers eg rail rover information/car hire discounts etc.
- Discount of up to 25 per cent can be obtained for groups of ten or more travelling together on standard tickets. In addition, if your company is organising a conference, notably at the NEC in Birmingham, you can obtain help with planning and bulk ticketing by phoning 021 643 3014.
- If you need to refer to Continental train information on a regular basis it is worth buying a copy of the *Thomas Cook International Timetable*.

Accommodation

Whether you are booking accommodation in the UK or abroad, for business travel you are better confining your choice to a hotel in one of the well-known hotel groups eg Holiday Inn, Inter-continental, Hilton, Trusthouse Forte, Sheraton, Marriott, Ramada and Best Western International. Standards are known and trusted, the services are designed for the business traveller and there are London-based reservations offices to handle bookings worldwide. A list of hotel reservation offices, addresses and phone numbers can be found in *Travel Trade Gazette* – or you can phone a London hotel in the same group and ask for their international reservations number. You can also obtain information through your travel agent or on Prestel, and some airlines operate a hotel booking service, eg British Airways. Another invaluable book, which gives details of hotels in a variety of towns and cities worldwide, is the *ABC Worldwide Hotel Guide*. Equally, *Michelin Guides* are indispensable for information on hotels and restaurants in Europe.

If your boss is going to a British town where there is no well-known hotel, then refer to the *AA Handbook* or *Hotels and Restaurants in Great Britain*; or ring the local Tourist Board. Most hotels are grouped by star categories – the more stars the better the facilities. Below three stars is not usually suitable for executive travel. In the same way you can contact the Tourist Boards of small towns abroad, eg the local *Syndicate d'Initiative* in France, to obtain a printed list of hotels in a particular area – although you may have to translate some of the information given about the facilities available!

Bear in mind that the needs of a business traveller are different from those of the holidaymaker. A swimming pool and tennis court are not as valuable as an 'any hour' check-in service, tea/coffee making facilities in the room, early morning breakfast facilities, and good dining/meeting rooms. Car parking may be essential – if your boss is travelling to the hotel by road *do* remember to check this! Many hotels are waking up to the fact that more and more business travellers are now women – to whom a trouser press is less important than a good hairdrier! A group campaigning actively for good facilities for female travellers is the Business Women's Travel Club Ltd. Telephone them on 071 384 1121 for information if you have female executives in your organisation.

Hints and tips on organisation

- Always confirm your reservation in *writing* – preferably by telex, not fax (there is no proof of receipt with a fax). If you do use fax, ask the hotel to fax back confirmation. This is particularly important in some parts of the world where hotels are far more laid back about keeping reservations!
- Provide your boss with the names, addresses and phone numbers of alternative hotels in the area just in case!
- Enquire if the hotel has no-smoking rooms if your boss is a non-smoker.
- Be aware that a twin room has twin beds and a double room has a double bed.
- Check if the rate is per room or per person and whether breakfast is included. (In the USA, for instance, there is one room rate regardless of the number of people the room holds and the price never includes breakfast.)
- If your boss will be arriving after 6 pm make sure the hotel knows, so that it won't relet the accommodation.
- If the hotel is one you have not used before check if credit cards are acceptable. If the hotel is abroad remember that the words *Barclaycard* and *Access* mean nothing – you must use the terms **Visa** and **Mastercard**.
- Another American idea now being adopted in Europe is the 'all-suite' hotel – based on the idea that many business travellers need more space than is traditionally provided in a single room. In a 'suite' the definition can vary, from two (or more) spacious rooms, to one main room with areas for working, sleeping and even eating.

Hints and tips on cost

- Many international hotel chains (especially in the USA) operate schemes similar to those available to frequent fliers eg Honored Guest or Gold Pass. If your boss is in one of these privilege programmes try to make bookings at these hotels and give the membership number when making the reservation.
- If you are on the mailing list of hotel chains you will be sent details of their special offers.
- First time business travellers should be aware that the cost of their

stay will soar if they take advantage of the mini-bar in their rooms, as prices are frequently exorbitant.

- It is far cheaper to phone the office using an international telephone credit card (obtainable from Post Office Telecommunications) than to use a hotel phone which is usually subject to a considerable surcharge.
- If you need to cancel at the last moment bear in mind that the hotel cannot charge you immediately for the cost. They have to try to relet the room first. Unless the rate was clearly quoted as room only, if it fails to relet it can bill you only for two-thirds of the account. It must deduct one third which is the amount officially allowed for food.

Travel insurance

Two important points to note are firstly, standard holiday cover is not sufficient for business travellers – a good on-going policy is needed which covers any number of trips. Secondly, although EC countries now have reciprocal arrangements with Britain provided you have obtained form E111 (available from a Post Office), the medical care is provided by the state sector, and standards fall far short of the NHS in many countries. In addition costs have to be paid on the spot and reclaimed later. It is therefore wise to take out additional medical insurance for all countries.

Policies are available from insurance companies, banks, building societies, brokers, major travel agents and the AA. Cover should include the following.

Medical expenses To cover medical treatment (including hospitalisation), a special air ambulance home and an ambulance to and from the airport in both countries. £1 million is recommended for worldwide cover.

Personal liability £1 million, to cover accidental injury to people or property.

Cancelling or early return Should cover the full cost of the trip. Acceptable reasons should include illness or death of self or business associate/fellow traveller, redundancy, disasters at home/work (eg fire), being a police witness or on jury service.

Belongings and money To cover personal items and company equipment or samples taken abroad. 'Money' should include travellers' cheques and tickets, not just cash.

Delayed luggage At least £75 to cover emergency purchases.

Delayed departure If delay is more than 24 hours through bad weather, strikes or transport failure then the full cost of the trip should be covered.

In addition other features can include the expenses incurred in obtaining a duplicate passport and cover for legal expenses. Aim for a nil excess policy, which means the full amount of any claim will be paid, without deductions.

Hints and tips

- Obtain a copy of the policy document (*not* the advertising blurb) and read the exclusion clauses carefully *before* taking out the insurance. For instance check the limit on individual valuables – and exactly what goods are classed as valuables.
- Photocopy the policy for the traveller to take with him.
- If your boss has a charge card or gold card, business travel insurance may be included. If so, check *exactly* what cover is given. Don't automatically assume it will be sufficient.
- If you cancel the trip and are claiming on the insurance policy get a cancellation invoice from the travel agent *plus* written proof as to the reason.
- Make sure your boss knows to keep all receipts of any extra travel/accommodation/medical costs incurred.
- Check the policy to ensure what events must be reported to the police immediately for claims to be valid. Get written confirmation from the police that this has been done.
- In some countries medical treatment will not be started until the insurance has been checked. Make sure your boss knows the emergency number to ring for help.
- If the trip is curtailed because of a delayed departure then you need the details confirmed in writing by the airline.
- If baggage is missing then the traveller should complete a Property Irregularity Report – obtainable from the airline. Ask the airline to confirm the loss.
- Make sure the insurance company is aware of any on-going medical condition. If there is any doubt about cover ask for a doctor's letter to certify fitness to travel and send this, plus any other details to the insurance company, so you cannot be accused of 'withholding material fact'.
- Bear in mind that if your boss is a woman who is pregnant, cover may not be provided at all – or only during the first six months of pregnancy.
- Many insurance policies insist that valuables must be kept in a hotel safe.

CHECK IT YOURSELF
- Look through a copy of the latest *AA Guide* and note the facilities offered against the different star categories. What does the percentage figure quoted indicate?
- Call at one or two of your local banks, building societies and insurance companies and obtain literature on travel insurance. Check the cover offered and work out which is the best value for money.

Card safe protection/insurance

An increasing number of companies are now offering a service to cover the loss of credit cards at home or abroad for a yearly premium. The service greatly simplifies the procedure involved if cards are lost or stolen, as only one phone call is required and the card agency does the rest. The facilities vary from one company to another. Check that you are offered:

- cover for fraudulent use before notification (though the owner is usually liable for the first £50)
- the facility to make reverse charge calls from all over the world (to notify the loss)
- an emergency cash advance worldwide
- a replacement airline ticket worldwide (repayable later).

Companies will also record details of other valuables, eg passports, share certificates etc and keep these on computer so that the information is readily available in case of loss or theft.

Hints and tips

- Bear in mind that if a card protection policy is paid by credit card then the small print of the agreement will probably include automatic renewal. *You* have to notify *them* if you want to change – don't expect them to check with you every year before renewal.
- Keep a list of all emergency telephone numbers and give your boss a typed copy. If there is an emergency card safe number then put a copy of this in an unusual place so that if the wallet or handbag is stolen the number to ring hasn't disappeared too!

Finance abroad

Travellers abroad have a variety of methods of paying for goods. The first rule is to keep to a minimum the amount of cash taken – for obvious reasons. However, some currency is obviously required for small day-to-day needs. This should be ordered from the bank seven days in advance – especially if the currency is an unusual one. Note that for some countries, eg Morocco, you can only obtain currency upon arrival. In other cases the amount of cash that can be taken out of the country on departure is restricted. Alternatives to cash include Eurocheques, travellers' cheques, credit cards, gold cards and charge cards.

Eurocheques are only used in European and Mediterranean countries and to be of any use the traveller also needs a Eurocheque card which guarantees the cheques up to £100 (or more in some cases). If the traveller has a PIN number, (only available at present with the NatWest Eurocard) the card can also be used to obtain money from cash dispensers abroad which display the distinctive red and blue EC logo. The bank can supply a list of cashpoints in Europe in an illustrated booklet which also shows how to use the different types of cash machines found in different countries. Allow ten days to get a Eurocheque book and card and bear in mind commission is paid on all cheques debited to the account.

Travellers' cheques are available in sterling and several other currencies as well. A commission charge is levied by the bank when you buy the cheques and, if they are sterling cheques, a further commission is charged when they are cashed. Both dollars and sterling are known as 'hard currencies' and are acceptable in many countries in the world. Travellers' cheques are ordered from the bank and the *traveller* must sign each one on receipt. On encashment the holder must produce his/her passport and sign the cheque(s) again. The list of cheque numbers and the cheques themselves must be kept safely in separate places for security and the list of numbers produced if the cheques are lost or stolen. In the case of loss or theft a refund can be obtained – theoretically straight away but it may be more problematic in practice, especially in unusual places with no correspondent ('link') bank.

Today the most usual method of paying for items abroad is by using credit cards or charge cards. Indeed in some countries, eg the USA, this may be the only acceptable way to pay in some situations. Credit cards are Mastercard and Visa cards – to date Visa cards have more outlets abroad. Credit cards offer better rates of exchange than the local tourist rates although some Visa companies add on their own fee (including Barclays and Midland). The major problem with credit cards abroad – especially for business travellers – is the credit limit. In some countries hotels protect themselves by asking for the card on arrival and then processing it for a much larger amount than the quoted hotel bill (in case damage is caused or the guest runs up a tremendous restaurant bill). Whilst only the amount spent is actually charged to the card at the end of the stay, in the meantime the card will be useless for other purchases if it has reached its limit. The highest credit limit can be obtained with a British Airways Visa card which carries a credit limit three or four times higher than most other cards. The card can also be used to obtain the equivalent of £100 a day in cash from any Visa linked bank in the world.

Another way around this is to carry charge cards – and many business travellers subscribe to either Diners Club or American Express. A charge card is different from a credit card in that the account must be paid in full at the end of a pre-set period (between 45 and 60 days) or a late payment penalty is levied. There is *no* pre-set spending limit. There is an annual fee and Diner's Club also charge a joining fee. Corporate cards can be purchased and issued under the name of the company. A breakdown account is issued to the company giving the expenditure for each charge card so that expenses can be checked. The advantage is that charge cards can be used for air tickets and additional hotel stays if the trip is unexpectedly extended or the executive is re-routed halfway across the world. Other benefits include automatic travel insurance and automatic emergency replacement if the card is lost or stolen. A new Corporate charge card is the Thomas Cook card which can be used wherever Mastercards are acceptable and which gives the same service as other charge cards plus air travel, hotel and car savings. In addition holders receive privileged treatment in any Thomas Cook office world wide including the use of their telex machines.

A gold card is similar to a charge card but often with more facilities, perks and higher fees. Many gold cards offer comprehensive travel benefits, eg travel insurance, emergency assistance and guaranteed hotel reservations. The holder has to earn at least £20 000 a year to qualify – more with some cards.

The banks also offer services which can be used either to set up a bank account abroad or to transfer funds abroad in an emergency. A letter of credit is a letter of introduction to a bank so that the holder can cash his/her own UK cheques. This service is rather outmoded today with more modern methods of currency exchange. It is more likely to be used if a person will be working abroad for a long period and wants to open an account in a foreign bank. The company can then send out funds regularly, by Standard International Transfer, and these are paid into the bank account. The person working abroad then has all the facilities of a normal current account holder in that country. If money is wanted urgently then an Urgent International Transfer form can be completed and the British bank will forward the funds onwards to a nominated bank and the person concerned can collect the funds upon proving his/her identity.

Hints and tips

- Keep a note of currency regulations in countries your executives frequently visit, plus banking hours and other useful hints and tips about money.
- Always make sure your boss has some small change for tips, taxi fares or even a cup of coffee on arrival. You can do this by keeping in a safe place the small change he/she brings back and reissuing it on the next trip to the same country.
- It is usually cheaper to buy larger amounts of foreign currency at one time – check with your bank. If this is the case then try to 'batch' your orders and keep spare currency in the office safe.
- Make sure first-time travellers know to avoid obtaining currency at airports and railway stations where rates are usually poor or commission charges high.
- No traveller abroad should ever be reliant on just one credit card. If the card company makes a mistake, or the limit is reached then funds could be drastically curtailed!
- Shop around for exchange rates on currency and commission charges on currency and travellers' cheques. Do bear in mind that what seems to be a good buy may not be once the commission charges are included.

- Try to avoid selling back currency a business traveller brings back – otherwise you are losing money both ways. It is far better to keep it for next time.
- Make sure your boss has a BT Chargecard for making calls back to the UK.
- Remember that your boss may return with unused travellers' cheques. If these are sterling or dollar cheques they can be used anywhere on subsequent business trips. If you have purchased specific currency cheques they can only be used in the country to which the currency relates.
- Dollar travellers' cheques can be used as cash in the USA; therefore make sure your boss has some in small denominations, eg $10 and $20.
- Many airlines, petrol companies, hotels and car hire firms issue their own charge cards. Holders of these are often eligible for discounts so if your boss uses any of these services regularly it is worth obtaining more details. (See also Car hire.)

A final word on costs and expenses

Throughout this section we have been concerned with the costs of business travel – and for very good reasons. A recent survey revealed that nine out of ten companies considered their travel costs were increasing faster than their turnover. Of these costs about 46 per cent are on air fares and 24 per cent on accommodation – therefore any savings in these areas can help considerably.

However, to keep an eye on costs properly, it is important that every organisation operates a well-organised expenses system, especially in relation to cash advances to business travellers. Company credit cards or charge cards can reduce this need and enable expenditure by type, department or individual to be checked. However, day-to-day expenses may still be required and extra allowances granted, eg for clothing required for very hot or very cold countries, and these should be monitored closely.

Monitoring can be done on a basis of average cost per country or city. Any expense claims which are much higher than this figure should be investigated. In a recent survey undertaken by *Business Traveller*, the dearest city in the world in which to stay is Tokyo, where almost £290 a day is required just to eat, sleep and do a small amount of entertaining. Paris is the next most expensive at £240 a day, whilst London is close behind at £236 a day. Inflation must also be taken into account – remember this varies from one country to another. At present prices in the Far East have been rising rapidly and therefore any 'league table' of countries must be updated regularly.

Finally you should be aware that your company can claim tax relief on travel expenses which their employees incur 'necessarily' and 'in the performance of' their duties. Either dispensation for deductible items on specific trips has to be arranged in advance with the tax office or your boss has to enter deductible benefits on his tax form P11D every year. All travellers should keep a record of expenses and benefits received.

Putting it all together – designing the itinerary

There are basically two types of itineraries. One is a simplified list of travel arrangements which may be typed out on an A4 sheet – or summarised – on a small card (which is easier to keep handy). The second type is a more detailed schedule which covers events and functions being attended, contact names etc. This second type is dealt with in the next section.

There are a few simple, basic rules to follow when drawing up a standard itinerary.

- Type the dates covered, the destination and the names of those involved clearly at the top.
- List the arrangements in date and time order and *always* use the 24-hour clock.
- Include all important information, eg times of departure/arrival, flight numbers and terminals for airline reservations; name, address, telephone number and fax/telex numbers of hotels or car hire firms. Remember *all* travel arrangements must be covered, including getting from home/office to the airport and return.

An effective way of presenting this information is to paperclip it to a wallet folder in which are placed all the confirmation documents – again in date/time order. Tickets should be kept separately. An example travel itinerary is shown below.

ITINERARY FOR MS MARGARET SAHAMI
VISIT TO PARIS
<u>26 – 28 February</u>

<u>Monday 26 February</u>

```
0530   Company car from home to Birmingham airport
0615   Check-in for flight to Paris
0715   Depart Birmingham flight BA 968
0925   Arrive Paris (Charles de Gaulle) To be met
       by Mr Lefevre, Paris rep
       Accommodation booked at Hotel Sevigne,
       6 Rue Belloy, Paris 75016. Tel:(010 331)
       47.20.88.90 Tlx: 610219
```

<u>Wednesday 28 February</u>

```
1700   Depart Paris office for Charles de Gaulle
       airport (company car)
1825   Check-in for flight to Birmingham
1925   Depart Paris flight AF 962
1935   Arrive Birmingham
       To be met by company car for journey home
```

TEST YOURSELF

One of the biggest tests for a PA is when, despite all the planning, something goes wrong. Below are ten problems which could occur, at home and abroad. For each one write down the action you think you should take immediately *and* any action you could take to prevent the problem occurring again. Check your answers with the key at the end of this section.

1 Your boss rings you from Orly airport to say that at the Hertz desk they have no record of the car you reserved.

2 Just as your boss's car is about to collect him to take him to the airport you discover you can't find the flight tickets.

3 A young representative with your company rings you from Rome to say he has lost his passport and air ticket home.

4 Your boss has her handbag stolen in New York – it contains credit and charge cards, travellers' cheques and foreign currency.

5 You are asked to collect the hire car you ordered for your boss. Five minutes later you are involved in a crash. You are uninjured but the car is badly damaged.

6 Your boss was attending a meeting in Shrewsbury then travelling to London by train and finally flying to Paris. She rings you from Heathrow airport to say that her train was delayed and she has missed her flight.

7 Your boss telephones you from his hotel in Geneva to say that he is expecting to take delivery of his hire car at any moment but has just discovered that he has left his driving licence in his desk drawer.

8 Your boss rings you from the Ambassador hotel in Karlsruhr, 70 miles from Frankfurt airport. On her arrival in Frankfurt on the afternoon BA flight her baggage was missing but an identical case was left on the carousel. Assuming that her case had been taken in error by the person whose suitcase was left, she reported the situation to the BA desk and handed over the case. She was assured that BA would contact the person concerned, exchange cases and deliver her case to her hotel. That was five hours ago. Despite constantly phoning Frankfurt airport she is getting no reply. She has an important dinner to attend that evening and has arrived wearing a casual outfit.

9 Your boss is taken ill the day before an important trip abroad. At the last minute the MD agrees to go in his place.

10 Your boss rings from the airport to say that the airline has overbooked the flight for which he has a reservation and he is being transferred onto the next flight three hours later. He is furious with the airline and worried that he will not be able to meet your company's representative at Vienna airport as arranged, nor be in time to attend an important meeting that evening.

Individual/group tasks

Case study 1

Your organisation has recently decided that it can reduce the costs of travel substantially if planning trips becomes a centralised function within the company. You have been given the job of senior travel planner and a budget of £500 to set up your new office. You will have two junior assistants to help you.

1 Executives in your company travel mainly by rail in the UK and by air to overseas destinations.

   a Make a comprehensive list of travel books you would like to buy to help you plan trips effectively.

   b Make a comprehensive list of the contents of each for your two assistants.

   (For information, see also Chapter 2, Researching and retrieving information, page 75.)

2 Contact your local travel agent and obtain details of its business travel service. Summarise these in a memo to your new staff.

3 Obtain as much information as possible on different travel insurance policies. Select the one you think would be most suitable and notify your boss, with the reasons for your recommendation.

4 Make out a comprehensive 'emergency action' sheet which you will issue to all business travellers with their tickets.

5 List the duties you consider your staff could undertake, and the training they will require. Note any specific areas where they must check with you before taking action.

Case study 2

You work for a small computer consultancy in Leeds. One director, Dave Wilkinson, frequently makes trips abroad and tries to combine these into an overall business visit to save money. His one insistence is that, as he is a relatively heavy smoker, you keep domestic USA flights as short as possible because no smoking is allowed on these flights. He also refuses to travel by British Airways on UK domestic flights for the same reason.

Six weeks next Tuesday he wants to travel by rail to London, for a meeting with your distributor. After staying overnight he then wants to fly to Rome where he will stay for two days. His next stop is in Denver, USA, where he will be for the next week, before moving on to Melbourne for six days. He will then return home via Singapore where he will be staying for four days. He knows that it can be cheaper to book a 'round the world' ticket (ie to keep travelling in the same direction) and has therefore decided that he could take advantage of this by breaking his trip and staying in Hawaii for the weekend.

1 Plan his journey to London using a current British Rail timetable. If possible try to find a suitable Pullman train.

2 Plan his flights, being aware of his requests. Make sure you are clear on days and dates, bearing in mind the time zones he will travel through. Submit your plan for his approval.

3 Assuming he agrees with your plan, draw up a comprehensive itinerary with dates and times. Clearly state terminals, names of airports and check-in times.

4 Assuming this is the first trip he has made to these particular countries, find out what visas are required and whether he needs any vaccinations or inoculations before he leaves – and the timescale which must be allowed for these. Detail this information in a memo.

Key to Travel problems

1 Immediately – your boss should have a copy of the reservation confirmation detailing the type of car and the telephone number of the office where the arrangement was made. Otherwise fax this through to Hertz desk at Orly. If arrangements were made through a travel agent you could contact them or, for speed, contact Hertz headquarters and ask them for help. In the meantime your boss could enquire with other car hire desks at airport or ask the airline for help – particularly if travelling First or Business Class. Have you a Paris agent or Paris office who could help? Final resort – taxi to hotel/company/city centre and make different arrangements, eg through hotel or French Tourist Office.

In future – Check executives always carry copy confirmations with them, plus a list of emergency telephone numbers.

2 Immediately – you should have noted the ticket number. If not, you still have the travel details on the itinerary. Ring airline (at airport) or travel agent and explain. Duplicate ticket can be issued for collection at airport against computer reservation. You may have to pay for this until the airline knows that the original ticket hasn't been presented for use.

In future – design a better system for ticket storage, and stick to it. If your boss has lost it then change the arrangements; only hand it over at the last minute.

3 Immediately – advise him to contact local airline office (or you contact UK office). Replacement procedure will be similar to that given under question 2, above. For passport he should report loss to local police and obtain police statement. Then take this and three passport photos and some identification to the nearest British Consulate or Embassy or High Commission. Claim the cost of the replacement and the charge for the emergency passport back from your travel insurance company.

In future – why not type out a list of 'what to do in an emergency' for all your company's travellers?

4 Immediately – tell her to report the loss to the local police and obtain a copy of the statement. This will be needed for insurance claims. Cancel the cards by ringing the card issuers' emergency numbers or by contacting your card protection agency. Check with each card company their procedure for sending replacement cards abroad (if you don't know this already). Charge card companies are often better at this than credit card companies.

The booklet given with travellers' cheques states the nearest bank; contact them to report the loss and give the cheque numbers. Until replacements arrive your executive is without funds. Ring your bank and ask them to express funds to her; if you give the address of her hotel they will be able to send them to their nearest correspondent bank. Tell her where the bank is: she should take her passport for identification. In a dire emergency – no funds, no ID etc – head for the British Embassy.

In future – as for question 3, above.

5 Immediately – presumably the car was covered for both drivers: you and your boss. Take the names, addresses and car numbers of those involved and details of witnesses. If anyone is injured call the police. Keep an accurate record of the accident and notify the company immediately. You should be able to obtain a replacement car, but may have to pay additional insurance charges.

6 Immediately – she should go to the airline desk and tell them the situation. They will usually do all they can to get her on the next flight out, especially if she belongs to their frequent flier programme. If this is completely impossible you may have to investigate alternatives, eg rail/hovercraft links. In a real emergency, with a top executive and a very valuable contract at stake it may mean chartering a plane! Notify contacts at the other end of the revised travel plans. Check your insurance policy for cover – note that at present British Rail's Condition 25 absolves them from responsibility, though this may change in the future.

In future – little you can do unless you didn't allow enough time in the schedule for possible (reasonable) delays.

7 Immediately – fax a copy to the hotel. Providing he shows ID (eg his passport) then this should be sufficient. Alternatively you could use Datapost to send it to him overnight. This means it will arrive quickly and you will be covered if it is lost in the post.

In future – design a check list of everything he will need for his trips and go through this methodically with him before he leaves (see section 2).

8 Immediately – check all travel details and make sure you have the bag tag number(s). Ring the airline office at your nearest airport, explain the problem and give all travel details and other relevant information. Ask them to chase up Frankfurt and keep you informed. They can telex their baggage handling office direct. Keep your boss informed. Check the travel insurance; she can probably buy a replacement outfit but she must keep her receipts *and* her check-in baggage tags. She will also need a letter from the airline confirming the loss.

In future – if her suitcase is a common make she could put on some jazzy stickers to personalise it and make this less likely to happen.

9 Immediately – Notify your travel agent or the airline. Don't just send the MD along with the same ticket without checking – usually it isn't transferable.

   In future – if 'switching' people is a regular feature of your organisation check if the airline operates a ticket on departure system. You reserve the seat in the company's name, they make out the ticket on departure and issue this at the airport in the name of the traveller. Or ask your travel agent for help.

10 Immediately – reassure him you will contact the representative with the revised information. Action on the meeting depends on whether your boss's presence is crucial, if so could the start be delayed/could the meeting be rescheduled – could the rep help? If your boss was going for information purposes only, the rep could go on ahead and they could meet up later. Your boss could get a taxi from the airport. Note that if you direct your boss to the Executive lounge he should be able to contact your rep direct (which would be best) and also have a drink to calm himself down!

   In future – Note that a confirmed reservation gives a traveller a legal entitlement to a seat, but not necessarily on the flight booked. Only if the delay is 'unreasonable' is the airline liable, and three hours wouldn't be considered unreasonable for a flight from London to Vienna (whatever your boss thinks!)

   It is therefore sensible to allow enough time between the arrival time of a flight and the start of an event if attendance at the latter is *vital*. Alternatively, you should make a 'contingency plan' – which includes giving your executive a list of emergency numbers to contact/knowing what action he would want you to take in an emergency such as this.

Section 2 – Planning and organising business visits

Whilst travel arrangements undoubtedly must be well organised and well planned, the *type* of organisation required may well depend on the sort of visit being made. Not only are outward visits made for a variety of reasons, but your organisation may regularly welcome visitors from other parts of the UK and abroad. These may be regular customers or those seeking to do new business with your company – and the arrangements you make may be critical to a successful outcome.

Define the objectives

Business visits are always made for a reason. This is often to generate new business or to rectify a problem. In the first category are visits by your boss and other executives in the company to particular organisations, trade fairs and exhibitions, company agents and representatives abroad, conferences and seminars. Attendance at the latter may have something of a PR role – your company is wishing to heighten its profile – and obviously good organisation and planning is vital for this to be achieved. The trip may be made by one or several executives, in your organisation – depending on the importance of the visit. A sales team may be despatched to try to secure an important contract, with various specialists to represent the company on technical aspects. Attendance at a trade fair or exhibition will undoubtedly mean making multiple travel arrangements, often so that the sales office remains covered at the same time as there is representation at the exhibition.

'Rectifying problems' often entails last minute emergency arrangements being made – possibly for technicians or engineers. Different company procedures are likely to be involved than, say, in arranging travel for the MD, and you must know these and abide by them. The period of stay may be longer, and frequently return travel may be open-dated if the difficulty is not known. It is also worth bearing in mind that this can mean sending people out to 'trouble-spots' and/or getting them home again quickly. Every organisation should have contingency plans for dealing with this and a system for keeping relatives informed. When it comes to mounting a rescue operation, cost should be a minor consideration, and the role of the Foreign Office can be invaluable.

You should also note that there will be a difference in the level of support/information you should give the new or inexperienced traveller from that required by the veteran – who may be insulted by being given basic facts he/she has known for years!

Visit briefs

A **visit brief** defines the objectives of a visit; several may have to be prepared, one for each appointment. If the visit is for a particular country or region, it is useful to have an opening section which defines the area and, say, its market needs and potential and any import/export restrictions. Such detailed information should have been obtained before the visit is planned as it is obviously no use spending money on a trip which has no potential. The Department of Trade and Industry (DTI) is the best source of information for companies wishing to enter new markets. Other sources include Chambers of Commerce, Trade Associations, Export houses, commercial banks and the company's intermediaries – agents, distributors and subsidiary companies overseas (see below).

Information on particular companies to be visited should include needs, usual practices, past history, characteristics, special problems (which may include finance and transport), strengths and weaknesses. This part of the brief may include details of the main products in which the company has shown an interest and the discount/credit facilities which can be offered as an inducement. It is usual for a sales team to discuss a visit brief thoroughly before the trip and note down the best strategies to be used and the follow-up procedure should the visit prove successful or unsuccessful.

A visit brief to a new company should not only include the names of the people who will be seen but also a phonetic version of their names, so that no mistakes are made in pronunciation. Note also whether each person is male or female, to save embarrassing mistakes.

You should note that visit briefs are usually more involved for countries which have different cultures/economic systems to our own. For instance, a sales trip to Russia may include a detailed sheet on the different State Planning Agencies involved and the contacts in each, together with the procedures to be followed – which may be quite complex – in the event of a sale. Similarly a brief for some countries may include the names/designations of prominent officials who need to be persuaded (financially!) before a deal can be negotiated, if this is customary practice in that part of the world.

Contacts overseas

Intermediaries

A company which exports its goods has a variety of options in relation to the scale of its operations. On a scale of low to high penetration it may do the following.

- Use an export house to do all its selling.
- Appoint a UK based representative to cover the area. Linguistic skills are vital for success, as is a good knowledge of the culture and customs of the region and frequent visits to maintain contact.
- Appoint a foreign agent in the country or territory concerned. The agent knows the territory well and is usually paid on a commission basis. He/she is usually a foreign national experienced in the local market.
- Appoint a distributor who stocks the company's goods and generates sales within the designated territory. There may be an exclusive contract so the distributor can sell your company's goods only.
- License companies abroad to produce your company's products or use your company's process. This gets round import/tariff barriers and is often used when the product would be too bulky and expensive to transport. Your company would be paid royalties by the licensee who would have a defined territory.
- Set up a joint venture with a foreign national company in the market concerned.
- Set up its own offices, or subsidiary company, abroad. This can give a company the 'edge', especially in countries where contracts are mainly won by companies who provide employment in that country.

With the possible exception of licensees, *all* the above are valuable sources of information in relation to their particular territory. You should never attempt to organise a trip to an area which has a subsidiary office or an agent without their involvement. They know their own area as well as you know yours – and will stop you making fundamental errors as well as helping to plan most of the visit for you. Make friends with your contacts overseas; help them, keep them informed and respect their judgement and you should find that they will offer you the same courtesy.

Existing customers

Whilst any agent, representative or distributor will obviously be in touch with your organisation's existing customers, it is likely that you or your boss may liaise with the customer directly when a trip is being planned. This is especially true if your organisation has a longstanding relationship with the company.

A visit brief may be less important here, unless someone from your organisation is visiting them for the first time. Instead, a **customer record** should be compiled which gives a summary of past transactions/ terms offered, details of contacts and history, plus a synopsis of recent correspondence. You should note that in some cases your boss may wish to take with him/her a meeting brief, particularly if he/she is representing others. This should include full details of the items to be addressed and relevant papers should be attached in the order in which they will be discussed.

In some cases executives may become very friendly with their opposite numbers abroad (and with agents overseas). A visit (in either direction) can then have a fairly large social content. Equally the 'tone' of your messages overseas – especially those written on behalf of your boss – should reflect this relationship.

Contact lists

You should draw up a comprehensive list of contact names, addresses, telephone, fax and telex numbers for your executives to take with them. If someone is visiting a customer for the first time you can include an informal information column for the main contacts, eg very anti-smoking, vegetarian, likes to eat in the early evening etc. This can smooth the path of the first-time visitor and help to prevent potentially embarrassing moments.

You also need a contact list – probably of PAs or secretaries, but certainly of other people in the organisations to be visited with whom you can liaise and communicate easily, both before the visit and during the visit itself, so that you can leave messages for your boss. You therefore need a contact who either speaks English or can talk to you in a language you understand. Note that your boss will also need this person's name if he/she is the most likely person to answer the phone when his/her opposite number is out of the office.

You are wise if you get to know your opposite numbers well, so that you can liaise with them about the arrangements being made and gain their confidence. They can give you lots of local information and, if they become your friends, they won't mind answering odd requests at strange times – provided you don't abuse this and become a nuisance!

Meetings in a rush

If your boss has only a few hours to spare in a city – or his/her contact has – then it may be possible to set up a meeting at the airport. Many airports have meetings rooms or offices available so if there is a tight schedule you could investigate hiring one of these in which to conduct the meeting.

It is also worth noting that British Rail have meetings rooms available which hold up to ten people, in Edinburgh, Leeds and Newcastle. These can be booked for a day or half-day.

Major sales trips

A major sales trip, which may involve one person or a sales team, may necessitate a considerable amount of preparation and detailed checklists as to the equipment and documentation which must be taken overseas.

Equipment

You may need to arrange an export licence for some items of equipment, and an import licence for the goods to be allowed into the country concerned. Check everything is properly insured and that you have a record of the serial and model number(s). Electrical equipment will require travel adaptors – or different plug fittings. Transporting equipment is more likely to be necessary if your company is participating in an exhibition and this may be the responsibility of your Shipping Department or Section. You will not usually need to think in terms of presentation equipment as this can be hired locally.

Samples

Depending on the product made by your company, taking samples of your stocks abroad may again mean acquiring an export licence for this country and import licence(s) for the countries being visited. Again you need to check with your Shipping Section or, failing that, the DTI. Another invaluable guide which gives a vast amount of useful information is *Croner's Manual for Exporters*.

Facilities

Sales presentations are usually carried out in an hotel, the company being visited or the office of an overseas subsidiary. You need to draw up a list of all the equipment and facilities you require, eg slide and/or overhead projector, video, tape recorder, microphone(s), lectern etc. Make sure everyone involved contributes to or sees the list before you send it off, so that you are not solely responsible for any omissions.

Documentation and presentation aids

You may be asked to make slides or overhead 'foils' (which can be designed and printed on a DTP package with a laser printer). You may also need to have translations available – contact a translation bureau and fax them the wording for speed. Note that you cannot prepare anything yourself if the language needs a different keyboard, eg the Cyrillic (Russian) alphabet.

The company may have its own sales video, in a range of languages. Pack *two* copies, in case one is damaged in transit or in an unfamiliar machine. Check that the format of your tape (eg VHS) – and speed – is compatible with the video machine being supplied.

Sales documentation, too, may need to be specially prepared and/or translated. If your company uses an advertising agency then they will usually be involved. Some specialise in technical documentation and artwork and will arrange all translations and printing. Your main task will be to draw up a schedule for receiving the printed material, and to make sure this is adhered to.

It is useful to collate 'packages' of literature per person, usually in folders or binders printed with the name of your organisation. These may include brochures, catalogues, price lists, leaflets and information about the company. Make up more sets than you think will be needed – too many are better than too few.

All your team should take a good supply of visiting cards; these may be printed in foreign languages or even set out differently to make them easier for foreign businessmen to read and understand.

Conferences

If your boss is attending a conference he/she will have already received an invitation and a programme of events, which you should include in his/her travel folder.

If he/she is making a speech then you will have to type this. Always use double or even treble line spacing – with single line spacing it is easy to lose your place when making a speech. Pack at least two copies, preferably in different places, eg one in the briefcase, another in the suitcase. Make sure the hotel is on fax – and you know the number – in case of an emergency.

Again you may be involved in making up visual display materials, and packs of information for each delegate.

Country fact sheets

Whilst a visit brief will give details of the market and potential/actual customers, much more information than this is needed if the visit is to run smoothly and be organised properly. For each country visited you need to have a variety of facts at your fingertips, eg:

- when are banks open and what are the currency regulations, if any?
- what dates are public holidays when visits should be avoided?

- what is the climate like – what clothes should be packed?
- what credit/charge cards are acceptable?
- what are the driving regulations which must be borne in mind?
- what are the tipping conventions?
- what is the cuisine and nightlife like and where are the best places to entertain business customers?
- what customs should be observed/known?
- where is the British Embassy/Consulate?

The best way of acquiring this information is from standard reference sources and by talking to people who have already visited that country. Useful standard sources of reference are the DTI booklets *Hints to Businessmen*, *Croner's Guide for Exporters*, Tourist Information Offices/Consulates for the countries concerned (usually situated in London) and the magazine *Business Traveller* which often focuses on a particular country, as well as including information on climate and holidays. (See also Chapter 2, Researching and retrieving information, page 75.)

Always encourage people to add to your fact sheets after they have visited the country. A visitor just back from Japan, for instance, may tell you that the Japanese believe in showing their enjoyment of food by eating noisily eg slurping their soup. In addition, because a visitor may be taken to a traditional Japanese restaurant – where he/she will be expected to sit on the floor – appropriate clothes should be packed. Short, tight skirts are not ideal, neither are trousers which will bag at the knee for the rest of the trip. Type up your findings under clear headings and photocopy the pages for first-time travellers to that destination.

You will find that the content of your facts sheets will vary quite considerably in terms of emphasis. For instance, one on the USA may have only a short section on customs and culture, whereas one on a country in the Middle East would be much longer. Such information can be critical. One businessman, about to leave his Hong Kong hotel after breakfast was surprised to hear a strange noise but ignored it and proceeded to the company he was visiting. On arrival he was the only one there. The sound had been a cyclone warning instructing everyone to stay indoors!

On the following pages are given extracts from facts sheets for both the United States and the Middle East, so that you can see how these can be compiled.

Checklists

The type of visit, and your boss's own personal requirements, will determine what he/she packs. Whilst personal articles are obviously not your concern, a good PA will have a detailed list against which to check that everything from audio tapes to vaccination certificates has been remembered. Eventually both boss and PA will come to know the list off by heart. In some cases, if an executive travels frequently and has short 'turn round' times, a spare set of the main items can be made available, to save time.

TEST YOURSELF

Starting at 'A' and working through the alphabet, list as many items as you can think of which would be useful on a sales trip abroad. Compare your list with ours at the end of this chapter.

FACTS SHEET – UNITED STATES OF AMERICA

Capital: Washington DC. President: George Bush. Official language: English. Currency: US dollar = 100 cents (dime = 10 cents, quarter = 25c and nickels = 5c). Current exchange rate $1.72 = £1.

Travel

Mainly by air – serviced by all major airlines. No smoking on US domestic flights. Latter cheap relative to European flights. If flight is overbooked on American airlines then travellers offered monetary inducements to leave plane and take later flight. When travelling from major Canadian airports, US immigration procedures take place on Canadian soil to facilitate speedy processing in US.

Many cities have several airports – some quite a distance apart, eg San Francisco/Oakland airports. Avoid JKF (NY) if possible – hectic and crowded.

Tipping

Expected everywhere – staff insulted if not tipped. Space on bills for gratuities – min of 15% expected.

Driving

Pay for hire car by credit card. Hire cars cheap compared to Europe. Main differences to UK include:

- flashing traffic lights – red = like stop sign so cross with caution, amber = go but give way, green = give way to pedestrians
- normal to turn right against a red light
- a parking offence to stop with nearside wheels against the kerb
- maximum speed limit in most states = 55 mph.

Interstate highways (motorways) – odd numbers north to south (eg I25) and even west to east (eg I6).

Phones

Police/Fire/Ambulance = 911. Local calls free. For

long distance dial '1' first. Directories subdivided into areas – residential directories white, business yellow. To call UK from pay phone dial 011 44, then UK area code without the 0. Cheap rate 6 pm and 7 am.

Climate
Varies considerably with latitude/longitude. South eastern states more humid. Mountainous areas cold in winter. In summer buildings/cars air conditioned so business dress similar to UK (see below).

Dress
Business dress more formal than in UK – suits/ties the norm for men. Women dress formally – 'power' dressing, eg tights not bare legs, suits and jackets, high heeled shoes.

Shopping
Prices in shops do not show total selling price. Must add GST (General Sales Tax) – rate about 7.5%. Some states/cities add a local sales tax too.

Banking and currency
Banking hours 9 am – 3 pm weekdays (6 pm one day) and 9 am – 12 noon Sat. Maximum $10 000 can be taken out of the country without being declared to customs. Low denomination dollar travellers' cheques accepted as cash. Credit cards universal.

Eating and drinking
Wide range of cosmopolitan food, large helpings, cheaper than UK. Salad served as separate course before main meal unless requested with main course. Coffee black as standard. Don't understand term 'white coffee' – use term 'with cream'. Bars not pubs. Minimum age to drink alcohol = 21. Don't pay for individual drink orders – pick up tab at end of night.

Customs and culture
Keen on health/fitness – fitness rooms in office blocks. Most areas no smoking including hotels/public buildings/restaurants. Specify if smoking area/smoking room required. Hours of work different to UK – start earlier, eg 8 am and work later, eg to 6.30 pm or 7 pm. Good hosts. In some areas entertaining at home rare.

Public holidays

January – 1st, 15th; February – 12th + third Monday
May – last Monday; July – 4th
September – first Monday, 9th
October – second Monday
November – 11th, fourth Thursday
December – 25th

EXTRACT FROM FACT SHEET ON MIDDLE EAST

Culture and customs

The Middle East can be divided into relatively relaxed and strict areas.

Relatively relaxed areas

Dubai (public places to drink)
Bahrain and Oman – alcohol by licence

Strict areas

Saudi Arabia, Qatar, Kuwait – all dry (alcohol illegal).

During holy weeks, eg Ramadan, no smoking or drinking is allowed in public in any country by men or women.

Driving

As in America but women forbidden to drive in strict areas.

Dress

Men should be conservatively dressed. Shorts should not be worn in town or on a Friday. Women should cover their legs and their arms to the elbow. No low cut blouses or dresses. Be prepared to cover the head, ie carry a scarf or shawl.

Segregation

A man is not allowed to be with any woman other than his wife (even on business). In strict areas segregation is total, eg women only banks. Women are not included on any business talks or allowed to participate in evening entertainment outside the hotel.

Photography

Never photograph public places/buildings or holy places or police will confiscate film.

Visitors to your organisation

If you are involved in making arrangements for overseas or British visitors to your organisation then your aim is to make the visit go smoothly and help your visitors to feel at home. The first point to check is how many people are coming and whether businessmen/women are bringing their partners. In this case you may have to make arrangements to occupy the other partner whilst business is being conducted, as well as arranging an entertainment programme.

Check on their travel arrangements – unless door to door arrangements have already been made transport will be needed from the station or airport to your company. The type will depend on the level of visitor – from chauffeur driven limousine to a taxi. Your company may have its own transport department through which you make these arrangements. If you have to meet someone yourself whom you have never met before, then either wear something which identifies you as representing your organisation or carry a clearly printed notice showing the name of the visitor. If you have arranged for a hire car to be available, don't forget to reserve a parking space in your company car park.

You should have reserved accommodation and chosen the hotel with care. Warn them of any special dietary requirements in advance. Bear in mind that after a long journey most people want to freshen up and unpack before starting to do business. They may need a day's rest if they have travelled far and are suffering from jet lag.

Be aware of cultural differences. For instance, in Japan flower arrangements are significant in that different types of flowers/arrangements give a certain 'message'. You could therefore cause problems simply by ordering a basic bouquet to be delivered on arrival – unless you know what you are doing. You can always ring the Embassy of the country concerned (or the DTI) for information.

If the visitor(s) speak little or poor English arrange for an interpreter to be available (check your *Yellow Pages* or ring the Embassy for information). Make sure your visitors know how to telephone home; ask British Telecom for some copies of their leaflet *How to call home from the UK* and give a copy to your guests.

Have information available on banks, places of interest in the area, hints and tips etc (ie facts sheets on the UK). It is a good idea to include the name, address and phone number of a local laundry (especially one which offers an express service) for long-stay visitors. If your visitors will be shopping during their stay, they can reclaim the VAT they have paid if the goods are taken with them when they leave the UK. Contact your local department store or VAT office for details.

If you have to book for special events, anything from Wimbledon to the Dublin Horse Show, or for theatre tickets at the last minute, you are often better contacting a booking agency which may have tickets available, although you will be charged a booking fee over and above the price of the tickets.

Be prepared to talk to visitors and be sociable yourself! Start by expressing an interest in the area from which they come and remember to avoid sensitive or confidential business matters. *Do* make sure you can correctly introduce people, (see Chapter 3, Reception, page 162).

Finally, you should have prepared for your boss a detailed programme of the visit and allowed time for additional unspecified events, particularly if your visitors are planning to see other companies or tourist attractions in the area. It is now your job to make sure the programme operates to schedule right through until the time they depart. This way you will have contributed in the best way possible to the success of their trip.

Organisation and paperwork

When you make any arrangements for business visits whether inward or outward, or concerning one person or several, do make sure that you are always properly organised in relation to the paperwork. It is usual for a visit to be organised in several stages.

1 The basic outline plan – which may be subject to a feasibility study in terms of costs/benefits.

2 Confirmation that the visit will go ahead – full discussion of dates/times/proposed programme.

3 Pencilled travel plan/visit programme – if approved then bookings are made. Note there may be modifications at this stage if some plans cannot be realised (eg clashes of appointments, minimum connection time difficulties etc).

4 Final programme – when all arrangements are confirmed.

Your actions at each stage are given below.

1 Open a visit file (clearly labelled with heading/dates) which contains the preliminary documents. Blank out the dates in pencil in your diary and in the diaries of those concerned (see Chapter 7, Organising work schedules, page 352).

2 Add notes or minutes from any meetings at which the visit is discussed. Include notes on your boss's preferences regarding the trip, who else is going, their designations/extension nos etc. Include copies of relevant correspondence/faxes etc.

3 Draw up two documents: a plan of travel or visit programme and a checklist of action required if approved. Check all details carefully. Submit for approval.

Upon approval, start to make arrangements. Clearly note down when each sector of the programme is confirmed and keep confirmation documents (plus invitations etc) in file.

Keep a separate list of any modifications which have to be made, why and what action was taken.

4 Draw up a detailed itinerary and visit programme. Clip it to the front of the new folder. File your own copy. Within the folder keep all confirmation documents in chronological order. Behind this put all customer files which will be required.

Make sure all details are posted to relevant diaries. Make copies of itineraries/programmes for other directors/your boss's partner and anyone else who should be informed.

Go through it with your boss the day before departure. Check contingency plans/points of contact throughout trip and note these down for both of you. If necessary, include the UK Direct number for a country (details from BT) so that your boss can get straight through to the BT international operator and avoid any potential language problems.

5 *After the visit:* check that all the arrangements (both for travel and visit schedules) went smoothly. Find out if there was anything which went particularly well or anything which didn't, so that you know what to do/not to do next time.

Travel and visit programmes

These go under a variety of names; they may be called itineraries, detailed itineraries, programme itineraries, agendas or travel/visit programmes! The style of these will also vary from one organisation to another although the main features are usually the same:

- a detailed list of all travel arrangements from leaving home to returning home
- a list of all visits arranged, where, who with, contact names/numbers, documents provided
- additional notes re contacts/free days/entertainment/social functions etc
- notes *within* the programme relating to additional documents, eg meeting agendas, conference programmes, invitations, contracts etc
- notes on any possible alternatives requested plus alternative/emergency contact numbers.

An extract from a travel programme to the United States is given on page 223. Compare the level of detail in this against that in the itinerary shown in section 1 of this chapter.

Whilst your boss is away

The lazy PA often thinks this is a time when she can relax and take things easy. The optimistic PA thinks this is a time when the filing can be brought up to date. The realistic PA knows that this is a time of greater responsibility – as she is the main contact person both for the travelling executive and others inside and outside the company during the period of absence. Indeed, if the event arranged has involved several people from the department, or if several people are off in different directions at the same time, then the PA is the main anchor between them all. The basic rules for good coordination are as follows.

- Have a daily regular contact time plus (always) an emergency number.
- Bear in mind time differences! If your boss has travelled east then he/she may have to ring you at home if something critical comes up in a morning. By the time you get to work your boss could be involved in a series of meetings. Equally, don't ring your boss in New York the second you arrive at the office one morning!
- Open all mail. Have an agreement as to what you should do with anything marked *Personal* – especially if it's also marked Urgent!
- Divide all incoming mail and messages into three groups:
  1 that which is urgent and needs your boss's comments/approval
  2 that which is non-urgent and needs your boss's comments/approval
  3 that which you can deal with yourself.
  Put every document, in every group, into priority order.
- At contact time *always* have your notebook to hand. If he/she is in a rush check what to do with group 1 only. If there is more time you can go through group 2. Normally you won't mention group 3 until he/she returns.
- Bear in mind that if you don't get to group 2 on one particular day, some messages in that group may have to be transferred to group 1 for the next day.
- If a complicated or long message is involved then fax it to the hotel first – for later discussion. Don't expect your boss to be able to take it all in at one reading over the telephone.
- If your boss has gone to a remote part of the world, with few fax machines and difficulties with the telephone network, do remember you can 'talk' to each other over telex.
- Don't forget that messages can be left on electronic mail systems at any time (see Chapter 1, Communication systems, page 64).

After contact time you will have plenty to do, clearing all the documents in group 1 (and perhaps group 2 as well), before the next day. It is useful to write 'holding letters' – even on relatively non-urgent matters – rather than let your existing customers think they are being ignored.

Finally, don't forget your boss's family. In some cases he/she may be in constant touch anyway, but in some parts of the world contact is difficult to make once a day let alone twice.

When you have done all this and sent all the letters and faxes on your boss's and your own behalf, made any outstanding telephone calls and updated anyone who needs to be kept informed then you can get your filing straight – and even, perhaps, put your feet up for ten minutes!

Upon your boss's return

Allow for jet lag when planning the diary, which may necessitate your boss taking the following day off. Schedule at least one 'quiet' day for catching up.

You can save time if you type out a resumé of everything you have dealt with in his/her absence and also a list of urgent matters which have to be attended to. Make sure all papers to be dealt with are in priority order beneath this list and try to protect your boss from unnecessary interruptions.

TRAVEL PROGRAMME FOR JAMES TAYLOR
VISIT TO JAPAN   10 – 13 JUNE 199–

Monday 10 June

1300	Company car from office to airport
1430	Check in Heathrow, Terminal 3
1530	Depart flight VS900

Tuesday 11 June

1055	Arrive Tokyo. To be met by **Mr Kumagai**, Tokyo Agent.
Hotel	For nights of 11 and 12 June only
	Rate 24 000 Yen (£105) approx per night
	Palace Hotel, 1-1 Marunouchi 1-chome, Chiyoda-ku, Tokyo, Japan
	Tel: 010-8133-211-5211
	Fax: 010-8133-211-6987
	Confirmation No 182971 (attached)
1400	Meeting with Sumito Corporation
	Mr T Hirachi Tel 010-8133-294-1611
	Re: Supply agreement (see contract attached)
1730	Dinner – to be confirmed by Mr Kumagai

Wednesday 12 June

all day	Meeting with Sukiyu AG (with J P Fisher)
	Mr T Hashimito Tel 010-8133-5486-6206
	(Contact Dr T Suki)
	Re: Licensing contract (see customer file)
1730	Dinner at Oshaya Hotel. Black tie.
	Invitation attached.

Thursday 13 June

1055	Depart hotel for airport with Mr Kumagai
1155	Check in Tokyo airport
1255	Depart flight VS901
1730	Arrive Heathrow Terminal 3.
	Company car arranged for transport home.

£800 in US Travellers' Cheques
£100 cash in Yen

Group/individual tasks

Case study 1

You work for a company whose executives and representatives frequently travel abroad. Your boss is concerned that several new employees are ill-prepared for the climate and pack the wrong clothes. In two cases representatives returned with very bad colds and in one case with heat stroke.

He has asked you to design a fact sheet on the climate in Italy, Finland and Japan. As a basis he has passed you the article below, but wishes you to research further to produce more detailed information.

CLIMATE

Climatic zones can be divided into five areas for visitors – minimum clothing zone, one layer, two layer, three layer and maximum clothing zone. The amount/type of clothing depends on two factors – temperature and relative humidity (RH). If the RH factor is high (eg above 75 per cent) then it will be hot and sticky. This is typical in equatorial regions. Physical exertion becomes exhausting. There is heavy rainfall all year. A typical example is Singapore.

Almost as hot, but less humid, are tropical areas. North of the equator they are characterised by moderate to heavy summer rainfall and a slightly cooler and drier winter season. South of the equator there is rain all year and tropical storms in summer – hurricanes, cyclones and typhoons. A typical example is Hong Kong.

Desert areas have persistent sunshine. Temperatures may be well over 35°C but humidity is low. Loose/light clothing is worn and protection needed for the cold nights. A typical example is Dubai.

The Mediterranean can be classed as a one layer clothing zone. Hot, dry summers are followed by quite warm, wet winters. Nearness to sea will moderate high temperatures. A typical example is Cyprus.

Britain is a typical two-layer clothing zone with warm summers and cold winters, whereas Norway qualifies as a three-layer zone with a short, cool summer and intense cold in winter. In a maximum clothing zone it is always very cold. A typical example is Northern Canada.

Note that the wind affects temperature, (the windchill factor) as does altitude.

Case study 2

Your boss is enthusiastic about the idea of building up a series of fact sheets on different countries. The only one he has available at present is on the United States.

Choose any other country – perhaps one you have visited yourself – and design a comprehensive fact sheet. As well as researching information also ask other people you know who have visited the area for their help. He suggests the layout should be similar to that on the USA (see page 216).

Case study 3

You work for Jayne Shackleton, Sales Director of a large drug company. She is visiting the States next week. From the information given below, design a comprehensive visit programme.

Extract from letter from travel agent

Flights have been confirmed as follows:

Sunday 9 June	– Depart LHR 15.00, terminal 4 BA 185
	Arrive Newark at 17.45
Wed 12 June	– Depart Newark 15.10, CO225
	Arrive San Francisco 18.30

Please note that we have wait listed you on the earlier flight at 13.10, arriving at 16.30, as requested. Flight number CO223

Thurs 13 June	– Depart San Francisco 18.30 BA286
	Arrive LHR, terminal 4, 12.40 Fri 14 June.

Please note check-in is one hour for all flights.

Fax from New York office Fax No 0101–617–923–1982

Hotel booked for stay in New Jersey Marriott, 105 Davidson Avenue, tel 0101–900–500–0900, fax 0101–908–560–3118. Avis hire car available at Newark.

Fax from San Francisco office Fax 0101–415 266 1092

Avis hire car reserved at airport. Lunch at Stanford confirmed – please collect Lisa Chowley at Sheraton hotel at 18.45. Your hotel Holiday Inn, 500 Airport Boulevard, Burlingame, San Francisco. Tel: 0101–415–340–8400, fax 0101–415–340–0199.

Note from Jayne

Please arrange $1200 in travellers' cheques (some in small denominations) and $500 cash.

Extract from diary

Mon 10 June	0930 Klineman Inc, Bloomfield – contact Dr Jack Glover – tel 0101–215–704–2910. Re R & D programme
	1330 KWN Corp, Midway – tel 0101–201–628–0110. Contact Dr Alfred Hubert. Re Licensing agreement
Tues 11 June	All day in NY office – meeting with Dan Williamson et al
Wed 12 June	0900 Glenby International Corp – contact Dr Simon Oates. Tel: 0101–201–831–3271 Re antibody research programme
Thurs 13 June	0900 Phila Inc, tel 0101–415–340–8201. Contact Dr Peter Farthing – re anti-coagulant drugs
	1230 lunch at Stanford University – Prof Larry McDermott et al – tel 0101–415–723–0198

Documents:
1 Beatty's test report for Klineman
2 Copy of licensing contract for KWN
3 Research papers for Glenby

Note from Jayne

Whilst you were at lunch the travel agent phoned – my wait list has come up! I've checked with San Francisco – the hire car will be available earlier.

Fax from New York

Have managed to arrange the plant tour you wanted of Technofusion Inc. Have arranged this for Tuesday am – starting at 0830. We can have lunch on site and return to the office by 1300 – should be no problem completing discussions by 1900 as planned as we can do most of the preliminary paper work before you arrive. Contact name at Technofusion is Warren Gallagher – tel 0101–201–831–0014, fax 0101–201–831–8839.

Regards, Dan

Key to checklist

A Audio tapes
B Batteries (spare – for razor, dictating machine etc)
Briefcase
Baggage labels (spare)
C Calculator
Car keys
Car documentation
Credit/charge cards
Confirmation documents
D Diary
E Emergency phone numbers
Eye mask
Eurocheque book and card
F Foreign currency
Flight bag
Floppy disks
G Guide books
H House keys
I Insurance documents
International driving licence
Itinerary
M Maps
Medical packs
P Passport
Phrase book
Phone card
S Sunglasses
Sterling
Spectacles (and spares!)
Sales literature
Speeches
Samples
Suitcase
T Tickets
Travellers' cheques
V Vaccination certificates
Visa
Visiting cards

Managing problems

The only reason a lobster is stuck in a trap is because it never looks up . . .

There are always some days when you will feel beset with problems – nothing seems to go right from morning to night. True problems – as opposed to minor difficulties – are often caused by people. Not deliberately, but because they have a different way of seeing the world than you do and therefore operate in what might appear to you to be unexpected or illogical ways.

RULE 1

All problems have two aspects

* technical
* social.

You must think about both to find a solution.

There are a variety of different types of problems you will encounter at work, including:

* conflict between people with whom you work (or between yourself and another person)
* crises and emergencies
* those created by conflicting objectives within the organisation
* those you have created for yourself!

Each of these can create a real problem which needs to be coped with by developing a deliberate strategy or technique.

RULE 2

Never act in haste to solve a problem without first identifying all the key aspects.

Rational thinking

Many books on problem solving will give you a simple four-step approach to finding the answer

1 Define the problem.
2 Choose a solution.
3 Implement the solution.
4 Check it has worked.

This is perfectly acceptable if the problem is **localised**, ie you are trying to find a difficult piece of information, sort out when everyone can attend a meeting or work out a difficult travel itinerary. It will *not* work if the problem is widespread, involves several people or is very complicated. Instead you may be simplifying it to an extent where you simply make matters worse.

In many cases, doing the first thing that comes into your head has the same effect. Consider the following scenario. A junior colleague of yours is making life difficult for you by not giving you the information you need when you ask for it. You complain to your boss who promptly hauls her over the coals. Now she gives you the information on time, but not in sufficient detail for it to be of any use . . .

Did you solve the problem? No. Did you make it worse? Yes. Because you can hardly go running back to your boss again (without appearing to be unable to cope yourself), you still haven't achieved what you want and there is now open antagonism between your colleague and yourself.

The irony is that you may have used this approach before quite successfully, with a similar problem, and this led you into the dangerous belief that you could use this strategy again.

RULE 3
Never assume that a problem is similar to a previous one. Each is usually unique in relation to the people, the timing and the context. Each therefore needs a different solution.

A different approach

A more successful way of problem-solving is usually to change your own way of thinking. We all get trapped into our own ways of viewing a situation which blinds us to other ways.

 TEST YOURSELF
Go back to the scenario above and write down the action *you* would take to solve the problem. Don't spend more than five minutes searching for an answer.

Changing your thinking

There are several ways in which you can approach this. One is to develop a form of lateral thinking when you reject the obvious solutions and search around for alternatives before you act. You can only attempt this if you start by redefining the problem itself.

1 Find the key factors

Start by writing down every key factor associated with the problem. A list of those for the scenario above could be:

- you
- your boss
- the type of information required
- the atmosphere at the office
- the relationship between your colleague and yourself

- the historical perspective (eg your predecessor was unreasonable or never asked for this type of information)
- the time span between request and delivery

and several others!

2 Look for related areas

Now try to find 'sub-areas' which fit with the factors you have listed. If you think of other areas then don't discard them. Simply make a note of them elsewhere – they may come in useful later. Examples under 'you' could be:

- the way you ask her
- your job description doesn't give you the right to ask her for this information
- you never show appreciation
- you ask for too much, too often
- you've never shown her what you really want
- again several others could apply too!

3 Analyse your notes

Go through your notes methodically and honestly checking which factors are likely or unlikely. Don't strike out anything which could be even marginally possible.

4 Group the factors you find

Try to link the factors you highlight under certain headings. In this case you may end up with three headings, eg Training, Timescale and (even) Miscellaneous.

5 Find another perspective

If possible, at this stage, talk through your ideas, preferably with a true and trusted friend. The chances are that yet more possible or relevant factors will come to light.

6 Find some common ground

With every problem concerning another person there is always some common ground – even though it may not be very large! This is your basis for negotiation and moving forward. It is a good idea to define

a what the best possible solution is, and
b what is the least you can live with.

Whilst you might start off aiming for **a**, you may find the realistic solution is to settle for **b**!

7 Open communications

Now is the time to start to talk to the other person involved. Your style of communication is very important. Whilst you must be assertive so that your protagonists know your feelings, you must be prepared to acknowledge their perspective of the situation – and not simply dismiss their views as irrelevant.

RULE 4

Don't expect to get all your own way – a common approach which goes half way towards a solution has a much better chance of success than one which appears to solve it outright but involves total capitulation by one party.

---

8 Move forward slowly

Don't expect miracle results. So long as the general trend is forward you are making progress. Remember that the solution may lie in other areas – such as your own time management, people or communication skills – and everyone (including you) will need time to adapt.

 TEST YOURSELF

Go back to the previous scenario and work through this from steps 1 to 8. At stage 5 pool all your ideas and information with the rest of your group and discuss it between you. You will be surprised at some of the different ways of thinking this highlights! Then decide on a joint approach to taking action.

Now compare this with the quick answer you first thought of when you did the first exercise on page 228. How does it compare? Hopefully this exercise should have opened your eyes to how easy it is to over-simplify a problem.

Doing nothing

Another approach to problem-solving is, believe it or not, to do nothing! This makes sense once you realise that acting in haste can make problems worse. Doing nothing at least stops you from doing that. Will it solve anything? Possibly. Some problems – especially those which are loose and woolly – change and take shape as time goes on. Others solve themselves. Much will depend on the other problems you have to deal with at the time. If you are too busy to get around to it at once then by the time you do it may have simply gone away.

RULE 5

In certain circumstances procrastination can both solve and improve problems. Always consider whether a problem can be kept 'on ice' for a while until more information comes to hand.

 TEST YOURSELF

Again go back to our original scenario. Try to write down at least *five* events which could occur which will simply solve the problem without your doing anything. Now compare your ideas with the rest of the group. How many suggestions have you listed altogether?

Owning your own problems

Finally, if you want to be considered a good leader, don't offload your problems on to someone else and expect them to be solved for you. Equally don't try to act as the office 'agony aunt' and solve other people's problems for them. Yes, you can act as a 'help-mate' and listen to their ideas and comment on them. No, you can't offer a solution because what would suit you won't necessarily work for them.

RULE 6

A problem shared is a problem halved *only* when the one who does the sharing is the one who eventually takes action.

Once you have taken action, and consider the problem solved, don't forget what you have learned – or throw your notes away. There are often connections and interrelationships between different problems, and a fresh insight into one area can lead you on to revolutionary ideas in another.

5 Preparing and producing documents

Section 1 – Producing text from oral and written material

No matter what other skills you may or may not possess, when you venture out into the world as a secretary or PA, this is the most crucial of all. Whilst employers may be understanding and helpful as you develop your knowledge of meetings procedures and find your way around organising their travel, they will take for granted *at the outset* your ability to prepare and produce immaculate and well-presented documents at a moment's notice. It will not matter that the notes are barely legible and were scribbled on a fast moving train, or that the audio tape is almost incomprehensible because the dog was barking in the background. First-rate keyboarding, communication and presentation skills are your stock-in-trade and anything less will severely jeopardise your ability to survive in a secretarial job, let alone progress to greater things.

Keyboarding equipment

Life is obviously made easier if you have at your disposal either a dedicated word processor or a microcomputer with a high quality word processing package. The danger, however, is that your boss now feels free to ask you to amend every document you produce, because it is so easy to change odd words or phrases.

Second best is a good electronic typewriter with a quite lengthy memory, especially if you prefer to leave proof-reading until the end. The type with a window display is usually the easiest to use and a good range of basic functions is essential.

Don't be misled, however, into thinking that the era of the electric or manual typewriter is dead. If you work for a small business or charity organisation you may find that the machine you are expected to use may be better placed in the local museum. Whilst you can *suggest* that an update is in order there is no guarantee anyone will listen or that the organisation can afford the expenditure that would be required. There is, of course, also the problem of power cuts, which can render every electrical appliance in the office useless. As your boss remembers the old manual typewriter stored in the basement, so that you can carry on regardless, it is worth remembering that a good PA should be a like a good driver – capable of handling any model, from a mini to a Porsche!

Word processors and microcomputers

The difference between a dedicated word processor and a microcomputer is that the former can *only* be used for word processing, whereas the latter can use a whole range of software, including word processing, spreadsheets, databases, accounts, and desktop publishing.

With the current trend for integrated and/or compatible packages, where the user can transfer documents from one package to another at the touch of a key, and the advent of powerful word processing software incorporating a vast array of functions, few companies are finding it cost effective to purchase dedicated word processors.

Computer systems

The micro you use may be a stand-alone or part of a networked system. The latter is more likely if you work for a large organisation. A stand-alone system means what it says. You have your own VDU, CPU (processor), keyboard and printer. With luck you will have a CPU containing a hard disk on which is installed the software you use regularly. This saves the problem of having to load a program via a floppy disk each time you want to use it. It also means you can create a series of directories on the hard disk in which to store your documents so that they can be found easily and rapidly. You can also switch from one program to another in a matter of seconds. It does *not* mean that you won't have to use any floppy disks as you will need to back up your documents on floppy disk in case your hard disk develops a fault. Failure to make regular back-ups is guaranteed to result in chaos at the first sign of a machine fault, as the 55 page report you have spent the last two weeks keying in is lost forever.

An alternative system is a series of networked microcomputers where all the micros in the organisation are linked together either over a **local area network** (LAN) or a **wide area** (geographically dispersed) **network** (WAN). With a networked system all computers within the organisation have shared access to the company information.

If your micro is part of a network then the software available to you is stored on the network itself, although it is possible to keep additional packages on your own computer hard disk (or load them via your floppy disk drive). You will only be able to access the network, ie **log on**, by means of a personal password, which you should remember and not write down! On many networks you need to change your password frequently as an additional security measure. Forgetting your password can be embarrassing as you then need to admit your predicament to the Computer Department or Local System Administrator who then has to go through a laborious procedure to reactivate your security authorisation.

Network jargon can be very confusing. The main terms are:

Baseband cabling May be used over short distances to transmit data over the network from one computer to another. Because it is a single channel system usually only one device can transmit data at a time.

Broadband cabling Used in larger organisations to transmit data quickly. Can be used over long distances. Because this is multi-channel different communications can be transmitted simultaneously on different frequencies, eg data, voice and video.

Compatibility   The ability of one terminal or computer system to understand and 'talk' to another.

Computer support   A centralised unit of computer support staff whose function is to assist network users, resolve difficulties and instigate network development.

Data communications   The use of communications equipment to transfer data from one computer terminal to another.

Electronic Data Interchange (EDI)   The ability to transfer information eg orders and invoices from one computer to another by means of a communications network. For EDI to be effective users must agree on certain standards for formatting and exchanging information.

File server   The hard disk micro, mini or mainframe computer which coordinates and controls the storage of shared data for the network. It carries out the dual functions of organising and prioritising all file related tasks received by the network at tremendous speed.

Gateway   A device to enable users to pass from one network to another, eg from UK to international data transmission services.

Global Network Service (GNS)   A networking service, managed by BT, which interconnects IPSS and other international networks.

Internetwork (also known as **Internet**)   Two or more networks linked by gateway devices.

International Packet Data Service (IPDS)   Mercury's international packet switching service which transmits data worldwide.

International Packet Switching Service (IPSS)   BT's international packet switching service.

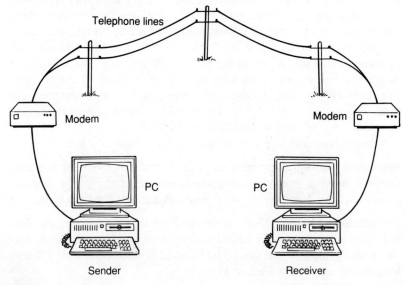

Modem A communications device which enables a computer to transmit information over a standard telephone line by converting computer digital language into analogue signals which can be transmitted via the telephone system. One is required at each end of a remote system. The executive with a modem and PC at home can access the company's computer system and log on to the network.

Network configuration There are three ways in which your network may be laid out or configured – a **bus** network, a **ring** network or a

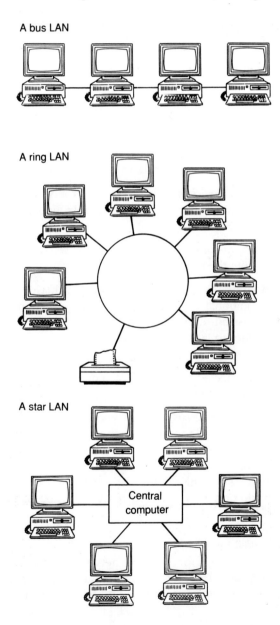

A bus LAN

A ring LAN

A star LAN

Central computer

star network. The difference is purely in the way the devices are connected. A bus network is linear, a ring network forms a loop and a star network radiates from a central hub.

Network domain (also referred to as **network segment**) In a large organisation, where more than about 50 stations share the network, it is likely that the stations will be subdivided into groups called domains or segments. Each domain is a part of the total network which represents, say, one department or one floor of a large building. Each will have its own file server(s) and manager station.

Optical fibre Transparent, hairsbreadth tubes with virtually limitless bandwidth. They are the fastest means of transmitting information.

Packet switching A technique for delivering messages by means of small units of information (**packets**) which are relayed through stations in a computer network along the best route available at that time. Because a packet switching network handles information in small units and breaks long messages into multiple packets which are reassembled at the point of destination, the network is fast and efficient. (See also *X25*, which is an international standard for packet switching networks.)

Printer server A device which controls a group of shared resource printers on the network. In some networks this function is carried out by the file server. (See also *Spooling*.)

Spooling A system sometimes used by printer servers whereby data is stored on disk until the printer is free to process it.

Value Added Network (VAN) A network which is 'value-added', ie which offers additional services besides communications connections and data transmission, eg message routing, resource management and conversion facilities to link incompatible computers.

X25 An international standard which specifies one way in which computers are connected to packet switching networks so that they are compatible with each other.

On some networks you may find that you have no CPU and even no printer. A network linked to a mainframe computer will probably result in your having a **terminal** in your office which is purely a slave device connected to the mainframe computer. It therefore doesn't need a 'brain' ie a processing unit, as this aspect of the work is undertaken centrally. If your printer is a shared resource it, too, may be situated some way from your office, although as secretary/PA you have a good argument for a printer of your own, especially if you are involved in typing confidential information.

Some of the more sophisticated networks link more than just computers. A wide variety of office equipment can be interlinked – including fax machines, photocopiers and telex machines. Additionally your photocopier may be of the 'smart' or 'intelligent' variety which can hold a variety of document formats in memory. Therefore with true compatibility you can design a document on your PC and send it straight to the photocopier for printing or display it on a video monitor in reception!

An ideal set-up, where everything is interconnected and compatible

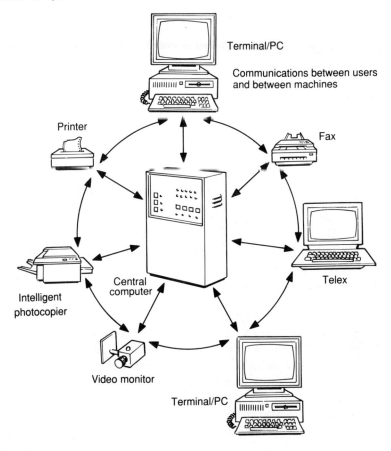

In addition to centrally held word processing software, you may have access to a central database of customer/supplier names and addresses, and your organisation will probably have its own electronic mail system (see Chapter 1, Communication systems, page 64). If your organisation is really up-to-the-minute you may have a complete integrated management information system with an electronic diary and meetings planner so that you can access electronically the movements of all the executives in the company.

Word processing software

The aim of all word processing software is to enable you to create, store and print documents and retrieve and amend them as you wish. All such software will enable you to:

- underscore, inset paragraphs, embolden, justify and centre text automatically
- identify blocks of text to copy, move or delete
- search for key words and replace these throughout a document (ie globally) if you wish
- print out in different line spacings and with different margin settings
- insert headers and footers at the top and bottom of specified pages
- mail merge, ie merge standard documents with a list of variables to be inserted, eg names and addresses.

The more sophisticated and expensive packages include facilities to:

- insert footnotes or endnotes in a document
- create a contents page or index
- type in vertical columns
- rule tabulations and displays both horizontally and vertically
- spell-check your document
- find synonyms for words you have used by means of a thesaurus
- carry out mathematical calculations
- store and insert graphics
- type in a range of fonts, ie different typefaces and styles (eg Helvetica, Times, italics, outline and shadow) and sizes (providing your printer will support these)
- print on either A4 portrait or landscape paper.

Understanding your system

The problem for both PAs and administrators is the wide variety of both hardware and software on the market. Murphy's Law usually prevails in that both the system and the software installed in your organisation are totally different to that which you mastered at college or in your last job.

Hints and tips you may find useful to learn to use a new system quickly include the following.

- If possible, try to learn on an IBM-compatible system. You will then find that most systems you work with are at least vaguely recognisable.
- Jot down the key points you need to remember to log on (or access) the system (and log off again!).
- In Chapter 9, Office resource administration, page 424, reference is made to the 80/20 rule. This rule applies to software as it does to nearly everything else. 20 per cent of the commands you will use 80 per cent of the time. These usually include bold, underscore, centre text, inset paragraphs, justification, block move/delete/copy, retrieve/save a document, list/display directory and print. Learn these well.

- Invest in a *short*, simple, purpose-written book which tells you how to use your software quickly. It will usually be easier to understand than the manual. Make sure it has a good index.
- Don't bother ploughing through a tutorial system in which you have to produce dozens of fake documents to master one simple facility.
- Learn how to use your 'help' facility.
- Never forget to read your screen. Most software packages include prompts to help you when you get stuck. In addition your screen display will give you information on your 'status', ie name of document, page number, position on screen etc.
- Whilst you get to grips with your merge facility (which can be very complicated on some packages and marvellously simple on others), remember that you can easily produce individual letters by inputting the text as a master document and simply typing in individual names and addresses on each one. Try to keep variables *within* the body of the letter to a minimum in the early stages. Save all the individual documents on disk – at least until after you've checked them prior to despatch.
- Be well organised. Set up your own directory system with different directories for documents relating to different topics and files. Enter as much information about each document as possible, to enable you to find and retrieve documents easily. Back up each directory on a separate, clearly labelled, floppy disk.
- Look after your floppy disks. Store them neatly in a proper disk box, away from heat, damp and anything magnetic. Label them clearly (make out the labels *before* sticking them on the disk so that you don't have to press on to the disk itself). Delete unnecessary files at regular intervals – or purge the whole disk if the material on it is no longer needed.

If you are given any choice about the software you can use, then select one of the high quality, industry standard word processing packages available, eg WordPerfect, Word, Wordstar etc. The top software producers are intensely competitive and new versions of the main packages are being released all the time. The latest version is always the one suffixed with the higher number. Useful functions include:

- a switch facility – so you can toggle between two documents on screen at the same time
- a ruling facility – to draw *both* vertical and horizontal lines
- a font facility – so that you can type variations of text when required. If you frequently type in other languages choose a package which will enable you to insert the symbols you may require.
- a spell-check – invaluable not only to save you hours with a dictionary but also as a 'first-time' proof-reader (see page 251)
- a thesaurus – for when you can't think what to say next, or don't want to use the same word twice in a sentence.

Your choice of software may be restricted by other users either in your own or other organisations. If you regularly exchange information on disk with another office or company then obviously you need compatible software. You may also be constrained in relation to other software you wish to use, eg if you want to use word processing and desktop publishing packages you need two which are compatible with each other.

Computer hardware

If you are given a choice on hardware, then you may be better choosing an IBM-compatible system so that you have less chance of having to relearn all your skills if you change jobs. The most well-known business hardware which is not IBM-compatible is the Apple Mac system. Expensive, but well-known for its reliability and user-friendliness, it is ideal if you need a system which easily incorporates both graphics and dtp on a regular basis. However, you will find that a wide range of commonly used database, spreadsheet and accounts packages cannot be used on this system.

Always select a high quality printer. The various types available and their advantages and disadvantages are given below.

Dot matrix printers   The cheapest type on the market, they are not usually suitable for correspondence at PA level, even if the most advanced (32 pin) machines are used in NLQ (near letter quality) mode.

Daisy wheel printers   These are quite expensive and losing ground to ink jet printers.

Ink jet printers   These can support a wide range of styles and sizes of print as well as having the capability to reproduce graphics. The snag with these is that the ink is still wet when the print-out first appears and can be smudged if handled carelessly. Copies taken out in the rain can become unreadable!

The copies are produced by means of ink being sprayed through nozzles onto the paper and a new ink cartridge is required after about every 500 pages. These can be quite expensive to buy, so if you are a poor proof-reader you could find these printers an expensive option!

Laser printers   If you regularly use a dtp package you are better investing in a laser printer. Modern desktop laser printers are reasonably priced and much faster than in the past. You will spend more, however, if you opt for a **postscript** laser printer, as this can support a huge range of graphic and font capabilities. Even if you haven't much to spend initially, it is usually wise to choose a laser printer which can be upgraded to postscript later. Otherwise you will find that you are unable to achieve many of the effects you want. (Desktop publishing systems are dealt with in more detail in the next section, see page 267.)

Instead of the ink cartridge required for the ink jet printer you now need a toner cartridge – which is even more expensive. Again, therefore, careless use of the machine can prove costly.

All computer systems and printers have several drawbacks. They are usually poor at printing envelopes and labels and it can be nearly impossible to insert text accurately in a pre-printed form. In all these cases it can be easier and quicker to use a standard typewriter.

Whichever equipment you choose you *must* learn how to use it properly. Keep the manuals close at hand at all times. Learn what to do in an emergency, eg how to stop printing immediately if there is a paper jam. All manuals contain a 'trouble-shooting' section and it is worth photocopying this page and keeping it close at hand. Additionally, follow the manufacturers' advice regarding the type of paper to use (this can be critical for laser printers)/software compatibility and care and maintenance of the equipment. On a standard computer system *always* check basic connections, the power supply and screen control settings *before* you ring for help.

Electronic typewriters

There is a tremendous variety of electronic typewriters on the market today, and prices have fallen rapidly. However, the more you spend the greater the range of functions available on the machine you buy. At the top end of the market you will find a sort of 'mini word processor' on offer, with screen, spell-check and full editing facilities. Always try to choose a machine which offers you some form of window display or editing, even if it is only one line. The larger the memory the better, as you can then scroll back through your document and mistakes can still be edited without difficulty. The best machines offer you the ability to reprint the entire document, from memory, if you wish. This is invaluable if you find mistakes on four lines on the first page of a 10 page document only after you have printed it. The more you pay, the faster the printing is likely to be, and vice versa.

The type of features to be found on virtually all electronic machines include:

- a choice of pitch selection – usually 10 point (pica), 12 point (elite) and 15 point (micro). (Use 10 point if you want to match standard computer printers, 12 point for long documents or tabulations as you can fit more on to one page. 15 point is rarely used for external work but can be useful if you have to fit a large amount of text into a very small space, eg on a pre-printed form.)
- automatic paper insertion and removal
- a choice of line spacing
- a repeat function on selected keys
- a relocate key to take you back to the point at which you were last typing, and a line return key to take you back to the beginning of the line you are currently typing
- automatic centring, emboldening, underscore, inset left margin and right hand margin justification
- ordinary and decimal tabulation settings

- automatic correction over a varying number of characters
- a variety of pressure settings
- (on some machines) the ability to store in memory standard sentences, paragraphs, addresses etc.

The golden rules for using an electronic typewriter include the following.

- *Never* use it as you would a normal typewriter, ie:
  - always insert/remove paper using the keys/commands required – not manually
  - always move up and down the page using the key commands – again not by turning up the paper manually.

  The reason for this is simple. An electronic typewriter *remembers* every key stroke (including those involved in inserting and turning up the paper). It therefore knows exactly where you are on the page, which page is inserted and so on. It can therefore correct what you want by relocating *on the basis of its memory.* You defeat the object of this entirely if you start moving the paper up and down manually (or even worse, take it out and start again by the same method!).
- Go through the manual and make a list of the main commands you will need to use, especially where these involve multiple keys. Keep your list beside you at all times until you know it by heart. Remember the 80/20 rule and refer to the manual for any less frequently used functions.
- Some machines automatically rule up tabs both vertically and horizontally. The problem with this is that as you move backwards and forwards through your document it is likely that at least one problem will occur and you *may* not use the correct method to rectify it. Your ruling will then go wrong. Unless you have terrible problems with tabs it is usually better to rule them yourself (see section 2, page 265).
- Use good quality ribbons and lift-off tape. Take care when changing these *and* when changing or handling the daisy wheel.
- If you work for a specialist, eg a mathematician, linguist or scientist, choose a machine where you can change the daisy wheel for another with specific characters or symbols. Bear in mind that international keyboards have different functions to the standard English keyboard and you may prefer to buy one where you can change from one keyboard to another at the touch of a key.

Electric typewriters

Rapidly becoming obsolete, these machines were introduced purely to take the drudgery out of continually pounding the keys of manual machines. Whilst the touch is similar to that used on an electronic machine the functions are not, although later machines did incorporate several pressure options and the use of a correction tape. This removed the need for the more traditional forms of correction (see below).

You can produce very good work on these machines provided that your knowledge of keyboarding is sound and you *think* before you type. If you are using one for the first time then test it out – especially the repeat keys. If you are not used to the fact that marginally greater pressure on keys such as 'x', '.' and '-' will result in a whole line being printed you may have some early disasters. A final point is always to check you have the shift lock down *before* aiming for the underscore – otherwise you will end up with a row of hyphens or 6's across the page!

Manual typewriters

Not to be scorned! In an emergency – and in the hands of a good typist – they can be a life saver and excellent documents can still be produced. They are still invaluable where there is no local power point and notes have to be typed out quickly.

Remember that the *feel* is different – and the position of your wrists should change to suit the slope of the keyboard and the pressure you need to exert to *hit* (rather than 'stroke') the keys. Tap the keys smartly yet firmly and then release for the best and most even effect.

Correcting errors

You need a good range of correction materials, even if you regularly use an electronic typewriter, mainly because of the problems inherent in correcting carbon copies. You also need to know how to use these properly. Generally it is always better to correct errors 'as you go' rather than at the end of the page, as then it is easier to miss some.

Correction ribbons

If you use a machine which takes a 'one-time' ribbon then you will need a *lift off* correction tape. This is coated with a sticky surface to lift off the carbon impression put on to the paper. Alignment is therefore critical for the impression to be removed properly, so it really is essential that you spot the mistake before you remove the paper from the machine.

If you use a standard reusable fabric ribbon (rarely in evidence today on modern typewriters) then you will need a *cover up* tape which puts a chalky substance over the incorrect image. These are less satisfactory for two reasons.

1 The chalky surface of the tape creates dust inside the machine.
2 If the incorrect image on the document is rubbed the chalk can be removed, showing the error underneath.

The same disadvantages can apply to correction paper (see below).

Correction paper

This is used to cover up mistakes if you are using a fabric ribbon on a machine without a correction tape. If the image still shows through it is probably because the platen roller is too far from the keys for the impact to be solid. Compensate for this by using your correction paper two or three deep. Then type the correct letter over the top, more than once if necessary to get an even 'tone'.

Correction fluid

Always use this *sparingly*. The reason most people struggle with correction fluid is that they paint it on rather as if they were painting the side of a house. For *really* top class results, start by *gently* rubbing the mistake with a soft typing eraser, then smooth the paper the way of the grain. Finally put on a *small* amount of fluid, again brushed the way of the paper grain and *wait for it to dry* before typing over it. *Don't* allow your fluid to thicken or become lumpy – keep the brush clean, the top tightly fastened when not in use and throw the bottle away if the liquid starts to thicken and can't be thinned down.

SPECIAL NOTE

It is amazing how many typists happily waste paper by the ream yet practise incredible thrift when it comes to replacing old bottles of correction fluid or buying new packets of correction paper. Efficiency dictates that the reverse should be true – lumpy correction fluid is worse than useless and a portion of correction paper, once used, *cannot* be used again as there is no chalk left!

Carbon copies

The problem with any form of automatic – or manual – correction to top copies is the resulting mess on carbon copies. If possible, forget carbons altogether and photocopy any extra copies you require from your (corrected) top copy. If you are using a word processor or an electronic typewriter with a reprint facility then you can simply print out any additional copies required.

If you are in the position where you have no option but to take carbon copies then correct your top copy whilst your document is still in the machine and worry about your copies later. Correct these *out of the machine*, using the eraser/liquid paper technique described above. Then reinsert each one in the machine and type in the correct letters or words where required. Try to realign each one correctly. This gets easier as you become more used to a particular machine. Learn how to squeeze up a word to insert an extra letter, or how to spread it out to replace it with a word of fewer letters. Practise realignment, you never know who may be looking at your carbon copies one day – or your files – and your reputation will be ruined for ever if they are scruffy, smudged and illegible! For the same reason *never* overtype *anything!*

Work stations and layout

The health and safety regulations on office equipment for typists and VDU staff are about to change following new European Community guidelines (see Chapter 10, Health and safety at work, page 497). Not only must all new equipment sold after 1992 conform to the new standards but any old equipment must be modified by 1996.

Seating   All chairs must be capable of swivelling up and down and on a movable base (ie castors). You need a chair which is comfortable and has an adjustable back rest. Make sure it gives you the support you need.

VDU desks   Must not reflect light and must be 68 cm high (not 72 cm as at present). The desk needs to be large enough to hold all the equipment plus any paperwork.

Keyboards   Must be separate from VDUs and adjustable to lie flat or slope upwards. The layout of keyboards varies considerably and a new keyboard can be confusing at first. The keys should have a matt finish. The function keys (F1, F2 etc) may be down one side or across the top. There may be also special purpose keys at the right or left hand side.

If you have a keyboard with a far right section of cursor and function keys note that this is usually linked to the number lock facility. To be usable on a wp package the number lock must be *off*. (It is usually sensible to ignore this section of the keyboard when word processing and use the cursor keys nearer to the main part of the keyboard.)

VDU screen   Must be adjustable in terms of the angle at which it is positioned and the brightness and contrast of the screen. The screen should be non-reflective and flicker-free. A variety of colour combinations is available and many software packages enable you to change the colours you have displayed on screen. Many people prefer white characters on a blue background as being the most restful for the eyes and yet clear to read.

Most screens today hold a full line of text for an A4 portrait type page but only a section of the page can be shown vertically at any one time.

In addition, for VDU operators, there are further regulations in relation to lighting and glare, noise, temperature, humidity, eye tests and breaks away from the screen (see Chapter 10, Health and safety at work, page 497).

Any work station should be designed so that all key elements of the system are within easy reach. This applies just as much if you are typing text from a manuscript on to a manual typewriter or from audio equipment on to a computer. The science of **ergonomics** relates to the organisation of the work area in relation to the type of job being done, on the basis that the more closely these are related the more efficiently is the work carried out and the less fatigue is experienced by the operator. This has resulted in 'systems furniture' with filing units built in and trunking or cable management to ensure that all wiring is both safe and kept out of view.

It is useless having the correct furniture or equipment if you don't use it properly. Slouching in a chair will result in backache regardless of the design of the chair and typing with the heel of your hands resting on the edge of the desk will cause muscular problems as well as inaccurate typing. It is therefore up to *you* to sit up straight, hold your hands and arms correctly and position both your VDU and your copy so that you can see both clearly and without straining your head or neck. Legislation cannot force you to do this – but ignoring such advice can be disastrous for your own long term health.

Care and maintenance

No matter what type of equipment you have in your office unless you care for it properly you cannot expect it to function properly.

Computer systems Static on your screen will attract dust; use anti-static screen wipes or a *damp* cloth to wipe over this regularly.

Special cleaning materials are available for the outside casing of the machine. Dust between the keys with a soft brush.

Follow the manufacturers' instructions for keeping printers in good condition. Full directions are usually given in the manual.

Electronic typewriters Keep the keyboard clean as above. If you decide to clean your daisy wheel remove it first and then brush it *gently*, supporting each petal carefully as you brush it. If you use any force you will break off the petal and the daisy wheel will be useless.

Keep the transparent plastic gauge clean by frequently wiping it with a soft or damp cloth. Be careful not to bend the gauge outwards or you may break it.

Electric/manual typewriters You can brush the type bars in these machines quite vigorously with a stiff brush to remove excess deposits from the ribbon. Pay special attention to characters such as 'o', 'p' and 'g' as the holes in them can become solid with ink. Special fluid is available to help to remove these deposits but must not be used on the outside casing or it will dissolve the plastic! *Never* allow rubber dust to fall inside the machine.

Business documents

The type of business documents you may be asked to produce can include letters, envelopes, memos, standard forms, labels, reports, summaries, displays, tabulations, minutes of meetings and itineraries – to name but a few! The range of documents you are required to produce will vary from one organisation to another, and the layout will often depend on the 'house-style' of the company.

Every single document you produce is composed of two aspects:

- the layout and presentation
- the accuracy.

Other relevant considerations for your boss are the length of time it takes you to produce each one – and whether you produced the most urgent document *first* or let everyone wait until you got round to it!

Layout and presentation is covered in the next section of this chapter. So far as accuracy is concerned this is dependent on:

- the source of the text and its accuracy and legibility
- your expertise in solving any problems you encounter with your source text
- your proof-reading skills
- your knowledge of the English language
- your attention to detail.

Remember that every document you produce is your personal advertisement. If it has your name (or initials) on it and it is badly typed or presented, then you tell everyone who handles it just how poor a PA you are! You also give a very bad impression of your boss and the company which employs you. As the complaints and problems start to land on your boss's desk, you may even find yourself having to scan the situations vacant column to look for another job!

Written sources

These can range from a draft typescript, to a hastily scribbled manuscript, to a few notes jotted on the bottom of a letter or memo out of which you have to compose a sensible, grammatical business communication. Remember – people don't write rubbish; if you are reading something that does not make sense then you are not reading it correctly! If you cannot make head nor tail of what is written then you must check what is required with the originator before going on!

Draft typescripts

These are the easiest to follow, provided they are in double-line spacing and your boss has good handwriting and has clearly indicated where he/she wants each alteration. Otherwise you may be struggling to make sense of some of the comments.

If you are having problems then read the original text to see where alterations should logically be inserted. If you cannot check any dubious points immediately, type the text as you think it should be written, but mark problem areas clearly (with a light pencil cross in the margin) and resubmit the document for your boss's attention before taking a final print-out.

Manuscript

If you regularly type up documents from manuscript then you should get used to your boss's writing.

- Read through the document *before* you start, to get the sense of it.
- Make sure you can differentiate between any explanatory notes to you and the text which must be typed.

- Underline any difficult-to-read words in pencil and read on for a few lines to try to get the meaning from the context. Look for similar letter patterns to give you a clue.
- Make a note of phrases, technical terms and abbreviations your boss uses regularly.
- If you are still having problems, and you are using a word processor, type the document and print it out in draft first. Again mark any doubtful passages or words for clarification.

 SPECIAL NOTE

The number and type of errors you should correct yourself and those which you should refer back to your boss will depend on three factors:

- his/her ability to write good English
- your ability to do the same
- how touchy he/she is about having work altered.

Generally, if a mistake is obvious – whether it is one of grammar, punctuation, spelling or inconsistency – then you should make the correction. Often these are not worth mentioning to the originator of the document, who may have put it together in a rush and be grateful for your care and attention.

There are cases, however, when you may not be sure what was meant or the inconsistency could be deliberate. In this case make a note of it and ask your boss later. You may find that as you proceed with the document all becomes clear.

When pointing out a mistake, however, remember two things:

- be tactful – not triumphant!
- be sure that you are right!

Notes for expansion

The ability to write a good, well-constructed business letter or memo is an essential weapon in the armoury of any professional secretary, PA or administrator (see Chapter 6, Processing correspondence, page 298).

If you are given a list of notes in reply to a document remember that:

- the order of the notes may not be the best order for the finished document
- you are *not* expected merely to join together the notes with a few well-chosen conjunctions!
- the tone of the letter must be correct bearing in mind the topic and the recipient.

It also helps if you are given the original document to which you are replying. Try to train your boss always to pass this to you – you then have the means of checking the recipient's correct name and title, the address and any other details you may require, such as reference numbers which must be quoted in reply.

Verbal sources

One variation on the theme of written notes are the verbal notes dictated to you. These may be even more random and sketchy than written notes, depending on how much of a hurry your boss was in when he/she gave you the information! They are also likely to contain several asides to you, and phrases about the recipient that your boss does not want incorporating into the document itself.

Make sure you write down everything you are told, and repeat the main points to make sure you have listed everything. The chances are your boss will expand on some of the information during this 'repeat' session. Query anything you are not sure about – especially if your boss is on the way out of the office and wants you to send off the document in his/her absence. It is far better to check this now than risk the problems inherent in sending out a totally inappropriate document.

SPECIAL NOTE

One special attribute of a first rate PA is to prevent her boss from sending out communications he/she will later regret. This usually happens towards the end of a bad day when, to top everything, a disaster occurs caused by another member of staff or even an outside company. In his/her fury – and haste – you may find yourself being instructed to send out a letter or memo which has been written or dictated when all sense of judgement and discretion seems to have temporarily disappeared. If the wording is particularly abusive or makes you feel uncomfortable, type the document, then save it for the following day. The next day, use the excuse of having missed the post and ask your boss to give it a final check. The chances are that it will be completely redrafted – or consigned to the shredder.

Audio dictation

There is a wide variety of portable audio equipment – often known as 'pocket memos' – on the market. The aim of these machines is, in theory, to enable the high-flying and well-travelled executive to be able to dictate correspondence at virtually any hour of the day or night, no matter where he/she is at the time. The problem with this idea is that the tapes on which you learned and practised your audio skills in college can bear little resemblance to those you are expected to transcribe at work. The departure lounge at Heathrow airport or the M25 in the rush hour do not make for meaningful and literate dictation.

To get the best out of the system it is essential that *both* of you know the basic rules for audio dictation and transcription.

Train your boss to:

- start by identifying him/herself (especially if you regularly receive tapes from several people)
- indicate what is going to be dictated before starting on the text proper (At least you then know which type of paper to use. Some clue as to the likely length and any copies required is a bonus.)
- make it clear whether the document is a draft or whether you are supposed to type it in its final format and, if your boss is away, send it out in his/her absence

- give a clear distinction in his/her voice between instructions to you and the actual material you should type (Otherwise you can end up with totally unintelligible documents.)
- speak clearly and at a steady pace and with a sense of rhythm so far as sentence construction is concerned
- hold the microphone relatively near his/her mouth *all the time*
- remember not to move around, eat or drink whilst dictating, and reduce or eliminate background noises (this includes sneezing and coughing mid-way through a sentence)
- spell any unusual names or words, preferably at the point at which they are dictated
- state when new paragraphs are expected/or required
- stop dictating if disturbed, ie someone knocks on the door, the telephone rings etc and when the out-of-tape audible warning signal is heard
- avoid asides, eg 'ah, yes, where were we?' and other distractions you might find yourself typing in error
- clearly indicate when one document is finished and another begins.

For your part you should:

- be prepared to put up with the untrainable boss who ignores all your hints and advice on how to dictate properly (or practise your newly-found assertiveness, see page 348)
- listen to each piece of dictation first – especially to pick up the key piece of information left until the end, eg 'forget that letter – I'll ring him tomorrow'
- use the best layout for the work required (don't expect or ask for advice from your boss on this – it's your job to be able to produce good business documents, not his/hers)
- have a good knowledge of his/her usual phrases and style so that you can substitute suitable words for mutterings and incoherent noises
- spell, punctuate and type the document so that it is 100 per cent accurate
- know how to get the best out of your transcribing machine by knowing all the functions it can carry out, eg automatic search control, variable automatic backspacing and last word repeat, tape speed control etc.

The advantages of using audio are considerable. You can listen to the tape over and over again if necessary, and are not reliant on your own scribbled and sometimes incomprehensible notes. In addition, if you both have access to dictating equipment then you can use the system for leaving recorded messages for one another. This is especially useful if your boss is only due in the office after hours and will then be away for several days to come. Try to keep the tone of any verbal messages relatively formal and stick to the facts you wish to convey – in priority order.

The main disadvantage with audio is that it is difficult to type the documents in priority order, unless your system is such that it is easy for your boss to indicate which document you should access first – *and* it is equally easy for you to find this on the tape.

! **SPECIAL NOTE**
In *all* documents you are expected to type from notes or audio, have a rule whereby *either* you *or* your boss inserts or dictates punctuation. If you both do your own thing you have a recipe for total confusion. Bosses usually fall into two categories – those who require commas everywhere, or those who leave them out completely. Find out how pedantic/knowledgeable he/she is about punctuation and act accordingly. If you do make regular corrections to dictated instructions for punctuation then you are wise to keep these to yourself.

Proof-reading

The first rule to remember is that *all* typists make mistakes. However, the difference between a good typist and a bad one is that the first spots her errors and the second doesn't. Sending out documents which contain typing errors or – even worse – mistakes which keep the staff laughing for weeks can ruin your reputation completely. One harassed PA sent out a memo to the MD which started 'We have just received your daft proposal for a new computer unit to be situated in this department . . .'

The second fact to remember is that nobody likes proof-reading and no one is born to the task. It takes time to learn how to do it properly, is always tedious and boring, and is the first thing you are likely to skimp if you are under pressure or overworked.

If you are using a word processor then complete your document and run through a spell-check as your first test. This will highlight the first type of errors (you'll probably be surprised how many!) ie words which are completely mistyped and make no sense at all. Do remember that a spell-check will not pick up many transpositions, eg 'form' not 'form', and 'stain' not 'satin' because the alternative is a valid word. Equally, homophones will also remain undetected (check not cheque, revue not review, draught not draft etc), or words with the wrong ending, cause not caused, standing not standard etc.

Give the document a second read, *one word at a time* (read it as if it is an instruction on how to dye the most expensive dress in your wardrobe). If the document is long then give yourself a break mid-way through, or enlist the help of a friend – you read and she checks and then swap over. Use a ruler whenever figures are involved to avoid jumping a line and read digits in *pairs*. Remember to take more care over these as there is no 'meaning' to help you and a mistake in a critical figure could be disastrous.

For *very* important documents enlist the help of a colleague and ask him/her to check it for you with fresh eyes. A variation on this theme is to read through your documents once again later in the day before submitting them to your boss – when they are 'hot off the press' you are still apt to miss even obvious mistakes as you read what you think should be there, not what you have actually typed. When you can approach documents 'cold' you are more likely to notice any errors.

Danger areas include

- word substitution (form/from, is/it, as/at, our/your/you etc)
- letter substitution/transposition (r/t, i/e, n/m, u/y, etc)
- faulty spacing and inconsistency in presentation (eg 24 and 12 hour clock times, words and figures, capitalisation etc)
- forgetting to expand abbreviations (or expanding them wrongly)
- names, addresses and figures
- words transposed or omitted – or even *lines* of text missed out.
- wrong endings to words – eg 's' omitted from plurals, 'ed' instead of 'ing' etc.

Again mark each error in pencil in the margin. The number of crosses (and the scale of the error) will determine whether you can correct them or whether you will have to retype the page.

SPECIAL NOTE
Enlist your boss's help with proof-reading. There's a happy medium to be struck here – if too many errors are found your boss will consider you incompetent. However, on the basis that he/she is likely to find some occasionally you don't lose your reputation if your boss thinks he/she is helping you rather than finding fault. (The other bonus is that psychologically we all find perfection frightening – he/she will probably find it quite comforting to find the odd error you have made!) Apologise and alter the offending word or phrase immediately.

Bear in mind that the danger with this approach is that, having found the error, your boss may now feel free to make other alterations to the document which may mean the whole thing has to be retyped.

Confidentiality
The higher you rise in the secretarial world the more likely it is that the correspondence and other documents you type will be confidential. There is a whole range of procedures of which you need to be aware if this is the case.

- If you are in the process of typing a confidential document on a VDU and someone enters the room then turn the brightness control down immediately so that no one can read it on screen.
- Better still, position your desk or angle your computer screen so that your work cannot be read by visitors to your office.
- If you have to leave the room, either lock your door or close down the system and lock away the disk.
- Lock both the documents and any related computer disks away at the end of the day.
- If you are using a typewriter and you need to leave the room, either remove the document or lock your door. If security is paramount then, after the work is complete, you will also need to destroy the ribbon or any carbon paper used – as both are readable.

- Remove tapes containing confidential information from the audio machine and lock them away the moment you have finished transcribing them.
- Keep confidential documents in a folder on your desk and close the folder when someone enters the room (the office gossip is often adept at reading upside down!).
- Make a note of those people who have received confidential documents and always despatch the papers in sealed envelopes, clearly marked CONFIDENTIAL.
- Destroy any spoiled copies in the shredder.
- Do not discuss the content of the document with anyone. If pressed, deny having had anything to do with it and feign ignorance.
- Keep the keys to your office, desk and filing cabinet on your person *at all times*.
- If you are involved in highly confidential work and you find anyone snooping around your office or behaving suspiciously then inform your boss *immediately*.
- Take care if photocopying – at least ten per cent of users regularly leave the original on the glass of the machine!

Schedules and priorities

Probably the most fundamental difference you will experience when you are working rather than training is prioritisation. In a training environment you will often be given documents to type in a specific order and left to complete these in your own way and in your own time. There may be some constraints on the latter, but it is doubtful whether you will be regularly interrupted or suddenly asked to break off from one job and start another.

In the real world, one of the main difficulties with a top level secretarial job is that of fragmentation – and again Murphy's Law prevails. No sooner have you become involved in creating a long and complicated tabulation than the telephone rings, someone calls into your office with an urgent message and your boss suddenly wants you to type an urgent memo. Even if you have a word processor and can simply exit from your original document and save it until later, you have the problem of losing your concentration and forgetting what you were going to do next.

Constant interruptions are the name of the game and you will have to learn to deal with these – or change your job! Learning prioritisation skills can be more difficult and take longer. Whilst organising your own work schedule is covered more fully in Chapter 7, Organising work schedules, page 369, basic tips specifically for producing documents include the following.

- Learn through experience when your quietest times are likely to be and save complicated documents until then. This may vary according to times of the day and days of the week. The day before your boss sets off on a two week trip to America is not the time to start the most intricate typing job you have had to do in months.

- Learn to cope with completing work in stages. This may be frustrating but is often essential. You simply cannot afford to ignore what is going on at the moment and blindly continue with what you first started.
- Don't even attempt to type documents in the order in which they were received. As a general rule type letters *first* on the basis that you need to get these in the post. Contracts, urgent reports (often left until the last moment before being written at all) and other important outgoing documents should come next. Memos are usually last – being internal they can go out later in the day and, if desperate, you can even telephone urgent information through first.
- Always be prepared to jettison your schedule because something more urgent crops up. Don't sulk or react as if this is an exception. Treat it as the norm and be pleasantly surprised if you keep to your schedule at all!
- Learn to 'read' your boss. The longer you are with a company, and the more you learn about the job the easier this becomes. You can then develop a sixth sense in relation to urgency.
- Try to train your boss to avoid interrupting you when you are doing one urgent job to replace it with another! (See Managing your boss, page 291.)
- Scan written manuscripts, notes and jottings to make sure you don't miss important clues as to urgency, eg 'I will telephone you tomorrow, 24 March, to see if this is convenient'.
- If you take shorthand notes then give each document a 'star' rating on urgency. Three stars means type immediately, two stars means as soon as possible, and so on – or use A, B and C.
- Preview an audio tape (or the enclosed notes) for hints as to priority.
- Tick off everything you type as you go, then no matter how much you have to alter your schedule you still know where you are and what still needs to be done.

Finally, keep your temper and learn to stay calm in the face of adversity. There is no place in a busy office for a temperamental PA who goes to pieces the moment a crisis occurs. *You* are the one who should be smoothing your boss's ruffled feathers on a bad day – not vice versa!

ACTIVITY SECTION

Individual tasks

1 From the notes your boss has scribbled at the foot of the following letter, compose and type the documents required.

JGK INTERNATIONAL plc
Platbury Gardens
MILTON KEYNES
MK4 5JL

Tel: 0908 687392   Fax: 0908 610012

14 May 199_

Mr G Sharpe
Sales Director
Copyquick plc
Branch Road
MANCHESTER M4 6DA

Dear Sir

COPYQUICK 500K COPIER

As you may be aware, 2 months ago we took delivery of 10 of
the above copiers for installation in our UK offices. Both
your advertising material and your representative assured us
of the speed, quality and outstanding performance of these
machines.

I would advise you, however, that during the last 4 weeks your
service engineers have had to attend to the machine at this
office on 3 occasions and I also understand that at least 5 of
the other machines we purchased have a similar fault record.

Quite obviously we find this state of affairs quite
intolerable. It would appear that either the machines are not
up to the standard we require or your service engineers are
incapable of rectifying the fault. I should therefore be
grateful if you would take steps to solve the problem
immediately. Alternatively I will have no option but to ask
the machines to be removed from all our offices.

Yours faithfully

P. L. Douglas

P L Douglas
Office Services Manager

Pse reply immediately!
1) Apologize
2) Explain I'm investigating matter thoroughly – both
faults and why not specified 1st visit.
3) M/c in their office will be replaced immediately.
4) Will contact him again – in next few days – when
details are to hand.

(He's a valuable customer!!)

Send memo to Paul Entwistle, Service Mgr – mark it
urgent. Ask him what's going on, for heaven's sake.
(want full details on my desk tomorrow by
9 am or heads will roll!

2 Since your company installed a new laser printer your boss is concerned about the number of calls users are making to the Computer Department for help over even minor problems.

Using a laser printer at your college or workplace as your model, and the accompanying manual as your reference document, design and type a tabulated trouble-shooting guide which can be given to all users to rectify the problem.

3 Your company has recently employed a new Office Manager, Paul Midmarsh. He is young, extremely computer-literate and considered a 'whiz kid' by the management. You have now discovered that he plans to jettison all electronic typewriters owned by your company, plus the two old manuals kept in the cupboard on the ground floor. He considers they are all outdated and useless and that all typing work should now be carried out on word processing equipment.

You feel it would be a great mistake to throw out every typewriter in the building, as there are several occasions when they are invaluable.

Write a memo to Paul Midmarsh, from you, pleading your case. Detail exactly why you consider the typewriters to be so useful. You may invent any additional details you feel would make your memo more realistic, but your factual information must be correct.

4 Test your proof-reading skills! In the extract below are 20 errors. Find them all and type a corrected version of the document.

After the Second World War the British coal mining industry introduced technicaly revolutionery methods of cole cutting. The industry was re-equipped with expensive machinery. Being now a much more capitol-intensive industry it's economic performance depended very much upon high utilisation of the coal cutters, conveyers and powered suports. In the 1950s, Lord Robens, then Chairman of the the Naitonal coal Bord, was concerend that so many miners wiere consistently working four shifts instead of the regulation five, and that absenteism was a public issue. A news-paper recorded the following exchange betweeen the Chairman of the Board and one workign miner:

Lord Robens, 'Tell me, why do you regularly work four shifts instead of the regulation five?

Minor: 'I'll tell you why I regularly work four shifts; it's because I can't quite manage on the money I earn in three.'

(Checkland P B, Systems Thinking, Systems Practice, Wiley, 1981)

Individual/group tasks

Case study 1

You work for John Barton, Sales Director of J P Holdings plc, a thriving company which sells moulded plastic components both in the UK and abroad. The sales department has a team of ten sales representatives responsible for various UK territories and eight overseas sales representatives. Your company has recently opened two branch offices in Europe, one in Paris and the other in Dusseldorf.

Following every visit to an existing or potential customer, it is the representative's responsibility to make out a short report on the visit and highlight any follow-up action required by the sales department. It is your job to coordinate the receipt of these reports, make sure they are typed out by the sales office and then passed to your boss.

In the last few weeks it is obvious that this system is not operating effectively. Many reports are late arriving with the result that sales have been lost because of poor follow-up by your office. Of those reports which do arrive several are illegible and there are constant complaints from the typists. On at least four occasions representatives are claiming that their reports were sent on time, but you have no record of their receipt.

To solve the problem John Barton is considering installing either a centralised dictating system in the company, so that representatives can telephone their reports direct on to the audio equipment or issuing each representative with his/her own pocket dictating machine and each typist with a transcription unit.

He has asked if you will undertake the following tasks.

1 Investigate the comparative benefits of each of the above systems to
   a the company
   b the dictator
   c the typists
   and list these in a short report.

2 Draft out the format of a one day training programme which could be held within the company, for all representatives and typists, so that problems both in using the system and in dictation and transcription would be minimised.

3 Draw up a headed and ruled sheet with specific columns which you could use as your master document to keep a close check on the progress of the reports.

Case study 2

Your new office junior, Ailsa McDonald, has just started to use the company word processing system for the first time. She attended a short course held by the supplier of the equipment last week and, on interview, claimed she had learned word processing during a clerical course although she has no formal qualifications.

So far as you can see she now seems thoroughly confused by the whole system. Yesterday she left two floppy disks on a radiator with the result that they were unusable and today she panicked when her work scrolled off screen as she thought it was lost for ever.

You have now come to the conclusion that it is time to take her in hand and make sure that she is clear on at least the basics of word processing.

1 Compose a short dictionary which she can regularly use which contains the main word processing terms and a short sentence for each stating the definition. Make sure this is clearly laid out and easy to read.

It is essential that you include the following terms, although you should add to these any others you feel are appropriate.

cursor, scrolling, Wysiwyg, hard disk, CPU, kilobytes, mouse, wrap-around, hard returns, scrolling.

2 Make out a short do's and don'ts list for handling floppy disks. Add any illustrations you consider may make it easier for her to understand.

3 Type out a short memo to her, from you, explaining what you are enclosing and why. It is important that this is tactfully worded so that she will accept your help positively and not feel as though you are patronising her.

Section 2 – Presenting narrative, graphic and tabular information

Today many of the old, pedantic rules about layout and presentation have been buried for ever. Whilst this is not a moment too soon, it is still a truism that a really good, professional keyboard operator, starting work on a blank sheet of paper, is the equivalent of an artist with an empty canvas. How she creates and sets out the document will determine how pleasing it is to the eye of the recipient. For that reason her layout and presentation skills should be first-rate. You may never have thought of yourself as being in a similar role to a graphic designer but you are – and whereas he/she works with shapes and designs, your tools are text and pre-prepared graphics.

To do this part of your job well, you need to master several skills:

- a sound knowledge of modern typing conventions and layouts
- the ability to put these into practice quickly and easily on a variety of equipment
- the ability to *convert* and *adapt* these to an organisation's specific house style
- the ability to use modern software packages to help you – including desktop publishing systems
- an eye for balance and detail.

Typing conventions and layouts

Virtually all secretaries will have attended a keyboarding or typing course at some stage in their career to master to basics of touch-typing and the rules to follow when setting out business documents. The problem is that some become too hidebound with formal theory and find it difficult to 'loosen up' afterwards and create documents spontaneously. A typical example is tabulations. There is no place in a busy modern office for the typist who takes hours painstakingly to calculate a tabulation both vertically and horizontally. Therefore, although it is essential to have learned the basics to know what you are doing, you must know how to use these to develop shortcuts which you can use on a day-to-day basis.

For that reason, below you will find an 'alternative' typing glossary to which you can refer as you wish. The main typing terms are included, and rather than notes on the basic conventions you will find comments on what to do in actual practice – suggestions that your usual typing book may not contain!

The alternative typing glossary

Abbreviations   *Standard abbreviations* are those you will find at the end of a good dictionary, eg VAT, UK, ie, nb. Easier and quicker to type using open punctuation (ie as shown above with no full stops).

Bear in mind that some abbreviations should only be used in certain circumstances:

- only with figures – am and pm, abbreviations for measurements and weights (kg, mm, ft etc) and %
- in specific cases, &, Ltd, plc.

Longhand abbreviations are shortened versions of ordinary words, eg th = that, sep = separate, wl = will, etc. A list is issued for RSA typing exams.

Don't expect your boss to know or use any of the official versions except for basic ones such as Thurs, Feb etc. More likely are written notes such as 'aka' (also known as), 'wef' (with effect from) and 'tba' (to be arranged) and a few more invented on the spot! Note these down and *always* expand them in formal communications.

Accents   Those signs in foreign language words you always mean to write in afterwards and keep forgetting. Many wp programs have these as optional extras but even on a typewriter there are some shortcuts you can use. Type a comma under a c for a cedilla (eg garçon) and quotation marks "for an umlaut (eg Zoë). Other accents you need to insert in black ink afterwards. To stop yourself forgetting, at the point you see where the first accent should be inserted get out your black pen and either put it behind your ear or between your teeth. Leave it there until you've finished the document, *then* you can't possibly forget.

Boxes and spaces   An typical example of this type of document is an estate agent's sheet where spaces have to be allowed for photographs of the property to be inserted later. *Read your instructions on photograph size carefully!* The greatest calamity is to leave too small a space (for obvious reasons). In addition you will have to allow for a margin *around* the photograph.

Life is easier if you draw a box in the position you want to place the photograph. You can then type merrily around it. If you *can't* do this officially then you certainly can in pencil – and then rub it out later.

Cards and labels   *Both* require skill in typing on small sizes of paper and card can present problems of its own if it is too thick.

Forget automatic line spacing and do everything manually – there is less likelihood of anything slipping (this is one occasion when manual typewriters had the edge!). If you are dealing with perforated labels or cards *don't* separate them until after typing. Check lines low down on the card or label are aligned with your alignment scale and adjust as necessary. Go slowly – the moral of the tortoise and the hare story applies here.

Charts   The main types you will be asked to type are flow charts and/or organisation charts.

First rule – practise typing rectangles so that you can *always* place the text exactly in the middle. (Remember to turn down twice as many spaces after the top line as you do before the final line.) Work out what your widest rectangle will be and, if you are creating a vertical chart, type them all this size for simplicity (ie start at the same left hand margin point).

If you have any other shapes to create (eg diamonds, triangles etc) then type the rectangles *first* then *draw* in the other shapes and type the text in last.

Don't forget to finish off your chart by drawing in the connecting lines at the end!

Circular letters (and tear-off slips)   Note whether an external address is required so that you know how much space to leave. Standard date lines are – 'month and year' or 'date as postmark'. Note your salutation – whether a generic name is required (eg clients, customers, parents etc) or a blank space must be left.

The ending may or may not require a signature. If none is required it is usual to *type* the name of the signatory *midway* between the complimentary close and the name/designation.

A tear-off slip requires an *edge-to-edge* row of *hyphens* (not dots!). The form should be in double line spacing and rows of dots should be typed for completion. Any white space should be immediately above the tear-off slip – not below it! Calculate this easily by counting the lines required for the tear-off slip then add the space at the foot of the page (6 lines for 1″) and the cut-off line. Divide this by 6 (to give you the size in inches). Don't worry if it won't divide exactly – round it slightly upwards for safety, eg 27 lines = $4\frac{1}{2}$ inches. Make a pencil mark at this point above the bottom of the page and that's where your hyphens must be typed. (Don't forget to rub it out afterwards.)

Consistency   Is essential throughout any one document. Pitfalls include:

- *Time* – either use the 24 hour clock throughout (1700 hours – note there are no full stops) or the 12 hour clock (5 pm). Don't type useless zeros, eg 5.00 pm.
- *Words and figures* – eg the figure 2 on one page and the word two on another (unless the latter starts a sentence). Apart from starting sentences you are better to stick to one in words and everything else in figures – *always.*

- *Names* – don't refer to someone as Tom Smith on one page and Mr Smith on another.
- *Dates* – don't date a letter as '14 June' and refer to next Tuesday as 25th June in the text.

Continuation sheets   It is doubtful whether any company in existence has ever used the time-honoured practice of typing the name of the recipient, the page number and the date on continuation pages of business letters. Make life simple for yourself and simply type the figure at the top left margin, then turn down two or three spaces and continue typing. Don't forget to use plain paper!

With formal reports and anything where lists of numbered points are involved, a figure at the top of the page can be confusing. It is then better to opt for bottom of the page, centre position.

A point to remember in multi-page documents are what are known as **orphans** and **widows**. These are single lines of text at the end of one page and/or the start of the next where the rest of the paragraph is on the other page. They look sad and lonely and need joining up – so do so.

Combination characters   Few are actually used in business today as most electronic typewriters incorporate the main options (eg degree signs, equals etc). They can be fun to practise but in reality, if you regularly need to type a square root sign, buy a daisywheel on which this is an option (or a wp package which includes it).

Copies   Usually the distribution of letters is never shown on top copies except in examinations! It is far more usual to type a circulation list (initials only) just on the copies (what text books call 'blind carbon copies'). Memos are different. If you have more people to write to than you can fit in the space allocated simply type the words 'see below' after the heading 'TO' and type the circulation list at the bottom.

Don't forget to tick off the copies or you won't know who has one and who hasn't.

Correction signs   Unless you work for a publisher it is doubtful if you will ever meet these at work – apart from obvious ones such as NP.

Curriculum vitae   Your personal advertisement – see Managing your career, page 534.

Decimals   Must be aligned throughout – if you are on an electronic machine and have to do a decimal tabulation learn how to do this using the correct commands. Five minutes with the manual will save you hours of messing about.

Degree sign   In typing exams you will be taught to type this with a space between the figure and the degree sign, eg 20 °C. Now look at the weather forecast in your local paper. You will either see 20C or 20°C! The latter version is the more common in the business world – correct or not.

Diagrams   Frighteningly elaborate diagrams of office and other layouts may be included in advanced typing exams. It is doubtful whether you will ever see one of these at work. In the exam just draw the shapes first (as near as possible to match the draft) and then type in the information. Again the critical thing is to make sure the shapes are large enough.

Division of words at line ends   Quite simply, don't! It looks old-fashioned and isn't needed with a justified right margin.

Draft copies   Should be *clearly* marked 'draft' so nobody posts it by mistake.

Display   Rarely done at work unless you type the canteen menu every day. Vary the weighting of lines with underscore, capitalisation, emboldening etc and, if you want to centre each one, use the automatic centring feature. Go easy on any fancy edges, borders and tailpieces. Modern displays are plain and easy to read.

Professional display layouts are today produced using dtp systems – see page 267.

Ellipsis   Used to signify missing words. Quite simple . . . just use three spaced dots.

Enclosures   Although essential both in memos and letters in exams, at work no one is likely to notice whether you put 'Enc' on the document provided that you actually remember to include them! In minutes or reports containing several enclosures use the dot method instead for ease (see Chapter 8, Servicing meetings, page 402).

Enumeration   In other words, numbered points. Line these up properly and use a consistently inset left hand margin for clarity. If you need to use decimal points

1 The first main point goes at the left hand margin.

   1.1 Line up a decimal at a new inset point.

   1.2 Make sure your spacing is even

      1.2.1 both within each point

      1.2.2 and between points.

Envelopes and postcards   Always start half-way down and a third the way across so the address is roughly in the middle. Don't measure or calculate it! Put a small pencil dot at the right place to start until it becomes second nature. Better still, use window envelopes.

Financial statements   Nothing like as hard as they seem *provided* you understand what they are saying! Keep columns and tens and units aligned and type your total lines accurately so that the figure is in the middle. Learn to understand why a figure is carried to the next column so that you type it correctly, eg

	£	£
Income		3000
Expenditure		
Rates	500	
Rent	500	
Food	800	
Clothes	400	
	<u>350</u>	
		<u>2550</u>
Savings		<u>450</u>

Practice typing the double underscore at the end by means of your variable line spacer or interliner to get the gap right – or buy a word processing package that will do this automatically!

So far as commas or spaces are concerned, commas are generally old-fashioned but still preferred by some companies. They are usually inserted only in 5 digit numbers and over, eg 10,000 or 10 000 (though some organisations prefer 4 digits and over). Internationally, the modern convention is to use neither space nor comma up to 9999, then group in threes, leaving spaces from the right. Look through the files and see what the convention is where you are working – and be prepared to change if you move jobs. Wherever you are, *always* align all tens and units!

Footnotes   If several are required forget your asterisk and use figures. On a typewriter these should be raised half a line space in the text with no space between the word and the footnote, eg today[1]

The footnote itself should appear at the bottom of the page to which it relates – see below. (If you put it at the end of the document it is technically called an 'end note'.) The figure now goes on the line and there is one space between this and the explanation. It is usual to type a solid line, *margin to margin* between the text and the footnotes so that you don't thoroughly confuse the reader.

Forms   See *tear-off forms* above. *Always* use double spacing and leave a long enough line or no one will be able to complete it. Use equal margins and aim for a balanced appearance.

Fractions   You can mix and match between those which are on your keyboard, eg $4\frac{1}{2}$, and those which aren't, eg 5 3/16.

Headings   After a main heading text still looks better with two clear spaces between (ie turn down three). If you have a sub-heading then simply turn down two after your main heading, then (again) three before starting the main text.

Use shoulder headings rather than side headings – they're quicker and you won't forget to inset your text and return to the left margin by mistake.

Horizontal centring   You should know the width of your paper by heart and be able to use the centre function on your electronic typewriter or word processor. At work only centre anything if absolutely necessary – block everything you can at the left hand margin.

Inset material   Use the automatic inset function on an electronic typewriter or set a temporary left hand margin on your wp. The cardinal sin is to drift back to the left hand margin in error. Learn the difference between a left hand margin inset and an inset which is

equally inset from both the left and the right hand margins.

---

[1]   as shown above

Invitations   Buy them and *write* in the gaps, create them on a dtp package or have them professionally printed.

Itineraries   See Chapter 4, Arranging travel, page 204.

Justification   Always looks better than a ragged right hand margin. You'll also need to use a flush right hand margin for the internal address of personal letters (see below).

Leader dots   Forget fancy versions, use continuous dots for ease. Always remember to leave a clear space before they start and after they finish.

Letters   If you can't type a standard business letter you shouldn't be reading this book! You should know *by heart* the main components and where these are typed. Most textbooks today will tell you to turn down a standard two spaces between each component, apart from where the document must be signed. Many bosses hate this layout and insist on a variety of styles and formats (see *House style* after this glossary). In addition the printed layout of your letter-headed paper may make this an impractical option.

If you have to sign letters in your boss's absence find out how you should end the letter as there are a variety of ways of doing this – either

a   write the letter on his/her behalf (eg Mr Bloggs has asked me to write and thank you for your letter . . . etc). In this case you would use your own name and designation at the bottom of the letter.

b   write the letter from him/her. In this case you can:

(**i**)   sign it as below

Yours sincerely
T L PETTIGREW LTD
L. Cappitello
pp John Bloggs
Sales Manager

or

(**ii**)   opt for this version

Yours sincerely
T L PETTIGREW LTD
L. Cappitello
Dictated by John Bloggs and signed in his absence

You may often be expected to type personal letters for your boss and he/she may not have printed headed paper. Always type personal letters with the address at the top, with a flush right hand margin. Turn down 2, type the date at the left margin and then continue as usual.

Meetings documents   See Chapter 8, Servicing meetings, page 388.

Memos   The standard headings can vary greatly from one company to another. Be consistent in style – don't write to Bill Rogers from J P Jenkins. Either include titles for both sender and recipient or miss them out completely.

If you are *composing* memos stick to one topic for each memo and keep them short. People lose interest after the first paragraph.

Numbers   *Ordinal* denote order, ie first, second, third – stick to words in continuous text as they're easier to understand than 1st, 2nd, 3rd.

Roman numerals are rarely used these days and can now be aligned from the left or the right, eg

(iii)   (iii)
(iv)   (iv)
 (v)   (v)

the latter is more up to date and easier to type. It helps if you know which number you are typing. The greatest danger is not leaving enough space for the longest number, eg viii.

Cardinal are standard figures. Clearer and easier to use a figure for everything except the number one (see *Consistency*).

Pagination   See *Continuation pages*.

Paper   Comes in different sizes, types and weights. You should know the difference between the various sizes and why they are used – ie A3, A4, A5 and A6 – and the difference between portrait and landscape.

You should be typing top copies on bond paper and carbon copies on bank paper. Good quality bond paper is watermarked and has a right side and a wrong side (the latter is slightly fluffy). You will know when you are looking at the right side because you can read the watermark. Insert the paper into your typewriter or printer with *this* side on the top, or else you defeat the object of using top quality paper!

Paper weights are dealt with in the next section of this chapter.

Paragraphing   Usually block style, though if your boss *wants* 10 space indented paragraphs in every letter, and he is paying your salary, who are you to argue?

We doubt if anyone uses hanging paragraphs in business today – or has even heard of them.

Rearrangements   Be methodical. No matter how easy your list may seem to be to start with *always* mark it up first and tick off as you go. Otherwise at the first interruption you will have to start all over again.

Reports   Simple provided you know the basic rules of paragraphing, headings, pagination and enumeration and are *consistent throughout.*

Tabulations   Think of these as a large-scale, divided rectangle, which you want to appear roughly in the middle of the page. At work, if you are typing from previous typescript then you can easily cheat by drawing the box the same size as it was before and then typing in the information!

If you are typing from manuscript then work out the width carefully and then guestimate the length for vertical centring. If you get this wrong keep going and then photocopy your tabulation on to another sheet of paper. Reposition it (centrally) on the glass just before you take the copy.

Don't forget to draw in all the vertical lines!

Vertical headings   Again rarely used except in typing exams. Easier to use the modern version of

T
O
D
A
Y

than the older version where the text is typed side on (although it takes up more room). The side on version is impossible to do on a wp anyway.

House styles

It is a secretarial phenomenon that you can spend years learning how to type correctly, pass all your typing examinations with flying colours, and then get a job where you are asked to set out documents that bear absolutely no relation to anything you have ever seen in your life before. The huge variation in styles and layouts is apparent immediately you examine incoming mail for more than three days in succession.

The basic rule to remember is that 'he who pays the piper calls the tune'. If your boss wants the letters typed upside down you should go ahead – unless you feel very secure in your job you are usually ill-advised to say that the company house style is 25 years out of date. If you are lucky you will work for a boss who has no interest whatsoever in how you set out any document as long as each one is clear, accurate and neatly presented.

The golden rules for coping with different house styles include:

- look in the files upon your arrival at a new company to see how letters, memos etc are set out in this organisation
- know the alternatives available, eg:
  – full punctuation (and all its variations)
  – semi-blocked style where the date is typed alongside the reference and ends at the right hand margin, indented paragraphs are used and the complimentary close is centred on the page
  – blocked style which is like the above except that the paragraphs are blocked
- if you are working in a large organisation then you may find that they have a manual containing examples of the layouts they require. Whatever you think of these, as a new employee you are hardly in a position to comment!

Desktop publishing systems

If you want to create documents which contain a mixture of text and graphics or need a professional look to their display, then it is unlikely that you can do this unless you have access to a dtp system.

There are several dtp packages on the market, some of which are quite complicated to learn. They are usually well worth the effort, however, as the effects which can be achieved are superb.

The first fact to remember is that a dtp package is *neither* a graphics package *nor* a word processing package. It is a package which enables you to *put together* text and graphics to produce a variety of documents which look 100 per cent professional – notices, posters, reports, presentations, 'newspapers' etc. You can, however, use the dtp package itself to design simple graphics, eg shaded boxes for title pages. Apart from these basic graphics and simple lines of text, other graphics and text are created using other types of software and then 'imported' into the dtp package where they are then integrated into one document, usually referred to as a **publication**.

Text
This is usually input via a compatible word processing package and then saved. The file can then be accessed from the dtp package later and the text imported to the publication being created.

Graphics
These are usually input via a **document scanner**. This may be a full scale scanner into which you simply feed the document containing the illustration you require, or a **hand-held scanne**r, which you move slowly down the illustration – in a straight line! In both cases you will need to 'clean up' your image on screen as any dirty marks on the page will also have been 'read' by the scanner.

Scanners operate in conjunction with **optical character recognition (OCR)** software, so that all dark lines are 'read' by the scanner. Most OCR packages also give you the option to amend graphic areas by means of a mouse, eg to extend or reduce lines, add shading, enlarge or reduce the image etc. Good quality scanners will also enable you to scan photographs.

When you are satisfied with your graphic image you should save this under a specific file name which you can then access later via the dtp package.

Desktop publishing
Virtually all dtp systems operate by means of a mouse and drop down windows from which you choose your options by clicking the correct mouse button. If you have never used a mouse before then practise getting used to the feel of it. On the basis that it takes skill to manipulate this properly, *always* use the hand with which you normally write to control it.

When you first load the software you will have to select the type of publication you are going to create, eg is it multi or single page, will it have columns, what other features do you want throughout the document – types of headings etc. Most packages operate a system of rulers which are only visible on screen, not when you print, so that your headings and other features are always correctly aligned.

There will usually be a tool box option which will enable you to draw a number of shapes and shade these in as required, as well as enlarging or reducing the image on the screen for 'fine tuning'.

You may start with a simple heading at the top of your publication and on a dtp package you will have a choice of font styles and sizes. Remember that you can only choose those which your printer can support. If you are fortunate enough to have a postscript laser printer attached then you can choose virtually any option, and any size, but don't get too carried away or the heading will be out of all proportion to the text which follows!

You can now import the graphics you saved and position these in the most effective place. You will have the facility to move, cut and trim, enlarge and reduce these until you are satisfied with the result. An important technique to learn is how to keep the illustration in proportion – as you adjust its size you may make it go out of shape (fatter, thinner etc). With a photograph this can have devastating results and may result in less than cordial working relationships with some staff later.

Finally you can import your text. You may want to alter this slightly, eg enlarge the first letter in a paragraph, embolden headings and create sub-headings or move the text around to get the best, most balanced effect. When you really know what you are doing you can position the text irregularly around a graphic for maximum impact (see illustration opposite).

SPECIAL NOTE

Be careful what you copy on to your dtp or you could be in danger of infringing copyright! You *cannot* just copy large chunks from a book or magazine and then scan in all their illustrations too. See Chapter 2, Researching and retrieving information, page 108, for information on copyright law .

Design hints and tips

Graphic design is a special field in its own right. The following hints are given to stop you making some basic mistakes, but eventually your designs will rest very much on your own creativity and imagination! However, it can be great fun experimenting and that is the best way to learn.

1 Aim for clarity and impact. *Never* put too much information on one page – it simply looks confusing to the reader.

2 Sketch out your layout on paper first and see how visually appealing it is. (If you aren't sure, ask someone else for their opinion.)

3 Keep an eye on proportion, ie the size of a graphic or heading in relation to the page. Nothing should be so large it overwhelms everything else.

4 A formal look can be achieved by using conventional layout and putting a border around the page. An informal look requires a different, more unorthodox layout. A legal document, such as Health and Safety regulations, should be set out totally differently to a supermarket handout!

5 Balance can be boring! Unequal left/right or top/bottom margins can create interest. So, too, can the use of white space around text or artwork – or graphics irregularly placed on the page.

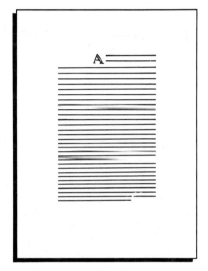

6 Organise each page around a single dominant visual element – the headline, a large graphic or block of copy.

7 If you are designing a two-page publication both pages must balance and not fight for attention. Design them both as one unit rather than separate entities.

8 Don't go for more than three columns except on special occasions and five is the most at any time! Columns *don't* have to be the same length.

9 Use your margins effectively (overleaf, left).

10 Start text low down if there is a small amount of reading matter and use white space for effect (overleaf, right).

11 If you are creating an informal publication then use a typeface or style which will reflect the document you are creating, eg IrReGuLaR GrApHiCs!

12 Insert subheads where you think they will be effective and make them stand out by setting them in bold or large type.

13 Insert captions on graphics where required but keep them short and to the point. Use a small typeface so the captions don't compete with the main body copy.

14 Use white space to make design elements stand out. White space provides a background which emphasises whatever it surrounds (see illustrations). However, avoid white space in the middle

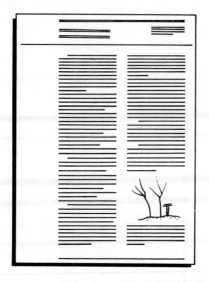 

of a page, eg in the middle column, as this creates a hole in your design.

15 Accentuate text or graphics with the use of boxes – shade these for impact or to create an edging to the box.

16 Avoid short lines of type at the tops or bottoms of columns (orphans and widows again).

17 Adjust your line spacing for added emphasis where necessary.

18 Don't forget to proof-read! Your publication will lose all its impact if text is wrongly spelt or there are typing mistakes.

ACTIVITY SECTION

Individual activities

1 Your new junior has great problems when typing tabulations. She takes hours and hours to calculate where these should be positioned on the paper and even then never produces one which is actually usable.

On four occasions recently you have helped her by quickly typing the offending document so that it can be sent out as required. Full of admiration at your skill and expertise she has asked for your help.

Design a short, easy-to-understand list of points which she can follow to ensure that she will never go wrong again.

2 Your boss has given you the following document to produce. He needs it for a meeting in 20 minutes. Unfortunately, at the last minute he has changed the way he wants it displayed. Can you cope?

	Jan £ 000's	F	M	Ap	M	June
Europe	248	624	187	283	496	205
Australia	105	208	602	412	110	486
USA	96	84	105	108	73	68
South America	54	60	42	30	84	20
Far East	35	40	22	25	61	86
Total						

Sorry! pse rearese so months are vertical and countries across top. Pse total and rule up.

Ths.

Individual/group activities

Case study 1

You work for Ms Marjorie Stevens, the Health and Safety Officer of a large mail order company. Your organisation is very aware of the legislation which relates to VDU operators. From next month all VDU operators will:

- receive a free eye test at regular periods
- have regular rest breaks away from their machines.

In addition the main office areas where VDUs are sited have been redecorated and new lighting and new workstations have been installed.

To make sure that all employees know why these measures have been taken, and other important aspects of working with VDUs and health and safety, Ms Stevens has decided to hold a short training session for all VDU staff tomorrow afternoon.

She has asked you and your colleagues to
a Carry out your own research on this subject.
b Prepare a booklet which simply and clearly gives the relevant facts to the staff. She has asked that you design and illustrate this as appropriate, preferably using the company's desktop publishing system.
c Prepare a short (10 minute) presentation to highlight the main points.

Case study 2

Your company has recently changed from using mainly electronic typewriters to a networked system of microcomputers. All staff have access to the company's database of customer names and addresses and details of their accounts, in addition to a range of other software including word processing packages and spreadsheets. Only accounts staff have access to the payroll package and only personnel staff and senior management have access to staff records.

Whilst a system of passwords is in operation for all network users, and your company is registered as a user on the Data Protection Register, your boss Mike Cummings is worried that the company is still not complying correctly with the provisions of the Data Protection Act 1984 and that there could be problems if information on either customers or staff is freely available.

He has therefore asked you to

a Research the requirements of the Act thoroughly and find out which aspects apply to your company. (You may like to start by referring to Chapter 2, Researching and retrieving information, p 84.)

b Detail these in a short report for his attention. Clearly outline any procedures he should check to make certain that the requirements of the Act are being met.

Section 3 – Organising and arranging the copying, collating and binding of documents

There are many occasions when multiple copies of documents are required – from a memo which needs to be sent to various members of staff to an 80 page report which has to be copied, collated and bound for presentation to a client. The quality of reproduction for such documents *must* be superb for the preservation of your company's image. Anything which is slipshod or amateurish is totally unacceptable in today's highly competitive business world.

For this reason, many organisations spend a great deal of money on top quality equipment to produce such documents. *Your* task is to know their functions and how to use each one to your advantage. Even if your organisation operates a centralised print room or, as a PA, you are no longer expected to use the equipment yourself, a good knowledge of what can be achieved, and how, will help you when planning and scheduling how such work should be carried out to best effect. *And* you never know when an emergency may occur – if the offset-litho machine operator is off with flu just when she should be producing an urgent report for your boss, you may become the star of the show if you can turn your hand to actually producing the copies required.

Methods of reprography

Strictly speaking, reprography refers to any type of equipment which can produce multiple copies. For that reason, even a fax machine can be classed as reprographic equipment. This section, however, concentrates on the principal methods by which organisations today undertake their printing requirements.

Generally you will find you have three choices of reproduction.

1 Take multiple copies on a computer printer.

2 Photocopy the document(s).

3 Duplicate these on an offset-litho machine.

The type of equipment an organisation chooses to buy, and whether this is offered as a centralised or local facility will depend upon:

- the documents being produced
- the frequency with which they are required
- the quantities required
- the level and sophistication required in relation to graphics, drawings, illustrations and colour work
- the corresponding cost of having documents and brochures produced by outside printers
- the capital cost of establishing an in-house print room facility
- the running costs of the above
- the space available
- the availability of printing staff and/or training requirements.

The equipment, either purchased or rented, will therefore depend very much on the individual requirements of a particular company.

Computer printers

These are dealt with in more detail on page 240. Whether you decide to select this option for copying a particular document will depend on:

- the speed of your printer
- the quality of work it produces and the reason for which the document(s) are required
- the number of pages involved.

Most software packages now allow you to work on one document whilst printing out another, which obviously saves time. However, many good quality printers are not particularly rapid, so it may be much quicker to print one master copy and then put this on to the photocopier if multiple copies are required. Much depends on the number of pages involved.

In certain cases, it is considered inappropriate to send out photocopies. A CV is a typical case in point. Wherever possible you should *only* send out a top copy CV – not a photocopy which may give the impression that you regularly send this to any company in which you are vaguely interested! The same argument may apply to a survey or report your organisation is presenting to a customer.

SPECIAL NOTE
Never try to fax a document which has been produced on a dot matrix printer – the text can easily break up in transmission and be unreadable on receipt.

Copying systems

Photocopiers are a feature of all offices, although their size and complexity varies considerably. Their major attribute is their ability to produce an exact replica of a document in a matter of seconds.

There are three types of copier on the market today:

- black and white copiers
- colour copiers
- 'smart' or 'intelligent' copiers.

The first type operate by means of the electrostatic process, the second and third owe their existence to modern advances in laser technology.

Black and white copiers

These are available in a wide variety of shapes and sizes, from the small desktop variety to the huge, multi-function machines more commonly found in centralised print rooms. The difference is not only in the range of functions, but in the number which can be undertaken *automatically*, with minimal work for the operator. In addition, the speed of the large machines can be two or three times that of smaller, cheaper machines.

Many of the smaller machines are bought outright from a local dealer, and then a separate maintenance contract will be negotiated. Larger copiers are more usually rented, and paid for on a copy cost basis. Such rental agreements include a servicing agreement to cover call-outs in the case of machine breakdown. Prompt service is essential for a company which depends heavily on a large volume copier for most of its reprographic needs. The other advantage with a rental agreement is that, as more advanced and sophisticated copiers come on to the market, the company can trade in its old machine for a more up-to-date model.

CHECK IT YOURSELF
List the number of copiers in your organisation (or college) and find out whether each one was bought outright or has been purchased on a rental or service agreement. For any copiers covered under the latter, try to establish:

- the amount paid per copy
- any additional charges
- the length of the agreement

The electrostatic process

Knowing how a copier works means that not only does the layout *inside* the machine start to make sense but you are also more knowledgeable about the consumables you need (types of paper, toner etc) *and* what type of faults can occur and why.

All basic photocopiers work by means of an electrostatic process – and the term 'static electricity' should be familiar to you. If you comb your hair rapidly then you can usually pick up several bits of paper if you hold the comb close to them. Believe it or not, it is upon this phenomenon that electrostatic copiers are based.

Inside the machine is a drum or plate, usually coated with selenium. An electrically charged grid moves across the drum to charge the coating with positive electricity.

When you place your original on the glass of the machine you will notice that this is illuminated by a bright light. The illuminated image passes through a lens system on to the coated drum, and because the latter is light-sensitive the positive charges disappear in all the areas which have been exposed to light. The pattern of charges left on the drum is now exactly the same shape as the dark part (the print) on the original document.

Negatively-charged toner powder is now dusted on to the drum. This sticks only on to the charged areas (remember the paper and comb) to give a **mirror image** of the original document.

The sheet of copy paper is now brought in contact with the drum and, at the same time, receives a positive charge of electricity. The paper therefore attracts the powder from the drum, forming a **positive image**. This image is softened and fused into the paper, usually by heat, to create an exact copy of the original document (which is why your copies are warm when they first appear).

CHECK IT YOURSELF
If you open a copier you should be able to identify:

- where the new toner is stored, and how this should be replenished
- how the used toner is stored, and how often this container should be replaced
- where the fuser unit is situated. This is usually at the extreme left hand side of the copier and can be dangerous to touch as it becomes extremely hot.

Health and Safety

The major considerations to be borne in mind are:

- site the machine so there is a free flow of air around it
- do *not* stare at the illuminated light if, for some reason, the lid is not in place
- make sure that the plug is properly wired and earthed
- do not touch hot parts of the copier (this particularly applies to the fuser unit)
- keep liquids away from the copier
- if you get toner on your hands or clothes use *cold* water to wash it off – otherwise it will set

- do not operate the copier if any part is damaged until it has been checked by the service engineer
- apart from standard faults, eg a paper jam or misfeed, never try to disassemble the copier or repair it yourself.

Copier functions

Most of the basic desktop machines today usually enable you to:

- adjust the density control for light or dark originals
- enlarge and reduce (though a limited number of pre-set ratios will be available)
- stack paper (often up to 100 sheets) in a paper tray for automatic feed
- insert coloured card, overhead transparencies, labels etc by means of a by-pass or supplementary paper tray
- take up to 99 copies in a single print run
- place books and thick manuscripts on the glass plate, as the rubberised lid is either detachable or hinged to allow for this
- carry out double-sided copying (**duplexing**) *manually* by re-feeding paper printed on one side so it now prints on the opposite side (the trick is to remember to keep the paper the right way up!)
- operate the machine by means of a counter so that the number of copies taken is logged automatically.

Whereas desktop copiers can be ideal as 'back-up' local machines for urgent copies, they do have their limitations – not least in terms of speed and lack of automaticity, and long or complex jobs may be tedious and time-consuming to complete. For this reason, most organisations have at least one large, multi-purpose copier which can carry out a range of functions including:

- copying automatically from a range of originals of:
  – different sizes
  – different types of paper (eg continuous computer print-out)
- copying on to different sizes of paper
- adjustable zoom and reduction ratios – on some very sophisticated machines the copier *itself* can calculate the best zoom or reduction ratio for the work in relation to page layout and consistency within a multi-page document
- automatic tray switching so that jobs aren't interrupted whilst a paper tray is refilled
- automatic collation, stapling and thermal binding
- automatic duplexing (from double or single sided originals), with automatic margin adjustment for left and right hand pages
- a programmable memory for similar or identical jobs (eg the monthly sales report); specific functions (eg card inserts, reduction/ enlargement, collation and stapling) can be preset in the memory
- an automatic document handler for multi-page originals

- an editing facility which enables you to delete confidential or selected sections of a document
- automatic machine diagnostic panel – on the more advanced machines the copier *itself* contacts its service department and details its own fault when something goes wrong!
- pre-programmable user codes with a print-out of the usage against each code at the end of a specified period (and a lock-out facility if the allowance is reached before a specified time).

SPECIAL NOTE

'Cutting and pasting' is the name given to the technique where a number of graphic or text elements are combined from separate sources on one sheet of paper before being copied. The technique is now becoming outdated as, with dtp software and the font/graphic capabilities of some wp packages, this type of work can usually be undertaken on screen.

However, there are still occasions when it may be quicker or easier to create your master page from cutting out information and piecing this together manually.

There are a few simple rules to bear in mind:

- keep the design simple and use white space effectively (see design elements on page 268).
- carry out any reduction/enlargements required on single elements *first* – then position these (without sticking them down) on your master page and check for an overall balanced look
- either use the edge of the paper as a guide or rule very faint pencil lines as your guide lines when positioning your work. Otherwise you may find that some of your cut outs are crooked on the page! Don't forget to rub out your pencil marks before copying
- either keep sellotape to a minimum (and make sure it is clean!) or use the special spray mounting adhesive used by graphic designers. This takes a little time to set, so giving you the opportunity, if necessary, to adjust your cut outs before pressing them down
- keep your master safely stored away, especially if it took you some time to prepare. Keep one of your photocopies in your general file so that *this* can be used at a later date if more copies are required.

Colour copiers

There are now small desktop copiers available which can operate in several colours. On other machines 'two-colour' copying is possible. This is undertaken by means of removable (or dual) toner cartridges. On the basis that toner is the photocopier equivalent of ink, then by changing the colour of the toner it is easy to change the colour of the copies produced. You may like to note that on many machines dual colour copying is achieved by feeding through the original(s) twice so that on the first pass, with one toner cartridge in place, you perhaps print the border and a few selected lines of text. Then with the contrasting colour cartridge in place you feed through a second original with other lines of text *in the correct positions to align with the first original*. The result is a two-colour copy.

This, however, is not the limit of colour copying. Developments in laser technology have now enabled full colour copiers to enter the market which can produce from A4 to A1 copies from a range of originals – drawings, photographs from magazines and books, even original photographs and slides. Needless to say, these are slower than standard copiers and *very* expensive. As yet there are few organisations which could justify the six-figure investment still required for one of these, but access can be had via a print shop or printing bureau, and cost per copy then becomes a far more credible option.

> **CHECK IT YOURSELF**
> Check if any print shop or printing bureau near you operates a full colour photocopying service. Find out if they will let you see it in operation and explain how it works. (You can, of course, have some copies made yourself, but aim to pay approximately £1 for each A4 copy you have produced.)

Smart copiers

These are almost a cross-breed between a laser printer and a photocopier and are frequently available as a networked resource for computer users. The laser technology undertakes the same type of function as in a laser printer, but on a much larger scale. Data received from computers, in the form of text, graphics, charts or even handwriting (eg signatures) can be stored in memory and printed on demand. You can therefore design your own forms and print them out professionally at the touch of a button. Companies which operate a technical drawing facility will be likely to link their printing technology to **Computer Aided Design (CAD)** or **Computer Aided Manufacture (CAM)** software so that three-dimensional drawings can be rotated, scaled and modified for the document(s) being produced.

The company's letter and memo headings (and logo) can be stored in memory and printed out as required on any document and other text can be scanned in to the system, rather than keyed in to save time. In addition a wide range of fonts and type sizes is available. Rather than a key pad these machines usually function by means of a touch-sensitive screen, so that all pages of a document can be modified (or combined) as required. You can even instruct the copier to print out an envelope automatically for every letter you produce and print!

Needless to say, such a printer will be a centralised resource, serving many different computers at the same time. For that reason all users are given an access code or password which the computer logs automatically. The costing of work can then be allocated to different individuals or departments as required.

Centralisation

The price of many of the sophisticated, multi-purpose machines is such that they are only cost-effective if they are operated as a centralised resource for a large number of users. Generally, they may be supplemented by a small number of orthodox, desktop copiers for one-time-only or urgent tasks. The organisation then has the best of both worlds – the flexibility to produce small numbers of documents quickly and easily and the facilities to produce top quality, professional presentations as required.

Other advantages of centralisation include:

- a well-trained staff who understand the equipment well and can obtain maximum benefit from the facilities available
- a centralised costing system which allocates costs to users throughout the organisation
- cover for specialist staff who may be absent or on holiday so that through-put is maintained
- standardised quality printing throughout the organisation
- centralised purchasing of printer consumables to minimise errors, problems or discrepancies.

The disadvantages can include:

- difficulty in by-passing the 'system' for urgent jobs to be undertaken
- reliance on one machine can create severe problems in the case of a breakdown
- lack of communications between specialists and users so that documents are not produced to user's requirements or specialists are not given the freedom to produce documents in the best way possible.

Duplicating systems

Generally, you will find that duplicators are also mainly offered as a centralised resource – not because of their expense but because of the expertise required in their operation. The difference between duplicating and copying is that for any duplicating system a **master** must be prepared from which the copies are made. Again masters may be prepared centrally, using special equipment, rather than handwritten or typed.

There are three types of duplicating process:

- spirit duplicating (old-fashioned and poor quality and today rarely used)
- ink duplicating (better quality but really only suitable for internal copies; relatively cheap and easy to use)
- offset litho (top quality, if used correctly).

Ink duplicators use masters called **stencils** which can be typed or, more often, produced on an electronic scanner. The latter enables both text and graphics to be copied.

Offset-litho duplicators use masters called **plates**. Paper plates are for short runs and can be typed or produced on most photocopiers. Metal plates are for long runs and are produced via a photographic process. Because the offset-litho process is the only one commonly found in business, this section will concentrate only on this method of duplicating.

The lithographic process

The word **lithography** means 'stone writing' and is so-called because its inventor, a Bavarian printer called Senefelder, discovered that when he wrote on a stone with a greasy pencil, water would cling only to the surface of the stone which was not covered by the writing. This is a similar phenomenon to one you may have encountered as a child if you ever wrote a 'magic message' with a candle on a piece of paper. If you wet the paper then water will run off the greasy message leaving it clearly visible.

Senefelder then discovered that if he rolled ink over the stone this would stick to the greasy marks but *not* to any of the wet areas. The basic principle of lithography, therefore, is that oil and water do not mix. (Think of puddles which have oil floating on the top.)

A lithographic plate is therefore prepared by starting with a greasy image which is put on to the plate (a carbon ribbon in a typewriter is suitable, as is the standard photocopying process). The plate is then dampened with water which sticks only to the non-image areas. The ink is then applied and sticks to the areas which are not damp, ie the image areas.

The master plate made from a
thin sheet of aluminium or paper

An image is formed on the plate,
using a greasy medium

The plate is damped
with water from a roller,
which only adheres to the
ungreased areas

The plate is inked,
but ink only adheres to greasy areas

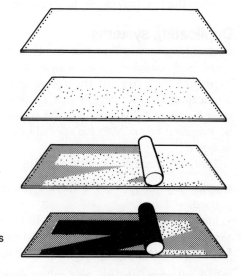

Offset lithography

Offset lithography is based on the principle that a reverse print of a reverse print is legible. On an offset litho machine there are therefore *three* cylinders.

- The first cylinder holds the plate (the plate cylinder).
- The second cylinder (the blanket cylinder) then takes the offset (mirror) image.
- The paper is then fed between this cylinder and a third (the impression roller) and the paper receives the print the right way round.

There are also two small rollers at the top, a dampening roller and an inking roller.

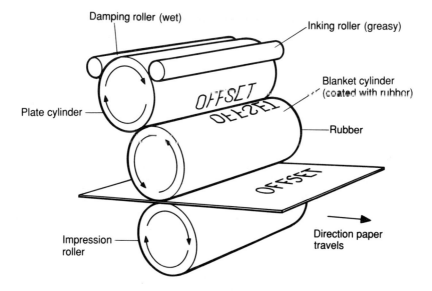

If you watch the machine being used you will see that the operator:

- applies etch to the plate to make it **lithographic**, ie ink will be attracted to the image areas
- fastens the master to the plate cylinder
- dampens the master with **fountain solution**, a mixture of water and an additive, usually available as a concentrate (The fountain solution is applied by bringing the master in contact with the dampening roller.)
- inks the plate by bringing the inking roller into contact with the plate cylinder to apply a thin layer of ink to the image areas
- transfers the image to the blanket cylinder (This is a metal cylinder covered with a rubber blanket. Only two or three revolutions are required for the image to be transferred and offset onto the blanket cylinder.)
- fans the copy paper (to prevent it sticking together) and places this in the paper tray
- takes a trial copy by feeding one sheet of paper between the blanket cylinder and the impression cylinder
- makes any minor adjustments to the position of the copy before duplicating the required number

- after use removes the plate and also removes the image from the blanket cylinder by means of a blanket wash lever which is held down whilst the cylinder goes through several revolutions.

SPECIAL NOTE

Special 'copier-duplicator' machines are available which *automatically* receive a typed copy, produce a paper plate and make the copies via the offset-litho process, rather than electrostatically.

The role of photographic processes

Companies which use offset-litho machines for in-house printing will probably find that the range of images which can be produced by typing or photocopying on paper plates is insufficient for their needs. For one thing, paper plates have a limited life and are not suitable for storing or for long runs. The print quality may also not be of the standard required for graphic images.

Instead, the company may have its own dark room where metal plates are produced by a photographic process. Originals such as diagrams, photographs, detailed line drawings and maps can be easily transferred to metal plates and the result is copies of very high quality. Up to 50 000 copies can be produced from metal plates and these can be kept and re-used in the future. The company can now undertake all its own printing requirements and, with some machines, can produce multi-colour copies. In this way not only can advertising literature and brochures be produced in-house, but the company can also print its own letter headings – complete with logo – plus its own company handbook, presentation documents etc.

The disadvantages of the offset-litho process include:

- skill is required for advanced applications – even for basic work a trained operator is required
- each machine needs cleaning down at least once weekly – a chore not welcomed by general office staff
- separate runs have to be made for each colour, plus the machine must be cleaned down between each colour run; colour printing only then becomes cost-effective if separate machines are *permanently* set up with specific colours
- all masters *must* be grease free – ie have no dirty marks or smudges.

Print-room equipment

Once the copies have been duplicated or photocopied then, unless you have a very sophisticated modern copier, you will be left with the job of the 'finishing work'. This is likely to include:

- collating the pages into sets
- jogging the pages so that they are even
- fastening these together – either by means of a stapler or a binding machine.

Collators

Most large-volume photocopiers have their own collator attached, but usually only up to about 20 'bins' are available. Each bin holds a completed set of documents, so that for runs longer than 20 the bins must be emptied and the job run through again.

Anyone producing multi-page documents *without* a machine with an attached collator will need a separate collator to sort the copies into sets.

Collators look so simple to use they almost appear idiot-proof! Unfortunately this is not the case. It is true that all you have to do is to stack the sheets in each bin and press a button. Problems which can arise, however, include:

- sheets stacked in the wrong order
- unpaginated sheets – so you don't know which one should be where
- back-to-back copies which are placed the wrong way round
- sheets stacked upside down
- the collator missing a page during a run
- overloading the bins so that a paper jam occurs.

Miscollated documents are obviously a total disaster. If page 7 comes before page 3, page 10 is upside down and page 15 missing altogether, then it doesn't matter how professional the copying has been – the document is useless. Decollating and recollating multi-page documents is a tedious and laborious chore. For that reason *always* take a trial copy and stop the collator at random intervals and sample the last one produced to make sure all is still going to plan.

Joggers

Joggers are usually built in to collators. The bins will therefore jog from side to side to straighten up the paper so that it is evenly stacked.

Guillotines and rotary cutters

If paper must be trimmed to a specific size then either a guillotine or a rotary cutter will be used. The former come in a range of sizes, from large industrial guillotines which can cut thousands of sheets of paper at one time to small desktop models. Instead of a guillotine blade, a rotary cutter has a small circular wheel which is moved down the length of paper to be cut. They are more of a precision instrument than a guillotine *but* can only cut accurately through small quantities of paper at once.

Staplers

There are four basic types of stapler – the hand-held variety, the long-arm stapler, the electric stapler and the heavy duty stapler. All can cause a nasty accident if you don't watch what you are doing.

With the **hand-held** type of stapler *always* use it on a flat surface – don't hold it in mid-air and expect your staple to go where you want it;

it might change direction entirely and end up through your fingers! A **long-arm** stapler is used to position staples in the centre of wide pages (similar to a book fastening). An **electric** stapler saves time and effort, though it can take a little practice always to aim the paper in exactly the right place for consistent stapling to be achieved. A **heavy duty** stapler takes both thicker staples and thicker quantities of paper than ordinary staplers.

Golden rules for using staples are as follows:

- don't obscure the text at any point in the document
- don't try to fasten too many sheets of paper in an ordinary stapler.

Punches

Heavy duty punches and electric punches are available for making holes in thick stacks of paper. A punch is again a precision instrument as the marks and settings allow you to punch different numbers of holes with different distances between them. You *must* be able to use any punch so that all of the holes in one document are *precisely* aligned.

Binding machines

There are two types of binding machine commonly used in offices.

Plastic comb binding machines These machines are cheap to buy and easy to use and 'thread' a plastic comb through punched holes at the edge of the pages. The number of holes and the distance between them is variable, as is the thickness (depth) of the binding. Comb binders are useful if a problem occurs as the combs can be taken out and put back again, eg if a new page needs to be inserted at a later date.

Thermal binders Equally cheap and even easier to use, thermal binders give a professional appearance to finished documents by fastening the pages inside the cover by means of heat. This melts the thin coating of adhesive already inside the spine of the cover. Covers are available in a wide variety of thicknesses, designs, colours and finishes.

The major points to watch for are that the pages are all knocked into position inside the spine, all are aligned correctly, and the bound document is left alone until it has had chance to cool.

Reprographic costs

The costs of reprography, as in other areas, can be divided into **fixed** and **variable** costs. The fixed costs of reprography relate to:

- the purchase or rental costs of the equipment
- the wages of the operator
- additional costs in operating reprography, eg lighting, heating, rent etc.

As you may appreciate, you have little opportunity to influence any of the above! You have, however, considerable influence when it comes to the variable costs which relate to:

- the number of copies taken
- the type and cost of the materials.

Wastage

In the average day, the number of wasted copies produced by each company is tremendous. Typical causes include:

- dirty, poor quality or totally unsuitable originals
- carelessness by the operator (eg pressing 'print' without putting the document in position first, incorrect quantity specified, wrong reduction or enlargement ratios specified, no adjustment for copy density etc)
- 'personal' copying
- additional copies taken 'just in case'.

Materials

Care *must* be taken in relation to the materials used – and the main one of these by far is paper. Cheap, cut-price paper may not only be unsuitable but cause paper jams which need an experienced mechanic to rectify. *All* paper should be removed from photocopiers both at night and (especially) at weekends as it becomes damp, loses its shape and will jam in the machine. Operators who forget to do this can end up with reams of unusable paper in the course of a month.

The **weight** of paper, as well as its size is significant. Paper thickness is expressed in **microns**: 1 micron = 0.001 mm. It is usually shown in terms of gsm or g/m^2 (grams per square metre). This refers to the weight of each sheet and the higher the figure the heavier (ie the thicker) the paper. If you are buying card you can specify the weight, in microns, that you require. Thin card starts at about 150 microns. Copier card is about 200 microns (165 gsm). Card weighing 280 microns is often known as **pasteboard**. Card weights continue up to thick card at 750 microns and mounting boards are in the region of 1250 microns.

If you are ordering paper, you will see that this is quoted only in gsm. The lightest paper, bank paper for carbon copies, is 45 gsm. Bond paper (for typing top copies) is sold in four weights – 60 gsm, 70 gsm (usually not watermarked), 80 gsm and 85 gsm. The latter is watermarked letter quality for prestige work.

Duplicating bond paper, for offset work (plus the slightly absorbent ink duplicating paper) comes in two weights – 70 gsm for single sided work and 85 gsm for double sided work.

Printer paper starts at 60 gsm and various weights are available up to 90 gsm.

You should note that many types of paper have special finishes, or are specially treated for their use and it is not recommended that you therefore mix and match. For example, copier paper is specially treated during manufacture to be impervious to the heat it encounters during the copying process. It is also specially treated to lie flat. Ordinary bond paper is therefore not suitable for use with most photocopiers (as well as being more expensive). However, if you use a laser printer then you will usually find that premium bond paper is recommended – any paper less than 80 gsm may be too light.

Finally, if you are involved in producing overhead transparencies on a photocopier, do make certain that you buy the special heat stabilised polyester film – at around 100 microns in weight. Any other type is likely to melt inside your photocopier and cause tremendous problems!

It is important that you note down the main points about paper types and weights in relation to the equipment you use regularly, ie:

- what type of paper is recommended
- what weights are acceptable (maximum and minimum).

You *must* make sure that any paper or card you order or use on the equipment falls within the acceptable parameters.

Supervising reprographics

The difficulty for the PA or administrator can be in relation to supervising others whose job it is regularly to use reprographic equipment. Considerations are likely to be mainly in relation to:

- monitoring/reducing costs
- monitoring work flow
- health and safety
- liaison between support staff undertaking copying/duplicating and users of the system
- copying confidential documents
- motivation of staff.

Costs are dealt with in the section above. Staff cannot be expected to keep these to a minimum if training is haphazard, formalised procedures are the same and monitoring of copying is non-existent. However, the PA who starts to introduce such measures into a previously uncontrolled area cannot expect to encounter no resistance. Sloppy work habits may be unacceptable but they also make for an easy life, and anyone trying to 'tighten up' such slackness may find entrenched resistance in some areas!

Good training of support staff is the first requirement so that they know the equipment well *and* know what is expected of them in terms of output and quality. Even in the case of a copier with a few simple buttons to press, junior staff will need help in learning how to schedule and prioritise work, how to 'clean up' unsuitable originals, and how and when to refer requests back for clarification.

A sensible turn-around time for producing documents is essential. Users will frequently try to beat any system by pleading emergencies, disasters or even their own incompetence! The difficulty for a PA is in devising a system which minimises disruptions and yet allows for genuine emergencies. One method can be to log such pleas in the early days, and comply with as many requests as possible. An objective view of the log at a later date will highlight those who operate on a last minute basis as their norm.

Genuine large-scale emergencies can sometimes be coped with by closing off one copier from general use for a few hours whilst involved or complicated work is completed.

Good communications are essential between support staff and those using the system to ensure that working relationships are harmonious and neither side is unnecessarily inconvenienced by the other. Users have a responsibility to make sure that their requests are reasonable, their originals are of good quality and their instructions unambiguous. Support staff have a responsibility to undertake the work carried out within the time specified, to produce work of high quality, and to keep the user informed if there are any problems or delays. You have the task of liaising between both, clarifying situations when necessary and, on occasion, arbitrating between conflicting demands or instructions.

Monitoring copy usage is essential *but* this is only effective if a realistic copy allocation is allowed per user – and this may vary from one person to another. It is hopeless trying to expect people to cooperate if the number they are allocated is well below their realistic requirement to do their job effectively. You are better served by minimising *wastage* than reducing actual copy allocations (and will often save more in the long run).

Confidential documents should be copied behind locked doors. In a busy area this may only be possible in the early morning or after hours – and this is a good reason why each PA should have access to a desktop machine which she can use in private when necessary.

Finally, every supervisor should be aware that constant copying or duplicating is not the most fascinating of jobs. The work can be boring, monotonous and even dirty. Staff need all the support you can give them – recognition for a job well done (rather than a constant stream of complaints for any minor faults) is a good first step to take. Encourage all reprographic staff to take a pride in their work and help them to realise their value to the organisation. Without them, all the elaborate typing, graphics and sales talk may be worthless. Your influence will be valued if you regularly support your staff and show a genuine appreciation of their efforts.

ACTIVITY SECTION

Individual tasks

1 From an office equipment catalogue, list the main office consumables required by a centralised print-room. Detail the type of paper/card required for both photocopiers and offset-litho duplicators, the various weights

available and the current cost of each type of paper that you list (plus VAT). Assume that your company purchases each month:

- 500 reams of 70 gsm copier paper
- 250 reams of 70 gsm offset paper and 200 reams of 85 gsm offset paper
- 50 reams of 70 gsm bond paper and 50 reams of 85 gsm watermarked bond paper
- 50 reams of 80 gsm printer paper for the laser printers.

a How much will the company spend on paper each month?

b If 10 per cent of this is wasted each month, what will be the saving to the company if you reduce wastage by 25 per cent?

2 Design a record form which will enable your organisation to monitor usage of *either* its photocopying or duplicating facilities on a monthly basis.

Draft out a short memo which could be completed by print-room staff to notify users if they were in danger of exceeding their specified copying allowance.

3 Your organisation has just purchased a new offset-litho duplicator and staff have recently been on a one day training session at the supplier's premises. On their return, you are alarmed to find that although they know how to operate the machine, they appear to have little consideration of health and safety issues.

a Make a list of the main considerations they should be aware of when operating the equipment.

b Photocopy your instructions on a piece of card which can be placed on the wall in the offset litho room.

Individual/group tasks

Case study 1

You are PA to Janice Hollins – recently appointed as Office Manager in your organisation. The company has two large photocopiers situated near the General Office and operates a centralised system of photocopying for all staff. In addition, separate desktop photocopiers are available for PAs wishing to carry out confidential or emergency copying.

Mrs Hollins is concerned that working relationships between the support staff in the copying room and the users in the sales department are poor. Many of the reps have complained about the system in operation saying that it is totally unsuitable for their needs. Their major complaints include:

- originals returned as 'unsuitable' without any warning whilst they (the reps) are out of the office, resulting in unacceptable delays in the eventual copying
- delays through constant equipment malfunctions – at least one copier always seems to be out of order
- no prioritisation by the copier staff so that urgent (but complicated) work is left whilst non-urgent, but more straightforward work is carried out immediately
- work received which is of poor quality and unsuitable for sending out to clients.

You have talked to the girls in the copying room. Rather than sympathise with the sales staff they have their own list of complaints:

- unclear instructions which are either unreadable or do not make sense

- reps who are not available or too busy to see them when they try to clarify instructions
- reps whose every piece of work is always urgent and who constantly harass the staff to copy it immediately
- one member of the sales staff who becomes abusive when work is delayed, of poor quality or not carried out in accordance with his instructions.

Mrs Hollins has decided to solve the problem by:

a devising a new system which will attempt to reconcile the conflicting demands of both staff

b calling two meetings next week, one for all sales staff and the second for all copier staff so that the situation can be clarified.

She has asked for your help as follows.

1 Design a clear form that the sales reps will complete when submitting their work for copying. The form should allow for all the common areas of misunderstanding which have been voiced by all staff.

2 Design a list of guidance notes for the reps, to accompany the new form.

3 On the basis that one machine is five years old and is in constant need of repair, investigate a suitable replacement which could cope with multi-page documents and offer a wide range of supplementary functions, eg duplex copying, automatic stapling and binding, a wide range of reduction and enlargement ratios etc.

   Detail your findings and recommendations in a memo to Mrs Hollins.

4 In a separate memo, detail your ideas for monitoring work through the department, so that both you and Mrs Hollins can see at a glance the progress of the various jobs which are received in the copying room.

5 Write a short list of standard procedures which the copier staff must follow from now on, to prevent problems occurring with poor quality printing, lack of prioritisation skills and inadequate communications. Clarify the type of issues which should be referred either to yourself or Mrs Hollins if there are continuing problems.

6 Mrs Hollins has considered that the matter should be dealt with in two separate meetings of staff, rather than one large meeting of all staff.
   a What advantages do you think there are in this approach? Are there any disadvantages?
   b Do you consider that a joint meeting would have been more effective? Justify your decision.
   c Draft out an agenda for both meetings, for Mrs Hollins' approval.

Case study 2

A new junior member of staff has recently been employed by your company to help with a range of reprographic requirements. You, as his supervisor, will be responsible both for his training and for monitoring his progress.

He has had some experience of operating a copier at college but the machine was totally different from the one which is used in your organisation. He has no idea how to cope with standard machine maintenance, nor how to rectify paper jams.

1 Write out a clear and precise list of instructions for him to follow when undertaking each of the following tasks:
   a refilling the paper tray
   b rectifying a paper jam
   c replenishing the toner and emptying the used toner
   d taking double sided copies.

2 Last week your new junior was involved in copying several papers for you. One document was a report following a disciplinary interview your boss had recently held with a member of staff. To your horror you have just heard on the grapevine that the details of this interview are now all round the building.
   a How would you approach your junior about this problem?
   b How would you respond to your boss, who holds you responsible?
   c What precautions could you take to prevent this type of problem recurring?

3 Several multi-page documents you produce require thermal binding. Note down the key points of this process and clearly and simply demonstrate how this is undertaken so that your junior can carry out this procedure on his own in future.

4 As you are responsible for ordering office supplies for your department, you find that the quantity of copier paper being used is now double what it was six months ago. Your boss wants to know the reason.
   a What investigations would you carry out before you meet your boss to discuss the matter?
   b What measures could be taken to lower the quantity being used, and how would you recommend that these are implemented?

Managing your boss

In order to win the war, it is first important to learn that it may be essential to lose the occasional battle . . .

Broadly speaking bosses can be divided into two categories:

- those who work *with* their PAs, support them, delegate as much responsibility as they can and encourage them to develop their knowledge and their skills
- those who don't!

In the latter category are many types of boss: some appear to have culti-vated the art of being deliberately difficult, and some are as yet 'untrained' – all they need is the guiding hand of a good PA to teach them how to get the most out of a good boss/PA relationship. If you are unfortunate enough to encounter a difficult boss then read the tips below. It may be, though, that in the final analysis all you can do is put it all down to experience – and move on. Learning when to cut your losses can be vital!

RULE 1

Good working relationships are like all relationships – they need to be built up over time and have to be worked at on a daily basis.
Two prerequisites are **mutual trust** and **respect**.

Most bosses *mean* well – and some can be terrific. It is up to you to try to bring out the best in your boss and to help to build up a good working relationship between you.
The benefits are tremendous:

- you will *both* accomplish more
- the atmosphere will be positive and friendly
- you know you can rely on each other – especially in a crisis.

It seems ridiculous that, with so much to gain, developing a good working relationship is not everyone's priority. There are many reasons for this – 'personality clashes' where you just *cannot* get on with some-one, a lack of communication, or simply not knowing where to start.

RULE 2

No boss was made in heaven – but neither were you! Don't let unrealistic expectations get you off to a bad start!

Every boss you will ever work for will have strengths and weaknesses, plus foibles, idiosyncracies and annoying habits – but will feel exactly the same about you! It is part of your job to be able to cope with these, use them to your advantage where possible and develop an *honest*, relationship where you can talk about things which are worrying you.

No list of 'types' of bosses is all-encompassing but below are some common 'types' you may find.

The female boss

She has usually worked hard to achieve her position and will therefore have very little patience with sub-standard work or sloppiness. Generally you can expect less sympathy for minor problems eg 'female' complaints, and possibly less praise because she will have high expectations. Don't expect her to eulogise, therefore, because you've tidied out the filing cabinet one afternoon.

On the positive side you may find she is highly supportive of your efforts to do well and climb the ladder yourself and easier to talk to about a genuine problem. Loyalty, discretion and hard work are *essential.*

RULE 3

Never try to bluff or charm your way past a female boss – she will see straight through your efforts! Don't forget, she's probably tried this one herself in the past!

All bosses are different. Therefore the characteristics below could apply to any boss, male or female.

RULE 4

Always try to identify the key traits of your boss before deciding what action to take.

Retired into the job

A doddle to work for – provided you're not ambitious! On the basis that a secretary's status is usually determined by that of her boss, if you stay with this boss then you will have to be happy with your achievements to date. There will be little pressure, and still fewer deadlines. You *could* hang on, on the basis that he/she will be gone in a couple of years and the successor might be more ambitious . . .

The laid back boss

Similar to the above, but usually younger. May have given up all hope of promotion (or be frantically searching outside the company). Will probably get on as your organisation will give this boss a fantastic reference just to get rid of him/her. Only too happy to delegate (probably everything!) and will never lose his/her temper with you or spell out how to do a job. Ideal for your first job, provided you realise that this boss is a 'one-off'.

The procrastinator

Puts off everything he/she doesn't want to do until the very last minute – and leaves you to take the flak. May take it out on you personally for reminding them (the 'shoot the messenger' syndrome). You *may* win, if you're skilful, by sheer bribery. Hold back something your boss wants until he/she has done something he/she doesn't want to do. If your boss is incorrigible you will have to decide where your priorities lie – if you defend him/her you may be labelled similarly yourself. If you are desperate you could appeal to one of his/her colleagues to have a word in private. If you are not bothered about the job or ruthlessly ambitious, then, in a final dramatic act, you could 'shop' your boss to a superior.

The pragmatist

Lets you think you are excellent in every way, whilst either damning you with faint praise outside his/her inner sanctum *or* making sure that nobody else in the organisation recognises your abilities. Will take the credit for your good work and blame you (to outsiders) for any mistakes (whether yours or not). The rationale is simply to hang on to you at all costs – and this will work if nobody else thinks you are any good at all. You may gain some consolation from the fact that usually other people are more aware of your boss's characteristics than you perhaps realise and may know that you are being deliberately undersold.

In the worst scenario, this boss will cheat and lie to keep you, eg giving you a bad reference if you want to move on. No easy answer. If you work for a large organisation you could try making your name known outside your own office, eg as Staff Social Committee chairman or organiser. One thing is for sure – if your boss goes down he/she will have no scruples about taking you down too.

The go-getter

This type of boss is ambitious and very image-conscious. It is vital you always play to his/her self-esteem. Never even *remotely* criticise your boss in front of others or put him/her on the spot, eg by asking tricky questions in a meeting he/she is chairing. Work hard and make your boss realise he/she won't get half as far without you as with you and you're probably on your way . . .

The high flier

Similar to the above although his/her image may be less important. Will probably be moving rapidly from company to company and you're more likely to 'acquire' than 'inherit' this type of boss. Make yourself indispensable (for the first few months) by demonstrating that you know the politics and the people of the organisation backwards. After that you're on your own – though if he/she sprints upwards you could gain promotion too.

The worrier or fusspot

Would probably like to be 'retired into the job' but his/her conscience won't allow it. Frets about every small detail *plus* what others say. You can help enormously by listening, keeping calm, giving support. Try to control the fussing, eg OK in front of you, not in the MD's office. You can easily make yourself indispensable by *never* letting your boss down, eg making sure all the right papers are available at the right time. He/she will be so reliant on you he/she will do anything for you –

including singing your praises to anyone who will listen. Normally a sweetie to work with (because he/she will also worry about you, too!), provided you can take some of the weight off his/her shoulders. Probably extremely conscientious and utterly supportive.

Professor Higgins

Wants to teach you everything he/she knows. Sees you as 'wasted' and wants to help you to get on. Probably very competent and totally secure in his/her own job. The best boss of all – listen and learn!

The status conscious

Very conscious of the fact that he/she is an executive and you are 'only' a PA or administrator. Views all PAs as glorified filing clerks and constantly reminds you of the difference in your status. Makes marginal changes, as a matter of principle, to everything you do. May play nasty tricks, like keeping you hanging on at the end of the day, just to prove who's boss. Difficult to deal with – hopeless if you're status conscious yourself! You may take quiet satisfaction out of outwitting him/her, eg put a minor error in every document so that your boss can happily point them out! Consider this type of boss a good motivator for really getting on in the future so that you can visit him/her later to show how important you have become.

The totally disorganised/incompetent/ruthlessly ambitious

Tolerate the situation only as long as it takes you to find another job.

The office Romeo

> **RULE 5**
> *Never*, for one second, think that you should have to put up with anyone's unwanted advances, just because you work for them.

This man is a pest – and *extremely* difficult to deal with if you are young and in your first job. Basically there are three facts you should consider:

- is he married or single?
- how much of a pest is he?
- how much do you like the job?

If he is single and the attraction is mutual then your actions are up to you. However – a word of warning – you are *always* better keeping your private life and your business life separate. It is very difficult to continue working for someone with whom you once had a close relationship if this has now ceased – with all the attendant bitterness which can be caused.

The *real* problem character is the one whose advances either embarrass or frighten you. You can, of course, complain officially of sexual harrassment, but this knowledge is of little use if you work for a one-man band or you would far prefer to resolve the situation amicably.

First stage

1 Talk a lot about your jealous boyfriend or strict father.

2 If he is much older than you, tell him how much he reminds you of your father (or grandfather, if you want to be really nasty).

3 Avoid being on your own with him and don't be silly and encourage him by making innuendoes yourself, wearing very short skirts etc.

If the above (ie gentle hints!) fail, then you will have to take your courage in both hands and practise assertiveness (see Chapter 6, Managing Communications, page 345).

Second stage

1 Say, firmly, that you would like to speak to him alone for a few minutes towards the end of the day. *Don't* give him any warning what it is about.

2 Sit down opposite him. Be business-like in tone, manner and voice. Tell him that you find his behaviour (eg constant innuendoes, touching you when he passes etc – be specific, give examples) unacceptable and that you genuinely feel that you cannot continue to do a good job for him if the situation continues. Say that if necessary you will leave but you would rather not. Ask him which he would prefer.

3 Expect him to be alarmed, and to refute your allegations (eg you're imagining it, he was only joking, you have no sense of humour).

4 *Don't argue with his assertions.* Say that you apologise if it is all your imagination but you would prefer to have no further incidents on which your imagination can run riot (or no more 'jokes' since you obviously haven't a sense of humour).

5 Thank him for listening and then get up and leave the room. *Don't* enter into any discussions. If you've timed it well and it is time to go home, then *go* and let him sleep on it.

6 Don't expect grovelled apologies – remember he has to save face (ie by treating it as a joke). Next day be calm and business-like and never mention the topic again, unless he persists – in which case either report him or leave. It just isn't worth the hassle to stay.

Training the untrainable

With *any* boss, aim to have certain 'minimum' standards upon which you insist. If you have a new, untried boss then introduce these slowly and gently, one by one.

1 Always ask for help, don't demand it (eg 'could you please do me a favour and . . .')

2 Be tactful, but firm (eg I'm sorry I can't do that for you now, I'm still trying to finish the urgent contract you gave me yesterday.')

3 Give praise when it is due.

4 Flatter your boss when things are going your way – you can afford to!

Standards to aim for	Strategy to try
Minimal interruptions when your boss knows you are already very busy	Look fraught. Make mistakes and apologise – say it happened when you were interrupted. Next time, smile sweetly and ask if you can come in and see him/her as soon as you've finished this important job. Say you're frightened of making mistakes again . . .
Planned workload to prevent havoc and unnecessary out of hours working	Have a busy week or two so you can't *possibly* stay, much as you'd like to. Pile up a few jobs, throw up hands in despair and ask your boss to prioritise them for you. Do as often as necessary.
Answers telephone when you are very busy or out of office *and* takes coherent message	Ask your boss to take over when you are doing the next vital job needed very quickly – if he/she refuses, miss the deadline – say you couldn't cope because of phone . . . *Don't* follow up incoherent messages – shrug, smile and say 'never mind – if it's vital I'm sure they'll get back to us'.
Understands filing system and will use it	Lose an important paper, ask your boss to help you find it. Put it somewhere obvious and give lots of praise when it is found. Your boss will then consider that he/she knows the system better than you do . . .
Delegates interesting jobs	Say you are attending a course to maximise your potential. You need help to give you challenges you can write about as course work. First job given, ask for help at certain points. Thank effusively. Progressively ask for less help so that your boss only gradually realises you don't need any . . .
Tells you what is going on, involves and includes you in key events	Make a key mistake based on lack of information. If he/she misses you out from key events send your boss off with a file with

ambiguous/muddled information or important paper missing. Apologise afterwards – if only you had been there . . .

Respects your abilities and gives you praise when it is due

Align your success and abilities with his/hers. Talk about how you have read that bosses get the PAs they deserve . . . only they hold the key to unlocking their PA's potential . . .

Dictates at a sensible pace

If your boss speeds up too much at a critical point, gasp and drop your notebook on the floor. That will hold everything for a few seconds. Alternatives include sneezing, coughing and deliberately breaking your pencil. Watch for your boss reading from notes. Cure by asking for the document 'so that you can copy type it' (to save your boss the time and trouble of reading it out). (See also Chapter 11, Shorthand transcription, page 510.)

RULE 6
Never become so enthusiastic about enlisting your boss's cooperation that he/she understands your job backwards. How can you be indispensable if the office runs just as smoothly when you are away?

In the final analysis, your boss needs your support just as much as you need his/hers. If he/she 'forgets' to help you out, then you can quietly look disappointed, and give a few gentle reminders.

Visibly appear to 'improve' as your boss starts to play things your way – and give him/her the credit. That way you might be losing the odd battle, but you should certainly win the war!

6 Processing correspondence

Identifying and responding to correspondence for your own action

Throughout the course of this book, emphasis has been placed on the difference between someone who carries out notetaking and keyboarding duties in an office and a PA. One of the most important differences you will note (or have already noted) is the way in which you are asked to deal with correspondence. As a junior you are normally expected to transcribe accurately the notes either dictated to you or given in the manuscript form and to display them in the required format. As a PA you may be the one who is doing the dictating! Even if you are not, there will certainly be occasions where you have to prepare the correspondence either on your own initiative or – at best – from brief written or verbal instructions.

To undertake this task you need a mixture of different skills. You must be capable of making a range of different decisions in relation to the type of document, the priority level and even the legal implications of your actions. You must be able to differentiate between the different types of correspondence and be capable of composing documents which are effective in a wide range of situations. Not least, you need the 'tools of the trade' – the ability to produce documents which are not only grammatically correct, but which are accurate in terms of punctuation and spelling. If you are in any way worried about your abilities in this area, then you are advised to turn to page 321 and work on the final part of this chapter first. If you are more confident of your skills then you can use it as a reference section at any time in your career.

Preparing the correspondence

One of your first tasks may be to decide what type of document is required. In some cases you may have no choice – your boss asks you to write a letter of reply to a complaint he/she has received. In other cases, however, you may have to decide whether a report or a memo, a notice or a letter etc is the most appropriate form of communication. Indeed you may decide that a written form of communication is inappropriate and that a telephone call will suffice.

Factors involved in choosing the correct document

Factors which could affect your choice of written medium include

Urgency In this instance you may query whether *any* written document is the correct form of communication and choose instead to use the telephone. There are occasions, however, when an urgent written communication is required, particularly when the information it contains is too long or complicated to be transmitted verbally, eg:

- details of current price lists and product information to a sales representative who needs them to close a deal
- a last minute request for information from a senior executive who needs it for a top level board meeting or conference or to send to an important client.

In such cases the use of fax or telex is obviously advisable.

Volume   A short item of information can be contained in a memo. A longer item may have to be contained in a report.

Cost   A ten minute transatlantic telephone call or expensive fax may be necessary on occasions (where urgency outweighs cost) – but only on occasion! Where possible use a cheaper method of communication such as a letter. You must remember, however, that there are 'hidden costs' in any written document, eg:

- preparation – gathering together the material and drafting out the reply (although even a telephone call requires some preparation)
- transcription
- proof-reading
- preparation for mailing
- stationery – letterhead/envelope/photocopy etc
- postage.

Accuracy   Normally any communication containing statistical or financial information should be in writing – there are too many opportunities for error if this type of information is transmitted verbally.

Image   This factor is often linked with that of cost. A handwritten note to a colleague is cheap and effective – so is a brief telephone call. Sales literature intended for use in a high profile sales presentation requires a more sophisticated approach. So, too, does a communication to a valued customer who would expect a well-presented letter.

On occasion your boss may want to write in the salutation and subscription on a letter. This indicates to the customer that he/she is held in regard by your boss. A completely handwritten item of correspondence from a senior executive to a client or colleague is also regarded as a mark of esteem.

Confidentiality   A notice on the staff noticeboard is not a suitable method of informing members of staff that they are to be made redundant or that certain individuals are going to get a pay rise!

Legal issues   Certain documents may have legal implications. If so, they should be in writing and couched in formal terms – a letter, a memorandum or a report rather than a brief note.

Preparation of correspondence   At this stage in your career or training you should be familiar with the standard layouts for all types of correspondence (see Chapter 5, Preparing and producing documents, page 259). You should also be capable of dealing with your boss's mail and of making decisions as to what is:

- to be dealt with by him/her
- to be handled by someone else
- your responsibility.

Some bosses are more than willing to let you make such decisions; others are more cautious. Normally the longer your working relationship with your boss and the greater the trust shown in your judgement, the greater will be your responsibility in this area.

If you are given this responsibility, in the early stages you should be able to rely upon your boss to help you by checking with you some of the decisions you have made. After that initial stage you need refer back only matters about which you are uncertain.

 TEST YOURSELF

You work for the Managing Director of a company which manufactures garden furniture. The following items of correspondence have appeared in his in-tray. Classify them into:

- those items with which your boss should deal directly
- those with which you can deal independently
- those with which you can deal initially but which then require reference back to your boss
- those which you can hand over to others.

1 A letter from a shareholder asking whether the annual company report will make any reference to company policy on the employment of disabled workers.

2 A note from the Office Manager asking for a copy of the departmental staff holiday list.

3 A memorandum from the Catering Manager asking for details of the catering arrangements required for the next lunchtime meeting of the Board of Directors.

4 A letter from a large supplier apologising for a delay in supplying some raw materials and asking if a further two week delay is acceptable.

5 A letter from a company offering a reduced rate telephone cleaning service on a monthly basis.

6 A letter from an irate customer complaining that one of your company's chairs she had bought from a large department store has become rusted and unusable after only a month's use.

7 A letter from the owner of a chain of small furniture stores asking for an up-to-date catalogue and price list.

8 A letter from an unemployed labourer asking if there are any vacancies.

Establishing priorities

You must be able to prioritise the order in which you deal with and reply to correspondence in exactly the same way as you prioritise your other work (see Chapter 7, Organising work schedules, page 374).

Working in chronological order through your boss's in and out trays, through your shorthand notebook or through an audio-dictation tape is not a good idea. You should sort out the correspondence in the mail trays into urgent and less urgent items both for your attention and that of your boss. As you were being given dictation you should have been annotating items to indicate their importance or the need for an urgent response (see Chapter 11, Shorthand transcription, page 523). Dictation on an audio-cassette is less easy to re-sort. In this case try to impress upon your boss the need to:

- dictate the items in order of importance (which may be rather a forlorn hope!)
- leave a space at the beginning of each cassette so that at the end of the dictation he/she can use it to give some indication of urgent items
- attach a note to the cassette with similar indications.

TEST YOURSELF

In your boss's out-tray are the following pieces of correspondence.

1 A reminder that a notice should be sent to all sales representatives giving them details of the price increases on the new summer range of products.

2 A note asking you to refuse on his behalf an invitation to an official banquet at the Town Hall next week.

3 Notes for a letter to accompany an article for a business magazine – the deadline for receipt of which is this coming Friday.

The items on the dictation machine are:

4 A letter to a customer demanding *full* payment of an outstanding account.

5 A memorandum to the Managing Director giving him details of the press release which is to be sent to the major newspapers in the next few days.

6 A reply to the Health and Safety representative who has queried the way in which some dangerous substances are being stored in apparent contravention of the COSHH regulations.

Your notebook contains the following items:

7 A report intended for circulation to the members of the Joint Consultative Committee before next month's meeting.

8 A letter replying to a request for a donation from a charity.

9 An 'in sympathy' letter to the wife of an ex-employee following his recent death.

List the order in which you will deal with each item (from 1 – 9) and give reasons for your decision.

Quality control

Quality control is another 'in' word. In this context all it means is that you should institute a system which prevents substandard correspondence leaving your office.

In some organisations a senior executive has the overall responsibility for all quality issues within that company. One of his/her duties is normally to keep a check on the standard of correspondence and in some cases he/she may ask for a number of 'sample' copies of correspondence which have been issued by each department each week. This can cause problems, however, and you may find that you are acting as a buffer between this executive, your boss and your staff.

A more usual method is for you either to set your own standards as to layout and style or to ensure that the company 'house style' is followed.

Questions you should ask are:

- Have *all* the original instructions been carried out?
- Has the most suitable form of communication been used? Have you, for instance, written a memorandum, which on reflection you feel should have been a report?
- Has the correct paper choice been made?
- Has the correct layout been chosen?
- Is it dated? (The date is almost always included on a letter or memo but quite often forgotten on a report or notice – where it should appear at the foot of the document.)
- Are the enclosures mentioned in the correspondence actually enclosed?
- Have the requisite number of copies been taken?
- Should it be marked 'Personal', 'Confidential' etc?
- Have any specific mailing instructions been included?
- What is the overall impression? Can you see any errors in grammar, punctuation and spelling? (If you're not sure, turn to page 321!) Does it 'read' well?
- Have any 'follow up' reminders been placed in the appropriate system?
- Has it been signed or initialled?

SPECIAL NOTE
It may be company policy that:

- your boss signs all correspondence
- you sign some items on your boss's behalf, eg Susan Carpenter, Personal Assistant to Mr F Charteris, Managing Director
- you sign your boss's name but add your initials.

Whatever method is chosen, note the legal effect of a signature. It is binding. (See also Chapter 5, Preparing and producing documents, page 264.)

Legal implications

A letter or other written document may look innocuous. In some cases, however, it can cause endless legal problems. Your boss should be aware, for instance, of the law relating to copyright, defamation and negligence. So should you.

Defamation

It is defamatory to publish, ie to put in writing for someone else to read, anything about a person which could 'lower him/her in the eyes of right thinking people'. If, therefore, you write something defamatory you may be accused of libel (if you write it down) or slander (if you communicate it by telephone). Before setting light to everything in your filing cabinet, however, remember that you have certain defences.

- You can claim 'justification', ie that the statement is true (bear in mind, however, that if you do use this defence and repeat what has been said, the damages awarded against you will be increased if you lose the case).
- A safer defence is that of 'qualified privilege'. It is accepted, for instance, that letters of reference are a necessary part of business life. Consequently, if you provide a reference you are entitled to be blunt, eg 'She is incompetent'. You must not, however, make the statement maliciously. If malice is proved, ie that you intended to damage that person's reputation rather than give your honest opinion to the person to whom you are writing, then your defence crumbles.

Negligence

If someone suffers damage as a result of a careless statement made by you, you may be liable in negligence. In one case a bank was asked to give a reference about the creditworthiness of a particular company. It was negligent in supplying the information (it actually gave information about the wrong company) which resulted in a loss of money for the company which had asked for that information. In the first instance, the bank was held to have been negligent. However, it had taken the precaution of putting a **disclaimer** in its letter and was therefore able to escape liability.

Remember this case when writing a letter of reference – a disclaimer is a very useful 'escape mechanism'!

Types of correspondence

The standard list from which you would normally choose includes

- a letter
- a memo
- a report or factsheet*
- a notice
- a bulletin/newsletter/house journal
- an invitation
- a press release
- minutes of a meeting*.

(* for further information see Chapter 2, Researching and retrieving information, page 127 and Chapter 8, Servicing meetings, page 394.)

Letters

Given that by now you are likely to have typed a large number of letters you will probably already have realised that the most acceptable structure for most letters comprises:

- an introduction or opening paragraph which should state the reason for writing
- the 'body' of the correspondence. Remember that it is usual to:
  - use a number of short paragraphs rather than one long one
  - give the most important information first, the least important last
  - move from the 'known' (ie information both parties already have) to the 'unknown'
  - list advantages and disadvantages separately where relevant
  - list information in chronological order
- the closing paragraph which should:
  - state the desired outcome
  - if relevant, give an indication of the time at which this action should take place.

The major types of business letter can generally be classified into those which:

- make or answer an enquiry
- give or request details of goods, products or services
- issue an order/statement/tender
- make or answer a complaint
- seek settlement of a debt or payment of an account
- check financial status or creditworthiness
- authorise credit advances
- outline interview arrangements
- offer or refuse employment
- outline conditions of employment
- give references.

Less frequently required letters include those which:

- give thanks
- give sympathy
- offer congratulations
- issue or reply to invitations
- reply to charitable appeals.

Given the relevant information you should be able to compose a suitable letter for most occasions. Certain types of letters, however, need particular attention, eg:

- because they are 'selling' your company and you want therefore to present the best possible impression
- because they are dealing with a topic, the potential repercussions of which could be either very beneficial or very harmful to your company
- because you need some urgent action to be taken.

In such cases it may be helpful for you to have to hand a skeleton outline of the way in which such information should be presented (or requested).

Sales letters

There are several formats recommended for sales letters. One approach is AIDA ie:

- every sales letter should gain the reader's **A**ttention
- their **I**nterest should be aroused and held
- their **D**esire should be kindled
- they should be persuaded into taking some **A**ction.

An alternative American method is divided into four similar stages:

- 'Ho Hum!' – the opening gambit designed to attract attention
- 'Why bring that up?' – answers designed to point out the benefits of the proposition
- 'For instance?' – claims are supported with examples
- 'So what?' – the request for an order, a signature etc.

Another approach is to remember the three P's:

- **P**icture – what the thing you are selling is like
- **P**romise – what it will do for the buyer
- **P**ush – now buy it!

Examples

Opening paragraphs

How to be safe rather than sorry!

How many work hours did you lose last year because of injury related illness?

Body of letter

Let our company solve all your problems by advising you on the correct safety equipment for your particular organisation – and all the up-to-date UK and EC legislation.

The benefits to you
– fewer accidents
– increased production
– higher morale
– NO legal repercussions

Closing paragraphs

Why not telephone us . . . and ask for Peter Clark. He will be happy to give you more details, without any obligation whatsoever on your part.

Hadn't you better get in touch with us right away?

Our representative will be in your area next month and will phone you before then to arrange a mutually convenient appointment.

Complete the enclosed pre-paid reply card if you want further details of our service.

May I come along and tell you more about this service?

TEST YOURSELF
Many organisations prefer to end their sales letters by retaining the initiative, ie they do not give the customer control over the next move to be made in the selling game. Can you identify which of the above closures loses the initiative and which retains it?

Acknowledging orders

It is relatively simple to acknowledge an order when you are able to supply the goods. It is a different matter if, for some reason, the goods cannot be supplied. To help you, examples are given below which cover both alternatives. Do remember not to promise anything you cannot fulfil. If you know there is no hope of supplying the goods within a certain period don't let the customer think there is. In the long run it will do more harm than good to customer relationships.

Opening paragraphs
Many thanks for your first order. We look forward to being of service to you and appreciate your interest in our products.

Thank you for your first order which we received today. It is a pleasure to welcome you as a new customer and we look forward to doing business with you.

Thank you for your order No . . . dated 16 October . . .

Body of the letter
a if the goods can be supplied

The order will go out by parcel post next week and should reach you well before the date you specify.

We are putting your order into production immediately and shall let you know its date of despatch as soon as possible.

The goods ordered can be supplied from stock and will be sent to you on . . . .

The goods will be sent within . . . days/weeks.

b if the goods cannot be supplied

Every item on your order except . . . will be sent to you from stock within the next few days. The rest of the order will be sent as soon as possible, certainly within 14 days.

Unfortunately we are unable to meet your requested delivery date. The response to the advertisement has been so overwhelming that we are having difficulty in keeping up with demand. However, we hope to be able to supply you with the goods by the end of the month.

Unfortunately the item you have ordered is no longer in stock. Could we suggest that an alternative might be . . . .

Closing paragraphs   We look forward to hearing from you.

Thank you again.

If we can be of assistance to you in the future please do not hesitate to contact us.

SPECIAL NOTE
As a PA you may not be expected actually to prepare statements, invoices or accounts. Nor are you likely to have to draw up tenders. What you may have to do is to check that:

- they have been sent out
- they have resulted in a response.

CHECK IT YOURSELF
Either at work or from the NVQ Level 2 Financial Administration handbook check that you know the steps to be taken in the ordering and invoicing of goods and the way in which a statement of accounts is drawn up. Check also that you understand clearly the difference between a quotation, an estimate and a tender.

TEST YOURSELF
You work for the Managing Director of a company which manufactures fireplaces. One customer is always submitting incomplete orders and tends to describe what he wants in imprecise terms, eg he will say that wants 'one of those Victorian style fireplaces' rather than indicating the order number specified in the catalogue. As a result he tends to argue about what has actually been supplied and takes little notice of the invoice. He often disputes the statement of account and delays payment as long as possible. Draft a letter for your boss to sign which:

- emphasises the necessity for a correct order (and for payment on time)
- outlines the company's invoicing procedure.

Credit checks
Although payment on credit is a common business transaction it is

open to abuse and it may be that you are asked to refuse credit terms to a particular customer. Be careful! Although the decision to refuse credit is not likely to be yours, the way in which you write the letter can either calm or exacerbate the situation!

Opening paragraph	Thank you for your letter in which you ask for credit facilities.
Body of letter	While we are not at the moment in a position to comply with your request, we hope it will be possible for us to do so at a later date.
	Unfortunately, however, as you have in the past tended to be rather slow in paying invoices we feel that at the moment it would be wiser to continue our dealings on a cash only basis
	Note Remember defamation – be *very* careful!
Closing paragraphs	We are sorry to have to refuse you credit but feel that, as a businessman yourself, you will appreciate our position.

Outstanding payment

If you are asked to remind someone of an outstanding payment, be prepared to write a series of letters at intervals of 10 to 15 days. Remember always to bear in mind the desired result. However tempted you may be to send off a series of increasingly abusive letters you may find this counter-productive – at least at first when persuasion rather than threat is to be advised. Even a final demand in which you state that legal action will be taken need not necessarily be rude. Persistence is the key!

Recommended stages

First reminder	May we remind you that there is a balance due on your account.
	Note In the US it is common to use a 'humorous' tone on a first reminder – often in the form of a printed reminder card, eg:

> Your bill's overdue
> I'm surprised at you!
> Please pay at once
> We know you're no dunce

	It's supposed to work, anyway!
Follow-up(s)	Do you recall our sending you a reminder about your overdue account?

Possibly our reminder about your overdue account has escaped your attention. If it did, may we remind you again to send you the payment within the next few days.

We are disappointed to note that despite several reminders you have still not settled your outstanding account.

Your account has now been outstanding for a considerable period. We must therefore insist that we receive full payment from you within the next seven days.

Final reminder

Unfortunately, you leave us no choice but to withhold further deliveries until this amount is paid. *(If you are able to do that)*

We regret that we have no option but to hand the matter over to our legal advisers.

SPECIAL NOTE

Bear in mind that at any stage of the correspondence it is possible that your letter and their payment may cross in the post. For this reason it is wise to include a proviso in case payment has just been sent, eg:

If you have already sent the payment please accept our thanks.

Remember, however, that a claim that 'the cheque is in the post' is a very common delaying tactic! Remember also that some payments arrive in instalments. Keep going but acknowledge the part-payment.

Finally, don't forget to distinguish between a letter of reminder to an individual asking him/her to fulfil an obligation and one in which you are reminding him/her to do you a favour, eg supply some information. Again persistence is the key. Consider such phrases as 'At the risk of being a bore, may I ask you to . . .' or 'I know how busy you are but dare I remind you . . .'

TEST YOURSELF

As light relief, prepare an American-style reminder card for your own organisation. Use verse and an appropriate illustration or logo.

Complaints

Making complaints

Be specific and give facts rather than vague generalisations. Make reference to back-up information. Remain polite even though you may feel you have been driven beyond endurance. Start gently – do not use up all your ammunition at the first stage. Decide on the best person to whom to address your complaint – the easy answer is to say that it should be addressed to the Managing Director, the Chief Executive etc. It might be a good idea, however, for you to keep this as your last resort. Otherwise you risk antagonising more junior personnel with whom you may have later dealings.

Opening paragraph	I do not often have cause to complain about your organisation but for the second time in three weeks an order has been delivered in which several of the items were missing.
	I must complain about the unsatisfactory way in which my enquiry about possible job vacancies was dealt with by your reception staff.
	Since you installed my central heating system last May, it has broken down on three occasions.
Body of the letter	I give below a detailed list of the shortages in the order . . .
	When I arrived at the reception desk I was asked to wait. This I did for 20 minutes but eventually asked the receptionist if she could help. She told me she could not and that if I did not wish to wait any longer I could always leave.
	Your maintenance engineer has been called out on each occasion but has been able to effect only temporary repairs.
Closing paragraphs	I should be grateful if you would look into this matter.
	I must insist on some further action being taken without delay.
	Unless I hear from you within the next few days I shall take the matter further.
	I have complained many times. This is the last.

Responding to complaints

Check and double-check the facts. Answer all the complaint, not just one part (although concentrate on the stronger part of your response). Say sorry – you'd be surprised how often this disarms even the most irate customer.

Opening paragraphs	I was concerned to hear that you had not received the goods you ordered.
	We do apologise for the apparently offhand treatment you received when you called in to our office last week.
	I am concerned to hear that you are so dissatisfied with our after-sales service.

Body of the letter	I shall make sure that the goods are delivered to you without delay and that no further mistakes are made.
	I have investigated the matter and find that during the period in question the senior receptionist was off duty.
	I have discussed the problem with my senior engineer who assures me that the system is now in full working order.
Closing paragraph	I apologise again.
	I hope that the matter is now resolved.
	Please let me know if you have any further problems/require any further information.

SPECIAL NOTE

Even if you are 100 per cent sure that you are at fault, it might still be a good idea for you not to admit *complete* liability because of possible legal repercussions. Words and phrases such as 'apparently', 'it may have appeared', 'a misunderstanding' etc are useful.

Note also that if you feel the complaint is unjustified (or that the writer is a regular or 'professional' complainer) you can take a slightly different approach. Remain polite – you have nothing to lose – but do not put yourself in a false position. Use sentences such as 'while we are very sorry that you are upset about . . . we must point out that . . .' or 'I am sorry but rather surprised that you were annoyed by my letter' etc.

TEST YOURSELF

You are the PA to the Managing Director of a chain of bookshops. You receive a letter from a customer who complains that he has tried unsuccessfully to order several books over the past few months. On the first occasion he was told that an ordering service was not available. On the second occasion he was asked to complete a form with the details of the book he wanted. Although he was told that it would be in stock within three weeks, two months later it has still not arrived. Last week he tried to order another book but was told that it was pointless because 'the ordering system is in chaos' and he would be better writing to the publisher direct or going to another bookshop.

You make enquiries and find that on the first occasion it was a new Saturday-only assistant who dealt with the matter. The book the customer ordered on the second occasion is a best seller, is in reprint and the publishers have promised to send a new supply by the end of next week. No one admits to having been involved on the third occasion!

Write a letter of reply for your boss to sign.

The circular letter

You may be asked to prepare a circular letter to be sent to a large number of people who may be from different backgrounds and also unknown to you. In such circumstances the way in which the letter is written has to differ from a letter from one correspondent to another.

- There must be a more general salutation, eg Dear colleague, friend, subscriber.
- As this communication is normally unsolicited, it should be brief and eye-catching as well as informative.
- The tone should be friendly and informal.

TEST YOURSELF

In many cases, circular letters are sales promotion letters. However, they can also be used on other occasions. Suggest some.

Alternatives to the standard letter

Cost is always a factor which has to be taken into account. There is little point, therefore, in composing a full reply to a letter when a cheaper written alternative may suffice.

A 'blitz' reply

Where a letter requires either a 'yes', 'no' or 'noted' answer you may wish to use the option of writing this reply on the original letter, taking a photocopy of it and sending back the original. This method can also be used to 'buy time', eg by writing a note such as 'will reply in full in the next two weeks' or 'information to be sent out within 10 days' etc. Organisations which receive a large number of requests for information use this method – many of them have special rubber stamps specially printed for this purpose.

TEST YOURSELF

Even in cases where a very brief answer is possible, in what circumstances would it *not* be advisable to use the 'blitz' method of replying?

Quick reply forms

Another cost-saving device is the use of a quick reply form which is normally printed in triplicate, in three different colours on NCR paper. It is divided into a left hand and right hand section. If used as a letter it is printed in the same way as a letterhead.

The sender of the letter writes the message on the top copy and sends it, together with the second copy to the recipient, and keeps the third copy for temporary reference. The recipient writes the reply on the top copy, keeps it for reference and sends back the second copy. The temporary file copy can then be destroyed.

The advantages are considerable, eg:

- replies are normally short
- certain information need not be repeated
- an immediate check can be made that all points have been answered.

You should note, however, that because of the increased use of fax this method of communication seems to be decreasing in importance.

CHECK IT YOURSELF
Either in your own organisation or in your work experience placement, check to see if any department or section operates a quick reply system.

Form letter

More frequently used are form letters which come in a variety of designs. They are normally pre-printed to give the recipient a number of options of replying. The advantages include:

- a number of specific options can be outlined which makes any subsequent action needed easier to identify
- the fact that the sender or recipient need only tick a box or circle an entry rather than make a written response may encourage a response.

Examples include

- letters which highlight discrepancies in invoices, eg:

You have not
sent the required number of copies ☐
signed the copies ☐
given the current discount ☐

- letters pointing out mistakes made in the writing of cheques, eg:

You have
failed to sign the cheque ☐
failed to date the cheque ☐
filled in the incorrect amount ☐
mismatched the written amount
with the amount given in figures ☐
etc.

Overseas correspondence

If you work in a company which has a number of overseas clients, you should be aware of company policy on the way in which correspondence should be handled. In large multinational organisations there will be a team of translators to deal with the correspondence. Smaller organisations may call upon the services of translators provided through various agencies. Alternatively, the organisation may employ bilingual PAs.

In such circumstances you will have to do little more than give details of exactly what is required. When any replies are received you return to the same sources for translation.

If, however, you want to send a letter overseas which is written in English (in the expectation – or hope – that your correspondent can read it or will be prepared to have it translated) you should remember to:

- write in short sentences
- use simple language
- avoid colloquialisms or jargon
- give the meaning of any abbreviations
- avoid any over-long introductory or closing paragraphs.

Remember – even if you are sending correspondence to someone in a country such as the USA, you should nevertheless try to avoid the use of words which have different meanings in both countries. (See Chapter 1, Communication systems, page 36.)

Memoranda

The memorandum – or memo as it is more usually known – is a document for internal use and can therefore normally be couched in more informal terms than correspondence which is intended for external use. It is a useful way in which to remind staff of certain jobs or to keep them in touch with current developments.

Points to note are given below.

- Apart from the usual memo heading – To/From/Date/Subject – no salutation is necessary. Neither is a complimentary close. It is usual for a memo to be initialled rather than signed.
- Although most memos are likely to be brief and their subject matter contained in a couple of short paragraphs, this is not always the case. Some memos can be quite long, particularly if they are explanatory (eg outlining new mailroom procedures) and in such circumstances can become akin to a report.
- Memos are usually sent through the internal mail or – if urgent – delivered by hand. Most memos from head office to branch offices are normally treated as letters although if the company has an electronic mail network then they will be sent by this method for speed and economy (see Chapter 1, Communication systems, page 64.)
- Multiple circulation of a memo can cause problems. Assuming there is no electronic mail network then you have the choice of either sending a separate copy to each individual concerned (with all names being typed on the top copy and ticked off individually) or one copy may be routed with an attached circulation slip.

  You can distinguish between those recipients by whom some action must be taken and those who have received the memo for information purposes only by putting FIO (for information only) or FYI (for your information) after the appropriate name.
- Be careful to use both name and job title if there is even the slightest

possibility of confusion. In a large organisation there may be a number of J Smiths. Where necessary, include room location.

- One problem of protocol which can arise is the order in which names should be listed. You have the choice of typing them:
  – alphabetically
  – by location
  – according to rank
  – according to job priority.
- Be careful when dealing with confidential memos. Most memos are not in envelopes – confidential memos must be. You should be particularly careful about transmitting confidential information over an electronic mail system unless there is an effective password system. Remember to store mail you wish to keep – or take a hard copy – if your particular system purges mail automatically after a certain period. You must also remember that if you or your boss has prepared a hasty or ill thought out memo it can be recalled easily from an out-tray. On some electronic mail systems you can retrieve it only if the recipient has still to read it – on others you can't recall it at all!

TEST YOURSELF

1 Look back at the different methods of listing names. Discuss as a group the advantages and disadvantages of each one. What method would you recommend?

2 You work for the Head of a Business Studies Department in a college. It is departmental policy that all full-time students should undertake at least two weeks' work experience each year. Because of the large number of students in the department, however, there have been certain problems in finding suitable placements for them all. It has been suggested that a part-time clerical officer be appointed to undertake this task. Another suggestion has been that work experience placements be spread out more evenly throughout the year, although tutors have made the point that to do so may involve clashes with examination schedules and final assessments of coursework. One tutor has suggested that consideration be given to the idea of sending students out on a one day per week basis (possibly to coincide with groups of part-time students attending college so that employers may be more willing to take a student replacement on those days). Your Head decides to discuss the matter at the next meeting of her senior team of six Divisional Managers. She wants them to have this information before the meeting (to be held on Wednesday of next week) and asks you to prepare a memo outlining the main points for discussion.

SPECIAL NOTE

An even more common form of written communication within an organisation is a scribbled note. There is nothing inherently wrong with this method but it has its drawbacks. It can get lost easily and its importance may be overlooked because of the way in which it is presented. In such circumstances you should consider the use of action slips which can be produced in small packs of brightly coloured paper with or without a printed heading. In some organisations each department has its own colour; in others, the executives use individually coloured slips so that messages from them can be identified at a glance.

You may also like to consider the use of pads, the sheets of which are held attached at the top by adhesive and which, when separated, retain some of that adhesive, eg Post-it notes. The messages are then easier to attach to desktops, typewriters etc.

Notices

You may be asked to communicate the same information to a large number of people within the organisation. To communicate directly with everyone is both a lengthy and an expensive process and in some cases it may be better to display the information in notice form.

Points to note are given below.

- Check that the notice board(s) on which the notices are to be displayed are:
  - well sited (not at the end of a long little-used corridor)
  - large (the norm is to have one to every 50 employees – more are preferable)
  - attractive (clean, in bright colours etc).
- Organise the boards to accommodate various types of notices, eg permanent notices, notices about events held at regular intervals, 'one off' notices etc. Remember that permanent notices should be laminated (to prevent their becoming dirty and fingermarked) and displayed separately.
- Write the notice so that *everyone* can understand it (if you write a letter or other document to a named individual, you normally have some idea of the type of person likely to read it. With a notice, you have not.)
- The language should be clear and simple. The style should normally be informal (unless it is a permanent notice outlining details of disciplinary procedures etc). Avoid saying 'May I draw your attention to the new opening hours of the canteen'. Say instead 'ATTENTION ALL CANTEEN USERS – note the new opening hours!'
- Be brief. Few people read notices anyway – *very* few read long notices.
- Check whether or not it is company policy to have notices signed. Normally they are. Remember always to date a notice – this will help your junior if you delegate to her the job of checking notice boards regularly to remove out-dated material.

 TEST YOURSELF

As a group:

1 Identify the circumstances in which a notice would not be a suitable form of communication.

2 The following information has been received. It is your job to write and prepare attractive and eye-catching notices. Group these appropriately either on an actual noticeboard or on a suitable sized piece of card.

- The Staff Welfare Group want to know if anyone is interested in becoming a member of the local health and fitness club – reduced rates are being offered if a group of more than 20 people apply. Expressions of interest to Louise Inman (ext 324).
- Joseph Akinwumi in the Accounts Department (ext 532) has been given a set of garden gnomes as a birthday present. He doesn't want them and will accept offers from £15 onwards.
- Up-to-date information about changes to the existing pension scheme is now available from Kathleen Lambert in the Personnel Department (ext 335).
- Peter Ellington (Purchasing Department) is now the proud father of a little girl (Mary Elizabeth).

Bulletins and staff newsletters

There are certain jobs in an office which are passed from hand to hand but which somehow always end up as part of the PA's job description. The preparation of a bulletin or the staff newsletter tends to fall into this category. If it is intended to be an informal document containing short items of information and 'gossip' you should have little difficulty (other than making the time to collect, prepare and edit the material).

Points to note are given below.

- The frequency of production – if you have to prepare one each week you need some assistance, or at least relief from other duties.
- The format required. The normal procedure is to collate the information in numbered points under a heading such as 'Staff Bulletin w/e 25 March' etc. Note that some bulletins have an on-going numbering system so that one copy of the issues for the entire year can be kept for reference purposes.
- The type of information. Examples include:
  - information about certain company activities, eg the opening of a new branch office; promotions; transfers; new appointments; launch of new products; references in the press; extracts from AGM reports
  - general information eg changes in car parking arrangements; new security arrangements
  - 'fun' items, eg who has become engaged/married, had a baby, achieved the Duke of Edinburgh's Award.

Remember that it is always advisable to check that the personnel concerned in the last item will actually appreciate their names being mentioned – and to double check that the facts are correct! Be wary also of mentioning someone's age – many people (of both sexes) are very sensitive to public announcements of this. You could make an enemy for life if you confirm what the office staff have suspected for ages – that Mr Parker, who prides himself on his youthful image, is really ten years older than he has always claimed to be!

Bear in mind that some organisations pride themselves on their good industrial relations and, to foster that image, spend time and money on the preparation of a House Journal which, in effect, is an up-market version of the staff newsletter or bulletin. In such circumstances you may be asked to make a contribution but are unlikely to be in charge of the entire production.

Advertisements

A job you may have to undertake is the preparation of advertisements – particularly secretarial job advertisements. (Unless you work in a small organisation you will probably find that other advertisements will be dealt with centrally.)

Although you should be able to get some guidelines from the newspaper or journal in which you place the advertisement, bear in mind that this is a form of communication in which cost is a major factor.

You should first of all carry out the following procedure.

- Check on a number of possible outlets; obtain details of costs, types of layout, distribution area, numbers of entries etc. Consider specialist journals, eg if you are advertising for a PA to the Personnel Manager an obvious outlet would be the Journal of Personnel Management. Consider also the use of Job Centres.
- Check with your boss where the advertisement should be placed (although if you have carried out sufficient research you should be able to give some advice in this respect). Check on the amount he/she wishes to spend.
- Check whether your boss wishes the name of the organisation to be included in the advertisement or whether he/she prefers a box number.
- If required, draft out the advertisement. It should be:
  - factual
  - informative but brief
  - eye-catching but in line with your company image. A traditional organisation may want to 'play it straight'; a modern one might prefer a 'Hey, are you just what we're looking for?' approach.
- If the advertisement is to be inserted in several different outlets, make certain that you ask applicants to state where they read the advertisement. You can then assess which outlets are the most useful.

Invitations

The normal rule is that 'like must match like'. If you receive an invitation which is in letter form, you should reply in the same format. Similarly, a formal invitation should be given a formal response, eg:

```
                                    Oakworth House
                                       Saddleworth
                                   4 October 199–

Mr and Mrs R Samuels have pleasure in inviting
you to the 21st birthday party of their
daughter, Rebecca, to be held at their home on
Saturday, 3 November 199– at 8 pm.

RSVP
```

Points to note:

- It used to be customary to have invitations typed on plain cards of A5 paper. Nowadays pre-printed cards are more popular.
- If the name of the recipient is to be included it is normal to handwrite it rather than type it, eg:

```
Mr and Mrs R Samuels have pleasure in inviting
..........Mr T Raphael...........
to the 21st birthday party of their daughter ...
```

etc.

- The information should be complete, ie:
  – the date, day and time of the function
  – the venue
  – the purpose.
- The third person, ie 'Mr and Mrs R Samuels' should be used in preference to the first person, ie 'We'.

If, therefore, your boss asks you to reply to such an invitation, you would use the following format.

```
                                   24 Kenilworth Road
                                             Farnham
                                     17 October 199–


Mr T Raphael has much pleasure in accepting
Mr and Mrs R Samuels' kind invitation to the
21st birthday party of their daughter, Rebecca,
to be held at their home on Saturday, 3 November
at 8 pm.
```

If your boss wanted to refuse the invitation, the refusal should be couched in the same terms although it is usual to give a reason for the refusal, eg another engagement etc, eg:

```
Mr T Raphael regrets that he cannot accept Mr and
Mrs R Samuels' kind invitation . . . He is out of
the country on a business trip on that date.
```

Don't forget to distinguish between a personal and a business invitation. In the latter case the address given would be that of the organisation. Remember, too, to check whether your boss's partner is included in the invitation. If so, you should reply for both of them.

Press releases

On occasion you may be asked to prepare a press release for either your local or a national newspaper – if someone is retiring after 30 years' service; if your company is launching a new product or opening a new annexe; if it is celebrating its centenary etc. Sometimes such a press release forms part of an advertisement feature (in which case you pay for the insertion). In other cases it forms part of the general news section and is a channel of free publicity. In the latter case in particular therefore you should try to assist the sub-editor by setting out the information in a specific form, ie:

- Use A4 paper and a clear and concise heading (but don't be upset if the sub-editor changes this!),
- Since the article may have to be cut, it should be written so that it can be 'pruned' from the last sentence upwards. Make sure, therefore, that you put the most important information *first.*
- Be factual rather than imaginative – the sub-editor should attach the appropriate captions and 'jazz up' the style if necessary. Be very careful to check and doublecheck the facts. Even the mildest person can become irritated if he sees his name mis-spelled or, having given you permission to say how old he is, finds that he has aged ten years because you typed 70 in place of 60! If you have any doubts as to the technical accuracy of an item of information ask an expert to check it for you.
- If you are sending the article to several newspapers, alter each version slightly. Papers tend not to like copies of a release which has been sent to their competitors.
- If you include a photograph, make sure that the appropriate caption or information is written on a label which is then attached firmly to the reverse. *Never* write directly on the reverse of a photograph – the pressure shows through and the photograph cannot be used for printing.
- Always include a name, telephone number and extension number of someone the press can contact for further information.

Tools of the trade

When you accept a job as a PA or administrator you will be *expected* to have certain skills. One such skill is that of being able to put together a grammatically correct piece of work with no spelling or punctuation errors.

It may be difficult for you, however, to determine just how good you are. The following section is designed therefore to:

- act as a brief 'aide memoire'
- allow you to test your proficiency
- give you a few ways of avoiding certain difficulties.

In order for you to test your proficiency and then work onwards without any difficulty, you should note that the answers to all the Test *Yourself* sections of this part of the chapter are given on page 342. For ease of reference, therefore, each of the *Test Yourself* sections is numbered.

Grammatical construction

There is not enough space in this book to detail all the rules of English grammar – nor do you really need them. What you *should* know is contained in the list below. If you want to read further on the topic look at standard reference texts such as *The Complete Plain Words* by Ernest Gowers or *Modern English Usage* by H W Fowler.

 TEST YOURSELF 1

Spot the genuine mistake in each sentence! Award yourself two points for each correct answer.

1 I would be delighted to see you on 25 May.

2 Due to an unavoidable delay, they were late for the meeting.

3 Miss Lyons, my PA, who you met yesterday, will take you round the showrooms.

4 I apologise for him not contacting you at the time you expected.

5 I think it is wise for you and I to meet next week.

6 Do you wish the colour scheme to be different to the one illustrated in the brochure?

7 The profits must be divided between the three departments.

8 Every one of the articles are of top quality.

9 Looking forward to hearing from you.

10 Please remember to carefully check the draft.

Now check your answers with the key on page 342. If you scored 20 out of 20 you can skip the rest of this section. If fewer than that, perhaps you should read it with a little more care.

Rule 1

The difference between note and sentence form

The usual method of explaining the difference between a sentence and a phrase (or note) is to say that a sentence has to have a **verb**. If you went to a school where formal grammar was not taught, you may still have difficulty in deciding whether or not you have included a verb. Look at the following examples.

Note   Delay in sending the goods.
Sentence There will be a delay in sending the goods.
Note   Looking forward to seeing you.
Sentence I am looking forward to seeing you.

Alternative If you are in any real doubt – copy. Look at a previous piece of correspondence on the topic which seems to read well and try to imitate its construction. If you do this often enough you will find that you are writing in sentence form almost without realising it.

TEST YOURSELF 2
Complete the following.

1 **Note** Thanking you for your order.
   Sentence
2 **Note** Apologies for the delay in replying.
   Sentence
3 **Note** Have the goods in stock. Shall send them to you by the end of next week.
   Sentence

SPECIAL NOTE
A common mistake in sentence construction is to write:

Passing the shop, a large flower display was visible from the doorway.'

The sentence does not say *who* was passing the shop. Say instead:

As I passed the shop, I noticed that a large flower display was visible from the doorway.'

Rule 2

Matching up the verb with its subject

Again, if you do not know which word is a verb and which a subject, you may have difficulty in matching them up. Look at the following example of incorrect matching.

Details of the new car is to be found in the latest catalogue.

The subject of this sentence is 'details' which is a **plural** word. The verb therefore should also be plural, ie 'are' not 'is' and the sentence *should* read:

Details of the new car are to be found in the latest catalogue.

It may help if you cross out (either mentally or actually) the material between the subject and the verb. If, for instance, you read the word 'details' and then the word 'is' immediately afterwards you will realise that it sounds wrong.

TEST YOURSELF 3

Complete the following sentences with the correct verb. (Remember to ignore the words between the subject and verb.)

1 The girl, who was with some friends, . . . late. ('was' or 'were'?)

2 His knowledge of Accounts, Computer Services and Economics . . . good. ('was' or 'were'?)

3 Long and complex items of information . . . difficult to assimilate. ('is' or 'are'?)

SPECIAL NOTE

Examples of variations on this theme are given below.

- If you start a sentence with 'either', 'neither', 'each', 'every' or 'any' you should use a singular verb because you are talking about a single person or entity, not a group, eg:

    I think neither is suitable for the job.

    Everyone who applies has to be over 18.

    Each of them has the opportunity to do well.

    Although it has been held traditionally that 'none' should be followed by a singular verb, it is now more common to use the plural verb because it reads better, eg:

    None were aware that their overtime pay would be reduced.

    reads better than

    None was aware that his overtime pay would be reduced.

    Remember also that where a collective noun is used (such as 'committee' or 'jury') you can use either the singular or the plural verb – but not a mixture of both, eg:

    The committee is scheduled to report its findings to the Board at the next meeting.
    or
    The committee are scheduled to report their findings to the Board at the next meeting.
    but not
    The committee is scheduled to report their findings to the Board at the next meeting.

- The words 'either' . . . 'or' and 'neither' . . . 'nor' are word combinations which again require a singular verb, eg:

    Neither the Office Manager nor her secretary was aware that the telephone call had been made.

Either the Personnel Manager or his assistant is required at the reception desk.

- If you want to use an opening such as 'This is one of the documents . . .' relate the verb to 'documents' not 'one', ie:

    This is one of the documents that are to be circulated at the meeting.

- Remember to match up pronouns (eg we, I, you, our, one) as well as subjects and verbs. Do not say:

    I feel that we shall be able to accept the offer.
but
    I feel that I shall be able to accept the offer.
or
    We feel that we shall be able to accept the offer.

Rule 3

The difference between 'who' and 'whom'
The rule is that 'who' is used as the subject and 'whom' the object, eg:

    This is the candidate who has been selected by the committee.
or
    This is the candidate whom the committee has selected.

Alternative   If you are in any doubt in this situation you can normally find another way of writing the sentence, eg:

    This candidate was selected by the committee.

Avoid also the common mistake of using 'him' for 'his' and 'you' for 'your', eg:

    I am disappointed at his refusing to see me.
not
    I am disappointed at him refusing to see me.

Alternative   If you are unsure, write instead:

    I am disappointed at his refusal to see me.
or
    I am disappointed that he refused to see me.

You should also note the difference between 'whose' and 'who's'. 'Who's' is merely an abbreviation for 'who is', eg:

    Who's coming to the party tonight?

'Whose' is used to indicate possession, eg:

    The young man, whose qualifications were very impressive, was disappointed at not being given the job.

    Whose bag is this?

Rule 4

The use of 'I' or 'me'; 'we' or 'us'

It is sometimes quite difficult to decide whether a phrase should read 'You and I' or 'you and me'. A simple way of resolving the problem is to translate it into 'we' or 'us' – that normally gives you an indication of which version is correct, eg:

> You and I (*ie we*) should make arrangements for the Paris trip as soon as possible.

> Mr Brown wants to see you and me (*ie us*) as soon as he arrives back from lunch.

Note that if you want to end a sentence with either 'I' or 'me' and are not sure what version to choose, again mentally add a verb at the end of it. If a verb reads correctly then 'I' should be used; if not, 'me', eg:

> He can deal with that question better than I (*can*).

Alternative Avoid using 'I' or 'we' at the end of a sentence. Say instead:

> He is the better person to deal with that question.

Rule 5

The difference between 'should' and 'would'; 'shall' and 'will'

'I' and 'we' are followed by 'shall' or 'should', eg:

> I shall be pleased to see you.

> We shall be pleased to send you details of our current stock.

but

> You will hear from us next week.

This rule is followed *unless* you wish to indicate a definite intention or determination, eg:

> I *will* get away by 4 pm no matter what happens.

> What I *would* like to do is to go to Disneyland.

Use either 'shall' and 'will' or 'should' and 'would' in the same sentence, not a mixture of both, eg:

> I should be grateful if you would (*not will*) call in.

> If you will consider this matter as urgent, I shall (*not should*) be grateful.

Try to not confuse 'would' and 'could'; 'would = willing to; 'could' = able to, eg:

> Could you complete this job any earlier?

> Would you be prepared to work late tonight?

Rule 6

The 'split' infinitive

It is inadvisable to write a phrase in which the word 'to' and a connecting verb is split by an intervening word, eg 'to boldly go', 'to hurriedly decide' etc. This rule is not applied as strictly as it used to be but it may be as well not to include many split infinitives in a document – it is unlikely, but you may have a purist boss who picks up such errors.

TEST YOURSELF 4

Rewrite the following sentences to avoid splitting the infinitive.

1 The Managing Director decided to immediately call a meeting.

2 He promised to urgently deal with the matter.

3 We advise all our clients to carefully consider these new developments.

Rule 7

The use of prepositions

Again it is considered ungrammatical to end a sentence with a preposition (eg 'to', 'of', 'with', 'about' etc). Avoid therefore constructing sentences such as:

> I give below, details of a number of problems we are dealing with.

say instead

> I give below, details of a number of problems with which we are dealing.

Note that nowadays, however, there is a relaxation of the rule in cases where to avoid putting the preposition at the end of the sentence would result in a very awkward construction, eg:

> What do you want to see me about?

rather than

> About what do you want to see me?

Again, though, be careful if you have a boss who likes all the niceties to be observed!

TEST YOURSELF 5

Rewrite each sentence to avoid placing the preposition at the end.

1 She is a client I have always had difficulty with.

2 I can find no one whom I can apply for information to.

3 What reason do you want this information for?

Rule 8

Prepositions at the end of phrases

Some phrases are always followed by a preposition, eg:

<pre>
acquiesce in   relevant to
dependent on   compatible with
</pre>

Remember in particular that 'similar' is followed by 'to' and 'different' is followed by 'from'.

Rule 9

The use of 'only'
Where possible place the word 'only' next to the word it modifies – otherwise the whole meaning of the sentence may be changed. Look at the following sentence.

> We offer an annual maintenance contract.

'Only' can be placed in several different places, each conveying a different meaning, eg.

> Only we offer an annual maintenance contract (ie we, and no one else, offer such a contract).

> We only offer an annual maintenance contract (ie you are not obliged to accept this offer).

> We offer only an annual maintenance contract (ie not a monthly *or* weekly one or that's all we offer, so tough!).

> We offer an annual, maintenance-only. contract (ie we offer a maintenance service and no other).

TEST YOURSELF 6
Use the word 'only' in three different positions to give three different meanings to the following sentence.

> I want a cup of coffee.

Rule 10

'Pairs' of words which are often mis-used
- **Not only/but also**
  Make certain that the whole sentence links together eg:

  > I want to know the price of the car not only for this year but also in future years.

  not

  > I want to know not only the price of the car at present but in future.

- **Due to/owing**
  'Due to' is used after words such as 'to be' (is/are), 'seem' or 'appear'. Otherwise use 'owing to', eg:

  > It is due to an operational failure.

  > Owing to an operational failure, the train was 30 minutes late.

Alternative   In most cases you can use the word 'because' eg:

Because of an operational failure, the train was 30 minutes late.

- **Alternative/option**

'Alternative' means a choice of two.

'option' means a choice of more than two.

You have the alternative of choosing either the black or the white model.

Of the three options, he preferred the first.

- **Between/among**

'Between' is used if only two people/items are concerned; 'among' if more than two, eg:

Divide the takings between the two of you.

Divide the takings among all three.

- **Less/fewer**

Use less for an uncountable amount; use fewer for countable numbers, eg:

There was less space in the reception area

but

There are fewer examination successes than in previous years.

- **There/their**

'There' is used either to refer to a place or in conjunction with the verb 'to be', eg:

Put the parcel over there.

There is plenty of time to catch the train.

'Their' is a possessive pronoun such as 'you' or 'our', eg:

Their commitment to the cause was absolute.

Are you going to give them back their answers?

TEST YOURSELF 7

Retest yourself by rewriting the following sentences to see whether you have improved!

1 Neither of my colleagues were there.

2 You and me must fly to New York.

3 The foreman failed to fully read the instructions.

4 She is the supervisor who the office juniors dislike.

5 I was surprised at them leaving so early.

6 Less than a dozen requests have been received.

7 This is a meeting which he must come to.

8 I shall be pleased if you would provide the information I require by Friday.

9 Who's errors are these?

Punctuation

The compilers of the rules for modern typewriting examinations may have assisted you at the time you were taking your examinations by allowing you to use 'open punctuation' (ie minimal punctuation) in all the correspondence you produced.

However, even nowadays, very few companies have a 'house style' which obviates the need for the use of any punctuation and even when you use open punctuation for addresses, salutations and complimentary closes, you *still* need to insert punctuation in the body of the letter for it to make sense to the reader. The basic rule here is to keep it simple. Master the use of the full stop, the comma and the apostrophe. The question and exclamation marks are unlikely to cause you much difficulty. The colon and semi-colon can be effective but you can live without them. Inverted commas (or quotation/speech marks) may be needed – but normally only on infrequent occasions.

TEST YOURSELF 8

Punctuate the following sentences

1 The Chairman who had a particular interest in the issue agreed to raise it at the shareholders meeting in a weeks time

2 At the meeting he observed I am pleased that the companys profits last year were so high

3 He appreciated one shareholders concern at the increase in the cost of goods labour and transport

4 What more could I have done to solve the problem he asked

5 The new product Fastflow had proved cheap to produce simple to package and easy to sell

6 It should improve the organisations financial position in a few years time

Check your work with the key on page 343. If you experienced any difficulties, read on!

Rule 1

The full stop

Use

- at the end of a sentence (although not at the end of a heading)
- traditionally after abbreviations (B.A., e.g., enc.)

However, you should note that it is more usual nowadays to omit full stops in abbreviations even in otherwise fully punctuated documents, eg ITV, LLB etc.

TEST YOURSELF 9

On what other occasions would you expect to use a full stop?

Rule 2

The comma
Use

- to separate words or phrases, eg:

  You will require a pen, a pencil and a notebook.

  Note that to be strictly accurate you should not use a comma before an 'and' in such a list.

- after introductory words or phrases, eg:

  Having discussed the matter with my colleagues, I am now able to give you a decision.

- to separate phrases mid-sentence, eg:

  Miss Matthews, the Senior Accountant, will give you the relevant information.

- to introduce a quotation, eg:

  As Tiny Tim observed, 'God bless us.'

- if required (ie company house style) to separate names, addresses and dates on a letter, eg:

  Mr. L. Brookes,
  32 Sunningdale Crescent,
  SHEFFIELD,
  SH4 2YD
  24th January, 199-

  Dear Sir, . . .

  Yours faithfully,

  Margaret Lammack,
  Purchasing Director

Note that you can alter the meaning of a sentence by the mis-placing of a comma, eg:

Frank, Lenny and I who are good friends, went to the cinema (ie Lenny and I are the good friends).
compare with
Frank, Lenny and I, who are good friends, went to the cinema (ie Frank, Lenny and I are all good friends).

Rule 3

The apostrophe
Many people have a mental blank about apostrophes. In reality the rules are quite simple.

Use

- in the place of a missing letter or letters, eg:

    You'll be sorry

means You will be sorry (with the apostrophe taking the place of the first part of 'will').

Remember this rule when writing 'its' or 'it's'. Use the apostrophe *only* when you mean to say 'it is', eg:

    It's cold outside.

Otherwise use 'its', eg:

    Its major function is to keep out draughts.

- to indicate possession, eg:

the work of the organisation becomes

    the organisation's work ('s)

the work of the organisations becomes

    the organisations' work (s')

Alternative   If you are in doubt, you may be able to use the longer version, eg if you are worried about where the apostrophe is to be placed in 'the organisations work' use instead 'the work of the organisation' or 'the work of the organisations'. Be careful, however, to check that the construction is not too awkward (the reason for having an apostrophe in the first place!).

A rule of thumb method is to put an apostrophe and add an 's'. However, if the word already ends in 's', you don't need another, eg:

    St Thomas' Church

In the case of plural words which do not end in 's', you have no option but to write the apostrophe and then the 's', eg:

    children's books, men's hairstyles etc.

Remember that certain words change from singular to plural which could affect the use of the apostrophe, eg:

    secretary's skills *becomes* secretaries' skills

The apostrophe is not used with words such as ours, yours, theirs, hers. The exception is 'one's', eg:

    One must fulfil one's obligations.

Note also that it is a common error to forget to put apostrophes in phrases relating to time, eg:

    two years' time or one week's time

Rule 4

Hyphens

Use

- in what are known as 'compound' nouns and adjectives, eg:

  semi-detached house
  up-to-date information

- after certain prefixes, eg:

  pre-Christmas sales
  anti-war demonstrators
  vice-chairman

Rule 5

The dash

Use

- to indicate a break or interruption or to precede a list, eg:

  English summers are renowned for the amount of rainfall – but this year has been an exception.

  She had all the qualities necessary for a PA – intelligence, tact, charm, technical ability.

Note that in formal correspondence a dash should not be used. Use a colon instead.

Rule 6

The colon

Use

- to introduce a list of items or a quotation, eg:

  Please check the items you require: computer disks, daisywheels, stationery.

  Hamlet said: 'To be or not to be, that is the question.'

Rule 7

The semi-colon

Use

- to link two parts of a sentence where the intended pause is not as long as that indicated by a full stop or as short as that indicated by a comma, eg:

  The goods ordered are of two kinds; one is suitable for outdoor use and the other for indoor use.

  Alternative When in doubt, use a full stop, eg:

The goods ordered are of two kinds. One is suitable for outdoor use and the other for indoor use.

Rule 8

The question mark
Use
- If there is a *direct* question eg:

    What time is it?

    but *not* if the question is *indirect*, eg:

    He asked what time it was.

Rule 9

The exclamation mark
Use
- In informal correspondence, sales or promotional literature, eg:

    Cheapest goods in town!

Rule 10

Quotation marks or inverted commas
Use
In certain limited circumstances only. Where they are used, however, the rules are simple:

- to separate direct speech from the rest of the sentence, eg:

    The speaker observed, 'Our business is suffering because of the recession.'

Note that is now seems acceptable to put a full stop either before or after the final quotation mark (although the norm would be to put it before).

- to enclose direct quotations, eg:

    It may be said that 'there is no smoke without fire.'

- to indicate a trade name, a title of a book, film or play etc, eg:

    'Oliver Twist', 'Hoover' etc.

Again the modern trend is to omit quotes in these cases.

- to indicate a colloquialism (slang term), eg:

    This colour scheme is 'in' this year.

- for a quotation within a quotation (in this case use double inverted commas), eg:

    The speaker told his audience, 'The most useful piece of advice I have ever been given is "Moderation in all things".'

Rule 11

The capital letter

Use

- in the main at the beginning of a sentence

- for titles, eg:

    The Princess of Wales

- for proper names, eg:

    New Kids on the Block
    Panorama
    Georgian architecture

- for headings, eg:

    Report into Crowd Violence at Football Matches

    Note that although traditionally all words except prepositions (of, to, etc) and conjunctions (but, and, etc) require an initial capital, modern usage is to reduce the number of capitals in headings.

- at the beginning of direct speech (in the middle of a line), eg:

    He said, 'You must be congratulated on your efforts.'

Rule 12

Brackets (or parentheses)

Use

instead of commas, usually to add a comment eg:

    Popular items (such as the tie-necked blouse) are sold out.

    When I was young (many years ago) I went to seek my fortune.

TEST YOURSELF 10

Retest yourself by punctuating the following passage – correctly, we hope!

under a new law and order initiative young offenders will be sent to an adult prison for 24 hours the shock treatment never before tried in the uk is an attempt to halt the increase in the crime figures among young people ministers worried that offenders still regard probation and community service as a soft option hope that the short sharp shock of spending time in a prison cell will have a deterrent effect giving them a taste of prison life locking them up in a cell making them experience the smells the noise and the slopping out should have a dramatic effect one official said they are not likely to want to return prison reform groups have protested that it is a very short sighted approach they say that if the scheme is put into effect there would be a significant increase in the number of prison suicides in a years time

Spelling

The advent of the word processor has meant that most PAs can rely to a certain extent on the spell-check facility it often contains. Remember, however, that although few people will notice if you use a comma instead of a semi-colon or if you split the occasional infinitive, they will notice if you mis-spell a word – and your image will be somewhat dented. More importantly, the document containing those spelling errors may not be taken as seriously as it might have been if its spelling was impeccable.

Note that even if you have little difficulty with spelling, the same may not be the case with your juniors. They are not likely to have to compose correspondence but they may be asked to type from a handwritten script in which certain words are either mis-spelled or illegible or audio tapes where the ability to spell correctly is critical. You should therefore make sure that they can spell – otherwise you will have to proof-read every piece of correspondence they type. The basic rule is that where in doubt (and in the absence of a spell-check) you should refer to a dictionary. This is of little use if (as your juniors might easily say) you do not know that you are mis-spelling the word. There are certain rules for you to follow, eg:

'i' before 'e' except after 'c' eg piece, ceiling or unless the word sounds like 'a', eg reign and weight

but there are so many exceptions to them that you may confuse yourself. It may be better, therefore, for you to familiarise yourself with some of the more commonly used words in business correspondence. We realise you've heard this many times before but it *is* true – the more you read, the better you will spell. You pick up the correct spellings automatically.

 TEST YOURSELF 11
Choose the correctly spelled word to complete the following sentences. Note that the number of dots is not significant.

1 .... makes the heart grow fonder. (*absence/absense*)

2 The two men are .... (*aquainted/acquainted*)

3 Make sure the .... for the job is put in tonight's paper. (*advertisement/ advertisment*)

4 The sub-......... comprised a number of financial experts. (*committee/commitee*)

5 Could I have the .... on the Derbyshire file. (*correspondance/ correspondence*)

6 He is very .... (*conscientious/concientious*)

7 I hope that the MD is not going to be too .... that his PA is leaving. (*dissapointed/disappointed*)

8 Check the number of your .... who want to take advantage of the new creche. (*colleagues/colleages*)

9 Do we have any details of the cost of ....? (*maintainence/maintenance*)

10 We met together .... to discuss matters of policy. (*occasionally/ occasionnally*)

11 This is becoming a frequent .... (*occurrence/occurence*)

12 It is a great .... to be asked to speak at this conference. (*priviledge/ privilege*)

13 Can I .... the chocolate cake. It is delicious. (*reccomend/recommend*)

14 Pack each item .... (*seperately/separately*)

15 .... this is the action we should take (*undoubtedly/undoubtedley*)

TEST YOURSELF 12

Correct the spelling mistakes in the following passage. (Remember that typing it out and running it through your spell-check is cheating!)

The situation has become agravated by the number of adolesents who felt embarassed by the way in which they were treated. A conserted effort by a group of them, in liason with a number of wellfare societies, has resulted in some reforms. Psyschologically, they gained an advantage when they pursuaded a number of senior personel to support there cause.

Vocabulary

Knowing how to spell a word is one skill; knowing what it means and where best to use it is another. If, as is likely, you are expected to compose letters and other documents for your boss you should take care to choose the most appropriate vocabulary and should try to avoid making any obvious errors in that choice. Watch in particular that you do not 'mix up' the meanings of words which both look and sound similar, eg:

accept/except
I accept the compliment.
I like all sweets except chocolate.

affect/effect
Too high a pollen count affects my hay fever.
What effect has this price rise had on sales?

complement/ compliment
The flowers complement the colour scheme. (Remember the word 'complete'.)
May I compliment you on this excellent piece of work.

discreet/discrete
A good PA is discreet enough never to reveal any confidential information.
Structure the report into five discrete units.

formally/formerly
Interviews for senior posts are normally conducted more formally than those for junior posts.
He was formerly in the army and now works for the local authority.

practise/practice
It is now normal practice for a child to learn a foreign language.

How much time should each child be given to practise that skill?

Note that practice is a noun (eg choir practice): practise is a verb (eg to practise playing the piano). Similar considerations apply to advice/advise; licence/license

passed/past

He has passed all his examinations.

In the past too much attention has been paid to learning by rote.

personal/ personnel

Personal skills are of the utmost importance for a PA.

Please make sure that all company personnel are aware of the provisions of the Act.

stationery/stationary

Remember to order adequate supplies of stationery. (Note – stationery – think of 'e' for envelope)

Was the car stationary or moving at the time?

CHECK IT YOURSELF
Check the meanings of the following pairs of words:

1 alternate/alternative

2 comprehensive/comprehensible

3 respectfully/respectively

4 uninterested/disinterested

5 continuous/continually

TEST YOURSELF 13
Complete each sentence with the correct word.

defer/differ

1 I shall have to .... that decision until I receive last month's sales figures.

2 We shall have to agree to ....

eminent/imminent

3 The .... politician was invited to make the opening speech at the conference.

4 Rain looks ....

impressionable/impressive

5 It is surprising that at his age he is so ....

6 One cannot help but find the Taj Mahal ....

lose/loose

7 The tape around that parcel looks rather ....

8 Be careful that you do not .... the contents.

tolerant/tolerable

9 At school it is not always the .... teacher who gets the best results.

10 The headache became .... after she had taken an aspirin.

Style and meaning

Look at the following extract from the Employment Protection (Consolidation) Act 1978.

> 'If provision is made by Northern Irish legislation (that is to say by or under a Measure of the Northern Ireland Assembly) for purposes corresponding to any of the purposes of this Act, except sections 1 to 7 and 49 to 51, the Secretary of State may, with the consent of the Treasury, make reciprocal arrangements with the appropriate Northern Irish authority for coordinating the relevant provisions of this Act with the corresponding provisions of the Northern Irish legislation, so as to secure that they operate, to such extent as may be provided by the arrangements, as a single system.'

All that information and only one full stop! In this case, of course, style is irrelevant, absolute precision being the only requirement. When preparing non-legal documents, however, you should bear in mind other factors. Some people dress with style – it comes naturally to them. Others have to work at it. The same applies to writing style. If you are good at expressing yourself in writing you will probably find it difficult to understand why anyone has any problems in this respect. Good mathematicians have equal difficulty in understanding the problems of those who cannot add up. Nevertheless, there are certain basic techniques for you to remember. Bear in mind the following points:

- **the reader and the reason for sending the document**
  In a brief memorandum you can afford to write in a relaxed style; in a letter to an important client you cannot.
  Note that an informal style has been used throughout this book. If it had been written as a PhD thesis to be submitted to a university its style would have been very different.
- **the use of abbreviations**
  It is all right for you to use 'don't', 'I'll' etc in an informal piece of correspondence – but not in more formal documents. Remember that 'all right' is acceptable – 'alright' is not.
- **the use of cliches or stereotypes**
  Try not to use over-used or hackneyed expressions – 'time alone will tell'; 'least said, soonest mended'; 'my lips are sealed' etc. If your boss

likes them you can either try to limit the number which are contained in one document or use the old device of putting them in inverted commas (to indicate that they are used in a semi-humorous fashion) eg I must warn you that 'silence is golden'.

- **business jargon**

  If you work in a specialised or highly technical area, some jargon is unavoidable. If, for instance, you work in a company specialising in the selling of computer software you would expect to use a somewhat esoteric vocabulary. Even so, you would have to distinguish between information which is to be sent to other computer experts and that which is to be sent to 'lay' personnel.

In general terms it is unlikely that you would ever be tempted to use any of the following phrases. Even if you are, resist the temptation! Try to persuade your boss to do the same.

- as and from the first of next month
- at the present time *or* at this moment in time
- at your earliest convenience
- beg to acknowledge your letter
- enclosed please find
- in the not too distant future
- kindly advise
- the writer

Remember also to avoid **tautology**, ie using two words or phrases with the same meaning, eg:

- This is a once only, unrepeatable offer
- Finally and in conclusion

Although it is customary to say that correspondence should be as short as possible this does not necessarily mean that it will always be short. Some documents must, of necessity, be quite long because of the subject matter they contain. What is advisable, however, is to chose short words and phrases rather than a longer equivalent.

TEST YOURSELF 14

1 Look back to the list of phrases above. Suggest a suitable alternative for each one.

2 Rewrite the following sentences more simply.
   a We shall endeavour strenuously to assist you.
   b The Sales Manager was made the recipient of a gold watch.
   c The new edifice is very imposing.
   d Could you give me an inventory of the damage caused by the recent conflagration?

SPECIAL NOTE
Recognition that a good writing style is necessary is illustrated by the number of training courses which are now available not only for junior staff but also at

senior management level. On one senior executive course, a three hour session out of a two week course on management skills is devoted to this topic.

Moral   Do you want your boss to know more than you?

ACTIVITY SECTION

Individual tasks

1 You have been engaged in a series of correspondence with a customer with whom you have provided a delivery of knitting wool but who has settled only part of his account. Generally he is a good payer and has been a regular customer. His business tends to be seasonal and you feel that he may be able to pay his bills on time in the future. However, your boss is very worried about his cashflow and wants to have as many accounts as possible settled. Write the appropriate letter.

2 You work for the Managing Director of a company which specialises in making dried flower arrangements. A customer who is about to open a small chain of health food shops sends in the following order from your catalogue (which contains details of over 400 arrangements).

Order number	Description	Quantity
342	'Heliotrope' arrangement	4
356	'Delphinium' arrangement	6
393	'Carnation' arrangement	3

She needs these arrangements within seven days (the week before the actual opening of the shops). You check with the Production Manager who tells you that Item 393 is out of stock (and is too complicated to be produced within the time period specified). There is a sufficient number of Item 342 but there are only two left of Item 356. It is probable, however, that there will be a sufficient number of Item 356 available by the end of the week. Write to the customer informing her of what you can do.

Note that she may turn out to be a regular customer if you treat her properly! Repeat business is a distinct possibility here.

Case study 1

A typist, Netta Dixon, who has worked for the company for five years, wishes to take maternity leave. She intends to return, however, and you arrange for a temporary clerk to take her place. Netta sends the following memo to you.

```
M E M O
TO  . . . . . . . . .  (you)
FROM  Netta Dixon
DATE  13 May 199–
MATERNITY LEAVE

I really do want to come back after my baby is born but I'm not
sure of what I should do to let the Personnel Manager know that I
intend to return. I'm also a bit worried about my replacement –
suppose she is so good that they don't want me to take over when
I do come back? Can you help please?
```

You obtain the necessary information from the Personnel Department (see document below) but you think it may be rather complicated for Netta to follow. Send a memo to her answering her specific queries.

EMPLOYMENT RIGHTS FOR THE EXPECTANT MOTHER

The right not to be dismissed

A woman who is expecting a baby and who has worked for her employer continuously for at least two years has the right not to be dismissed because of pregnancy or for a reason connected with her pregnancy unless her condition makes it impossible for her to do her job adequately or her continued employment would be against the law. In these circumstances she must be offered a suitable alternative job if one is available.

The right to return to work

a An employee is entitled to time off work to have a baby and to return to her job at any time up to 29 weeks calculated from the beginning of the week in which her baby was born. Should her job no longer exist she must be offered a suitable alternative if one is available.

b An employer who takes on a temporary replacement should advise the replacement in writing at the time of the engagement that his or her employment will be terminated when the original employee returns.

c A woman has the right to return to her job and to receive statutory maternity pay only if she continues to be employed until the 11th week before the baby is due and has at that time been continuously employed by her employer for at least 104 weeks. She should give her employer three weeks' notice in writing of her maternity absence. She must also tell him at least 21 days before the day on which she proposes to return. The employer is entitled to be shown a doctor's or midwife's certificate of the expected week of confinement and he can write to her not earlier than 49 days from the beginning of the expected week or date of her confinement asking her to confirm her intention to return to work after the birth.

Individual/group activity

Case study 2

A group of you has decided to get together to run a cleaning agency. You intend to offer a general cleaning service to both private households and offices. In addition you will offer an upholstery and carpet cleaning service. You will all be involved in the business side of the agency but intend to employ both full and part-time staff to carry out the cleaning duties. At one of your first meetings you decide:

- to draw up an advertisement for both the local evening paper and the Job Centre giving details of the cleaning staff required (including rates of pay). Note that one of you has volunteered to visit the Job Centre to look at the vacancies already on display and to check on current rates of pay for

cleaners; another has volunteered to look through the evening paper for similar information.
- to prepare a circular letter suitable for a mailshot to local businesses and small companies containing details of the services you intend to offer.
- to draft out an invitation to the official opening of the agency in six weeks' time which you intend to send to local dignitaries and business people.
- to prepare a press release for the local paper, giving details of the services you intend to offer, the reasons for the setting up of the agency and also some background information about the personnel involved (ie you!).

Prepare the necessary documents ready for a second meeting in a week's time.

Key to Tools of the trade

Test yourself 1

1 I should be delighted to see you on the 25 May.
2 Owing to an unavoidable delay, they were late for the meeting.
3 Miss Lyons, my PA, whom you met yesterday, will take you round the showrooms.
4 I apologise for his not contacting you at the time you expected.
5 I think it is wise for you and me to meet next week.
6 Do you wish the colour scheme to be different from the one illustrated in the brochure?
7 The profits must be divided among the three departments.
8 Every one of the articles is of top quality.
9 I look forward to hearing from you.
10 Please remember to check carefully the draft *or* Please remember to check the draft carefully.

Test yourself 2

1 Thank you for your order.
2 I apologise for the delay in replying.
3 We have the goods in stock and shall send them to you by the end of next week.

Test yourself 3

1 was
2 was
3 are

Test yourself 4

1 The Managing Director decided to call a meeting immediately.
2 He promised to deal with the matter urgently.
3 We advise all our clients to consider carefully these new developments.

Test yourself 5

1 She is a client with whom I have always had difficulty.
2 I can find no one to whom I can apply for information.

3 For what reason do you want this information? *or* Why do you want this information?

Test yourself 6

1 Only I want a cup of coffee (no one else wants one).
2 I want only a cup of coffee (ie not a pot).
3 I want a cup of coffee only (ie not a cup of tea).

Test yourself 7

1 Neither of my colleagues was there.
2 You and I must fly to New York.
3 The foreman failed to read the instructions fully.
4 She is the supervisor whom the office juniors dislike.
5 I was surprised at their leaving so early.
6 Fewer than a dozen requests have been received.
7 This is a meeting to which he must come.
8 I should be pleased if you would provide the information I require by Friday. (*or* shall/will)
9 Whose errors are these?

Test yourself 8

1 The Chairman, who had a particular interest in the issue, agreed to raise it at the shareholders' meeting in a week's time.
2 At the meeting he observed, 'I am pleased that the company's profits last year were so high.'
3 He appreciated one shareholder's concern at the increase in the cost of goods, labour and transport.
4 'What more could I have done to solve the problem?' he asked.
5 The new product, 'Fastflow', had proved cheap to produce, simple to package and easy to sell.
6 It should improve the organisation's financial position in a few years' time.

Test yourself 9

1 After initials, eg Dr. L. Robinson, P. L. Harmsworth & Co. Ltd. (but *not* if open punctuation is used).
2 Between hours and minutes with the 12 hour clock, eg 10.30 am, 1.30 pm. With the 24 hour clock punctuation should never be used, eg 1030 hours or 1330 hours.

Test yourself 10

Under a new law and order initiative, young offenders will be sent to an adult prison for 24 hours. The shock treatment, never before tried in the UK, is an attempt to halt the increase in the crime figures among young people. Ministers, worried that offenders still regard probation and community service as a 'soft option', hope that the 'short, sharp shock' of spending time in a prison cell will have a deterrent effect.

'Giving them a taste of prison life, locking them up in a cell, making them experience the smells, the noise and the slopping out, should have a dramatic effect', one official said. 'They are not likely to want to return.' Prison reform groups have protested that it is a very short-sighted approach. They say that if the scheme is put into effect there would be a significant increase in the number of prison suicides in a year's time.

Test yourself 11

1 absence	**9** maintenance
2 acquainted	**10** occasionally
3 advertisement	**11** occurrence
4 committee	**12** privilege
5 correspondence	**13** recommend
6 conscientious	**14** separately
7 disappointed	**15** undoubtedly
8 colleagues	

Test yourself 12

aggravated	welfare
adolescents	psychologically
embarrassed	persuaded
concerted	personnel
liaison	their

Test yourself 13

1 defer	**6** impressive
2 differ	**7** loose
3 eminent	**8** lose
4 imminent	**9** tolerant
5 impressionable	**10** tolerable

Test yourself 14

1 from the first of next month
  at present *or* now
  as soon as possible
  Thank you for your letter
  I enclose
  soon
  let us have
  I or we

2 a We shall try to help you.
  b The Sales Manager received a gold watch.
  c The new building is imposing.
  d Could you give me a list of the damage caused by the recent fire?

Managing communications

I really don't know what you mean . . .

Communications are a vital part of all our relationships yet frequently they are the cause of the majority of misunderstandings. Written communications in business are dealt with fully in Chapter 6, Processing correspondence. This section deals exclusively not only with verbal communications but with the difference between what we mean to say and what we actually are perceived as saying by our 'receiver'.

RULE 1

All communications involve at least two parties – the sender and the receiver. Only when your receiver receives the identical impression in his/her mind, to the one in yours, have you been successful in transmitting your communication.

If you think about it, it is amazing how many times we misinterpret communications we receive from very good friends and colleagues or even our own family. And yet these are the people we know best! Misinterpretations can occur because of:

- the situation and the timing – people are too busy, too harassed or too stressed to listen to what we are really saying
- the mood we are in – we vent our feelings most on those we know best (who we know will forgive us later!)
- the words, phrases and gestures we choose – which are often ambiguous or inappropriate under the circumstances
- the tone we use – which may give a totally different impression from the one we meant to convey
- the fact we expect people to be semi-psychic and know what we really mean and how we really feel.

Transactional analysis

Transactional analysis (TA) is a technique you can use to analyse the way in which you speak to people (and the way in which they speak to you!). It has many applications – eg learning how to speak to a client when you are in a difficult situation, knowing how to address your boss to give the *real* impression you want to convey, and realising how you often speak to people and create problems by mistake!

RULE 2

Resist the temptation to speak on impulse about anything which may be in the least contentious. Putting your brain into gear before engaging your voice is a sensible lesson to learn! If the outcome could be really serious, sleep on it before taking any action.

Transactional analysis was developed by a man called Eric Berne[1] who considered we all act and speak on three levels:

- as a child
- as a parent
- as an adult.

Within each of those main sections there are sub-sections which characterise our behaviour and our communications (both verbal and non-verbal). The chart below shows the sub-personalities Berne analysed.

The child

According to Berne, although we all start off when young as a *Free Child*, we progress to become the *Adapted Child* (to gain approval) and its opposite (when thwarted) – the *Rebellious Child*. Child-like behaviour is always characterised by being rather 'over the top' – either by being rather too goody-goody or by being silly to gain attention. At work, the Adapted Child is the 'yes-man' employee or the one who is deliberately avant garde to gain attention.

The parent

Many older people may react with you in *Parent* mode. On one hand they are seen to be helpful, giving you advice which they feel you should take to heart – and this is genuine and well-meant. However, should you choose to disregard this then the *Critical Parent* may surface; you will be told that it is all your own fault that things turned out the way they did, if only you had listened to them . . . etc etc.

SUB-PERSONALITIES

Mode	Sector	Characteristics
Adult	Rational	Making a decision, collecting information, assertive
	Primitive	Intuitive – sensitive to 'vibes' and sixth sense
Parent	Critical	Judging people, critical, domineering, paternalistic
	Nurturing	Protective, helpful, giver of advice (for your own benefit!)
Child	Free	Emotional, playful, curious, wanting own way, excitable
	Adapted	Wanting to please, clinging or attention seeking
	Rebellious	Devious, jealous, stores up 'slights' to get own back later on.

[1] Berne E (1963), *The structure and dynamics of organisations and groups*, Grove Press, New York

The adult

The *Adult* mode is not subdivided in every book on TA and can be examined in one category. Basically the adult is objective and analyses facts unemotionally before making a decision. The benefit of highlighting the *Primitive Adult*, however, is considerable. This is the behaviour which is characterised by an 'inner voice' which tells us – often – that 'something is wrong'. Some people never seem to hear (or heed) that inner voice – to their peril. Others are so acutely aware of it that they feel powerless to act in many situations.

How can TA help you?

Knowing about TA can help you analyse your own reactions to a situation (and other people's reactions to you). This is not to say you can alter other people's behaviour – you can't. It is conditioned by many factors, including their previous experiences of dealing with you. What TA can do is enable you to select, perhaps, the correct mode for a particular person or situation – or at least help you to analyse where you went wrong in an encounter.

As an example try the following.

TEST YOURSELF

Your boss returns from a meeting where everything has gone wrong. His proposal for a new computer system, on which he has been working solidly for the last two weeks, was rejected. His staff were criticised by two members of the committee for not passing on urgent information when it was needed. The MD informed everyone that budgets will be reduced – and targets increased – next year. Your boss comes into your office in a foul mood. Which statement are you most likely to greet him with?

a Oh, dear, never mind – put your feet up and have a rest while I make you a nice cup of coffee. Then you can talk about it if you want.

b I told you those proposals would never get through, not with the mood the Board are in at the moment.

c Never mind – when you're on holiday in Hawaii next year none of this will matter.

d Let's talk about it. I'm sure things can't be as bad as they seem.

e I'm not staying here if you're going to be like this – I'm going home.

f What can I do to help? Make a drink? Tidy up? What would you like me to do? Just say the word.

g Say nothing immediately. Make a cup of coffee, give it to him and *perhaps* add 'do you want to talk about it?'

Try to identify, for *each* of the statements above, the 'mode' the speaker is in. Discuss as a group the likely *reaction* you will get to each comment before you read on.

Crossed transactions

One of the reasons that we don't appear to 'see eye to eye' with people is that we often have a crossed transaction. That is, your 'modes' are non-complementary. If your boss wanted to be pampered after his meeting he would have appreciated reaction **a** as then you would be acting as Nurturing Parent to his Child. If he regularly likes to act as a Parent to your Child then he would have preferred reactions **c** or **f** (the Free Child or the Adapted Child). It is doubtful whether he would have appreciated reaction **b** (the Critical Parent) or **e** (the Rebellious Child) – as neither mode is what most executives require from their PA.

Adult modes really require an adult response. Statement **d** is the Rational Adult, whereas **g** is the Primitive Adult – more sensitive to mood swings. Your boss would only appreciate these if he felt like being rational himself – but with option **g** you give him the choice whether to discuss the matter or not. However, if he was not being rational he might perceive either of these responses as critical!

RULE 3

There is no straightforward answer to 'how to react'. This will depend on the circumstances, the person and your past relationship. You are far better to judge each situation on its own merits.

Ambiguous messages

You should be aware that you give away the 'mode' you are in not only by your verbal communications but also by your non-verbal signals! As an example, imagine your boss sends for you about a problem which has occurred involving you and your staff. Although he sounds as if he believes your side of the story he is tapping his foot, stroking the side of his face and slightly grimacing. He is also leaning away from you as opposed to towards you. The signals he is giving are those of disbelief – and therefore you would return to your own office feeling uneasy. What has happened is that he has reacted to you on the surface as an Adult, but subconsciously his gestures reveal a Parent to Child transaction. If you have only responded as an Adult (ie given him the facts of the situation) you have not reacted to the underlying transaction. Had you suddenly reverted to the Child mode yourself – or reacted to him on this level – you may have done better (ie, 'Oh, dear, what do you think we can do about it?' or 'I need your help to be able to cope with problems like this.').

RULE 4

Give out consistent messages yourself! Don't say one thing and let your non-verbal gestures tell a different story – you will only confuse, annoy or upset your listener.

Assertiveness

One of the 'buzz' words at present is assertiveness. This is the ability to say what you honestly feel without upsetting anyone around you – which is far from easy! Not only do your message and your non-verbal gestures have to be coordinated, but you will also need to choose your moment with care. Acting assertively is acting in Rational Adult mode – and won't go down well if your boss is in Parent or Child mode!

If something upsets or worries you then there are two basic options with regard to what you can do:

- nothing – and hope it will go away
- say something.

If you choose the latter then you have to decide what to say. Let's assume a tricky situation.

Your boss is, by nature, disorganised and frequently asks you to stay on in an evening to help him get straight. Sometimes, after half an hour, he decides it's all a waste of time and abandons the effort anyway. On other occasions the odd fax or telex message does get sent after hours. You are fed up with this. Night after night he asks you to wait sometimes for up to an hour – and yet criticises you if you are two minutes later than him in a morning. You feel it is unfair. Last week you decided to put an end to the matter and made a variety of excuses as to why you couldn't stop late. He sulked all week and is now muttering about finding a new PA who is more committed to the job. What are you going to do?

Remember, this situation won't go away if you don't say anything. When your pool of excuses runs dry you are in a mess – and the requests to stay late will resume. You therefore need to talk to him.

TEST YOURSELF
From what you now know about TA, can you identify which 'mode' you are in if you start the conversation with each of the following statements?

1 I have a problem I'd like to talk to you about. Can you spare me a few minutes some time today?

2 I can't carry on like this any longer. Do you realise what an awful position you're putting me in? I'm not doing it any more.

3 You know I always like to help you when I can. I'm finding it difficult to cope with working late every night – but if you really want me to do so I can make suitable arrangements.

4 I'm fed up with staying late every night – and you making me feel guilty if I don't. If *you* were better organised this wouldn't happen.

5 Work, work, work – it's all you think about! I like to escape from this place and live it up after hours!

TA and assertiveness

Let's analyse the responses given above. There are three 'child' responses. Number 2 (the Rebellious Child – the ending 'so there' fits well after the statement given), number 3 (the Adapted Child – will do anything to please), and number 5 (the Free Child – escapism is all!).

All these responses are likely to result in a (Critical) Parent reaction from your boss. You can imagine the kind of statements which could ensure!

The only way in which a 'child-like' opening could help is if he often operates in a Nurturing Parent mode. Then you could open the conversation with 'Please can you help me – I've a dreadful problem I really can't solve on my own.'

Response number 4 is putting yourself in Critical Parent mode! Unless he is prepared to act like a guilty little boy it is doubtful that this would succeed.

There is also another key problem with responses 2 and 4. Both put the onus on him as the guilty party (read them again!), but he hasn't got the problem, you have. Only response number one shows you owning your own problem and approaching him as a Rational Adult. This should trigger a Rational Adult reaction – and in this mode he is more likely to see that his behaviour is unreasonable.

RULE 5

Own your own problems! Assertive statements contain the word 'I', rather than the word 'you' (which signifies aggression).

There is a very fine line between assertiveness and aggression. Aggressive statements are responses 2 and 4 where you have shifted the onus on to your boss – and attacked him for causing your problem! People who are attacked go into defence mode – or attack back!

The basis of assertiveness, therefore, is to be able to stand up for yourself by reacting as a rational adult, and staying in this mode despite the provocation to change. The urge to change – and revert back to Child mode – is very strong and often pre-conditioned from our childhood. As an example think of the following situations.

- You order a meal in a restaurant which, when it arrives, is inedible. You pluck up the courage to complain. The waiter replies 'Oh, no, madam – you must be mistaken – our chef is one of the best in this area.'
- A friend asks if she can borrow your favourite dress one evening. You really don't want to lend it to her. She counters with 'Oh, please, you can't let me down now.'
- Your boss criticises the lack of detail in an investigation you carried out for him. You explain that this was because he asked for it in a hurry and you were very busy with other things at the time. He replies with 'Well, to top it all, there were two typing errors in it as well.'

In each one of the above cases you have initially tried to be assertive, and stated your case clearly and unemotionally. Each time the person you are talking to has countered your reply. How will you cope?

The temptation is to resort to child-like behaviour – ie either give in *or* become aggressive and lose your temper. Neither is suitable and in both cases you are likely to lose. What you must do is to press your case by sticking to Rational Adult behaviour.

 TEST YOURSELF

1 Discuss as a group how you could reply in each of the scenarios given above so that you *remain* assertive.

2 Each person in the group should write down a similar scenario where it is difficult either to be – or to remain – assertive. The group as a whole should discuss and decide the best reaction in each case.

RULE 6

Assertiveness takes patience, practice and courage! It also requires the ability to stand up for yourself and yet, at the same time, be sensitive to the reactions of others.

The benefits from being assertive are tremendous and will help you in many situations both at work and in your private life. If you are interested in the topic, then you are strongly recommended to read about it in greater depth (see Further reading section).

7 Organising work schedules

Section 1 – Managing appointments

The diary

Although you might not recognise the importance of the office diary at first glance, you will find out just how important it is if you lose or mislay it! It is the focal point of the office and should be your primary aid in planning and organising both your work and that of your boss. It is not only a means of recording appointments but also the basis of your office planning system.

In some offices you may find that you have one diary and your boss has another. In addition he/she may keep a personal diary. In such circumstances you must accept that it is your responsibility to update and coordinate all three diaries – otherwise you run the constant risk of double bookings or missed appointments. With some bosses you may find that the personal diary becomes the bane of your life – he/she may try to sneak in appointments behind your back and without telling you about them. Try to make an agreement that the diary is handed over to you at least every two days so that you can make sure your version is up to date.

If possible, therefore, consider using one diary only, with *all* appointments made by you. It is also good practice to try to persuade your boss, if he/she is asked to agree to an appointment while out of the office, to suggest that you and your opposite number PA liaise over appropriate dates and times. You can then remain in control of the situation. Note also that you can photocopy a page of the diary each day which your boss can use as an aide memoire when travelling. The more advantages there are in letting you be in charge of the diary, the less likely he/she is to sabotage – accidentally or deliberately – your efforts.

TEST YOURSELF
The advantages of recording all the information in one diary are outlined above. In some circumstances, however, there are corresponding disadvantages, ie:

- lack of immediate availability to anyone who may need access (eg your office receptionist)
- difficulties in keeping certain items of information confidential
- problems of theft or loss.

Discuss what steps could be taken to overcome these problems.

Types of diary

There are very many commercially produced diaries from which you can choose, according to your own particular needs. Alternatively you may find that your organisation uses a standard diary bearing the company's logo and that these are issued to both staff and clients. Outside organisations may also supply your company with complimentary copies of their diaries. If, on the other hand, you work in a specialist area you may find that the appropriate professional Institute (eg the Chartered Institute of Marketing etc) supplies its members with diaries designed around particular needs. These are likely to contain useful additional pages of information, eg on business travel, public holidays overseas etc, which you may find helpful.

If you cannot find a diary which meets your specific needs you may be able to create one for yourself. One approach is to use a ring binder in which you can insert customised diary pages designed specifically to meet your own requirements. Remember, however, to avoid a 'home made' appearance and to maintain your professional image; if you want to take this approach make sure that the binder is top quality and the sheets are produced on a desktop publishing system (see Chapter 5, Preparing and producing documents, page 267).

Whatever diary you use, you should check on the presence of certain essential features, ie:

- it should be of adequate size (though not so large that it is difficult to carry)
- there should be at least one page for each day
- in normal circumstances it should run from January to December
- there should be an appropriate number of time indicators. This can vary from a page divided into 15 minute intervals to one which is divided into morning, afternoon and evening. (Note that unless you are working in a specialist area such as a dentist's or a doctor's surgery, it is normally advisable to have as few sections as possible to allow you more flexibility when making appointments. See page 357 for details of an electronic diary.)

CHECK IT YOURSELF
At college, in your workplace or from examples found in stationers' shops or bookstores, list at least four examples of different diary layouts.

Scheduling procedures

Buying the diary is the easy part! As PA/supervisor, you are responsible for *scheduling* the appointments in the most effective manner and for linking the information in the diary with that contained in other planning systems (see page 363 for information on planners etc). Bear in mind, too, that other people may wish to have access to the information in the diary.

One of your most important first steps is to *talk* to your boss about personal preferences in relation to the planning of appointments. The more experienced a PA you become and the more longstanding the relationship between you and your boss, the easier it will be for you to 'second guess' him/her. In the early stages, however, (or if, – regrettably – your boss tends to be somewhat of a law unto him/herself) try to make time (or to make your boss have the time) to discuss certain general principles, ie:

- the general pattern of the day's work – does your boss like a 'quiet hour' either at the beginning or the end of a day? Does he/she like a regular lunch break? Is he/she prepared to have a working, lunch, dinner (or breakfast)?
- the general timing of appointments. Does your boss like to get through appointments in one block, eg every morning between 9.30 am and 12 noon? Or does he/she prefer to have them spread out so that he/she has some breathing space?
- is your boss very anxious that appointments should not overrun? (If so, you must get some specific guidelines – what if the client is important or the member of staff is particularly worried or upset – do the same rules still apply?)

SPECIAL NOTE
At this stage it may be advisable to discuss various methods to 'speed up' visitors who outstay their welcome. Are you to use the tactic of the telephone call, the note placed on the desk or the verbal reminder of the next appointment? Some executives have a concealed buzzer or other signal which indicates to anyone in the outer office that they need rescuing – and quickly!

Using the diary

Having agreed the ground rules you can then turn your attention to the use of the diary itself.

Basic procedures

First of all you need to establish certain basic procedures for both you and your junior staff to follow, ie:

- that handwriting should be clear and that the names of non-regular visitors should be *printed*. (You would also remind your juniors to obtain a first name and telephone number in case arrangements have to be changed.)
- that, where necessary, the visitor's status or title is indicated (eg Councillor/Managing Director etc)
- that, where relevant, an appointment made over the telephone is confirmed in writing
- that a brief note is made of the business of a meeting (bearing in mind that some matters are confidential)
- that all appointments are entered into the diary as soon as possible. (If, on the first of the month, your boss mentions that he/she will be away on the 28th, don't wait until the 27th to enter the information in the diary!)
- that there is some forward planning – regular meetings or appointments can be entered in the diary weeks in advance or even for the full yearly cycle

- that provisional appointments are pencilled in so that they can be altered more easily (or erased altogether) should this be necessary. (Alternatively you may want to use certain abbreviations or signals [eg square brackets] to indicate that an appointment is provisional. Whichever method you use, make sure that everyone knows what it is and what it means.)
- that if the diary is to be used as an aide-memoire or reminder system, those using it all follow the same approach. (For instance, everyone should be aware that it is office policy that reminders about collating papers for a meeting should be made a week in advance etc.)
- that the habit is adopted of crossing out entries immediately after the appointment has taken place. You can then tell at a glance what remains to be monitored, what has to be rearranged and what has to be checked up on (if, for instance, an important client has not appeared).

Danger areas!

Some aspects of diary scheduling can cause problems which you should try to anticipate and prevent.

- The timing of appointments is all important. Try to calculate how long each appointment will take. You may be helped by a boss who tells you that he/she will be back at a certain time or that an appointment in his/her office is scheduled for a certain period, but even this may be an optimistic rather than a realistic assessment. In the early stages in particular, over-estimate – too much time between appointments is better than too little.
- Do not overbook unless absolutely unavoidable. Try to maintain some 'blocked out' time to enable both you and your boss to get on with your own work. This is particularly important if he/she has just returned from or is about to go on a business trip or undertake some other work outside the office. It allows for both thinking time and time for reflection!
- If your boss has his/her own diary make certain that entries in both diaries coincide. Methods you can use to remind you to move appointments you have already entered include placing an asterisk by the entry, using a different colour of pen or adopting a similar approach to that relating to provisional appointments. Remember, however, to use this stratagem sparingly – a diary full of too many abbreviations or signals can become very confusing!

 SPECIAL NOTE
You will find that executives vary considerably in their ability to calculate travelling time to and from appointments accurately. Some consider that they are a modern day version of Nigel Mansell and believe it enhances their image if you think they can travel from London to Manchester in well under three hours. The opposite is the executive who plays safe and allows for three punctures and a two hour traffic jam in every journey. Only experience will tell you how much

time realistically to allow and this can depend on time of day, road conditions and weather. You will do both of you a favour if you read the road works reports in one of the national newspapers each morning and notify your boss of any adverse conditions on the route he/she may be using.

The needs of others

Remember that it is not only your boss's schedule which you have to consider when arranging appointments. Other people will also have commitments which have to be taken into consideration. If the personnel involved are all members of the same organisation there are fewer problems – particularly if your boss is the senior person. Even then it can take some time to coordinate your diary with those of the other PAs. If you need to schedule an important or urgent meeting you may find that it is almost impossible to allocate sufficient time within the standard working hours of 9 am to 5 pm. In this case you have a choice between:

- holding the meeting out of hours
- trying to persuade one member to change an appointment
- holding the meeting without some members (particularly if these are not key people at the meeting).

More problems can arise if the appointment to be arranged is with someone outside the organisation and there are other people involved too. If you find that such an appointment clashes with another, then after discussions with your boss you will have to decide which takes priority. (See below for details of how an electronic diary can take care of some of these problems.)

TEST YOURSELF

1 Your boss, the Managing Director of a department store, would like you to make the following appointments during the course of today. How long would you estimate each appointment should take and what additional factors, if any, should you take into account?
   a Your boss has a dental appointment at 3 pm (for an inspection only).
   b The Marketing Manager wants to discuss the cost of advertising the store's pre-autumn sale.
   c The weekly meeting of the Departmental Managers has to be fitted in some time during the day (it has been moved from its regular spot which was originally at 11 am yesterday).
   d Both the Personnel Manager and the Company Accountant want to see your boss but both are available only between 11 am and 2 pm.
   e The Managing Director of a company which supplies the store with a lot of discount price furniture is calling in for a 'flying visit' before catching the 10.30 am train.

2 You have been asked by your boss to arrange a meeting for him today with the Personnel and Assistant Personnel Managers, the Training Officer, the Chief Administrative Officer and the Head of Computer Services. He wants to discuss the computerisation of the personnel records system and thinks the meeting should last about an hour.

You contact all the people concerned to find out the best time for the meeting and collect the following items of information:

- your boss is booked up between 11 am and 1 pm
- the Assistant Personnel Manager is away all afternoon on a training course
- the Training Officer has a lunchtime appointment and another at 5 pm
- the Chief Administration Office has an appointment from 1.30 pm to 3 pm
- The Head of Computer Services is not free until 3 pm.

Decide the most suitable time for the meeting. Justify your decision by stating the factors which made you come to this conclusion. Note down any additional action you now need to take.

The electronic diary

Many offices today pride themselves on being 'electronic offices' and operate integrated computer networks with shared access to information (see Chapter 5, Preparing and producing documents, page 233). If your company operates such a system then you should either make use of or investigate the possibility of obtaining an electronic diary facility. One example of such a system is given below.

| WAMCAL.FIL | | | | | | | Friday, March 8, 1991 | 1:59pm |

Sun	Mon	Tue	Wed	Thu	Fri	Sat
17	18	19	20	21	22	23
24	25	26	27	28		

March 1991

					1	2
3	4	5	6	7	8	9
10	11	12	13	14	15	16
17	18	19	20	21	22	23
24	25	26	27	28	29	30
31						

April 1991

Friday, March 8, 1991

Memo

Appointments

To-Do List

1 Date; 2 Options; 3 Print; 4 Auto-Date: – (Tab Next Window; F3 Help; F7 Exit)

The illustration shows the basic calendar screen. Note its four main features, ie:

The calendar   You can select the date you require by moving your cursor key to the appropriate point.

The memo section   Use this section for reminder notes – the section will expand to incorporate all the notes you want to make.

The appointments section   Appointment times can be entered in this section – a 'window' will open for you to fill in the start time, the end time and the purpose of the meeting (see illustration below).

There is a 'zoom' option which allows you to see all the appointments for the day at a glance. Note that you will find it difficult

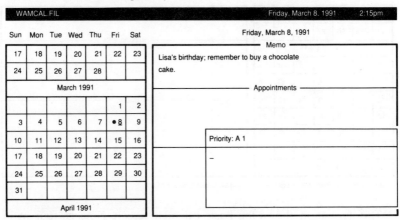

Friday, November 3, 2000

Sun	Mon	Tue	Wed	Thu	Fri	Sat
22	23	24	25	26	27	28
29	30	31				

November 2000

				1	•2	3	4
5	6	7	•8	9	10	11
12	13	14	15	16	17	18
19	20	21	22	23	•24	25
26	27	28	29	30		

December 2000

| | | | | | 1 | 2 |

Memo

Appointments

Time: 3:30pm   Ending Time: 4:15pm

F1 Cancel; F4 Copy; CTRL-F4 Move; F6 Bold; F7 Exit; F8 Unrlin; Shft-F10 Paste;

to double book appointments because the system will indicate to you where there is any overlap.

The 'to-do' list   You can list a number of actions you wish to take and, if necessary, have these prioritised. If, for instance, you enter two items and then decide that a third item takes precedence, the system will re-sort the list into priority order (see illustration below).

Friday, March 8, 1991

Sun	Mon	Tue	Wed	Thu	Fri	Sat
17	18	19	20	21	22	23
24	25	26	27	28		

March 1991

					1	2
3	4	5	6	7	•8	9
10	11	12	13	14	15	16
17	18	19	20	21	22	23
24	25	26	27	28	29	30
31						

April 1991

Memo

Lisa's birthday; remember to buy a chocolate cake.

Appointments

Priority: A 1

F1 Cancel; F4 Copy; CTRL-F4 Move; F6 Bold; F7 Exit; F8 Undrlin; Shft-F10 Paste;

Other facilities

- A recurring appointment need be entered once only. If, for example, you have a staff meeting at 10 am every Monday morning, you need enter the appointment once only and it will appear on your calendar during the entire time period you specify.
- You can be reminded of appointments as they are about to occur by the sound of an alarm buzzer.
- The memos, appointments or 'to-do' lists can be merged into your word processing system if you require the information for, say, an invitation or an itinerary.
- The diary can also be combined with a small database containing

names, addresses and telephone numbers of clients etc. You could therefore call up on your 'to-do' list the name of a person to telephone plus his telephone number.

Scheduling of meetings

You may be given the responsibility for arranging a meeting for your boss which involves a number of people. A great deal of time can be spent telephoning round and making provisional bookings before a universally agreed time and date are fixed. The scheduling feature of your electronic diary system removes much of this work from your shoulders.

The illustration below shows a computer screen on which is displayed a 'request' box and an 'organised' box. The request box lists the events your boss should attend. The organised box lists the events you have organised for him/her.

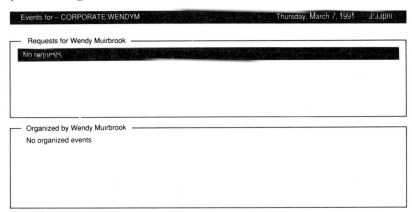

If you move to the 'month' screen (see below) you will see that the calendar window on the left hand side has a bullet (●) on every day for which you have an event scheduled. The window on the right shows the events for the day against which the cursor is positioned.

Sun Mon Tue Wed Thu Fri Sat   Thursday, March 7, 1991

		March 1991				
					1	2
3	● 4	5	6	● **7**	8	9
10	● 11	12	● 13	14	15	16
17	● 18	19	20	21	22	23
24	● 25	26	27	28	29	30
31						

		April 1991				
	● 1	2	3	4	5	6
7	● 8	9	10	11	12	13

8:00 am
8.30 am Review Susan Ward's Portfolio
9:00 am Interview Susan Ward
9:30 am
10:00 am
10:30 am
11:00 am
11:30 am
12:00 pm
12:30 pm Lunch with Enzo and Eric
1:00 pm
1:30 pm
2:00 pm Conference Planning Meeting
2:30 pm
3:00 pm
3:30 pm
4:00 pm
4:30 pm
5:00 pm

1 Date; 2 Sched: –   (Shift-F1 Setup; Shift-F3 Week; F3 Help; F7 Event)

If you want to arrange a meeting for your boss with a number of people, you would key in the information relating to the event, the people involved, the place, the date and the length of the meeting. The information can then be transmitted to all the people on the list.

If someone is unable to keep that appointment because of another engagement, a bullet will appear to indicate a 'busy' time. You can then, if you wish, use the computer to search for an available time within a certain period.

Personal organisers

Your boss may wish to make use of a portable electronic diary (often known as a **personal organiser**) with features which include:

- word processing facilities
- a database including diary and calendar facilities.

Info Bank, for instance, works as an address/phone book and a diary with a clock and basic calculator. When information is keyed in, the Info Bank itself sorts addresses alphabetically and puts diary dates in chronological order. It allows 'sensitive' data to be protected by a password. Another alternative is the AgendA which contains a diary, calculator and file spaces for addresses. It also functions as a database and has a search facility which will find a file from any word entered into it.

You should note that unless your boss's personal organiser is compatible with your computer system in the office, and information can automatically be relayed and sorted between the two, a personal organiser can present the same sort of problems (and in some cases worse ones!) than the personal diary – especially if your boss takes it away on long distance business trips and makes notes, jottings and appointments in it – but forgets to tell you on his/her return!

CHECK IT YOURSELF
The Business Equipment Digest often contains advertisements for personal organisers and has an easy reference system of relevant names and addresses of suppliers. Check through some recent copies and send off for any relevant information.

Advantages and disadvantages of the electronic diary

Most of the advantages are self-evident, ie:

- reduction of paperwork
- reduction of time spent in contacting people
- reduction in the number of excuses about being 'engaged' at certain periods and unable to attend meetings!
- ability to combine a number of functions, eg appointments/database
- greater confidentiality (compared with the diary left on the top of a desk)

- on a networked system the receptionist can have automatic access to a chronological list of expected visitors.

There are, however, certain disadvantages, ie:

- possible equipment breakdown or malfunction
- less room for manoeuvre if your boss wants an excuse for not attending a meeting!
- less persuasive than a telephone call.

Other planning aids

Although the diary is an important tool it can be supplemented by other planning aids. Some make it easier for you to plan ahead. Others make it less easy for you to forget to take certain important actions!

The list

Don't despise the making of lists! They can be the key to much of what happens in an office. After all, your filing system is no more than an elaborate list, so, too, is your database.

It takes only a few moments to make out a list of jobs to be done at the beginning of each day (or at the end of the previous day) but such a list can be invaluable. Don't overlook the psychological effect of being able to tick off or draw a line through certain jobs as they are completed, even if they are as simple as ordering coffee and sandwiches for a meeting. Most PAs learn this stratagem early and a 'sure-fire' method of picking them out from the rest of the office workforce is the notebook they carry with them constantly. If you want to be considered part of the electronic age then you may like to consider the use of a personal organiser. Their only drawback is their lack of portability when compared to the ubiquitous notebook.

SPECIAL NOTE
It is no use carrying a notebook around unless you have a pen or pencil constantly on your person. Choose a pen which writes horizontally – many a PA has been given important instructions when walking down the corridor and the only suitable surface to rest on is the nearest wall!

Permanent and temporary lists

Distinguish between lists which are temporary 'one-offs' and those which are permanent and act as constant reminders. Temporary lists are those which are changing all the time as you carry out urgent jobs and cross them off, and add new ones. Danger areas to watch for are:

- constantly avoiding doing jobs you don't like. (You can spot this if you find yourself making out a new lists and regularly transferring one or two particular items!)
- doing the jobs in the order in which you write them down, rather than prioritising these into the order in which they *should* be done

- forgetting to add new jobs – especially when you receive the information from an unusual source or in an unusual place
- not crossing jobs off as you go, so that by the end of the day you don't know where you are.

Make yourself feel better by starting the day by doing one or two jobs you really hate. Having got these out of the way you can now work through the rest of the day with a clear conscience!

In contrast, because permanent lists are reminders, if you are going to cross off items as you go, then take a photocopy first. Examples of permanent lists include:

- arrangements for meetings (actions to be taken before/during/after the event etc)
- arrangements for regular visits abroad
- Post Office services (which delivery services are faster, which are more expensive/economical etc)
- holiday arrangements for staff.

TEST YOURSELF

1 Discuss what other types of 'permanent' check lists you could use in an office.

2 Once having prepared these checklists, what factors would you have to bear in mind to ensure that they are always helpful?

The card index

You may find a card index system helpful as a reminder which you can check each day as part of your daily routine. Use one guide card for each day of the month (or month of the year) and place any reminders to yourself behind the appropriate number. If, for instance, you want to remind yourself that your boss's car tax expires in August, place a reminder to that effect behind the August guide card. If you know that your boss is attending an important meeting on 23 March, you could place a note behind, say, card 16 to remind you to collect together all the relevant papers he will need.

This system can be more useful than writing reminders in a diary which is already full of appointments, meetings and travel details. Equally, if you are suddenly given a letter during dictation with the instruction 'put that on ice for a couple of weeks and remind me to write to them again then' you can not only jot down the details on the relevant card, but also attach a photocopy of the letter to the index card so that you have all the details to hand when the couple of weeks has elapsed.

The strip index

A more complex, commercially produced system is the 'strip' or 'busy person' index by which reminders are entered on to individual strips which are then fixed into position in a strip index container for your boss's personal use. The information is seen at a glance and can be put in a container small enough to be carried in a briefcase. You would be wise, however, to have your own copy and to make frequent cross checks (in the same way that you cross check diaries).

Pre-printed forms

Don't assume that you are being extravagant if you decide to buy your requirements from outside suppliers. Make use of those organisations which specialise in preparing business forms which not only save your time (and therefore the company's money) but also act as built-in reminders. Bought-in forms also have the advantage that they are frequently printed on NCR (no carbon required) paper, so that copies can be taken easily and quickly.

Examples of frequently used pre-printed forms include:

- lateness records
- sickness and absence records
- holiday report forms
- holiday rota schedules
- suggestions forms

- message forms
- routing slips
- petty cash vouchers
- purchase requisition forms.

CHECK IT YOURSELF
A number of office supplies companies specialise in producing such forms. Contact at least one of them to obtain an up-to-date catalogue of what they have to offer.

Planners

Planners can be of considerable assistance to you particularly if you use them in conjunction with your diary and other planning aids.

As the standard time span in most organisation is one year (which normally runs from January to December) if you want to take a systematic approach to the planning of the work of your office you should take the annual cycle as your starting point.

Note that even if your organisation works to a three or five year plan you will still be able to incorporate the information into your annual planner by means of a carry forward system each year.

TEST YOURSELF
- In some instances the 'standard' year will be from April to the following March or from August to the following July. In what types of organisation (or departments within an organisation) are you likely to operate these two different time spans?
- Look in an office supplies catalogue to find examples of 'perpetual' or 'rolling' planners to see how these operate.

Scheduling tasks

Once the yearly cycle has been established you can then subdivide it into monthly, weekly and daily cycles to meet your own requirements.

Tasks which can be planned on a yearly basis include:

- the annual general meeting
- the annual sales conference
- dates of sales trips
- dates of quarterly reports
- directors'/governors'/councillors' meetings
- financial activities relating to the year end
- Health and Safety Committee (and other regular) meetings.
- publicity campaigns.

Those which can be planned on a monthly basis include:

- a transfer of the relevant items from the yearly planner, eg an annual general meeting entered on the yearly planner for August would have to be included in the monthly planner
- meetings with Trades Union representatives
- monthly reports from departmental managers
- training courses
- interview arrangements
- production scheduling meetings.

TEST YOURSELF

1 Either by using your own workplace as an example, or your experience on work placement, add to the list of tasks which you think could be included in a yearly or monthly planner.

2 Given that the diary is the obvious alternative to the use of the weekly planner in particular, when might you find it more convenient to use the planner? Factors to consider include:

a the need to keep the information in the diary brief and uncluttered

b the fact that more than one person may want to have access to the diary at any one time during the day

c the advantages of seeing the week's events at a glance.

Devising your planner system

You have the option of creating your own planners (particularly if you have access to a desktop publishing system – remember they don't need to be complicated, see opposite).

If, however, you feel that the planner system is likely to be a major factor in your overall planning strategy you should consider using one of the many commercially prepared **visual planning charts**. Some of

Year planner 19--/19--

JAN	FEB	MAR	APR
MAY	JUN	JUL	AUG
SEPT	OCT	NOV	DEC

Monthly planner 19--

Week beginning 21/12	
7/1	
14/1	
21/1	
28/1	

Weekly planner
Week beginning.....................

MONDAY	
TUESDAY	
WEDNESDAY	
THURSDAY	
FRIDAY	

these are designed to fit your general requirements. Others are more specific – if you work in a school or college you may require a timetabling planning chart; if you work in a production unit a production scheduling chart is useful, and many sales departments use a 'perpetual' or 'rolling' planner so that the next 12 months is constantly on view.

The advantages of such charts include:

- their appearance – if displayed on a wall or screen they look effective both to members of the organisation and also to visitors, particularly if use is made of accessories such as labels/coloured flashes etc
- their flexibility – many of them are re-usable.

They do have some disadvantages, however, ie:

- they can become over-complicated (too many different coloured labels and signals can be confusing)
- they can be time-consuming to set up (although you should beware the false economy of neglecting to spend a couple of hours sorting out a system which is 'user-friendly' in favour of a system which can be set up within a few minutes but which nobody can understand or operate)
- if you use sticky labels they are usually there for good, whether you like it or not. Magnetic rubberised strips, which can be cut to shape are better, but make sure they are large enough to hold on to the board. If they fall off on the floor it is doubtful if you will have much idea where they should go! (And beware the 'helpful' member of staff who, seeing them on the floor, adds them to the chart wherever they would appear to look best!)

ACTIVITY SECTION

Individual tasks

1 You have been away on a week's training course on Time Management. You return to find that a series of notes has been left on your desk by a not-very-efficient stand-in secretary. You have to sort out your boss's diary for the following week (bearing in mind that you also have several regular appointments already scheduled).

State how you would deal with any obvious overlaps.

Regular appointments
Weekly Heads of Department meeting – Monday 9 am
Research and Development meeting – Friday 3 pm

Notes from temporary secretary

Norma Fairhurst coming at 9.30am on Monday to discuss final details of contract (must be away by 10.30am)

Don't forget – 21st Birthday Party – Sat 7.30pm for 8.

Fri to foll. Tues – International Energy Conservation Conference, Brussels. Leave office no later than 10.30am for airport!

Asif Patel rang – OK for lunch at 1pm Thurs – Providential Hotel.
(Golf Lesson – Thurs 2.30pm!)

Jacques Lapitte – Paris Office – urgent tel. call – needs advice asap. Can be contacted in office between 9am & 11 Monday.

2 Complete a standard page of a diary dated Monday, 19 August with the following entries and add any supporting information you think is relevant.

- Your boss has to go to London on 20 August to attend a meeting at the London Chamber of Commerce and Industry. Normally he travels on the 8.30 am train from Manchester Piccadilly to London Euston.
- Denise James, a chief reporter with a technical journal, is coming from Glasgow by train to interview your boss at 10.30 am on 19 August.
- There is a monthly meeting of Departmental Heads next week and you will have to contact them to see if they have any items to put on the Agenda.
- This evening your boss will attend a Rotary Club dinner. Evening dress is required. Guests are requested to be there at 7.30 pm for 8 pm.
- A member of the Computer Services Department is coming to check your computer terminal at 9.30 am.
- Your boss has a lunch appointment at the Berlioz Hotel at 1 pm and wants to go straight from there to a building site in Didsbury to check over the findings of the surveyor with the Site Manager.
- Jim Robinson has an appointment to see your boss at 4 pm to discuss a building contract about which there has been substantial correspondence.

3 The PA of an important client telephones to say that her boss will be in town on Wednesday and would like to lunch with your boss. He must be away by 3 pm for a meeting with another supplier. You check the diary and find that your boss is in a board meeting at 11 am and has a lunch appointment at 12.30 pm with an important local councillor. What do you do?

Case study 1

You work for Terry Gregory, Sales Director of a large company which exports textile machinery all over the world. The Sales Department comprises a Sales Office Manager and ten Area Sales Managers – each responsible for a different territory, eg UK, Europe etc. In addition your company has agents and/or small branch offices both in the USA and most capitals in Europe. Mr Gregory is frequently away for several days at a time, during which period you liaise with the Sales Office Manager about any queries which may arise.

Mr Gregory is away at an exhibition in London. One of the Area Sales Managers, who was with him yesterday, has brought back notes for you.

I appear to have some problems looming up for Tuesday, the 24th. Whilst I'm down here can you please try to sort out my diary for that day?

- You know that I want to travel to Paris that day but with all the other commitments it'll have to be an evening flight. Can you check what is available from Manchester?
- I know I'm due at the monthly Managers' meeting on Tuesday, but before that I must visit Production to see the new machine trials (for only about 20 minutes). I've also got to see the Area Sales Managers for about half an hour to discuss current sales positions.
- I need to have a separate word with Robert Evans and Barry Duerden. Bob sets off for Sydney on the Thursday and I think Barry leaves for Los Angeles on the Wednesday. 15 minutes with each will be enough.
- Fix up a meeting with Eileen Briggs in Personnel about the vacancy for Sales Coordinator – either in my office or hers.
- Can you confirm with Liam Neill of Dewey and Main that I can see him for about half an hour mid-afternoon to discuss the Canadian agency?
- If Farouk Aziz telephones let him know the best time for him to drop in with some samples he wants testing – he'll only take a few minutes.
- Donna Edwards wants to have a word with me about that computer program she's organising on sales statistics. She wants to demonstrate one or two things and is free either between 10 am and 11 am or after 3 pm. She says she'll need half an hour but you know her – try and make it longer.
- I'll need a breather – could you possibly schedule me to be in my own office between 2 pm and 3 pm – preferably seeing only internal people. If you arrange a snack for me at tea time we can go over the Paris stuff then – I'll go straight to the airport from the office. I won't be taking my own car so arrange a driver will you?

After having read the instructions:

1 Draw up the draft diary Mr Gregory requires.

2 At the right hand side of the page note down all the jobs you would have to do that day to make sure everything runs smoothly.

Case study 2

You work for three partners of a small company which specialises primarily in catering for children's parties. Prudence Towers is responsible for finances, Andy Walenski is in charge of marketing and sales and Maureen O'Brien takes care of the catering arrangements (including the supervision of five catering staff, all of whom are employed on an hourly basis, depending on the amount of work available each week).

Prudence likes to work at home at least one day a week. Maureen spends most of her time in the kitchen or food preparation area, although she is also responsible for the delivery of the food to the customers. Andy is away on frequent selling trips (sometimes for a period of two or three days) but he also spends some time in the office talking to both prospective and regular customers.

Obviously, coordinating the activities of the partners is difficult and you have already encountered some problems in the following areas.

a You are expected to arrange regular meeting times for the partners.

b You have to keep a record of the hours worked each week by the kitchen staff, which varies according to the current workload.

c There is a considerable amount of repeat business but it is company policy that, unless requested, the same menu will not be provided twice to the same customer.

d One of your duties is to keep an eye on the prices charged by competitors and you contact them regularly for price lists and other details.

State how you would attempt coordination in each case and give details of the planning aids you could use to assist you. Include illustrations where appropriate.

Section 2 – Organising your own work schedule

As a PA/supervisor you have to be both a short term and a long term thinker. You have to create a working environment for yourself and your boss which allows the majority of the work to be carried out on a planned and foreseen basis and which can therefore take into account any unexpected eventualities. If, for instance, you have organised your filing system effectively, you can find a file at a moment's notice. If you have given some thought to the duties you and your junior staff will be undertaking during the course of a day or a week, you can build into that plan sufficient flexibility to enable you to deal with any emergencies which may occur.

Organising the office

The office environment

One of the first steps you can take to assist you in such plans is to organise your physical surroundings; don't believe the old slogan that 'a tidy desk is the sign of a sick mind' – it isn't. It's the sign of a good PA or a good administrator. At the other extreme, a messy desk implies a messy mind and sloppy work. At the very least your desk should be cleared every night so that you have a clean start each morning.

Start with your work area. It is not always possible to influence where you are situated but ideally your work area should be:

- as near to your boss's office as possible (preferably in an anteroom). If the office is open plan then your desk should be closer to the traffic flow than that of your boss and, if possible, he/she should be screened from visitors
- adequately lit, heated, ventilated (and air conditioned where necessary)
- well decorated and furnished.

Don't feel that you are being too demanding in asking for such conditions.

You won't work to your full capacity, and neither will your boss nor your staff, if the working area is too hot, too cold or everyone is constantly suffering from headaches or eyestrain. Psychologically, too, you will work better (and visitors will be more impressed) if your surroundings are attractive and colourful.

Remember, however, that self-help is important; if you know the office is likely to be cold at certain times, dress accordingly and remind your juniors to do the same. If the office is too hot in summer, make sure that the blinds are adjusted to prevent direct sunlight, and so on.

It goes without saying that you will make sure that the office is clean (put pressure on your boss if the cleaning staff are obdurate) and as quiet as you can make it given the unavoidable presence of office equipment, the ringing of telephones, the constant flow of visitors etc.

TEST YOURSELF

Some PAs share an office with their boss. What do you think may be the advantages and disadvantages of this arrangement?

Office layout

Unless you work in a very large open plan environment you should have some control over the way in which your office furniture and equipment are organised. Bear in mind certain key points.

- Have as large a desk or working area as possible (provided everything placed on it is within easy reach).
- Make sure your filing system (unless centralised) is near to hand (see Chapter 2, Rearching and retrieving information, page 75). Try not to have too many files on your desk at one time – only those concerned with the job upon which you are working at that particular time.
- See that your telephone is positioned properly (depending on whether you are left or right handed) and that your keyboard is a help and not a hindrance to the rest of your work. An L-shaped desk is particularly useful as the keyboard can be positioned on the side attachment leaving the rest of the working space free.
- Pay attention to details such as desk accessories – pen holders, filing trays etc – but don't clutter your desk with non-essential items, however stylish. Once you have positioned all the items, keep to that arrangement so that even when in a hurry you will automatically find what you want, eg your diary and notebook.
- Check your own chair – if you feel at all uncomfortable it could be that your chair is too low, too high, the back is not positioned correctly or the arms impede your work.
- Remember that a notice board is useful provided you keep a check on it to see that the material is not overcrowded, untidy or out of date.
- Unless there is a separate reception area, make sure that there is a suitable arrangement of furniture to allow visitors to sit in comfort when waiting for your boss.

TEST YOURSELF

Look at the list of standard items of office furniture, equipment and office aids given below. Assume you are in a 'green field' situation and are setting up a new office. Put an A against the items you would need on the first day, a B against all the items you would require within the first month and a C against those which you could obtain as and when required.

Address book
Adhesive tape dispenser
Air cleaner and ioniser
Anti-static and other products
    for keyboards
Ashtrays
Badges (for visitors)
Batteries (for calculators etc)
Binders/binding systems
Bins
Blotters/deskpads
Book/magazine racks
Calendar
Calculator
Cash and security boxes
Coffee percolator (plus
    crockery/fridge etc)
Clipboards
Clock
Coat racks/stands
Computer (+ acessories)
Desk top accessories
Diary
Dictation equipment
Dictionary
Duplicator/photocopier
Fax machine
Filing equipment and card index boxes

First aid kit
Furniture
Guillotines/trimmers
Indexing equipment
Key cabinets
Labels/label makers
Laminating machine
Noticeboards
Paper clips and pins
Planners
Pencils/pens/sharpeners
Perforators/punches
Post-it notes
Postroom accessories
Safe
Scissors
Screen dividers
Shredder
Staplers
Steps
Stamps
Stationery
Telephone/switchboard
    answering machine
Trays (filing etc)
Trolleys
Typewriter/Wordprocessor

Desk layout

Some executives don't like using a desk. Instead they use a large square table on which all their work can be laid out. In theory they should have no need for a more traditional desk with drawers – you are paid to organise all their paperwork for them. You can follow suit if you wish but remember that you may have more need of a standard desk with drawers in which you can keep a number of frequently used items.

Office equipment suppliers have catalogues which illustrate a wide variety of desks. Most of them, however, have standard drawer layouts comprising a left hand set of three or four drawers of the same size and a right hand set of two drawers, the bottom one being large enough to be fitted with lateral files if desired. Various locking systems are available.

1		4
2		
3		5

1 Your desk contains the above set of drawers. You wish to keep the following items off the top of your working surface. Assume that only drawer three locks.

Put the number of the appropriate desk drawer against each of the following items to indicate where it will be stored:

eg office stationery 4

paper clips	drawing pins
bottle opener	pens/pencils
computer labels	confidential documents
scissors	sellotape
stamps	stapler
staple remover	aspirins
petty cash	needle and thread
treasury tags	telephone directories
safety pins	screwdriver (a must!)

2 Discuss as a group the personal items you would want to keep in your drawer in case of emergencies.

 SPECIAL NOTE

The personal items you keep may not just be for yourself! A steadfast PA may have an 'emergency' drawer to help her boss out. Typical items can include: a spare set of car keys, the horrendous desk calendar given by an important customer last year (for when he visits!), the key code number to the changing room at the golf/squash/any other club, breath freshener and a packet of mints, plasters, a spare toothbrush and tube of toothpaste, emergency telephone numbers and a list of family birthdays and the presents you helped choose for them last year. Your list may vary slightly if you have a female boss but many of the above still apply!

Organising the office systems

You have cleared the decks for action and your office environment is organised in just the way you want it. Your next step therefore is to organise the time you spend in the office.

Time management is 'in' – for the PA or administrator it has never been out (see Managing time, p 381). Remember, however, that although you should 'manage' your time as far as possible, your major problem is that, by the very nature of your job, you are often expected to work at the pace of your boss rather than at your own, and to complement his/her method of operation. This can make forward planning problematic and a good working relationship with your boss is therefore of the utmost importance.

Try to establish your boss's preferences as to working arrangements and the general pattern of the day and week. Persuade him/her to cooperate by pointing out that the time taken in such a discussion will be more than offset by the time saved later on. If your boss is still unwilling to give you any clear guidelines try to find another experienced PA who may be able to give you some advice (see also Managing your boss, page 291). Your boss's previous PA, if available, is an ideal source – unless she gave up completely.

The information you gather should then act as a basis for all your future planning. You may like to note that if you are already a PA/supervisor there is still some benefit to you in periodically reviewing your office procedures and working practices to see what can be improved or amended. In some cases you may not be aware of up-to-date labour- and time-saving devices. Look through business journals from time to time to see if there are any articles on new approaches which could be taken.

Winning the paper chase

Because a good PA never gives the impression of disorganised chaos a good first move is to review the systems in operation for coping with the plethora of paper which arrives each day. 'A place for everything and everything in its place' is a truism which will save you time and worry – and help you to keep your sanity when things are hectic.

Start by setting up systems of work which suit your job and then *stick to them*. If they aren't easy to keep to then redesign the system, not the idea. A suggested system is shown below – adapt it to your needs as necessary.

1 Make out a file folder for each main area of work for which you regularly have 'work in progress' (WIP).
2 Make out a pocket or envelope wallet (in a bright colour) labelled 'miscellaneous two minute jobs'.
3 Have a set of trays – In, Out, In Progress, Pending and Filing.

As you receive work put it in *either* the correct folder or the correct tray (or the wastepaper bin). Don't leave single papers lying around.

4 Keep your WIP file folders in *priority order.*
5 Given time to concentrate on a current job, start with the top folder. If you are interrupted put the papers back again and return the folder to its tray.
6 If you only have five minutes, take out two jobs from your pocket wallet and get them out of the way.

Beware the filing and the pending tray – they should not be a halfway house to the wastepaper basket. If you *know* something is totally out of date or will never be required then throw it away – don't hoard it. (But don't make judgements like this until you've been doing the job for a few months!)

One idea to cope with papers which *may* be needed in future, but have no real place in your system, is to start a **deferral** file. In this you put anything which doesn't fit anywhere else. If you go through it every two weeks you should find you are able to throw most of the items away.

Task management systems

Once you have had discussions with your boss and set up your own systems for dealing with the paper you receive every day, you will then be able to take further steps.

1 List all the tasks you have to undertake and make a similar list for your boss and your junior staff (if you have one, use your job specification as a basis for this exercise).

2 Classify these tasks into:
   a those which are infrequent and which can be anticipated and planned well in advance, eg an annual general meeting
   b those which occur more frequently but which can also be anticipated, eg monthly updating of price lists
   c those which occur regularly but which cannot be identified precisely, eg word processing, dealing with visitors, taking dictation.

Then introduce a time element, ie what you can plan on a yearly, monthly, weekly and daily basis. Planning on a yearly or monthly basis is generally straightforward provided you use the most appropriate planning aids, ie diaries, planners and follow-up systems (see page 361).

Planning on a weekly or daily basis requires more skill and at this stage you have to bear in mind certain additional factors.

• You have to allow for unforeseen eventualities – planning for the unexpected is one of your more exacting tasks!
• In order to do this you must establish a set of priorities for both yourself and your staff which are sufficiently precise to be helpful but not so rigid that they cannot be re-organised in an emergency.

When you are new to the job it is a good idea consciously to make a list each week of:

• work which *must* be done – this is normally on-going and sometimes increases as the week progresses
• work which *should* be done – eventually, of course, this turns into work which must be done
• work which *could* be done – although this is normally wishful thinking rather than a genuine expectation!
• work which could be delegated to others.

Delegation

Your boss will expect you to take the responsibility for developing the skills of your junior staff – firstly to keep them interested and motivated in the work that they do, secondly to enable them to keep the office going if you are ill or on holiday.

You can only do this if you *involve* them in what is going on, where you can, and *delegate* work to them so that they can learn more about the skills required to become a PA. It is totally unfair to expect your junior assistant to be able to take minutes at a meeting when you have rushed off to help out at an exhibition, when you have never even involved her in meetings procedures at any stage of her career.

Delegation is an art. It takes nerve, patience, skill – and courage. If you are a supervisor then you have the opportunity to delegate the *job itself* but *not* the responsibility for that job. If she does well, then you should be the first to praise her. If she does badly then *you* get the blame – hence the need for courage!

This is one of the reasons people fail to delegate. Others include the belief that:

- 'the only one who can do a good job around here is me'
- 'it's quicker to do it myself'
- 'I haven't time to show her'
- 'she may make a better job of it than I could – and where does that leave *me?*'

So why does anyone delegate? Basically because the pluses are greater than the minuses. If you do it properly then your staff will be well motivated and more productive, the working atmosphere and relationships in the office will improve, your section will be seen to shine and *you* will get the accolades – from your staff and your boss.

SPECIAL NOTE
Fifteen minutes spent training someone properly how to do a job will repay itself a thousand fold by the end of the year.

How to delegate

The golden rules of delegating include:

- explaining *clearly* and *simply* what is required and the standard of work expected at the start
- allowing your staff the freedom to decide how to carry out the task (though you could ask them to clarify this for you in the early stages)
- checking your instructions are understood by encouraging discussion about the task and how to do it
- being realistic about what you expect them to do and the timescale
- being alert for signs that there are problems, but only intervening if absolutely necessary
- making certain that your staff know they can always come to you for help, advice and encouragement.

- Giving praise where it is due and *constructive* criticism only if necessary.

And *don't* give out just the boring jobs you hate doing yourself! Identify the tasks which could be delegated by asking yourself: 'If I were on holiday for the next three weeks, what tasks would really *have* to wait until my return?' *Those* are the only jobs you should hang on to!

Prioritising and organising for emergencies

One of the most difficult skills to learn is that of prioritising the tasks you have to carry out. Although experience is an enormous help here, there are methods you can use to help you to identify how quickly something must be done.

There are two key aspects of a job which mean it is top priority – its **importance** and its **urgency**. Tasks which are *both* should be at the top of your list. Tasks which are neither should be ignored, or even better, jettisoned completely.

For those which fall in between, urgency will usually rule the day. However, you will find that the better organised you become the less you are trouble-shooting and trying to cope with lots of things which were all wanted yesterday. When you find that most of your time is spent working on important jobs which are not yet urgent, then you know you are starting to win!

Tips to help you cope include:

- learn to allow for contingencies and emergencies, eg:
  - when a job takes longer than you thought
  - when your boss overrides your priorities with a sudden emergency of his own
  - when other staff are away and you have to take on extra work
- if a job is new, allow 20 per cent more time for it than you first estimated.

 TEST YOURSELF

Read the following list of tasks you have prepared for Monday, 25 March.

- Carrying out routine safety checks on office equipment
- Receiving visitors
- Taking dictation
- Filing
- Obtaining information for a report required for 29 March
- Checking the diary and follow-up systems
- Keyboarding of urgent correspondence
- Updating databases
- Organising training schedules for junior staff
- Preparing new wall planners
- Making arrangements for your boss's trip to Scotland on 5 May
- Discussing day's work with boss
- Checking telephone answering system

- Listening for instructions on dictating machine
- Ordering office supplies (which are getting low)
- Checking the fax machine
- Opening and distributing the mail
- Taking notes at a meeting to be held at 2 pm
- Dealing with routine correspondence
- Circulating documents for meeting to be held on 10 April

1 Re-categorise them into:
   – tasks which *must* be done
   – tasks which *should* be done
   – tasks which *could* be done.

2 Place an asterisk by those tasks which you think you could delegate to an office junior.

The daily routine

Remember that there are certain crucial parts of the day to which you should pay particular attention.

Arrival at the workplace

- Forget about the lark/owl syndrome (unless your boss is of exactly the same mind as you); even if you are by nature an owl and want to work late at night rather than early in the morning you should still try to arrive at the office before your boss. Otherwise chaos could reign.
- If you do arrive before your boss remember there is nothing wrong with having a slow start and relaxing for a few moments with a cup of coffee. Treat this as your 'thinking time' and if it puts you in the right frame of mind to greet your boss, your junior staff and any early morning visitors, so much the better.
- Carry out certain routine tasks (unless you have delegated them to your junior), eg check the fax machine, the telephone answering service etc.
- Make a physical check to see that all areas are clean, tidy and of the right temperature (if they are not, make a note to speak to the cleaner or to whoever else is responsible for office maintenance). Check also for any potential health and safety hazards or security risks – rooms left unlocked by the cleaners etc.
- Check the diaries – remind reception of the arrival of any visitors.
- Either open or supervise the opening, sorting and date stamping of the incoming mail. Decide what you can do and what needs your boss's attention. Find and attach any relevant papers.
- Draw up or check the list of jobs for your junior staff.
- See your boss as soon as possible (or as soon as he/she allows) to discuss the day's programme.

During the day

- Much depends on the day. During the periods when your boss is away from the office or involved in a meeting or other appointments you can deal with the lists of jobs which must and should be done. If your boss is away all day, you may even be able to do some work from the list of jobs which could be done.

- Remember, however, to keep a general check on the work going on in the office and in particular, the work of your junior staff. Much depends on how experienced your staff are – if they are, don't irritate them by constant checks; if they are not, keep a closer (but not too close) eye on what they are doing.

At the end of the day

- Check the outgoing mail and deal with any last minute requests.
- Check on the work of your juniors to see whether they have left anything important outstanding.
- Check the diary for the following day and highlight the priorities. Sort out any documents which may be required for early morning appointments. Remember to check with your boss whether he/she is coming into the office or going straight to his/her first external appointment.
- Make end of day checks on security; see that equipment is switched off, that confidential papers are locked away, that filing cabinets are made secure. Check that the fax machine and telephone answering machines are left switched on.
- Check your list of jobs for the week to see whether any on the 'could be done' list have now to be moved to the 'must be done' list and adjust the following day's work accordingly.
- If your boss is staying on to work late, check that all the documents he/she needs are available, and – if you really want your boss to think well of you – offer to make a cup of coffee before you go!

TEST YOURSELF

Various pitfalls can occur throughout the day. Look at those listed below. Put a tick against the one listed in each category which you would find the more difficult to avoid. Then discuss with your tutor the best ways of overcoming them.

1 Acting without a plan

Adhering too strictly to the day's plan

2 Being too optimistic about what you can achieve during the day

Being too pessimistic about what you can achieve during the day

3 Being so engrossed in your work that you resent any interruptions from your boss, your juniors or visitors

Having an 'open door' policy so that you make time to listen to everybody but have no time to do your own work

4 Spending too much time chatting

Never having any time to chat

5 Doing everything yourself

Delegating everything to your juniors

6 Constantly proof-reading and making other checks on the work of your juniors

Leaving your juniors to it

7 Being indecisive

Letting no one else but you make a decision

8 Working in chaos

Constantly tidying up

9 Making too many draft outlines of tasks to be carried out during the day

'Dashing something off' within minutes

10 Not having the appropriate materials available – reference books, stationery, computer disks etc

Being unable to start a job unless all the materials are to hand

11 Spending a long time each day doing the filing no matter what else happens

Letting the filing accumulate

SPECIAL NOTE
Remember that although it is essential that you do take responsibility for organising the work schedule of the office, you do not have to bear that burden uncomplainingly – or on your own. Don't be a martyr – if there are problems ask for help from your executive or another PA. Try to make sure that your relationships with your junior staff encourage a two-way process of consultation and discussion. You may be the focal point of the team but you are still a member of that team (see Managing stress, page 414).

ACTIVITY SECTION

Individual/group tasks
1 You take up a new appointment and arrive on the first day only to find that your office looks as if it has just been vandalised. It is dirty, the floor is uncarpeted and the vinyl covering is torn and stained. All the working surfaces are dusty. There is an old kettle and some unwashed crockery on a table in the corner of the room and the nearest washing up facilities are at the end of the corridor. The gas-fired central heating seems adequate and there is some central fluorescent lighting which is bright but rather harsh. The windows look out on to a busy street. There is no space for visitors to sit. There is only one vertical filing cabinet which is so full that the drawers are half open. Its key is nowhere to be found. The only photocopier you can find is one which is situated a floor down from your office and is used by so many other clerical staff that there is always a long queue. Your desk is small and its desktop is virtually taken up by a typewriter, some filing trays and a few unmatched containers full of office sundries such as pencils, rubber bands and paper clips. Your chair is a standard upright model. You have one office junior whose desk is even smaller than yours.

You have one telephone between you. Some out-of-date planners are stuck on to the wall with sellotape.

Discuss as a group the steps you would take to effect improvements (and the order in which you would take them).

Case study 1

You are the assistant to the PA of Joan Fletcher, the Managing Director of a company of toy manufacturers. You have just returned to the office after a week's holiday and find that your PA has been called away unexpectedly because of her mother's illness. She has left you the following note.

'Sorry to land you with this but mum is quite ill with an angina attack and I can't leave her on her own. I'll get in touch with you when the doctor arrives and I find out what has to be done.

Joan's diary is pretty straightforward apart from the fact that I think she may have slipped in a lunchtime appointment without telling me – on Friday I overheard her talking on the phone to Frank Adams of Monks Ltd and I think she arranged a lunchtime meeting then. She dashed off immediately afterwards and I didn't get the chance to check with her.

She did promise Margaret Phillips, the union representative, that she would provide some information about the proposed new job grading scheme for the next Joint Consultative Meeting this coming Friday. She is waiting for some information from Jim Lancaster in personnel – could you chase him please?

A word of warning – Beattie Murphy has now filed an official complaint that she sprained her ankle because she fell over a bucket left by the cleaner at the entrance to the staff canteen. I think the union representative may try to see Joan today on the grounds of a breach of Health and Safety. Try to warn her first thing and look in the Health and Safety file for any relevant information.

Joan is giving a speech at the Toy Manufacturers' Association Annual Dinner this evening – it is formal and she will have to wear evening dress. Her husband has been invited but on Friday he was still trying to get out of it! The organisers must know by lunchtime at the latest whether he is going.

Just a reminder – the Electricity Board officials will be coming today some time to check on all electrical appliances to see whether or not they are in need of repair. Ask the staff to cooperate even if they are busy – we'll be in trouble with the Health and Safety Committee if we don't comply.

Julia Maynard was trying to see Joan all last week about publicity for the Christmas Fair in Bath. She needs to know certain basic information such as what products are to be promoted and at what price. Her final deadline is Wednesday and she needs to see Joan today (she claims the meeting will last at least an hour!).

The next Board meeting is a week on Thursday – I don't know whether or not I shall be back in time to circulate the notice and agenda but they need to go out some time today.'

You know that Joan will be in the office in half an hour's time. List what action you will take before she arrives and how you will deal with any potential problems. (Assume that there are no other appointments booked in the diary.)

Managing time

Give me just a little more time . . .

If you think about it, the English language is full of phrases to do with time – and most of them are misnomers! We talk about 'finding' time or 'making' time when we obviously can't do either! And we certainly can't 'manage' time in the literal sense, as this would imply being able to alter the clock whenever we felt like it.

Yet there are dozens of books written and management courses held about time management – so what is their aim? Quite simply, it is to enable you to identify how you spend your time so that you can control its usage more effectively. Good time management doesn't only relate to your work life, but also enables you to protect what the Americans call 'quality time'. This is the time you need for yourself – no matter how busy you are. Make time to spend with your family, or your friends, to pursue a hobby or merely to relax – in order to recharge your batteries for the following day.

RULE 1

Learn to value your time – it is your most precious resource. It is the only one which is completely irreplaceable.

Time wasting

If time is so valuable, then wasting it must be a crime! If you waste an hour – and have to work late to catch up – you have eaten into your 'quality time' which you could have spent doing other things. So the pay-off for reducing time wasting activities is tremendous!

Which of the following apply to you?

- making unnecessary journeys (eg twice to the photocopier in ten minutes)
- spending ten minutes looking for a document you should have filed last week
- gossiping to colleagues (who call into your office, you meet on a corridor etc)
- chatting on the telephone
- shuffling papers – because you can't decide which job to start next
- daydreaming – because you just aren't in the mood for work that day.

Most of us – especially on bad days – are guilty of some of the above. Problems occur when we *regularly* waste time in these activities.

RULE 2

You won't stop all your time-wasting activities overnight. Step one is to be *aware* of when you are wasting time; step two is to change your working habits.

The role of the boss

The problem for a PA or secretary that even if *she* is organised and doesn't waste her time, her boss might. At the very least he/she will usually expect the PA to be at his/her beck and call and to drop whatever she is doing when she is needed.

RULE 3

Standard time management rules cannot be applied to a PA/ secretary as her boss is often the key controlling factor on her time.

If you are very busy, and your boss constantly interrupts you or distracts you then you have to make a decision – is it that he/she doesn't *know* how busy you are – or doesn't *care?* If it is the former, then you need to be able to point this out, firmly yet politely (see Managing communications, page 345.) An executive normally wants his/her PA to do a good job – after all, it is in his/her own interests that she does. You should therefore find that your boss will do everything possible to help you if there is an urgent job to be done, and you need a quiet hour to complete it – providing that you *tell* him/her.

If you have the type of boss who seems impervious to reason then you have a greater problem. One possibility might be to list all the jobs you have to do and ask your boss to prioritise them for you – he/she would then take responsibility for anything not completed. However, this is fairly drastic action and there is often a better, more tactful method (see Managing your boss, page 291).

Other time stealers

How many of these are familiar to you?

- procrastinating – ie putting off jobs which are boring or you don't want to do. Then getting irritable as the deadline gets closer . . .
- flapping about – piling all your work in the in-tray and then dithering over what to do first
- darting about – trying to do three jobs at once and not doing anything properly
- taking on too much, from too many people, in an effort to please everyone – and ending up totally overloaded
- having a schedule that goes to pieces the minute an emergency occurs

and

- realising with a sinking feeling that the piece of paper you now have in your hand should have been posted two days ago!

Techniques for time management

Learning to control and manage your time is a *skill* and like all skills it has to be practised. Therefore don't expect to be an expert in five minutes. Expect to slip back into your old ways now and then – but remember, you have nothing to lose and much to gain from taking yourself in hand and trying again.

The areas to concentrate on are:

- office organisation and systems of work
- planning
- prioritising
- people
- self-discipline.

The first three of these areas are dealt with in Chapter 7, Organising work schedules (see page 369 to page 379). This short section therefore concentrates on the *people* who may disrupt you – and how to deal with them – and the techniques *you* need to manage your time effectively.

People

There are three categories of people on which you should concentrate if you want to manage your time better.

- your junior staff – to whom you can delegate work (see Chapter 7, Organising work schedules, page 375)
- time wasters – who may or may not be deliberate in their intentions!
- the 'just-do-me-a-favour' sort.

Time-wasters

Be ruthless with the time wasters in your life (unless it's your boss!). This does *not* mean being rude to anyone!

Most time wasters are colleagues who visit your office for some reason or another:

- try to train them to phone you rather than visit
- if they phone, and you need an excuse to ring off, say your boss is buzzing you on your other line . . .
- if the caller arrives in person, politely explain that you can't stop as you'll be in trouble if you don't finish the job you're doing in the next 5 minutes . . . or

- keep a calculator on hand and a set of figures. When the caller arrives, frown and mutter to yourself. Say you can't talk or you'll forget where you are . . .
- work out an emergency routine with your boss for *real* problem characters who can't take a hint. Arrange to be able to rush into his/her office with an 'urgently wanted file' so you can escape if necessary. (A variation on this routine also works well in reverse when your boss needs rescuing.)

The 'do me a favour' sort

Another type of problem person you will meet is the one who will ask you to do jobs 'as a favour'. Because most of us like others to think well of us we tend to say 'yes' in situations like this. **Don't** – unless there's a very good reason why you should (eg you're up for promotion and this person would be your next boss!).

Learning to say 'no' is very hard to do – but often essential. If you are asked to do something then ask yourself two questions.

1 Have I the time to do a good job, without jeopardising anything urgent or important?

2 Could it do me any good in the long run?

If the answer to both is yes, then go ahead. Otherwise say 'no' (see Managing communications, page 345).

RULE 5

It is not heartless to work out 'what's in it for me?' – simply cold business logic. However, don't think in terms of money! Building up favours can be far more useful – as you can call these in when you need help yourself!

Self-discipline

Probably the hardest part of all! We are all creatures of habit and it is therefore extremely difficult for us to change the way we operate. This is why you must 'stick at' time management if you want to see results – and not give up the first time something goes wrong.

- Eliminate time wasting methods of working:
  - reduce the time you spend walking around the building. Group jobs which have to be done or delivered elsewhere and do them in one journey
  - don't put on the coffee machine and sit and watch the coffee filter through. You could do about three small tasks in that time
  - file *whenever you have a spare few minutes.* Don't wait for a chunk of time before you start it.
- Don't put off jobs which you don't like doing. Do them *first* – then give yourself a treat (a cup of coffee?) as a reward.

- Don't throw out your systems because you had a bad day. We all have days where we go solidly backwards now and then.
- Don't allow yourself to be lazy or idle! Set your own deadlines and challenge yourself to achieve them!
- Remember that a job well done doesn't come back to be redone tomorrow! Carelessness ruins both your image and your time schedules in one go.

RULE 6

Don't expect miracles. Time management is a bit like going on a diet – you may slide back from time to time but if you keep at it you see the benefits later.

A final word of warning – and advice

Many people are hesitant about practising time management because they are frightened that if it works *too* well then they will have nothing to do. The extreme of this, of course, is that your job is seen as superfluous.

It is true, and rather sad, that if someone walks into your office while you are sitting staring into space, they are unlikely to believe your explanation that you were deep in thought about the best way to present the next monthly sales report. Instead they are likely to hurry away, comment to your boss that you have nothing to do, and he/she will feel honour bound to find you something.

Experienced PAs never *quite* operate time management to this extent but always keep one or two non-urgent tasks to do at quiet times. This prevents a disaster occurring as the MD decides to visit your particular patch on the very first day in the year that you have had very little to do. Remember that deferral file? In moments of extreme crisis retrieve it and shuffle the papers, frowning at those you are holding. If you decide to wander around the office to see what is going on, carry a file or two with you. Remember that work in an office is always one of extremes and enjoy the reprieve – tomorrow will probably be hectic!

8 Servicing meetings

Section 1 – Organising and preparing for meetings

Why have a meeting?

Having a meeting is only one of many ways to communicate in an organisation. Sometimes it can be replaced by a report, a memo requesting ideas or information, a series of telephone calls or even an informal chat with one or two people over a cup of coffee. A meeting should therefore be called only when it is obviously the most appropriate form of communication for the purpose intended.

Some forms of meeting (such as statutory meetings) are more elaborate and formal than others and consequently more time consuming. If, for instance, the meeting is to be an Annual General Meeting many formalities have to be observed. Other meetings such as departmental meetings can be more informal as the number of members can be kept to a minimum, the amount of paperwork reduced and the order of business made more flexible.

Types of meeting

Informal meetings are held all the time. They range from a discussion between two people on a specific topic to a regular get together by a group to talk about on-going matters which affect the work of that group. In some cases they are called **working parties**. You may or may not be asked to take notes of the proceedings.

Formal meetings tend to be more frequent the more senior you become in the organisation. If you are a director's secretary or PA you may have to prepare for, attend and take notes for the following meetings:

Board meeting

A body such as a limited company must act through its Board of Directors which is responsible for managing the company's affairs. The first board meeting must be held as soon as possible after the appointment of the first directors and the receipt of the company's Certificate of Incorporation.

Business at subsequent meetings might include both policy making and routine business transactions, such as:

- development of the company's business
- means of acquiring additional capital
- acquisition of another company
- receipt of reports from various committees
- sanctioning large amounts of capital expenditure
- the organisation of the company
- the appointment of senior staff.

Committee meeting

If allowed by the Articles of Association (the rules by which a company is governed under the Companies Acts 1948–1989), the Board of Directors can delegate powers and duties to a committee or committees which carry out certain tasks and report back to the Board.

The principal forms of committee are:

- **Executive**   A committee with **plenary** power, ie one which can make a binding decision provided it acts **intra vires** (within its terms of reference). If it acts **ultra vires** (outside its terms of reference) its decision will not be binding.
- **Advisory**   A committee which gives advice and makes recommendations but which does not have the power to make binding decisions.
- **Standing**   A committee which is permanently in existence with business conducted at regular intervals
- **Ad hoc**   A committee formed for a particular task. Having achieved its purpose it then ceases to exist.
- **Sub**   A committee formed as part of another committee which can be either standing or ad hoc.
- **Joint**   A committee formed for the purpose of coordinating the activities of two or more committees. Again it may be standing or ad hoc.

Annual General Meeting

Unless the company is a private company, it must hold an AGM each year to which all shareholders must be invited. The business transacted is that specified in the Articles of Association, eg:

- to receive the directors' and auditors' reports
- to examine the accounts and balance sheets
- to sanction the dividend
- to appoint or re-appoint directors
- to decide on the auditors' remuneration.

Other business may be transacted provided its nature is clearly stated.

Extraordinary General Meeting

An EGM is normally called to transact business which cannot conveniently be held over until the next AGM.

Other less frequent meetings

These include:

- **Class meetings**   Held principally in connection with the variation of rights and privileges attached to different classes of share
- **Meetings of creditors**   or classes of creditors in connection with any form of reconstruction or on the winding up of the company.

Meetings documents

Most meetings are conducted in accordance with their **Standing Orders** – the rules which provide for the way in which the meeting should be run. In such circumstances it is important for you to be aware of the appropriate paperwork you may have to prepare in order to comply with those rules, ie:

- **Notice**
- **Agenda**
- **Chairperson's agenda**
- **Supplementary papers**
- **Minutes**

Notice

You must let the members of a meeting know when it is going to happen and where it is going to take place. If the meeting is informal all you may need to do is to type a brief memo or even make a telephone call (although cautious PA's rarely rely on verbal communication!). If the meeting is formal, however, certain procedures must be observed.

The notice must be sent to all members. If it is not this may affect the **validity** of the meeting, ie whether or not the decisions made at that meeting have any binding effect. However, if you do forget to send a notice to a member all may not be lost – your omission may be excused if:

- the rules provide for **waiver**, ie where the members of the meeting are allowed to overlook the mistake
- everyone *entitled* to be present *is* actually present – they may have heard about the meeting on the office grapevine! – and agrees to what is being done
- those to whom a notice has not been sent are 'beyond summoning distance' ie abroad or too ill to attend.

The length of notice required is normally provided for in the rules or Standing Orders of the meeting. If not, reasonable notice must be given. Unless otherwise provided, it is implied that the number of days stated are **clear days** ie exclusive of the day of serving the notice *and* of the day of the meeting.

CHECK IT YOURSELF

1 Look at the example of a notice opposite and check that the following details are included:

- place of meeting
- date, day and time of meeting
- the business to be transacted

- the date of notice
- the signature of the person convening the meeting (normally that of the meetings secretary and only included in formal notices).

NOTICE

Derby Ceramics Ltd
King Street
DERBY
DF3 1AA

12 June 199–

The next Board meeting will be held in Committee Room No 1 at 1430 hours on Tuesday, 27 June.

Anne Davies

Secretary

---

2 There is a difference between a private secretary, who arranges and takes the notes at a meeting, and a Company Secretary. Check on their different duties.

Agenda

No one should be expected to attend a meeting without having some clear idea of what is to be discussed at that meeting. Think of the agenda as a compass which is intended to indicate the direction the meeting must take.

The items on the agenda should therefore be arranged according to the rules of the meeting and if these do not specify the order it is up to you to arrange the items logically – normally with the routine business first so as to leave more time for the other more specific business of the meeting.

Fortunately there are a number of guidelines for you to follow.

Look at the example of an Agenda below.

Note:

The heading   This must indicate what kind of a meeting it is and when and where it is to be held. It is usual to send the notice out with the agenda so that the information is not given twice. Only when time is short and an agenda is not yet completed is a separate notice sent out.

Apologies for absence   This item allows for the recording of the names of those people who have indicated that they cannot attend.

Minutes of the previous meeting   This allows members the opportunity of pointing out any factual errors in the minutes.

Matters arising   This enables members to comment on and query any action taken as a result of the discussions at that meeting.

Correspondence   This item can be used to draw the attention of the meeting to a communication of general interest, eg a request from a charity for volunteers for a flag day etc.

Specific item(s)   There can be as many items of specific business as you or the chairperson thinks fit given the meeting's terms of reference.

Any other business   This item allows members to ask for discussion on a matter which has arisen too late to be included on the agenda.

AGENDA

Derby Ceramics Ltd
King Street
DERBY
DF3 1AA

12 June 199–

The next Board meeting will be held in Committee Room No 1 at 1430 hours on Tuesday, 27 June.

Anne Davies

Secretary

A G E N D A

1 Apologies for absence
2 Minutes of the previous meeting
3 Matters arising
4 Correspondence
5 Display of company's products at autumn
  exhibition
6 Staff welfare
7 Any other business
8 Date and time of next meeting

> **Date and time of next meeting** This is usually the final agenda item. However, it is often useful for the chairperson to discuss this item before the actual business of the meeting begins. This overcomes the problem of members who have to leave before the end of the meeting.

SPECIAL NOTES

1 A word of warning! It is a common error, particularly for a new meetings secretary, to 'overload' the agenda. You will naturally want to clear as much business as possible but be realistic – you will probably know how long the meeting is scheduled to run so try to avoid the possibility of the discussion of important items being curtailed because of lack of time. In the early stages you should be able to rely on your chairperson to check the agenda with you to see whether you have achieved the right balance. (You may have to bear in mind, however, that he/she may have reasons of his/her own for curtailing a particular item or placing it at a particular stage on the agenda – and that decision rests with the chairperson alone!)

2 It is usual for the chairperson to ask members for items for *Any other business* at the beginning of the meeting. It is then possible for a decision to be made as to their importance – should they be discussed immediately, should time be left at the end of the meeting for discussion or should discussion be deferred until the next meeting, when the item may be given its own 'slot' on the agenda?

Chairperson's agenda

From the very beginning you will realise that your main role as the meetings secretary is to support and assist your chairperson. Of particular assistance to him/her is any quick and easy source of reference to use during the course of the meeting. The normal agenda is usually insufficient for this purpose and what you should therefore do is to provide the chairperson with an annotated or extended version (see pages 392-3).

SPECIAL NOTES

1 It is likely that your chairperson will use the chairperson's agenda to make notes as the meeting progresses and these notes may help you when you are preparing the minutes. An example of such notes is shown on page 410. Be careful, however! It is advisable that once the minutes have been prepared and accepted by the members that the chairperson's agenda is destroyed – otherwise there could be problems if the chairperson's notes (which may have been made in a hurry and not corrected at a later date) do not coincide with the actual minutes. This is one of the few occasions when you are actually encouraged *not* to keep a record.

2 At formal meetings you may be required to:
 • use the full notice heading instead of the abbreviated form used above
 • provide the actual wording of the motions the chairperson will speak, eg *I move that the Meeting accepts the report of the Auditors for the year under review.*

CHAIRPERSON'S AGENDA

Meeting: Board Meeting

Date/time: 1430 hours, 27 June 199-

Place: Committee Room No 1

AGENDA ITEM	NOTES
1 Apologies for absence John Brooks still in hospital – meeting's best wishes for a speedy recovery.	1
2 Minutes of previous meeting	2
3 Matters arising	3

Questions may be asked
on:
- final cost of
  refurbishment to
  reception area –
  £27 500
- progress on launch
  of new christening
  mug
  - Press conference
    2/7/– information
    to follow
  - Article in 'The Lady'
    7/7
  - Advertising campaign
    10/7 onwards

Supplementary papers

Most meetings require you to prepare additional documentation depending on the items to be discussed. Try to avoid the following problems!

- It is common for too much paperwork to be produced, which deters all but the most determined member from reading it. How enthusiastic would you be to read a 30 page document relating to just one item on a ten item agenda?
- Equally annoying to members is receiving a document on the morning of the meeting – although this may provide a good excuse for some of them to give up even the pretence of having read it!

4 Correspondence   4
Letter of thanks from
local college for
company's response to
request for work
experience places

5 Display of company's   5
products at autumn
exhibition
- to be held at NEC
  Birmingham
- Sales Manager to
  provide members with
  report. Information
  pack already
  circulated

6 Staff welfare   6
Staff Welfare Committee
anxious to hold staff
dinner dance. Advise
Board to recommend that
Committee be asked to
provide further details
at next meeting.

7 Any other business   7
Comments on selling
trip to USA

8 Date and time of next   8
meeting
Avoid 7-14 July -
Conference in Brussels

- Wherever possible try to avoid **tabling papers** (ie producing them at the time of the meeting) – given that your hands may be tied if you are waiting for your chairperson or another senior member of the organisation to produce the relevant documents.
- Try to adopt a layout for these papers which is easy to read and to which the members will become accustomed. Unlike the rest of the meetings documentation there is usually no set format for you to follow. Consider the use of:
  – headings and subheadings
  – numbered paragraphs, sections and sub-sections for easy reference
  – tables, graphs and illustrations.

Make sure that *every* paper is properly identified and linked to the relevant agenda item. Ensure too that the reproduction of the documents is of a high standard – you are trying to *tempt* members to read them.

Minutes

It is always wise to have a written record of any business transacted, even at an informal meeting. In some cases it is a legal requirement.

MINUTES

Minutes of the Board Meeting held in Committee Room No 1 at 1430 hours on 27 June 199-.

PRESENT

Mr Ernst Heilberg	Chair
Mrs Linda Hargreaves	Purchasing Manager
Mr John Wright	Personnel Manager
Miss Veronica Olonde	Secretary
Mr David Jones	Sales Manager (Coopted)

1 APOLOGIES FOR ABSENCE

Apologies for absence were received from Mr John Brookes. The Chairperson was instructed by the meeting to send him best wishes for a speedy recovery.

2 MINUTES OF THE PREVIOUS MEETING

The minutes of the previous meeting were taken as read, agreed as a true and correct record and signed by the Chairperson.

3 MATTERS ARISING

The Chairperson reported that the final cost of the refurbishment of the reception area was £27 500

He also outlined the publicity arrangements made for the forthcoming launch of the new christening mug.

The Purchasing Manager confirmed that the maintenance contract for the computer equipment had been renewed for another year.

4 CORRESPONDENCE

The Secretary read out the letter of thanks from the college for the organisation's participation in its student works experience

---

Although the format to be followed can vary and often depends on 'house rules', the more formal a meeting is, the more likely it will be that you have to record the proceedings in a standardised manner.

CHECK IT YOURSELF
Look at the set of minutes below. There's a checklist of information to be included on page 396.

scheme. It was agreed that this was a useful way of furthering industry/college links.

5 DISPLAY OF COMPANY'S PRODUCTS AT AUTUMN EXHIBITION
The Sales Manager referred to the report which had been circulated previously to members. The exhibition was to take place at the National Exhibition Centre, Birmingham, and involved a team of 5 members of staff who had received specific training in the techniques required for mounting such an exhibition. A full statement as to the cost would be presented at the next meeting.

6 STAFF WELFARE
The Chairperson reported that the Staff Welfare Committee was anxious to hold a staff dinner dance. Discussion took place about the cost of such a proposal and it was agreed that the Committee should be asked to prepare a report for the Board's consideration at a later meeting to cover not only the question of cost but also that of venue.

7 ANY OTHER BUSINESS
The Chairperson gave a brief outline of his recent visit to the USA. A return visit was being planned by representatives of several large departmental stores in New York when it was hoped that some new business would be generated.

8 DATE AND TIME OF NEXT MEETING
It was decided that the next meeting should be held at 1430 hours on Tuesday, 20 July 199-.

(Signed) ....Chairperson

...........................Date

You must include:

- The name of the organisation, the type of meeting and the place, date and time of the meeting.
- The names of those present. It is usual to put the name of the chairperson first and that of the secretary last. It is also advisable to put the names of the rest of the members in alphabetical order – thus avoid-ing problems of status! You should also indicate whether any member is a **coopted member** (ie one invited for a special purpose as distinct from one who is a regular member of the meeting) or there **ex officio** (ie one who is entitled to attend by virtue of his/her position in the organisation).

   Note that if the meeting is particularly large (such as a shareholders' meeting) you need record only the *number* present.
- A brief note of what has been discussed and decided using an acceptable form of wording. Items should be numbered, and if possible, should follow the numbering of the Agenda (see also **Special Note** below).
- The date and time of the next meeting. From what you already know, how should this item have been dealt with – bearing in mind that the meeting might have lasted a long time?
- Space for the chairperson to sign and date the minutes once they are agreed as a correct record at the next meeting.

SPECIAL NOTE

- The more senior a secretary you become the greater the possibility will be that you will be required to produce minutes which contain more formal language than that used in the illustration above. Look, for example, at item 6 which summarises the discussion and the decision about the organisation's annual dinner dance. In a more formal context the item would have to be re-written to include the word **resolved** (because a decision was made) and to reduce the discussion, ie

   It was resolved that the Staff Welfare Committee be asked to report back to the Board of Directors on the possibility of holding a staff dinner dance.
- Numbering systems for minutes vary – some organisations use the minute number followed by the year, ie 23/93 would be the 23rd item discussed and minuted for that committee during 1993. Check the system in operation where you work.

Meetings procedure

Informal meetings

At an informal meeting the atmosphere tends to be relaxed (at least at the beginning!) and much depends on the way in which the chairperson wants to handle matters although it is always advisable to:

- set a time limit or **guillotine** on the length of the meeting
- follow the agenda without too many diversions
- have a clear consensus as to what has been decided.

The meeting then proceeds as follows:

1 The chairperson will open the meeting, welcome new members and receive apologies for absence. He/she should then check on the

items to be raised under **Any other business** to see whether any of them are so urgent that they must be dealt with immediately. Otherwise time might run out before that agenda item is reached. He/she will then (unless the meeting is very small and informal) ask whether the minutes of the previous meeting can be 'taken as read' (otherwise you will have to read them aloud).

2 The chairperson then asks whether the minutes can be agreed 'as a true and correct record' – this is where you hold your breath. If there are any corrections you must note them and make reference to them in the next set of minutes.

3 The items of business, as listed on the agenda, will then be discussed in turn and the decisions taken will be noted for the minutes (see illustration above).

Formal meetings

In more formal meetings, however, (such as those held by Local Authorities, the Civil Service or the Trade Unions) there is normally a set procedure (sometimes known as **the order of business**).

1 Before the meeting actually begins you must check that a **quorum** exists, ie the minimum number of people required to be present in order for the business of the meeting to be validly transacted. If an insufficient number of people arrives the meeting cannot be held. Note that you must also be careful to check *throughout the course of the meeting* that a quorum remains. If some people leave in the middle of the meeting it is easy for it to become **inquorate** without anyone realising it at the time. Only when a quorum has been mustered can the chairperson open the meeting.

2 The next stage of the procedure is as given in points 1, 2 and 3 under Informal meetings.

3 Other business of the meeting will then be discussed with each item possibly involving one or more of the following procedures.

- Any proposals which are made at the meeting are normally referred to as **motions**.
- The rules may expect each motion to have a **proposer** and a **seconder** ie someone who puts forward the proposal and someone who supports him/her. If no one is prepared to act as seconder the motion can go no further. (In most cases, however, you will find that the proposer of a motion has already asked someone to be its seconder before the meeting begins.)
- Sometimes the proposer of a motion realises in the course of the discussion that the motion is not likely to be successful or has been overtaken by other suggestions. In this case it can be withdrawn and no further discussion need take place.
- Once a motion has been discussed it may then be put to the vote and a **resolution** (ie a decision) reached which either accepts or rejects it. Note that a difficulty for the secretary may be that during

the discussion someone may propose an **amendment** to the motion in order to improve it by certain alterations. There is a set procedure to be followed which may confuse you at first if you are trying to follow a number of different arguments at the same time (see below).

TEST YOURSELF

Suppose the original motion had been

I propose that we hold the annual staff dinner dance on Saturday, 12 December, at the Royal George Hotel.

One of the younger members of the meeting might protest that there should be a visit to a nightclub afterwards. A married member might want the start and finishing times included for the benefit of those who require babysitters. Someone else might object to the term *dinner dance* and want it altered to *get-together*.

How do you think the chairperson should deal with these suggestions?

a By allowing general discussion to take place followed by a general agreement as to what changes should be made

b By allowing discussion on one suggested amendment at a time, followed by a vote on each amendment in turn

c By allowing discussion on one suggested amendment at a time, followed by a vote on each amendment as it affects the original motion.

Discuss your ideas with the rest of your group before reading on.

Correct procedure

What the chairperson should *not* do is to allow all the proposed amendments to be discussed at the same time. The procedure to be followed is **c**. Each amendment is discussed in turn and then each amendment is voted on – *in the order in which it affects the original motion*. Therefore the suggested amendment from staff dinner dance to staff get-together would be voted on first, the insertion of the times second and the proposed visit to a nightclub third.

Assuming that the amendment to include a visit to a nightclub was rejected but the other two accepted, the motion (now known as a **substantive** motion) would read:

I propose that we hold the annual staff get together from 8 pm to 12 mid-night on Saturday 12 December at the Royal George Hotel.

4 Note the difference between an amendment and a **rider**, which is an addition to a resolution after it has been passed.

5 During the discussion you may hear the chairperson or other member remind the meeting of a **point of order**. This normally means that one of the rules of the meeting has not been followed, that the discussion has become irrelevant or that the language used is unacceptable or open to innuendo or misrepresentation.

6 If, for some reason, the meeting cannot continue – because, for instance, some relevant information is not available or the meeting has become too unruly – the chairperson can call a motion to

adjourn the meeting. Normally the motion includes a time, date and place for its continuance. If it does not, it is said to be adjourned **sine die** (without another date having been arranged). Note the difference between postponing a meeting (which has not begun) and adjourning a meeting (which has begun, but has been discontinued).

7 After discussion has ended it is normal for the motion to be put to the vote. There are five main methods of voting:

- by voice (in very small meetings)
- by show of hands
- by poll (by the marking of a voting paper where a member may have more than one vote, ie a vote for each share held)
- by division (the procedure in Parliament and, in some cases, in local government where members go into separate rooms according to whether they are for or against the motion)
- by ballot (where members mark their voting papers and deposit them in a box which is afterwards opened and the votes counted).

After the voting has taken place the chairperson normally declares the result. In formal meetings it is declared in formal terms, ie:

The motion is carried	It is agreed
The motion is lost	It has been rejected
The motion is carried unanimously	Everyone is in favour
The motion is carried **nem con**	No one voted against but some have abstained (ie not voted for or against).

CHECK IT YOURSELF
Some of the procedures given above may seem very confusing. The best way to clarify how these work is to see a formal meeting in action. Try to attend a Trade Union or other formal meeting held in your organisation. If this is impossible, watch a televised union meeting (eg those held at the Trades Union Congress) to see the system in operation.

Role of chairperson

A good chairperson – one who is competent, tactful, impartial and firm – can make your life much easier. Such a person will:

- be fully conversant with the standing orders of the meeting
- start the meeting punctually
- insist that all who speak **address the chair** ie talk to the meeting as a whole rather than to each other
- explain clearly the topic to be discussed and, having given the lead, then keep quiet and allow discussion to develop and ideas to be formulated
- see that everyone has the opportunity to speak and to keep those who do speak to the point

- decide when the discussion has gone on long enough and ensure that a summary of the discussion is given before a decision is taken – this is particularly vital for your minutes!
- ensure that any motion is clear and worded in such a way as to stand the best chance of gaining general agreement. (Try to avoid allowing a motion to be negative, ie it is more acceptable to propose that something be done than to propose something should not be done.)
- leave no one in doubt as to what has been agreed
- close the meeting promptly and formally so that everyone is clear that the business has been concluded.

In order to be able to carry out these duties efficiently the chairperson is likely to have been given certain powers by virtue of the Standing Orders of the meeting:

- to maintain order
- to decide points of order as they arise and to give rulings on points of procedure
- to give a **casting vote**, ie a second vote where there is an equality of votes. (Although the chairperson can vote either way he/she will normally vote to preserve the status quo, ie the existing state of affairs.)
- to adjourn the meeting.

The meetings secretary

In this context – as in many others – you must be a good organiser. For best results you should work closely with your chairperson but certain tasks are your specific responsibility. Remember that there is a regular cycle of tasks for meetings and you must therefore keep a checklist of tasks to be done for each meeting you attend. Ensure also that you have a first class filing system to deal with all the paperwork.

If your organisation regularly holds meetings off the premises it is useful to keep a record of suitable external venues in your area which can provide the facilities required by:

- your company as a whole or particular committees/working parties
- those organising meetings which require visiting speakers
- those organising special presentations
- overseas visitors who may be invited to attend
- any disabled members
- anyone with special dietary requirements.

Keep such a file up to date and include price details so that proper comparisons between venues may be made quickly and easily.

Before the meeting

- Book the appropriate accommodation making sure that you allow for sufficient time (at least 15 minutes) before and after the meeting.

- Prepare and circulate the necessary documents – notice, agenda, chairperson's agenda, minutes of previous meeting, supplementary papers.
- If required, obtain any statements from members who cannot be present but who may wish to have their views made known about certain items to be discussed.
- If necessary, prepare a seating plan of the meeting for the chairperson and provide him/her with background notes on any new members. (He/she may chair a large number of different meetings and need a reminder as to who everyone is around the table.) It may be a good idea to prepare name places, particularly at formal meetings.
- Prepare an attendance list (so that members can sign it on the day of the meeting. It saves you a job and, in some cases, is a legal requirement.).
- Check that the seating arrangements are appropriate and that there is a supply of pens/paper etc.
- Have ready a spare supply of agendas, minutes of the previous meeting and supplementary papers; someone always turns up without them.
- Check on any equipment which is to be used, eg cassette recorder or video equipment. If it is being moved to an external venue list the serial numbers and check it will be insured in transit and covered whilst in the hotel.
- Check on refreshments. If a buffet or full meal is being served take note of any special dietary requirements. Many people today are now vegetarian or vegan or may have to follow a certain diet because of their religious beliefs.

Unless it is absolutely unavoidable *do not* put yourself in the position of having to serve tea or coffee during the meeting – you have too much else to do. On the odd occasion when you find that you have to do so, try tactfully to make sure your chairperson does not carry on with the meeting but calls a halt in the proceedings until refreshments have been served.

- Check on whether or not the area is 'no-smoking' and, if so, warn smokers beforehand. Otherwise provide ashtrays.
- If necessary, make the appropriate car parking arrangements.
- Check whether any interpreters are needed.
- Inform reception of the date and venue of the meeting and make sure someone has been delegated to take phone messages on the day on behalf of those attending.

On the day of the meeting
- Confirm arrangements with reception and the switchboard.
- Nominate someone to take messages for those attending the meeting (the switchboard may be too busy). The person concerned should

know how to handle requests that the meeting be interrupted to pass on an urgent message. If such a disturbance is inevitable, then the messenger should write down the message and hand it to the person concerned, rather than pass on the information verbally.

- Check on accommodation and cleanliness/heating/lighting/seating arrangements.
- Arrange for the relevant papers, files and correspondence to be brought to the room.
- Be there first to welcome members.
- Check that the attendance list is being completed.
- Sit next to the chairperson (to be able to give reminders of certain points if necessary and to pass relevant papers).
- Take notes of the proceedings (trying, if possible, to keep a separate list of actions promised by the chairperson so that you can act as memory-jogger later).

SPECIAL NOTES

1 In many organisations the minutes are composed with an **action column** to the right hand side. In this are recorded the initials of each person who agrees to undertake a specific task, alongside where the task is mentioned in the minutes.

2 Enclosures with minutes can present special problems unless you are very well organised. A good method is to abandon the usual procedure of typing *Enc* at the foot of the minutes and substitute a short line of four dots in the left margin *each time* an enclosure is mentioned. At the end you need simply check the number of times you have typed dots against the number of enclosures.

After the meeting

It is easy to breathe a sigh of relief after a meeting and to turn your attention to the next job. Try to avoid this temptation and take follow-up action as soon as possible.

- Check your notes for any urgent action promised by your chairperson.
- Draft the minutes and check them with your chairperson and other relevant members of the meeting before arranging for their repro-duction and circulation.
- Draft any letters of thanks if necessary (eg to people invited to a meeting for a particular purpose).
- Prepare any other correspondence arising from the meeting.
- Check that all papers used at the meeting have been returned to their original files.
- Enter the date of the next meeting in your diary and that of your chairperson.

Individual activities

1 Although in most meetings voting is by a show of hands, why do you think:

  a many people prefer voting by means of a secret ballot?

  b the 'voice' method of voting is only used at very small meetings?

2 Complete the following sentences with the appropriate word or phrase:

  a As only five people were present the meeting could not begin because of the lack of a . . .

  b 'Although I support the motion in principle I should like to propose the following . . .'

  c The . . . . . . Committee, formed to make arrangements for the Lord Lieutenant's visit, has now been disbanded.

  d Because possible redundancies were being discussed at the next meeting it was decided to invite the Personnel Manager to attend as a . . . . . . member.

  e 'I wish to . . . the motion and trust that someone will . . . it.'

  f As a suitable date and time could not be agreed the meeting was adjourned . . . .

3 A junior member of staff has been appointed as your assistant to help you organise and service the meetings in your company. The idea is that eventually he will be able to deputise for you when you are absent through illness or on holiday. Bear in mind what you know about the basic rules of delegation (see page 375).

  a Can you state:

  - the duties you would give him *initially* to help you to prepare for a meeting
  - the duties you would allow him to undertake whilst the meeting is in progress
  - the duties you consider he should undertake once the meeting is over?

  b Draw up a schedule to show how you would extend his role over the next 12 months.

Individual/group tasks

1 A colleague has been appointed as Chairperson of the Safety Committee of your organisation for the next 12 months. She is not familiar with meetings procedure.

  Bearing in mind that these meetings are relatively informal, with safety representatives from various Departments present plus the Health and Safety Officer in an ex officio capacity:

  a Draw up a schedule which will show her at a glance how each meeting should progress and her role in the proceedings.

  b Make out a list of 'Chairperson's do's and don'ts' which she can read before her first meeting to enable her to run it more smoothly and cooperate fully with her meetings secretary.

2 There are certain personality traits which are very easy to identify during the course of a meeting, especially:

  - the non-stop talker
  - the digressor
  - the mumbler

- the one who is slow on the uptake
- the silent one
- the one who persists with his/her viewpoint or idea despite lack of support or even despite active opposition from the other members
- the sycophant who always agrees with the boss
- the one who knows all the rules (down to the last page and paragraph number).

Discuss (if you are working with a group) and/or make notes on how a good chairperson would deal with each of these personalities at a meeting.

Group task

You are your group's student representative on the student committee. You have been receiving complaints from them about people smoking in the refectory area. There have also been complaints about the poor quality of the food which is cold, expensive and of insufficient variety. The vending machine, which is supposed to operate when the refectory is closed, frequently breaks down or is vandalised. In addition some students have complained about the lack of a pay telephone for student use.

1 Get together as a group of student representatives, appoint a chairperson and a secretary (or you can all act as secretary and compare notes afterwards).

2 Prepare a notice and agenda.

3 Hold the meeting and prepare a set of minutes.

4 Note down the ways in which you think the chairperson successfully guided the meeting and areas which need attention.

Individual group tasks

Case study 1

You work for Toptree Paper Products plc – a large company which makes paper for the office stationery market. The directors are concerned about the future of the industry in view of the volume of cheap imported paper currently flooding into Britain. They have decided to hold a planning meeting next weekend at a local hotel. The draft schedule is as follows:

- Friday evening – 6 pm start: welcome by both Chairman and MD. Overview of weekend. Dinner 8 pm
- Saturday 9 am – noon: video on paper industry plus follow up slides on sales figures, competitors etc. Presentation by Sales Director, Martin Broome and guest speaker from local Business School – Arif Choudry
- Lunch – 12.30 pm – 2 pm
- Saturday 2 pm – 4 pm: Appraisal of Toptree Paper Products in terms of strengths and weaknesses plus presentations of pre-prepared papers by department
- 4 pm – 6 pm: overview of findings by MD. Dinner 8 pm
- Sunday 9 am – noon: 'think tank' session by directors working in groups. Lunch as Saturday
- Sunday 2 pm – 5 pm – ideas brought together. Final plenary session hosted by Chairman and MD.

1 Type up a draft programme for the weekend using the information given above.

2 Note that Arif Choudry will attend for dinner on the Friday night and leave after Saturday lunch. Make out a *comprehensive* list of all the duties you will need to undertake before the weekend takes place and all the arrangements you will have to make with the hotel.

3 Draft a letter to the hotel confirming the details.

4 The MD has asked you to be present at the hotel for the final session on Sunday afternoon, to take notes.

   a Why do you think you have been asked to attend *this* particular session, and not the others?

   b Bearing in mind this is not a usual type of meeting how would you set out your notes and how would you head them?

Case study 2

You have recently started work at JDP Information Systems Ltd – a small computer consultancy – as PA to one of the (two) directors. Once a month sales meetings are held in the board room, to which all 12 sales representatives are invited. The aim of the meetings is to report on progress to date with prospective and actual customers, highlight and clarify queries, discuss new product development and sales techniques, identify are as of weakness in sales reporting methods (if any), and discuss future prospects.

You attended the first meeting with the 'outgoing' PA and were horrified to find:

- On arrival at the board room everyone had to wait outside because the last meeting was over-running – not that this mattered very much as your director, who chaired the meeting, arrived ten minutes late.
- No notice or agenda had been issued so the discussion was something of a 'free for all'.
- Two reps didn't turn up – but nobody knew why not.
- Two errors in last month's minutes were never recorded – the PA merely made a pencilled alteration on her set of papers.
- Representatives frequently talked amongst themselves which made minute taking difficult, if not impossible.
- Most reps had forgotten to bring their copies of last month's sales report, which should have been discussed during the meeting. This item was therefore abandoned.
- The meeting ran out of time long before major items had been covered and the next group to use the board room were already waiting.
- There was a gap in the notes for the minutes where the PA had to jump up to serve coffee.
- The meeting was interrupted four times for reps to take urgent telephone calls. Each time a junior member of staff simply opened the door and called the information across the room.
- Several belligerent members 'shouted down' the suggestions of the others and once the rep for North Wales started on his pet theme of Welsh language publicity material no one could stop him talking.
- An fierce argument broke out between a non-smoker and a smoker when the latter lit a cigarette.

- Later that day you noticed that several confidential matters, brought up at the meeting, were being freely discussed by the other office staff.

After the meeting the director took you on one side. He said that he acknowledged that the meetings were chaotic but the company had grown very quickly in the past two years and none of the employees were knowledgeable about correct meetings procedure – including himself. He added that one of the reasons you were appointed to the job was because of your meetings expertise and he therefore thought that you could help to reorganise them! He has therefore asked you to:

1 Outline for him the procedures he should follow – and why – to be an effective chairperson. He would like these particularly to relate to the present problems he is experiencing at sales meetings.

2 Make out a brief checklist of your own responsibilities to ensure that subsequent meetings run more smoothly.

3 Note down how meetings *should* be interrupted should this prove necessary.

4 State the importance of confidentiality in terms of meetings and the ways in which this can be achieved.

5 Draw up a draft notice and agenda for the next meeting – to be held four weeks from today at 1400 hours – from the topics usually discussed at these meetings.

6 You are lucky in that the director is very honest about the situation and will be supportive of you in your efforts to bring about change.
   a It is still important that you do not hurt his feelings by being tactless in the way that you present the problem *and* your suggested solutions. Make out a list of 'do's and don'ts' – for yourself – in relation to the way in which to handle the situation in a diplomatic manner.
   b If your director had been unaware that there *was* a problem what difference, if any, would this make to your approach?

Section 2 – Administering and taking notes of meetings

It is surprising how many otherwise very experienced PA's are very reluctant to take the minutes of a meeting. If you are prepared to do so and prove that you can you are likely to be highly regarded in the organisation.

What is important to note, however, is that minutes are regarded as a permanent record of the proceedings of a meeting to be produced in court if necessary as evidence of what actually happened at the meeting.

You should, therefore, be prepared to spend time in ensuring that the minutes are:

- true, impartial and balanced
- written in clear, concise and unambiguous language
- as brief as is compatible with accuracy.

In order to ensure that this is the case you must first of all master the skills of note taking and it might be useful for you to consider the following points.

Hints and tips for minute taking

- Prepare your writing materials thoroughly beforehand. Have a supply of pens and pencils. Either use a shorthand notebook or A4 lined paper. The advantage of A4 paper is that you can put more on one sheet and can subdivide it into sections. You can also leave a wide margin (some secretaries draw a line down the middle of the page and use the left half only, leaving the right half for any alterations as the meeting progresses). If you are allowed to do so, consider the use of a cassette recorder as a back-up.

- Try to find a mentor. If you are lucky you will be working in an organisation where at first you will be taking minutes alongside another more experienced PA who will compare notes with you afterwards. If not, there may be someone in the organisation who is willing to give you some assistance over layout or subject matter plus background information about what normally happens in the various meetings.

- Check the level of detail you are expected to record. Many minutes these days are merely summaries of the discussions which took place, rather than details of who said what.

- Be selective about what you write down while it is being said. This saves having to plough your way through pages of notes later to find the parts that matter. It is also less of a strain on your note-taking skills than trying to write down every word! The more familiar you are with the topic under discussion the better – you should at least know what the chairperson is going to say about it.

- If you lose the thread of the discussion don't panic! Right at the beginning of the meeting make sure you know the names of all the members so that you can note who is contributing to a particular topic and, if necessary, query it with them after the meeting.

- If you are still unsure, do not risk recording inaccurate or confusing information. It is preferable to minute nothing at all rather than something which is incorrect.

- Draft the minutes as soon as possible after the meeting while the events are fresh in your mind. Keep your sentences short and your wording simple. Use the third person (rather than 'I', 'we' or 'you') and the past tense – you are writing about something which is over and done with (see below). Consider the use of an action column at the right hand side of the minutes for the names or initials of anyone who has been asked to take action on any topic.

- It is particularly important to check that the minutes are not defamatory as legal action may be taken for libel if a defamatory statement is made in writing, in print or some other permanent form (Defamation Act 1952).

- Until you become experienced, and sometimes even throughout your career, you may find it preferable to submit your draft minutes to the chairperson for checking. Even if you have recorded the information accurately it may be that the chairperson prefers a different emphasis at certain points (for a variety of reasons!). If you have typed up your minutes on a word processor it is then a simple matter to edit your text before printing out your final version.
- It is very important to make sure that the completed and signed minutes are filed away safely. Some sets of minutes are so confidential that they are always stored in a locked filing cabinet and any amendments made in ink and counter-initialled. Even less formal minutes are regarded as sufficiently important to warrant your looking after them with great care.

Note-taking skills

Believe it or not it can actually be a disadvantage to have a very high shorthand speed for minute taking, as then the temptation to write down too much is tremendous! You can even train yourself to write down minutes without any shorthand skills at all, providing you have developed some foolproof method of abbreviating key words.

The basic points to remember are:

- Any note-taking or shorthand system is not an art form but a means to an end! Don't worry about your outline or symbol being technically correct – so long as you can read it.
- Write neatly and space it out.
- Know the terminology of your 'trade' and the outlines/symbols/abbreviations you can use for all the technical terms you hear.
- Be aware that during transcription it is the short, simple words which usually cause the most trouble!
- Take advantage of respites in the meeting – the break for coffee or informal or humorous discussion – to check through your notes.
- If necessary, make notes to yourself, either in a separate column or in square brackets so that they are easily identifiable.

Transcription skills

It is very important that you can write minutes which are unambiguous and clear and are in the third person. There are several routine phrases which are often employed, eg 'After discussion it was decided that . . .' You should note that in *very* formal minutes you should always try to avoid using actual names. For instance, instead of saying 'Alison Lee proposed that . . .' you would use the term 'It was proposed that . . .'.

Remember to avoid slang and colloquial expressions which are often used in everyday speech. Report unemotionally whenever possible. For instance, the chairperson of a budget meeting may have ranted and raved about overspending in the previous financial period but in the minutes this can be simply reflected by the following statement:

The chairperson said that budget overspending, such as that which occurred in the previous financial period, would not be tolerated in the future.

Writing in the third person and past tense becomes easier with practice. Most people have no difficulty converting a sentence such as '*I think we should increase the sales budget*', *said the Sales Director* to *The Sales Director felt that the sales budget should be increased.* (NB – note the use of the word 'that' to introduce reported speech).

Difficulties, however, may arise in the following cases.

'Always true' statements

Consider the following: '*Bloggs plc is a very large company*' *said the Chairman.* If you convert this to *The Chairman said that Bloggs plc was a very large company* then you imply that Bloggs plc is no longer very large – which is (presumably) incorrect. Therefore the correct version should be *The Chairman said that Bloggs plc **is** a very large company.*

Questions

It is fairly easy to convert a sentence such as '*Can we extend the advertising campaign?*' *asked Mrs Andrews*, to *Mrs Andrews asked whether they could extend the advertising campaign* or *Mrs Andrews queried whether the advertising campaign could be extended.*

However, if the question is rhetorical then direct conversion is not suitable. In this case you need to show the meaning which was implied when the question was asked, eg, '*Am I going to have another set of inaccurate calculations?*' *asked the Sales Manager, annoyed.* This statement obviously means that inaccurate figures are not acceptable and should be rephrased to reflect this, eg *The Sales Manager commented that he did not expect to receive any more inaccurate calculations.*

Time

Remember that expressions of time change when reported speech is used, eg:

- *today* becomes *that day*
- *now* becomes *then*
- *tomorrow* becomes *the next day* or *the following day*
- *yesterday* becomes *the day before* or *the previous day.*

Therefore *I will be going there tomorrow* converts to *He said that he would be going there on the following day.*

TEST YOURSELF
Convert each of the following statements correctly into reported speech. Try to use alternatives to words such as *asked* and *said*, eg *queried, commented, suggested* etc.

Remember not to repeat slang expressions or include anything which could be defamatory!

1 'It's all very well to make that suggestion,' said Susan Bolova, 'but do you honestly think the staff will respond?'

2 'I visited the company yesterday,' said Paul Jenkins, 'and they said that they wanted me to call again next Tuesday.'

3 'A six-month trip to Australasia – that's an expensive venture you're suggesting. Are you sure it would pay off?' asked Malcolm O'Leary.

4 'I know it is a three-hour flight from London to New York on Concorde,' said Imran Patel, 'and the flight departs from Terminal 4.'

5 'OK, so we can't make a decision on this one yet until we get more information on the accounts. I intend to have a chat with John Turner anyway. If he paid as much attention to getting out the figures as he does to reducing his golf handicap we'd all be in a better position to know what we are doing,' said Graham Swift, the Chairman.

ACTIVITY SECTION

Individual tasks

Case study 1

Whilst you were absent last week the sales meeting went ahead as usual. As no one was free to take the minutes your boss, Martin Lewis, jotted down notes of what happened on his chairperson's agenda.

From these notes produce a summarised set of minutes.

CHAIRPERSON'S AGENDA

Meeting:	Sales Meeting
Date/time:	1000 hours, 14 March 199–
Place:	Board Room
Sales Team:	Martin Lewis (Chair), G Barton, C Edwards, P Hinchcliffe, T Marsden, F Paton, J Vines (In attendance – Paul Bailey, Technical Manager)

AGENDA ITEM	NOTES
1 Apologies for absence	1 Frank Paton (held up on M4)
2 Minutes of previous meeting	2 OK
3 Matters arising Questions may be asked on: • progress on McNaughton contract	3 ML reported – Meeting arranged with Jim Pascal, Sales Dir of MCN a week on Tues. to finalise penalty clause.

- date new advertising campaign starts on TV

  ML – starts Yorkshire on Anglia begins 21 March networked (national coverage) from 28/3

4 Customer reports
- Tom Marsden just returned from trip to Paris

  4 Saw Besseau & Cie – interested in new machine – 3 other bidders. Our prospects good. Board decision expected by 26/3.

- Check if problems at Micro Products solved

  No – PB reported 2 technicians visiting next Mon.

5 Advertising campaign
Report on progress to date

5 ML – Meeting with ad. agents last week. Some minor modifications still required to literature. Final proofs due next wk.

6 Technical modifications
Report by Paul Bailey on model 48X

6 Re D report on technical modifications tabled. PB gave overview. To be discussed in depth at next meeting.

7 Forthcoming exhibition
Olympia, London
14 – 21 October

7 CE – stand booked. CE/JV to organise/co-ordinate. ML's sec to book accomm. – check requirements with JV.

8 Any other business

8 PB reported strike at Evans Electronic now over. TM following up enquiry by Kent County Council

9 Date and time of next
Avoid 28 March – 3 April (Easter)

9 23 March 10am Board Room

Case study 2

You have acted as the secretary at the meeting of the Staff Welfare Committee held in the staff canteen at 1700 hours on Wednesday, 2 July, to discuss the arrangements for the staff dinner dance.

Other than you, those present included Mr William Sanderson (who chaired the meeting), Mrs Muriel French, Mr Henry Cartwright and Miss Barbara Atkinson. The agenda was as follows:

1 Apologies for absence

2 Minutes of the previous meeting

3 Matters arising

4 Correspondence

5 Proposed venue

6 Entertainment

7 Printing

8 Any other business

9 Date and time of next meeting

Given below is an actual transcript of the meeting. From this, prepare a set of minutes for the chairperson to sign.

Meeting transcript

Chair Good afternoon – thank you for coming. Might I give a special welcome to our new secretary who has taken over the job at rather short notice? Before we actually start the meeting can I take it that everyone has a copy of the agenda and the minutes of the previous meeting? If not, we have some spare copies available. Good. Next point. Have we any items for Any other business? Has anything urgent arisen since the agenda was sent out? No? Right. Let's get on. The first item on the agenda – Apologies – ah, yes – Frank Thomas is away on a selling trip and Angela Norman is on holiday this week. (*to you*) Can you make a note of that please.

The next item – the minutes of the previous meeting – can I take them as read and approve them as a correct record? (*all agree*)

Right – matters arising from the previous meeting. If I go through the Minutes page by page as usual, you can stop me if you wish to query an item.

Henry Can I query Item 5 on page 2? What has happened about getting the prices from the various hotels?

Chair We have the prices listed and the secretary will pass a copy of them to all of you when we reach that item on the agenda.

Any other queries? Can we then start on the main business of the meeting?

Barbara Is there any correspondence to be dealt with?

Chair I'm sorry, I should have dealt with that item – no, there isn't.

The next item is that of choice of hotels – remember we have to make a report to the Board giving our recommendations for the staff dinner dance and venue is something we must discuss. We have a list of prices from the various hotels (*you circulate them to everyone*). One or two hotels were late in responding to our request so we didn't have time to circulate them beforehand.

Muriel Could I make the point that I didn't like the hotel we went to last year – the 'Golden Hind' – the service was poor and the meal ordinary. Some of the girls in my office have asked me to say that they weren't too keen on it either.

Barbara I didn't think it was too bad but I'm willing to try somewhere else – how about the 'Boar's Head'?

Henry It's a bit far out – there may be transport problems.

Muriel What about the 'Royal George'? I've been there recently and quite liked it. They seem quite used to catering for large numbers.

Henry The new owner of the 'Imperial' is eager to expand his business and may be willing to give us good value for money.

Chair	Any other ideas? Well, it seems a straight choice between the 'Royal George' and the 'Imperial'.
Barbara	Why don't we try the 'Royal George' this year and the 'Imperial' next year, when we have more of an idea whether the new venture will be a success?
Chair	Can we decide on that? Do you all agree the 'Royal George' this year, then? (*all nod*) OK then it's agreed.
	(*to you*) Can you contact them to confirm the provisional booking? Tell them we'll confirm exact numbers and so on nearer the time.
	Next item. The entertainment. Henry – you were going to look into the matter, weren't you?
Henry	Yes, if you remember last time we had a small band which was popular with the older members of the staff but didn't go down too well with the younger element. One girl has suggested that we have some disco music to be played during the intervals which seems a good idea. If everyone is in favour of that then I can check with the hotel to see if it could be arranged.
Muriel	Wouldn't it be a bit difficult, trying to talk above that sort of music?
Henry	There is a separate bar at the 'Royal George' where anyone who wanted could sit during the intervals.
Muriel	If that's the case then I have no objections.
Chair	Has anyone else anything to say? Well, should Henry be authorised to go ahead and make the necessary enquiries? (*all agree*)
	Last item, as we have no items to discuss under AOB. The problem of printing. The in-house reprographic unit is under some pressure at the moment and may not be too willing to cooperate with us about the printing of menus, invitations etc. Should we think about contacting local printers to see how much they will charge us?
Barbara	What do you think the Board's reaction will be?
Chair	I don't suppose they'll want to spend a huge amount of money but they do look upon the dance as a good public relations exercise and of benefit to the staff, so they may be willing to pay a printer rather than risk the event looking as if it has been poorly organised.
Muriel	Why don't we obtain some prices as you suggest and let the Board decide – we can make it a strong recommendation from this committee but it is up to them eventually to decide what they want to pay.
Chair	Is that acceptable to everyone? (*everyone agrees*) (*to you*) Will you get together some prices for the next meeting please.
	Before you all go, let's fix a date and time for the next meeting – pretty soon I suggest. How about 3rd August? The same time? 1700 hours?
	(*general agreement*)
	Well, it only remains for me to thank you for coming.

Managing stress

If anything else goes wrong I will s-c-r-e-a-m !

Have you ever noticed how:

- things never go wrong in 'one's'
- some days you wish you had never bothered getting out of bed
- when you are in a hurry, or doing something very important, Murphy's Law always prevails, ie if anything can go wrong, it will?

Many factors in our lives lead to stress, such as:

- people – who can put us under pressure by their demands, their moods, their actions or even just by being talkative and delaying us
- change – whether good or bad, in our personal life or at work, puts us under strain
- time – when there never seems to be enough of it.

Work scheduling and time management is dealt with on page 352 and 381. This chapter is to help you to cope when all seems to be going wrong in your world and you begin to feel it's all getting too much for you.

RULE 1

Ironically we all need *some* stress in our lives to help us to function. Imagine a life with no challenges, nothing to achieve or complete. We would feel worthless and in that situation many people take up hobbies and interests to provide the interest and focus lacking in their lives.

It is therefore an *excess* of stress which leads to problems – not stress itself.

Type A or type B?

The American team of Friedman and Rosenman undertook research and isolated two main types of personality which they categorised as type A and type B. To find out which you are do the short quiz below.

Answer *Always, Sometimes* or *Never* to each of the following:

1 I hate being late.
2 I live for my job.
3 I eat quickly.
4 I am impatient.
5 I play to win.
6 I am ambitious.
7 I hide my feelings.
8 I talk rapidly.
9 I feel I have to hurry.
10 I feel guilty when I am not working.

Give yourself two points for each *Always*, one point for each *Sometimes* and no points for *Never*, then add up your score.

A high score indicates a Type A personality – who will experience considerable stress. A low score means you are a Type B personality – easy-going, patient, casual and unlikely to suffer from very much stress. The irony is that whilst type As are usually more successful on the climb to the top in an organisation (though not necessarily at the top) they are also more prone to heart disease and heart attacks.

RULE 2

Stress is the result of *you* upsetting *yourself*!

Whilst other people and factors outside your control may contribute to a situation in the first place, it is your reaction to that situation which creates undue stress.

What can stress do?

In addition to leading to heart attacks, stress can also cause a whole range of physical symptoms – high blood pressure, skin rashes, bodily aches and pains, migraine, ulcers, and arthritis, as well as tiredness, exhaustion and depression.

The initial symptoms of stress are even more diverse and often very personal – the effects stress triggers in me will be different from those it triggers in you. These can range from sleeplessness to forgetfulness, a 'tic' developing on your eye or mouth to irritability, biting your nails to over-eating/over-drinking.

You need to learn to observe *yourself* and to identify those symptoms you develop which mean you must take action to prevent the problem becoming any worse.

Many working days are lost each year because of employees reporting sick with stress-related symptoms – and even if you manage to carry on working you are unlikely to be effective or efficient and may upset others by losing your temper or just being snappy or unreasonable.

RULE 3

Bear in mind that we all differ in our tolerance of stress.

Even a small amount can be too much for some people, whilst other people can cope with much more.

Learn your own tolerance levels – and try to be aware of those of any staff for whom you are responsible.

How to cope

There are a variety of coping strategies recommended for when we feel things are all getting too much. The best idea is to try different ones out and find out which works best for you.

1 Identify the cause

If you feel stressed and wound up it is important to recognise why – and not 'pin the blame' on the first thing that comes to mind.

Areas to think around include:

- **Work overload**

  Probably the most obvious cause is too much to do and not enough time to do it – but also work which is too difficult or too demanding or even actually unpleasant.

- **Role conflict**

  This includes not being sure what people expect of you, with different people making different demands – often the case if you work for more than one boss – and/or finding junior staff difficult to control or cope with and not having the power to do much about it.

- **Change**

  Another American team, Ruch and Holmes, discovered that all changes in our life create stress – even 'pleasant' changes such as getting married, Christmas and holidays. Unpleasant changes, eg death of a close relative, being made redundant, getting divorced, score very highly indeed. Ruch and Holmes came to the conclusion that we can all stand a certain number of life or career changes but they have a very stressful impact on us if *too many* changes happen *too quickly*.

- **People, politics and personalities**

  Whilst this covers areas such as a personality clash with someone with whom you work, it also relates to your *own* personality – whether, for instance, you often take things personally and become upset about them (such as your boss being in a bad mood) where another person might just shrug them off.

  Office politics can also create stress – keeping on the right side of the group or doing what they expect you to do (or else risking being ostracised and isolated), two people you know trying to get the better of one another with you acting as a reluctant referee or a 'sympathetic ear'.

- **Work/home conflict**

  This covers everything from conflicting demands in both places at once, to an uncooperative partner, to having to take work home on a regular basis and feeling that you are neglecting the family.

> **RULE 4**
>
> Always bear in mind that what seems catastrophic today is usually more tolerable in a week, a vague memory in six months and relegated to history in two years!

2 Face up to the problem

Having identified the problem you need to analyse:

- what aspects of it you find stressful, and why
- who or what is involved
- what you can (or can't) do about it
- what you actually *want* to do about it (and be honest with yourself!).

RULE 5

Clarify your thoughts by

- making a list of what's bothering you (even if you tear it up later)
- talking to a friend (a good old moan session if you want) – but choose your friend carefully!

At this stage you should have reached one of two conclusions:

a you can do something about the problem (eg reschedule your work, talk to the person who is causing you problems)
b you can do nothing about the problem – either because:
  - it is unchangeable (bereavement obviously comes into this category)
  - the solution is out of your hands or not feasible (eg giving in your notice at work if you need the money and there aren't any alternative jobs available).
  - the other person(s) involved are just not approachable.

RULE 6

Can't sleep?

- Physically tire yourself out – spring clean a room or dig the garden or go for a *long* walk. Then have a pleasantly hot bath, a warm milky drink and get into a warm bed with a good (but not too exciting book). Turn the lights down low and read until your eyes start to close . . .
- Still no good? Then get up and walk about a bit, read the paper – *don't* lie there worrying about it. Have you ever read how many hours sleep hospital doctors get – and they still manage!

3a Something can be done

This may mean tackling somebody senior to you to talk to them about the problem. Learning assertiveness can be helpful here (see page 348). Putting your problem as objectively and as unemotionally as possible is important – often the other person might be quite stunned to realise how you feel.

Be positive! If you think that change is needed, eg in work practices, then come up with some suggested solutions – not just a whole load of problems!

3b Nothing can be done

This is the conclusion that can lead to a continuation of stress unless you take some positive action for yourself. However, before you give up hope of changing the situation there is one final thing you should check – your way of defining and thinking about the problem.

Ways of thinking

It is often the case that we get trapped into ways of thinking. For instance, we feel happier thinking about small adjustments to an existing situation rather than redefining it from scratch – yet this can often give us a new perspective on the problem. As an example think about the adult returner who has started work after five years of being at home with the children. She finds the conflicting demands of home and work too much – even though her husband helps her in the house. No matter how much they talk over the problem at home it seems that the only solution will be for her to give up work until the children are older.

Whilst there are no easy solutions to this problem, the couple should avoid the temptation of simply making small changes to the way they operated when the wife was at home all the time. It is significant that her husband refers to 'helping' her around the home – not doing jobs just because they need doing. They may gain a fresh insight on the problem if they forget how they have coped over the last five years and rethink their problem from scratch – for instance:

- list what needs doing (and what can be left or ignored!)
- consider how many people (eg teenagers) can be involved, when and how
- work out whether time schedules can be changed around
- calculate whether they can afford to 'buy in' some help.

If this still does not help then you will need to develop a method of taking your mind off the problem or making yourself feel better.

RULE 7

People under stress lose their sense of humour. One way to reduce stress is to try to see the funny side of something. A good laugh – especially with someone else – can make you feel better physically and help you to put a situation more into perspective.

Options to try

- Take up a hobby – anything which will distract you from going to the cinema to playing tennis or learning a musical instrument.
- Get the 'angst' out of your system – write a hate note and then tear it up, have a good cry, scream and shout and thump the pillow, swear loudly.

- Give yourself a treat – have a day (or evening) off. Go shopping (window shopping if you're broke), go to a sauna or for a swim, buy and read a good book, have a long lazy bath, have your hair done.
- Plan something super for the future – a weekend away, a holiday abroad, a day out with a really good friend. Get lots of brochures and daydream.
- Cuddle and/or stroke something or someone – partner, cat, dog, rabbit or even an old moth-eared teddy-bear.
- Learn to relax – go to classes if necessary or buy yourself a relaxation tape or a soothing record and curl up by the fire.
- Give yourself a lecture – tell yourself how good you are, argue with yourself if you start to become negative, list all your strengths and ignore your weaknesses, tell yourself how lucky people are to have you as a colleague/friend.

RULE 8

Don't take to drink or chain smoking to cure your problems – you'll only add to them! *Reducing* alcohol and cigarettes and improving your diet (eg by reducing the fat content) will also help you to cope better both physically and mentally.

---

4 Practice what you preach

Remember – you are not the only person who has to cope with stress! As a supervisor you should be alert to any of your colleagues who may have problems.

- Be a good listener – don't just brush off their problems because you are having a bad day.
- Make sure people who are responsible to you know exactly what job they have to do and what is expected of them.
- Be supportive – stick up for your staff.
- *Reduce* conflict – never add to it.
- Recognise type A behaviour and don't encourage it.

RULE 9

Always be alert to signs of stress – in other people as well as yourself.

---

9 Office resource administration

Section 1 – Maintaining office supplies

The responsibilities you are expected to undertake in relation to the maintenance of office supplies can vary tremendously from one organisation to another. Ironically, the number of tasks with which you are involved may be greater in a small organisation than a large one, where the storage, maintenance and control of the majority of the stock and equipment is the responsibility of a centralised division. In this situation a PA is likely to be responsible for maintaining departmental supplies, in addition to ordering special items required by her boss.

In a small organisation, however, a PA operating in the role of office administrator may have to undertake the full range of responsibilities in relation to office supplies and to devise a system which incorporates not only ordering and storage procedures but also keeping comparative notes on suppliers and monitoring usage as well as costing and valuing stock for auditing purposes.

Why have a system?

Many small organisations grow up without any specific system for stock. Consumable items and even office equipment may be ordered on a 'needs must' basis in the early days, when both the range of requirements and the quantities needed are only small. Stock may be stored randomly where there is some space, the area is open access and stock is available on a first-come first-served basis.

Even if staff and management are complacent about this slapdash approach their accountants are unlikely to take the same view. *All* stock has a close relationship with office accounts, although this differs depending on whether the stock is for resale or for use by the organisation itself. Office supplies clearly fall into the latter category but are equally important because they represent an expense and must be listed as such in the company's accounts. Capital expenditure (eg on office equipment) is also important. If equipment is bought outright, rather than leased, an allowance has to be made for **depreciation** because the machine will obviously wear out over a number of years and have to be replaced.

TEST YOURSELF

Imagine that you have started work in a small company which operates no recognisable stock control system. Working in groups try to think of:

a the type of problems which may result from this approach
b the possible financial consequences for the organisation.

Compare your group's list with those made by others *before* you read further.

The importance of cost control

All organisations who wish to remain in business for any length of time monitor their costs very carefully in *all* areas – from raw materials for manufactured goods to the size of their electricity or telephone bill. To see why, you need to understand how an organisation's profit figure is calculated – and your contribution to this.

$(P - C) \times V$ = gross profit

where

P = selling price of an item
C = cost price of the same item
V = volume

This much is easily understood. The only way gross profit can be increased is by the company:

a increasing the selling price (but then customers may reject their goods in favour of those made by a competitor)
b increasing the volume sold (easier said than done if the market is competitive plus the additional costs attached to this option must be considered, eg advertising)
c reducing the cost of making the item (eg by using cheaper components or re-evaluating the design).

Not only is the last option the *only* one which is under the direct control of the company, but a cost reduction will have a greater effect on profits than the same percentage rise in sales. For this reason a company will be very concerned about the cost of making a product or supplying a service.

Gross profit – expenses = net profit

Once the gross profit has been calculated, the accountants are concerned with working out the total expenses of running the company. The largest item by far is usually the wage bill, but *every item counts* – electricity, rent, depreciation, expenditure on stationery, telephone, fax line etc. The higher the expenses then, obviously, the lower the net profit. In a small organisation which is struggling to survive in a competitive market the difference of only a few thousand pounds may be crucial to survival. Therefore in an area which may seem as mundane as office supplies, you are making a direct contribution to your organisation's profitability by your actions (or lack of them!).

The penalties of a lack of control

If a company has no system whatsoever, any of the following may result. (Check this list against the one you made earlier – note that the following are not exhaustive and you may have thought of some good points not shown below.)

- Wrong or damaged stock is delivered but not noticed and is therefore paid for.
- Goods are ordered in error – they must be paid for although they are of no use to the company.
- The company is paying too much for stock; there is no system to take advantage of discounts through bulk buying, special offers etc.
- There is wastage through deterioration or poor storage; stock becomes obsolete yet it is neither used up nor written off correctly.
- Invoices are unchecked so may be incorrect when paid or invoices are not paid on time so that no advantage is taken of prompt payment discounts and all suppliers are hesitant to deal with the company in future.
- Haphazard storage and ordering procedures mean that staff can't find goods they need – they either order more unnecessarily *or* supplies run out at critical moments thus endangering customer relationships.
- Over-ordering and/or lack of control means more capital is tied up in stock than is necessary.
- Pilfering and misuse may be rife.

Every single item listed above will *add* to the organisation's costs whereas it should be your aim to reduce these wherever possible.

Devising a system

It is important to define the scope of a good stock system, ie whether it should encompass purely ordering and storage procedures or be more comprehensive in its coverage, such as the areas detailed below. Only if the system is devised to operate as a whole, rather than everyone 'doing their own thing' can it be expected to function properly. Not only that, but one which is effective will also incorporate elements for coping with the unexpected.

Determining operational requirements

Whilst the final decisions in this area will be made at management level, as a PA you may be involved in collecting information and making your recommendations in relation to:

- which supplies should be held in stock and which (if any) should be bought only as required
- the maximum levels and minimum quantities to be held in relation to budgeted allowance for stock, storage space available, projected usage and lead times for supply
- the method of stock control to be used, ie manual or computerised
- the range of goods to be encompassed by system, eg whether to include equipment, special requirements at director level etc
- the method and frequency of audit and the costing procedure to be employed

- the degree to which emergencies may occur which could not be served by the planned system – and how these should be handled
- the frequency with which operational requirements should be overviewed and updated.

Monitoring procedures

When a system is devised there must be some way in which it is controlled. In a comprehensive system this does not mean merely completing stock record cards as this is only one aspect of a total control mechanism. To be effective it should incorporate:

- the total stock control system operation and the details which must be recorded
- the scale of the operation and staffing requirements (bearing in mind the range/quantities of goods in stock, usage etc)
- the frequency of usage reports to be issued and the method of analysis to be employed
- the frequency of inventory reconciliation and audits
- the method of valuation, usually **AVCO** (average cost system) or **FIFO** (first in first out)
- other reporting procedures and frequency.

Determining storage and access to stock

This should include:

- the site and layout of storage for consumables
- whether additional storage areas are required, eg for hazardous substances, confidential items or valuable goods and equipment
- key holders and their responsibilities
- the requisition or order system to be instigated before stock can be obtained and authorisation procedures
- the availability of stock for staff (eg constantly, daily, twice weekly, weekly etc)
- the method of retrieval and issue, ie **FIFO** (first in first out) or **LIFO** (last in first out)
- the procedures for dealing with obsolete or spoiled stock
- possible deviations from standard systems and estimated frequency and accepted method(s) of coping with these.

Determining suppliers/buying procedures

At the outset, the company should consider:

- the importance of quality versus costs *for each particular item*
- possible discounts available (which may affect the cost-effective operational levels of stock)
- which items can be supplied in-house (eg should the company undertake its own printing or buy in ready printed forms, letterheads etc)

- whether to operate a policy of 'cultivating' particular suppliers or 'shopping around' to take advantage of competitive prices
- the degree to which reordering can be undertaken automatically, ie which items and/or level of expenditure are subject to management approval
- the procedure for checking orders prior to despatch and determining those staff who are to have official authorisation to order on the company's behalf
- the system for checking goods and invoices upon receipt and who should be authorised to pass these for payment
- the procedure for monitoring total expenditure in this area as an on-going management information item.

Operational requirements

Much will depend on the work carried out by the company as to the type of supplies to be held in stock. All organisations require standard items, eg paper, envelopes, pencils and pens, filing materials, printed materials and office sundries such as punches, paperclips, disk boxes etc. Today a wide range of computerised items may be held in stock, from disk boxes, printer leads and cartridges to computers themselves, if, for instance, laptop computers are held in stock for executives to take abroad or for use at exhibitions etc. It is usually easier to start by defining straightforward consumable items which require no special treatment.

You can categorise these items into those relating to everyday needs, where a high level of turnover and demand is expected, and those which are required on a more infrequent basis. The technique for doing this is known as **Pareto Analysis** and is described in this chart.

PARETO ANALYSIS

The easy way to understand Pareto analysis is to relate it to yourself first. Unless you are very unusual you will find that:

- you wear 20 per cent of the clothes in your wardrobe 80 per cent of the time
- 20 per cent of the tasks in your job description take up 80 per cent of your time
- you access 20 per cent of the files in your filing cabinet 80 per cent of the time

The **80/20 rule** (as it is known) can be applied to many areas; sociologists often say that 80 per cent of the world's wealth is held by 20 per cent of the population.

Items which are used most of the time are known as **Pareto items**. If the items which make up this 20 per cent can be identified, isolated and given special attention then it is logical that major benefits will flow automatically. The remaining 80 per cent can be virtually ignored. Or, in other words, concentrate on 20 per cent of the items 80 per cent of the time!

If you have to rationalise stock requirements and movements and project usage, then your first step should be to itemise all items currently kept in stock and note alongside each item the usage to date. Now divide your stock into **highly active** (Pareto) items, **less active** (less frequently used) and **non-active** (rarely used) items. Then note down any factors which could create variances from the situation you have at present, eg proposed projects and their effects, seasonal requirements and so on. This will show you whether the level of demand is likely to be static or fluctuating over a period of time and will help you to plan ahead.

For all non-active items examine the lead times from suppliers, ie the length of time it normally takes from order to delivery. Many companies now are changing to 'JIT' systems of working. The acronym JIT stands for **just-in-time** and if your organisation subscribes to this philosophy it will prefer *any* item which is used infrequently and can be obtained quickly and easily to be purchased only as needed. This immediately reduces the amount of capital which must be tied up in stock and the amount of storage space required.

For all items the obvious basic rule is that you will need a higher level of buffer stock for goods which take a long time to deliver than those which do not. Now prioritise your active list into essentials and those items of lesser importance. Letter headings, for example, are critical – and may take longer to print and deliver than, say, shorthand notebooks. The former should therefore be higher on your list.

Alongside each item enter two figures, your **minimum stock** (ie the lowest possible amount you will always need to keep in stock) and the **maximum stock** you consider you should hold, given the constraints of space and the budget you have been allocated. You should note that you will actually reorder goods before the minimum stock figure is reached, to allow for delays in the new stock reaching you and the fact that whilst the stock is still on its way people will continue to need supplies.

Once this exercise is completed, calculate the full value of all stock which would be held if all items were at maximum level. Work this out at cost price – you can ignore VAT as the company will claim this back on expense items. Your final total is the amount of capital you are asking the organisation to commit to stock. It is a good idea to be slightly below budget so that you have some flexibility in relation to emergency requests and changing needs over the next 12 months. It is now time to check this figure with your boss.

During the discussion session you should be prepared to negotiate and adjust your initial forecast. There may be additional items required which you have not included and your boss's views on priority may differ slightly from yours and you will have to allow for this. At this stage, if not earlier, your boss may wish to discuss capital expenditure, eg on equipment and your role in this area. You should note that records of such items are usually kept separate from consumables, but you may still have a role to play in relation to usage, maintenance agreements and monitoring costs.

Monitoring procedures

The proposed control system for stock needs to be discussed and costed. If you already operate a microcomputer then a stock control package can easily be purchased and installed; you may however like to note that these are often linked to accounts packages and much may depend on the accounting system currently operated by your organisation. Nevertheless, given that you can operate most stock control packages independently, there are many advantages to having your system on computer, rather than operated manually (see below for a comparison of both systems). The major benefit of a computerised system is that of on-going management information at the touch of a key as reports on usage, cost etc can be generated quickly and easily. This facility needs to be linked with the requirements of your organisation in relation to the following.

- Physical stock checks – how frequently must a stock inventory be undertaken and the quantities in stock compared to the stock records?
- How often will a full audit be carried out and what system of costing will be used – and who will carry this out?

  A full audit means working out exactly how much has been spent in a specified period (usually a year) by:
  - carrying out a stock inventory
  - calculating the value of the stock currently held
  - calculating the quantity of issued stock and its cost
  - noting any discrepancies or adjustments (eg between issued stock *plus* current stock and the total ordered over the year) and costing these.

  There are three systems of costing stock of which FIFO is the most common for consumables. FIFO refers to 'first in, first out'. In this system not only is stock *issued* in this way (so that the oldest stock is used first) but stock is also valued on the same basis. (See opposite.)
- What system should be instigated for coping with – and making adjustments for – damaged, missing or obsolete stock? These are easy to record on any stock control system but what you need to establish are company procedures and reporting requirements, eg:
  - what level of damage or 'loss' must be reported to management and what level is 'acceptable' (eg minor damage through carelessness, mislaying small items etc)
  - the degree to which you will be consulted and/or informed if any stock is about to become obsolete (to enable you to use it up quickly). In many cases obsolete stock can be given an alternative use (eg out-of-date forms converted into scrap pads or resold cheaply to staff). You need to establish whether you can instigate such measures yourself or whether you would need to check with your boss beforehand.

COSTING STOCK

There are three ways of costing stock for valuation purposes, **FIFO**, **AVCO** (average cost system) and **LIFO** (last in, first out). Only the first two are used for consumables, with FIFO being the most common.

FIFO (first in, first out) means that stock is both costed and used in relation to when it was received.

AVCO (average cost valuation) means that the cost of stock is averaged out over a given period, eg a year.

Two examples should suffice.

1 A company takes delivery of bond paper twice a year; on both occasions 100 reams are received. The first time the cost is £500 and the second time (because of inflation) it is £600.

2 The company also buys two laptop computers for executives travelling abroad. The first cost £2000 and the second (which is identical) £2500.

At the end of the year the stock left is 50 reams of bond paper and two laptop computers.

Under FIFO it is assumed that the cheaper paper was used first, so the 50 reams remaining were bought at the higher price. The stock valuation is therefore £300. If AVCO is used then the *average* cost for the year is calculated – in this case £1100 ÷ 200 = £5.50. The stock is therefore valued at £275.

With the laptop computers neither of these is consumed in the same sense as the paper. The total cost was £4500 and this is therefore their valuation under either system. However, if one is damaged and written off then under FIFO it would be valued at £2000 and under AVCO it would be valued at £2250. If LIFO was used then the valuation would be the *last* amount spent, ie £2500.

On the basis that the Inland Revenue will not accept LIFO as a public method of accounting it is unlikely that this system would be adopted. Similarly it is also required that a company's system of valuation is consistent. You may therefore be instructed to follow the same system which is used for valuing any stocks of goods which are held by your company for resale.

Once basic procedures have been established, so that you know which areas are your specific responsibility, the final fact to ascertain is how often the system is going to be reviewed. Obviously the needs of the company will change over time and therefore stock evaluation should be on-going. Your boss may suggest that you prepare a report on your system, together with your recommendations for changes every six months. By detailing your views first, he/she can then think over your proposals before the two of you meet to agree on any changes which must be made.

Stock control systems

Manual stock control

With this system a series of record cards is created, one card for each item in stock. (See below.) These may be index cards, stored in a cabinet, or visible edge record cards, stored in special visible edge folders. The advantages are that they are easy to complete (and amend) and can be taken from place to place (which may also be a disadvantage!). However, it does mean that you could take them home to examine if you so wish.

Stock issued is booked out on the card and incoming stock is also recorded, so that a running balance is available for each item. You can obviously adapt the style of card shown below for your own use, eg if you have three stock cupboards to monitor, it would be sensible to include a heading for 'location'. This can also include the shelf number in a large area to guide the stock control clerk.

STOCK RECORD CARD

Item A4 Bond paper (white) **Max** 100 reams
                                  Min 20 reams

Supplier Office Supplies Ltd **Units** reams

Date	Received	Issued	Department	Order No	Balance

The difficulty starts when you want to analyse stock movements or usage, as the only way this can be done is by ploughing through all the cards methodically, noting down relevant facts. Other types of analysis, such as the frequency with which you use certain suppliers, may be almost impossible from this source and more easily compiled by examining invoices over a given period.

Computerised stock control

A computerised stock control package is simply a database designed to record, calculate and report on stock. A stock card similar to the one above will appear on your screen. If the package is designed to record stock which will be resold (as most are) then you will have to ignore certain areas if you are using this purely for in-house consumable items. For instance, there are likely to be spaces where you can insert the cost price (useful), and the percentage mark up required (not so useful). The latter column means that the computer can automatically calculate the selling price of each item – a feature which is irrelevant for your needs.

There are usually other useful headings, eg 'Quantity currently on order'. This stops the computer reminding you to reorder something when you are still waiting for it to be delivered.

The package is accessed to record outgoing and incoming stock and the current balance is automatically shown on each card. A report can also be generated which details usage further – though you might find that this goes under the heading of 'Sales analysis'! If your package has this facility then you *must* have an area on the stock card to nominate a department, person or office, as it is under these headings that usage will be grouped.

It is in the area of reports that a computerised package definitely has the edge for anyone who is trying to monitor and control stock. In addition to 'usage' reports you can also ask the computer to give you:

- a print-out of all stock at cost price (ie an instant stock valuation)
- a list of all stock which needs to be reordered
- a list of all items and the number currently in stock with a blank column at one side. (This column is completed during a physical stock check (inventory) and the number actually in stock recorded for comparison against the stock shown by the computer.)
- an audit trail. This logs all the computer entries which have been made – and is useful if you want to analyse what your junior could possibly have done to end up with the balance currently showing of 5 million paperclips!

You should note that the computer will enable you to make adjustments to stock levels (though these too will be recorded on the audit trail). The computer will want to know why you want to make such adjustments (to satisfy your accountants at a later date). Valid reasons may include a correction of an incorrect entry or because stock is damaged, lost or now obsolete.

Reporting procedures

It is useful to discuss with your boss the reports you should generate, how frequently, and whether or not you should show them all to him/her or operate a system of 'management by exception'. On this basis it's a question of 'don't tell me if it's OK, just tell me if it's not.' Whilst this is normally much easier for both of you, some initial parameters need to be set as to what is meant by OK! If you consider that the sales department are still operating normally if they use 20 per cent additional stock one month, but your boss does not, then you will be operating at cross-purposes.

Once agreement has been reached you can then operate by means of, say, monthly 'exception reports' which only detail *differences* in usage or expenditure.

Determining storage and access to stock

Quite obviously you will have examined the site where your stock is to be stored (or should have done so!) before deciding on your maximum stock levels. The area you choose must be capable of being locked, be clean, dry and well-ventilated and have a range of shelves from floor to ceiling. Usually these are slatted to allow for air movement. Plan to keep all large and bulky items low down so that staff aren't involved in lifting heavy weights, and buy a safety stool for access to high shelves. Make sure that all fast moving items will be readily accessible.

Label all your shelves clearly and then work out what containers you need to buy, in which to keep small items (such as pens, pencils etc which would otherwise roll about). It is also a good idea to transfer small items which are supplied in large quantities into containers (eg paperclips) so that they are not issued in large quantities as this normally encourages wastage.

Hazardous substances

List any hazardous items you may need to store and bear in mind that under COSHH (**Control of Substances Hazardous to Health**) regulations 1988 you will have to have these items assessed by a competent person to ascertain the level of risk involved. (See also Chapter 10, Health and Safety at Work, page 494.) Dangerous chemicals must be kept in a separate area (eg a chemical safe or bonded store) with restricted access and all key holders must be listed. Items which are hazardous, rather than dangerous, can usually be stored with other consumables but it is advisable to keep these on a separate shelf. Typical examples are chemicals related, say, to offset litho duplicating. Most items are flammable, eg blanket wash and etching fluid, and others are even more volatile, eg MEK (methyl ethyl ketone) which is a blanket conditioner. All hazardous substances are marked with special hazard warning signs and a hazard data sheet can be obtained from the supplier. If the latter is difficult to understand then simplify it for any staff who may be handling the substance and check that your handling and storage arrangements do not contravene the supplier's instructions in any way. As a final safety measure draw up a list of emergency procedures, eg what to do if the substance is spilled, inhaled or gets into someone's eyes etc.

Valuable stock and security

If part of your remit is also to store equipment then you may have to decide whether or not a special secure area needs to be provided. However, it is worth noting that whilst, say, a camcorder or laptop computer may cost a considerable sum to purchase, it is likely that such items will be covered by the company's insurance. They may also be quite difficult for anyone to steal as, unless someone has a lot of nerve, it is not easy to sneak around the corridors with a laptop computer under one arm. Conversely, many consumable items are quite expensive to buy, very useful at home and can quickly be hidden in a bag or under a coat. As an example, a developer and toner cartridge for a laser printer can cost between £80 and £100 to buy, and your company's stock of audio or video tapes may be extremely desirable items. It is sensible to check whether consumable items are also covered against theft under the company's existing insurance policy.

The most sensible arrangement is for all stock to be stored in locked cupboards and for a limited number of key holders to be appointed, all of whom are responsible for undertaking the stock inventory at given periods and reporting on discrepancies. This does not mean expecting a ten page explanation because three paperclips have gone missing, but does mean invoking an atmosphere of collective responsibility and good communications so that you are informed at the *outset* if there are requests – by anyone – for deviations from the system.

Special items

Special items are those which are a specific requirement of your organisation or your boss and may not be available to every member of staff. These could be classified as 'confidential' – except that when any item is placed in a general stock cupboard it usually ceases to be confidential! As an example, consider the case where an MD obtains leather-bound desk diaries for senior staff but does not want these open to general use because of the cost – and may not want their existence to be discussed amongst the staff in case everyone thinks they deserve one! Even more 'confidential' may be gifts for clients at Christmas time, eg whisky or cigars, in addition to special items stored for commemorative occasions, eg cut glass items produced for an anniversary occasion etc. If you are involved in storing items such as these you are strongly advised to set up a separate system, in a cupboard that you and perhaps another PA knows about. Do train your boss to keep you informed if he/she takes items from it – or if you have responsibility for the contents you may have near heart failure one morning if you open it to discover it is half empty!

Special items which are also valuable may require storage in a safe. If you stock dollar travellers' cheques, for instance, you would be extremely foolish to place these anywhere else. For that reason many executive offices contain a small safe which can be used to store confidential papers, cash and small but valuable items.

Access to stock

The frequency with which stock can be accessed will depend mainly on the scale of operation and your staffing in this area. If you have a full-time stock control clerk and your organisation is fairly large (or needs constant flexibility) then you can cope with stock being available on a constant basis. More usually, however, stock is issued at either specific times of the day or on specific days of the week. However, the more infrequently you issue stock the more likely you are to be faced with emergency requests – so you need to take this into consideration when devising your system. A sensible compromise may be to have stock available for collection either once or twice daily.

In most companies stock is only issued against authorised requisitions and you need to decide your turn-around time between receipt of requisitions and stock availability. Stock is usually ordered on an internal stationery requisition form, the design of which may vary from one organisation to another. These are usually printed in pads of NCR (no carbon required) paper. Three copies are usually required; the top copy and second copy of the order are sent to the stationery section and the third copy is retained for departmental records. When the requisition is received and the order completed, the top copy is returned with the goods (and any items to follow or out of stock noted on it) and the second copy is retained by the stationery section.

Problems arise, however, when senior staff don't follow the system. If the MD suddenly rings you for a new signature book you would be very unwise to respond that there will be a delay of two days before this can be supplied and that you must receive a requisition form first! A simple way around this is to have a requisition pad in your own drawer which you can use in response to verbal requests by senior staff. The top copy of the requisition can be sent to the person concerned, together with their order, and you have the second copy for your records. It is from all these second copies that your junior can update the stock control system. Copies which relate to orders as yet incomplete should be kept in a 'pending' tray and only the items which have actually been issued logged as such on the stock record cards.

If your junior staff are responsible for issuing the stock then they must be aware of the importance of keeping the stock area clean *and* tidy and of locking it as they leave. They should know that unwrapped paper is likely to discolour and that it is sensible to store all items with their descriptive labels facing outwards, for ease of reference. You may find you have problems in persuading them to store new stock behind or below old stock (so that the oldest stock is used first) if this means taking off packets of heavy paper first. You can make life easier for them by devising a system where new stock is, say, always placed to the right of older stock and that which is positioned at the left is always used first, on the basis that it is easier to slide stock along a shelf then take it off and put it back on again somewhere else.

Make sure that you, too, establish a clear system of 'management by exception'. In other words – your junior staff don't tell you when things are going to plan but they *do* tell you when things aren't! This way, if they suddenly find that there has been a run on a certain item, or if something is missing, you will know in time to take the appropriate action. Do remember to avoid the 'shoot the messenger' syndrome. If your staff interrupt you with bad but important news when you are busy, and you are obviously annoyed with *them*, don't be surprised if they opt not to disturb you next time!

Determining suppliers and buying procedures

A large organisation is likely to have a centralised Purchasing section through which all goods must be ordered. In this case you may find you have to operate to a recommended list of suppliers and/or leave the choice up to them. However, if you feel strongly that another supplier would give better value you can, of course, make the *suggestion* that they may be worth evaluating – though the eventual outcome will be up to your company buyer.

In a smaller organisation, or one without a centralised purchasing section, you may have full responsibility to select a supplier and buy the goods you need.

When you are deciding upon a suitable supplier for a particular item of stock you have a variety of factors to take into consideration – and only one of these is the actual price of the goods. Other factors you need to think about include:

Delivery   How long will you have to wait for the goods? Does the company have its own door-to-door delivery service?

Reputation   How long has the company been established? How did you find out about them? Do you know anyone else who has used them? Are they known to be reliable and/or responsive in the event of an emergency?

Location   How far away are the suppliers? If they are very distant will you have to pay carriage charges and/or will there be difficulties in returning faulty or damaged goods? If equipment is involved, what arrangements would be made for servicing and/or maintenance?

Range of goods   Are standard, branded products available and if so what choice is there? Is the catalogue helpful or merely informative? Do you have an up-to-date price list?

Discounts   Does the company offer cash discount (for prompt payment) and/or trade discount (for bulk orders) and if so what are the conditions attached to these? Will your company require sufficient quantities to benefit from trade discounts? How do any cash discount terms fit in with your company's policy for paying invoices?

Credit   Assuming no cash discount is offered, what credit terms are available (especially on large orders or for items of equipment)?

You need to be able to weigh up the advantages of cultivating a local supplier, who will then consider you a good customer and give you priority service, against those of shopping around. The danger of keeping all your eggs in one basket is, of course, that you may be inconvenienced if the company you always use is itself out of stock or if it becomes complacent in relation to the business you put its way. In theory, if you use a company regularly, you should be able to expect a more sympathetic ear from its staff if you need goods in an emergency or your junior ordered some goods by mistake and you want to send them back!

A sensible compromise may be to develop a good working relationship with one or two suppliers in your own area, but keep your eyes open for other sources, possibly further afield. Change your supplier only if you are actually unhappy with the service you receive or if there is a substantial price difference. Then try out the new company with one or two minor orders and evaluate the service you receive before giving them more custom.

You will need to train your staff in both identifying the items which need reordering (unless your computer gives you this information automatically) and following the ordering procedures of the organisation. Do bear in mind that 'exception management' again applies – if your communication systems are good then you should be forewarned if anyone will be wanting large quantities of certain items in the near future for a special job. Such requests can mean that you increase the priority level of an item to ensure that stocks are always adequate.

If a centralised purchasing system is in operation then it will be your task to complete a standard office order form, send it to the Purchasing section and keep a copy for your records. If you have full responsibility for ordering goods then your order must still be made out on an official order form. You should note that if you telephone through an order to a company it is standard practice for them to ask you for your official order number. If you are not going to make out the order and send it off immediately, do make sure that you clip a note to it to remind you not to use it for anything else! In an emergency make out the order promptly and fax it through for confirmation. In normal circumstances, obviously, it would be sent by post.

Again it is useful if orders are pre-printed in NCR pads, so that the copies remain in the pad for reference.

Authorisation procedures for signing orders vary considerably and you need to check the policy of your company. At PA level you may have authority to make out orders for up to a specified level of expenditure or you may have to ensure that all orders are signed or countersigned by your boss. Check also whether it is company policy that the order form has to detail the *exact* amount of expenditure or whether an estimated amount is acceptable (provided this is within certain parameters, eg five per cent of the eventual invoice.)

Checking goods

When goods are received they must be checked carefully. If the goods have been despatched by the supplier's own transport a delivery note will be attached. If another method of transport has been used then you will receive an advice note with the goods and the delivery note will follow by post. Note that neither of these documents gives the amount due. In a large organisation the goods may be received (and even unpacked) in a central Stores section and be delivered to you with an internal goods received note attached.

You need to teach your staff how to check incoming goods carefully, ie:

- that nothing is missing
- that goods are not included which were never ordered
- that the correct goods have been received
- that no goods are faulty or damaged.

If any goods are missing then train your staff to examine the delivery note or goods received note as the next basic step. It may be that the goods are temporarily out of stock and will follow later, in which case they will be marked as such. A note needs to be made of these items so that they can be followed up later, if necessary, and a careful check made of the invoice when it arrives in case it includes these items in error.

Some companies automatically substitute out of stock goods with other similar lines. If you don't want these then you are quite within your rights to return them.

If there is an obvious discrepancy and either goods are missing or the wrong items are included then check the order before you telephone the company – just to make sure. You may have a problem if your junior wrote out the order with the wrong item code and this wasn't noticed, as you will have to rely on the goodwill of your supplier to take the goods back – he has no legal obligation to do so.

If goods are faulty, damaged or not as described in the catalogue then under the Sale of Goods Act 1979/Trade Descriptions Act 1968 you are within your rights to return them.

Once the goods have been checked they should be put into the store immediately to prevent loss, damage or accidents (eg if boxes are left lying around). The stock is then booked into the system against the delivery note or goods received note.

Paying for goods and monitoring expenditure

If you have bought goods which are subject to cash discount for prompt payment then do make sure you process the invoices for these in time to gain the benefit! The invoice should be the same as the delivery note except that this time the price is included. Do check that the two match and that all the calculations are accurate. If you are honest you will notify your supplier of *any* errors – no matter which of you would benefit!

At this point it is worth bearing in mind that the invoice should show a similar total amount due to that which you expected if you have done your homework correctly. If, say, you bought a new set of electronic postage scales and when the invoice arrived it was for a larger amount than you were quoted then you may be within your rights to return these under the Consumer Protection Act 1987. This is particularly the case if you were misled over the price.

Payment now needs to be authorised and again the policy for this will depend on the organisation for which you work. In a small company your next step may be to make out the cheque and present it to your boss for signing. In a large organisation only your boss may be able to authorise payment; the invoice is then passed to the Accounts section. In this case they will also be responsible for posting this payment to their accounts and, from this information, would be able to give you the total expenditure with any one supplier as and when you asked. However, this will show the total organisational expenditure with this company – not just that of your own department. If your boss wishes to keep track of your section's own expenditure against the allocated budget then you are advised to keep your own departmental records. Similarly, in a small organisation you will be expected to keep records of expenditure on consumables against budget, even if you are not doing the accounts work yourself.

Whether you track this expenditure by supplier or item is up to you and will depend very much on the type of information your boss requires. Again, a good computer package may be able to do much of the work for you if there are sections on the card where you include the cost price of individual goods and the supplier in each case. In this case you must ensure that your staff note down any *differences* in price which are shown on the invoice from the cost price currently held in the computer for that item.

If you keep up-to-date and comprehensive records of expenditure then you will find that much of the work which needs to be undertaken for the annual audit is already completed and the task isn't as overwhelming as you first thought it would be.

Capital expenditure

Many of the skills you have learned can be usefully applied if you are responsible for ordering or maintaining office equipment in your organisation. However, there are one or two differences of which you should be aware.

- If you are spending a considerable sum on an item of capital equipment, eg a photocopier, fax machine or computer, it is usual to start by contacting various competing companies for quotations. *Don't* accept an estimate as this simply gives a total estimated price rather than an itemised list. You cannot therefore hold the company to its quoted figures to the same extent.
- If you wish to obtain comparative figures on buying, renting and leasing make sure you specify this clearly. You will also need details of the terms of the rental or leasing agreement.
- Be aware that in certain areas (photocopiers being one), once you start making general enquiries you may find that you are inundated with representatives calling to try to persuade you to buy their product! This can be counter-productive, confusing or time-wasting and, at worst, tempt you to buy something you don't really want simply for the sake of peace. Because of this some organisations operate a system whereby they will only see representatives by

invitation and they specify this on their initial enquiry. If you are still pestered you could try the tactic of telling them that you routinely cross any supplier off your list if they unduly harass you for business!

- Make sure that you obtain full information on:
  - warranty periods (for which servicing and repair is free)
  - maintenance agreements (under which the warranty period is extended) and the terms/cost of these
  - routine servicing – how often, what work is carried out etc
  - emergency call out arrangements if the machine or equipment breaks down (in particular find out what time scale is likely to be involved)
  - whether essential supplies for the machine must be purchased from that particular company and if so, the cost
  - what training is provided for staff in how to use the equipment – and who provides this.
- It is usual for most PAs to make an initial assessment of the available equipment, its features and cost and then report back to their boss who will make the final decision on which particular item or model should be purchased. If you need to produce such a report then summarise the advantages and disadvantages objectively and attach relevant documents as your appendices (see Chapter 2, Researching and retrieving information, page 127).
- When the equipment arrives do supervise its installation. Book a day when you know you will be available so that you can make sure it's positioned where you want it and also that you receive all the necessary documentation – handbook, guarantee etc. With many machines (eg photocopiers, faxes etc) the person who installs it will set it up and then explain its functions to the staff. Make sure *you* are the person who receives this initial instruction then you can train your own staff. Make notes as you go and then reinforce your knowledge by teaching your juniors. Check the 'trouble-shooting' guide in the manual with the person who installs the machine to make sure you understand clearly how to rectify basic problems and for which faults you must call out an engineer.
- Devise a system for monitoring faults and problems, so that if there are any particular problems with the equipment you are aware of them. If you are ever in any doubt as to whether you will incur a call-out charge if you ring for help then check first – and do make sure that you really need assistance and you cannot solve the problem yourself.
- Use your 'faults log' to ascertain the value of possible maintenance agreements once the warranty expires. If the maintenance agreement would be very expensive and if the equipment involved is very reliable and/or not essential on a daily basis, it may be most cost effective not to take one out. If, on the other hand, the maintenance agreement is reasonably priced, the equipment is used intensively and a breakdown would be catastrophic then it is obviously a different matter.

With all items of capital expenditure the time will come when it is actually cheaper to buy a new machine than it is to keep servicing and maintaining the old one. However, do let your own judgement (and the figures in your faults log) be your guide, rather than the service engineer. Whilst he may be very honest and honourable, he may also have a vested interest in persuading you to update your equipment. If you have kept accurate records then the situation is easy to clarify and you have the basis of a factual, objective request to your boss for the replacement that you need.

ACTIVITY SECTION

Individual tasks

1 You are about to teach your junior exactly how she should complete a standard stock record card and book stock in and out.
   a Devise a clear list of instructions which she can use as a check list to help her to accomplish this task.
   b Three weeks later, you notice that many of the cards are incomplete or illegible. State clearly the action you would take to try to solve the problem.

2 In the past four weeks there have been two accidents in the stock room and one 'near miss'. Your junior fell over a box left behind the door and hurt her ankle, two days later she stabbed herself on some loose drawing pins on a high shelf whilst she was trying to reach some letter headings stored behind them. Yesterday another member of your staff narrowly missed being seriously hurt when a heavy box fell off the top shelf and landed a foot away from where he was standing. To your horror this morning you found that a delivery man who was unloading boxes in the area had lit a cigarette near the stock of flammable liquids.
   a Make out a list of safety regulations for staff working in this area and include guidance for staff on how to store stock so that the possibility of accidents is minimised.
   b Write a memo to your staff, which will accompany the regulations, detailing their responsibilities in this area and the importance of following standard procedures.
   c On a checklist for yourself, note down the ways in which your stock can be reorganised in the stock room to help to minimise accidents.

Individual/group tasks

Case study 1

You have recently started work as PA/Office Administrator for a relatively small company which has rapidly expanded over the last three years. One of your duties is to introduce a stock control system and to monitor expenditure on office supplies. The director to whom you are responsible, John Frankland, has given you a list of the items he knows the company used last year, although he doesn't think that this is exhaustive. The list doesn't include printed items such as letterheads, memo paper, printed forms, business cards and compliment slips and all quantities shown are approximate.

A4 bond paper (white)	50 reams
A4 bank paper	5 reams

paperclips	2000
brown manilla file folders	200
A4 photocopying paper	200 reams
carbon paper	1 box
fax rolls	20
blue biros	750
DL white envelopes (self-adhesive)	5000
C5 brown envelopes	2000
HB pencils	30
lever arch files	2
box files	15
envelope wallets	100
shorthand pads	500
punches	5
sellotape (large rolls)	30
bulldog clips	2
toner cartridges (for laser printer)	8
continuous feed printer paper	20 boxes

a Divide the list into active and non-active stock and note down suggested maximum and minimum quantities to be stocked in each case.

b Examine a current office supplies catalogue and list any other items you feel should be included and again add maximum and minimum quantities.

c From the price list which accompanies the catalogue calculate the cost of obtaining maximum stock levels for all the items you have listed.

d Analyse the list Mr Frankland has given you from the point of view of possible wastage, misuse or pilferage, ie note down any discrepancies in the quantities used which you think are suspicious or indicate that staff are not cost conscious.

e Detail *all* your findings and recommendations in a memo.

Case study 2

You are responsible for the ordering, recording and monitoring of all stock used by the Sales department for which you work. Although your organisation has a centralised Purchasing department and all accounts are settled by the Finance section, each department in the organisation is responsible for monitoring its own expenditure against budget for items such as consumables.

Because your department has a large requirement for stationery stock especially when major events occur, eg exhibitions, presentations, seminars etc, you keep separate stock records of all the goods you order and use and all expenditure by the department.

To help you in your task your boss, Ms Pamela Street, has agreed that the present manual system of stock control should be replaced with a software package you can run on your IBM compatible computer which, at present, you use only for word processing.

She has asked you to investigate at least *two* suitable packages and to find out the features of each and the price.

Carry out the investigation she requires and detail your findings in a memo. Include details on the method you would use to transfer the information from one system to another and the time-scale you think would be required for this. Include any *disadvantages* you consider there may be to operating the system on computer and the ways in which you consider these might be overcome.

Section 2 – Maintaining a petty cash system

Every office needs to have some method of coping with small items of expenditure which would be ludicrous to pay by cheque or on credit. There are a myriad of reasons why an organisation would want cash on hand for everyday expenses – to pay for taxis, emergency items of postage and stationery or to settle a small account with the window cleaner, newsagent, florist or milkman. The type and frequency of expenditure may vary but the principle never does – everyone needs to have cash available for certain types of purchases.

In a very small organisation – eg a sole trader – it may be tempting for the owner to dip into his till or back pocket to settle such debts instantly. The danger with this method of operation is that there is no record of the amounts paid out – and over the course of a year these may be quite substantial. When the accounts are produced at the end of the year there is no way in which these amounts can be recorded as valid business expenses. The net profit figure will therefore be higher than it should – and so will the tax which must be paid.

For this reason it is essential that businesses record *all* their expenditure – no matter how trivial – and it is usual to do this through the petty cash system.

The PA and petty cash

Many PAs are responsible for the operation of a petty cash system – either for their department or, in a small business, for the organisation as a whole. Frequently there is a junior assistant who can be a great help, but the *responsibility for* (as opposed to the *task of*) balancing the books – and the money – never rests with junior staff. Therefore, no matter which tasks you may decide to delegate, you must remember that it is *your* reputation which is at stake if the books and the cash in hand don't agree. For this reason you need to know the system thoroughly and understand the problems which can occur and the best ways in which to solve these.

Designing the system

It may be, of course, that you take over the job of petty cashier from a previous PA who has operated an efficient, established system for many years. In this case it is logical for you to follow her lead. In another situation you may be asked to initiate a petty cash system yourself. In either event, over time the requirements of the company will change – expenditure will probably increase (through inflation if nothing else) and certain procedures and components of the system will have to be reviewed. Therefore it is essential that you understand exactly what elements comprise a petty cash system, and why.

Your 'tools for the job' include packs of vouchers (obtained in pre-printed form from any stationer), a lockable petty cash tin and a petty cash book in which all expenditure is recorded and balanced.

It is sensible to recommend to your boss that you operate the **Imprest system**, whereby a fixed float is restored at specified intervals. This system also works as a security check, as the level of the float is known and the cashier should only be reimbursed when the petty cash book detailing expenditure for the previous period has been balanced and agreed by the main cashier.

Two aspects on which you and your boss need to agree are:

- the level (and type) of expenditure which is allowable before special authorisation must be obtained
- the size of the float.

Areas of expenditure to be covered by petty cash vary tremendously from one organisation to another. The fundamental criterion is whether or not the level of expenditure in one particular area is such that the company should receive monthly accounts from a supplier and settle these through the usual accounting system. For instance, a company which has a regular order with the local newsagent for daily papers and several monthly magazines should ask the newsagent to send in an account each month and this can then be settled in the normal way. Petty cash is not designed to pay out large sums of money to regular suppliers. If, on the other hand, papers or magazines are purchased only infrequently and only small amounts are spent then it would be unrealistic and unfair to expect the newsagent to send in an account and have to wait to receive payment.

Many organisations set a maximum value on the transactions which can be settled via the petty cash system. Employees who pay out more than this sum are expected to submit an expense claim form, rather than a petty cash voucher, and to be reimbursed separately from the main accounts section. A typical maximum value of a petty cash transaction might be anywhere between £10 and £20. This figure would have to be reviewed periodically to make sure that it is still realistic and generally acceptable. There are, however, occasions when cash may be required for payments considerably in excess of the agreed maximum and, depending on the area of expenditure involved, additional amounts may be sanctioned if prior authorisation is obtained. A typical example is money required to buy snacks or sandwiches for a small buffet. The local branch of Marks and Spencer is likely to look somewhat askance if you fill a basket with crisps, nibbles and sandwiches and then ask them to send in their bill! Yet, obviously, if you are entertaining several people the bill may be considerably beyond your standard maximum figure.

With this in mind you need to think carefully about the specific requirements of your own organisation and the system you will need to cope with these. Normally, the more 'exceptions' you find yourself having to deal with, the more inadequate is your present system.

The size of the petty cash float is, again, a very variable amount and will depend on the size and number of transactions and the period over which it is supposed to last. What is considered a ridiculous amount by some companies is regarded as chicken feed by another; the size of the petty cash float can vary from £50 to £500! It is useless having a float which is too small as time after time you will have to appeal to your cashier for emergency injections of cash. Having a float which is too large increases your responsibility *and* creates more work – as you have a larger sum of money to count and balance each time.

Finally, you need to decide over what period your petty cash accounting periods will operate. Usually your choice is between weekly and monthly (ie four week) periods of operation. The shorter the period the smaller the float required (and the less the temptation to put off balancing it for weeks on end!). Equally, if very few petty cash payments are made in the average week then you are simply making work again to opt for weekly periods. Let the number of transactions and the size of the operation be your guide.

Setting up the system

The first thing you need to do is establish the procedure for obtaining your float from the main cashier (or the bank, if you work for a small organisation). If you are liaising with the main cashier than it is likely that you will have to complete a special form for this purpose which states that a certain amount, say £200, has been allocated to petty cash. If you are responsible for withdrawing funds from the bank then again make sure that you make a special note on the cheque counterfoil that the cash was required for this purpose. This must be specified so that an appropriate entry can be made in the company's main cash book, ie a credit entry to the effect that cash has been moved from the cash account to the petty cash account.

Do make sure that you receive plenty of small change in your petty cash; ten £20 notes are a nuisance and a great deal of time and effort is wasted trying to find the right change for people.

Setting up the petty cash book

An extract from a petty cash book is shown opposite. The number of columns is variable, depending on the number of analysis columns/expenditure headings you require (see below).

- Column 1 is the debit column in which you enter the money received. This is the float with which you are issued originally and the reimbursements you receive at the end of your accounting periods. If you understand anything about double entry book-keeping you should realise that this debit entry is the *opposite* entry to the credit entry in the main cash book.
- Column 2 is the date column – both for receipts and payments.
- Column 3 is where you record details of expenditure.
- Column 4 is for either you or your junior to record the **voucher number**. In a small organisation entries in this column should show consecutive numbers – or you should want to know the reason for

PETTY CASH BOOK

Receipts £	Date	Details	Vchr No	Total payment £	VAT £	Expenditure headings			
						Travel £	Stat'ry £	Enter-taining £	Office Sundries £
200.00	3 May	Balance b/d							
	3 May	Coffee	223	3.50					3.50
	7 May	Art paper	224	11.75	1.75		10.00		
	10 May	Buffet lunch	225	42.00				42.00	
	11 May	Taxi fare	226	5.00		5.00			
	14 May	Flowers	227	15.00					15.00
	17 May	Poster adhesive	228	8.05	1.05		7.00		
	17 May	Milk	229	23.00					23.00
	21 May	Window cleaner	230	8.00					8.00
	22 May	Petrol	231	16.45	2.45	14.00			
	25 May	Sandwiches	232	8.50				8.50	
	26 May	Marker pens	223	2.35	0.35		2.00		
		TOTAL		143.60	5.60	19.00	19.00	50.50	49.50
	1 June	Balance c/d		56.40					
200.00				200.00					
56.40	1 June	Balance b/d							
143.60	1 June	Cash received							

the discrepancy. In large organisations different departments may have different blocks of numbers and the numbers may not be consecutive.

- Column 5 gives the **total payment** against each voucher.
- Columns 6 – 10 are where the expenditure is allocated to its own heading. If your company is registered for VAT there must also be a separate VAT column.

Your first job is to record your funds as a receipt, ie a *debit* entry and to put the money in your cash box. Decide on the best place to store this – remember that petty cash boxes are only light and very portable. It is no use thinking that it is secure purely because it locks! Remember that the vouchers must also be kept safely – in the wrong hands these could easily be misused!

Now decide on your expenditure headings. These are the headings under which you can group most items of expenditure. Choose one fewer than the number of available headings you can have and call the last column 'Office sundries' for all those items which won't logically go anywhere else. One method is to look back over previous types of cash expenditure and see if you can group these logically. Examples of typical headings usually include Stationery, Travel or Transport, Entertaining or Hospitality, Postage, and Casual wages.

You should note that you will probably be constrained in your choice of expenditure headings by the expense accounts shown in your organisation's General Ledger. Remember that when you have balanced your petty cash book the balances have to be *transferred* somewhere, ie your credit (outgoing) entries must be entered as a debit entry in an opposite account. What happens is that when you submit the petty cash book for checking at the end of each accounting period the totals of each expenditure column are extracted and entered in the appropriate account in the General Ledger, eg £56.50 in the Travel account, £27 in the Stationery account and so on. This system cannot operate if you design headings which don't match any recognisable account operated by the Accounts section – so once you have pencilled in the headings, check with that these will correspond with the main accounts system.

Petty cash and VAT

If your organisation is registered for VAT then you **must** have a VAT column in which you record any VAT paid separately. This is to enable your organisation to post this amount to the main VAT account so that all amounts paid out on VAT can be reclaimed when the VAT return is completed for that period.

For VAT to be reclaimable a VAT invoice must have been obtained from the supplier – and only suppliers who are themselves registered for VAT can issue such an invoice. The invoice must show both the supplier's VAT registration number and the tax point of the invoice (the date ownership of the goods is transferred).

On a VAT invoice the cost of the item and the amount of VAT are usually shown separately. The net price of the goods is shown first, then the VAT and finally the total amount. These details should be transferred to the petty cash book in the same way – the net amount only shown under the expenditure heading, the VAT entered in the VAT column and the total in the total payments column. Remember that some goods and services are either zero-rated or exempt from VAT – which is why no VAT is levied on travel (eg train fares or taxis), on food (unless it is a pre-prepared meal) and on books or magazines. In these cases, therefore, your VAT column will be blank.

In some cases, however, the amount paid on an account is *inclusive* of VAT. A typical example is petrol. Garages usually issue VAT inclusive receipts so that the amount of VAT which has been paid must be calculated then recorded in the usual way. Then, of course, only the net amount of the receipt is recorded under the appropriate heading.

CHECK IT YOURSELF
Anyone responsible for operating a petty cash system should have a copy of the latest VAT Guidelines close at hand so that they have correct and up-to-date information available in the case of queries. You can obtain a copy by contacting your local VAT office.

Calculating VAT inclusive amounts

These are calculated by using the following formula.

$$\frac{\text{rate of VAT}}{\text{VAT rate} + 100} \times \text{amount spent}$$

which obviously works no matter what rate of VAT is in force, to give the amount of VAT charged.

Note that you can save yourself much work if you know how to cancel down fractions! For instance, at the current rate of 17.5% VAT, the formula is

$$\frac{17.5}{117.5} \times \text{amount spent}$$

and if you are clever at cancelling down you will be able to work out that this is equivalent to

$$\frac{7}{47} \times \text{amount spent}$$

This is both far easier to remember and far easier to work with!

SPECIAL NOTE
If 7/47 gives you the VAT amount, then 40/47 *must* give you the net amount before VAT was added. Use this knowledge to carry out a 'double check' ie:

- enter the total into your calculator and calculate the VAT amount using the VAT formula
- deduct this from the total receipt to get the net amount (answer 1)

- enter the total again and calculate the net amount using the opposite formula (answer 2).

Both answers should obviously be identical or you have gone wrong somewhere. (Note that you may often have to round your answers up or down to the nearest whole penny. If you do this correctly for both amounts the total will be identical to that shown on the account.)

Operating the system

If you analyse the operation of the system properly, you should be able to subdivide the tasks into:

- those your junior can carry out on her own
- those areas which she should check with you (or upon which you should do spot checks)
- those areas which are your sole responsibility.

TEST YOURSELF

Below is given a list of tasks which may be carried out either routinely or non-routinely by anyone operating a petty cash system. Label each one either 'junior' 'both' or 'me' according to the category in which you think it falls.

1 Issuing vouchers only on request and only in numerical order.
2 Making routine payments against a completed voucher.
3 Checking vouchers for accuracy.
4 Paying out amounts which exceed the agreed maximum in the event of an emergency.
5 Attaching receipts to vouchers.
6 Filing completed vouchers.
7 Issuing advances to senior staff.
8 Calculating VAT on VAT-inclusive receipts.
9 Making an urgent payment which will effectively empty the petty cash box.
10 Requesting additional funds from the cashier (or obtaining authorisation to get these from the bank) in the event of an emergency.
11 Entering expenditure in the petty cash book.
12 Adding up the petty cash analysis columns regularly and checking that the amount spent plus the amount remaining in the petty cash tin still equals the original float.
13 Balancing the petty cash book.
14 Refusing payments where expenditure is unauthorised or there is an error or discrepancy on the voucher.
15 Agreeing the petty cash book with the cashier and obtaining the restoration amount for the new float.
16 Investigating discrepancies and errors.
17 Taking responsibility for all receipts and other records meeting organisational accounting and auditing requirements.
18 Analysing total expenditure against budget and reporting same.

Compare your list with other members of the your group before you continue.

Delegation and training

You may be surprised to learn that, if you train your junior correctly and have specific procedures for her to follow, *most* of the tasks given above can be delegated. The only areas which should be your sole responsibility are numbers 17 and 18. Areas she should check with you are those where it may be been impossible to lay down standard guidelines or when foreseeable exceptions occur. Of the tasks listed above, numbers 1, 4, 6, 9, 10, 14 and 16 may be ones where you expect her to check with you first, although in most of these, if there is a coherent and continuous policy she will know the action to take. So far as task 12 is concerned, a wise supervisor makes regular spot checks on the system – but not to the extent that hardworking and reliable staff feel they are under possible suspicion or constantly being monitored.

Basic procedures

The obvious first step is to delegate basic tasks which are concerned with making routine payments, recording these and filing both vouchers and receipts.

It is important that all staff realise the importance of keeping receipts – especially where VAT payments are concerned. These should be checked carefully against the vouchers and both totals checked. Authorisation procedures vary from one company to another, but usually a manager, executive or supervisor has to countersign a claim for petty cash. If this has been done, the voucher is for an allowable expense, has been completed correctly and the receipt is attached, then there is no reason why your junior should not be able to pay out the amount involved.

Make sure that your staff know that all vouchers should be marked as such when paid and both the voucher and receipt kept safely for recording into the petty cash book. Only when this has been done should the receipt be clipped to the voucher and both filed in chronological order.

The next stage is to teach your junior how to record items of expenditure in the petty cash book. A useful tip is to photocopy the page for the first few times and let your junior make the entries on the photocopied sheet. That way there can be no disasters in the actual book! Check that she fully understands the expenditure headings shown and that she knows which types of expenditure are entered under which heading. If necessary, draft out a checklist she can use with the main types of item listed under each heading.

Once the items have been listed make sure that she knows that she should go back through all her figures, to ensure that no amount has been omitted, transposed or written in the wrong column. Start with simple vouchers at first, either with no VAT listed or with the amount plus VAT. Allow her to enter VAT inclusive amounts only when you are quite sure she knows how to do this – and after you have checked her calculations are correct.

Security procedures and confidentiality

You must impress on all staff the importance of security, especially if you are responsible for a substantial petty cash float. Not only should the petty cash tin be locked away when not in use but its whereabouts should not be the subject of general discussion. It must never be left lying on a desk unattended, nor left out if the cashier is called away to do another job. It should be your job to ensure that it is locked away safely at night (no one else's). Because all vouchers and, usually, the pages in the petty cash book are numbered for security, staff must be aware that they cannot simply crumple up spoiled vouchers or rip out sheets from the book because they make a mistake, without notifying you first. The reason for the missing voucher or petty cash book page is noted – and this information will usually be required by your auditors.

Staff should be dissuaded from discussing how the system operates and the amount kept in the float when out of your office. Equally, petty cash claims are not a matter for discussion or speculation amongst staff – senior executives are unlikely to be pleased if they overhear junior staff commenting on the fact that they seem to travel everywhere by taxi these days!

Cashing up and checking petty cash

This activity should be done routinely, every few days, and *not* just be left until the petty cash book has to be balanced.

Quite obviously, at any point in time:

- the total amount on the vouchers should equal the total amount recorded as expenditure in the petty cash book
- the difference between this total and the original float should equal the amount of money in the petty cash tin.

If either is not the case then you have some searching to do to find the error.

Always encourage junior staff to try to find their own errors first. You should be the *last resort* when they are really stuck – not the *first*, so that they run to you the moment they have a problem. Try to train them each to become a mini-Sherlock Holmes and undertake their own investigations! The method you should teach them to use will depend on whether the discrepancy occurred at the first point above or the second.

An error at the first point is usually caused by faulty addition (of the vouchers or the petty cash columns) or incorrect copying. An incorrect VAT calculation would also affect the total, so would incorrect addition between the amount showing in the analysis column plus VAT. It is also important that all the vouchers have been included and that none are missing (or are missing from the page entry) – a quick glance down the voucher number column won't always show this ie if vouchers have been muddled up.

A problem at the second point may be harder to solve. As a first step the basic subtraction should be checked, then the money in the tin should be recounted. It is, of course, possible that an amount has been paid out wrongly and either too much, or too little, given to the recipient. This is usually the case if there is a 'round' amount difference, eg £1 or 10p. It is less likely to be the case if you are 26p out! Looking back through the vouchers may give you a clue, however, to what could have happened.

There is a tendency for staff to be complacent when they are 'up' and distraught when they are 'down'. The old maxim is that if it doesn't balance it won't do, no matter which way the error lies! In practice, however, it is obviously less of a problem if you are £1 up rather than £1 down, though nobody should be pleased about the fact. Indeed there may be a faint hope that by the end of the month everything balances out and the 'ups' cancel out the 'downs'. Although this may save the day it rarely happens and you are more likely to have to make an entry to note the problem and prepare an explanation for the cashier or your boss! If the discrepancy is a large one then it is important that you report it immediately to preserve your own reputation.

Balancing the petty cash book

This is one job which you should delegate only when you are completely certain that your junior can undertake it competently. Again, practising on a photocopy first is best, and you can then check the figures before they are written up in the book itself.

Explain how to balance simply by asking your junior to undertake the task in the following order and work through an example with her, eg by reference to page 443.

1 Total all the analysis columns and the VAT column.
2 Add up the total payments column.
3 Check that the addition of the analysis columns and the VAT column *equals* the amount of the total payments column. Only when it does should she proceed to the next stage.
4 Deduct the total payments amount from the amount received at the beginning of the accounting period and enter the *difference* as the balance carried down.
5 Add this amount to the total payments amount to give the imprest amount and rule off.
6 Bring down the balance of cash held to the next accounting period.
7 Then enter the amount received to restore the imprest (when this has been claimed from the cashier).

Note that it is at point 6 that the cashier should be approached to check the books and restore the imprest.

Problems and contingencies

One of your key tasks will be to devise a system to cope with the unexpected, which is always difficult. However, it helps if you can identify the *range* of problems you may have to cope with.

One area could be dealing with emergency claims – especially if the amount required is very large and exceeds either the agreed maximum or the amount held in the petty cash tin at that time. This possibility should have been discussed with your boss at the outset so that you know the range of requests you can deal with on your own. Equally you may need authorisation before you can approach the cashier for additional emergency funds. If your boss is away and a difficult situation arises, then you can always ask the cashier (or another executive) for advice – *and follow it*. This is a safeguard for you in case your actions are later criticised. Needless to say, if there are frequent emergencies, or the money is prone to run out regularly before it should do, then you need to review the system, the way it is used by people *and* the amount of the float with your boss.

'User problems' can include scruffy vouchers, lost receipts, vouchers and receipts which don't tally, requests for advances and requests for reimbursement when the money has already been spent on a non-acceptable expense. You therefore need to train the users as well as your staff! Two common complaints by staff are that:

- they have never been told what is allowable and what is not and
- the system is not flexible enough to cover their needs.

The first is easy to remedy. Prepare a clear list of instructions in relation to voucher requests and completion, keeping receipts, company policy on advances, the type of expenditure which is recognised as acceptable and the correct authorisation procedures. Circulate this to all staff.

However, do bear in mind that the rules for senior staff may vary. It may be part of your remit to allow discretionary advances for managers and/or directors and even complete the vouchers on their behalf but you must still chase up the receipt if you want your books to balance. A good idea is to do this through their PA, but if any member of staff continually makes life difficult for you in this respect then talk over your problem with your boss and enlist some help.

Refusing to make a payment can create problems and, unless the amount is a large one or the item was ludicrous in the extreme, it may be politic to make a discretionary payment but warn the person concerned that such a payment would not be tolerated a second time. The situation will very much dictate the most sensible action to take. There is a tremendous difference between reimbursing a junior £1 so that she can catch a bus home when she bought something which she shouldn't, than paying out £50 to a manager who should have known better. In the latter case you would be wise to inform your boss of the problem before taking any action.

Expenditure, budgets and audits

The total expenditure under each analysis heading for a year will be recorded in the General Ledger. However, if you keep departmental records, or work for a small organisation, your boss may want you to work out the expenditure at regular intervals so that a check can be kept on the actual amount spent in relation to the amount which has been allocated in the budget. There is little point in suddenly telling your boss two days before the financial year end that the department has overspent by £2000!

If you are expected to undertake this type of exercise then you should keep a month-on-month record in a separate book. On the basis that any annual allocation for petty cash can be quickly divided by 12 to show the approximate monthly allocation, it is easy to see at a glance whether the department is below, at or above target. If the latter is the case then your boss may want you to check on specific *areas* which are prone to overspending and where cuts may be made or a change of policy is required. You can only extract this information if your records show the total expenditure for each heading, as well as the cumulative total.

At the end of the year you will be asked to submit your petty cash book and your vouchers and receipts to the Accounts department. If you work for a limited company (public or private) then your accounts will be **audited** (ie examined) by a firm of auditors who will study every transaction and every entry. It is for this reason that any discrepancies noticed during the year must be logged properly and not ignored (or hidden!). Any problems uncovered during auditing which indicate any type of deliberate cover up will throw suspicion on both you and your staff, which could prove both unpleasant and embarrassing.

ACTIVITY SECTION

Individual tasks

1 Two junior clerical staff in your department have been assigned to assist you with petty cash, starting next Monday.
   a List the tasks you will give them during the first week, and the checks you will make to ensure they carry these out effectively.
   b Make out a list of the security procedures they must follow from the first day.

2 All staff in your office are allowed to claim petty cash against an authorised voucher provided that a receipt is attached. The system works well except that you have found that junior staff are not completing vouchers correctly.
   Draft a short instruction page, which contains an illustration of a correctly completed voucher, explaining exactly how it must be filled in and the correct procedure to follow when presenting it for payment.

3 For the first time your junior has been calculating VAT inclusive amounts from petrol accounts submitted by representatives. Check if the figures are correct in each case. If you find any errors then correct them.

   - Total account = £18.50   VAT £2.76, net amount = £15.74
   - Total account = £27.00   VAT £4.20, net amount = £22.80
   - Total account = £14.80   VAT £2.20, net amount = £12.60
   - Total account = £16.75   VAT £2.49, net amount = £14.25

Individual/group tasks

Case study 1

You have recently started work for a small organisation which is managed by three Directors, one of whom is Paula Rhodes, your boss. There is a total of 20 staff in the office. Upon your arrival you find that the petty cash system is virtually non-existent. All cash expenditure is entered in the main cash book which is getting overloaded with entries for each month. Your task is to instigate a petty cash system which will serve the needs of the company. As a start Ms Rhodes gives you a note of the type of expenditure which is paid for in cash. Although she only has details for the last two months she has added a few notes she thinks might help you.

1 Petrol is quite a substantial item; last month it came to £48.50 and the month before £52.10.

2 We pay the window cleaner, newsagent and cleaner in cash (total for the three about £120 per month).

3 We keep a float of stamps (about £20 worth) for emergency post, and usually pay cash for special items, eg registered or recorded delivery etc.

4 Taxis can add up to £30 in the course of a month.

5 We don't do much entertaining, but there's a Directors' lunch every week (sandwiches from the local sandwich bar!).

6 Tea, coffee, milk etc are all bought for cash. You'll have a better idea of price than I have! One day we'll get a vending machine!

7 Don't forget emergency stationery items – last month this came to £23! Perhaps now that you are here we'll be more well organised on this?

From the details given above, decide:

• the level of float you will need to operate on a *monthly* accounting system
• the analysis headings which would be the most suitable.

Detail your recommendations in a memo to Ms Rhodes and make sure you clearly justify your decisions.

Case study 2

You are employed as PA to Bjorn Carlsen, Regional Director for a company of Management Consultants. There is a small office staff of three Senior Consultants and seven office staff. However, the Consultants who operate within your region also use your office as 'base' when they are not at a client's premises.

Part of your responsibilities is to keep the petty cash system for the office. All vouchers must be signed as authorised by either the Regional Director or, in his absence, one of the Senior Consultants. Advances are only allowed for senior staff and the maximum amount allowable for items under petty cash, without special authorisation, is £20. You have a monthly float of £300. At the end of each month you can withdraw the money you need from the bank, although copies of all your accounts must be sent to head office for verification.

For the past two weeks you have been on a special training course organised by your company at its own training centre in Sussex. One of the junior staff, Katie, who you have been training for some time, has been keeping the system operational in your absence.

When you return to work you find that she is away with flu and has left out for you the petty cash page for the month, which she has tried to balance and a note (see documents 1 and 2).

Receipts £	Date	Details	Vchr No	Total payment £	VAT £	Travel £	Stat'ry £	Postage £	Office Sundries £
300.00	4 Oct	Balance b/d							
	6 Oct	Phone cleaning	620	12.50	1.86				10.64
	8 Oct	Newsagent	621	18.00					18.00
	11 Oct	Jug kettle	622	13.50	2.01				15.51
	12 Oct	Taxi	623	18.00		18.00			
	14 Oct	Stamps	624	20.00				20.00	
	18 Oct	Tea and coffee	625	7.20					7.20
	20 Oct	Advance to BT	262	80.00		80.00			
	21 Oct	Milkman	627	15.00					15.00
	22 Oct	Print cartridges	628	75.00	11.17		63.83		
	25 Oct	Datapost fee	629	16.80				16.80	
	28 Oct	Flip charts	670	19.00	2.83		16.17		
		TOTAL		295.00	17.87	98.00	80.00	36.80	64.35
	1 Nov	Balance c/d		5.00					
300.00				300.00					

Read her note carefully, then:

1 Check the petty cash page she has left to see if you can find the problem and amend any errors.

2 Preferably as a group, consider the implications of all the problems Katie has experienced. Then detail the action you think should be taken to prevent any similar recurrences in the future.

DOCUMENT 2

---

28 October

Sorry I won't be around to welcome you back but I am feeling so poorly at present that even this hasty note is almost more than I can cope with!

Attached is the petty cash book for the month. I really have tried very hard to balance it but have given up – I can't think straight at present anyway. No matter what I do I can't get it to cross-check. I must have made an error somewhere but simply can't find it. There's only £5 in the tin so I assume my total payments total is right and have completed the balance on this basis. Hope it's OK!

There was a bit of trouble whilst you were away which someone is bound to tell you about on Monday. Mr Jackson (the new Senior Consultant) was furious last week. He tried to reclaim a train fare of £75 but I told him there wasn't enough money as I couldn't get it out of the bank and both you and the Regional Director were away. He said the float was useless if we got in this mess every month. I told him it was because of the printer cartridges (these ran out last week and we had an urgent job to do). I told Mr Carlsen when he came back and he asked why I bought so many – but you only get the discount if you buy six at a time. He said I should have asked first but we were desperate.

I then got into trouble because of the advance to Bernice Taylor – the Consultant at present working at Bell & Watts – but when she called she was in a hurry and said she'd had advances before, so I assumed it was OK. She still hasn't given me any receipts or filled in a voucher though I've phoned to remind her three times. She won't be in the office again for at least another month!

PS (5 pm addition)

Incidentally when you look in the tin you'll find it's now empty! Don't have a fit – Sarah lost her purse this afternoon so I lent her the £5 so she could get home. I'm sure she'll repay it on Monday (I hope so because I've brought down the balance for that date, and if she forgets we won't have one!).   Katie

---

Section 3 – Ensuring the use of authorised banking procedures

The range of financial services offered today by both banks and building societies is considerable. So considerable, in fact, that knowing what is on offer, so that you can use the service which is the most appropriate for a particular situation, can be something of a headache. The whole area of financial services has changed out of all recognition over the last few years as, in some cases, has the manner in which banking transactions are undertaken. Today a customer does not even have to visit the bank as the latest innovations include telephone banking and computerised banking. Customers who use the telephone service quote a special ID number as well as their account number and can then give instructions to the operator to conduct a whole range of transactions, eg pay bills, transfer money between accounts, receive an up-to-the-minute check on the balance in various accounts, order statements or cheque/paying-in books, set up standing orders and arrange travel facilities etc. Most telephone banking services can also be accessed by talking to the computer directly, eg via an MF telephone where the numeric and the star and gate keys are used to enter information, or via a tone pad on non-MF telephones (see also Chapter 1, Communication systems, page 30).

Businesses with PCs installed have access to an even greater range of services. Via a PC (whether networked or not) and a modem any organisation can link directly to a bank computer. The special user-friendly software has prompts to guide users as they transfer money between accounts, settle accounts with suppliers, pay wages to staff, obtain information on their account balances, set up direct debits and standing orders and arrange for foreign exchange transactions etc. Generally this system is easier to use than the telephone, as well as being more comprehensive. Other benefits include the fact that the information is displayed on screen and details can be printed out for later reference. Therefore much of a company's banking requirements can be undertaken without ever leaving the office. Indeed, the only time it is actually necessary to visit a bank is to pay in or withdraw funds, as these actions require the time-honoured method of walking to the bank – unless the amounts being handled are large enough to warrant a collection/delivery service.

Cashflow

The rapidity with which banking transactions can be carried out is increasing all the time – and this is a major benefit to all businesses. Why? Quite simply because of the basic fact that if a company's cashflow is increased, the safer it then becomes in financial terms – and rapid financial transactions improve cashflow.

Imagine buying a house which is so expensive that by the time you have paid the mortgage you can't afford any food – or buying a very expensive car but not being able to afford the petrol. In both these cases you have put your money into **fixed assets** (ie the house and car) but have not left yourself any capital to work with (ie **working capital**). In our private lives we use working capital to pay for our day to day living expenses – heating, lighting, food, travel etc, and we need income to enable us to do this. If we have too many bills to pay one month, or don't receive any income (or, heaven forbid, both at once!) then we suffer and have to cut down on or can't afford what we consider to be even the basic necessities of life.

Businesses operate in exactly the same way. The **income** or **revenue** received by a business is generated by customers paying their accounts. Equally, the company has to pay its own bills and its suppliers (who are also concerned about their own cashflow) will be pressing for payment by the end of the month. The worst that can happen is that a company pays its own bills but the organisations which owe it money don't settle on time. In this case money starts to run out rapidly, as salaries and other overheads must be met.

There are several measures organisations can take to guard against this. Not least is to try and put off settling their own debts with suppliers until the last minute and to set up procedures so that revenue received is banked as quickly as possible. Then, if surplus funds are available, these can be transferred (even for as short a period as overnight if the size of the funds warrant it) into an income generating account where they will earn interest. The more efficient the company's money management programme the more profitable it will become – and both commercial banks and building societies have developed a range of services to assist organisations to achieve this objective.

An important development is the current move into 'instant banking' by telephone or PC. Surplus funds can be transferred to an income-generating account at the touch of a key or by means of a simple telephone call, incoming direct debit forms completed by customers can be processed in the office and the information sent directly to the bank computer, foreign exchange requirements for either executives travelling overseas or international transactions can be communicated immediately and so on. The speed of the transactions enables an organisation to maximise one of its most valuable resources – finance.

SPECIAL NOTE

The correct name for high street banks, with which you are most familiar, is **commercial banks**. This term is used to differentiate them from the two other types of banks in the banking system, ie the **central bank** (the Bank of England) and **merchant banks** which provide a different range of services for specialist customers.

The PA and company finance

The first criteria for any PA worth her salt is to be fully aware of the *importance* of finance to a business and the significance of cashflow. This is not an area to which mere lip service can be paid as it is critical to the survival of any company. If a PA has a dual role as an office administrator for a small company then she plays a very key part in helping to maximise financial benefits by the actions she takes. If she puts all her efforts into settling the organisation's outstanding debts with suppliers, rather than chasing up money owed to her company by its customers during a very bad month, she can hardly expect to be congratulated by her employer!

If she works for a larger organisation or has a supervisory role over junior staff involved in routine banking transactions, then an appreciation of the importance of this part of the business means that not only will she prioritise this side of her work correctly, but she will also give it the care and attention it justifiably deserves. No PA is ever likely to see eye to eye with her boss unless she displays considerable empathy on this topic. If there are financial problems in the organisation then the mood will be one of doom and gloom and she needs to understand why. Equally, she can then appreciate why her boss is so euphoric if a large contract is won – and join in the celebrations!

Banks and building societies

Today both these institutions offer a wide range of what are known as **current account services** (see below). Businesses are apt to favour banks rather than building societies because of the additional services they provide and the range of company finance and business loans available. You are therefore more likely to find that any commercial organisation which employs you still operates its business accounts through a commercial bank rather than a building society.

Bank accounts

There are two types of account which a business may have:

- a current account
- an interest-bearing account.

However, more than one account may be held in each case. If more than one current account is operated then you might find that these go under the name of 'Trading Account 1', 'Trading Account 2' etc and that different types of expenditure are settled through different accounts. Do note that in each case there will be a separate cheque book and paying-in book and it is important that you use the correct one for a particular account. From the outset you should realise that the charges on a business account are much higher than on a personal account. Each transaction is charged for, and there are quite high fees for such items as stopping a cheque or requesting a copy of a statement. You can therefore incur considerable additional expenses just by carelessness! The charges are very high if, for instance, your company exceeds its agreed overdraft or if a cheque has to be returned because there is not enough money in your company's account to pay it.

There are several different types of interest-bearing accounts but one rule applies to them all – the more instant the access, the lower the interest rate. For this reason your organisation may have more than one such account, with varying access terms and interest rates. Note that if you see the term 'on call' it means that the money is available instantly.

In addition, companies involved in exporting may have foreign currency accounts to enable them to invest surplus foreign funds immediately instead of having to convert them into sterling first (and pay for the privilege). This is very valuable for a company which is continually receiving and paying funds in foreign currencies as any surpluses earn interest and the currency is readily available for future use.

Banking services

The services and facilities most likely to be used include the following.

Audit certificates   These give details of all transactions in and out of a business account for use by an auditor/accountant.

Automated credit card processing services   The names of these systems vary, eg Streamline (Nat West) and PDQ (Barclays). Both are computerised services whereby credit cards are swiped through an electronic terminal and the card balance and transaction logged by the bank computer.

Automated salary payments   All banks offer an automated payment service for businesses which wish to pay their employees by means of **BACS/credit transfer** (see below). The names of specific systems vary, eg Autopay (Nat West) and Payflow (Barclays).

Bank giro See *Credit transfer*.

BACS (Bankers' automated clearing service)   The automated alternative to cheque or cash methods of payment. Data can be input direct to the computer system either via a PC or from the customer's own bank and transfers made automatically – usually within three days (see also *Credit transfer*).

Bankers' draft   A cheque made out on the bank itself and useful for paying suppliers who may be hesitant to make a substantial deal with an unknown customer. The bank cheque is always acceptable and the bank can reclaim the amount drawn from the customer's account (see also *Foreign draft*).

Bankers' reference   Banks will obtain a credit reference from the UK bankers of a potential customer on request (see also *Status report*).

Bulk cash/delivery service   The delivery or collection of large amounts of cash/cheques.

Business loan   A business loan enables a company to borrow an agreed amount over a fixed period. Some banks give the alternative of borrowing a fixed sum at the outset or 'rolling up' the amount borrowed over a period of time. Loans can often be obtained either with a fixed rate of interest or a floating (variable) rate so companies can try to hedge their bets against interest rate changes. Most loans (especially to small businesses) have additional insurance attached to cover the repayments in case of an accident or serious illness. In the event of death (ie of the proprietor) the loan is paid off in full.

Capital repayment holiday   A system whereby the initial repayments on a loan are for the interest only and do not include repayment of the capital sum borrowed.

A cash card   Used with a PIN number (**personal identity number**) to obtain money from an ATM (**automated teller machine**). Cash machines may also give the balance of account if required and enable the card holder to order a new cheque book or statement.

CHAPS (Clearing house automated payment system)   Used to transfer funds rapidly between accounts in the UK via a computer network which links the main commercial banks.

Cheque book   Contains unlimited free cheques. Cheques are available in various sizes for business customers and can be pre-printed with the name and address of the organisation and for several signatories.

Cheque card   Used to guarantee cheques though the amount varies from one bank to another – currently from £50 to £250. Also used to obtain cash from a different branch from the one where the account is held.

Cheque reconciliation service   Companies writing a large number of cheques per week can obtain a computer record of all bank statements to enable rapid cheque reconciliation to be carried out.

Commercial insurance   Banks offer a range of policies to protect business premises and stock etc from theft or fire and to cover visitors in case of accident.

Credit card   Most banks offer a business credit card service whereby all cards relate to one business account and expenditure is detailed each month in terms of individuals as well as for the company as a whole.

Credit transfer   The name often used for the bank giro system where sums of money are transferred automatically from one bank account to another upon completion of a form. This service is used by companies which pay their wages through the BACS system and is also available to anyone who calls in to a bank and completes a bank giro form to transfer money to another account.

Debit card   Used in conjunction with either the Switch or Visa network. When the card is swiped through an electronic cash register linked to the EFTPOS (**Electronic funds transfer at point of sale**) network the money is automatically credited to the supplier's account within three working days.

Deferred checking   The ability to leave large amounts for paying in with the counter staff for later checking to prevent company staff having to wait at the bank.

Direct debit   An agreement by the customer to the supplier (*not* with the bank) that a sum of money, to be determined by the supplier, can be withdrawn from the customer's account at periodic intervals. Safeguards regulate which companies can offer this service to their customers, and the latter must be notified when there is any change to the amount being charged or to the frequency of payments. The system is ideal for irregular payments and/or amounts as the customer does not have to notify his/her bank of any changes.

Economic information   Available on projected economic trends both in the UK and overseas.

EFTI (Electronic funds transfer initiation service)   Used to transfer money electronically from a UK account to another account anywhere in the world. Transfer is more rapid for sterling payments than for foreign currency.

Eurocard   Guarantees any card made out on the Eurocheque system for between £100 and £140 (depending on the country) and also enables cheques to be cashed for the same amount.

Eurocheque   Used to pay accounts in any country which subscribes to the Eurocheque system. The cheque can be made out in the relevant foreign currency as well as in sterling. Companies *receiving* payment by Eurocheque are charged a fee if the cheque is drawn on a foreign bank.

Foreign draft   Similar to a **bankers' draft** but made out in a specified foreign currency and therefore capable of being paid into any overseas bank account.

Forward transactions   An agreement to buy a specific amount of foreign currency at a future date at a pre-arranged rate of exchange. This protects the company if the value of sterling falls in relation to a specific currency in the period between the start and the payment date of a contract.

International payment order   A method of transferring money overseas where the company's bank instructs a local bank abroad to pay money into a named account in that country.

Letter of credit   A written undertaking by a bank on behalf of a buyer which agrees to pay the supplier within a specific time limit subject to certain conditions. Used to guarantee payment to foreign suppliers.

Night safe   Used to deposit money at any time during the day or night. The deposits are processed the next working day.

Overdraft   Withdrawing more than the balance in a current account. This is a cheap method of obtaining a temporary loan as interest is charged on the overdrawn balance on a daily basis only. Having an overdraft often means that additional bank charges are also incurred. Permission must usually be sought beforehand (or the charges are even higher) and the bank has the right to request repayment virtually on demand.

Paying-in book   A book containing paying-in or credit slips in duplicate (or triplicate). The slips are pre-printed with the account number/holder's name. The top copy is kept by the bank and the duplicate(s) retained by the company.

Safe custody Banks will store valuables (either specific items or documents) in their safe for a specified period.

Smart card A plastic card which holds electronically the balance of the account. This information can then be read and updated by the bank computer when the card is inserted into a cash point or swiped through a terminal.

Special presentation The bank will check if expected funds have been paid into an account before the normal three working days which it takes for a cheque to be cleared. This service is also known as **expressing** by some banks.

Spot transactions Buying foreign currency at specified exchange rates – usually the rate in force on the date of purchase (see also *Forward transactions*).

Standing orders Usually used to pay a supplier when the amount charged does not vary from one month to another. The account holder sends notification to his/her bank to pay a fixed sum into a different account at specified intervals. Any alterations must be made by the account holder. This system is declining in popularity and being replaced by *Direct debit*.

Status report Banks will carry out a status enquiry on any business worldwide and give their opinion on the financial standing of any potential trading partner.

Telegraphic transfer The most rapid method of transferring money abroad.

Travellers' cheques Obtainable in a variety of currencies for encashment abroad (see Chapter 4, Arranging travel, page 201).

Banking procedures and the PA's role

The type of transactions with which you are likely to be involved will depend on several factors – the size of the organisation for which you work, the type of business with which it is involved, the number of cash transactions daily, whether there is a centralised accounts office and so on. In some jobs you may have little or no contact with the financial institutions used by your company; in others your work in this area may be considerable. Although you are unlikely to be involved in negotiating the terms of a business loan you may find that, at the very least, you are expected to be able to:

- write cheques to pay for goods and services received or to withdraw cash to replenish the petty cash float (even if you haven't the authority to sign them)
- supervise the receiving and banking of cash and cheque payments
- oversee the correct procedure for payments received by debit or credit cards
- organise payment systems for customers, eg by direct debit or standing order etc and advise on queries in relation to more obscure methods, eg payment by Eurocheque

- obtain foreign currency and travellers' cheques for executives travelling overseas
- arrange for money to be transmitted to other parts of the UK or overseas, sometimes in an emergency
- oversee the security and confidentiality procedures in force (or even advise and/or instigate these yourself)
- train and oversee junior staff involved in this area and monitor their work for errors and discrepancies
- ensure that accurate financial records are kept for use by the company's accountants.

! SPECIAL NOTE

It is important that you realise that, when categorising payments, accountants will refer to payments by any method for a one-off purchase as a **cash** payment, to differentiate this type of payment from **credit** payments which are organised on an on-going basis. Indeed the whole structure of the company's accounts is divided between cash and credit transactions. Cash transactions are recorded in a **Cash Book**, whereas any organisation which has an account (ie credit facilities) with your company will have its own account in the **Sales Ledger**. Therefore if Mr Bloggs calls in to buy some goods and pays for them by cheque, this is categorised as a cash (as opposed to credit) transaction.

Making out cheques

Before you even reach for a pen to write out any cheques your first move must be to check the account you are paying. Check firstly that the goods have been delivered (or the service performed), secondly that there are no problems (eg the goods are not faulty or the service unsatisfactory) and finally that the account is correct in every detail. Once that part of the procedure has been carried out then it may be your responsibility to make sure that payment is made. Note that many invoices today have a remittance advice form attached which you simply detach and send with the cheque. Alternatively your company may have its own forms which must be completed.

A cheque is simply an order from you, to the bank, instructing the latter to do what you say. This requirement is important in terms of legal protection. The more precise you are in the wording of your instructions, the more you reduce any possibility of problems, misunderstandings, misuse or even fraud being perpetrated on the cheques you have written – and the more you put the onus on the bank for negligence if anything goes wrong.

If you are instructing your junior to complete a cheque for the first time it is important that you instruct her in the basic rules to be followed. She should understand that:

- the cheque should be completed in blue or black ink for clarity
- the date should be written in full, eg 1 June 199- rather than 1/6/9- (which is easier to alter)
- the payee's name (ie the person receiving payment) should be

written in full, ie Trevor Howarth rather than T Howarth
- the amount in words should be written clearly though the pence can be written as a figure, eg Two hundred and two pounds – 50p only
- the addition of the word 'only' (see above) after the amount in words gives added protection as it makes the written amount more difficult to alter
- the amounts in words and figures must agree
- amounts should be written to the *left* of the lines to make it difficult for additional words or figures to be inserted
- all blank spaces should be crossed through
- any alterations must be clearly signed (rather than initialled) by the signatory, as near as possible to the alteration itself
- the counterfoil must be completed *in full* – it is wise to include a note as to the reason for payment, in addition to the basic information of who, when and how much.

In addition make sure that your junior staff understand the markings on a cheque, ie which is the bank sort code, which the account number and which the cheque number and the different terms used, ie payee, drawee (the bank) and drawer (the person signing the cheque).

Cheque crossings

Virtually all cheques today are **crossed**, ie they are pre-printed with two parallel lines through the middle. A cheque without these lines is known as an **open cheque**. These cheques are extremely risky as they can be cashed at the bank where the account is held, whereas a crossed cheque must be paid into a bank account. Therefore open cheques are rarely used and certainly should never be sent through the post.

There are several variations on the basic two line crossing. You may find that a supplier has asked that you cross all cheques 'A/c payee only' or 'not negotiable'. In this case you simply write these words between the two parallel lines. In reality, neither give complete protection against fraud and only the words 'not negotiable' have any statutory meaning – and even then, probably not in the sense you think (see below).

Automated cheque production

Companies which require large volumes of cheques to be produced usually process these by computer. This means that payments are logged and sometimes even recorded in the accounts system automatically. Remittance advice forms are also usually printed at the same time. Rather than an executive signing vast numbers of cheques at the end of each computer run, a cheque-signing machine may be used for this purpose. Needless to say, the automated production and signing of cheques need to be closely guarded and the cheque signing machine locked when not in use. Frequently companies will authorise that cheques which exceed a specific amount must be signed manually and/or by two or three executives as a security measure.

A useful aid for all PAs is to keep an updated list of exactly who can sign cheques and for how much – so that in the absence of her own boss she is not trapped in a situation where no cheques can be sent.

Guarding against fraud

Fraudulent use of cheques is increasing – not merely with thieves stealing cheque books but mainly by fraudsters stealing cheques sent by post and paying these into their own accounts.

Problems arise in that the wording on a cheque enables a payee to order the bank to do something different with the cheque than the drawer first intended – hence the words 'or Order' at the end of the first line. In plain English the first part of the cheque is really saying 'pay the payee or carry out his orders'. This means that the payee can change your instructions. For instance, he could endorse the cheque by signing his name on the back and writing a different order, eg pay Joe Bloggs. The bank would then carry out this instruction. The law specifically says that the bank does not need to check that the signature on the back of a cheque is genuine nor does a bank have to check the identity of the payee. Therefore if, at any stage, a cheque is stolen it is a relatively simple matter for the thief to write the name of the payee on the back and pay the money into his own account.

You may think that if you add a special crossing you are protected, but this is not necessarily the case. For instance the A/c Payee only crossing has no force in law even though it is meant to prevent the cheque being paid into a different account from the one specified (ie the payee's account). In practice it simply means that the paying bank has a legal responsibility to ask a few questions. The words 'not negotiable' simply mean that if your cheque to a customer is stolen and the thief passes it on to a third person who accepts it in good faith, that person cannot sue you if the bank will not pay them. Indeed, in a recent Government report on Banking Practice it was stated that the words written on a cheque 'neither say what they mean nor mean what they say'!

According to the Banking Ombudsman the safest way to make out a cheque so that it cannot be misappropriated is to:

- add the word 'only' after the name of the payee
- delete the words 'or order' and ask the person signing the cheque to initial the change
- write the words 'not transferable' between the two parallel lines. (In other words this cheque *must* be paid into the payee's account.)

If the bank still allows the cheque to be paid into someone else's account then it is likely that it can be held liable for negligence.

Bear in mind that the above precautions should be used to prevent fraud with cheques you are in the process of writing. If the complete cheque book goes missing then you must inform the bank at once and put a stop on all cheques which are remaining in the book. Only when the bank has been notified do you cease to be liable for fraud – so don't delay.

A final point to note is that if a supplier reports that he has not received a cheque in the post then you should not only stop the cheque by telephoning the bank immediately but also reclaim the bank charge for doing this from the Royal Mail service, as they were guilty of non-delivery in the first place.

Cashing cheques

If you wish to obtain cash at the bank, eg to replenish your petty cash float, then theoretically you have to:

- substitute the word 'cash' for the name of the payee
- cancel the crossing by writing 'pay cash' (followed by the signature of the drawer) through the crossing lines.

In practice, however, you will find that many banks dislike this method because of problems of fraud and misappropriation. Needless to say, losing such a cheque on the way to the bank would be disastrous!

You are therefore better to negotiate a policy with the bank that you will make out the cheque in the name of the person who will present it to the bank and *then* cancel the crossing. Arrange for cheques to be cashed only upon proof of identity. If you add the words 'only' after the payee's name and cross out the words 'or Order' it will – with luck – prevent anyone who finds the cheque from endorsing it and then producing their own proof of identity in return for the cash.

It is important that you train your staff to undertake **cash analysis** before they cash cheques at the bank, as upon arrival they will be asked what denominations of notes and coins they require. If you need £200 for petty cash and your staff return with four £50 notes you have little likelihood of operating an efficient system until you have obtained a fair amount of small change! It is important that you not only instruct your staff how to analyse the number of coins and notes required, but also to follow a recognised procedure and double-check their work before visiting the bank.

Receiving payments by cheque

Make sure that all staff responsible for receiving payments by cheque know that they should examine closely both the cheque itself and the cheque guarantee card before they accept the cheque in payment. This, of course, only applies when the person paying the account is a private individual who calls in person, and does *not* apply to business organisations which send a cheque in settlement of their account.

The cheque must be examined in terms of:

- the date (after six months a cheque ceases to be valid so the wrong *year* can create a real problem)

- the name of the payee, which should be the official title of your company as shown on its bank account
- the amount in words and figures (which must agree)
- the signature.

In addition staff should check that the guarantee card is:

- for a greater amount than that stated on the cheque
- has not expired
- shows the same bank sort code as the cheque
- shows the same signature as that on the cheque.

Only then should they write the cheque card number on the reverse of the cheque and initial this (in case the identity of the person who dealt with the matter is needed later).

Your company will no doubt have a policy as to whether or not post-dated cheques are acceptable, ie cheques made out for a later date than when they are written. Usually these are not acceptable, but a small organisation, offered payment by a particularly slippery customer, may prefer this to nothing at all! The same argument may apply to payment for a greater amount than that shown on the cheque guarantee card – and many companies allow this to be exceeded provided the customer's address is written on the reverse of the cheque. Therefore don't be too arbitrary in your judgements – find out what action to take if a particular set of circumstances is somewhat unusual.

Problem cheques

Difficulties arise if a cheque is found to be wrongly completed or if a minor disaster has occurred when the post was opened (eg the cheque was torn in two!). Before you frantically telephone your customer and ask for a duplicate to be sent (and land your customer with extra charges for stopping the cheque you now have in your hand) *ring the bank and ask for their advice*. In many cases you can *still* present the cheque for payment, eg if the cheque is torn into two pieces rather than 25 it can be sellotaped, if the amount in *words* is correct – and is larger than the amount in figures – the cheque may still be acceptable.

Depositing payments received

It is usual for payments to be banked as quickly as possible, firstly to prevent problems of theft or loss (particularly if your company's insurance policy does not cover large amounts kept on the premises overnight) and secondly to facilitate cash flow. If a large sum of money is received, therefore, you should treat the banking of this as top priority; if such amounts are regularly received out of banking hours then consider the use of a night safe.

Do make sure that your junior staff know how to complete a paying-in slip correctly. On the basis that a busy bank cashier will not welcome a heavily crossed out and edited paying-in slip at any time, let alone when the bank is busy, make sure that your junior first prepares a breakdown on a separate piece of paper and balances the receipts, before transferring the information to the paying-in book.

Most company paying-in books have slips in duplicate or even triplicate. The bank takes the top copy. The second copy is either retained in the book or, if it is the second of three, can be sent to the accounts section for their records.

To cash up properly and *quickly*, cash receipts and cheques should first be separated and then the following procedure should be undertaken.

- The cash should be stacked in specific quantities, eg £1 coins in tens, 20p coins in fives and so on. The *height* of all the piles for each denomination should therefore be identical (apart from coins left over at the end).
- All notes should be stacked in specific denominations with the Queen's head to the right.
- The totals for each denomination of notes and coins should then be listed on a separate paper and then added together.
- The total must then be checked to ensure that it agrees with the expected amount. If the latter is not known, then as a precaution a second person should check that the procedure has been carried out correctly and the same figure is reached.
- The paying-in slip should be made out neatly, with cheques and postal orders listed on the reverse and carried forward on to the front and added to the total cash received. Note that it is usual for the name of the company's bank account and the account number to be pre-printed on each slip. If your company has several accounts then make sure the correct book is being completed!
- If the paying-in slip has a duplicate copy then the information is automatically recorded on this – provided the carbon paper is inserted the right way round!

The cash itself should be put into the special cash bags provided by the bank. These are clearly marked with the denomination required and are usually in different colours. Don't worry if a bag isn't full, eg if you have only £18 in £1 coins instead of the £20 specified, but don't mix coins in one bag – or you risk annoying the bank cashier.

At some stage you must, of course, make out a record of all the payments received *and why they have been made*. The latter information is essential in the case of any subsequent queries. Obviously the systems used by organisations differ – if dozens of payments are received daily then these will probably be entered on computer before any documentation or cash is processed for taking to the bank. In a small organisation a more basic system may be in force, possibly the recording of the details on a payments received sheet prior to entry in the company's Cash Book.

Depositing cash

You should note that the signature on a paying-in slip must be that of the person who is paying in the money. However tempted or busy you are it is never advisable to give junior staff the responsibility of taking money to the bank on a regular basis, unless the amounts are small and you allow staff to go in pairs. This is not so much a matter of trust, because discrepancies should be easily identifiable, but one of common sense and security. From what you have already read about cheques, you should realise that serious problems can arise if these are stolen on their way to the bank, especially if they are made out for large sums of money. The dangers of transporting cash are obvious.

If very large sums are involved then most banks offer a collection service (they also offer a delivery service if large sums of money need to be withdrawn from the bank). If the sums involved are less substantial then precautions should still be taken, including banking the money at different times each day and taking a different route. Most companies arrange for transport by their own security staff if possible. If you are personally involved then make sure you are accompanied – and driven there if the bank is not within short walking distance.

Be aware that if there are any errors in your counting or in the completion of the paying-in slip then the bank cashier may be prepared to rectify these only if the discrepancy is minor, eg a simple addition. If the slip requires major modifications expect it to be returned for you to sort out yourself! Do check the cashier stamps and initials your duplicate copy as well as his/her own, as proof that the money has been deposited. Mistakes can happen and if there are any queries at a later date your paperwork needs to be beyond reproach.

Many companies have streamlined their receipts system by asking customers to pay by standing order or direct debit. This removes the need for handling large amounts of cash or cheques *and* the associated problems of transporting this (see below).

Bounced cheques

Cheques which are returned to you marked R/D (return to drawer or refer to drawer) are those which the drawer has made out whilst there are insufficient funds in the account. There is, however, a 'half way' stage which some banks carry out. The bank will notify you that the cheque cannot be processed and state that it will represent the cheque for payment in a specified period. In this case you sit tight, wait and keep your fingers crossed! Equally, if the bank returns the cheque to you and asks *you* to represent it after a certain period then you must follow this procedure. Be aware there is usually a fee for representation.

The worst case is when the cheque is returned to you marked R/D and *you* have to take up the matter with the client. This means that not only are there insufficient funds in the account at the moment but that the drawer's bank does not expect more funds in the foreseeable future!

Most organisations have systems in place to deal with this situation – a key aspect being that not only should the customer be contacted immediately and *encouraged* (rather than threatened) to pay as soon as possible, but that anyone dealing with the categorising of customers in terms of credit worthiness is also informed promptly. At the very least no further goods should be sold to that customer until the situation is resolved.

Debit and credit cards

If your company accepts payment by debit cards then cash registers must be installed which link to the EFTPOS network. It is envisaged that this system will eventually replace the use of cheques for on-the-spot payments as not only is it quicker (thus reducing queues) but also the checking of the balance of the customer's account by the computer makes it impossible for a person to pay for an item he/she cannot afford.

The same is the case with credit cards if these, too, are swiped through an electronic terminal linked to a credit card centre. The terminal not only checks the acceptability of the card but also prints the sales voucher. If, however, your organisation still operates a manual sales voucher system then you must be certain that both you and your staff know the floor limit for credit cards, ie the maximum amount which can be accepted before a special check is made. This may be as low as zero or as high as £500. Above this limit a telephone call must be made to ascertain the authorisation code which guarantees payment. This code is then inserted on the sales vouchers in the space provided.

Manually produced vouchers are listed on a summary form which is handed to the bank within five working days of the vouchers being completed, together with copies of the vouchers issued. In this way the company is reimbursed by the bank for the money received from credit card payments, *less* a trade charge. The electronic system removes the need for vouchers to be taken to the bank as the information is transmitted electronically, rather than the vouchers themselves being processed.

Do make certain that your staff know that:

- customers must sign for both credit card and debit card payments
- the signature on the voucher and card must agree
- the card must be checked to ensure that it is still valid.

In addition, train your staff to deal tactfully and diplomatically with problem situations. If, for instance, a regular customer proffers a card and this is deemed as unacceptable by the terminal, then the situation must be handled sensitively. It may be that the computer or the bank is at fault, rather than the customer. Loudly proclaiming the fact that the card is allegedly over its limit in a crowded reception area is unlikely to do much for customer relationships!

Direct debit and standing orders

If your company offers any type of service to which customers subscribe on a regular basis then persuading them to convert to direct debit payments is probably the ideal situation. It reduces considerably staff time involved in monitoring payments received, issuing reminders and dealing with major problems if the rates or frequency of payments are changed.

You should note that banks will not allow all organisations to operate a direct debit system as a variety of safeguards is in operation to prevent fraud. This is essential for a system whereby an organisation is effectively given the power to levy charges on someone else's account as and when they are due. Less protection is needed in the standing order system because, in this case, the order comes from the customer to the bank and further notification has to be given each time there is a change to the existing (standing) arrangements. Whilst this can be annoying and time-consuming for the customer he/she obviously has greater control over what is happening on a day-to-day basis.

Under both systems the customer must provide various details, ie details of his/her bank including the name, branch, sort code number, bank account number and the name of the account to be debited. The form should also allow space for the inclusion of your company's name, address and bank details similar to those required of the customer. It is usual to assign a reference number in each case so that payments can be traced and monitored as required. The customer must know the amount you require and the frequency of payments and must obviously sign the document for authorisation to be agreed. A standing order form is returned to the bank by the customer whereas *you* would receive completed direct debit forms.

Assuming your organisation has the bank's authority to operate a direct debit system then there must be certain safeguards built in to your system so that customers are informed if any changes are made to the original instructions, eg in terms of the amount paid or the frequency of payments. Checks are essential here as the bank's policy is to refund amounts to customers who were debited with an amount which is not in line with the instructions given. If the fault lies with your company then the bank may withdraw the right for you to operate the system. It is therefore essential that a full monitoring system is in operation.

Apart from time saved in chasing up payments, processing cheques and completing a mountain of paperwork, a further advantage of the direct debit system is that via BACS a company can input details of the direct debits themselves by computer *or* deliver details to their local branch (either on paper or computer tape) for processing, which usually takes about three days.

With both these systems of payment the amount of income is predictable – the organisation knows the amounts it will receive, and when. Payment is received promptly, as it falls due, so that cashflow is improved.

Paying by standing order/direct debit

You may, of course, be paying accounts to other companies yourself by either of these methods, eg for insurance premiums, car leasing etc. Again, this saves you work chasing up executives to sign cheques as payments fall due. Do keep a file copy of any direct debit or standing order forms you complete, so that these can be checked against the bank statement at the end of each month.

Other payment methods

Depending upon the organisation for which you work, you may occasionally be offered payment by other means. For instance, if you worked in a large hotel you may find that visitors wish to pay by travellers' cheque or Eurocheque. The same may be true of any business which deals regularly with foreign visitors who may purchase goods or a service and pay in cash.

A large organisation will have specific policies to cover these contingencies, eg that travellers' cheques can only be cashed or accepted in payment upon production of a passport or that a Eurocheque can only be accepted if the amount is in sterling and it is within the constraints of a valid Eurocard. In a small organisation, however, you may find yourself having to make the rules as you go! For instance, assume you work as the PA to the owner of an art gallery. An Irish visitor wishes to buy a painting and offers you a Eurocheque. What do you do?

In an emergency it may be difficult for you to contact the bank for advice, and your boss may be no wiser than you! One basic fact to bear in mind is that banks charge fees for anything out of the ordinary – and as a rule the more out of the ordinary the greater the fee. You therefore need to bear in mind two facts:

- you must make sure that payment will go through satisfactorily, eg in the case of a Eurocheque that it is covered by the Eurocard
- check that the price of the goods is such that any profit isn't immediately wiped out by additional bank fees!

With a Eurocheque the charge depends on the bank on which the cheque is made out. Those drawn on foreign banks must be sent away and cannot be processed through the normal clearing system.

There are two systems by which Eurocheques may be processed:

By negotiation In this case the cheque is sent to the foreign bank but the bank advances the money to a customer (ie your company). You will be asked to sign a mandate to cover the bank, so that it can reclaim the money if the cheque is referred to drawer. This is not usually required for small amounts, eg under about £200.

By collection In this case the bank collects the money from the foreign bank first and then credits the customer's account.

Banks charge to send cheques away – usually a minimum charge and then a percentage fee on the size of the cheque (ie the larger the amount of the cheque the more you pay). If the cheque is written in foreign currency then the minimum charge is less but the payee takes a risk that the exchange rate may move against him/her (ie the value of sterling may go down).

Travel requirements

If your boss regularly travels abroad he/she may have his own Eurocheque book and Eurocard. It is, however, more usual for business executives to use either credit or charge cards and travellers' cheques/foreign currency when they are abroad. Note that in the case of travellers' cheques and foreign currency you can shop around to find the commission charges being levied by various banks and/or travel agents. There is no rule which says you must obtain either of these from your own bank! All these methods of finance abroad are dealt with in full in Chapter 4, Arranging travel, page 200.

Transmitting money within the UK and abroad

There are several services available which you can use to transmit money both within the UK and abroad. Money is relayed by the CHAPS system within the UK and by EFTI abroad (see glossary, page 458). Both are computerised systems and for foreign transfers there is a choice between standard and urgent methods – depending on the urgency. The service operates to any country in the world, although the more remote the location the longer the transfer may take. Before contacting the bank you need to know the name of the payee, the name and address of his/her bank and the amount to be paid. Don't worry if the payee uses a foreign or unusual bank – British banks pass the details to their nearest correspondent bank abroad and this bank then relays the money onwards.

If the person receiving the funds is an employee of your company and does not have a bank account abroad you can still use the service – but make sure that full details accompany the transfer and instruct the person collecting the money to take along a passport as identification.

Other alternatives include telegraphic transfers (in a real emergency), international payment orders and foreign drafts. Even travellers' cheques can be made available for collection.

Because banks differ considerably in the services they offer in this respect you are advised to telephone them first with your query and then weigh up the comparative advantages of speed and cost in relation to the options they give you and the specific circumstances at the time.

Security and confidentiality

Security is not simply confined to worrying about how money should be taken to and from the bank; it is a major factor in all aspects of handling money within the company. In terms of your own work role there are several aspects to consider:

● the degree to which *you* are responsible for cash receipts and transfers

- the degree to which you are responsible for others involved in this process
- the safeguards in place to protect you (and your reputation) as well as those designed to protect the company.

The worst possible scenario would be that you are responsible for large sums of money in, say, a small company which has no particular procedures for handling or storing cash. In this situation your position could rapidly become untenable – especially if you do not have the authority to instigate changes.

All organisations which handle cash payments must have recognised security procedures, eg a minimum of two key holders for the safe or vault, staff accompanied or supervised when handling money, proper recording procedures and thorough investigations of discrepancies. Safeguards you can introduce yourself are to ensure that entries or withdrawals you make from the main system are countersigned by someone in authority and that there is a standard procedure which can be followed in the case of queries or problems.

When you delegate any part of this task to junior staff you must remember that *you* are still responsible for the job as a whole. If there is a discrepancy later than this is your responsibility. For that reason, err on the side of caution both in what you delegate and what you check. Explain to your junior staff that it is as a safeguard for *both* of you that such checks are undertaken, rather than a monitoring process to check what *they* can do. Don't rush people involved in counting money; if there is an emergency then roll up your sleeves and join in! *Never* cut any corners with your recording procedures or you will live to rue the day.

It is also wise to check the limits of your personal responsibility if a discrepancy occurs. If there is ever the need for an investigation of any kind then it is in your interests to cooperate fully, so that any problems are uncovered and solved as quickly as possible and suitable preventative measures can be taken to preclude any recurrence.

Security is obviously heightened if staff involved in banking procedures are encouraged not to gossip about the work they carry out or the amounts of money they handle. Confidentiality is important to protect the reputations of both customers and staff and it is standard practice in most companies for cash to be handled in a secure area which is out of bounds to general office staff and all financial records to be locked away when not in use.

Financial record keeping

All financial transactions *must* be recorded by *all* organisations. Nowadays there is great emphasis on management information systems as well as traditional accounting requirements. Financial information is a legal requirement so far as both the tax authorities and the Customs and Excise VAT offices are concerned. Even companies which are not eligible for VAT need to keep an eye on turnover for the year (ie the total amount of sales) as, beyond a specific figure, they become liable to register. Limited companies must, by law, be audited once a year and financial information is obviously required by the auditors. Additionally, if any organisation applies for a loan from a financial institution it will be expected to produce its accounts for the last few years and its *projected* earnings for a certain period in the future.

The last item is particularly important. Traditionally, all financial accounting was undertaken on an 'historic' basis, ie the accounts were completed at the end of a year and the figures presented to the tax authorities. Whilst this satisfies the legal requirements it is of little use for a manager to find that six months previously the cashflow was particularly poor and this resulted in the company incurring an unauthorised overdraft with its attendant interest and bank charges. Had the information been available at the time then alternative action could have been taken which would have saved the company money (eg additional money could have been transferred to that account from another account).

For this reason, many companies now employ management accountants who are charged with the responsibility of producing accounts virtually on a daily basis, projecting trends into the future and analysing key financial ratios, eg the amount of profit to date in relation to sales etc. It is their task to give managers the necessary financial information to enable them to make decisions which are in the best interest of the company and to recommend corrective action immediately it is required.

As a PA, it is unlikely that you will be very involved with the company accounts unless you work for a small organisation in the role of office administrator. In this case you will need to learn the principles of book-keeping and accounting properly, which is beyond the remit of this book. However, even if you are only involved in routine banking procedures then you may be asked to check the bank statement and to carry out bank reconciliation procedures.

Bank statements

A company can specify to receive a bank statement at certain periods, eg weekly or monthly etc. The more transactions there are in the course of any given period, the more often you need to receive a statement.

The statement should be checked to see that:

- cash receipts and payments are as recorded on the paying-in slip duplicates and cheque counterfoils
- any requested transfers between accounts have taken place correctly
- standing order payments and direct debits are as expected
- the account is still in surplus (at roughly the expected figure)
- there are no unexpected bank charges.

At present both banks and building societies are in the process of formulating a voluntary Code of Practice. As part of this code bank charges must be clearly listed in a leaflet, although there is no requirement for a bank to notify you automatically when charges are changed nor to give you warning of charges before they are debited to the account. You may find 'unexpected' charges in a statement which obviously affect the final balance – the worst feature is that some charges are calculated on a daily basis and may be almost impossible to check.

Charges are particularly high if, for any reason, an account is overdrawn. They are much lower if permission to overdraw has been given beforehand (note that this applies to your own account as well as that belonging to your company!). If you have any queries then telephone the bank and ask them to explain the reason for the charges. You should then detail these facts in a memo to your boss. A bank manager has a considerable amount of discretion and it is often the case that if your boss contacts him to challenge the charge it may be revised. Your boss cannot do this if you don't give any warning first!

Bank reconciliation statements

No matter how accurately you record bank transactions the amount showing on the bank statement will usually differ from the amount showing on any internal records, eg the Bank account entry in the company's Cash Book. Why? Firstly the statement shows the *uncleared* balance of the company – it does not allow, for instance, for cheques which have been deposited in the past two or three days as these have not yet been processed. Other reasons include:

- some payments by direct debit and standing order may not have been posted in the Cash Book (or listed in your internal records)
- bank charges have not been recorded
- cheques sent to creditors may not have been presented for payment
- customers may have completed a bank Giro credit form at their own bank and paid by credit transfer. There is no requirement for them to notify you separately
- if the company has interest-bearing accounts, then interest paid to the current account will not be recorded in any internal records
- errors may have been made – by your staff, the accounts staff or the bank.

The basic rule for making out a **bank reconciliation statement** is to *keep it simple*. Major adjustments should be made in the Cash Book by the accounts staff or to your internal records. If the bank has made an error than they should be notified accordingly.

A straightforward bank reconciliation statement is shown overleaf. Remember that:

- it is usually easier to start with your Cash Book (or internal record) figure and end with your bank statement figure
- whether you add first and subtract later or vice versa is irrelevant
- statements should be kept for future reference – to show that the accounts were reconciled at a specific date

- if you work methodically then the task is relatively straightforward.

```
MICRO ELECTRONICS LTD

Bank Reconciliation Statement
as at 31 October 199-

Balance as per Cash Book                    £11975
Add        cheques issued, yet to
           be debited                         £425

                                            £12400

Deduct     cheques deposited, yet
           to be credited                     £950

Balance as per bank statement               £11450
```

Start by examining your records carefully and ticking off all the *payments* which are shown in both, eg cheques which have been processed and any other payments you have recorded. Note that in a small company you may be asked to tick off the cheque counterfoils at the same time to confirm that the cheques have been presented for payment.

Next mark all the *receipts* shown on the bank statement against those you have recorded in your internal records. Again you can work direct from your paying-in book, but should note that only the *total* deposit amount will be shown on the bank statement. If there is a query you will need to refer to either the reverse of the paying-in slip or a separate record which states the payments which comprise the total amount.

Identify the items on the bank statement which have not yet been ticked. In most cases these will need entering in the Cash Book or your internal records. If, for instance, you are showing a balance of £2000 in your internal records and the bank has levied charges of £25, then you need to enter these and adjust your balance to read £1975.

Because your internal records already include all cheques and payments (even if these have not yet been processed through the bank) then *your* figure is the one which accurately represents the balance in the bank at the present time (ie the cleared balance) *not* that actually showing on the statement.

Draw up a bank reconciliation statement as follows:

- start with your Cash Book figure or the one you have calculated on your internal records
- **add** any cheques you have made out which have yet to be presented for payment (eg from the unticked counterfoils in the cheque book)
- **deduct** any cheques which you have paid into the bank which have not yet been credited to your account (from your records or the paying-in book)
- the final figure will show the same figure as on the bank statement.

If you have any other payments or charges to include then add or deduct these in the same way.

There have been many arguments that banks should show two balances on their statements – both the cleared and the uncleared balance – but as yet there is no sign of any changes to the present system.

Note that you can, if you wish, start with the bank statement figure and end with your internal figure. In this case you must *deduct* cheques issued but not yet debited and *add* cheques paid in which have not yet been credited to your account.

The final step is to make sure that your boss is aware of both the uncleared and the cleared balance at the bank. The difference is important. Most companies attempt to keep the balances in their current accounts within certain limits: too low and there is a danger of being overdrawn and incurring punitive bank charges; too high and the money is lying idle. This can be transferred to an interest-bearing account where it can earn interest. If the amount is substantial then even overnight interest can be worth receiving. In most cases the money can be transferred by means of a telephone call or by instructing the bank by computer. Only by being vigilant and keeping your boss informed can you help to maximise your company's financial resources.

ACTIVITY SECTION

Individual tasks

1 Mrs Helena Cartwright of 24 Sunnymede Road, Farnborough has been a customer of your company for many years. She recently paid for a large order by cheque, made out for £1800. You banked this cheque several days ago but it has now been returned to you marked 'Refer to Drawer'. You know that she lost her husband recently and has been very distracted since. However, it is your job to contact her to explain the position and ask her when payment will be made.

You are aware that you could lose an important customer if you do not do this tactfully and, rather than telephone her you have decided to write instead.

Draft the letter required.

2 Your internal records show a balance at the bank of £7465 for the end of June. Your bank statement shows an uncleared balance of £5950.

When you investigate you find that:

- two cheques you made out, one for £1500 and one for £600 have not been presented for payment
- your latest deposits (made yesterday and the day before) for £1150 and £2250 are not shown on the statement
- the bank has levied charges of £15 for foreign currency transactions
- you have not included a direct debit payment for £200 to your insurance company on your internal list.

Adjust your internal records to allow for the additional outgoings and then prepare a bank reconciliation statement.

Individual/group tasks

Case study 1

You are employed as PA to Declan Murray, Chief Executive of a local cable television network. Your company has just reached agreement with the bank to enable it to offer a direct debit service to its customers from the end of this month. Previously the company has billed all its subscribers monthly and sent reminders out at regular intervals. After three reminders the service is disconnected until payment is received. Most customers pay by cheque when their accounts are due.

1 Write a memo to all staff outlining exactly how the direct debit system operates and the benefits both to them and to the company of the new system.

2 Your boss wants as many customers as possible to transfer to the new system. Draft a letter for his signature which will persuade your customers to do just that. If you wish, you could outline the benefits to them on a separate sheet, preferably prepared on a desktop publishing system.

3 Design a form (again preferably on a dtp system) which can accompany the letter and which customers must complete and return to the company in order that they can use the direct debit service.

Case study 2

You work as the PA/office administrator to a small company of interior designers. The company is doing well but is still finding its feet and is therefore concerned about improving its cash flow. Both you and your boss, Sue McCrossen feel that several measures could be taken to help and she has asked for your assistance in this area.

1 You are both concerned that the bank used by the company charges exorbitant fees for a variety of services. Sue McCrossen has asked you to obtain a bank charges leaflet from *each* of the main High Street banks and prepare a comparative table which lists the charges for each of these services:

   - stopping a cheque
   - sending a copy statement
   - providing a bank reference on an unknown company
   - providing a banker's draft
   - special presentation of a cheque
   - safe custody

2 She is also interested in installing PCs throughout the company so that bank transactions can be carried out by computer. Find out the details of the electronic banking service offered by *at least one* High Street bank and detail the main aspects in a memo to her.

3 In some cases payments to the bank have been delayed because of incorrect banking procedures followed by the junior staff. Prepare an easy-to-understand instruction sheet (together with illustrations) to enable juniors to complete paying-in slips accurately at the first attempt.

4 As a precaution against fraud, Sue McCrossen wants all company cheques to be completed as recommended by the Banking Ombudsman. Prepare a sample cheque made out in this way which can be photocopied as guidance for all staff.

Managing your money

Income £1, expenditure 99p, result happiness. Income £1, expenditure £1.01p, result – blind panic![1]

The last chapter concentrated on the company's assets and resources – and using these to the best advantage. However, to practise financial astuteness at work, and yet not in your own life is silly, especially when many considerations are so similar.

RULE 1

There is a tremendous difference between being financially astute and being a skinflint! In both cases you have money to spend but in the first case you spend it wisely and in the second you prefer not to spend it at all.

Unless you have inherited wealth or regularly rob a bank for a living, then you have two basic ways of acquiring money – either by earning it or by borrowing it. Unfortunately there are many ways of spending it – from paying essential bills, to buying clothes and paying for entertainment. On top of that, you may hope (though it may be a forlorn one!) to have some surplus cash to *save* for the future.

This section looks at managing your money in four ways. Managing:

- your income
- your borrowings
- your expenditure and
- your savings

The aim is to reduce your outgoings and increase your revenue – at whatever level you operate!

Because the subject is so vast, this section simply gives you basic hints and tips under each of the main areas.

Managing your income

Full-time students

1 If you are eligible for a grant then you may be eligible for other benefits as well, eg travel expenses, assistance towards child care costs etc. Check with the student counsellor at your college.

2 Don't open a bank account or take out a student loan with the first bank you see on registration day. Shop around (see below).

---

[1]with apologies to Mr Micawber! (Charles Dickens)

3 If you are working in your spare time, check you are not paying tax if your income is below the minimum earnings level *and* make sure that you are registered at your bank or building society as a non-taxpayer, so that your savings won't be subject to tax either.

Full-time employees

1 Make sure you understand how your salary *and* all your deductions are calculated. Check your pay slip each week or month.

2 As an employee you probably pay tax through the PAYE system. Your taxable income is determined by your tax code, which is calculated by the Inland Revenue on the information you provide on your tax form. Details are given on your Notice of Coding or Notice of Assessment which you can request from your tax office. If you think this is wrong then appeal *immediately* and ask for a postponement of tax at the same time (otherwise you will have to pay the tax and reclaim it later).

3 When you complete your tax form make sure that you are claiming all the tax allowances for which you are eligible. If you pay professional subscriptions or union dues than you can declare these expenses on your tax form. Some expenses incurred in your job *may* qualify for tax relief. If you are a working mother and are paying a child minder then keep up to date with budget changes which could be to your benefit.

4 If you are married and your spouse is unemployed or has low earnings then check that your tax arrangements are beneficial for you *both*. Under independent taxation each half of a married couple has an amount they can earn before tax is paid – so investigate the option of transferring some of your money to him (as a gift). In addition, if your husband's taxable income is less than his total allowances, the unused part of the married couple's allowance can be transferred to you.

5 Look on your P60 or ask your employer for the address of the tax office with whom your company deals with *and* the company's tax reference number. Quote this in any dealings you have with them.

RULE 2

Don't be frightened about contacting your tax office if you have a problem. Put your query calmly and reasonably and give a clear account of all the relevant facts. You have nothing to lose by asking!

Other work-related expenditure

1 Keep a record of any expenses you incur on behalf of your company and don't forget to reclaim these, eg travel allowance if you use your own car, expenditure which can be reimbursed from petty cash etc.

2 If you enter the money that your employer pays you for expenses on your tax return as part of your income, you must also enter the amount you have spent – otherwise you'll pay tax on everything as income. Note that an expense is only allowable against tax if the money has been spent *'wholly, exclusively and necessarily in the performance of the duties of your employment'* – check with your company accounts office if you think some of your expenses are allowable and you aren't claiming them properly.

Increasing your income

1 How does your salary compare with that paid to secretaries in other companies in your area? (Check the advertisements in your local paper to find out.) If you are paid well below the going rate then you should try to discuss this with your boss. Your salary is far more likely to be negotiable if you work for a small company.

2 If all else fails, then look around for another job (but don't give up the first until you've found a new one!).

3 If you're desperate to make extra money try:
- taking on *temporary* part-time work in an evening
- using a hobby, eg make a skirt for a friend or cakes for a local shop
- taking on some typing at home.

RULE 3

Never respond to any adverts for part-time work which involve you

- paying a deposit for the privilege (no matter what the promises)
- typing (eg envelopes) for a ludicrously low rate of pay.

---

4 Don't disparage your junk! In such a cash crisis turn out the attic. You may not have a Picasso stored away but you may have:

- paperbacks or records you can sell/exchange
- clothes to send to a 'nearly-new shop'
- coins or commemorative articles you were given (try local flea markets)
- goods your family no longer uses eg toys, bikes, sports goods.

RULE 4

Always try to raise money by selling something you'll never miss, rather than by borrowing. You'll also have the benefit of additional space after the clear-out!

Managing your bank account

1 Shop around and don't forget that many building societies offer the same type of services as the high street banks. Check:

- the availability of an *interest bearing* current account into which your salary can be paid and which does not incur charges if overdrawn. (One problem with interest-bearing current accounts is that they can be expensive if you go into the red – so check first.)
- that fully itemised statements will be sent to you each month
- that there are branches nationwide plus some close to your home and your workplace
- that there are ample cash machines
- that you will have access to a credit card, a debit card *and*, if possible, a £100 cheque guarantee card.

2 Beware of budget schemes where the bank will manage your bills for you – these are subject to bank charges. You are usually better to tighten your belt for a month, put the surplus into a savings account (which pays *you*) and pay your bills from this.

3 Make a record of *all* items of expenditure – complete your cheque counterfoils, keep your cash dispenser receipts and debit card counterfoils. *Check* your statement each month – banks do make mistakes.

4 If you have overdrawn for a short period by accident, and find that you have incurred interest charges *plus* a large bank fee, then ring up the bank and argue! Most of the charges are subject to the manager's discretion – if you are persuasive enough then they may be reduced (or removed altogether).

5 Keep a record of all your card numbers but *not* your cash card PIN number! If you lose any of your cards or if they are stolen notify the bank *immediately*.

6 *Always* get a receipt from a cash dispenser. Check the money you receive; if you have any problems note down the time, date and location of the dispenser. Ask someone in the queue to be your witness and get his/her name and address. Keep the receipt and complain to the bank as soon as possible.

RULE 5

Never send any letter of complaint, without finding out the name of the person to whom it should be addressed. Keep a copy. Follow it up if you haven't received a response within a few days.

Managing credit cards

1 Keep the number of cards you own to a minimum; to avoid the temptation of spending more than you can afford. If possible, try to opt for a card which does not incur an annual fee.

2 Use a card on which credit is charged from the statement date – *not* the transaction date – otherwise you will incur more charges than necessary.

3 Always try to pay off your debts in full every month to avoid interest charges. If you regularly owe money on your credit cards then go to your bank or building society and negotiate the best personal loan you can get. Pay off the cards with it – you will save on the interest you have to pay.

4 Avoid shop credit cards like the plague – not only is the APR (see below) higher in most cases but most charge from the transaction date too.

5 Make a note of your card numbers and the emergency number to phone if the cards are lost or stolen. Ring immediately if this happens; or register all your cards with a card protection agency (see Chapter 4, Arranging travel page 200).

RULE 6

If you need to borrow money, shop around for the lowest possible APR (annual percentage rate). This is the total amount of interest (plus administrative charges) you will pay in one year. Ignore any other misleading figures, eg 'only 2.5% per month'.

Managing your expenditure

1 Keep an eye on your bills! A budget account with a company where a fixed amount per month is withdrawn from your current account by direct debit is a good idea *but* there are drawbacks.f

- If all your bills are paid this way then you can easily under-estimate the amount required – and end up overdrawn at the end of the month.
- If the amount has been estimated incorrectly you may find that you are 'inadvertently' saving up with British Gas or your local Electricity Board!

So use the system but keep a close eye on what you are paying and when.

2 Don't buy on impulse – even in the sales. The item you like *isn't* a bargain if, at its full price, you wouldn't have touched it with a bargepole!

3 If you see something you *really* can't afford, and know you shouldn't have, sleep on it before making a decision.

4 Colour coordinate your clothes so that you can mix and match. Use black as a basic colour but, unless you have dark hair, keep it away from your face (or choose navy or grey as an alternative). Buy contrasting shirts, blouses and/or jackets. Don't buy clothes which won't fit into your colour scheme.

5 Know your consumer rights – it pays! Remember that if something you buy is not of merchantable quality, is unfit for the purpose for which it is intended or if the description was misleading then you can return the goods and *insist on a refund*. Faults do not have to appear instantly – if the soles start to come off a pair of trainers after only two months, they are not fit for the purpose for which they are intended. If you have problems getting satisfaction, consult your Trading Standards Officer.

6 Bear in mind that if you have paid for faulty goods by credit card and the supplier proves difficult, then under the Consumer Credit Act 1974 you may be able to sue both the supplier *and* the credit card company.

7 With some credit card companies, eg Barclaycard, there is purchase cover for a specified period against loss, theft or damage for goods which cost over £50.

8 Only shop around for bargains *sensibly*. If you are working full-time then you haven't time – just keep a weather eye open eg the cheapest garage for petrol *on your normal route* etc.

9 Keep coupons and other special offers. In many supermarkets these are taken in lieu of any goods. Don't disparage special deals – try to use them – but *only* if they won't mean you incur additional expense.

10 Buy economically, eg rechargeable batteries (and a recharger) if you regularly use batteries in a variety of appliances. Learn to haggle! If you are buying three pairs of shoes at once *ask* if there is a discount if you pay cash.

11 Use the telephone to ring round and haggle for a large buy! List the shops/stores which sell the product you want and ring round to find the price at each. It will save your shoe leather *and* your patience.

12 Shop for basic goods weekly or fortnightly and only buy perishables in between.

13 Analyse your expenditure and see if any areas can be reduced or eliminated, eg rather than pay someone, form a baby-sitting circle and sit for them in return (or do an alternative favour – walk their dog, give them a plant you've grown etc).

14 *Really* shop around for any type of insurance you need – car insurance, life assurance, house contents etc. Don't automatically renew policies. Both premiums and benefits vary enormously from one company to another. (Start by contacting a broker to save time.)

Managing your savings

Rainy day and interim savings

1 Probably the best deal at present are TESSAs (Tax Exempt Special Savings Accounts) where the interest on your savings is paid tax-free provided your capital is untouched for five years. However, before you buy check that:
- there are no penalties if you want to withdraw the *interest* you have amassed before the five year period expires
- you can transfer additional money into your TESSA at a later date (if your premium bond comes up!) – and whether this money can be transferred from another TESSA account
- what the interest rate will be if an emergency occurs and you need to withdraw your capital before the five year period is up.

2 Compare savings accounts for:
- interest paid (gross and net if you are a tax payer)
- withdrawal penalties.

Open the one which pays the best interest and yet suits your needs in terms of withdrawal facilities.

3 If you are saving with friends for a special event, eg a holiday, you will gain if you open a *joint* savings account. Because the capital will grow faster you will be able to transfer your money to a higher interest-bearing account more quickly.

4 If you are left a large sum of money, or acquire capital quickly, then get *independent* financial advice on how it should be invested.

5 If you suddenly acquire a small amount of money unexpectedly you could always try a flutter on the Premium Bonds. The minimum now is £100. You won't be paid interest (or have a hedge against inflation) but you will have a 110–1 chance in the monthly draw and have the chance of winning the £250 000 jackpot! (And if you already have bonds and have moved a lot, check there isn't an unclaimed prize waiting in your name – ask for the list at your main post office.)

Saving for the future – your pension

If you are only young, then you may think that a pension is something you don't even need to consider. Wrong! Almost before you know it you will need to start thinking about the future – and who wants to have to work all their life and then have nothing to look forward to?

If you are employed, your National Insurance contributions go towards a variety of State benefits. Two of these are the basic state pension and the SERPS pension (State Earnings-Related Pension Scheme). If you wish you can 'contract out' of SERPS by choosing either your employer's scheme or a personal pension plan (PPP).

1 You are well advised to take professional advice in trying to assess the benefits of various PPPs and comparing these with your employer's scheme before making a decision.

2 Generally an employer's scheme will be better – but not always. Most employers' schemes link your pension to the salary you will be receiving immediately before retirement. There may be other benefits too such as life insurance or provision for early retirement due to ill health.

3 A PPP may be better if you intend to change jobs frequently, work abroad for several years or take a career break.

4 If you take out a PPP check the annual statement you receive from your pension company carefully to ensure that the correct amount has been transferred by the DSS from your National Insurance contributions.

RULE 7
The earlier you start to contribute to a pension scheme the better – the money put in at the start of the scheme has many years in which to grow, that invested later has not.

Coping in a crisis

If, despite all your efforts at money management a disaster occurs, you may end up with the situation where you are faced with several bills which you can't pay. What do you do?

1 *Don't* ignore the problem and hope it will go away – contact everyone to whom you owe money *in writing* and keep copies of your letters.

2 Visit your local Citizen's Advice Bureau. Help them by taking copies of your bank statements, outstanding bills etc and be honest – nobody can help you if they only know part of the story.

3 Don't borrow money to pay off your debts unless you are advised to do so by the CAB advisory service.

4 Check with the Department of Social Security that you are obtaining all the benefits to which you are entitled.

5 *Realistically* estimate your future income and expenditure.

6 If there isn't a local CAB office near you, then ring the National Debtline on 021–359–8501 for help.

RULE 8

Whatever your financial position, it is well worth reviewing your finances each year to ensure that your money is working for you *as effectively as possible.* Over the years both your financial situation and your needs will change – and what is best for you now may be far from the best for you in the future.

---

10 Health and safety at work

The size of the problem

It has been estimated that somewhere in the UK there is an accident at work every $3\frac{1}{2}$ seconds. Every year, about 600 of these accidents are fatal. Of the rest some are minor – sprains, cuts and grazes – whilst others result in major injuries, eg permanent disfigurement or disability.

Ironically the figures are rising at a time when most people are more concerned than ever before with their own health and safety. For instance, you may fill a car with lead-free petrol, plant a tree to help the environment and buy food which is additive free. If you then ignore the environment in which you work *you* risk becoming an accident statistics.

Many people who have accidents at work can pursue a claim for compensation through the courts. In addition, employers who contravene Health and Safety legislation can be fined by magistrates. Employers have a legal duty to set up and continually revise health and safety policies and procedures. It makes sense for employers to comply with this, not just because of the law but because of the effects of accidents on the businesses which employ people. Even minor accidents can mean a half-day or day off work for medical checks. In addition, all employees have a legal duty to cooperate with their employer in maintaining a safe environment.

PAs, administrators and supervisors all have a responsibility to monitor the situation on a day-to-day basis and should therefore be aware of Health and Safety legislation and its effects on working practices. They should also be able to recognise and control the risks involved in their own working environments ie the offices in which they are normally to be found.

Health and Safety legislation – the major Acts

Acts of Parliament relating to health and safety include the Health and Safety at Work Act 1974, the Factories Act 1961, the Mines and Quarries Act 1954, the Offices, Shops and Railway Premises Act 1963, the Nuclear Installations Act 1965, the Agriculture (Safety, Health and Welfare Provisions) Act 1956 and the Fire Precautions Act 1971.

The two main Acts relating to health and safety in the office are:

- the Offices, Shops and Railway Premises Act 1963
- the Health and Safety at Work Act 1974.

The latter is by far the most far-reaching, and is an **enabling** Act which lays down certain principles but does not go into great detail. This means that additional Regulations and Codes of Practice can be added at any time to keep the law up to date. Recent examples include:

- the Reporting of Injuries Diseases and Dangerous Occurrences Regulations (1985) [RIDDOR]

- the Control of Substances Hazardous to Health (1988) [COSHH]
- Electricity at Work Regulations (1989).

The Act is an 'umbrella' Act over all existing health and safety legislation.

EC Directives also affect health and safety requirements in the UK.

THE OFFICES, SHOPS AND RAILWAYS PREMISES ACT, 1963

1 Applies to all offices, shops and railway premises and the health and welfare of those who are employed there. Exemptions include businesses employing only close relatives/open for fewer than 21 hours per week.

2 Main requirements are in respect of:
   - cleanliness
   - work space – to prevent overcrowding (400 cu ft per person)
   - temperature (min 60.8° F after first hour)
   - adequate ventilation and lighting
   - suitable and sufficient washing facilities and lavatories
   - accommodation for clothing
   - adequate supply of drinking water
   - seating facilities
   - eating facilities
   - machinery guards and safe positioning of equipment
   - safe lifting procedures
   - fire precautions (a fire certificate is required if there are more than 20 employees).

3 To deal with accidents there should be:
   - first aid box provision, plus a trained first aider if more than 150 employees
   - written notification sent to the local authority if an accident results in the death of an employee or if he/she is disabled for more than three days.

THE HEALTH AND SAFETY AT WORK ACT, 1974

1 Applies to all work premises. Anyone on the premises is covered by and has responsibilities under the Act – employees, supervisors, directors or visitors.

2 Requires all employers to:
- 'as far as is reasonably practicable' ensure the health, safety and welfare at work of their employees. This particularly relates to aspects such as:
  - safe entry and exit routes
  - safe working environment
  - well-maintained, safe equipment
  - provision of protective clothing
  - safe storage of articles and substances
  - information on safety
  - appropriate training and supervision
- prepare and continually update a written statement on the health and safety policy of the company and circulate this to all employees (if there are five or more of them)
- allow for the appointment of safety representatives selected by a recognised trade union. Safety representatives must be allowed to investigate accidents or potential hazards, follow up employee complaints and have paid time off to carry out their duties.

3 Requires all employees to:
- take reasonable care of their own health and safety and that of others who may be affected by their activities
- cooperate with the employer and anyone acting on his behalf to meet health and safety requirements.

Enforcing the law

Under the Health and Safety at Work Act a new enforcement agency was created – the **Health and Safety Executive** (HSE) with its own Inspectorate and Advisory Service. The HSE is directly responsible to the **Health and Safety Commission** (HSC), also established in 1974, which comprises Advisory Committees on a variety of subjects and industries. It is their responsibility to consider and reach agreement on proposals for new Regulations.

Whilst industrial premises are monitored by the HSE, offices and shops are the responsibility of the local council – and this duty is usually undertaken by the Environmental Health Officer(s).

An inspector can visit any premises, without warning, either to investigate an accident or complaint or simply to inspect the premises and question the employees. If dissatisfied with the working practices of the company the inspector can issue:

- an **Improvement Notice** requiring the employer to put matters right within a specified time, or

- a **Prohibition Notice** to stop operations immediately if the workers or the general public are felt to be in immediate danger.

On receiving a notice the company has the right to appeal to an **Industrial Tribunal**. If the appeal is lost and the company fails to comply with the terms of the notice then the organisation can be fined or the owner imprisoned.

TEST YOURSELF
Despite the legal safeguards and enforcement procedures, some companies still continue to operate – and get away with – unsafe practices. Why do you think this is the case? Write down your ideas under the following headings.

1 The number of Health and Safety Inspectors/Environmental Health Officers v the number of companies
2 The vagueness of the term 'reasonably practicable'
3 Small companies
4 Companies employing non-unionised labour
5 The difficulties associated with making a complaint
6 The size of fines (average £500 in 1990)

Planning for health and safety

Planning for health and safety is carried out at two levels:

- By architects when designing a new building or work area
- By designers or office staff when considering how best to use the space they have.

Architectural design

Architects, too, are constrained by the law – mainly the Building Regulations Act 1985 and Fire Precautions Act 1971. Plans for new buildings (or extensions or alterations to old buildings) must be drawn up in line with the requirements of the Building Regulations and submitted to the local authority for approval. If the plans contravene the Building Regulations, are incomplete or unsatisfactory then they will be rejected.

The Building Regulations incorporate regulations about fire precautions and escape, hygiene, hot water and sanitary conveniences, safe entry and exit (particularly where stairways are involved) and facilities for the disabled. The local authority will liaise with the fire authority regarding the proposed means of escape in the case of fire.

Designing public access areas

The diagram below shows some factors an architect will take into account when designing a building to accommodate members of the public. Such buildings, and those where more than 20 people are employed (or ten in some circumstances) need a fire certificate from the fire service. The fire officer classifies all buildings into categories of risk and will survey the building if it will be used by the general public.

Fire Prevention Officers undertake regular inspections to ensure that the premises continue to be safe, fire fighting equipment is maintained in efficient working order and employees know what to do in the case of fire.

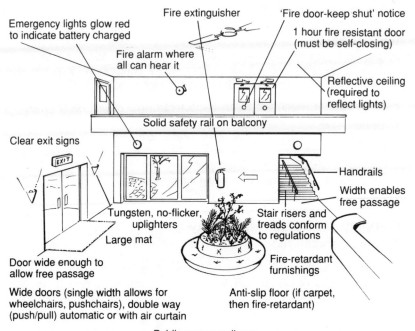

Emergency lights glow red to indicate battery charged

Fire extinguisher

'Fire door-keep shut' notice

Fire alarm where all can hear it

1 hour fire resistant door (must be self-closing)

Reflective ceiling (required to reflect lights)

Solid safety rail on balcony

Clear exit signs

EXIT

Handrails

Width enables free passage

Tungsten, no-flicker, uplighters

Large mat

Stair risers and treads conform to regulations

Door wide enough to allow free passage

Fire-retardant furnishings

Wide doors (single width allows for wheelchairs, pushchairs), double way (push/pull) automatic or with air curtain

Anti-slip floor (if carpet, then fire-retardant)

Public area usually on main escape route

CHECK IT YOURSELF
- What colour of fire extinguisher denotes
  - foam
  - dry powder
  - water
  - carbon dioxide
  - halon?
- On what type of fire should each one be used?
- How often are checks on the equipment in your company carried out, and by whom?
- What happens in your building if the lights fail, and what measures are taken to ensure emergency lighting/signs are maintained?

Violence – the additional hazard

A hazard frequently in the news today for those who work in public access areas is that of possible violence from members of the public. Various measures are now being implemented to protect employees from the possibility of attack. People who work alone, and those who handle money are particularly vulnerable, not just because of possible robbery, but also because a client can blame *them* for a problem connected to the organisation. The problem is likely to be exacerbated if the client has been kept waiting a long time, has been drinking, is mentally unstable or is in a large group (eg a gang of football hooligans).

Measures of physical protection include:

- improving communication systems (eg installing panic buttons) so staff can call for help quickly and unobtrusively
- installing glass screens
- changing staffing arrangements and manning levels to ensure staff do not work alone in a high risk area.

In addition, many companies are reviewing their procedures for cash handling, and providing training for all employees in *tactfully* relating to the public and a recognition of the danger signals. Self-defence is seen as the last resort; the aim of training is to enable staff to defuse a potentially dangerous situation.

Designing office areas

Offices are generally of two main types – **closed** or **open plan**. Closed offices are usually small areas situated off a main corridor whereas an open plan office accommodates many staff, often with the whole area landscaped with the use of acoustic screens, seating arrangements, plants etc.

There are different implications in *each case* in respect of health and safety. The major difference between the two is that, in an open plan area, *the actions of one person affect others.* Such an area is, of course, also more hazardous if a fire breaks out and fire regulations reflect this fact. The smoke from the variety of furnishings, acoustic screens etc can be extremely unpleasant and quickly overcome staff trying to leave the area.

Sick building syndrome

Sick building syndrome is the term used to describe buildings which are considered to cause illness in staff. A wide variety of symptoms have been reported including skin ailments, headaches, dizziness, nausea, fatigue and lethargy, respiratory problems and eye irritation. The problem has been receiving a great deal of attention and publicity lately because of the effect on staff morale, productivity and attendance.

The cause of sick building syndrome has been diagnosed to be related to a variety of factors including:

- faulty or poorly maintained air conditioning
- inadequate ventilation
- chemical emissions from photocopiers and laser printers
- office chemicals, eg correction fluids
- dust build up in carpets and soft furnishings (often made from man-made fibres)
- large expanses of fluorescent lighting
- chemicals in cleaning products
- VDU radiation.

The problem is more noticeable in old buildings where ceilings have been lowered, windows made airtight and ventilation restricted. In such a situation the amount of fresh air allowed into the building has been reduced – often because it is cheaper to recirculate air which has already been warmed. If only recirculated air is being breathed then not only does the air itself become stale but the range of emissions from synthetic materials and office machines increases the pollution. Smoking makes the problem even worse. Practical steps which can be taken include repositioning office equipment, reappraising ventilation and air conditioning systems, installing filters to control dust and smoke and humidifiers and ionisers to purify the atmosphere.

SPECIAL NOTE
The Control of Substances Hazardous to Health (COSHH) regulations, passed in 1988, are often considered to have little relevance to the office. Not true! Photocopiers give off formaldehyde fumes, cleaning staff use chemicals and solvents, felt tip pens emit benzene gas and it can be extremely unpleasant to work near an office that is being painted or decorated.

All hazardous, flammable or noxious materials should be stored safely, well away from office areas. Clear hazard warning signs should be in position and staff should be kept well informed of any dangerous substances stored and the procedure to follow if a problem should occur. (See also Chapter 9, Office resource administration, page 430.)

CHECK IT YOURSELF
Is the building you work in 'sick' or 'healthy'? Draw up a checklist using the main factors listed above, then walk around and 'score' your environment on each aspect. Check with the people you work with. How many of them suffer from any of the ailments listed?

Information technology and health and safety

The increase in the number of microcomputers and VDUs (now often referred to as DSEs – display screen equipment) in offices has brought with it widespread concern about the health and safety issues involved in operating such equipment. Initially there were concerns about radiation emissions from VDU screens and dangers to pregnant women, though this particular case is still unproven.

The focus now is on health risks connected to:

- **eye strain** (resulting in tired eyes, headaches or migraine)
- **fatigue and discomfort**
- **stress**
- **tenosynovitis** and **repetitive strain injury** (RSI).

Eye strain

One of the biggest problems for VDU operators is glare – either **direct** from:

- the screen (contrast too high or low, reflections from window or lighting, small/indistinct characters or – worst of all – flickering characters)
- the keyboard (glossy keys or bright indicator lights in field of vision)
- the copy (on glossy or very white paper)
- the windows

or **reflected** – from the desk or keyboard or even from walls or ceiling.

Because the work is visually demanding then good lighting is essential – diffusers can be fitted to lights to reduce glare. Windows should have blinds which can be easily adjusted. The positioning of workstations is important – VDU screens should be positioned at right angles to a light source.

Shiny work surfaces should be avoided and walls should be painted in matt pastel colours.

Copy should always be clear and easy to read.

The VDU itself should have non-reflective glass and be easy to rotate and tilt. The brightness contrast should be simple to adjust. The image on the screen must be stable with no flickering.

Fatigue and discomfort

Fatigue and discomfort are common if operators are working at badly designed work stations.

The study of working environments to minimise discomfort and other problems is called **ergonomics** and in relation to VDUs is concerned with the layout of a work station (which includes the desk, chair, terminal, printer etc) to avoid back and posture problems.

The work desk should be large enough to allow for a flexible arrangement of the equipment itself, the copy and additional items such as a document holder. There should be adequate leg space. The chair should be stable but allow easy freedom of movement, with an adjustable seat and backrest. A footrest should be available if required.

High levels of fatigue and discomfort result in lower efficiency, more errors and high staff turnover. It is therefore in an employer's interest to ensure staff operating computers are not only positioned correctly but are also educated to know how to use the whole of the work station with their own wellbeing in mind.

Stress

Stress at work is covered in a separate section, Managing stress, page 414. However, it is mentioned here because VDU operators who perform repetitive, monotonous and sometimes highly pressurised jobs are very vulnerable to stress. The hours a VDU operator works may be unsocial if a company wants to make full use of its equipment, high levels of productivity can be demanded and problems with machine downtime can add to the pressure. The problem is exacerbated if staff have received little or no training, if there is conflict between workers (or between supervisor and workers), if a VDU operator is expected to work in relative isolation or if external noise levels are unacceptably high or distracting.

The technique of reviewing job design is an important part of improving this situation and will take into account the actual work done, the pace of the work and *additional* skills which could be added to the job to make it more interesting and enjoyable. The ideal is to blend the work of a VDU operator with other jobs which involve moving about and thinking skills. The job shouldn't be one which has been designed in isolation, with no career progression or prospects. Any output monitoring must be done with care and any speed or quality expectations should be realistic in relation to the experience of the operator and the amount of training he/she has received.

Tenosynovitis and RSI

There has been a marked increase in musculoskeletal injuries (eg neck and shoulder pains) and RSI with the increased use of computer keyboards. **RSI** relates to an injury caused by constantly making repetitive or awkward movements. **Tenosynovitis** (teno for short) refers to inflammation of the tendon sheaths in the hand, wrist and arms, and with VDU operators and typists is caused by repeatedly hitting the keys of a typewriter or keyboard. The initial symptoms of teno are aching, tenderness or numbness in the hand, wrist or arm. As the swelling increases, movements become more restricted and painful and the ability to grip is lost. By then the pain may have spread to the neck and shoulders. Left untreated teno may cause irreversible damage and permanent disability.

Teno is an officially recognised industrial disease, which means that sufferers can get DSS benefit if they have medical support for their case. They could also claim negligence against their employer, especially if there were no improvements after the complaint had been made. Anyone who thinks they may be suffering from teno should notify their union or safety representative and see their doctor without delay. As the only usually satisfactory treatment is rest their employer should try to find alternative work for them in the interim period. Anyone dismissed from work because of having teno may then win a case of unfair dismissal against their employer provided they claimed within three months of dismissal.

Obviously prevention is better than cure and again there is a range of precautionary measures which can be taken by both employers and employees. Good work station design is important and keyboard design and positioning is critical. Keys should be concave to reduce the risk of fingers slipping off them *and* to reduce the shock on the fingertips, fingers, wrists and arms.

The keyboard should be easy to move around the desk, yet stable enough to withstand movement during use. The *angle* of an operator's upper and lower arm should be between 70 and 90 degrees and allow for slight flexing of the wrists. The angle of the keyboard should be between 10 and 15 degrees.

Supervisors can avoid undue pressure on staff by ensuring that:

- there is an adequate number of staff for the work to be carried out
- staff are given regular rest breaks
- only a limited amount of compulsory overtime is worked
- there is, wherever possible, job rotation and an inclusion of non-keyboarding duties.

SPECIAL NOTE

The latest EC Directives reflect the increasing concern of VDU work and become law in Britain at the end of 1992. The directives include the right for VDU operators to:

- have a free eye test prior to VDU work and regularly thereafter
- have regular rest breaks
- be involved in the evaluation of workstations

and also give the standard to which all work stations must conform before they can be used.

Employers are also required to take a variety of measures to avoid or reduce the dangers of back injury related to heavy lifting.

Management of health and safety

Effective health and safety doesn't just happen – it must be planned, organised, monitored and controlled. To an extent, the management of health and safety is covered under the Health and Safety at Work Act but, as in so many other areas, a socially-conscious organisation will go much further than the letter of the law in ensuring that health and safety is comprehensively covered in its policies of operation.

Safety policies

The Health and Safety at Work Act requires employers of more than five employees to draw up and implement a safety policy.

Its contents should include:

- a statement of overall intent which should include an acceptance by management of a responsibility to apply and enforce current and future safety legislation
- an explanation of the organisation, ie:
  - the names, job titles and safety functions of the personnel involved
  - the chain of responsibility from top to bottom
  - the role of the supervisors
  - the functions of the safety adviser, occupational health personnel (if any), the safety representatives and the safety committee(s)
- the arrangements for ensuring that the policy is being implemented, eg:
  - the training and instruction given
  - the company rules for safe systems of work
  - emergency arrangements (fire, first aid etc)
  - accident reporting and investigation
  - identification of risk areas
- the signature of the senior manager.

The statement must be revised when appropriate – when new legislation is introduced, when personnel changes occur, when new technology is introduced etc. It *must* be brought to the attention of all employees.

CHECK IT YOURSELF
- If you work for a company which has more than five employees, obtain a copy of your organisation's safety policy and identify the various sections with those given above. If you work for a small company, try to see a copy from another organisation by asking a friend to obtain one for you or if you are at college, ask your tutor to show you a copy of the college policy document.
- Obtain a copy of the free leaflet HSC 6 from the HSE, entitled *Writing a safety policy statement: advice to employers.*

Safety representatives and safety committees

The Safety Representatives and Safety Committees Regulations were introduced in 1978. These gave a legal right to trade unions to appoint safety representatives in the workplace *provided* that the union is recognised by the employer for negotiations. The representatives are elected by union members (*not* the employer). After the union has approved the election the name of the representative is submitted to the employer. The number of safety representatives varies from one workplace to another, depending on the size of organisation, type of work carried out, potentially hazardous areas etc.

If an employer is requested in writing by at least two safety representatives he must institute a safety committee.

Duties of a safety representative

You may find that at some stage in your career you have to consult a safety representative, attend a safety committee meeting or even take on the job yourself. Whatever the situation you will need to know what is expected of you.

The Health and Safety at Work Act gives details of the duties to be undertaken by such representatives and provides for paid time off work to carry them out. They include:

- investigating potential hazards and dangerous occurrences at the workplace and examining the causes of any accidents (see page 501).
- investigating complaints by any employee relating to that employee's health, safety or welfare at work
- making representations to the employer on matters arising out of the first two points above
- making representations to the employer on general matters affecting health, safety and welfare
- carrying out inspections (at least every three months)
- representing the employees in consultations at the workplace with inspectors of the HSE and of any other enforcing body
- receiving information from those inspectors
- attending meetings of safety committees

To be a *good* safety representative you should regularly liaise and consult with your colleagues to involve them in your work. Take note of staff suggestions and try to implement them where you can so that staff realise it is worth consulting you. *Don't* take the credit for super ideas which came from someone else or their help and cooperation will be very short-lived.

SPECIAL NOTE
The very fact that the safety representative has direct contact with the HSE Inspectors acts as a potential safeguard against any attempts by unscrupulous employers to circumvent the provisions of the Act.

Work of the safety committee

The committee must:

- monitor local accident performance trends as shown by statistics and recommend preventative action
- consider reports of selected accidents and promote action to prevent recurrence
- consider suggestions and reports on safety matters and make recommendations to management

- promote local safety publicity and organise safety competitions and incentive schemes
- promote local applications of accident prevention techniques.

An *effective* safety committee can always be judged by the way in which it promotes change and negotiates improvements. An *ineffective* committee can be identified by the number of times the same issues come up on the agenda – with nothing ever being done about them.

Monitoring health and safety

Remember accidents can occur even in small organisations – a clerk can strain his back trying to pick up a heavy box of paper. All companies should have specific procedures laid down which staff must follow in the event of an accident or emergency. It may seem strange to talk of planning for an emergency, but this is exactly what is needed. Every organisation should evaluate objectively the *type* of incident which could occur in their industry – whether minor or major – such as explosion, electrocution, flood etc and make specific plans in relation to:

- raising the alarm
- procedures to follow until specialist help arrives
- evacuation procedures and nearest safety points
- rescue equipment required
- names of coordinators and controllers
- essential procedures to make the workplace and processes safe, eg shutting down a factory.

From these plans it should be possible to identify areas where specialist advice (eg from the fire authority) or staff training is required.

Recording accidents

When accidents happen, companies are required by law to record these, and safety representatives have a legal right to investigate the accident and make recommendations to management. All employers with more than ten workers must keep an accident book and records must be retained for at least three years.

Employees must report accidents to their employer or they may find that they are debarred from any DSS benefits to which they would otherwise be entitled. Their report must include their full name and address, the date and time the accident happened and the place where it occurred, and the cause and nature of the injury. If the person reporting the accident is doing so on another person's behalf then he/she must also give full name, address and occupation.

An accident which causes serious or fatal injuries or leads to more than a certain period off work has to be notified to the HSE under RIDDOR – the **Reporting of Injuries, Diseases and Dangerous Occurrences Regulations** 1985. Also, under RIDDOR, employers must keep records of all notifiable injuries, dangerous occurrences and diseases. Safety representatives and safety committees must be given access to this information.

Accident investigation

If you are a safety representative, and an accident occurs, you should get to the scene of the accident as soon as possible. Obviously it is important that you ensure that any injured people receive first aid or specialist attention immediately.

If possible make sure that nothing is moved or disturbed from the scene of an accident before a representative from the insurance company arrives *unless* it is to safeguard against a further hazard. If anything must be moved then make a note of the changes.

Details of the accident should be recorded by taking photographs, drawing sketches and taking measurements and witnesses should provide statements whilst the incident is still fresh in their minds. The statement should be written *in the witnesses' own words*, in ink, to prevent any later charges that you misled the witness or altered the record. You should then carry out a detailed accident inspection in relation to the working environment (lighting, noise, layout etc) at the time of the accident, the person involved, the level of supervision and equipment being used, to help to identify the underlying causes and assist the injured person if there is a claim for damages.

It is also your job to ensure that the HSE or environment officer has been informed and to check that all the appropriate records have been accurately completed, eg Accident Form and Accident Book. Following your investigation, if you have any specific proposals to make to management you should be make these in writing and finally make sure that any injured staff are advised of their legal rights.

Accident monitoring

The records of accidents should be analysed to:

- compare the accident rates in one organisation with the figures issued for the industry as a whole
- identify areas of particular concern
- monitor improvement/deterioration in standards
- identify if any new initiatives (eg a change in staffing levels) have affected accident statistics
- check that any recommended remedial action has been taken.

It is, however, not sufficient just to record *actual* accidents. *Near-miss accidents* should also be recorded. A pile of heavy files falling from a great height may miss the nearest worker – and therefore cause no injury – but from this incident it is easy to identify a potentially dangerous practice which could result in serious injury next time.

For this reason, near-miss accidents should be processed through the normal accident reporting system and investigated in the normal way.

First aid

Originally first aid requirements for companies were based purely on the number of employees. Under the Health and Safety (First-Aid) Regulations the number of first aiders is based on the type of industry and organisation, the size of the organisation and location of the employees; and where the organisation is situated.

The term 'first-aider' is used to denote someone who has been on an approved training course and been awarded a certificate to prove they are competent at administering first aid. An occupational first-aider is someone who has received additional training to cover additional hazards which may occur in a specific workplace, ie electrocution, poisoning etc. To remain a first-aider a person must take a refresher course and be re-examined every three years.

An *up-to-date* list of first-aiders should be easily accessible in every part of the organisation, together with the contact telephone number. It should never be the case that all first aiders are unavailable at the same time.

SPECIAL NOTE
First-aiders should be aware of any members of staff who suffer from diabetes or epilepsy. In most cases the Personnel Department should be able to supply that information.

First aid boxes

Guidance Notes to the Regulations give details of what should be kept in first aid boxes and the quantities required. Drugs are *not* kept in first aid boxes, or administered by first-aiders, because of the risk of adverse reaction by the patient.

In addition to the usual items of bandages, burn dressings and so on, larger equipment may also need to be stored nearby, eg stretchers and blankets. All should be regularly checked and replenished as necessary.

Identifying hazards

The *type* of hazards which can be identified in a workplace depends very much on the industry, the nature of the organisation, its location etc.

Although it is obviously true that an office is a safer environment than a factory, accidents still happen, basically because the common denominator in all these environments is *people*. Therefore, even when you have designed totally safe systems of work, have insisted on tidiness and 'good housekeeping' throughout, provided up-to-date and 'safety-conscious' equipment, someone will still rush around the corner and fall – because someone else has forgotten to move the box they put down five minutes ago.

SPECIAL NOTE

Although in large organisations formal safety procedures will be in existence, in smaller organisations you may have to take some responsibility in initiating and administering them. This is especially true if you work in a small office attached to an industrial unit.

The main categories of accidents, ie falling and slipping, show the degree to which people's own carelessness, thoughtlessness or being distracted play a part. To improve the accident rate in your office, your first job must therefore be to make – and keep – your colleagues aware of the potential hazards in their environment and the fact that *they* are a major contributor to the problem!

ACTIVITY SECTION

Individual/group activities

Case study 1

Janet Morrison started work at Derby Ceramics Ltd as office administrator in the Purchasing department. During her first few weeks of employment she noticed that:

- the fire door exit to the fire escape was blocked by a filing cabinet
- spoiled photocopies stored in black bags prior to recycling were stored next to the photocopying machine
- the floor covering of the visitors' waiting room was in need of attention
- the newest clerk never remembered to put on protective gloves when using the offset litho machine
- lighting generally was poor, but was particularly poor in the inner office where the VDUs were sited
- the small kitchen area was always untidy and no one had taken the responsibility for ensuring that crockery was washed and put away after use
- no one knew the procedures which should be followed in the event of the fire alarm sounding, or could remember when there had last been a fire drill.

Janet pointed out the dangers to the rest of the staff who, in the main, thought her over-anxious and fussy about safety. She also spoke to the Purchasing Manager on several occasions but dropped the matter when she saw he was becoming irritated. Eventually she became as casual about safety as the others.

Janet is a friend of yours and has asked you for advice.

1 Identify the areas in which there is obvious non-compliance with the Health and Safety at Work Act 1974.

2 What *effective* action do you think she could take to:
  a persuade her colleagues that she was acting in their best interests in her concern for health and safety
  b persuade her boss to view the situation differently?

3 Assuming she was unsuccessful in **2** above, state the course of action she should take if:
  a she works for a large company with unionised labour
  b she works for a large company with non-unionised labour.

Janet later tells you that she has been appointed Safety Representative for her department and has been asked to convene the first Safety Committee meeting for the company.

4 Draw up a checklist for Janet to use on her first inspection under the following headings:
  - Temperature
  - Lighting
  - General housekeeping
  - Machinery and equipment
  - Floors/stairs/entrances/exits
  - Accident recording
  - Fire
  - Noise
  - First aid
  - Welfare
  - Space
  - Training

5 Draft the agenda for her first safety committee meeting.

Case study 2

Ian Parker is General Manager of Southern Glass Ltd, a large company about to move premises from a town centre area to a new industrial estate. The new premises will have large open plan offices in which, except for senior management, all staff will be housed.

The company is spending a considerable amount of money landscaping the new office areas, which will contain a variety of equipment including telex and fax machines, photocopiers and computer terminals and VDUs.

Southern Glass is a very safety conscious company and Ian Parker is concerned that he may not have considered all the health and safety issues implicit in the move. He has asked you, his assistant, for your help.

1 Produce a check list of factors Ian Parker should consider under each of the following headings:
  - noise
  - heating
  - ventilation
  - fire risk/escape procedures
  - lighting
  - planning of 'walk-through' areas
  - hazardous/flammable substances.

2 Open-plan offices are sometimes described as 'office factories'. What reasons can you advance for this description? List the factors you consider can be incorporated into:
  - the way jobs are designed

- the way work is organised, and
- the surrounding environment

to improve the quality of working life in such surroundings.

3 The company has had a relatively tolerant attitude to smoking, prior to the move, as most of the staff who do smoke have their own offices. There is now unease amongst the staff that in the new open plan areas, unless a no-smoking policy is introduced, all staff will be affected by 'passive smoking'.

    a List all the factors you can think of both *for* and *against* a no-smoking policy.

    b What measures could Ian Parker take to minimise resistance from hard-line smokers to the introduction of a no-smoking policy?

Case study 3

Mary O'Connell is a freelance Systems Design Consultant who has been contracted by Meridian Electronics to redesign their offices in the light of the new EC Directives on VDUs. You are her assistant and your knowledge in this area, and her policy of always developing her staff as much as possible, means that you are often involved in assisting her on such projects.

Meridian Electronics employs 20 VDU operators, all female, on a two shift system, 8 am to 4 pm and 4 pm to midnight. Staff are allowed regular rest periods of 15 minutes every two hours, but have to work hard to keep to their deadlines and their output is closely monitored by a supervisor whose salary is linked to the output of the operators. Staff turnover is high and the supervisor is constantly complaining about the problems of recruiting new staff. Because of pressure of work, she hasn't the time to instigate proper training.

Management are concerned that any change in work practices will reduce productivity and will result in a backlog of work. Their problems are exacerbated by the fact that Meridian is struggling to stay in business at the moment in a highly competitive market.

1 From what you know about VDU work, list *all* the factors you consider are contributing to the staff problems at Meridian.

2 What changes do you think Mary will recommend, and why?

3 How do you think Mary could convince management that these changes should be made bearing in mind their own problems at the moment? (Note: *It may help you to do this if you list all the costs and benefits associated with the changes first.*)

4 Assume the recommendations have been accepted and Mary is about to hold a staff training session for all VDU operators. She is covering the topics of:
- workstation layout and design
- tenosynovitis and RSI
- job design
- the law and VDU operators.

She has asked you to help her. Select *one* of the topics and, in addition to studying the notes in this chapter, undertake further research to make sure that you know your topic well, then

    a make a short (ten minute) presentation on your chosen subject (with prepared visual aids) and/or

b design and produce a short booklet to give to the VDU operators highlighting what they should know.

Case study 4

You work as PA to Winston Harris, Personnel and Training Manager of Whitegate Studios. The company employs a large number of graphic designers and office staff and has a wide range of reprographic equipment installed.

One of your duties is to record and monitor accident statistics for the company and both you and Winston Harris are concerned that in recent months the number of accidents has increased alarmingly. In many cases these are not serious – last week a junior member of staff was trying to mend a stapler and stapled two of her fingers together. Yesterday, however, a typist was seriously injured when she fell on a slippery floor whilst carrying a laser printer. The printer was damaged beyond repair.

1 On the basis that work practices have not changed in recent months, what reasons could you advance for the increase in accidents?

2 Design an accident report form which not only complies with the information which must be collected by law, but which also enables full details of 'near-miss' accidents to be recorded.

3 List the forms of action Winston Harris could take to counteract staff complacency and help to reduce the number of accidents.

4 Design a comprehensive safety checklist which could be displayed in all areas to remind staff of the procedures to be followed at all times, eg using a safety stool to reach high shelves, correct procedures to be followed when operating/moving equipment etc.

5 Write a memo to all staff to inform them of the checklist and why it is being instigated. Make sure that your memo relates to the necessary contribution of all staff and appeals to them effectively for their cooperation.

Managing change

God grant me the equanimity to accept the things I cannot change, the courage to change what I can – and the wisdom to know the difference.

The first thing to remember about change is that it can be very stressful (see page 414). Even positive changes in our personal life, such as moving house, getting married or having a family can put us under stress. Negative changes – especially those which are imposed upon us – can create distress, confusion and worry.

The problems in a working situation can be summarised as follows.

- Organisations have to change to survive.
- Most changes are imposed upon an organisation by forces outside its control, eg new legislation, technology, actions by competitors, social changes, etc.
- People vary in their ability to welcome or cope with change.
- For many people change is threatening – in terms of their lifestyle, their status or even their job.
- Change can be *managed* so that people can cope more easily – but often this is mishandled or even ignored.

RULE 1
Learn to differentiate between basic change and fundamental change.

Basic change

This relates to changes to basic operating procedures which may create short-term hassle and annoyance but can be managed relatively easily. Such changes are **task-centred**.

Examples include changing the design of forms people complete, changing the rules for expense claims, changing a filing system.

Fundamental change

This relates to more far-reaching changes which can cause long-term anxiety, worry or distress and can only be managed with difficulty. Such changes are **people-centred**.

Examples include increasing the responsibilities of a job, changing the hours people work, changing the structure of an organisation (ie how many departments, who should work where and for whom etc).

RULE 2
Treating a fundamental change in the same way as a basic change usually makes the problem worse, not better.

Identifying fundamental change

Usually the change is fundamental if it involves any of the following:

- **job security** (eg redundancy, less money)
- **status** (eg loss of perks, 'distance' from the boss greater)
- **prestige** (eg loss of self-identity or self-worth)
- **social ties** (eg social life disrupted because of shift changes, etc)
- **personal anxiety** (eg cannot cope with/dislike new job).

Our natural reaction when threatened is one of 'fight or flight'. Therefore if such changes are imminent the reaction of employees may range from outright aggression/militancy to absenteeism.

> **RULE 3**
> Good management of change will lessen problems not create them.

TEST YOURSELF

Your company has recently reorganised its offices. Joanne, a typist who worked in the Sales office with three other girls, has been upgraded and given the job of coordinating the sales reports received every week from the sales representatives employed by your company. She has her own word processor and her own small office. To your surprise, after four weeks in the job, she comes to you to tell you that she is miserable in her new role and wants to go back to the Sales office.

a Think of *as many reasons as you can* why Joanne may be unhappy in her new job. (If possible do this as a group exercise.)

b For each reason listed, what advice would you give to Joanne?

c Assuming her main problems are loneliness and a fear of coping with the new job, what suggestions would you make to your boss to solve the problem?

d How do you think the problem could have been prevented in the first place?

Planning for change

The biggest problem when planning for change is that the planners concentrate on the tasks involved and not on the people. It is all very well to make suggestions about how *you* think a job should be done, but if you are not the person doing it then the suggestion could well fail.

> **RULE 4**
> Whenever possible, consult the people who are doing/will be doing the job *first* – never automatically think that you know best!

Remember that the biggest demotivator for staff is the feeling that they have no control over what is happening to them. *Listen* to what they have to say even if you don't like what you are hearing! Staff may be genuinely unhappy if they feel they can't cope with the work, or if they consider suggestions are unworkable. This may mean implementing staff training sessions or redesigning the job specifications.

> **RULE 5**
> Introduce change gradually and be prepared to modify your ideas.

Coping with change yourself

We have dealt with change as if you have the ability to affect some of the decisions which are being made. However, it is likely that the most fundamental and far-reaching changes will be decided above your head. You will then have the double problem of helping your staff to cope with change *and* coping with it yourself. Although you may be against some of the ideas there may be little you can do about it.

> **RULE 6**
> No changes are all wrong! List all the benefits from the change that you can think of (ask your staff to join in) and remember that to ignore change means you won't survive (think of the dinosaur!).

Communications are vital at this point – both with anyone affected and with your boss – to clarify worries, problems and even minor difficulties. If you think someone (or yourself) will be adversely affected, or if you consider that the change could be introduced in a more beneficial way try appealing to your boss who may be glad of your contribution if it contains ideas and solutions and not just problems and moans.

It may be the case that at the end of the day you – and your organisation – are considerably better off. Your working relationships and systems of work may be more streamlined and your organisation more profitable. If you seem beset with problems or even lose your job, you could be fatalistic and consider that something better is round the corner.

> **RULE 7**
> Learn to cultivate a positive attitude towards change – look upon it as a challenge with new opportunities, rather than as a threat.

If you approach change from this point of view then you will develop a good working relationship with both your superiors and those below you. You will also be more flexible and adaptable in your own ways of working and more creative in terms of making suggestions yourself.

From this point it is but a short step to learn to use change for your own benefit – to help you to increase your performance and your achievements and reap the benefits later when your talents are recognised.

TEST YOURSELF

Your boss wants to introduce a computerised stock control system for all stationery supplies. The two stock control clerks are against the idea and consider the existing record card system works very well indeed.

a What other reasons might the clerks have for resisting the change?
b What benefits do you think there might be to your organisation in implementing a computerised system?
c What measures would you take to reduce the clerks' anxiety/resistance and ensure their commitment to the change?

11 Shorthand transcripton

Producing documents from shorthand notes

One of the rather disappointing side-effects of modern developments in office technology is the relative demise of the high speed shorthand writer. The future of shorthand has been hotly debated for many years. Rationally and economically it can be argued that the audio machine is more cost-effective since it can be taken from place to place cheaply and easily (something which could not easily be done with a shorthand writer!) and it enables work to be carried out in two places at once; whilst the executive is dictating a letter or report, his/her PA can be gainfully employed in typing one he/she prepared earlier.

Whilst these arguments are valid so far as they go, they completely ignore the true added value of a shorthand writer. A first-rate PA or administrator, with good shorthand speeds, is not only invaluable in relation to straightforward dictation – where she can prompt, remind, suggest and comment as necessary – but also for other forms of notetaking. Minutes of meetings can be produced fluently and easily, details stated over the telephone are noted quickly and accurately and notes of discussions can be jotted down in an atmosphere of informality – as opposed to everyone freezing because a tape recorder was switched on at the outset!

Despite advances in modern technology, two facts are still significant. Firstly, senior executives who have experienced the benefits of having a PA with good shorthand speeds rarely like to settle for less afterwards (and indeed, may consider they have been downgraded if they are presented with an audio machine). Secondly, the jobs with the highest salaries are usually still those which require good shorthand speeds. This fact is either not widely known or ignored by many of those who aspire to be high level PAs and it is regrettable that even in cases where shorthand is studied, few writers seem prepared to persevere and challenge themselves to see just how fast they could write if they keep practising. It is so much easier to give up at about 70 or 80 words per minute!

This chapter is *not* a mini-shorthand theory section, although you may find one or two tips on outlines which may help you. Rather, it is to encourage you to keep working towards higher speeds and to give you practical tips on how to do this. If you take accept these ideas and are successful you will find that not only will your speed increase, but so too will the range of jobs for which you can apply. You should find a considerable difference not only in the variety of work you are asked to carry out but also in your pay packet!

Which system?

Most shorthand writers today write either one of the Pitman systems (New Era or, more probably, 2000) or Teeline shorthand. What is the difference? A purist would say quite a lot; a realist would comment that it doesn't particularly matter as all shorthand systems are simply a means to an end. No executive will ever be bothered about which hieroglyphics you create so long as you can read them back afterwards!

Generally, the more complicated the system the more reduced the outlines eventually become and therefore the faster the speeds which can be achieved. In the heyday of New Era shorthand many writers strived for 200 words per minute and beyond. Indeed such speeds were necessary for verbatim court reporting, which is now more frequently written using machine shorthand. Pitman 2000 is a rather easier system to learn – more 'user friendly' – but the outlines are longer so that the speeds achievable are usually rather less. Teeline, too, is a fairly recent innovation and was originally developed for use by journalists. Based on the letters of the alphabet it is probably the easiest system of all to learn but, again, has the drawback that unless the outlines are shortened considerably it can be difficult to reach speeds in excess of 120 or 140 wpm. Other systems, which seem to be less commonly used nowadays, are Pitmanscript, Speedwriting and Gregg shorthand.

Whichever system you write, there are certain basic principles you can follow to make the most of your abilities and to develop your speed and your own personal style. The fascinating part of building up shorthand speed is that, unlikely though it may seem to you at present, it can become almost an addiction. If you really believe that you will never make a high speed writer, then as you start to move upwards it becomes quite exhilarating, like climbing a mountain and never knowing when you will reach the top! So read on – and surprise yourself!

Developing your skill

The atmosphere for learning

Before you become involved in the details of speed development consider one basic question. Do you enjoy learning shorthand, or not? If not, why not? Are (or were) your lessons boring? Did you miss several lessons at the beginning and never really get the hang of it? Or did you not bother about practising so that everyone else in your group was writing faster than you? Two facts are important: firstly we all enjoy doing things at which we are successful (and hate doing things at which we are conspicuous failures!) and secondly if you *don't* work at it in the early days you will never make a good shorthand writer. Shorthand is a skill, and just as you don't expect Boris Becker or John McEnroe to play superb tennis without a lot of practice, neither can you expect to write good shorthand just because you want to! However, hard work *can* be fun (honestly!) and there are several ways in which you can make practising shorthand more enjoyable. Even if it is impossible for you to attend formal speed classes – or you feel you need to refresh your memory on the basics first – it is quite possible to do this yourself at home, provided that you can spare about an hour a day.

- If you are hazy on some of the basics then get yourself a good basic textbook on the system you know and start at Chapter One. Buy one with a key in the back but use this to check your work, rather than cheat. If your theory is simply rusty, or if you weren't listening properly the first time round, you'll be surprised at how quickly it all comes back. Writing shorthand is like riding a bike – you never completely forget how to do it!

- Whatever anybody tells you, *don't* drill an outline for hours in the vain hope that you may then remember it! Your writing will become sloppy and scrawly and after number 20 the outline will only bear a passing resemblance to the shape it was at the outset. In addition you will get fed up and before long give it all up. If you don't know an outline learn it by writing it half a dozen times *repeating* it to yourself each time and concentrating hard. Do this each night for three days and you'll never forget it again.

- Make your own tapes. Dictating shorthand is easy – all you need is a watch with a second hand and some dictation material counted in tens. Practise for a bit before you start to record. If you hate the sound of your own voice on tape then you can always play it back over a personal stereo so that no one else can listen to it but you!

- Get a copy of the 700 common word list; something like 80 per cent of all dictation contains these words so knowing these outlines well is the equivalent to giving yourself an instant boost on the speed run. Tape a simple passage (using words from this list) which lasts for about a minute or a minute and a half at about four speeds: your current speed then + 20 wpm + 40 wpm and + 60 wpm. If you are now writing at 80 wpm then your top dictation passage will be 140 wpm!

  Play it at your base speed and write it out (for *how* to write at speed see below). If you are stuck on any outlines then review them as given above. Repeat the passage, then try it at the next speed, treating each jump as a challenge. Stretch yourself in terms of the number of words you are holding in your head when the dictation ends! Try it again at the same speed – it will become easier each time. After about three attempts move up a level. If you keep on like this, before you know it this will be a 'pet' passage that you can easily write at your top speed. Now develop another pet passage, and so on.

  When you are particularly fed up because you feel you are not getting on as fast as you'd hoped, play one of your pet passages to reassert your confidence.

- Forget taping passages which don't comprise business-related material and don't try taking live dictation from the television or the radio – it's usually far too fast.

- Every so often put on tape some early exercises from your textbook, which have been devised to practise a particular point of theory. Use these as revision. You'll normally find you can write these quite quickly even from the outset.

- Practise with a friend. Record a tape each (or borrow a pre-recorded tape from college) and write your notes together. Don't make it competitive unless you are both operating at roughly the same base speed. Again use the 'pet passage' and building up speed idea. Compare any short cuts or special phrases either of you have developed (see later notes).
- Train for 'getting behind'. Read a sentence to each other but make it a rule that the writer can't start to write until the sentence has been completed. Then see if you can remember it accurately. Start at 15–20 words per sentence and then extend to 30 or upwards if you can manage it.
- Keep all your practice sessions short and intensive! Just like a work out – you should feel tired but exhilarated at the end. If you keep going beyond about 45 minutes you'll start to flag and go backwards so at this point you are better to stop. Little and often is the golden rule.

The tools for the job
First question: what do you write with and what do you write on? Nobody can develop a skill properly without the right tools for the job – and again, to use the tennis player analogy – just as top class players don't stint on racquets and shoes, neither should you stint on your writing materials!

- You need a notebook with *good quality* paper. Fluffy paper which catches your pen or pencil is worse than useless – it must be smooth. The book should have a hard cover, spiral binding and *not* be jumbo sized! If it is too thick then the position of your wrist will make your hand ache. The lines should not be too wide (or this will encourage you to write very large outlines) and there should be a margin at the left hand side. Write with the book *open* and the page flat.
- A pen is preferably to a pencil. Purists will say Pitman's shorthand should never be written in biro – but it often is and at quite high speeds! Pencils can break and cause havoc in office dictation (unless you have a spare one behind your ear!). If you have to keep your notes over a period of time, pencil may fade yet pen does not.

    However, the *quality* of your pen matters! A 10p bargain from the cut price shop will blob, smudge and only write if the point is held down. Buy a good quality, *lightweight*, ballpoint pen which writes smoothly and easily, has a fine point and can be used horizontally.

Are you sitting comfortably?
Believe it or not, posture is important. So is your working area and even your grip on the pen. If you are going for speed, every little helps!

- Sit with your feet flat on the floor. Try not to cross your legs, it puts you in a more 'relaxed' frame of mind – which isn't the idea! Forget any films you have seen showing a glamorous PA with her notebook on her knee. Put your book on the desk where it won't slither about. Keep the book *straight* – don't write at an angle.

- Make sure your weight is on the *opposite* arm to the one you use to write (ie on your left arm if right-handed and vice versa). If you *lean* on the arm with which you are trying to write it is rather like driving a car with the brakes on. The forearm of your writing hand should be on the edge of the desk and the little finger of your writing hand – not your wrist – on the notebook. If you can't see daylight below your wrist then the brakes are on again!
- If there's a top on your pen then take it off and put it on the desk – not on the barrel of the pen. Hold the pen *lightly* and try to keep your fingers straight. You can test your grip by getting someone to pull the pen unexpectedly. They should be able to take it from you easily. If you grip it hard then your fingers and hand will soon start to ache, and you will impede the freedom of movement needed to write at speed. If you can write with a short grip, ie your fingertips quite near the point of the pen, so much the better.

Using your notebook

- Always use a margin. This may seem a waste of time during practice sessions but it becomes *essential* during office dictation. You should always note your own comments in this space, either immediately after dictation or before starting transcription (see below). Some PAs draw an *additional* margin down the right hand side for their boss's comments and keep the left margin for their own notes.
- Date each page at the *bottom* so that you can easily check where you are by flicking through the pages.
- Some PAs use a rubber band to hold back the pages for the previous day, so that they can easily flick backwards and forwards through current dictation as they work.
- Make sure each piece of dictation is clearly headed and draw a line across the page when it is finished.
- Start special work at the top of a new page.
- Immediately dictation has finished – or immediately before transcription – read through your notes and make any notes you need in the margin. A tip here is to check the 'little' words – many is the time you will find a long but difficult outline very easy to read but stumble over a small 'joining' word such as 'of', 'on', 'to' etc.
- Cross out work clearly when you have transcribed it.

Using your pen

Knowing how to use a pen is a skill often thought old-fashioned nowadays. Far from being bunkum, your skill at *handling* your pen can add several words a minute on to your speed almost from the outset.

- *Always* write with light, hair strokes; keep pressure to a minimum as it slows you down.

- Practise 'flicking' outlines – *never* draw them. You will know when you are doing this properly because your outlines will be a little fainter or lighter at the end than at the beginning.
- Keep the size of your outlines under control! This is easier if your writing is naturally small. If you are a sprawly writer then discipline yourself; aim for 12–14 words a line maximum.
- Probably the best tip of all – *deliberately* exaggerate curves. Make straight strokes really straight and curved strokes *very* curved. This makes your shorthand much easier to read and prevents confusion between outlines such as 'not' for 'quite' (Pitman) and 'of' for 'to' (Teeline).
- In the same way, exaggerate doubled or lengthened outlines so that there can be no possible confusion between this outline and one which is normal size
- Use a smooth action and try to *glide* your hand along the page – don't write in a series of short, sharp jerks.
- Complete all circles or loops properly and show 'inner' circles clearly, eg 'school' (Pitman) or 'asked' (Teeline).
- Write at speed from the beginning – shorthand was never designed to be written slowly! Practise achieving the right 'feel' even in the early days, by writing out early sentences in the book very quickly.

Punctuation

It is astounding how many shorthand writers don't write a full stop. The danger lies when you are dictated a couple of sentences such as 'We have continued to make satisfactory progress during the year trading conditions have been difficult . . .' and then haven't a clue where each sentence begins and ends. You have two basic options.

- Train yourself to write the correct sign! If you write Pitman shorthand learn to write a cross without lifting your pen, ie   . If you write Teeline *don't* be tempted to write your full stops downwards as then you are no longer heading in the right direction, ie from left to right.
- if you *know* you will always miss out full stops when pushed for time then stop fighting the inevitable, and design your own system for coping. Leave a specific gap for a new sentence and a larger gap for a new paragraph – or drop down a line. The only problem with this method, of course, is that you have to differentiate your deliberate gaps from accidental ones! So long as you can do this without difficulty you are at least working with your instincts rather than against them.

Learning the basics

Shorthand basics are the equivalent of the foundations of a house. The structure can never be secure unless the foundations are solid. It might seem tedious at times, but it is absolutely *vital* that you don't cut corners on any of the following.

- Learning your short forms (Pitman) or special outlines (Teeline). These are designed so that *very* common words will require the minimum of writing and become completely automatic.

  Learn these by writing them on small cards with the answer on the back. Shuffle the cards and select a word at random – then write the outline. Check with the back of the card. Each time you learn new ones in class add to your cards (and if you learned shorthand some time ago and are rusty start by making out some cards and seeing if you still know the correct outlines to write).

  This can be done as a game if there are two of you: select 12 for your partner, let her select 12 for you and see who goes wrong first!
- Knowing your special outlines (Pitman) and distinguishing outlines (Teeline). Otherwise you can expect to write 'howlers' every now and then, eg:
  – He has to work hard to separate (support!) his wives (Pitman)
  – I was amused (amazed!) by his latest proposal (Teeline).
- Practising your basic phrasing (Pitman) or word groupings (Teeline) so that these become second nature. The fewer times you raise your hand from the paper, the fewer seconds are wasted – and they all add up! If you ever find yourself writing phrases such as 'as soon as possible' or 'we have' or 'there is' as separate words then you should be *really* cross with yourself! It is a far greater sin to omit a simple joining than to forget a long, fancy phrase! (Tip – always learn phrases as 'one unit', not as two (or more) words 'joined together'.)

During note-taking

- *Concentrate* on the sense of the passage and what is being said. Your memory can help you to an enormous degree during transcription if you have been listening to what is being said. If your mind starts to wander you are taking up 'thinking time' and this reduces the speed at which you can process the words you hear and convert them into outlines.
- Forget outlines which have passed; if you think you've written one wrongly it's too late now, if you dwell on it you'll miss something else. Wait for the next pause and scribble a note in the margin.
- Try to write neatly but *do* aim to get something for everything no matter how scruffy it is. You might struggle with a wayward outline but you certainly can't read a gap!
- Never write over your notes if you make a mistake – jot your outline in the margin instead.
- Don't be tempted to write initials of proper nouns, eg 'He has recently travelled from P to A.' could mean Perth to Adelaide, Paris to Athens and several other places as well! If you are desperate scribble a longhand abbreviation, ie the word with the vowels omitted, eg Prs to Athns would do.
- Don't panic if the speed gets quite fast – try to become a robot and get into a rhythm. It helps if you completely cut out any other unrelated thoughts which suddenly come into your mind.

- Train for 'getting behind' by trying to remember sentences of more and more words (remember your practice sessions?). Don't lose your concentration when the dictation stops but carry on until you've put down all the words you are remembering. (At work train your boss not to speak to you until you've stopped writing!)

Transcribing notes

You may have heard the claim that people are poor at written communications or spelling because they don't read as much as they should. There is a definite link between *reading* and knowing a language – and shorthand, in this sense, is a language. The more you read shorthand, the better you become at both transcribing and writing it. Practise by reading shorthand every day (come on, ten minutes won't kill you!) and always take some time to read your own notes, whether or not you are asked to transcribe them. *Don't* just try the first few sentences when your shorthand was immaculate! Only by seeing what you start to do under pressure can you get to know your own style of writing – and start to take this into consideration if you are having difficulty in transcribing a particular outline.

A good sequence to follow is given below.

- Read through your notes on a particular document *first*. Tidy up notes in the margin where necessary. If you can't read an outline don't panic, just pass over it for now.
- Type out your transcript. Be careful of making silly mistakes (like repeating a word) when you pause over an outline.
- Consider any blanks in context afterwards. If you are on a word processor you can type out the whole passage with spaces for the blanks and go back afterwards. On an electronic typewriter your ability to do this will depend on the memory available and whether you can adjust text on screen at all and then reprint later if necessary (see Chapter 5, Preparing and producing documents, page 241).
- Try the following seven-point plan for a blanks:
  - type (or write) as many words of the sentence as can be deciphered with certainty. Whatever you do, *trust your notes* – never alter a whole sentence, or add to it, to fit in an uncertain word
  - consider the context carefully; read back through previous sentences
  - look for any other clues in the rest of your notes, eg see if the same outline (or a similar one, which may be a derivation) appears again, eg Spain and Spanish
  - experiment with vowels, especially initial or final vowels
  - imagine, if you had been the writer, what you would have said at this point
  - analyse the outline 'crossword' fashion; write down what you *know* is there and then try substituting letters for the vague bits

– finally, the memory test. Think back – can you remember what was being talked about at the time and what might have been said? (See also office dictation and transcription, page 522.)

● Transcribe *sense* – nobody dictates rubbish. And if they did, and if you were concentrating during dictation, wouldn't you have noticed it anyway?

The ups and the downs of speed development

The irritating thing about learning shorthand is the fact that no one progresses steadily. Instead, you will find that your ability to write at speed develops in fits and starts. For a few weeks you may feel really perky: you can see a definite improvement and are starting to achieve speeds you never thought possible before. Then, for no apparent reason, you seem to come to an abrupt halt. Week after week goes by and you seem completely stuck at a certain level. It is at this stage you may be tempted to lose hope and give up.

Don't! Shorthand teachers the world over know this as the 'plateau phase', and you will go through a range of plateaux before you reach the top of your particular mountain. *Where* you reach them differs from one person to another, but if you expect them, and know that they are a standard occurrence, then you will find them easier to cope with. The answer is to keep practising and wait for each one to go away – as it surely will, eventually. You will then romp ahead for a few weeks until you meet your next plateau, and so on!

Having fun, finding shortcuts and developing your own style

Shorthand seems to consist of two types of writers: the purists and – for want of a better word – the realists. The purists like shorthand to be written by the book and to be as technically perfect as possible. The realists just get on with the job of writing it. Occasionally, their memory of an outline fails them or they have to write a word they've never met before. Rather than hesitate they scribble something which is the nearest thing they can think of and carry on. Over time, their shorthand becomes peppered with hybrid outlines so that after a number of years they are writing a system which may not be instantly recognisable in a formal sense but which they can read back perfectly! In addition, they might have developed a few outlines and shortcuts of their own which, unless they know the system backwards, may break one or two rules in the process. Some systems are less rigid in this respect than others, but if you are using shorthand to earn a living there are two facts you should never forget.

1 It is absolutely useless being the writer of perfect notes that you cannot read.

2 Shorthand is purely the means to an end – it was never designed to be an art form.

For that reason it can be fun to experiment, provided you have learned the basics thoroughly. You can also develop shortcuts for your boss's favourite phrases which he/she uses on a daily basis, and for technical terms used by your company. For instance, if your organisation deals with metals, you may find it quicker to write the chemical symbols, eg Al for aluminium, Zn for zinc than to try to work out the correct outline.

Advanced phrases

Advanced phrases fall into two categories – those which take advantage of certain techniques to reduce the amount of writing, eg the principle of omission, using one stroke or sound to do the work of two etc, and those which are a bit of a novelty (but not much use if your executive never uses these phrases!).

Developing your skills – Pitman

Please note that these outlines do not conform to real Pitman theory and would not be found in any Pitman shorthand textbook.

- Develop the number of intersections you use, eg:

  - 'ns' for necessary,

  - ....   it is necessary

  ....   it will be necessary

  - 'dm' for memorandum

  ....   recent memorandum

  - 'tv' for alternative

  ....   there is no alternative   or   ....

  ....   I have no alternative   or   ....

- Develop your phrases, eg use 'n' hook for 'in' eg:

  get in touch with me   ....

  keep in touch with me   ....

- Let one sound do the work of two, eg:

  ....   take exception

  ....   satisfactory results

- Omit syllables, eg:

.... satisfactory conclusion

.... we have no objection

- Or even omit a whole word or words, eg:

.... again and again

.... I have come to the conclusion

.... I am sorry to say

.... whether or not

A tip to learning these is to think of the phrase as it is written, eg 'I have no tiv' or 'I have clusion'.

There are many advanced phrase books on the market but remember to be selective in the phrases you learn – only choose those which you know you will use regularly or which relate to the particular area in which you are working.

Developing your skills – Teeline

There is more scope with the Teeline system for 'doing your own thing' – provided, once again, that you have learned the basics of the system properly. Indeed many Teeline advocates would say that there is not one correct outline for a word, but may be several, depending on the interpretation of the writer.

However, as it stands, Teeline is a longer system to write than Pitman shorthand and to reach a speed of beyond about 110 or 120 wpm you are probably going to have to invent a few shortcuts, for instance:

- Reduce the amount you write for common phrases, eg:

....X....	we expect	....O....	may be
....	we think	....	would be
....	in this way	....\....	during a
....	at all times	....	over and above
....	I would like	....	we would like

- Reduce disjoining for speed, eg:

.... it is important

.... it is most important

.... it is impossible

- Let one stroke or sound do the work of two, eg:

.... some measure

.... better results

.... this seems

- Develop a few distinctive phrases, eg:

.... semi detached

.... come to the point

.... accident black spot

Bear in mind these lists are not exhaustive but are intended to illustrate the type of principles which you can apply, once you become an expert at your particular system. Again a good phrase book is the best starting point; from then on you can develop your own to cope with your particular work and the terms and phrases that you use regularly.

TEST YOURSELF
Finally, see how imaginative you are. Overleaf are given some common expressions and phrases which have been developed quite ingeniously in some cases! Look through both lists and see if you can work out which outline belongs to which phrase!

The real thing – office dictation and transcription
There is a considerable difference between practising writing shorthand in a classroom and writing it for a living. For one thing, no boss on this earth dictates shorthand at a steady speed over a precise number of minutes! Unless your boss is adept at dictation (and in the early days you may hope that he/she isn't!) you will find that at work you are faced with a range of problems you haven't met before.

List 1 – Phrases

1	let the matter drop	**6**	I am under the impression
2	all along the line	**7**	all over the world
3	all things being equal	**8**	correct me if I am wrong
4	line of least resistance	**9**	last but not least
5	99 times out of a 100	**10**	in the long run

List 2 – Outlines

	Pitman	**Teeline**
A		
B		
C		
D		
E		
F		
G		
H		
I		
J		or	

- The speed varies tremendously between when your boss knows what to say (and is worried about forgetting it unless it is said quickly) and when he/she gets stuck (when your suggestions for an alternative word or sentence might be valued).
- Interruptions (eg the telephone ringing) will cause a distraction so that when your boss returns to dictating you will immediately have to read back the last two sentences.
- You may find yourself jotting down instructions or asides to you by accident, if your boss doesn't change the tone of his/her voice enough. Note down instructions *either* in the margin or in square brackets in the text so that you know these don't belong to the dictation proper.

- No punctuation, paragraphing or capitalisation is likely to be dictated.
- You may be expected to insert bits and pieces on your own, for which you will need to leave gaps, eg 'You may recall that I wrote to you on – now when was it . . . look it up will you – about the matter of . . .' Again note down these comments in square brackets, eg [check date] so that you don't leave a gap which may confuse you later. (Obviously the words 'check date' would be in shorthand, not in longhand!)

You should be delighted to know that, once you get used to it, this style is much *easier* to cope with than examination style dictation. With luck you will develop a good working relationship with your boss which will enable you to check doubtful parts easily (though *never* do this by interrupting when he/she is in full flow!) and without feeling guilty. Whilst there is obviously a limit as to the number of times your boss will expect this to happen, you will find that as you become more used to his/her style, phraseology and the technical words used by your organisation you will be able to make a far more intelligent guess as to the correct word to use if an outline defeats you. Life is even better if you have a boss who doesn't mind which word you substitute so long as the document makes sense and faithfully represents what he/she wanted to say. Bear in mind that the grammatical ability of executives varies enormously. If your boss dictates something which is obviously incorrect change it later – *don't* correct him/her at the time!

During dictation it is useful to 'code' each set of notes for priority, eg A, B, C. When you start to transcribe it is a straightforward matter to type all the notes coded 'A' first. It is also sensible to take advantage of respites and interruptions by reviewing the last few lines and tidying up your notes rather than staring out of the window. You are then ready when your boss asks the inevitable 'where were we?' afterwards. If dictation is too fast ask him/her (nicely) to slow down – (don't huff and puff or sigh – it's annoying and distracting). And remember that you are not paid to look annoyed if your boss suddenly remembers there are two more letters to write just as you were leaving the room!

Try to collect all the paperwork relating to the shorthand notes you have to transcribe; frequently, any blanks can be solved just by reading your boss's notes or the original document(s). The same applies to names. If you have scribbled 'Dear Mr A', all is revealed once you have the original letter to hand!

A final word of advice – if you are ever asked to take notes at evening meetings, or on special occasions, when the drink may be flowing, *be very careful*! Assuming you are not driving, you may be tempted to treat this as a semi-social occasion but beware – alcohol and shorthand don't mix. After about two drinks your outlines will become uncontrollable and will be virtually unreadable the following morning – especially as your concentration will also not have been all it should!

Individual tasks

1 Select *three* passages which contain business material from your relatively early theory work, and tape these at four speeds – your base speed (average speed on an average day), then + 20, + 40 and + 60 wpm. Try to choose passages which don't last longer than one minute at the top speed.

Follow the instructions given in this section on posture, holding your pen, gliding your hand and writing professionally and practise each passage until you are writing it easily at the top speed.

2 Make out a series of small cards containing short forms (if you write Pitman) or special outlines (Teeline) on one side and the key on the other. Test yourself by seeing how many you can write correctly without cheating and looking on the back!

3 If you are working, make a list of the phrases your boss uses regularly. Some of these may be standard expressions, eg 'as a matter of fact', others may be technical terms. Now work out the *shortest possible way* in which you can write these and yet not confuse them for anything else. Practise these special outlines until you know them by heart. (Tip – a quick way of writing 'as a matter of fact' is to think of it as 'smatteract'!)

Group/individual activities

Case study 1

Below is a script which highlights the incompetent PA's approach to shorthand dictation – despite a competent executive! *Either* rewrite the script yourself to show how a good PA would respond in the same situation or (as a group) re-enact the scene on video for the use of more junior students. Prepare a questionnaire which will enable students who watch the film to identify the errors the PA makes and a key to help them to check their work afterwards.

E (*rings through – long pause*)

PA (*enters – nothing in hands*)

E I'd just like to go over the morning mail – can you come in a moment?

PA Sorry – I've forgotten my book. Hang on a moment. (*pause – re-enters with book*)

E Can we make a start then? I've rather a busy day ahead of me.

PA OK. (*looks on desk for pencil, finds one eventually*) Yes?

E Let's go through the mail then. Have you sorted it out for me?

PA No. I didn't have time this morning what with one thing and another. Sorry.

E Well, let's take one thing at once then. Let me see. (*picks up one document*) Oh, this is an invitation to attend a reception at the Town Hall next month on the 12th. I suppose I ought to go. Have I got anything else on that evening?

PA I don't know. I can't remember.

E Have you checked the diary?

PA No, I forgot to bring it in. Shall I go and get it?

E Never mind now. Just check it later will you. What's next? (*picks up a letter*) Oh yes. I'll reply to this right away. (*starts dictating*) It's to The Manager, Northern Publishing Company, 23 High Street, Nottingham. Dear Sir, Thank you for your letter and enclosed list of new publications. I feel sure that some of these books will be of use to our sales staff and should be grateful if you would send one copy of each of the following to me. 'The Business of Selling' by A B Carter and 'Packaging for Profit' by R J Black. If this arrangement is agreeable to you – (*pause*) – no, I seem to have lost the thread. Can you read back that last sentence?

PA (*hesitates*) Er – 'The Business of Selling' by A B Carter and 'Packaging for Pleasure' by R J Black.

E Are you sure?

PA Just a minute – it looks like that.

E (*consults letter*) 'Packaging for Profit' surely?

PA (*with relief*) Yes, that's it.

E Let's carry on then. If this arrangement is agreeable to you, our cheque for the total amount, plus postage will be forwarded to you as soon as I have had – *breaks off* – what's the matter?

PA I've broken my pencil. (*looks in bag*) I think I've got another one. Yes, OK. Ready.

E I've forgotten what I was saying.

PA The last thing I have is 'if this arrangement'.

E Right. If this arrangement is agreeable to you, our cheque for the total amount, plus postage will be forwarded to you as soon as I have had an opportunity to inspect the books. Yours.

PA Yours what?

E How did I begin?

PA Dear Sir

E Well, surely its Yours faithfully then.

PA Yes, OK.

E I think we'll leave the rest of the dictation – in fact I might put it on tape for you. Are you better at audio dictation?

PA I'm not bothered – I'm pretty good at both.

Case study 2

The following script highlights the errors made by an incompetent dictator (who fortunately employs a good PA!).

1 Identify all the mistakes the executive makes.

2 Make notes on the course of action you would take to 'train' this executive to dictate properly *without* creating friction. (You may find it helpful to refer back to the sections on Managing your boss, page 291, and Managing other people, page 178, before you decide what to do.)

3 Note down any ideas you may have on organising your own work and your time to enable you to cope if he resolutely refuses to change!

4 Discuss your suggestions with the rest of your group and produce a group 'plan of action' to cope with the situation.

5 As a challenge, try to type a correct (and acceptable!) version of the letter the executive dictates!

PA   Have you time to go through the mail now, Mr Cartwright? I've sorted it out for you.

E   (*looking out of window – long pause – turns reluctantly*) I suppose so. What's first then?

PA   You've been invited to a reception at the Town Hall on the 12th of next month. You did say you would like to attend. I've checked the diary and you've no other engagements that evening.

E   I didn't say I would *like* to attend. I said I would *have* to attend – there's a world of difference you know. (*pause*) Oh, all right then – I suppose so. Anything else?

PA   You did say you wanted to reply to the Northern Publishing Company about those books. Here's their letter.

E   (*glances through it, looks puzzled*) Did I ask for this? I can't remember. Oh, leave it till later – I can't be bothered at the moment. I'll tell you what I have to do though – reply to this letter. (*picks it up from the desk, starts dictating very quickly*) The Manager, Star Supermarket, Market Way, Wolverhampton. Dear Sir, no – Dear Mr Lane – no, that's not right – Dear Sir. (*pauses*) Did I give you the address? Yes I did. Right. (*gets up and dictates the rest of the letter while staring out of the window*) Thank you for your letter which I received – was it some time last week – I can't find the date – yes here it is – last Wednesday. I – no – my staff – my colleagues – and I are at a loss to understand your difficulty in selling our goods – our product – and are very reluctant to allow your entire stock to be sold at the very reduced price you mention without further investigation. May I suggest that one – no, before that, put in a bit about first class products.

PA   Where exactly?

E   (*irritably*) Where appropriate of course. I'll get one of our advertising staff – just stick in any name there will you – to visit you and give you a hand with your display. How about Monday morning. Yours sincerely.

PA   Do you want to give him a time?

E   A time for what?

PA   For the visit.

E   Oh, just put in anything vague – gives us more room for manoeuvre. Sign it for me will you. I'm going out now.

Managing your career

Travel the road to success with care. Keep checking what's behind you and remember that overtaking is the most tricky manoeuvre of all.

As you come towards the end of this book, we hope that you have found its contents interesting, informative and useful – rather than overwhelming. If you are taking an NVQ 3 qualification then the knowledge you have gained should take you far in assisting you to achieve the necessary competencies for success. More than that, we hope to have inspired you in your performance of your own job, and enabled you to see aspects of it which you may not have thought about before. But finishing this book should not be the end of the road. Rather it should be the beginning; as you now stand back and review your skills you should be thinking 'What now?', rather than 'Thank heavens that's over!'

Planning your career

It is quite possible that, for domestic or other reasons, you simply want a part-time, straightforward office job, near to home, and have no personal aspirations for the future. If this is *genuinely* true, then you can probably skip this section. But think carefully: there is a vast difference between some part-time jobs and others – and you never know when circumstances may dictate a change of plan.

For some, having a career is something that happens to other people, not themselves, simply because they don't know where to start.

Others are eager to do well and succeed; they want to find out just what they are capable of achieving and are willing to work hard to achieve their goals.

RULE 1
Achieving success in life is not just a matter of luck! It takes planning, determination, hard work and commitment plus the ability to cope with setbacks and learn from them.

CHECK IT YOURSELF
Think hard and then write down the job you would like to be doing in five years' time. Be honest and realistic. You are unlikely to be able to become the MD of ICI in that time! *But* if you are female beware of the 'glass ceiling', ie the limits (real or otherwise) upon female executives reaching the very top of the career ladder. (Some believe that these are self-imposed because many female executives just cannot believe they can reach the top, others consider that these certainly exist as we live in a society where the majority of executives are still male. This section is not the place to debate the issue!)

> **RULE 2**
> Be wary about sharing your ambitions with others. Nobody likes
> power-hungry PAs or administrators and placing your trust in others
> unwisely can be disastrous.

Devising your career plan

Consider this under several headings:

- staying put versus changing jobs
- personal self-development
- projecting the right image
- applying for jobs and interview technique.

Staying put versus changing jobs

No one can make this decision for you, but there are several factors
you should bear in mind to help you weigh up the most favourable
action for you to take *in your own particular circumstances.*

Staying put

Stay where you are if:

- there is a reasonable chance that you could move up a notch before
  too long
- you are on good terms with your boss *and* the person whose job
  you want (in case they have a hand in choosing their successor)
- you have a good 'feel' for company politics and have learned how to
  use these to your advantage
- feedback from the grapevine and/or your junior staff (when they are
  not trying to humour you!) tells you that you are well respected and
  have a good reputation
- there are good opportunities in the company for which you work
- someone above you (your boss?) is helping you to develop your
  talents and is supporting you in your attempts to get on.

Moving on

Move on if:

- you have a dead-end job
- there are no prospects of a suitable vacancy in the foreseeable future
- you are not getting the credit (or salary) you deserve
- company reorganisation has downgraded you
- you are not perceived as worthy of promotion.

> **RULE 3**
> Don't put off making a difficult decision or expect something to fall
> in your lap. Waiting for an opportunity which never occurs can
> leave you frustrated and disillusioned.

The main benefit of changing jobs is to broaden your experience, which will make you a more valuable asset in the future. However, do be careful of being labelled a 'job hopper' or you will have a great deal of convincing to do at your next interview! Even the very ambitious aim for at least two or three years' experience at each level.

Personal self-development

This should be never-ending! Indeed the most interesting older people to meet are those who have open and enquiring minds, have developed a wealth of experience and interests over the years and have never stopped in their quest to gain new knowledge. They have a vitality of life which is second to none.

CHECK IT YOURSELF
Identify the areas which you really should develop to help you work towards your goal and the skills and knowledge which will be needed which you don't as yet possess.

Self-development areas

To progress towards your goal you need to enjoy responsibility and to be looking for new challenges. You should want to take the responsibility for your own development – as a first step – and be keen to meet the challenges these present. Areas to consider may include:

- developing your personal skills, eg dealing with people, diplomacy, assertiveness etc
- developing your supervisory skills
- developing your office skills eg increasing your shorthand speed
- developing *additional* skills, eg IT appreciation or a foreign language
- developing your business knowledge.

The latter is very important. If your boss enters the office and complains that 'the pound has fallen' you are unlikely to be worthy of any type of promotion if you start hunting on the floor! Do you listen to (or, even better, read) the news and realise how the state of the economy affects your organisation? Or political changes and initiatives? Or international changes and developments? Or is it all very confusing and a good excuse to switch off the TV when the newsreader reaches the 'boring' bits? This isn't very wise if you are a voter/taxpayer yourself as you are *personally* affected by most of that boring stuff!

Even if you work full-time, call in at your local college one evening during enrolment and see what's on offer to help you. Retake a GCSE that was a disaster, learn French or German, take an A level just to see if you can do it (economics? politics?), do an accounting course in the evenings.

Keep your eyes open for any short courses offered by either your local college or private companies. See if your organisation will sponsor your attendance. If not, consider paying the fees yourself!

RULE 4

Don't expect handouts to help you to get on! Treat any you receive as a windfall! Anticipate paying for your own self-development and look upon it as an *investment* (which should pay dividends) rather than expenditure.

Projecting the right image

There is an adage that to be worthy of promotion you have got to look as if you would be more at home in the next job than the one you have at the moment! In other words you must show, by your words, actions and image, that you should be 'one-step on'.

RULE 5

From tomorrow, act as you would if you were in the next job up from the one you currently hold. If you have a suitable role model then watch this person to see how he/she operates and use him/her as a guide.

In many cases the problem is one of image. If you were still a rather impulsive young thing when you first entered the organisation for which you currently work, there may be very little hope that they will ever see you as the mature person you now strive to be.

At the same time note that whilst you may apply for a job and promote your image on paper (see next section), your overall appearance and 'look' could hold you back.

CHECK IT YOURSELF
What did you wear for work today? And yesterday? What is your current hairstyle? Do you consciously try to dress more formally if there is an important occasion at work in which you are involved?

Image can be considered in two ways – in terms of your reputation and in terms of your appearance. Basically, you are considering how other people see you – and this is a tricky one as it is doubtful if anyone will give the right (or same) answer. Even if they do, you probably won't believe them if it doesn't suit you to do so!

Your reputation

Aim to develop a reputation where you are known for:

- toeing the party line on critical issues rather than kicking against the traces. This does *not* mean becoming a 'yes' man, but the hard facts of the matter are that if you become your department's main staff agitator you are very likely to reduce your chances of promotion.
- being loyal to your boss *always*. If you have reason to be seriously concerned about his/her behaviour in any way then you should raise this discreetly with a senior member of the organisation – not gossip about it.
- being loyal to your company when it is discussed – *especially* outside work – and not being disparaging about its systems and practices to the world at large.
- being helpful and cooperative with everyone you meet, no matter what their status. (They do say you should make friends with those you meet on the way up – as you may meet them again on the way back down!)
- listening as well as talking – so that you are seen as understanding, perceptive and knowledgeable rather than a know-all or chatterbox.
- supporting your juniors through thick and thin. They will then give you a vote of confidence if, before a promotion interview, your boss quietly asks them for their opinion of you.

Your appearance

It is fashionable to argue that in the days of equal opportunities and a progressively meritocratic society[1] people should be able to dress as they please at work. Usually this is rubbish – though it obviously depends to a great extent on the job you hold and the image your company wishes to project.

Despite the emergence of some trendy companies which encourage jeans and T-shirts as the norm (usually to be found in the media), by far the vast majority of organisations have traditional expectations and requirements in relation to the image of their organisation, and expect their employees to dress accordingly – especially those on the way up! However, there is a great deal of difference between a jumper and skirt (or sweater and slacks) and a suit and blouse (or shirt)! In one you give a low grade employee image, in the other the image of a top PA/junior manager/supervisor.

Upgrade your image by choosing smart outfits, and forget the knitted cardigans and sweaters which look unprofessional. A female PA or executive can totally transform a simple coat dress by the use of accessories, eg a belt, scarf or jewellery. (But don't wear a belt if your waistline isn't what it should be!) A young male executive, on a limited budget, can manage very well indeed with just two suits (in different shades of the same colour – not blue and brown!) and several shirts and ties which go with both.

---

[1] If you don't know what this means, look it up! Consider it the first stage in your self-development plan!

> **RULE 6**
> Whether you are male or female go steady on the jewellery at work!
> Go for a few *good* items, worn effectively – or none at all.

Try to choose colours which look professional, especially for jackets and suits *but* do choose colours and shades which harmonise with your own natural colouring. People need to see *you* first not what you are wearing! You may like to note that red is considered a 'power' colour and is claimed to give confidence in your ability (though too much can overwhelm).

Neutral colours are your best investments for the more expensive items of clothing. Avoid garish colours which will soon go out of fashion.

> **RULE 7**
> Fashion comes and goes but style never dates! Go for fewer, more
> expensive and more stylish clothes which you can wear for years
> and build these round a colour scheme of perhaps three or four
> colours which go well together.

Wear suitable shoes, especially on formal occasions, rather than sandals or trainers. Bear in mind that neutral colours will go with most outfits. Your shoes must tone with your outfit – not be the first thing that everyone sees!

If you are female, and especially on formal occasions, tights are essential! Never have bare legs – regardless of the weather. If you are short in stature wear colours which tone with your hemline and shoes as this will make you appear taller. If you are tall you can wear hosiery in a complementary colour. This will break up the line and you won't look too 'leggy'.

If you are returning to work after several years then it is worthwhile reassessing your make-up. Make-up which is too heavy, too trendy or non-existent is out. Make-up which is dated will add years to your looks. Buy a few magazines specially aimed at career women and examine carefully the look they project. Learn how to apply your make-up correctly. (Go to a professional and watch and learn. Even if you don't like the end result you can adapt the techniques to suit you.)

Your hair should be neat and tidy and in a style which suits you. Have it cut regularly – every six to eight weeks. It *must* be clean – choose a style which you can manage easily yourself so that you can wash it regularly. If you have long hair *don't* think that long flowing locks will enhance your image at work – they will enhance one image, but it won't be the right one!

Applying for jobs and interview technique

This section is valid even if you want to stay put! Many organisations have a system which requires internal candidates for a job to apply and be interviewed against external opposition and you must be equal to the occasion.

Your specific application will vary from one vacancy to another. Some organisations want you to write a letter and attach a CV; others send you an application form and ask you to complete it and attach a letter justifying your application.

RULE 8

Before you start to put together an application for a job put yourself in the shoes of the person who will be selecting the interviewees. What do you think he/she will want to read? Study the advertisement or job description again and note down any clues as to what they *really* want.

Letter of application

Forget anything you were taught at school – if your handwriting is awful then *type* it and show just how well you can display such a document! (Don't forget Enc for the form or CV.)

In a straightforward letter your aim should be that:

Paragraph 1 States clearly the position for which you are applying and where you saw it advertised.

Paragraph 2 Gives a few brief but relevant facts about yourself, ie what you are doing at present/have just done. Refer to your CV.

Paragraph 3 The tricky one! – says why you are particularly interested in that job. Refer to relevant experience you have had, a liking for that particular type of work, the opportunity to develop your knowledge and experience etc. This is the paragraph that sets you apart from the others!

Paragraph 4 States when you are available for interview (preferably any time).

If the letter is to *support* a standard application form then obviously your first paragraph would be different, ie thank them for the form, and your second paragraph will refer to the form, not your CV.

In this type of letter your third paragraph needs extending considerably – possibly into paragraphs 4 and 5 as well!

 TEST YOURSELF
Read the job advertisement shown below. Imagine that you have obtained an application form. Write out a letter in support of your application and ask your tutor to comment on your work.

OFFICE ADMINISTRATOR

Small but expanding computer consultancy requires experienced secretary/PA who wishes to take on the responsibility of running a hectic office and supervising the executives and the junior staff.

Essential are
- excellent communication and secretarial skills
- a recognised secretarial qualification (NVQ Level 3 or above)
- a minimum of 3 years experience as a junior administrator, personal secretary or PA.

Whilst a basic knowledge of office accounts and related software is desirable, training will be given if necessary.

Application forms are available on request and should be completed and returned no later than Friday, 4 June 199-, together with a supporting letter.

DP COMPUTER SYSTEMS LTD
Oak House
Miller Road
MIDCHESTER

Tel 0781 584787

Your CV

You should aim to have a running CV all your life so that updating it is easy and important facts are not omitted.

Your CV is your personal advertisement and must be beautifully produced and presented. Remember that you have a tremendous advantage over people wanting to progress in other fields – you can type your own CV (and – presumably – save it on disk). Many people have to pay agencies considerable amounts of money for the same service!

RULE 9

Never send a photocopy: use top quality bond paper and always keep your CV to a maximum of two A4 pages no matter what your age or experience, so that you retain the reader's interest throughout.

Break up your CV into sections with suitable headings, eg personal details, education (forget anything pre-secondary school) and qualifications, work experience and a final section including interests and whether you have a driving licence etc. Also give two referees.

SPECIAL NOTE
If you do not want your current employer to know about your application, then you are within your rights to ask that the organisation to which you are writing does not contact anyone at your workplace at this stage. Indicate that you would be willing for them to contact your employer if your application is successful.

The final touches

Use a good quality, white DL envelope. Address it carefully and include the postcode. Give the impression of being ultra-efficient and organised, even at this stage.

The interview

Only masochists enjoy interviews. Normal mortals hate them and consider that they are nerve-wracking experiences not to be undertaken lightly. For that reason you need to prepare for one carefully.

- Buy a good book on interview techniques and read it (there are many good paperbacks on the market).
- Read up about the organisation (see Chapter 2, Researching and retrieving information!)
- Plan what you will wear and make sure it is clean and pressed. Check that your shoes are clean and not down-at-heel and your hair is in one of its good phases!
- Work out the distance from home, route to take, time to leave to allow for journey etc.
- Think of the likely questions you might be asked and the type of replies which would be expected.
- Think of sensible questions you can ask.
- Assemble the materials you may need if they want you to take a short test (horrors!). Don't forget your emergency supplies, ie shorthand notebook, pen/pencil, bottle of liquid paper and a calculator.
- Ask a friend to give you a mock interview the day before.

On the day itself give yourself plenty of time to get ready. Keep paraphernalia (shopping bags, umbrellas etc) to a minimum. Read the headlines in the paper just in case a momentous event has just occurred about which you should be aware.

RULE 10

Female interviewees should remember to keep their handbag on the *left hand side* (either over/under the arm or over the shoulder). That way it is possible to shake hands easily with the right hand as you are introduced *without* the handbag getting in the way (or worse, falling off one shoulder or down one arm!).

Male interviewees should remember to take their hands out of their pockets – and keep them out!

Smile when you are introduced; sit down and put down anything you are holding so that you don't fiddle about with it out of sheer nerves. Try to restrain yourself from crossing your legs and *don't* lean back. Either sit up straight or lean slightly forward to denote interest. Keep your hands *still*. *Don't* avoid making eye contact or you'll look shifty.

Normally there will be a warm up phase before the questions start in earnest. Deal with each one as it comes. Give honest and concise answers; the interviewer(s) will ask for more information if necessary. If you don't know the answer to something *say so*. Equally, if you want someone to repeat the question or you haven't a clue what they mean, ask them to elaborate – better that, than bewildering the interviewer completely by answering a question which was never even asked!

At the end collect your possessions, be prepared to shake hands again and leave the room in a dignified way. Then cross your fingers!

If you get the job then go out and celebrate. If you don't then put it down to experience – though this is easier said than done if you really wanted the job. If it helps, think positively – something better is around the corner and you are meant to mark time until then!

Dealing with setbacks

Learn one basic fact early – life isn't fair! There are many occasions when things go wrong and you may feel like throwing in the towel. A colleague may let you down badly or betray your confidences. Your boss may blame you for something which wasn't your fault. You may do a super job on a special project to see another person claim the glory. Someone may be really hurtful, tear a strip off you and leave you in tears. Or you may have set your heart on a job which you don't get.

All these situations are difficult to handle. If you feel hurt and wounded you are in no position to go out and fight a few more battles. Rather you want to hide away and have a good weep. Do that first – you'll feel better afterwards. And then get annoyed – how dare anyone else make you feel like this? Rediscover your own self-confidence and finally, when you are in a more reflective state of mind, consider what you can learn from the experience. Was your strategy at fault in any way? Should you do things differently next time?

RULE 11

Life's achievers are those who deal with setbacks by licking their wounds, gritting their teeth and then living to fight another day. It isn't easy but then nothing worth achieving ever is.

Review your goals

Finally, as you start to move towards and achieve your goals, stand back and reconsider the goal you first set yourself. Is it still appropriate or have you changed your mind now? Have you broadened your horizons still further?

A wise man would probably add that the final secret of success – and happiness – is to realise when you are well off and when you are successful. Constant striving can wear everyone down and there is more to life than work. However, most people need to feel that they have achieved something which is totally and unalterably *their own* – and fulfilling your own potential can be very rewarding.

On your journey – with luck – you will have worthwhile experiences, meet new people and gain new friends. You will also become an achiever, and one day be in a position to encourage others to do the same.

Bon voyage!

Further Reading

If you wish to follow up any of the topics raised in the managing sections in this book, then you should start by reading a book which deals with the subject in which you are interested in more detail. Below is given a list of books which fall into this category, although you should note that most general management and business studies books cover topics such as motivation, leadership, change etc. Start by choosing books which look user-friendly and are easy to read!

Adair J, *How to manage your time*, Talbot Adair, 1988

ASTMS, *Occupational stress: a policy for prevention*, 1983

Argyris C, *Increasing Leadership Effectiveness*, Wiley & Sons, 1976

Atkinson P, *Achieving results through time management*, Pitman Publishing, 1989

Back K and Back K, *Assertiveness at Work*, McGraw Hill, 1990

Berne E, *Games People Play*, Grove Press, 1964

Blick Time Systems, *Guide to time management*, 1989

Cole G A, *Management, Theory and Practice*, DP Publications, 1986

Consumers Association, *Understanding Stress*, 1990

Consumers Association, *Which? Way to save tax*, (published annually)

Donkin S W, *Fit for work – A practical guide to good health for people who sit on the job*, Kogan Page, 1990

Friedman M and Rosenman R, *Type A behaviour and your heart*, Knopf, 1974

Garratt S, *Manage your time*, Fontana, 1985

Goffman E, *The Presentation of Self in Everyday Life*, Penguin, 1971

Handy C, *Understanding Organisations*, Penguin, 1976

Lakein A, *How to get control of your time and your life*, Gower, 1984

Lifeskills Associates, *Time management now*, 1989

Pugh, Hickson and Hinings, *Writers on Organisations*, Penguin, 1984

Ruck L O and Holmes T H, *Scaling of Life Changes: Comparison of Direct and Indirect Methods*, Journal of Psychosomatic Research, vol 15, 1971

Stewart R, *The Reality of Organisations*, Pan, 1970

Willis L and Daisley J, Springboard – *Women's Development Workbook*, Hawthorn Press, 1990

Index